Literatures of the Middle East

Literatures of the Middle East

From Antiquity to the Present

Edited and with introductions by

Willis Barnstone
INDIANA UNIVERSITY

Tony Barnstone
WHITTIER COLLEGE

Prentice
Hall

Upper Saddle River, New Jersey 07458

Library of Congress Cataloging-in-Publication Data

Literatures of the Middle East: from antiquity to the present / edited and with
   introductions by Willis Barnstone, Tony Barnstone.
       p.   cm.
    Rev. and abridged ed. of: Literatures of Asia, Africa, and Latin America, 1999.
    Includes bibliographical references and index.
    ISBN 0-13-046437-6
       1. Middle Eastern literature—Translations into English.   1. Barnstone, Willis (date)   II.
    Barnstone, Tony.   III. Literatures of Asia, Africa, and Latin America.
    PJ409.L58 2003
    808.8'00956—dc21   2002025140

Editor-in-Chief: Leah Jewell
Senior Acquisitions Editor: Carrie Brandon
Editorial Assistant: Jennifer Migueis
Managing Editor: Ann Marie McCarthy
Production Liaison: Fran Russello
Project Manager: Linda B. Pawelchak

Prepress and Manufacturing Buyer:
   Sherry Lewis
Interior Design: Delgado Design, Inc.
Cover Design: Robert Farrar-Wagner
Cover Image: Willis Barnstone
Marketing Manager: Rachel Falk

This text is derived from *Literatures of Africa, Asia, and
Latin America* by Willis Barnstone and Tony Barnstone.

Acknowledgments begin on page 480, which constitutes
a continuation of this copyright page.

This book was set in 10/12 New Baskerville by Lithokraft II
and was printed and bound by Courier Companies.
The cover was printed by Phoenix Color Corp.

© 2003 by Pearson Education, Inc.
Upper Saddle River, New Jersey 07458

Printed in the United States of America
10   9   8   7   6   5   4   3   2

ISBN 0-13-046437-6

Pearson Education LTD, *London*
Pearson Education Australia PTY. Limited, *Sydney*
Pearson Education Singapore, Pte. Ltd
Pearson Education North Asia Ltd, *Hong Kong*
Pearson Education Canada Ltd, *Toronto*
Pearson Educación de Mexico, S.A. de C.V.
Pearson Education—Japan, *Tokyo*
Pearson Education Malaysia, Pte. Ltd
Pearson Education, *Upper Saddle River, New Jersey*

This book is dedicated to
Reza Baraheni

C O N T E N T S

Section 1 ▪ Sumerian, Akkadian, and Ancient Egyptian Literatures   7

Section 2 ■ Biblical Literature: Old Testament, New Testament, and Intertestament   55

Section 3 ▪ Early Arabic Literature   227

Section 4 ▪ Poems of Arab Andalusia 302

Section 6 ■ Modern Arabic, Hebrew, Turkish, Alexandrian Greek, and Persian Literatures 350

CONTENTS BY GENRE

Poetry

SECTION 4 ■ POEMS OF ARAB ANDALUSIA

SECTION 5 ■ PERSIAN LITERATURE

SECTION 6 ■ MODERN ARABIC, HEBREW, TURKISH, ALEXANDRIAN GREEK, AND PERSIAN LITERATURES

Fiction

SECTION 1 ▪ SUMERIAN, AKKADIAN, AND ANCIENT EGYPTIAN LITERATURES

SECTION 3 ▪ EARLY ARABIC LITERATURE

SECTION 6 ▪ MODERN ARABIC, HEBREW, TURKISH, ALEXANDRIAN GREEK, AND PERSIAN LITERATURES

Prose Nonfiction

PREFACE

Literatures of the Middle East has been designed to present teachers and students with a textbook representative of the finest works of this province of world literature, one that is amenable to many different teaching approaches. This book includes a wealth of materials, so as to give teachers choices that they can tailor to their own preferences, needs, and expertise. This capaciousness will allow students to read around in authors, periods, and traditions that particularly excite them, supplementing assigned reading and providing an essential source book for their individual research. Teaching such a broad spectrum of texts may be challenging, and with this in mind we have supported the literary texts with a full apparatus: a general introduction, section introductions, and extensive headnotes. These supporting materials provide broad and specific contexts, placing literary texts within important cultural, linguistic, and historical movements. In addition, the headnotes include up-to-date bibliographies to guide students for further research.

Translations have been selected primarily for their literary quality because we firmly believe that it is a disservice to students, professors, and authors to present a great work of literature in an English translation that does not read as literature. The depth and quality of these texts demand excellent translations, so that students and professors may encounter them in a form that preserves their artistic integrity and delight. The translators featured here are among the finest in their fields, and many are themselves prominent writers. They include Richard Burton, Ezra Pound, Chana Bloch, Stephen Mitchell, Denys Johnson-Davies, Robert Pinsky, Robert Alter, Daniel Halpern, and Paul Bowles, among others. Our one rule has been to include no translation that is merely adequate. In a sense, then, this text is a showcase for the art of literary translation, and our hope has been to compile an anthology that students will want to take home with them and to read around in long after the course is completed.

In addition to literary texts, *Literatures of the Middle East* includes selections from religious and philosophical texts that have literary merit, such as the Old Testament, the New Testament, the Dead Sea Scrolls, Gnostic and other intertestamental scriptures, and the Quran, as well as Sufi poems and teaching stories. These beautiful works also provide a cosmological and cultural context for literary texts. Extensive headnotes and introductions trace out religious movements and influence, giving students a broad overview of world religions, which have often inspired and been an essential part of world literatures.

In dealing with many literatures written in many languages, a special problem is presented by the question of orthography. Generally speaking, we have chosen to use those transliteration systems that are best designed for the general, nonspecialist reader, for whom a more scholarly orthography would prove less informative.

We would like to thank the scholars who have contributed to the project: Richard Serrano and Ariel Bloch for suggestions and comments on the selections. We would also like to thank Richard Serrano for helping us regularize and simplify the orthography for the Arabic sections, and especially to thank Ericka Embry, David Livingston, and Ayame Fukuda for their essential help in research, typing, organization, and in the thousand small tasks that a project like this entails. Ayame Fukuda provided essential research help and also co-wrote several introductions. We would also like to thank Carrie Brandon, who had the vision to see the need for this book to see light.

We would also like to acknowledge the following reviewers: Ali Jimale Ahmed, Queens College; Peter Edmunds, Lansing (MI) Community College; Lydia Liv, University of California, Berkeley; Michael Palencia-Roth, University of Illinois; Herman Rapaport, University of Iowa; and Lois Parkinson Zamora, University of Houston.

—WILLIS BARNSTONE AND TONY BARNSTONE

Literatures of the Middle East

General Introduction

■

Literatures of the Middle East brings together literary, religious, and philosophical traditions from the many great civilizations that emerged from these fertile and ancient lands. This region has given us important writings, some of them dating back as far as the third millennium. Although Europe and the West are the children of ancient forebears in North Africa, Moorish Spain, and the Middle East, until recently, historically speaking, we have been essentially ignorant of the many major writers outside the West. Even the Bible, appropriated from the East as *the* foundation book of Western morality and thought, has scarcely been thought of as an Asian book.

Although the Bible is normally included only in anthologies of Western literature, in this volume we have attempted to contextualize the Bible in its Asian setting, showing its Sumerian, Babylonian, and Egyptian roots. We have also included a substantial selection of Jewish and Christian intertestamental scriptures, such as the Dead Sea Scrolls, which affirms the continuous writing of holy scriptures between the Old and New Testaments. It is also enlightening to read the Quran alongside the Bible, since the Quran is deeply informed by biblical figures and traditions. Despite history's sectarian distinctions, we have emphasized cultural affinities.

To compensate for the absence of non-Western writers, earlier world anthologies represented the non-Western world with a few Chinese, Persian, and Indian texts. A century of assiduous translation, however, has made the larger world accessible to the West, reconnecting us to an enormous past and present world literature. Particularly in our multicultural society, with peoples of every background, it is vital to reveal the great traditions of the Middle East, and to do so in fresh, excellent literary translation. *Literatures of the Middle East* presents a larger view of literature and civilization. The picture that emerges is of an antiquity in a ferment of creativity and of a migration of languages and literary forms.

The great written documents of antiquity root us as readers in a past of cultural particularity, cultural marriage, and universal themes and have offered superb new models for modern and postmodern writers. The interpenetration of the world's literary traditions has profoundly changed the ways that writers write. We live in a time when it's no less common for an American poet to write an Arabic *ghazal* than a sonnet, and when a well-known American novelist such as John Barth publishes a major novel based on the Arabic classic *The Thousand and One Nights*. In the current ferment of translation, a well-read lover of literature is as likely to be a fan of the

Persian poet Rumi as of William Blake, as likely to be reading the novelist and Nobel laureate Naguib Mahfouz as Ernest Hemingway. As in the Spanish saying "the world is a handkerchief" (*el mundo es un pañuelo*), all major literatures are now intimately accessible.

A few words about our criteria for inclusion and our rationale for ordering the texts here. There are thousands of authors competing for, and worthy of, inclusion, and we have had to make difficult choices. Although this anthology has an immense geographic and temporal range, we have represented writers and traditions in depth rather than number. We wished to present a comprehensive view of each literature. So, in addition to primary literary genres and forms, we have included key religious and philosophical texts, particularly those that have intrinsic literary value, such as the moral precepts of the Persian Sadi and selections from biblical and quaranic scriptures. In most cases, we've ordered the texts within each section chronologically and arranged individual sections according to a model of influence.

Though the term "Middle East" delimits an area of Southwest Asia and Northeast Africa, we thought it best to have an inclusive approach in this anthology, and to include important Arabic and Hebrew texts from Northwest Africa and Arab Andalusia. After all, the literatures of Sumeria, Babylonia, Egypt, Ancient Israel, Persia, and the Arabic-speaking countries, including medieval Muslim Spain, were intimately connected by influence and chronology and by a series of great empires. The countries of the Middle East ultimately gave the West its major religions (Judaism, Christianity, and Islam), its major myths, and its models for literature and art. So, this anthology's major movement goes west from the ancient Near East through Africa and represents a sequence of great civilizations from the ancient to the modern Middle East.

This large schema needs to be qualified. Islam, for example, spread east as well as west and penetrated south into parts of sub-Saharan Africa. The Moguls conquered most of India in 1526, bringing in Islam and Persian and Arabic language and literary forms. Today, Islam is the religion of much of Asia. Furthermore, influences are inevitably multidirectional, and each of these cultures has ancient indigenous traditions that predate the major religious and literary migrations. Still, it is essential to understand the global movements of culture and how outside influences have interacted with indigenous traditions.

The Middle East is often the unacknowledged source of much of Western civilization: columned Egyptian temples and sculptures were models for Greek temples and early statuary; Sumerian and Babylonian flood stories were retold in Genesis; and the story of baby Moses on the river derives from the Akkadian "Legend of Sargon"; Hebrew, the language of the Old Testament, is an Asian language, and the Greek of the New Testament was written in Asia for an Asian audience; the Asian deities Jehovah (Yahweh) and Jesus (Yeshua) were the foundation of Western Judeo-Christian religions. Even the essential activity of writing itself, of using alphabets and scripts, was imported from the Middle East. Without a writing system, we must remember, any development in European cultures would have been radically limited and, outside of surviving artifacts, unrecorded and destined to disappear. The Middle East gave us writing, and thus gave us literature, which is a bridge linking us to the civilizations of the past.

The process of writing, as far as we know, began in Sumerian Mesopotamia, which lies between the Tigris and the Euphrates Rivers in present-day Iraq—the same area that gave us Eden's Adam and Eve and was the homeland of Abraham and the Jews before their entry into Canaan. Well before the third millennium, Mesopotamian merchants and farmers communicated rudimentary trade information between towns by sending clay balls (bulls) that held inside them numbers and pictures of animals and merchandise. The oldest writing in the world is now thought to have survived in this mercantile correspondence. Soon there was communication to many cities, especially to those occupied by Phoenician traders on the coast of Asia Minor. The Sumerians also developed an elaborate system of pictographic writing in which each character represented a different idea or thing. In the world's first complete writing system, the Sumerians recorded their great literary and religious documents. These characters, known by the Latin term *cuneiform*, were inscriptions on wet clay tablets made with wedge-shaped wooden styluses (Latin *cuneus* means "wedge"). The system spread and soon all the main nearby languages adopted cuneiform characters as their writing system, including Akkadian, Elamite, Hittite, and Old Persian.

In second millennium Egypt, the Egyptians were developing their own hieroglyphic system of writing. As in Chinese and Mayan characters and Sumerian cuneiforms, the Egyptian hieroglyphs conveyed primarily meaning, rather than sound, thereby requiring thousands of different characters to express a full vocabulary. But then, independently, the Sumerians and Egyptians developed much simpler phonetic syllabaries consisting of about twenty-six letters, and modern writing began. Meanwhile, the Phoenicians—a term the Greeks invented to distinguish the Canaanites of the coast from Canaanites of Palestine—were preparing their own alphabet. The Greeks called this trading and seafaring people Phoenicians because of the famous purple cloth they made ("purple" in Greek is *phoenicia*). Around 1200 B.C., the Phoenicians devised a phonetic alphabet based on Egyptian cursive, which spread to Greece. The Cretan Greeks had an earlier alphabet, the so-called "linear B," but with the Dorian invasions around 1100 B.C., the Cretan script disappeared. From the Phoenician-inspired Greek script came the Roman alphabet in Western Europe and the Cyrillic alphabet in the Slavic-speaking countries to the north. "You can never step in the same river twice," writes Heraclitus, the pre-Socratic Greek philosopher. Time is such a river, but so is language, which flows from our mouths and is the medium of culture and society. To the Middle East, the West owes its ability to write, and thereby detain, the evanescent essence of human communication—language.

Like the Irish bog men preserved for centuries in peat or the marvelously conserved mummies of Egypt, humanity is preserved by writing. And there is wonder in what reaches us from antiquity. Like a bead of amber containing a prehistoric insect caught in mid-crawl, each word deciphered from cuneiform or Chinese, Sanskrit, or Quechua is precious. Ancient coins unearthed still retain monetary value, but we esteem them even more for their worth as microcosms of vanished worlds. This is the value to be found in ancient writing as well. There is an inexpressible pathos in reading the intimate words of the Israeli poet Yehuda Amichai, writing poems in search of an elusive peace in the war-ravaged Middle East. There is a shock of connection and understanding that comes from reading two women from very different cultures—Dahlia Ravikovitch from Israel and Forugh Farrokhzad from Iran—both writing about how their cultures reduce them as women to mechanical "dolls," and there is a universality to the grief of Gilgamesh, the Sumerian king, who confronts his own mortality after the death of his friend Enkidu.

In *Literatures of the Middle East,* we have gathered together the writings of the most ancient civilizations, against which the innovations of North America and Europe seem relatively recent. These texts stretch from antiquity to the present and, despite cultural differences, throughout reveal the universality of life-and-death experience. In every century and in every place, writers have recorded visions of the origins and end of the world, of the supernatural permeating ordinary life and afterlife, as in *The Egyptian Book of the Dead,* and the intertestamental apocalypses. Writers, religions, and philosophies have always tried to answer basic questions of origin, presence, and destiny and at the same time have given us intimate records of the self and the phenomenal world. The world's authors have observed the known and speculated on the unknown. *Literatures of the Middle East* is a record of their questioning and achievement. It encompasses a vast precinct of human knowledge, given to us by the writers of antiquity and by their heirs, our contemporaries, who continue to extend, and innovate, from Casablanca to Istanbul.

Introduction to
Section 1

■

Western Asia's civilizations mingled directly with those of North Africa and Arabic Spain and, for purposes of tracing the great historic movements of culture, one can consider these affiliated parts of Asia, Africa, and Europe as a kind of great bridge. Its peoples and cultures formed a bridge connecting Asia and Africa over which passed myth, religion, philosophy, literature, and even the art of cursive writing. North Africa's Egyptian, Persian, Hellenistic, Roman, Arabic, and Ottoman Turkish pasts make Africa, like Asia, Europe, and the Americas, a continent possessing ancient highly developed civilizations whose written traces come to life across the millennia with undiminished force. The same bridge area was a profoundly influential source of culture in Europe, the Americas, and the Far East.

The cultures of Western Asia are among the oldest and most advanced of the ancient world, with a written literary tradition going back more than four thousand years, beginning with the first writer whose name we know, the Sumerian moon priestess Enheduanna (c. 2300 B.C.). This region of fluid borders, inhabited by multiple ethnicities, has been the home of many cultures—Sumerian, Akkadian, Babylonian, Assyrian, Phoenician, Egyptian, Jewish, Persian, Arab, and Turkish, among others. The region was conquered time and again by the great empires of the West, the Greeks, Romans, and Ottomans, as well as by the crusaders and by Mongol invaders from the East. It is a place that saw millennia of religious ferment and development, culminating in three great, interrelated religious traditions—Judaism, Christianity, and Islam. The roots of these religions can be traced back to the ancient religions of Mesopotamia. Out of the polytheistic religions of the Sumerians, Babylonians, and Assyrians developed a belief in a supreme God. From Mesopotamia came stories of genesis and divine retribution that reappear in the Old Testament as versions of the fall of Adam and Eve from Paradise and of Noah and the Flood. The Flood in the Bible is similar to the version in the Babylonian text of the *Epic of Gilgamesh*, which is itself one of many versions in Hittite, Elamite, and Hurrian, all ultimately deriving from Sumerian compositions about a thousand years earlier. From Persian Zoroastrianism came many of the central elements of Christian cosmology.

Though Christianity originated in the Middle East, it migrated to Europe and became a largely European religion. Nonetheless, Christian peoples such as the Copts and the Maronite Christians have maintained a continuous presence in the Middle East since the first century A.D. Christians, Jews, and Muslims had lived in relative harmony in the region for thousands of years, in large part because of the historically tolerant nature of Islam, which sees Christians, Jews, and Muslims all as "people of the book," that is, the Bible. Thus, until the rise of Western-styled nation-states and of the concept of nationalism, religious oppression was relatively rare in the Middle East, though not unknown. Jews, Muslims, Christians, Arabs and Armenians, Kurds and Turks, all often lived in harmony in what we would now call multicultural conditions. The twentieth century's history of warfare and atrocity, between Palestinian and Jew, Persian and Arab, Turk and Armenian, is a late and lurid chapter in a history of frequent tolerance and heterogeneity.

1

Sumerian, Akkadian, and Ancient Egyptian Literatures

■

THE DEVELOPMENT OF CIVILIZATION IN SUMERIA

Mesopotamia, meaning "between rivers," refers to that section of the Middle East located between the Tigris and the Euphrates Rivers. Though the land here is dry and inhospitable today, it once was a rich and lush region, known as the "Fertile Crescent." In the Persian Gulf delta in the south of Mesopotamia, this fertility drew three peoples: the Ubaidians, a neolithic farming culture that settled the region dating to around 5000 B.C.; the Sumerians, who supplanted them and who may have come from southcentral Asia; and, later, waves of Semitic nomads from the deserts of Syria and Arabia, who merged with the Sumerians. The term *Semite* (meaning descended from Shem, one of Noah's sons) came to designate a number of peoples—Arabs, Akkadian Babylonians, Assyrians, Canaanites, Ethiopians, and Jews—whose languages derived originally, it is thought, from an ancient root language, Semitic.

In the south, the Sumerians developed an agricultural village culture, supported by an extensive fertilizing canal system. By 3000 B.C., a number of Sumerian dynasties developed around urban areas, such as Ur, Kish, and Erech. Sumerian civilization evolved into a highly developed urban culture, with massive architecture, skilled metalwork, sculpture, and pottery. The Sumerians were also advanced in mathematics and astronomy, which included estimates of the value of π (pi) and the division of the hour into sixty minutes. A number of different factors led to the urbanization of Sumerian culture and to the development of civilization. The Sumerians discovered how to use mud bricks created in forms and strengthened with reeds to build large structures. They mastered the fickle rains, snowmelts, and surrounding rivers through canals, dikes, and water conduits. This, in turn, assured regular crop yields, which supported larger populations in a small area. Agricultural surplus encouraged the exchange of goods and services and the beginnings of complex commerce, and, subsequently, the specialization of people into trades. More complex social structures developed to administer and plan flood control, the construction of large-scale projects such as complex irrigation systems, and immense architectural structures such as the gigantic terraced pyramids called ziggurats, built to appease the gods and ward off natural devastations. A complex social order developed, stratified into kings, aristocracy, priests, middle-class artisans and merchants, and slaves.

Sargon, the most famous of all Mesopotamian kings, was a Semite royal in the city of Akkad, north of Sumer, who established the Akkadian dynasty (c. 2340 B.C.) that united the many city-states of Mesopotamia into an empire for the first time. This dynasty also marked the domination of the Sumerians by the Semites. Later great Mesopotamian empires included the Babylonians and Assyrians, who owed much to the Sumerian written and religious traditions, although by the time of the first Babylonian empire, the Sumerians had all but died out. The spoken language was Akkadian, a Semitic tongue, though Sumerian language and literature survived as the formal academic language upon which the educational curriculum was built. The Babylonian empire had two incarnations, first, with King Hammurabi (c. 1792–1750 B.C.) of the city of Babylon, from c. 1800 to 1600 B.C., and later around 600 B.C. with Nebuchadnezzar's New Babylonia. Hammurabi was a great statesman and military leader but is best known for the Code of Hammurabi. The three hundred laws of this code were inscribed in thirty-six hundred lines of cuneiform around a stone column that was erected in public as a visible symbol and explanation of the law. Although it was often quite a harsh code, and although different classes were judged by different rules, it is among the most important early examples of an attempt to order social behavior according to a fixed standard.

The earliest examples of the symbolic representation that was to evolve into writing came from the Middle East as early as the ninth millennium B.C. Ancient people there used clay tokens to keep accounts, but by the fourth millennium B.C., they began drawing pictures of tokens on clay. Later, the Sumerians began depicting objects in clay pictographs (in which, for example, the symbol for fish would be a drawing of a fish). These pictographs, in turn, developed into a more complex form of writing known as cuneiform, which evolved ideographs (in which symbols stood for concepts) and also an alphabetic system that allowed for phonetic transcription of words. Cuneiform was inscribed with a stylus upon clay tablets, which were then hardened through baking or drying. It was adopted by later civilizations, such as the Babylonians, Assyrians, Hittites, Elamites, and the ancient Persian Achaemenids. By 2500 B.C., Sumerian cuneiform was so complex that writing became a profession, and the first formal schools were established to teach scribery. These became intellectual centers, where students studied literature, mathematics, linguistics, and botany. The literature of Sumeria survives in beautiful love songs, exhortations to the gods, myths, dirges, histories, proverbs, essays, fables, and most important, *The Epic of Gilgamesh,* which is among the oldest and still most impressive works of world literature. Sumerian literature is the oldest great tradition of written literature.

—Ayame Fukuda and the editors

THE DEVELOPMENT OF CIVILIZATION IN EGYPT

The largest cache of extant literature from the Asian Middle East and North Africa comes from Egypt. The powerful empire, with its large royal dominion and its gigantic pyramids constructed to glorify its man-god Pharaohs, was accompanied by an exuberance in the visual and literary arts. Its rich, complex culture was revealed through immense temples and pyramids, beautiful tomb paintings, and sculpture. In writing, conserved largely in hieroglyphic texts, are cosmologies and cosmogonies, prayers, parables and proverbs, philosophy, poetry, and fiction. By the Middle Kingdom (c. 2040–1780 B.C.), we even have compelling and sophisticated detective and ghost stories, the oldest examples in those genres.

There were some elemental factors that made the phenomenon of Egyptian civilization possible. The great civilization of ancient Egypt had its origins along the life-giving Nile, the longest river in the world. Through annual flooding, the river deposited silt from the Ethiopian highlands on the Egyptian floodplain. This natural system of irrigation and fertilization sustained civilizations in Egypt from as early as the late fourth millennium B.C. Thereafter, dynastic Egypt of the Old, Middle, and New Kingdoms was to dominate neighboring North Africa, the Eastern Mediterranean, and parts of Mesopotamia for many centuries.

The vast land of pharaonic Egypt, more than 750 miles long and containing diverse peoples with their singular cultures, was unified under a theocratic dictatorship headed by a god-king. The god-king came out of elaborate myths, with roots all over Mesopotamia, in which the gods fashioned the universe into being. Osiris and Horus, the key figures, had human counterparts in the living Pharaohs. Osiris was killed by his brother Seth and was patched and sewn together by his faithful wife Isis. Thereafter, Osiris's son Horus became the reigning king of the gods and Osiris became the Lord of the Dead. Following this division of power in the Egyptian theogony (the making of the gods) among humans on the earth, each living all-powerful Pharaoh was Horus and each dead one was Osiris.

Ancient Egypt had a unified kingdom accompanied by a spectacular literature for three thousand years. Around 3100 B.C., the kingdom was unified under the Pharaohs. The Old Kingdom, during which the great pyramids were built, is usually dated 2700 to 2200 B.C. The Middle Kingdom is usually set at 2000 to 1786 B.C., and the New Kingdom down to the last pharaonic dynasties lasted from about 1570 to 332 B.C. Egypt, which was to be the cultural bridge to early Europe, was also a bridge across which roared invaders and settlers from Western Asia and western North Africa. Invasions came from western neighbors during the Libyan dynasty, 945 to 745 B.C.; up from the south when the Nubians prevailed, 745 to 718 B.C.; and from the east as a result of wars and conquests by Assyrians and Persians from the eighth to the fourth centuries B.C.

Alexander the Great conquered Egypt in 332 B.C. Over the next thousand years, Alexandria, which Alexander founded, became successively the heart of Hellenistic culture, the Greco-Roman center of the Roman Empire, and a site for early monastic and theological Christianity. After the Greek conquest, the pharaonic culture went into precipitous decline until it effectively disappeared. The Pharaohs were replaced by Greek Ptolemaic monarchs who ruled the country. The last of the Ptolemaic rulers were Cleopatra (consort of Antony) and her son Ptolemy XIV (47–30 B.C.), whom Octavius (Emperor Caesar Augustus) put to death. Despite the formal demise of classical Egyptian civilization, its spirit survived in its influence on the Greeks and later Romans. Euclidian geometry was developed by an Alexandrian Greek, Euclid, but he based his formulation on the geometry practiced for thousands of years by master Egyptian builders. Egyptian art pervasively influenced Greek architecture and sculpture.

Alexandria became the magnificent Hellenistic city of the Mouseion, a great library-museum-university complex. Alexandrian Egypt contained a cross-section of the main currents of the classical world. In Alexandria were the learned philosophers, geometers, grammarians, and historians, as well as famous poets and sculptors. It was a syncretistic civilization that saw the merging of many cultures into a new Hellenism. So Philo of Alexandria (20 B.C.–A.D. 50?), a Jew, was the major Neoplatonist of his day, giving us the four ladders of being that were to provide a way for later Jewish, Christian, and Muslim mystical writing, and Plotinus (A.D. 205–270?), an Egyptian, was one of the great metaphysicians of antiquity. The city was also the inspired center of religions and gave us scriptures by Greeks, Jews, early Christians, and Gnostics. The Septuagint Bible was translated in the third and second centuries B.C. for the Jews of Alexandria who could no longer read Hebrew; the Septuagint remains the Bible of the Greek Orthodox and Russian Churches in Eastern Europe. The ascetic form of Christian monasticism was initiated by the hermit Saint Anthony of Egypt (A.D. 215–c. 350). Equally important theologically were the seminal mystical texts ascribed to the Egyptian god of wisdom, Thoth the Thrice Great, whose name in Greek translation was the celebrated Hermes Trismegistus. And Alexandria was also a great center of Gnosticism, the widespread religion derived from Judaism and early Christianity, which believed in gnosis (self-knowledge) rather than faith and in introspection rather than a clergy, and considered Eve, who gave us knowledge, a hero, in contrast to the Judeo-Christian tradition that condemned her as a sinner. In 1945, fifty-three Gnostic texts, translated from Greek into Coptic (the contemporary form of old Egyptian) were found in the ancient Egyptian town of Chenoboskion. These are the Nag Hammadi Gnostic scriptures, whose discovery is as significant to religious history and thought as were the Essene Dead Sea Scrolls found two years later at Qumran by the Dead Sea.

In the lands of dynastic Egypt, with their endless sun, time appears to stop. In Memphis, their city on the Nile, with its eighty pyramids that extended for a hundred miles on the horizon, it is said that the Pharaohs, who were god-king dictators, conveyed to their subjects a sense of permanence and eternity. The religion stabilized the Egyptian theocracy, lending its rulers divine authority, but placing a philosophical emphasis not on development but on repetition. This unchanging permanence was called the *ma'at*. So the Nile died and was reborn each year, as did the sun each day, and the dynasties of god-kings were also repeated for millennia. The pyramids and tombs were built to preserve the *ma'at*, the stability of the regime, but they also preseved the human soul, the *ba*, that continued to need sustenance even after death and mummification. Hence the tombs were painted with pleasant, uplifting murals and filled with all kinds of food, beer, and reading material, the latter being the source of discovered papyrus manuscripts.

The art of writing in Egypt is legendarily of divine origin. The gods recorded their creations and magical activities in small marks on stone, walls, or papyrus and bestowed on their subject priests the secret of deciphering these meaningful squiggles. So writing began. The Egyptian language was originally written in hieroglyphs, a form of picture writing deriving from some 604 essential pictures. There were also hieroglyphs used as ideograms (pictures conveying ideas) and phonograms (pictures conveying sounds, as in the owl representing the sound *m*). In the Middle Kingdom, the hieroglyphs used pictorially gave way to a cursive system called the "hieratic," and by the New Kingdom to an even quicker form called the "demotic." The hieratic and demotic use of hieroglyphs depended on the phonograms, the sound symbols, which became the Egyptian alphabet, excellent for literature and letters, and which the Phoenicians made into their influential writing system. The Egyptian cursive alphabet was adopted and changed by the Phoenicians, whose alphabet was in turn adopted and changed by the Jews into the Hebrew alphabet and by the Greeks into the Greek alphabet. From the Greek came the Roman and Cyrillic (Slav), which is to say, the alphabets of Europe. In the early dynasties, the literature, limited by the expressive problems inherent in hieroglyphic writing, was normally centered on praising the Pharaoh's accomplishments and majesty. By the Middle Kingdom, however, the hieratic cursive system allowed Egyptian writers to develop revolutionary genres and diverse forms of the short story.

The chance survival of a literary work depends on several factors, all present in Egypt: the recognized importance of the culture and the writer and the durability of the document itself. Egypt, a key to the origins of Western civilization, had the fame that led later scholars to uncover temples and tombs, to decipher difficult hieroglyphic texts (an iconic form of writing that, like the world's arithmetic ciphers, conveys sense rather than sound), and to translate them into modern languages. The writings also survived because they were famous enough in their own time to warrant being copied and recopied, an activity essential for the preservation of almost all ancient literature. As for physical survival, the texts themselves were normally inscribed on stone and papyrus (from which comes the word "paper"). Unlike later parchment, papyrus was fragile and easily destroyed by dampness. However, the Sahara Desert and especially the Fayyum region, where many Egyptian and Ancient Greek texts were uncovered, has minimal rainfall. So the earliest and most beautiful writings from the ancient Egyptian and Greek worlds were preserved in the desert-dry trash heaps of antiquity.

Our discussion of ancient Egypt also includes Greek culture, since the Greeks were in Egypt from at least the sixth century B.C. Alexandria, the city of the geometer Euclid, the Greek Septuagint Bible of Alexandrian Jews, and the philosophers Philo, Plotinus, and Hypatia, was the center of Hellenistic culture where the greatest libraries of antiquity were established. The earliest manuscripts by the classical lyric poet Sappho were found in 1879 in the Fayyum near Crocodipolis; twenty odes of the narrative poet Bacchylides and Alkman's choral ode (the prototype of Western drama) were found at Oxyrhynchos; and the works of playwright Menander were discovered in a refuse heap near Aphroditopolis.

Since only a small fragment of Egyptian literature has survived, we cannot know how many Egyptian Sapphos and Pindars might have existed. It is unlikely that Egypt had epics or drama, however, since no fragments or references survive. We do have long religious documents, notably The Book of the Dead, as well as tales, poems, hymns, prayers, and diverse didactic literature, including prophecies ("The Prophecies of Nefertiti"), admonitions ("Admonitions of an Egyptian Sage"), maxims, and teachings, as well as abundant religious and mythological writings from the Egyptian Pyramid Texts.

Since Egyptian kings were thought to be divine, the writings in the Egyptian tombs, the "house of eternity," were necessarily sacred. However, from the earliest Old Period Kingdom (third millenium B.C.), we also have private tombs of high officials and their families, and on the walls of their tombs begins Western literature. These Sixth Dynasty writings take the form of prayers to the gods and autobiographies of the tomb inhabitants to assure the immortality of their earthly image. Some apparent Old Kingdom writings are preserved in revised Middle Egyptian papyrus versions from the Middle Kingdom (c. 2135 B.C.–c. 1650 B.C.); these are the religious instruction and prophetic pieces of Prince Hardjedef, Kagemni, and Ptahhotep. It is now thought the Old Kingdom attribution is pseudepigraphic; that is, these are really Middle Kingdom pieces falsely attributed to the earlier period in order to enhance their sacred prestige. Most Old Kingdom writings are predictable prayers and formulaic catalogues of virtues. Whereas works from the Pyramid Texts and the body of didactic literature are of historical, religious, and aesthetic value, it is not until the Middle Kingdom that we have surviving examples of poetry and prose that may be considered important imaginative literature. The Egyptian stories in our possession are extraordinary, succinctly and artfully told, and, as the Egyptologist Miriam Lichtheim writes,

> these few surviving prose tales speak to the modern reader, for they are creations of the universal storytelling impulse, and of an imagination that roamed and played upon experience, unfettered by the functional orientation of most Egyptian literary works.[1]

Like most early literature, the tales are wondrous, imbued with miracle and the supernatural. At the same time, they suggest historical reality, even autobiography, a favorite Egyptian genre. In the history of the narrative, the ghost and detective stories are also first encountered in Egypt.

Egyptian love poems, in their speech, tone, and passion, seem contemporary, and particularly so when they come to us in felicitous versions by Ezra Pound and Noel Stock. Echoes of these secular love poems may, some centuries later, be recognized in the biblical Song of Songs; and it is thought that in reality Egyptian lyric was the model for the Song of Songs, which has, in turn, probably been the most influential sequence of poems in Western literature, pervading secular and mystical literature.

The few stories that have survived are a marvel. The Egyptians, three thousand years before Edgar Allan Poe, gave us fantastic literature and the well-plotted detective story of intrigue and adventure. We have only a fragment of Egypt's writings, but enough survives from three and four millennia ago—Old Kingdom religious ascension poems, Middle Kingdom short stories, and pastoral love poems—to depict a great hieroglyph of one of the world's literatures.

---

1. Miriam Lichtheim, *Ancient Egyptian Literature*, Vol. 1, *The Old and Middle Kingdoms* (Berkeley: University of California Press, 1975), 211.

■ The Pyramid Texts (2464–2355 B.C.)
Egypt (funeral poems)

TRANSLATED BY TONY BARNSTONE AND WILLIS BARNSTONE

The Pyramid Texts are religious incantations or "utterances" inscribed on the walls of sarcophagus chambers and corridors in the pyramids of Saqqara. These utterances for the resurrection and well-being of the deceased kings constitute—along with Sumerian writings—the oldest body of literature in the world. The extant Egyptian writings are the actual hieroglyphs written on the pyramid walls, whereas the Sumerian cuneiform tablets, though deriving from equally ancient writings, are themselves much later copies from the first millennium. The Pyramid Texts follow the resurrection of the king and his ascent to the sky. In the tomb, the king awakens to eternal life from the sleep of death. Then the king ascends the sky and seeks admission to the company of his fellow immortal gods. In the tradition of mystical literature, which abounds in Alexandrian Greek, Hebrew, Sufi Persian, Arabic, and later European literature, from Plato, Philo, Hermes Trismegistus, and Plotinus to Rumi in the Near East and Saint John of the Cross in the West, the sequence of enlightenment outside of earthly time, going from awakening from darkness to ascent and union, follows the stages of the Egyptian Pharaohs. The extraordinary poetry and beauty of these patches of ancient Egyptian verse are epitomized in these songs about the dead king's ascent away from the gloomy underworld existence to which common mortals are fated after death. In "The Dead King Eats the Gods," the king entering the sky becomes a god in heaven and in fact conquers the other gods, eating their hearts, entrails, and the magic that swells their bellies. He exults in his holy rampage, in the mystical feast that makes him the omnipotent deity.

FURTHER READING: Lichtheim, Miriam. *Ancient Egyptian Literature,* 1975. Simpson, William Kelly, ed. *The Ancient Egyptians,* 1966; *The Literature of Ancient Egypt,* 1972.

The Dead King Flies into Heaven

The voyaging king soars away from the common people,
abandoning the earth for the firmament.
O God of the city, he stands before you.
He thrusts against the sky like a heron,
he kisses the air like a hawk,   5
and springs into heaven like a grasshopper.

Pyramid Text 467 (c. 2180 B.C.)

The Dead King Flies into Heaven

Like a mallard the dead king flies from us.
He tears his wings from the falconer
and gyres into heaven like a loose kite.
The king is free from those who plagued him,
soaring above his enemies.   5

Pyramid Text 573

The Dead King Eats the Gods

The sky is a dark bowl, the stars die and fall.
The celestial bows quiver,
the bones of the earthgods shake and planets come
        to a halt
when they sight the king in all his power,
the god who feeds on his father and eats
        his mother.   5
The king is such a tower of wisdom
even his mother can't discern his name.
His glory is in the sky, his strength lies in
        the horizon,
like that of his father the sungod Atum who
        conceived him.
Atum conceived the king,   10
but the dead king has greater dominion.
His vital spirits surround him,
his qualities lie below his feet,
he is cloaked in gods and cobras coil on
        his forehead.[1]
His guiding snakes decorate his brow   15
and peer into souls,
ready to spit fire against his enemies.
The king's head is on his torso.
He is the bull of the sky
who charges and vanquishes all.   20
He lives on the stuff of the gods,
he feeds on their limbs and entrails,
even when they have bloated their bodies with
        magic
at Nesisi, the island of fire.

---

1. Refers to the cobra diadem of the king which had the power to burn up his enemies.

The king is prepared 25
and his spirits are assembled
and he appears as the mighty one, Lord of
    Holy Ministers.
He is seated with his back to the earthgod Geb
and he passes judgment
with the One whose name is concealed 30
on this day when the Oldest Ones are slaughtered.
He dines on sacrificial meals,
binding the victims
in preparation for the feast.
The dead king eats men and lives on gods 35
and to carry messages he has couriers:
Kehau the Grasper of Horns lassoes them like oxen,
and Serpent with the Raised Head
oversees and drives the victims,
and Master of Bloody Sacrifice binds them. 40
The moongod Khons, Racer with Knives,
strangles them for the king
and draws out their entrails.
He is the courier the king sends to hold them
    bound.
Shezmu, the winepress god, slices them up 45
and cooks a supper for the king
in his evening hearth.
He is the one who feasts on their magic
and swallows their spirit.
The great ones are for breakfast, 50
the medium-size ones are for supper
and the tiny ones are for midnight treats.
Old men and women are burnt for incense.
The mighty stars in the northern sky
ignite fires under the caldrons 55
with the thighs of their elders.
The sky-dwellers take care of him and sweep
    the hearth
with their womens' legs.
He has traveled through the two firmaments
and walked both banks of the Nile. 60
He is omnipotent
and his power over the powerful is absolute.
He is a holy icon, the holiest of all icons
    of omnipotence
and he eats as raw meat
whomever he finds on his path. 65

He stands first on the horizon among the nobility,
    a god older than the oldest.
Thousands are at his feet,
hundreds sacrifice to him.
Orion, father of the gods, assigned him his deed
    of power.
The dead king appears again in the heavens,   *70*
the crowned Lord of the Horizon.
He snapped their backbones, drained their marrow,
and tore out the hearts of the gods.
He ate the red crown worn by the King of Lower Egypt.
He swallowed the green crown of the goddess Wadjet,
    guardian of Lower Egypt.   *75*
He feeds on the Wise Ones' lungs.
He is sated with their hearts and magic.
He won't lick the foul tasting substances
    of the red crown.
He flourishes and enjoys himself with the magic
    in his belly.
His dignities are inviolate.   *80*
He has swallowed the intelligence of every god.
The dead king lives forever.
His boundary is infinite.
He does as he pleases
since he inhabits the endless horizon.   *85*
Observe how their spirits fill his stomach.
Their souls belong to him.
He cooks the leftover gods into a bone soup.
Their souls belong to him
and their shadows as well.   *90*
In his pyramid among those who live on the earth
    of Egypt,
the dead king ascends and appears
forever and forever.

                                       Pyramid Text 273–274

■ Enheduanna (born c. 2300 B.C.)
Sumer (poems)

TRANSLATED BY ALIKI BARNSTONE AND WILLIS BARNSTONE

Enheduanna was a moon priestess, the daughter of King Sargon of
Agade (2334–2279 B.C.) who reigned over the world's first empire, extending

from the Mediterranean to Persia. Sargon is the first important leader to emerge from the half-light of prehistory into the full light of a written record; words attributed to him are recorded on cuneiform tablets from the early first millennium:

> *My priestly mother conceived me; secretly brought me to birth; set me in an ark of bulrushes; made fast my door with pitch. She consigned me to the river, which did not overwhelm me. The river brought me to Akki, the farmer, who brought me up to be his son. . . . During my gardening, the goddess Ishtar loved me, and for fifty-four years the kingship was mine.*

The detailed quality of this personal account also characterizes the writing of his daughter Enheduanna, who is the first writer, male or female, whose name and work have been preserved. Her personal history survives in highly politicized poems, which in their cosmic vision and ethical outrage recall Isaiah. In her poems to the Sumerian goddess of love Inanna, she speaks to a deity who has descended to earth as an ally, as a friend to help her in her need. The poems' sensuality, surprising metaphors, and intimacy recall Sappho's poems to her ally Aphrodite. We have a stone disk that contains a detailed likeness of the high priestess, revealing her particular features and dress, flanked by three of her retainers. The poems presented here, preserved on cuneiform tablets, are from a sequence of eighteen stanzas in a single poem, "The Exaltation of Enheduanna," addressed to Inanna. In addition, we have forty-two hymns to temples whose authorship is not in question, as well as many other poems and fragments that may be hers.

Our thanks to William W. Hallo, Laffan Professor of Assyriology and Curator of the Babylonian Collection at Yale University, for his help and suggestions. The poems that follow have been adapted by Aliki and Willis Barnstone from William W. Hallo and J. J. A. van Dijk, *The Exaltation of Inanna* (New Haven: Yale University Press, 1968).

FURTHER READING: Hallo, William W., and J. J. van Dijk. *The Exaltation of Inanna,* 1968.

Inanna and the Divine Essences

> Lady of all the essences, full light,
> good woman clothed in radiance
> whom heaven and earth love,
> temple friend of An,
> you wear great ornaments,
> you desire the tiara of the high priestess
> whose hand holds the seven essences.

5

O my lady, guardian of all the great essences,
you have picked them up and hung them
on your hand. *10*
You have gathered the holy essences and worn them
tightly on your breasts.

Inanna and An

Like a dragon you have filled the land
with venom.
Like thunder when you roar over the earth,
trees and plants fall before you.
You are a flood descending from a mountain, *5*
O primary one,
moon goddess Inanna of heaven and earth!
Your fire blows about and drops on our nation.
Lady mounted on a beast,
An gives you qualities, holy commands, *10*
and you decide.
You are in all our great rites.
Who can understand you?

Inanna and Enlil

Storms lend you wings, destroyer of the lands.
Loved by Enlil, you fly over our nation.
You serve the decrees of An.
O my lady, on hearing your sound,
hills and flatlands bow. *5*
When we come before you,
terrified, shuddering in your stormy clear light,
we receive justice.
We sing, mourn, and cry before you
and walk toward you along a path *10*
from the house of enormous sighs.

Inanna and Ishkur

You strike everything down in battle.
O my lady, on your wings
you hack away the land and charge disguised

as a charging storm,
roar as a roaring storm,   *5*
thunder and keep thundering, and snort
with evil winds.
Your feet are filled with restlessness.

On your harp of sighs
I hear your dirge.   *10*

Inanna and the City of Uruk

You have spoken your holy command over the city
which has not declared:
"This land is yours,"
which has not declared:
"It is your father's and his father's,"   *5*
and you have blocked its path to you,
you have lifted your foot and left
their barn of fertility.
The women of the city no longer speak of love
with their husbands.   *10*
At night they do not make love.
They are no longer naked before them,
revealing intimate treasures.
Great daughter of Suen,
impetuous wild cow, supreme lady commanding An,   *15*
who dares not worship you?

Banishment from Ur

You asked me to enter the holy cloister,
the *giparu*,
and I went inside, I the high priestess
Enheduanna!
I carried the ritual basket and sang   *5*
your praise.
Now I am banished among the lepers.
Even I cannot live with you.
Shadows approach the light of day, the light
is darkened around me,   *10*
shadows approach the daylight,

covering the day with sandstorm.
My soft mouth of honey is suddenly confused.
My beautiful face is dust.

Appeal to the Moongod Nanna-Suen to Throw Out Lugalanne, the New Conqueror of the City of Uruk

O Suen, the usurper Lugalanne means nothing to me!
Tell An: "Have An release me!"
If you will only tell An
"NOW!"
and An will release me.   5
This woman Inanna will carry off this young cock
Lugalanne.
Mountain and flood lie at her feet.
This woman is powerful as he.
She'll make the city expel him.   10
Surely she will forget her rage against me.
Let me, Enheduanna, pray to her.
Like sweet drink let me cry freely for holy
Inanna!
Let me call to her!   15

The Restoration of Enheduanna to Her Former Station

The first lady of the throne room
has accepted Enheduanna's song.
Inanna loves her again.
The day was good for Enheduanna, for she was dressed
in jewels.   5
She was dressed in womanly beauty.
Like the moon's first rays over the horizon,
how luxuriously she was dressed!
When Nanna, Inanna's father,
made his entrance   10
the palace blessed Inanna's mother Ningal.
From the doorsill of heaven came the word:
"Welcome!"

▪ *from* The Epic of Gilgamesh (c. 2000 B.C.)

TRANSLATED BY PIERRE GRANGE AND EMMA VARESIO

The Epic of Gilgamesh is the oldest known literary epic. The actual Gilgamesh was a king of Uruk (Erech in the Bible), a city-state in what is now southern Iraq. He probably lived in the twenty-seventh century B.C., and, though little evidence remains, later traditions describe him as a great warrior and the builder of Uruk's great walls. The Sumerians, and later the Assyrians and Babylonians, worshiped Gilgamesh as a god for more than two thousand years after his death; he was a god of the underworld, or its king, and figures of him were utilized in burial rituals. The epic itself derives from Sumerian compositions that were later adapted and transformed into a Babylonian work in the second millennium, and versions proliferated throughout the Middle East in Elamite, Hittite, and Hurrian. The epic took on what is now considered its standard form around the thirteenth century B.C.—eleven tablets with a twelfth appended, a work of approximately three thousand lines—but the text in which it is most complete dates from the seventh century B.C., was written in Babylonian in cuneiform script, and was discovered among the ruins of Nineveh. Though it is the oldest epic, it depicts concerns that are so universal that it will always be contemporary. It is the story of how the gods create Enkidu, "the hairy-bodied wild man of the grasslands" to be a companion to the young king Gilgamesh and to keep him from oppressing the people. Though they fight at first, they become deep friends and together kill the demon Huwawa. Then the goddess Ishtar falls in love with Gilgamesh and wants him to be her husband, but he rejects her, and she goes to her father, Anu, asking him to send the Bull of Heaven to punish Gilgamesh. Together, Gilgamesh and Enkidu kill the bull, but the gods curse them for this, causing Enkidu to sicken and die. Gilgamesh mourns for his friend and is confronted with his own mortality. He sets out to find Utnapishtim (source for the biblical Noah), who has survived the flood, seeking the secret of immortality. This quest is the burden of the first eleven tablets; the twelfth tablet recounts a similar tale in which Gilgamesh grieves over Enkidu, who dies trying to retrieve Gilgamesh's drum and drumstick, which fell through a hole into the underworld. Through the intervention of the god Ea, Gilgamesh is able to speak with Enkidu's spirit and question him about life in the underworld. In both stories, Gilgamesh, confronted with his own mortality, seeks answers to basic human questions: Why must I die? What happens after death? Can death be avoided?

FURTHER READING: Gardner, John, and John Maier, trs. *Gilgamesh,* 1985. Kovacs, Maureen Gallery, tr. *The Epic of Gilgamesh,* 1989. Pritchard, J. B., ed. *Ancient Near Eastern Texts Relating to the New Testament,* 1969. Sandars, N. K., tr. *The Epic of Gilgamesh,* 1972.

Tablet VI

I. ISHTAR PROPOSITIONS GILGAMESH

After Gilgamesh and Enkidu cut
off Huwawa's head they returned to Uruk[1]
and Gilgamesh cleaned his blade there,
washed out his long, matted hair,
then shook out the locks that hung down his back.   *5*
He pulled his soiled clothes over his neck
and dressed himself in a fresh
royal cloak that he fastened with a sash.
When Gilgamesh put the crown on his hair
the goddess Ishtar[2] raised her eyes   *10*
and stared at the beauty of his fresh
limbs and sang "Come here, Gilgamesh,
be my lover, let me taste your fruit.
Be my husband and I'll be your wife,
and give you a chariot of lapis lazuli and gold   *15*
with golden wheels and amber horns
pulled not by mules but by storm demons.
When you enter our house it will smell like cedar
and the floor and dais will kiss your feet,
and kings, lords and princes will bow before you   *20*
and offer the yield of mountains and fields in tribute.
Your goats will bear triplets, your ewes will twin,
and even loaded down your donkey will run
faster than a mule; no horse will outrun your chariot steeds
and your oxen in the yoke will run as if free."   *25*
Gilgamesh answered the goddess Ishtar,
"If I take you in marriage, what could I pay
in dowry? Should I give you body oil or clothes?
Should I give you food or drink when I know
you eat the food of gods and drink the wine of kings   *30*
and are dressed in heavenly clothing?
Can a man lust for a goddess for whom they sacrifice?
You are an oven frozen over with ice.
You are the back door that lets in the wind.
You are the palace whose roof caves in,   *35*
the elephant who shakes off its carpet,
the pitch that sticks the hand to the bucket,

---

1. The ancient Sumerian city of which Gilgamesh was king.

2. Ishtar was the Akkadian goddess of love and war, the daughter of the sky god Anu. Her Sumerian name was Inanna.

the waterskin that leaks on its owner
getting him wet all over.
You are the limestone crumbling   40
in a stone wall until it tumbles.
You are a battering ram that breaks
when the army is in an enemy state.
You are the shoe that bites the foot.
What happened to your other lovers   45
whom you said you'd love forever?
What happened to the shepherd bird?
Should I tell you where they are?
Your first lover, Tammuz, was slain
and each year they wail for him in the festival.[3]   50
You loved the many-colored shepherd bird
yet struck him and broke his wing
so now in the forest he cries 'My wing, my wing!'
You loved the lion for his pure strength
yet dug for him seven and seven pits.   55
You loved the mighty battle stallion
yet decreed from him the whip, the spur and the halter.
You made him run seven and seven hours,
made him drink water muddied by his own hooves,
causing his mother Silili to weep.   60
You loved the shepherd of the herd,
who always brought you cakes
and slaughtered kids for you,
but then you struck him and turned him into a wolf
and so his own herd boys chase him   65
and his own dogs nip at his shins.
You also loved Ishullanu, your father's gardener,
who brought you clusters of dates
so that your table overflowed.
You raised your eyes to him and came close,   70
saying 'O Ishullanu, let me taste your strength,
put your hand here upon my vulva.'
Ishullanu replied, 'What do you want from me?
Doesn't my mother cook, haven't I eaten?
Why should I taste your evil, cursed bread?   75
When it's cold, should I cover myself only in rushes?'
When you heard these words
you struck him and turned him into a frog

---

3. Ishtar's lover Tammuz is a nature god who dies each winter and comes to life again each spring. During the yearly festival in his honor his worshippers would wail in lamentation for the dying god.

who lives in the garden
unable to leap or to burrow. _80_
Now you say you love me,
but you would treat me just like them."

II. ISHTAR'S RAGE

When Ishtar heard this
she flew to heaven in a rage
and went before her father, the Sky God Anu[4]
and her mother Antum, wailing,
"Gilgamesh has insulted me, _5_
revealing all my despicable deeds,
my evil actions and curses."
Anu said to the glorious Ishtar,
"You have called this upon yourself,
and Gilgamesh has merely recounted _10_
your foulness and the curse
of your evil actions."
But Ishtar told her father Anu,
"Father, create for me the Bull of Heaven
to kill Gilgamesh in his home. _15_
Give me the Bull of Heaven
or I will smash the gates of the underworld
and fling them wide open
so that the dead may rise and eat the living
until there are more dead than living!" _20_
Then Anu spoke to glorious Ishtar,
"If I do what you wish
there will be seven years of empty husks
at harvest time in the lands of Uruk.
Have you gathered enough grain for the people _25_
and grown enough grass for the cattle?"
Ishtar spoke to her father again,
saying "I have gathered enough grain
and I have grown enough grass"[5]
Anu listened to Ishtar's plea _30_
and created the Bull of Heaven for her
and she loosed it upon the city of Uruk.

With its first great snort the Bull of Heaven
caused the river Euphrates to shake
and caused a vast pit to open into which _35_

---

4. Anu is the sky god and is called Father of the Gods.

5. The text is fragmentary here, but it seems that Ishtar convinces Anu to give her the Bull of Heaven.

a hundred young men of Uruk fell and died.
With his second snort he killed two hundred,
and with his third snort a huge pit yawned open
before Enkidu, but Enkidu leapt up
and seized the Bull of Heaven by his horns.   40
As they wrestled, the Bull of Heaven spewed foam
from his mouth and flung dung from his tail,
and Enkidu called to Gilgamesh,
"Friend, we have boasted of our strength
but can we slay this beast?   45
We must find strength to destroy it
with a sword thrust between the neck and horns."
Enkidu rushed at the Bull of Heaven
and grabbed the beast by the thick of his tail.
Then Gilgamesh approached with confidence   50
and with the precision of a butcher
thrust his sword between the neck and horns.
After killing the Bull of Heaven, they tore out its heart
placed it before the Sun God, Shamash,
and withdrew, bowing to Shamash.   55
Then like two brothers they sat down to rest.

Ishtar ascended to the top of Uruk's palisade
and in a posture of mourning uttered this curse:
"Curse Gilgamesh, who has slandered me and killed the Bull of
        Heaven!"
When Enkidu heard these words,   60
he tore off the Bull's thigh and tossed it in her face, saying,
"If I could reach you, I'd do the same to you,
and tie your arms with his entrails!"
Ishtar summoned her curly-haired priestesses,
the harlots and temple prostitutes,   65
and mourned with them over the Bull's thigh.

Gilgamesh called together the craftsmen and artisans,
who all admired the size of the horns,
each containing thirty pounds of lapis lazuli,
with hard casing two inches thick   70
and six barrels worth of oil inside
that he gave as a balm to his god Lugalbanda.
He hung the horns in the shrine of his ancestors.
The heroes washed their hands in the River Euphrates,
then clasped arms and rode through the streets of Uruk   75
As the people gathered around to see them
Gilgamesh spoke to the assembled men and women,
"Who is the bravest of men, the most valiant of men?
Gilgamesh is the bravest of men, the most valiant of men."

Then Gilgamesh gave a great feast in the palace   *80*
and the two heroes lay on the divans and slept.
Enkidu lay down to sleep and was troubled with dream
and when he awoke he told Gilgamesh his dream:
"Why are the great gods meeting in council?"

Tablet VII

I. ENKIDU'S DREAM OF THE COUNCIL OF THE GODS

As daylight first gleamed through the house
Enkidu turned to Gilgamesh,
murmuring, "Such a strange dream I had
last night! Anu, Enlil, and Shamash had gathered.[6]
Anu spoke to Enlil of how we killed   *5*
the Bull of Heaven and Huwawa. One of us
should die, he said, whichever one had cut
the cedar from the mountainside.
Then Enlil's voice rose, saying, 'Enkidu must die,
but not Gilgamesh!' Shamash challenged Enlil, saying, 'But I   *10*
commanded both of these companions
to enter that forest, to do my errand.
Why should this innocent companion to Gilgamesh
die?' Enlil's rage flared, as he angrily told Shamash,
'Daily you journeyed with them,   *15*
you were like their companion.'"

II. ENKIDU'S ILLNESS

Enkidu fell ill, lying in tears before his friend.
Gilgamesh murmured, "How could the gods lend
me forgiveness yet deny
my brother? Why should he die,
leaving me alive to mourn?"   *5*
Enkidu asked, "Will I soon only sit with spirits and ghosts,
far from the sight of my brother?"
Gilgamesh whispered, "Can I only sit just beyond
those dim shadows which press
outside the House of the Dead,   *10*
while Enkidu moves inside that place?"

---

6. Anu is the sky god, the father of the gods; Enlil is the god of the earth and the air; Shamash is the sun god.

VI. ENKIDU'S DREAM OF THE UNDERWORLD

Enkidu drifted through layers of hazy
half-sleep, his fists clenched, his stomach queasy.
At dawn he turned to Gilgamesh,
relating his dream. "Last night the cloudless
sky was broken by a low moan.   5
The earth howled its frenzied response, and I stood alone
between them. A figure rose before me,
a towering, darkened body,
formed from a lion's head and paws,
and an eagle's talons reaching to claw   10
my loose hair. I beat him, struggled with him,
but his body overpowered mine.
As he grasped me, I called to you,
Gilgamesh, but you were too
frightened, watching this man trample me.   15
But then he transformed my body,
and my arms grew feathered and as graceful as a bird's.
He clutched one of my wings and led me down
to Irkalla's[7] palace, the House of Shades.
Those who enter that place never return.   20
They walk down a road but never return.
They sit huddled in darkness, hidden from all light,
eating clay and mud, swallowing dust and dirt.
Like birds they cover their limbs with feathered clothes
and layers of dust settle on the door's thick bolt.   25
Scattered heaps of crowns clutter the floor:
dead kings who ruled the earth before
hover in the doorways, transformed,
waiting only to serve steaks brimming with red juice
and cool pure water to Enlil and Anu.   30
I entered the House of Ash
where I saw the high priest and the wailer,
the purification priest and the dervish,
and the priest of the Great Gods.
Etana[8] and Sumuquan[9] were there, and   35
so was Ereshkigal, Queen of the Underworld.
Belit-Seri, the Underworld's scribe,
knelt before her, reading aloud from her writing tablet
where everyone's fate is inscribed

---

7. Irkalla is also known as Ereshkigal, queen of the underworld.

8. This king, seeking a magic plant of fertility for his barren wife, was carried into the heavens by an eagle but he fell back down to earth.

9. The god of cattle.

Ereshkigal lifted her head, looked me in the eyes
and asked, 'Who has brought this man here?'"

40

V. THE DEATH OF ENKIDU

"Your dream is terrifying," Gilgamesh replied.
Curled on his bed Enkidu lay
growing ever more ill day after day.
On the twelfth day, he struggled to lift his head,
calling to Gilgamesh, "Friend, the gods are angry.
I am cursed, not even able
to die gracefully in battle."
Then Gilgamesh heard the death rattle
and he moaned for his friend like a dove.

5

Tablet IX

I. GILGAMESH'S GRIEF AND FEAR OF DEATH

Gilgamesh grieved Enkidu's death, roaming
through hills and desert plains, weeping and saying,
"Just as Enkidu died, I will die.
I feel sorrow and fear in my chest
and I am frightened of death."
So Gilgamesh set out for the far wilderness
desperately seeking Utnapishtim,
the son of Ubartutu, the only one
who might know how death could be avoided.

5

II. THE MOUNTAIN PASS

At night, slipping through the mountain passes,
Lions frightened Gilgamesh.
Lifting his eyes toward the moon,
he prayed to the moon god, Sin:
"Please protect me."

5

IV. THE GARDEN OF JEWELS

Gilgamesh emerged from the mountain trails once
the sun rose. He headed toward a garden of gem-encrusted stones,
and towering, fleshy bushes,
where vines bloomed with lapus-lazuli leaves,
and emerald trees spilled
ruby blossoms. Beyond the garden, the ocean sparkled like emeralds.

5

Tablet X

III. CROSSING THE WATERS OF DEATH

Gilgamesh lifted off the clothes that hung
close to his body, tethering
them to the mast,
so his boat could sail upon the waters.

IV. UTNAPISHTIM SEES GILGAMESH APPROACHING

Utnapishtim stood on the distant
shore, gazing at the hazy shape of the boat as it
slid across the waters of death.
He murmured to himself,
"Why have the stone images broken?   5
And why is Urshanabi not navigating the boat? I strain
my eyes, unable to see
who sails here toward me."

V. THEIR CONVERSATION

Urshanabi the ferryman asked Gilgamesh, "Why is
your face so sunken and weathered, your eyelids
smeared with shadows, your cheeks rough, haggard
and starved? Why are your clothes in tatters?
You look as if you've traveled for ages, hungry and lost,   5
seared by the sun and burned by frost.
Why are you mourning?
Why do you come here, searching?"

Gilgamesh asked Urshanabi, "Shouldn't I look haggard?
I am starved and lost, and battered   10
even more by an endless sadness.
I wandered in the wilderness
seared by ice and burned by the sun,
grieving for Enkidu, my brother, my soulmate, the one
who slew the panther in the wilderness   15
and in the mountains chased the wild ass.
Together we climbed the mountain
and fought and killed the Bull of Heaven.
We slew the demon Huwawa of the Cedar Forest,
and killed lions in the mountain passes.   20
My companion, the one whom I love beyond all
is dead. I could not leave his dead body, even for its burial.
But then maggots fell out of his nose,

and I grew horrified at his molding skin.
This is why I roam through the wilderness.   25
Enkidu is nothing but clay and dust,
and now I fear my own inevitable death.
Won't I be just like him? Lying pressed
against the mud, never rising? So I sought
Utnapishtim, the remote sage.   30
I traveled, hunting and skinning the bears, stags,
ibex, hyenas, and lions. I wrapped their skins around
my cold body, ate their flesh. The tavern keeper
slammed her door in my face, and I lay huddled
shivering in the dirt, the icy night air keeping me awake."   35

Urshanabi said to Gilgamesh:
"You have been created from the flesh
of the gods, and the flesh of humans,
born of a goddess and a man.
But is a house built so that it will never crumble?   40
Is a contract obeyed forever?
Do brothers always share their inheritance willingly?
Does hostility last forever? Does jealousy?
No: there is no permanence.
Rivers rise and flood, clogging the soil with rushing dampness.   45
Insects are shed from warm cocoons, only to flutter for a moment.
And how long can any person gaze at the sun?
No, there has never been any permanence.
How similar the sleeping and the dead appear:
the servant and the ruler's bodies reveal the same picture   50
when they are both dead.
Once the Anunaki,[10] the great assembly of gods,
gathered together. Mammetum, the Mother goddess,
the weaver of destinies, came with them. The Anunaki established
that life and death should be created.   55
Then they set the days of death, but keep these times hidden."

Tablet XI

I. UTNAPISHTIM RELATES HOW EA WARNED HIM
OF THE FLOOD

Utnapishtim turned to Gilgamesh, saying,
"I will uncover for you a secret hidden
by the gods. The city of Shurippak,[11] nestled

---

10. The Anunaki are the gods of destiny, the sons of the god Anu.
11. Modern day Fara.

on the banks of the Euphrates—
a place of which you have surely heard—   5
it had grown old, and full of the spirits of the gods.
The gods decided to unleash a flood
upon the city. They all gathered: Anu, their father;
Enlil, their counselor; Ninurta, the god of war;
Ennugi,[12] guardian of the canals; and,   10
clear-eyed Ea, the clever one.[13]
Ea's voice whispered through the thin reed walls of my room,
'You, reed hut, reed walls! Listen, pay attention:
Utnapishtim, tear down the walls of your house and build
a boat! Abandon your home, spurn wealth and   15
possessions, disregard evrything except for life! You must
bring a seed from each living being onto your boat,
safely past the threat of the approaching flood.
Construct your ship with careful precision:
Let length and width be equal to each other,   20
and let a roof shield it just as the deep abyss is covered.'
I leaned toward the reed walls, murmuring, 'I hear you,
I will honor you, but how should I respond to
the city, the people, the Elders?' And
Ea parted his mouth, whispering to me, his servant: 25
'You will tell them that Enlil's hateful wrath has consumed you.
Because of his spite for you, you cannot live in the city, you
cannot even set foot on his land.
Say you must find another god to protect
you, and that you will seek Ea in his abyss. And in Shurippak,   30
once dawn shimmers on the horizon, abundance
will rain down upon them: a flood of the harvest,
wild birds falling, rare fish tumbling from
the clouds, showers of glinting wheat-grains
and baked loaves hitting the surface   35
of the earth. Such copious torrents of all
these things—this you will tell the city and its people.'

II. UTNAPISHTIM BUILDS THE ARK

"As glimmers of dawn first appeared
all the people gathered to watch me build
my vessel. Children carried tar and gravel,
as other workers brought timber and whatever else I wished.
I sketched plans: six decks,   5
and each wall measuring one hundred and twenty cubits.

---

12. God of irrigation.

13. Ea is the god of the waters and of wisdom, patron of humanity.

We pieced each section together, hammered
the beams, and drove plugs into its frame to stop the flow of water.
I poured tar into the furnace, and spread
it to caulk the hull and the inner layer. I put oars on board,   *10*
and after all this I slaughtered bulls and sheep for the workmen.
We poured endless glasses of rich red and white wine,
beer, dark ales, a river of drinks. At sunset
on the seventh day, with the boat completed,
I spread fragrant lotions and oils on my hands.   *15*
I loaded everything I owned into it: silver, gold,
the wild animals in my fields. I brought my family,
gathered the workmen and their children with me,
and I took a seed of each living thing.
The launching faltered; we shifted our weight   *20*
and prodded everything into place, the boat groaning.
Two-thirds of it sank, submerged by the river.
We maneuvered it carefully to keep it from capsizing.
In the evening I heard Shamash saying:
'Soon it will shower abundance—   *25*
Come inside your ship, seal the hatches!'
So I moved inside, latching the gates against the downfall,
and let Puzumurri, the caulker,
have my worldly goods and palace."

III. **THE FLOOD**

"With the earliest glints of dawn
came a roiling dark cloud
with Adad, the storm god, roaring within.
Devastation and submission rode the wind
over mountains and grasslands.   *5*
Nergal, god of the underworld,
lifted the dams in his realm, and
Ninurta, god of war and chaos, broke down the dikes
so the floods could rush forth.
The Anunaki lifted their blazing torches,   *10*
but Adad's rage swept through the heavens,
turning the flaming light back into chilly dusk.
Adad smashed the vast land like a clay pot
and the streaming tempest raged like war
through the broken city.   *15*
Torrents of wind flew past the mountainsides,
and no man could see another
through the sheets of water.
The gods shrank, sobbing,
and retreated to the highest heavens.   *20*

They curled against Anu's walls,
huddled like dogs and shivering helplessly.

Glorious Ishtar's sweet voice howled
as though she were giving birth:
'Days have disintegrated into clay and dust.   25
Because of my evil demands from the gods,
I brought destruction and catastrophe to my people!
I gave birth to them and they are in the waters
like the spawn of fish!'
The Anunaki humbly bowed their heads   30
and wept with the Goddess.
The winds shrieked with the fury of childbirth,
and for six days and seven nights,
torrents of water flooded the land.
On the seventh day, the flood ceased,   35
the throbbing storm shuddered and calmed
like an army after battle,
everything becoming suddenly still.
I lifted the hatch, and sunlight fell on me.
Nothing moved on the silent sea.   40
It was flat as a clay roof
and all mankind had turned to clay.
I fell on my knees, and wept. All through the day,
I crouched and wept in the vast silence,
frantically scouring the stretch of waters   45
for some thing. And finally I glimpsed the dim
outline of an island beneath the water.
It was the peak of Mount Nisir
and my boat was grounded there
on its rocky surface. The ark   50
held its place for one day, two,
on Mount Nisir, three days, four,
for seven days, motionless."

IV. THE SECRET OF IMMORTALITY

"On the seventh day I sent forth a dove, but
she returned, finding no place to perch.
I freed a swallow, but she also found no perch
to rest upon, and came back to the ark.
I sent a raven aloft, who saw the sea receding.   5
I glimpsed her soaring, clawing the air, gliding
in perfect circles. But she never came back.
So I released all the birds from my boat,
and they scattered in all directions,
rising up through the wind.   10

I stepped on the shore, setting seven upon seven
vessels over a fire of myrtle, cane,
and savory cedar. I offered incense as sacrifice,
and the gods drew close to all this fragrance,
hovering around my altar like flies.   *15*

*   *   *

Enlil approached, spotting my ship,
and his body shook with the rage of gods.
'How could any mortal escape this deluge?
No living being should have survived that annihilation!'
Ninurta's lips parted, and he told Enlil,   *20*
'Who could create anything without Ea? Only
Ea, the cleverest god, understands such crafty plots.'
Ea replied, 'Valiant Enlil, how could you unleash this
flood without reflecting upon its effects?
Charge the transgression to the transgressor,   *25*
punish only those who offend!
Show compassion, never ravaging the lands indiscriminately.

*   *   *

Ea continued, 'I did not reveal the glorious gods' secret.
Utnapishtim glimpsed the truth in a dream vision.
How shall the gods respond to such wisdom?'   *30*
Then Enlil stepped inside the ark.
He grasped my hand, and made me kneel.
He twined his fingers into my wife's hand, leading her to kneel
beside me. He stood between us, pressing
our foreheads together and saying,   *35*
'You and your wife, once mere humans are now
transformed into gods. You will dwell at the mouth
of all rivers, the source brimming with liquid
for all the streams of the world.'"

Then Utnapishtim asked Gilgamesh,   *40*
"Now, who would assemble the glorious gods for you
so that you could also gather everlasting youth?"

*   *   *

Utnapishtim's wife asked him, "Gilgamesh is so weary,
his clothes tattered and his hair matted. What will you
give him so he can return to his city with honor?"   *45*
Gilgamesh overheard them as he rowed home,
and steered his boat back toward the shore.
Utnapishtim told him, "Gilgamesh, after your
exhausting journey, what should I give you?
Let me uncover a mystery of the gods for you: *50*
there is an underwater plant, with deep roots

spreading through the mud; its spikes and brambles wait
to prick your hands, the thorns will make
blood spring from your fingers
as when you seize it like a rose. Plunge into the waters,   *55*
and pull up the plant: it will give you everlasting life."
So Gilgamesh bound heavy stones to his feet,
while opening the sluicegates so the current
could pull him toward the deepest waters.
His hand encircled the plant, its thorns slicing his palms   *60*
and cutting the heavy stones from around his ankles.
Then the tide spilt him back upon the shore.

VII. Gilgamesh Speaks to the Ferryman

Gilgamesh told the ferryman, Urshanabi,
"This marvelous plant holds eternal life!
I will bring it back to Uruk, to the elders, to every person
in my city! I will tell them its name:
'The Aged-Man-Becomes-Young-Once-More.'   *5*
I will place part of it on my own tongue, for
swallowing it will spread virility and youth through my body,
keeping death far removed from me."

VIII. The Serpent by the Pool

Gilgamesh and Urshanabi traveled
twenty leagues, then broke their fast.
Ten leagues past this they stopped to rest.
Gilgamesh glimpsed a spring of fresh
lucid water and descended into the cool pond   *5*
to rouse his tired body, holding the magical plant
close to him. But a serpent danced
towards him through the flickering reeds,
breathing the flower's tempting fragrance,
and snatched the thorny plant,   *10*
shedding its rough skin as it rustled quickly away.

Gilgamesh realized what the serpent had done,
and wept. He grasped Urshanabi's hand, tears flowing down
his cheeks, choking, 'What should I do? I traveled through
the wilds, spilling my own blood,   *15*
destroying my own body, for what? For whom?
I have gained nothing. The serpent,

lion of the soil, stole the plant
from me, and dropped it into the rushing tides.
It must be twenty leagues distant already!   *20*
This is a sign telling me: abandon your search,
leave your empty boat on the shore."

■ Adapa: The Man (Second Millennium B.C.) *Babylonia* (myth)

TRANSLATED BY N. K. SANDARS

The name [Adapa] is not "a man" but "man," it is Adam; but the story of this Adam is of fooling and paradox. Unlike Utnapishtim, the Babylonian Noah who won eternal life for himself through obedience to a god, in Adapa, humankind was given the chance of eternal life and lost it through obedience to a god. The scene of the beginning is Eridu, in southern Mesopotamia. One of the oldest Sumerian cities, it stood on the edge of a great lagoon near the Persian Gulf and was sacred to Ea, the Sumerian Enki. The father of the gods, Anu, is still in this story the supreme authority in heaven. Of the two lesser gods, Tammuz and Gizzida, who stand at the East Gate of heaven, Tammuz has descended from Dumuzi, and Gizzida was a god of healing sometimes also connected with the Underworld. Gizzida was called Lord of the Tree of Truth, as Dumuzi—Tammuz was Lord of the Tree of Life—trees that were stars planted in heaven. Besides Anu's messenger or minister and the South Wind, these are the only protagonists.

The text is put together from three fragments; the oldest and longest was found in Egypt among the fourteenth-century archives, mostly diplomatic correspondence, of Tell el Amarna. The two shorter fragments were in Ashurbanipal's library at Nineveh. The el Amarna text has no metrical form, it is (presumably) prose; and the story (the sting in the tail notwithstanding) is nearest to a morality or *conte.* The morality cuts more than one way, and it is worth noticing that for one split second, before his ignominious return to earth, Adapa is allowed the vision of heaven. Though every kind of trouble lies ahead, this is something that belongs to Adapa; the vision cannot be taken away from man.

—N. K. Sandars

FURTHER READING: Sandars, N. K. *Poems of Heaven and Hell from Ancient Mesopotamia,* 1971.

In those days, in those years long ago at Eridu, the city which stands on a sweet lagoon, there was a man. He was wise like one of the gods. When he gave an order it was as though Ea,[1] the master himself, that subtle god, had spoken; for Ea is the master of subtlety, and he also controls the waters. Ea had made him a leader, a man to be followed. He gave him sagacity and intelligence enough to comprehend the design of the world: but he made him a dying man.

In those days, in those years, he was man's first pattern, scrupulous in his service to the temple, one with clean hands; the sage of Eridu was accounted wise even among the Great Gods. No one questioned his orders. Daily he stocked up the city with bread and drinking water, baking bread with the bakers of Eridu, steering the ship that fished for Eridu, going through the ritual with clean hands. Only *he* could set and clear the god's table.

In those days, while Ea lay at ease on his bed and this man Adapa was busy in the sanctuary, the household had need of fresh stores of fish. So Adapa boarded the sailing boat at the quay-side, the one which is sacred to the New Moon. It blew a following wind and he let the boat run before the gale. He steered with the oar, sailing out into the wide sea alone.

In the middle of the sea Adapa went about catching fish; the sea was calm as a mirror. Then the South Wind got up; it capsized him, and he plunged down into the world of fish. In his desperate anger Adapa yelled out a curse,

'South Wind, you rose out of malice, I will break your wing,' and as he spoke the wing of the South Wind shattered, and for seven days it did not blow on to the land at all.

Anu,[2] the god who reigns in heaven, called out to his servant Ilabrat,

'Why has the South Wind not blown on to the land for seven days?' Ilabrat answered,

'My Lord, the man, Ea's son, has shattered the wing of the South Wind in his arrogant fashion.'

When he heard this Anu got up angrily from his throne. He sent his messenger to Ea, because he is wise and knows the gods well. They spoke together, and Anu shouted,

'Fetch the man here!'

Ea gave the man a warning, for he knew the ways of heaven. He told him to go in rags and in mourning with his hair uncut and hanging loose.

'You must go up the road to the top of heaven and appear before Anu, the king. When you have reached the gate of heaven you will see two gods, Tammuz and Gizzida,[3] who stand there together. They will ask,

"Man, for whose sake do you look like this?"

---

1. Ea (the Sumerian Enki) is the god of sweet waters and wisdom, patron of the arts, one of the creators of mankind to whom he was generally kindly disposed, and the chief god of Eridu [Editor].

2. Anu (Sumerian An) is heaven, the sky and the god of the skies, the father of Ea [Editor].

3. Tammuz is the semitic name for Dumuzi. Gizzida, also Ningizzida, is "Lord of the Tree of Life," a god of fertility and healing, also connected with the underworld [Editor].

'Answer,
"Two gods have left our land, I mourn for them."
"What gods are they?"
"I mourn for Tammuz and Gizzida."
'Then they will smile at each other and say kind words to Anu; they will show you his *gracious* face. When you are standing in front of Anu they will offer the bread of death; do not eat it. They will offer the water of death; do not drink it. They will bring a garment; put on the garment; and when they bring oil anoint yourself. Take care that you do not forget this advice. Remember!'

The messenger from Anu came for the man. He led him up the road of the firmament; he approached the East Gate of heaven. Tammuz and Gizzida stood at the gate; when they saw him they said,

'Heavens, Man! Why do you look like this? Whom are you mourning?'
'Two gods have left our land, I mourn for them.'
'What gods are they?'
'Tammuz and Gizzida, I mourn for them.'

They exchanged glances and smiled. Adapa approached the lord of heaven. Anu looked at him and said,

'You, Man, why did you break the wing of the South Wind?' The man answered,

'My lord, I was catching fish in the middle of the sea for the household of my master, Ea. The sea was a mirror but the South Wind got up, he capsized me and I plunged down to the world of fish, and in the anger of my heart I cursed him.'

Then Tammuz and Gizzida, standing beside him, spoke kind words. They soothed the heart of the king of heaven so that he said, speaking to them,

'What was Ea about to give knowledge of all nature to a wretch of a man, to make him like one of us, and with such a name for wisdom? But now that he is what else can we do? Fetch the bread of life and he shall eat it.'

When they brought him the bread of life he would not eat. When they brought him the water of life he did not drink it. When they brought him a garment he put it on; and when they brought oil he anointed himself.

Then Anu, the lord of heaven, looked at the man and laughed,

'Ah, Adapa, why did you neither eat nor drink, stupid man; perverse mankind; you will never now have eternal life.'

'My master Ea ordered me, "You shall not eat, you shall not drink,"'

Loudly Anu laughed again at the doings of Ea,

'Of all the gods of heaven and of earth, as many as there may be, whoever gave such an order! Who can circumvent the will of Anu?'

Then the man looked from the horizon of heaven to the meridian; he saw the majesty of heaven, and Anu gave the man his orders and he gave to the priests of Eridu the rule of their lives. But as for him, the man child of man, who broke the wing of the South Wind in his arrogant fashion, who went up to heaven—he brought on us the sufferings of mankind. He brought disease to our bodies that only the Lady of Healing can assuage.

May sickness depart. May there be no more disease; but as for him, let him not lie down in gentle sleep again, nor feel the happiness that men know in their hearts.

■ The Shipwrecked Sailor (c. 2040–1650 B.C.) *Egypt* (story)

TRANSLATED BY EDWARD F. WENTE, JR.

"The Shipwrecked Sailor" is Middle Kingdom fiction, probably written in Dynasty 11, c. 2040–1650 B.C. In its adventure and magical realism, it is a miniature quest journey such as that of Odysseus. But unlike with Odysseus, whose goal was return to Ithaca and recovery of his kingship, we are uncertain of the purpose and true meaning — if there be one — of this elusive and intriguing quest tale. Written in the first person, as an autobiographical memoir (surely a literary device) and with a story within a story within a story, we have the plights, frights, and excitement of a single person confronting unpredictable nature, supernatural gods, and the authority of the immediate sovereign who is the judge of the sailor's journey and accomplishments. Rich in realistic detail, the tale also provides specific information on everyday Egyptian life.

The astute lieutenant spoke: May your wish be satisfied, commander. See, we have reached home. The mallet has been taken, the mooring post driven in, and the prow rope set upon the ground. Praise has been rendered, God has been thanked, and every man embraces his companion. Our crew is returned safe without loss to our troops. Now that we have reached the limits of Wawat and we have passed by / Senmut, we have returned in peace, and we have attained our land.[1]

Listen to me, commander. I am devoid of exaggeration. Wash yourself; place water on your fingers. Then you can reply when you are interrogated and speak to the king with self-assurance. You will answer without [stammering]. For the speech of a man saves him, and his words gain him indulgence. / Act according to your judgment. Yet speaking to you (in this fashion) is wearisome.

---

1. A quarrying, mining, or military expedition has returned by Nile from the south, and its commander appears to be downcast at the prospect of facing the king after an unsuccessful mission. His chief aide tries to cheer him up. Wawat is northern Nubia, and Senmut is the island of Biggeh, just south of Aswan in the First Cataract region. The mission took place in the eastern desert or on the Red Sea. The expression, "our land," is not otherwise attested in Egyptian literature and may in fact have a patriotic nuance.

Let me tell you of a similar thing which happened to me myself.[2] I went to the mining country for the sovereign. I went down to the sea[3] in a boat 120 cubits long and 40 cubits wide.[4] One hundred twenty sailors from among the best of Egypt were in it. Whether they looked at the sky or whether they looked at the land, / their hearts were fiercer than those of lions. They could foretell a stormwind before it came and a downpour before it happened.

A stormwind broke out while we were at sea, before we had touched land. The wind was lifted up,[5] but it repeated with a wave of eight cubits in it. There was a plank which struck it (the wave) for me.[6] Then the boat died. And of those who were in it not a single one survived.

Next I was set upon / an island by the surf of the sea, and I spent three days alone, my heart as my companion. I slept inside of a cabin of wood;[7] I embraced the shade. I stretched forth my two legs to learn what I might put in my mouth. There I found figs and dates, and all excellent kinds of vegetables. Sycamore figs were there and notched sycamore figs. / And cucumbers as if they were cultivated. Fish were there and birds. There was not anything which was not within it. Then I ate to satisfaction, and I put (some aside) on the ground because of the overabundance in my hands. I cut a fire drill, lit a fire, and I made a burnt offering for the gods.

Then I heard the sound of a thunderclap, but I thought it was the surf of the sea. The trees were shaking / and the ground was quaking. When I uncovered my face, I discovered that it was a serpent coming along. He was thirty cubits. His [hood] was more than two cubits, and his body was plated with gold. His two [markings] were of real lapis lazuli, and he was coiled up in front.[8]

He opened his mouth to me while I was on my belly in his presence, and he said to me: Who is it who has brought you, who is it who has brought you, little one, / who is it who has brought you? If you delay in telling me who it is who has brought you to this island, I shall see that you find yourself as ashes, transformed into one who is not seen.

Although he was speaking to me, I did not hear it; when I was in his presence, I did not know myself. He placed me in his mouth, and he took

---

2. Here begins the story within the story.

3. The word for sea is literally, "the great green," and is used of the Mediterranean as well as the Red Sea. Since the mining country is either the Sinai peninsula or the eastern desert, since the serpent speaks of the land of Punt (a southern region in Africa or on the Red Sea), and since the produce is African (giraffe tails, etc.), the sea in our story is clearly the Red Sea.

4. The cubit is the Egyptian measurement of length, about 20.6 inches or .523 meters. The ship is about 206 by 70 feet.

5. Perhaps an idiom with the sense, "we traveled onward."

6. This passage difficult in the original.

7. Possibly the cabin of the boat, but conceivably a natural or man-made shelter.

8. The terms *hood* and *markings* have been interpreted in various ways by different scholars. The first is the usual word for beard.

me off to his rest house. He set me down without touching me, / and I was intact, without anything being taken away from me.

He opened his mouth to me while I was on my belly in his presence, and he said to me: Who is it who has brought you, who is it who has brought you, little one, who is it who has brought you to this island of the sea, the two sides of which are in waves? And I answered him, my arms bent in his presence, and I said to him: It is I (myself) who have gone down / to the mines on a mission of the sovereign in a boat 120 cubits long and 40 cubits wide.[9] One hundred twenty sailors from among the best of Egypt were in it. Whether they looked at the sky or whether they looked at the land, their hearts were [fiercer] than those of lions. They could foretell a stormwind before it came and a downpour before it happened. Each one of them, his heart was [fiercer] / and his arm more valorous than his fellow's, without a fool among them. A stormwind came forth while we were at sea, before we could make land. The wind was lifted up, but it repeated with a wave of eight cubits in it. There was a plank which struck it (the wave) for me. Then the boat died. And of those that were in it not a single one remained except for me. Behold me at your side. Then I was brought to this island / by the surf of the sea.

He said to me: Do not fear, do not fear, little one, do not turn white. You have reached me. Indeed, God has allowed you to live. He has brought you to this Island of the Ka[10] within which there is not anything which does not exist. It is full of all good things. See, you shall spend month after month until you complete four months within this island. / A boat shall come back from home with sailors in it whom you know. You shall go home with them, and you shall die in your village.[11]

How joyful is the one who relates what he has tasted after painful affairs are past. Let me relate to you something similar which took place in this island when I was on it with my brothers and sisters and the children among them.[12] We were seventy-five serpents, my children and my brothers and sisters. And I will not call to mind to you a little daughter who was brought to me through [prayer.][13]

Then a star / fell, and because of it these went up in fire.[14] It happened completely. Yet I did not burn, for I was not among them. But I died for them when I found them in a single heap of corpses.[15]

---

9. This kind of repetition of an entire section is frequent in all ancient literature.

10. An island of the spirit or enchanted island.

11. Burial in a foreign land was abhorrent to the Egyptians, a theme developed in Sinuhe as well.

12. Here begins the story within the story within the story.

13. This curious phrase has not yet been satisfactorily explained.

14. A meteor? In the historical text of Thutmose III from Gebel Barkal there is a description of a falling star.

15. Here the serpent's story ends. Like the sailor, he was a sole survivor.

If you would be brave, regulate your desire. Then you will fill your embrace with your children, you will kiss your wife, and you will see your house (again); for it is better than anything. You will reach the home in which you (once) were in the midst of your brothers and sisters.

As I was stretched out on my belly and touching the ground in his presence, I said to him: I shall relate your prowess to the sovereign, and I shall inform him / of your greatness. I shall have brought to you ladanum, *heknu*-oil, *iudeneb,* cassia, and incense for the temples with which to satisfy every god. I shall indeed relate what has happened to me through what I have seen of your prowess. You will be thanked in (my) town in the presence of the magistrates of the entire land. I shall sacrifice to you oxen as a burnt offering, and I shall wring the necks of birds for you. I shall have brought to you transport ships loaded with all the specialties of Egypt, as should be done for a god who loves the Egyptians in a distant land which the Egyptians do not know.

Then he laughed at me because of these things which I had said, out of the [craftiness] of his heart. / And he said to me: Myrrh is not abundant with you, although you have become a possessor of incense. Indeed, I am the Prince of Punt; myrrh belongs to me. That *heknu*-oil, of which you spoke about bringing me, why it is the main product of this island! Now it will come to pass that you will separate yourself from this place, and you will never see this island, since it will have turned into waves.

Then that boat came, as he had foretold before. I went and I set myself on a high tree, and I recognized those who were in it. I went to report it, but I found that he knew it. And he said to me: Farewell, farewell, little one, to your home! You will see your children. Place my good repute in your town: this is all I ask / from you.

I placed myself on my belly, my arms bent in his presence. And he gave me a cargo consisting of myrrh, *heknu*-oil, *iudeneb,* cassia, *tishepses, shasekh,* black eye-paint, giraffe tails, large cakes of incense, elephant tusks, hounds, apes, baboons, and every kind of precious thing. I then loaded them onto this boat. It then came to pass that I placed myself upon my belly to thank him, and he said to me: You will arrive home within two months. You will fill your embrace with your children. You will become young again at home, and you will be (properly) buried.

I went down to the shore / in the vicinity of this ship, and I called out to the troops who were in this ship. I gave praise upon the shore to the lord of this island, and those who were in it (the ship) did likewise.

We sailed northward to the Residence city of the sovereign, and we arrived at the Residence in two months, according to everything he had said. Then I entered before the sovereign, and I presented to him this produce which I had brought back from within this island. He thanked me before the magistrates of the entire land. I was appointed lieutenant, and I was assigned two hundred people. Look at me, / now that I have touched land, after I have seen what I have experienced. Listen to my speech. It is good for men to hearken.

He said to me:[16] Do not act the part of the astute man, friend. Who gives water to the goose at daybreak when it is to be slaughtered in the morning?

It has come, from its beginning to its end, as it has been found in writing, in the writing of the scribe excellent of fingers, / Ameny's son Amen-aa.

■ The Tale of the Doomed Prince (c. 2040–1650 B.C.) *Egypt* (story)

TRANSLATED BY EDWARD F. WENTE, JR.

"The Tale of the Doomed Prince" is, like "The Shipwrecked Sailor," a Middle Kingdom fiction from Dynasty 11. In this Egyptian fairy tale, a young crown prince is threatened prophetically with death from a crocodile, a snake, or a dog. The young prince goes abroad—a common theme—disguised as the orphan son of a simple chariot warrior. In the eastern margin of the delta, he comes to the land of the Prince of Nahrin. The prince has protected his daughter by placing her in a tower house seventy cubits above the ground. He makes it known that whoever can leap up that high will have the hand of his daughter. The doomed prince leaps up to the tower window, and the daughter of the Prince of Nahrin falls in love and kisses and embraces him "all over his body." The father, at first annoyed by the young prince's supposed low station, is soon charmed and won over and he too kisses the young man all over his body. Meanwhile the threat of death from the animals remains. By miraculous coincidences, the young groom survives encounters with the ferocious beasts, and while the tale is incomplete, the reader feels, as in an unfinished Kafka tale, that the process of escape from death will go on indefinitely, and the "doomed" prince in disguise is in reality a virtuous prince who will be compelled by fate of his good life, loving wife, and inevitable escapes from death to become the "blessed" prince. The Egyptian tale-makers loved the literary intrigue of masked heroes, allegorical beasts and god figures, fearful and suspenseful adventure, and quests whose ultimate meaning must never be revealed.

Once upon a time there was a king, so the story goes, to whom no son had ever been born. [But when His Majesty, re]quested a son for himself from the gods of his time, they ordered a birth to be granted him, and he went to

---

16. These are the commander's only words in the story.

bed with his wife in the night. Now when she [had become] pregnant and had completed the months of child-bearing, a son was thus born.

Presently the Hathors[1] came to determine a fate for him and said: He shall die through a crocodile, or a snake, or even a dog. Thus the people who were at the boy's side heard and then reported it to His Majesty. Thereupon His Majesty became very much saddened. Then His Majesty had [a house] of stone built [for him] upon the desert, supplied with personnel and with every good thing of the palace, so that the boy did not (need to) venture outside.

Now after the boy had grown older, he went up onto his roof and espied a greyhound following a grownup who was walking along the road. He said to his servant, who was beside him: What is it that is walking behind the grownup who is coming along [the] road? And he told him: It is a greyhound. And the boy told him: Have one like it obtained for me. Thereupon the servant went and reported it to His Majesty. Then His Majesty said, "Let a young springer be taken to him [because of] his heart's [disquiet]." And so someone [caused] the greyhound to be taken to him.

Now after days had elapsed upon this, the boy matured in all his body, and he sent to his father saying: What will the outcome be while I am dwelling here? For look, I am committed to Fate. Let me be released so that I may act according to my desire until God does what is his will. Then a chariot was yoked for him, equipped [with] all sorts of weapons, and [a servant was put in] his following for an escort. He was ferried over to the eastern tract[2] and told: Now you may set out as you wish, [while] his greyhound was with him. He went northward over the desert, following his inclination and living on every sort of desert game.

Presently he reached the Prince of Nahrin.[3] Now none had been born to the Prince of Nahrin except a [marriageable] daughter. There had been built for her a house whose window was seventy cubits distant from the ground, and he sent for all the sons of all the princes of the land of Khor[4] and told them: As for the one who will reach the window of my daughter, she shall be a wife for him.

Now after many days had elapsed upon this and while they were (engaged) in their daily practice, presently the boy passed by them. They took the boy to their house, cleansed him, gave fodder to his team, did every sort of thing for the boy, salving him and bandaging his feet, and gave food to his escort. They said to him by way of conversation: Where have you come from, you handsome lad? He told them: I am the son of a chariot warrior of

---

1. According to popular religious belief in the New Kingdom, there were seven such Hathor goddesses, who determined the fate of a child at birth; see "The Tale of the Two Brothers."

2. The desert edge forming the eastern margin of the Delta.

3. The land of the Mitannian kingdom, located east of the bend of the Euphrates river. Since this kingdom fell toward the end of Dynasty 18, the action of the story takes place at a time in this dynasty when Syrian princes owed their allegiance to Mitanni.

4. Here synonymous with Syria.

the land of Egypt. My mother died, and my father took for himself another wife, a [stepmother]. She came to despise me, and I left her presence in flight. And they embraced him and kissed him over [all his] body.

[Now after many days had elapsed upon] this, he said to the boys: What is this that you have become engaged in, [boys? And they told him: It has been three] full [month]s till now that we have spent time here [leaping up, for the one who] will reach [the] window of the daughter of the Prince of Nahrin, [he will] give her to him for [a wife. He] said to them: If I could but enchant my feet,[5] I would proceed to leap up in your company. They proceeded to leap up according to their daily practice, and the boy stood by afar off observing, while the eyes of the daughter of the Prince of Nahrin were upon him.

Now after (some while) had elapsed upon this, the boy came in order to leap up along with the children of the princes. He leapt up and reached the window of the daughter of the Prince of Nahrin. And she kissed him and embraced him over all his body. Then someone went in order to impart the news to her father and told him: Somebody has reached the window of your daughter. Then the prince inquired about him saying: The son of which of the princes is he? And he was told: He is a chariot warrior's son. It was from his stepmother's presence that he came in flight from the land of Egypt. Thereupon the Prince of Nahrin became very much angered. He said: Is it to the Egyptian fugitive that I should give my daughter? Send him back home.

And someone came to tell him: Please set out for the place whence you came. But the daughter seized hold of him and swore by God, saying: By Pre-Harakhti, if he is taken away from me, I shall neither eat nor drink but shall die right away. Then the messenger went and reported to her father every word that she had said, and her father sent men to slay him while he was still where he was. But the daughter said to them: By Pre, if he is slain, as soon as the sun sets, I shall be dead. I will not stay alive an hour longer than he.

Then [someone went] to tell it to her father. And [her father had] the [lad] and his daughter [brought be]fore him. The lad [came before] him, and his worth impressed the prince. He embraced him and kissed him over all his body, and he said to him: Tell me your background. See, you are (now) a son in my eyes. And he told him: I am the son of a chariot warrior of the land of Egypt. My mother died, and my father took for himself another wife. She came to despise me, and I left her presence in flight. Then he gave him his daughter for a wife and gave him house and fields as well as cattle and all sorts of good things.

---

5. Other scholars have rendered the clause by: "If my feet were not paining me so," but neither the traces nor the length of the lacuna support the restoration of the negative *bn*. The determinative of the verb favors "enchant."

Now after (some while) had elapsed upon this, the lad told his wife: I am committed to three fates: crocodile, snake, and dog. Then she told him: Have the dog which follows you killed. And he told her: [What a demand]! I will not let my dog, which I reared when it was a puppy, be killed. And she came to guard her husband very carefully, not letting him venture outside alone.

Now from the day that the boy had come from the land of Egypt in order to travel about, the crocodile had been his fate. . . . It appeared [from the midst of] the lake[6] opposite him in the town in which the lad was (living) with [his wife]. However, a water spirit was in it. Neither would the water spirit let the crocodile emerge nor would the crocodile let the water spirit emerge to stroll about. As soon as the sun rose, [they] both [would be] engaged [there] in fighting each and every day for a period of three full months.

Now after some days had elapsed upon this, the lad sat down and made holiday in his house. And after the end of the evening breeze the lad lay down upon his bed, and slumber took possession of his body. Then his wife filled one j[ar with wine and filled] another jar with beer. Presently a [snake] emerged [from its] hole to bite the lad, but his wife was sitting beside him without going to sleep. The [jars were thus standing] accessible to the snake, and it imbibed and became intoxicated. Then it reclined and turned upside down. Thereupon [his wife caused] it to be [split] into segments with her hand-axe. She then awoke her husband . . . him, and she told him: See, your god has delivered one of your fates into your hand. He will guard [you henceforth. Then he] made an offering to P[re], praising him and extoling his power daily.

Now after some days had elapsed upon this], the lad went out to stroll about for relaxation on his property. [His wife] did not go out [with him], but his dog was following him. Then his dog took a bite,[7] [saying: I am your fate. Thereupon] he fled before it. Presently he reached the lake and descended into the [water in flight before the] dog. And so the crocodile [seized h]im and carried him off to where the water spirit (usually) was, [but he was not there.

The] crocodile told the lad: I am your fate who has been fashioned so as to come in pursuit of you, but [it is three full months] now that I have been fighting with the water spirit. See, I shall let you go. If [my opponent returns to engage me] to fight, [come] and lend me your support in order to kill the water spirit.[8] But if you see the . . . see the crocodile.

---

6. The word used for "lake" is *ym*, "sea," used also to refer to the lake of Apamea; see Alan H. Gardiner, *Ancient Egyptian Onomastica*, 3 vols. (Oxford: Oxford University Press, 1947), 1:167*–68*, and Helck, *Beziehungen*, p. 307.

7. See Hildegard von Deines and Wolfhart Westendorf, *Wörterbuch der medizinischen Texte*, 2 vols. (Berlin: Akademie Verlag, 1961–62), 2:947. Other translators have rendered: "Then his dog took on the (power) of speech."

8. Or possibly rather: "and boast of me in order that [I] might kill the water-spirit."

Now after dawn and the next day had come about, the [water spirit] returned . . .

(The remainder of the tale is lost.)

■ The Book of the Dead (c. 1500 B.C.) *Egypt* (spells)

TRANSLATED BY RAYMOND O. FAULKNER

After the Old Kingdom Pyramid Texts, written in hieroglyphs (which, like numbers, convey meaning rather than sound), in the Middle Kingdom we have the *Coffin Texts* which used hieroglyphs, but in a cursive script called "hieratic" with an increasing number of phonograms (a hieroglyph, such as an owl, that represents a sound). In the late New Kingdom, we have a truly demotic cursive phonetic system, which eventually provided a model for the Phoenician cursive that is the basis of Semitic and European scripts. The last great collection of funerary texts, found on papyrus scrolls, is the New Kingdom "guides to the beyond" known as *The Book of the Dead,* written at first in semicursive hieroglyphics known as "linear hieroglyphics" and, finally, in pure demotic cursive. The literary quality of these spells is erratic to the modern reader, being most often of theological and historic rather than of literary importance. Yet there are extraordinary pieces, which can astound even today.

FURTHER READING: Andrews, Carol, ed. *The Ancient Book of the Dead,* 1972. Budge, E. A. Wallis. *The Book of the Dead: The Hieroglyphic Transcript of the Papyrus of Ani,* 1960. Lichtheim, Miriam. *Ancient Egyptian Literature,* vol. II: *The New Kingdom,* 1976.

SPELL FOR GIVING N'S HEART TO HIM IN THE REALM OF THE DEAD

My heart is mine in the House of Hearts, my heart is mine in the House of Hearts, my heart is mine, and it is at rest there. I will not eat the cakes of Osiris on the eastern side of the Gay-water in the barge when you sail downstream or upstream, and I will not go aboard the boat in which you are. My mouth will be given to me that I may speak with it, my legs to walk, and my arms to fell my enemy. The doors of the sky are opened for me; Gab, chiefest of the gods, throws open his jaws for me, he opens my eyes which were closed up, he extends my legs which were contracted; Anubis strengthens for me my thighs which were joined together; the goddess Sakhmet stretches me out. I will be in the sky, a command shall be made for my benefit in Memphis, I shall be aware in my heart, I shall have power in my heart, I shall have power in my arms, I shall have power in my legs, I shall have power to do whatever I desire; my soul and my corpse shall not be restrained at the portals of the West when I go in or out in peace.

Spell 26

SPELL FOR NOT EATING FAECES OR DRINKING URINE IN THE REALM OF THE DEAD

I am the horned bull who rules the sky, Lord of Celestial Appearing, the Great Illuminator who came forth from the heat, who harnesses the years; the Double Lion is glad, and the movement of the sunshine has been granted to me. I detest what is detestable, I will not eat faeces, I will not drink urine, I will not walk head downward.

I am the owner of bread in Heliopolis, bread of mine is in the sky with Re, bread of mine is on the earth with Gab, and it is the Night-bark and the Dar-bar which will bring it to me from the house of the Great god who is in Heliopolis. I am loosed from my windings, I make ready the ferry-boat of the sky, I eat of what they eat, I live on what they live on, I have eaten bread in every pleasant room.

Spell 53

■ Ancient Egyptian Love Poems (1554–1085 B.C.) *Egypt*

TRANSLATED BY EZRA POUND AND NOEL STOCK

These ancient love lyrics written in a woman's voice are outstanding examples of Egyptian literature. Beyond the speaker's voice, we are uncertain of gender and authorship. By contrast with Egypt, in Rome we have virtually no literature attributed to women. Although it was standard for the well-educated Latin woman to paint and write poetry, only seven poems by one Latin woman poet, Sulpicia, exist, and these were found at the end of the canon of the Roman poet Tibullus. Given Sappho's fame as the "tenth muse" of ancient Greek poetry, it is curious that from the abundance of classical Latin literature, no woman other than Sulpicia was deemed worthy enough to copy and thereby invite survival and recovery.

These love poems in ancient Egyptian, exquisitely and powerfully translated by Ezra Pound and Noel Stock, are a universal type of the lyric that appears in many literatures around the world. These earliest examples of the candid, erotic woman's love poem, with spiritual implications, have a counterpart in the pseudepigraphical biblical Song of Solomon (Song of Songs). It is generally assumed that the chaotic beauty of the fragments that comprise the biblical idyll of the Song of Songs is derived indirectly—or perhaps directly—from the tradition of these earlier Egyptian love songs, so similar in speech, spirit, and theme.

FURTHER READING: Barnstone, Aliki, and Willis Barnstone. *A Book of Women Poets from Antiquity to Now,* 1980. Pound, Ezra, and Noel Stock. *Love Poems of Ancient Egypt,* 1962.

from Pleasant Songs of the Sweetheart Who Meets You in the Fields

I

You, mine, my love,
My heart strives to reach the heights of your love.

See, sweet, the bird-trap set with my own hand.

See the birds of Punt,
Perfume a-wing   5
        Like a shower of myrrh
Descending on Egypt.

Let us watch my handiwork,
The two of us together in the fields.

II

The shrill of the wild goose
Unable to resist
The temptation of my bait.

While I, in a tangle of love,
Unable to break free,   5
Must watch the bird carry away my nets.

And when my mother returns, loaded with birds,
And finds me empty-handed,
What shall I say?

That I caught no birds?   10
That I myself was caught in your net?

III

Even when the birds rise
Wave mass on wave mass in great flight
I see nothing, I am blind
Caught up as I am and carried away
Two hearts obedient in their beating   5
My life caught up with yours
Your beauty the binding.

VII

Head out the door—
Is he coming?

Ears alert for his step,
And a heart that never stops talking about him.

A messenger: 5
"I'm not well . . ."
Why doesn't he come straight out
And tell me
He's found another girl.

One more heart to suffer.   10

VIII

I writhe so for lost love
Half my hair has fallen in grief.

I am having my hair recurled and set,
Ready, just in case . . .

from Garden Songs

I

The pomegranate speaks:
My leaves are like your teeth
My fruit like your breasts.
I, the most beautiful of fruits,
Am present in all weathers, all seasons,   5
As the lover stays forever with the beloved,
Drunk on "shedeh" and wine.

All the trees lose their leaves, all
Trees but the pomegranate.
I alone in all the garden lose not my beauty,   10
I remain straight.
When my leaves fall,
New leaves are budding.

First among fruits
I demand that my position be acknowledged,   15
I will not take second place.
And if I receive such an insult again
You will never hear the end of it. . . .

III

The little sycamore that you planted
       with your own hands
Moves its mouth to speak.

How lovely his branches, lovely
As they sway, and swaying, whisper,
Their whisper sweet as honey.   *5*

The branches bend with plump fruit
Redder than the blood-red Jasper,
Leaves like malachite.

They are drawn to you from afar
Who are not yet in your cool shade.   *10*
You entice a love-letter
From the hand of that young girl,
Daughter of the head gardener,
Who runs up to her lover, saying
"Let us go somewhere quiet."   *15*

The garden is in full splendour,
With tent pavilions;
And all for you.

My gardeners rejoice to see you.

Love Lyrics

I

Diving and swimming with you here
Gives me the chance I've been waiting for:
To show my looks
Before an appreciative eye.

My bathing suit of the best material,   *5*
The finest sheer,
Now that it's wet
Notice the transparency,
How it clings.

Let us admit, I find you attractive.   *10*
I swim away, but soon I'm back,
Splashing, chattering,
Any excuse at all to join your party.

Look! a redfish flashed through my fingers!
You'll see it better   *15*
If you come over here,
Near me.

II

Nothing, nothing can keep me from my love
Standing on the other shore.

Not even old crocodile
There on the sandbank between us
Can keep us apart.   *5*

I go in spite of him,
I walk upon the waves,
Her love flows back across the water,
Turning waves to solid earth
For me to walk on.   *10*

The river is our Enchanted Sea.

III

To have seen her
To have seen her approaching
Such beauty is
Joy in my heart forever.
Nor time eternal take back   *5*
What she has brought to me.

IV

When she welcomes me
Arms open wide
I feel as some traveller returning
From the far land of Punt.

All things change; the mind, the senses,   *5*
Into perfume rich and strange.
And when she parts her lips to kiss
My head is light, I am drunk without beer.

V

If I were one of her females
Always in attendance
(Never a step away)
I would be able to admire
The resplendence   *5*
Of her body entire.

If I were her laundryman, for a month,
I would be able to wash from her veils
The perfumes that linger.

I would be willing to settle for less   *10*
And be her ring, the seal on her finger.

2

Biblical Literature: Old Testament, New Testament, and Intertestament

■

INTRODUCTION

The Jews and the Bible (consisting of the Old Testament and the New Testament) are forever linked. The Bible is the early history of the Jews from Abraham through Jesus Christ, the last Jewish prophet and, for Christians, the Messiah foretold in the Old Testament. Hence the Jews have come to be known as the "people of the book." It must be understood that while the Jews do not read the New Testament as believed scripture, the New Testament is also a narration composed by Jews, whose central figure is Yeshua the Messiah, the Jewish charismatic rabbi. Yeshua the Messiah has been translated into English as Jesus Christ (based on the Greek translation of his Aramaic name). Thus, that group of Jews that split off from mainstream Judaism to follow the teachings of Yeshua have come to be known as

Christians, meaning Messianists. Although the Bible in its entirety is a book authored by and about Jews, Jews receive the Old Testament as their Bible of belief, whereas Christians receive both the Old Testament and New Testament as their Bible of belief. To this we should add the canonical Apocrypha (books of the Bible surviving only in Greek translation of the lost Hebrew original), which is accepted as canonically part of the Bible by Jews, Catholics, and Greek and Russian Orthodox, but not by Protestants.

In addition to Old Testament and New Testament scripture, including the canonical Apocrypha, which appears in varying degrees in Jewish and Christian Bibles, there is a vast body of scripture that did not find its way into the canon, much of it written during those centuries between the closing of the Old Testament at the beginning of the first century B.C. and the final selection of the New Testament, which was not canonized until the last decades of the fourth century A.D. The religious scriptures of this period, which include noncanonical apocrypha, gospels, apocalypses, acts, psalms, wisdom poetry, Dead Sea Scrolls, Gnostic texts, and writings under the general title of pseudepigrapha (falsely attributed scripture) compose the Intertestament. A selection from this abundance of literature is increasingly included in recent study Bibles. Among the most commonly included of such works is the Gnostic Gospel of Thomas, which may precede by two decades the Gospel of Mark, the earliest of the canonical gospels and the noncanonical apocrypha, and which is of extraordinary literary and theological importance. If we consider the Old Testament, New Testament, and Intertestament together, we have in effect an unbroken line of biblical scripture, which we might call the Greater Bible.

■ The Old Testament (Eleventh to First Centuries B.C.) *Israel*

The Bible (from the Greek plural of *biblion,* "book," a diminutive of *biblios,* "papyrus") is an anthology of sacred texts—histories, prophetic writings, wisdom literature—whose canon takes diverse forms for Jews and Christians. The Old Testament has been preserved in Hebrew, though parts of Daniel, Jeremiah, and Ezra are in Aramaic. For Jews, the Bible is the history and writings of the Jewish people, from between the eleventh or tenth century to the first century B.C. It is also called the *Jewish Bible* or the *Hebrew Bible,* referring in the first instance to people, the second to language, but the common designation in English is simply the Bible. In Hebrew, *Torah* refers to the first five books of Moses, and often Torah is used metonymically to mean the whole Bible.

The Bible of the Jews has been designated by Christians as the Old Testament; the Old Testament and the New Testament compose the Christian Bible. The term *Old Testament* reflects a Christian comparative notion of looking back at an older or earlier part of the Bible. For the Jews, however, this book is the entire Bible, and therefore not an old or early part of a composite document. The terms *Old Testament* and *New Testament* came into being in the fourth century A.D. when Jerome (c. 347–420?) translated the Bible into Latin from Hebrew and Greek, calling the parts *Vetus Testamentum* and *Novum Testamentum* ("Old Testament" and "New Testament"), which is a mistranslation of the Greek titles *Palaia Dietheke* and *Kaine Dietheke* ("Old Covenant" and "New Covenant").

The thirty-nine books of the Old Testament include Torah, Histories, Prophets, Wisdom Books, and the canonical Apocrypha. The fourteen books of the Apocrypha are accepted as secondarily canonical (deuterocanonical) by Jews, Catholics, and Greek Orthodox Christians and held to be uncanonical by Protestants. They appear in the famous Septuagint, a second-century B.C. translation into Greek of the Hebrew Bible for the Jews of Alexandria who could no longer read Hebrew. The name *Apocrypha* means "hidden away" in Greek, and these are the "hidden biblical books," meaning that the original Hebrew or Aramaic texts were "hidden away," that is, not available when the Bible was canonized. Since the original texts were lost, the authorship and authenticity of the texts was in doubt (Protestants have never overcome that doubt), and so in a more general sense, "apocryphal" has taken on the meaning of doubtful authenticity. With regard to the canonical Apocrypha of the Hebrew Bible, the loss was in part modified in 1947 with the discovery of the parts of the original Hebrew texts for Tobit and fragments of other Apocrypha.

The Hebrew Bible has its origins in Mesopotamia, both in story and theology: hence, Shinar, site of the tower of Babel, has been identified as Sumer, and the tower of Babel is a reminiscence of massive Mesopotamian structures called ziggurats, such as those at Ur and Khorsabad. Names of historical sites and even of God changed as cultures changed, moved, borrowed, and reinvented their past. Even the name of God reflects a historical confusion of intermingled traditions. Sometimes God is "El," sometimes "Elohim," which is the plural form meaning "the Gods," which may be a linguistic holdover from a polytheistic stage; sometimes God is "Yahweh" and sometimes "Baal." Baal was normally the God of the Canaanites and an enemy deity, but in the Psalms, Baal appears as a synonym for Yahweh. Elsewhere, the Old Testament shows its debt to the Middle East and North Africa: the Genesis Flood story has multiple earlier variants in Mesopotamia, including the Babylonian version in *The Epic of Gilgamesh;* the Book of Proverbs has its antecedents in Egyptian proverbs, recorded in hieroglyphs, of the wise man Amenoemope. Religious scripture is traditionally transmitted orally, later transcribed, and then worked over to improve, censor, and alter according to the needs of the compilers. So to a significant extent, the Bible is a compilation and adaptation of earlier Middle Eastern texts and oral traditions. Both in its prehistory and its present form, the Bible is a book of Asia. The Asian Bible (including the New Testament, which is also an Asian book) has been the most important non-European book in determining the cultures, theologies, and literature of Europe and indeed the globe. It is the world's most translated and migratory book.

Although the Hebrew Bible contains the legends, creation tales, parables, and wisdom literature of many earlier people, in its essence it remains the early history of the Jews and their encounters with Babylon, Egypt, Canaan, Persia, Greece, and Rome. Their recorded history began in Mesopotamia. They settled in the land of Israel in about the thirteenth century, and during the many diasporas that took them to Egypt, Ethiopia, India, and Asia Minor, North Africa, and Europe, the Bible remained the single document that held the "people of the book" together. It is good to look more closely at that history. Although we do have much information about the early Jews from Babylonian, Persian, Egyptian, Coptic, Greek, and Latin sources, obviously the Bible itself gives the fullest account of the history, literature, and theology of the Jews.

Jewish history begins with the family of Abraham and his linear descendents Isaac, Jacob, and Joseph. The word *Jew* derives from "Judah," who was the fourth son of Jacob, Abraham's great-grandson. The word *Hebrew*, also associated with both the ancient Jewish language and people, apparently derives from an earlier source, from the biblical figure of Eber (from *apiru* or *habiru* meaning "migrant," "transient"), who was the grandson of Shem, the son of Noah.

Abraham, the semihistorical patriarch of the Jews, was born perhaps in the eighteenth century B.C., in Ur of the Chaldeans (Babylonians) in southern Mesopotamia, in what is present-day Iraq. Paul calls Abraham the father not only of the Jews but of all who believe (Rom. 4:11). Abraham's father Terah brought the family from Ur to Haran in Syria. There, the Old Testament states, when Abraham was seventy-five, God (Yahweh) commanded him to go to Canaan (modern-day Israel and Palestine) and settle there. He also went to Egypt, where he stayed and prospered, but he then returned to Canaan. When Abraham was ninety-nine, God made a *covenant* with him. Yahweh would make him the ancestor of a multitude of nations, and this covenant would persist through all generations between God and Abraham's offspring. In return, Abraham would become circumcised, as would all future generations of Jewish males on the eighth day after their birth. God also told Abraham that he and his wife Sarah (who was ninety at the time) would have a son, and in nine months Isaac was born. From this covenant came the notion of a pact between God and humankind. (The New Testament, which in Greek is "New Covenant," reflects a *new* covenant between God and the followers of his Messiah Jesus.) Abraham is presented as the first historical Jew, and he is a model of the man of faith for whom salvation for himself and his people comes through God.

During a famine, Abraham's grandson Jacob and his son Joseph migrated to Egypt. Other Jews followed, and eventually Moses, in the period of Ramses II, led the Jews out of Egypt (which is celebrated in the Passover ceremony). On Mount Sinai in the desert, God delivered to Moses the Ten

Commandments; and after forty years of wandering, the Jews entered Canaan again. Thereafter, the nomadic tales recounted in the first chapters of the Bible take on a distinctly historical character as in the tenth century B.C. the Jews developed one of the powerful states in the Middle East. This state extended over significant territory and had an important and famous monarchy, though the nation was frequently conquered during the next thousand years.

The rule of kings Saul, David, and Solomon (who built the first Temple) was a relatively undisturbed time of prosperity and unified power. Then, the tribes of the north formed their own kingdom of Israel, and those of the south formed the kingdom of Judah (also called "Judea" and "Yehuda"). In 722 B.C., the Assyrian ruler Sargon II captured Samaria, capital of Israel, exiled its inhabitants, and the northern kingdom of Israel disappeared along with its people, who are often called the "lost tribes of Israel." Subsequently, the southern kingdom of Judah was taken over in turn by Assyrians, by Egyptians, and, most significant of all early conquests, in 586 B.C. by the Babylonians, who also destroyed the Temple. This was the first great diaspora, in which many were taken to Babylonia, as we hear in Ezekiel and Jeremiah. The Persians under Cyrus the Great defeated the Babylonians and freed the Jews in 538 B.C., permitting their return to Jerusalem, although many chose to remain in Mesopotamia. Sizeable old communities of Jews, dating directly back to the Babylonian Captivity and diaspora, lived in Iran and Iraq until 1948. The second Temple in Jerusalem was rebuilt by 516 B.C. and was to remain as the center of Second Temple Judaism until A.D. 70, when it was destroyed by Titus of Rome. After their return from Babylon, the Jews came under Greek rule and cultural influence. Later, there was a period of independence when in 165 B.C. Judas Maccabeus defeated the Greeks and recaptured Jerusalem. The feast of Hanukkah, which includes the lighting of candles, celebrates that victory. Later, Israel (a general name for the Jewish presence, not to be confused with the kingdom of Israel that was conquered by Sargon) came under Roman rule. In A.D. 66, the Jewish rebellion against Rome began. In A.D. 70, Titus conquered Jerusalem, destroyed the Temple, crucified thousands of Jews, and sent traditional Jews and Christian Jews into extended diaspora. By this time, however, the largest community of Jews was in Alexandria, Egypt, and spoke only Greek. Paul preached largely to the Greek-speaking Jews in the synagogues of Corinth, Thessaloniki, and Rome with the purpose of convincing fellow Jews that Jesus was indeed the foretold Messiah. By then the Jews were already widely dispersed in Asia Minor, North Africa, and southern Europe.

After Rome conquered Jerusalem, there continued to be centers of learning in Palestine, but the most important communities were in Babylonia, where Jewish academies produced the Talmud, an extensive commentary on the Bible. The Jews also migrated to central and western Europe. The golden age of diaspora Judaism occurred in Islamic Spain, under the Moors, from the eighth to the end of the fifteenth centuries. There, as philosophers, poets, and governors, Jews in Iberia enjoyed extraordinary freedom and cultural expansion. A knowledge of Aristotle and Plato in Arabic translation was present in the Spain of the Moors and Jews; indeed, a rekindling of classical philosophy came to Western Europe through Spain by way of translation under the Moors and later under Alfonso el Sabio in thirteenth-century Toledo. But in 1492, with the conquest of the Moors at Granada and unification of Spain under Isabel and Ferdinand, the Inquisition forced the Jews to convert to Christianity or go into exile. The Sephardic Jews of North Africa, Italy, southeastern Europe, and Turkey are descendents of the diaspora from Spain.

In other countries of Western Europe, the Jews suffered persistent persecution, murder, and frequent expulsion. They were expelled from England in 1290, from France in 1306, and from Germany through the fifteenth century in diverse persecutions. From Germany, they carried their native medieval German (Yiddish) to Poland and Eastern Europe, where they settled, lived in ghettos, and built thriving cultures. Holland welcomed the Jews from Spain and Portugal. The eighteenth-century philosopher Baruch Spinoza lived in Holland, and the family of the English prime minister Benjamin Disraeli came from that country. By the nineteenth century, the Jews of England, France, Germany, and Austria began to emerge from the ghettos, and there appeared Karl Marx, Felix Mendelssohn, Heinrich Heine, and Disraeli, whose price of acceptance, however, was nominal conversion to Christianity. In the twentieth century, most of the formal barriers had fallen, and Sigmund Freud, Albert Einstein, the French philosopher Henri Bergson, and other public figures were not forced into conversion. Then came the Third Reich, 1933–1945, under Adolf Hitler. During the war, the Germans under the Nazi party rounded up Jews, Slavs, Gypsies, homosexuals, and dissidents, and by 1945 some twelve million died in concentration camps. This broad holocaust included the execution of six million out of a worldwide population of sixteen million Jews. The centuries of diaspora came to an end for many of the surviving Jews with the establishment of the state of Israel in 1948.

FURTHER READING: *The Bible. The Holy Bible.* Alter, Robert. *The Art of Biblical Narrative,* 1981; *The Art of Biblical Poetry,* 1985. Alter, Robert, and Frank Kermode, *The Literary Guide to the Bible,* 1987. Gabel, John B., and Charles B. Wheeler, *The Bible as Literature,* 1985. Gros Louis, Kenneth R. R., ed., *Literary Interpretations of Biblical Narratives,* 1982. Barnstone, Willis, ed., *The New Covenant: The Four Gospels and Apocalypse,* 2002.

Genesis (King James Version, 1612)

The first line of Genesis, "In the beginning God created the heavens and the earth," is so rich in implication that theologies circle on its single words. Kabbalists (Jewish mystical interpreters of holy scripture) find meaning in its syllables and letters. Early Kabbalah reasoned that to create with the fiat "Let there be light," God had first to invent the verb to make his command heard; and even before the verb he had to create letters out of which words were made.

And who declared us into existence? Was it a single God or several? About the singularity or plurality of God the very first line of Genesis leaves us in grave doubt. Whereas the King James Version (1612) says "In the beginning God created the heavens and the earth," the word translated as God is in Hebrew *Elohim,* meaning Gods; *El* is God, *Elohim* is Gods; the suffix *ohim* pluralizes the noun. To counter a plural translation of Elohim, textual redactors used the singular form of *bara,* the verb for created, thereby suggesting a singular subject of the verb, that is one God, not several. Linguistic and theological explanations have been given to explain away this discrepancy, but it is clear that in earlier versions of Genesis (or in its immediate sources in Mesopotamia), the creator was multiple. As polytheism gave way to monotheism, the Hebrew verb was altered to its singular form to save the emerging tenet of monotheism. However, the invisible editors forgot to put God in the singular form and hence the endless ambiguity. Elsewhere in the Bible when the word *Elohim* is used, as in the Psalms, it means Gods. In most cases, the translation into other languages again disguises the existence of several gods by translating *Elohim* as "masters."

These fascinating questions abound in every line. Genesis (a Greek word meaning "born" or "beginning" given by the Septuagint translators) is the first book of the Torah or Pentateuch (Greek for "five books"), and the five books are traditionally attributed to Moses—although Moses' death is described in Deuteronomy (fifth book of Pentateuch). To explain Moses' foresightful knowledge of his death, conservative explicators attribute the passage to later editorial insertions, thus acknowledging a tampering with holy text. In reality, all authorial names in the Old Testament, New Testament, and Apocrypha are probably pseudepigraphical, that is, false ascriptions, with the exception of Paul (Saul), for whom half the letters ascribed to him are surely by him. But for purposes of reference, we will speak of the authors by their traditional names.

Genesis gives us two versions of creation: the Elohist one known as the E document, in which God is Elohim; and the Yahwist one known as the J document, in which God is Yahweh or simply YHWH (in Hebrew only the consonants are written). Formerly, Yahweh was translated as Jehovah. In Gen. 1–2:4a, Elohim creates the world in six days and then, despite his omnipotence, rests on the seventh day. In the second version of the creation, beginning with Gen. 2:4b, Yahweh creates the earth and heavens in a single day and on that same day forms a man out of the dust of the earth, breathes life into his nostrils, and also builds his abode in Eden. From Adam, Eve is made. Eve, hungry for knowledge, chooses the forbidden fruit, yielding to disobedience and sin, and ending innocence. Woman has in the Judeo-Christian tradition been the symbol of temptation, evil, man's downfall, and death. However, the later Gnostics (from *gnosis* in Greek, meaning "knowledge") held that Eve, urged on by the "good serpent," who was the first incarnation of the "luminous Jesus," gave us knowledge. So in Gnosticism, woman was not sinful but heroically good like Prometheus, who gave us fire. From these first profound and complex passages of the Hebrew Bible, and all the later conflicting interpretations, we see the future shape of Western thought and values, as Greek antiquity gave way to Judeo-Christian religious hegemony.

We do not know when Genesis was written down, but the Pentateuch, of which Genesis is book one, existed in some form when the Jews returned from Babylonian Captivity (597–538 B.C.). It is speculated that the oral material for the Yahwist version of Genesis may be from the period of the Judges and was recorded in a narrative during the first years of the Monarchy in the tenth century B.C. The Elohist version is perhaps from the ninth or eighth century B.C. Although Genesis appears at the beginning of Jewish and Christian Bibles and deals with the earliest figures and events of the Jews, several prophetic books were composed before Genesis. The Dutch philosopher Baruch Spinoza believed that Ezra (fifth century B.C.) gathered disparate stories of the creation together, leaving the book of Genesis unfinished and therefore jumbled. Its present form dates probably from the third century B.C., making it one of the last books of the Bible in its present composition.

FURTHER READING: Genesis. Clines, D. J. A. *The Theme of the Pentateuch*, 1978. Fokkelman, J. P. *Narrative Art in Genesis*, 1975. Jacob, Brenno. *The First Book of the Bible: Genesis*, 1974. Sandmel, Samuel. *The Hebrew Scriptures*, 1963.

The Creation of the World

Genesis (1:1–2:3)

In the beginning God created the heaven and the earth. And the earth was without form, and void; and darkness was upon the face of the deep. And the Spirit of God moved upon the face of the waters. And God said, "Let there be light": and there was light. And God saw the light, that it was good: and God divided the light from the darkness. And God called the light Day, and the darkness he called Night. And the evening and the morning were the first day.

And God said, "Let there be a firmament in the midst of the waters, and let it divide the waters from the waters." And God made the firmament, and divided the waters which were under the firmament from the waters which were above the firmament: and it was so. And God called the firmament Heaven. And the evening and the morning were the second day.

And God said, "Let the waters under the heaven be gathered together unto one place, and let the dry land appear": and it was so. And God called the dry land Earth; and the gathering together of the waters called he Seas:

and God saw that it was good. And God said, "Let the earth bring forth grass, the herb yielding seed, and the fruit tree yielding fruit after his kind, whose seed is in itself, upon the earth": and it was so. And the earth brought forth grass, and herb yielding seed after his kind, and the tree yielding fruit, whose seed was in itself, after his kind: and God saw that it was good. And the evening and the morning were the third day.

And God said: "Let there be lights in the firmament of the heaven to divide the day from the night; and let them be for signs, and for seasons, and for days, and years; and let them be for lights in the firmament of the heaven to give light upon the earth." And it was so. And God made two great lights; the greater light to rule the day, and the lesser light to rule the night: he made the stars also. And God set them in the firmament of the heaven to give light upon the earth. And to rule over the day and over the night, and to divide the light from the darkness: and God saw that it was good. And the evening and the morning were the fourth day.

And God said, "Let the waters bring forth abundantly the moving creature that hath life, and fowl that may fly above the earth in the open firmament of heaven." And God created great whales, and every living creature that moveth, which the waters brought forth abundantly, after their kind, and every winged fowl after his kind: and God saw that it was good. And God blessed them, saying, "Be fruitful, and multiply, and fill the waters in the seas, and let fowl multiply in the earth." And the evening and the morning were the fifth day.

And God said, "Let the earth bring forth the living creature after his kind, cattle, and creeping thing, and beast of the earth after his kind": and it was so. And God made the beast of the earth after his kind, and cattle after their kind, and every thing that creepeth upon the earth after his kind: and God saw that it was good.

And God said, "Let us make man in our image, after our likeness: and let them have dominion over the fish of the sea, and over the fowl of the air, and over the cattle, and over all the earth, and over every creeping thing that creepeth upon the earth." So God created man in his own image, in the image of God created he him; male and female created he them. And God blessed them, and God said unto them, "Be fruitful, and multiply, and replenish the earth, and subdue it: and have dominion over the fish of the sea, and over the fowl of the air, and over every living thing that moveth upon the earth." And God said, "Behold, I have given you every herb bearing seed, which is upon the face of all the earth, and every tree, in which is the fruit of a tree yielding seed; to you it shall be for meat. And to every beast of the earth, and to every fowl of the air, and to every thing that creepeth upon the earth, wherein there is life, I have given every green herb for meat." And it was so. And God saw every thing that he had made, and, behold, it was very good. And the evening and the morning were the sixth day.

Thus the heavens and the earth were finished, and all the host of them. And on the seventh day God ended his work which he had made; and he rested on the seventh day from all his work which he had made. And God blessed the seventh day, and sanctified it: because that in it he had rested from all his work which God created and made.

The Second Creation

Genesis (2:4–3:24)

In the day that the Lord God made the earth and the heavens, and every plant of the field before it was in the earth, and every herb of the field before it grew (for the Lord God had not caused it to rain upon the earth, and there was not a man to till the ground) there went up a mist from the earth, and watered the whole face of the ground. And the Lord God formed man of the dust of the ground, and breathed into his nostrils the breath of life; and man became a living soul. And the Lord God planted a garden eastward in Eden; and there he put the man whom he had formed. And out of the ground made the Lord God to grow every tree that is pleasant to the sight, and good for food; the tree of life also in the midst of the garden, and the tree of knowledge of good and evil. And a river went out of Eden to water the garden; and from thence it was parted, and became into four heads. The name of the first is Pison: that is it which compasseth the whole land of Havilah, where there is gold; and the gold of that land is good: there is bdellium and the onyx stone. And the name of the second river is Gihon: the same is it that compasseth the whole land of Ethiopia. And the name of the third river is Hiddekel: that is it which goeth toward the east of Assyria. And the fourth river is Euphrates.

And the Lord God took the man, and put him into the garden of Eden to dress it and to keep it. And the Lord God commanded the man, saying, "Of every tree of the garden thou mayest freely eat: but of the tree of the knowledge of good and evil, thou shalt not eat of it: for in the day that thou eatest thereof thou shalt surely die."

And the Lord God said, "It is not good that the man should be alone; I will make him a help meet for him." And out of the ground the Lord God formed every beast of the field, and every fowl of the air; and brought them unto Adam to see what he would call them: and whatsoever Adam called every living creature, that was the name thereof. And Adam gave names to all cattle, and to the fowl of the air, and to every beast of the field; but for Adam there was not found a help meet for him. And the Lord God caused a deep sleep to fall upon Adam, and he slept: and he took one of his ribs, and closed up the flesh instead thereof; and the rib, which the Lord God had taken from man, made he a woman, and brought her unto the man.

And Adam said,

"This is now bone of my bones,
>and flesh of my flesh:
She shall be called Woman,
>because she was taken out of Man."

Therefore shall a man leave his father and his mother, and shall cleave unto his wife: and they shall be one flesh. And they were both naked, the man and his wife, and were not ashamed.

Now the serpent was more subtil than any beast of the field which the Lord God had made. And he said unto the woman, "Yea, hath God said, 'Ye shall not eat of every tree of the garden'?" And the woman said unto the serpent, "We may eat of the fruit of the trees of the garden: but of the fruit of the tree which is in the midst of the garden, God hath said, 'Ye shall not eat of it, neither shall ye touch it, lest ye die.'" And the serpent said unto the woman, "Ye shall not surely die: for God doth know that in the day ye eat thereof, then your eyes shall be opened, and ye shall be as gods, knowing good and evil."

And when the woman saw that the tree was good for food, and that it was pleasant to the eyes, and a tree to be desired to make one wise, she took of the fruit thereof, and did eat, and gave also unto her husband with her; and he did eat. And the eyes of them both were opened, and they knew that they were naked; and they sewed fig leaves together, and made themselves aprons.

And they heard the voice of the Lord God walking in the garden in the cool of the day: and Adam and his wife hid themselves from the presence of the Lord God amongst the trees of the garden. And the Lord God called unto Adam, and said unto him, "Where art thou?" And he said, "I heard thy voice in the garden, and I was afraid, because I was naked; and I hid myself." And he said, "Who told thee that thou wast naked? Hast thou eaten of the tree, whereof I commanded thee that thou shouldest not eat?" And the man said, "The woman whom thou gavest to be with me, she gave me of the tree, and I did eat." And the Lord God said unto the woman, "What is this that thou hast done?" And the woman said, "The serpent beguiled me, and I did eat." And the Lord God said unto the serpent,

"Because thou hast done this,
>thou art cursed above all cattle,
>and above every beast of the field.
Upon thy belly shalt thou go,
>and dust shalt thou eat
>all the days of thy life:
And I will put enmity between thee and the woman,
>and between thy seed and her seed;
It shall bruise thy head,
>and thou shalt bruise his heel."
Unto the woman he said,

"I will greatly multiply thy sorrow and thy conception;
In sorrow thou shalt bring forth children;
And thy desire shall be to thy husband,
And he shall rule over thee."

And unto Adam he said, "Because thou hast hearkened unto the voice of thy wife, and hast eaten of the tree, of which I commanded thee, saying, 'Thou shalt not eat of it':

"Cursed is the ground for thy sake;
    in sorrow shalt thou eat of it all the days of thy life.
Thorns also and thistles shall it bring forth to thee;
    and thou shalt eat the herb of the field;
In the sweat of thy face
    shalt thou eat bread,
Till thou return unto the ground;
    for out of it wast thou taken:
For dust thou art,
    and unto dust shalt thou return."

And Adam called his wife's name Eve; because she was the mother of all living. Unto Adam also and to his wife did the Lord God make coats of skins, and clothed them.

And the Lord God said, "Behold, the man is become as one of us, to know good and evil: and now, lest he put forth his hand, and take also of the tree of life, and eat, and live for ever—" therefore the Lord God sent him forth from the garden of Eden, to till the ground from whence he was taken. So he drove out the man; and he placed at the east of the garden of Eden Cherubims, and a flaming sword which turned every way, to keep the way of the tree of life.

Cain and Abel

Genesis (4:1–5:5)

And Adam knew Eve his wife; and she conceived, and bore Cain, and said, "I have gotten a man from the Lord." And she again bore his brother Abel. And Abel was a keeper of sheep, but Cain was a tiller of the ground. And in process of time it came to pass that Cain brought of the fruit of the ground an offering unto the Lord. And Abel, he also brought of the firstlings of his flock and of the fat thereof. And the Lord had respect unto Abel and to his offering: but unto Cain and to his offering he had not respect. And Cain was very wroth, and his countenance fell. And the Lord said unto Cain, "Why are thou wroth? and why is thy countenance fallen? If thou doest well, shalt thou not be accepted? and if thou doest not well, sin lieth at the door. And unto thee shall be his desire, and thou shalt rule over him."

And Cain talked with Abel his brother: and it came to pass, when they were in the field, that Cain rose up against Abel his brother, and slew him. And the Lord said unto Cain, "Where is Abel thy brother?" And he said, "I know not: am I my brother's keeper?" And he said, "What hast thou done? the voice of thy brother's blood crieth unto me from the ground. And now art thou cursed from the earth, which hath opened her mouth to receive thy brother's blood from thy hand. When thou tillest the ground, it shall not henceforth yield unto thee her strength; a fugitive and a vagabond shalt thou be in the earth." And Cain said unto the Lord, "My punishment is greater than I can bear. Behold, thou hast driven me out this day from the face of the earth; and from thy face shall I be hid; and I shall be a fugitive and a vagabond in the earth; and it shall come to pass that every one that findeth me shall slay me." And the Lord said unto him, "Therefore whosoever slayeth Cain, vengeance shall be taken on him sevenfold." And the Lord set a mark upon Cain, lest any finding him should kill him. And Cain went out from the presence of the Lord, and dwelt in the land of Nod, on the east of Eden. . . .

And Adam knew his wife again; and she bore a son, and called his name Seth: "For God," said she, "hath appointed me another seed instead of Abel, whom Cain slew." And to Seth, to him also there was born a son; and he called his name Enos; then began men to call upon the name of the Lord. . . .

And the days of Adam after he had begotten Seth were eight hundred years: and he begot sons and daughters. And all the days that Adam lived were nine hundred and thirty years: and he died. . . .

The Flood

Genesis (6:1 – 9:29)

And it came to pass, when men began to multiply on the face of the earth, and daughters were born unto them, that the sons of God saw the daughters of men that they were fair; and they took them wives of all which they chose. And the Lord said, "My spirit shall not always strive with man, for that he also is flesh: yet his days shall be a hundred and twenty years." There were giants in the earth in those days; and also after that, when the sons of God came in unto the daughters of men, and they bore children to them, the same became mighty men which were of old, men of renown. And God saw that the wickedness of man was great in the earth, and that every imagination of the thoughts of his heart was only evil continually. And it repented the Lord that he had made man on the earth, and it grieved him at his heart. And the Lord said, "I will destroy man whom I have created from the face of the earth; both man, and beast, and the creeping thing, and the fowls of the air; for it repenteth me that I have made them." But Noah found grace in the eyes of the Lord. . . .

Noah was a just man and perfect in his generations, and Noah walked with God. And Noah begot three sons, Shem, Ham, and Japheth. . . .

And God said unto Noah, "The end of all flesh is come before me; for the earth is filled with violence through them; and, behold, I will destroy them with the earth. Make thee an ark of gopher wood; rooms shalt thou make in the ark, and shalt pitch it within and without with pitch. And this is the fashion which thou shalt make it of: the length of the ark shall be three hundred cubits, the breadth of it fifty cubits, and the height of it thirty cubits. A window shalt thou make to the ark, and in a cubit shalt thou finish it above; and the door of the ark shalt thou set in the side thereof; with lower, second, and third stories shalt thou make it. And, behold, I, even I, do bring a flood of waters upon the earth, to destroy all flesh, wherein is the breath of life, from under heaven; and everything that is in the earth shall die. But with thee will I establish my covenant; and thou shalt come into the ark, thou, and thy sons, and thy wife, and thy sons' wives with thee. And of every living thing of all flesh, two of every sort shalt thou bring into the ark, to keep them alive with thee; they shall be male and female. Of fowls after their kind, and of cattle after their kind, of every creeping thing of the earth after his kind, two of every sort shall come unto thee, to keep them alive. And take thou unto thee of all food that is eaten, and thou shalt gather it to thee; and it shall be for food for thee, and for them." Thus did Noah; according to all that God commanded him, so did he. And the Lord said unto Noah, "Come thou and all thy house into the ark; for thee have I seen righteous before me in this generation. Of every clean beast thou shalt take to thee by sevens, the male and his female; and of beasts that are not clean by two, the male and his female. Of fowls also of the air by sevens, the male and the female; to keep seed alive upon the face of all the earth. For yet seven days, and I will cause it to rain upon the earth forty days and forty nights; and every living substance that I have made will I destroy from off the face of the earth."

And Noah did according unto all that the Lord commanded him. And Noah went in, and his sons, and his wife, and his sons' wives with him, into the ark, because of the waters of the flood. Of clean beasts, and of beasts that are not clean, and of fowls, and of every thing that creepeth upon the earth, there went in two and two unto Noah into the ark, the male and the female, as God had commanded Noah. And it came to pass after seven days of Noah's life in the second month, the seventeenth day of the month, the same day were all the fountains of the great deep broken up, and the windows of heaven were opened. And the waters prevailed, and were increased greatly upon the earth; and the ark went upon the face of the waters. And the waters prevailed exceedingly upon the earth; and all the high hills, that were under the whole heaven, were covered. Fifteen cubits upward did the waters prevail; and the mountains were covered. And all flesh died that moved upon the earth, both of fowl, and of cattle, and of beast, and of every creeping thing that creepeth upon the earth, and every man. All in whose nostrils was the breath of life, of all that was in the dry land, died. And every living substance was destroyed which was upon the face of the ground, both man, and cattle, and the creeping things, and the fowl of the heaven; and they were destroyed from the earth: and Noah only remained alive, and they that were with him in the ark. And the waters prevailed upon the earth a hundred and fifty days.

And God remembered Noah, and every living thing, and all the cattle that was with him in the ark: and God made a wind to pass over the earth, and the waters assuaged. The fountains also of the deep and the windows of heaven were stopped, and the rain from heaven was restrained; and the waters returned from off the earth continually: and after the end of the hundred and fifty days the waters were abated. And the ark rested in the seventh month, on the seventeenth day of the month, upon the mountains of Ararat. And the waters decreased continually until the tenth month: in the tenth month, on the first day of the month, were the tops of the mountains seen.

And it came to pass at the end of forty days that Noah opened the window of the ark which he had made: and he sent forth a raven, which went forth to and fro, until the waters were dried up from off the earth. Also he sent forth a dove from him, to see if the waters were abated from off the face of the ground; but the dove found no rest for the sole of her foot, and she returned unto him into the ark, for the waters were on the face of the whole earth: then he put forth his hand, and took her, and pulled her in unto him into the ark. And he stayed yet other seven days; and again he sent forth the dove out of the ark; and the dove came in to him in the evening; and, lo, in her mouth was an olive leaf plucked off: so Noah knew that the waters were abated from off the earth. And he stayed yet other seven days; and sent forth the dove; which returned not again unto him any more.

And it came to pass in the six hundredth and first year, in the first month, the first day of the month, the waters were dried up from off the earth: and Noah removed the covering of the ark, and looked, and, behold the face of the ground was dry. And in the second month, on the seven and twentieth day of the month, was the earth dried. And God spoke unto Noah, saying, "Go forth of the ark, thou, and thy wife, and thy sons, and thy sons' wives with thee. Bring forth with thee every living thing that is with thee, of all flesh, both of fowl, and of cattle, and of every creeping thing that creepeth upon the earth; that they may breed abundantly in the earth, and be fruitful, and multiply upon the earth." And Noah went forth, and his sons, and his wife, and his sons' wives with him. Every beast, every creeping thing, and every fowl, and whatsoever creepeth upon the earth, after their kinds, went forth out of the ark.

And Noah builded an altar unto the Lord; and took of every clean beast, and of every clean fowl, and offered burnt offerings on the altar. And the Lord smelled a sweet savor; and the Lord said in his heart, "I will not again curse the ground any more for man's sake; for the imagination of man's heart is evil from his youth; neither will I again smite any more every thing living, as I have done. While the earth remaineth, seedtime and harvest, and cold and heat, and summer and winter, and day and night shall not cease."

And God blessed Noah and his sons, and said unto them, "Be fruitful, and multiply, and replenish the earth. And the fear of you and the dread of you shall be upon every beast of the earth, and upon every fowl of the air, upon all that moveth upon the earth, and upon all the fishes of the sea; into your hand are they delivered. Every morning thing that liveth shall be meat for you; even as the green herb have I given you all things. But flesh with the life thereof, which is the blood thereof, shall ye not eat. And surely your blood of your lives will I require; at the hand of every beast will I require it, and at the hand of man; at the hand of every man's brother will I require the life of man. Whoso sheddeth man's blood, by man shall his blood be shed: for in the image of God made he man." . . . And God spoke unto Noah, and to his sons with him, saying, "And I, behold, I establish my covenant with you, and with your seed after you; and with every living creature that is with you, of the fowl, of the cattle, and of every beast of the earth with you; from all that go out of the ark, to every beast of the earth. And I will establish my covenant with you; neither shall all flesh be cut off any more by the waters of a flood; neither shall there any more be a flood to destroy the earth."

And God said, "This is the token of the covenant which I make between me and you and every living creature that is with you, for perpetual generations: I do set my bow in the cloud, and it shall be for a token of a covenant between me and the earth. And it shall come to pass, when I bring a cloud over the earth, that the bow shall be seen in the cloud: and I will remember my covenant, which is between me and you and every living creature of all flesh; and the waters shall no more become a flood to destroy all flesh. And the bow shall be in the cloud; and I will look upon it, that I may remember the everlasting covenant between God and every living creature of all flesh that is upon the earth." And God said unto Noah, "This is the token of the covenant, which I have established between me and all flesh that is upon the earth." . . .

And Noah began to be a husbandman, and he planted a vineyard: and he drank of the wine, and was drunken; and he was uncovered within his tent. And Ham, the father of Canaan, saw the nakedness of his father, and told his two brethren without. And Shem and Japheth took a garment, and laid it upon both their shoulders, and went backward, and covered the nakedness of their father; and their faces were backward, and they saw not their father's nakedness. And Noah awoke from his wine, and knew what his younger son had done unto him. And he said, "Cursed be Canaan; a servant of servants shall he be unto his brethren." And he said, "Blessed be the Lord God of Shem; and Canaan shall be his servant. God shall enlarge Japheth, and he shall dwell in the tents of Shem; and Canaan shall be his servant."

And Noah lived after the flood three hundred and fifty years. And all the days of Noah were nine hundred and fifty years: and he died. . . .

The Tower of Babel

Genesis (11:1 – 11:9)

And the whole earth was of one language, and of one speech. And it came to pass, as they journeyed from the east, that they found a plain in the land of Shinar; and they dwelt there. And they said one to another, "Go to, let us make brick, and burn them thoroughly." And they had brick for stone, and slime had they for mortar. And they said, "Go to, let us build us a city and a tower, whose top may reach unto heaven; and let us make us a name, lest we be scattered abroad upon the face of the whole earth." And the Lord came down to see the city and the tower, which the children of men builded. And the Lord said, "Behold, the people is one, and they have all one language; and this they begin to do: and now nothing will be restrained from them, which they have imagined to do. Go to, let us go down, and there confound their language, that they may not understand one another's speech." So the Lord scattered them abroad from thence upon the face of all the earth: and they left off to build the city. Therefore is the name of it called Babel; because the Lord did there confound the language of all the earth: and from thence did the Lord scatter them abroad upon the face of all the earth. . . .

Joseph, the Interpreter of Dreams

Genesis (40:1 – 41:43)

Some time after this, the butler of the king of Egypt and his baker offended their lord the king of Egypt. And Pharaoh was angry with his two officers, the chief butler and the chief baker, and he put them in custody in the house of the captain of the guard, in the prison where Joseph was confined. The captain of the guard charged Joseph with them, and he waited on them; and they continued for some time in custody. And one night they both dreamed—the butler and the baker of the king of Egypt, who were confined in the prison—each his own dream, and each dream with its own meaning.

When Joseph came to them in the morning and saw them, they were troubled. So he asked Pharaoh's officers who were with him in custody in his master's house, "Why are your faces downcast today?"

They said to him, "We have had dreams, and there is no one to interpret them."

And Joseph said to them, "Do not interpretations belong to God? Tell them to me, I pray you."

So the chief butler told his dream to Joseph, and said to him, "In my dream there was a vine before me, and on the vine there were three branches; as soon as it budded, its blossoms shot forth, and the clusters ripened into grapes. Pharaoh's cup was in my hand; and I took the grapes and pressed them into Pharaoh's cup, and placed the cup in Pharaoh's hand."

Then Joseph said to him, "This is its interpretation: the three branches are three days; within three days Pharaoh will lift up your head and restore you to your office; and you shall place Pharaoh's cup in his hand as formerly, when you were his butler. But remember me, when it is well with you, and do me the kindness, I pray you, to make mention of me to Pharaoh, and so get me out of this house. For I was indeed stolen out of the land of the Hebrews; and here also I have done nothing that they should put me into the dungeon."

When the chief baker saw that the interpretation was favorable, he said to Joseph, "I also had a dream: there were three cake baskets on my head, and in the uppermost basket there were all sorts of baked food for Pharaoh, but the birds were eating it out of the basket on my head."

And Joseph answered, "This is its interpretation: the three baskets are three days; within three days Pharaoh will lift up your head—from you!—and hang you on a tree; and the birds will eat the flesh from you."

On the third day, which was Pharaoh's birthday, he made a feast for all his servants, and lifted up the head of the chief butler and the head of the chief baker among his servants. He restored the chief butler to his butlership, and he placed the cup in Pharaoh's hand; but he hanged the chief baker, as Joseph had interpreted to them. Yet the chief butler did not remember Joseph, but forgot him.

After two whole years, Pharaoh dreamed that he was standing by the Nile, and behold, there came up out of the Nile seven cows sleek and fat, and they fed in the reed grass. And behold, seven other cows, gaunt and thin, came up out of the Nile after them, and stood by the other cows on the bank of the Nile. And the gaunt and thin cows ate up the seven sleek and fat cows. And Pharaoh awoke.

And he fell asleep and dreamed a second time; and behold, seven ears of grain, plump and good, were growing on one stalk. And behold, after them sprouted seven ears, thin and blighted by the east wind. And the thin ears swallowed up the seven plump and full ears. And Pharaoh awoke, and behold, it was a dream.

So in the morning his spirit was troubled; and he sent and called for all the magicians of Egypt and all its wise men; and Pharaoh told them his dream, but there was none who could interpret it to Pharaoh.

Then the chief butler said to Pharaoh, "I remember my faults today. When Pharaoh was angry with his servants, and put me and the chief baker in custody in the house of the captain of the guard, we dreamed on the same night, he and I, each having a dream with its own meaning. A young Hebrew was there with us, a servant of the captain of the guard; and when we told him, he interpreted our dreams to us, giving an interpretation to each man according to his dream. And as he interpreted to us, so it came to pass; I was restored to my office, and the baker was hanged."

Then Pharaoh sent and called Joseph, and they brought him hastily out of the dungeon; and when he had shaved himself and changed his clothes, he came in before Pharaoh.

And Pharaoh said to Joseph, "I have had a dream, and there is no one who can interpret it; and I have heard it said of you that when you hear a dream you can interpret it."

Joseph answered Pharaoh, "It is not in me; God will give Pharaoh a favorable answer."

Then Pharaoh said to Joseph, "Behold, in my dream I was standing on the banks of the Nile; and seven cows, fat and sleek, came up out of the Nile and fed in the reed grass; and seven other cows came up after them, poor and very gaunt and thin, such as I had never seen in all the land of Egypt. And the thin and gaunt cows ate up the first seven fat cows, but when they had eaten them no one would have known that they had eaten them, for they were still as gaunt as at the beginning. Then I awoke.

"I also saw in my dream seven ears growing on one stalk, full and good; and seven ears, withered, thin, and blighted by the east wind, sprouted after them, and the thin ears swallowed up the seven good ears. And I told it to the magicians, but there was no one who could explain it to me."

Then Joseph said to Pharaoh, "The dream of Pharaoh is one; God has revealed to Pharaoh what he is about to do. The seven good cows are seven years, and the seven good ears are seven years; the dream is one. The seven lean and gaunt cows that came up after them are seven years, and the seven empty ears blighted by the east wind are also seven years of famine.

"It is as I told Pharaoh, God has shown to Pharaoh what he is about to do. There will come seven years of great plenty throughout all the land of Egypt, but after them there will arise seven years of famine, and all the plenty will be forgotten in the land of Egypt; the famine will consume the land, and the plenty will be unknown in the land by reason of that famine which will follow, for it will be very grievous. And the doubling of Pharaoh's dream means that the thing is fixed by God, and God will shortly bring it to pass.

"Now therefore let Pharaoh select a man discreet and wise, and set him over the land of Egypt. Let Pharaoh proceed to appoint overseers over the land, and take the fifth part of the produce of the land of Egypt during the seven plenteous years. And let them gather all the food of these good years that are coming, and lay up grain under the authority of Pharaoh for food in the cities, and let them keep it. That food shall be a reserve for the land against the seven years of famine which are to befall the land of Egypt, so that the land may not perish through the famine."

This proposal seemed good to Pharaoh and to all his servants. And Pharaoh said to his servants, "Can we find such a man as this, in whom is the Spirit of God?"

So Pharaoh said to Joseph, "Since God has shown you all this, there is none so discreet and wise as you are; you shall be over my house, and all my people shall order themselves as you command; only as regards the throne will I be greater than you. Behold, I have set you over all the land of Egypt."

Then Pharaoh took his signet ring from his hand and put it on Joseph's hand, and arrayed him in garments of fine linen, and put a gold chain about his neck; and he made him to ride in his second chariot; and they cried before him, "Bow the knee!" Thus he set him over all the land of Egypt.

Job (Revised Standard Version)

Job is a great work of world literature because of its intense narration, its poetry, and the complex and profound character of Job, whose duel with himself and with God remains an unfinished tale of debate and speculation. As in each biblical book, we have the problem of textual historicity: read the document as it is, or trace out an ur-text (an original) and separate it from probable additions and interpolations. In Job, these questions center on the poetry, the heart of the book, which is framed by a prose preface and prose afterward. Are the prose frames and the poetry truly related? Or is Job a book of deep human pessimism to which a later appended prose passage provides a pious ending of surrender, reconciliation, and holy reward? Is prosperous, powerful, righteous Job punished because, like Eve, he dares ask for knowledge, because he questions the justice of his unwarranted woes, and is the lesson that through silence, submission, and repentance happiness will come? Is Job the essence of impatience or patience? The vitality of this splendid, complex, astonishing poem, with its primeval darknesses, its sufferings, and its hope, has inspired every form of literature in many languages. It has given John Milton and William Blake speech. It is the dark side of Walt Whitman's Bible-inspired "Song of Myself." Its ethical dilemmas, economic and societal implications, and argument with God's bestowal of terrors and grace all leave an unfinished, unresolvable, and happily ongoing discourse.

FURTHER READING: Job. Gerald, Janzen, J. *Job*, 1985. Kahn, Jack. *Job's Illness: Loss, Grief and Integration*, 1975.

Then the Lord Answered Job out of the Whirlwind (38:1–39:8)

Then the LORD answered Job out of the whirlwind:

"Who is this that darkens counsel
by words without knowledge?
Gird up your loins like a man,
I will question you, and you shall declare to me.

"Where were you when I laid the foundation of the earth?
Tell me, if you have understanding.

Who determined its measurements—surely you know!
 Or who stretched the line upon it?
On what were its bases sunk,
 or who laid its cornerstone,
when the morning stars sang together,
 and all the sons of God shouted for joy?

"Or who shut in the sea with doors,
 when it burst forth from the womb;
when I made clouds its garment,
 and thick darkness its swaddling band,
and prescribed bounds for it,
 and set bars and doors,
and said, 'Thus far shall you come, and no farther,
 and here shall your proud waves be stayed'?

"Have you commanded the morning since your days began,
 and caused the dawn to know its place,
that it might take hold of the skirts of the earth,
 and the wicked be shaken out of it?
It is changed like clay under the seal,
 and it is dyed like a garment.
From the wicked their light is withheld,
 and their uplifted arm is broken.

"Have you entered into the springs of the sea,
 or walked in the recesses of the deep?
Have the gates of death been revealed to you,
 or have you seen the gates of deep darkness?
Have you comprehended the expanse of the earth?
 Declare, if you know all this.

"Where is the way to the dwelling of light,
 and where is the place of darkness,
that you may take it to its territory
 and that you may discern the paths to its home?
You know, for you were born then,
 and the number of your days is great!

"Have you entered the storehouses of the snow,
 or have you seen the storehouses of the hail,
which I have reserved for the time of trouble,
 for the day of battle and war?
What is the way to the place where the light is distributed,
 or where the east wind is scattered upon the earth?

"Who has cleft a channel for the torrents of rain,
 and a way for the thunderbolt,
to bring rain on a land where no man is,

on the desert in which there is no man;
to satisfy the waste and desolate land,
and to make the ground put forth grass?

"Has the rain a father,
or who has begotten the drops of dew?
From whose womb did the ice come forth,
and who has given birth to the hoarfrost of heaven?
The waters become hard like stone,
and the face of the deep is frozen.

"Can you bind the chains of the Pleiades,
or loose the cords of Orion?[1]
Can you lead forth the Mazzaroth in their season,
or can you guide the Bear with its children?
Do you know the ordinances of the heavens?
Can you establish their rule on the earth?

"Can you lift up your voice to the clouds,
that a flood of waters may cover you?
Can you send forth lightnings, that they may go
and say to you, 'Here we are'?
Who has put wisdom in the clouds,
or given understanding to the mists?
Who can number the clouds by wisdom?
Or who can tilt the waterskins of the heavens,
when the dust runs into a mass
and the clods cleave fast together?

"Can you hunt the prey for the lion,
or satisfy the appetite of the young lions,
when they crouch in their dens,
or lie in wait in their covert?
Who provides for the raven its prey,
when its young ones cry to God,
and wander about for lack of food?

"Do you know when the mountain goats bring forth?
Do you observe the calving of the hinds?
Can you number the months that they fulfil,
and do you know the time when they bring forth,
when they crouch, bring forth their offspring,
and are delivered of their young?
Their young ones become strong, they grow up in the open;
they go forth, and do not return to them.

---

1. Constellations.

"Who has let the wild ass go free?
　　Who has loosed the bonds of the swift ass,
to whom I have given the steppe for his home,
　　and the salt land for his dwelling place?
He scorns the tumult of the city;
　　he hears not the shouts of the driver.
He ranges the mountains as his pasture,
　　and he searches after every green thing."

JOB (40:15–41:34)

"Behold, Behemoth,
　　which I made as I made you;
　　he eats grass like an ox.
Behold, his strength in his loins,
　　and his power in the muscles of his belly.
He makes his tail stiff like a cedar;
　　the sinews of his thighs are knit together.
His bones are tubes of bronze,
　　his limbs like bars of iron.

"He is the first of the works of God;
　　let him who made him bring near his sword!
For the mountains yield food for him
　　where all the wild beasts play.
Under the lotus plants he lies,
　　in the covert of the reeds and in the marsh.
For his shade the lotus trees cover him;
　　the willows of the brook surround him.
Behold, if the river is turbulent he is not frightened;
　　he is confident though Jordan rushes against his mouth.
Can one take him with hooks,
　　or pierce his nose with a snare?

"Can you draw out Leviathan with a fishhook,
　　or press down his tongue with a cord?
Can you put a rope in his nose,
　　or pierce his jaw with a hook?
Will he make many supplications to you?
　　Will he speak to you soft words?
Will he make a covenant with you
　　to take him for your servant for ever?
Will you play with him as with a bird,
　　or will you put him on leash for your maidens?
Will traders bargain over him?
　　Will they divide him up among the merchants?
Can you fill his skin with harpoons,
　　or his head with fishing spears?

Lay hands on him;
> think of the battle; you will not do it again!
Behold, the hope of a man is disappointed;
> he is laid low even at the sight of him.
No one is so fierce that he dares to stir him up.
> Who then is he that can stand before me?
Who has given to me, that I should repay him?
> Whatever is under the whole heaven is mine.

"I will not keep silence concerning his limbs,
> or his mighty strength, or his goodly frame.
Who can strip off his outer garment?
> Who can penetrate his double coat of mail?
Who can open the doors of his face?
> Round about his teeth is terror.
His back is made of rows of shields,
> shut up closely as with a seal.
One is so near to another
> that no air can come between them.
They are joined one to another;
> they clasp each other and cannot be separated.
His sneezings flash forth light,
> and his eyes are like the eyelids of the dawn.
Out of his mouth go flaming torches;
> sparks of fire leap forth.
Out of his nostrils comes forth smoke,
> as from a boiling pot and burning rushes.
His breath kindles coals,
> and a flame comes forth from his mouth.
In his neck abides strength,
> and terror dances before him.
The folds of his flesh cleave together,
> firmly cast upon him and immovable.
His heart is hard as a stone,
> hard as the nether millstone.
When he raises himself up the mighty are afraid;
> at the crashing they are beside themselves.
Though the sword reaches him, it does not avail;
> nor the spear, the dart, or the javelin.
He counts iron as straw,
> and bronze as rotten wood.
The arrow cannot make him flee;
> for him slingstones are turned to stubble.
Clubs are counted as stubble;
> he laughs at the rattle of javelins.
His underparts are like sharp potsherds;
> he spreads himself like a threshing sledge on the mire.

He makes the deep boil like a pot;
> he makes the sea like a pot of ointment.
Behind him he leaves a shining wake;
> one would think the deep to be hoary.
Upon earth there is not his like,
> a creature without fear.
He beholds everything that is high;
> he is king over all the sons of pride."

Songs of David (Psalms)

TRANSLATED BY WILLIS BARNSTONE

The Psalms (Songs) is an anthology of Hebrew poems that follows the tradition in Middle Eastern literature, specifically Ugaritic and Syro-Palestinian writings, of gathering together diverse poems of lament, distress, supplication, and praise for God. After the Book of Psalms, this tradition continues in the Dead Sea Scroll Thanksgiving Psalms, and the splendid pseudepigraphical[1] Psalms of Solomon and the Jewish/Christian/Gnostic Odes of Solomon. The biblical psalms also carry on a personal speech with God about the meaning of all things, earthly and spiritual, of being, death, God, and justice. The essential metaphysical questions of ethics, pleasures, life, and death are the subjects of these great poems. Dating and authorship as always are guesswork. Some psalms may go back to the period of David in the tenth and ninth centuries B.C. Most are from after the First Destruction of the Temple in 586 B.C. The frequent superscription "a psalm of David" is a later addition. In their entirety, the psalms reflect perhaps five centuries of monologue and speech with God.

Traditionally there are 150 Psalms, divided into five books, perhaps reflecting the division of the Five Books of Moses. The collection in Hebrew is entitled *Tehillim,* meaning "Praises," from *hallel,* "to praise." Our cry of *hallelujah,* meaning "praise the Lord," also derives from *hallel.* Usually, the poems are divided into genres, and more specifically into what Robert Alter, in his essay on Psalms[2] calls "liturgical or cultic occasions," such as an annual enthronement ceremony. But Alter rejects the strict frame of genre and occasion as too limiting for author poets who may begin with a category of supplication or praise, but go well beyond formulaic utterances. In the opening lines of Psalm 121, "I lift my eyes to the mountains./ Where does

---

1. *Pseudepigraphical* means false ascription. It refers to the practice of ascribing texts to the names of great biblical patriarchs and prophets so as to gain acceptance for that text into the canon as "authentic" biblical scripture. So the assignment of the Song of Songs to Solomon or the Psalms to David is an example of pseudepigraphical ascription.

2. Robert Alter, and Frank Kermode, *The Literary Guide to the Bible* (New York: Basic Books, 1985), p. 26.

my help come from?," these first words of raising one's eyes to the Lord are common. Yet in context, the lines are memorable and convey the utter trust and companionship of the speaker with the Lord, who, with eternal powers, never sleeps, guards every step, protects from sun and moon, and the shadow of death. The translations of the psalms are legion. In fact, the first book published in America in English was the *Bay Psalm Book*, published in Boston. The influence of the psalms on the work of our great poets, who transformed their spirit and images (as did George Herbert, John Donne, and Gerard Manley Hopkins) is of equal import, for in their emotional range, beauty, terrible despairs, and joys, they have shaped poetry in English and many other languages. The Psalms have also been frequently set to music. A famous example is George Frederick Handel's glorious setting of Psalm 139, containing the line "If I take the wings of the morning, and dwell in the uttermost parts of the sea."

FURTHER READING: The Psalms. Alter, Robert. *The Art of Biblical Poetry*, 1985, chap. 5. Gunkel, Hermann. *The Psalms: A Form-Critical Introduction*, 1967.

Song 23[1] (of David)

The Lord is my shepherd, I will not be poor.
　　He makes me lie down on green pastures,
he leads me by the waters of stillness.
　　He restores my soul.
In his name he leads me along a straight path.

Though I walk through the darkest valley,
　　I fear no evil.
For you are with me.
　　Your rod and staff, they comfort me.

You prepare a table with food before me
　　in the presence of my enemies.
You anoint my head with olive oil,
　　my cup overflows.
Only goodness and kindess will follow me
　　all the days of my life,
and I will live in the house of the Lord
　　through all the hours of my life.

Song 100 (of Thanksgiving)

Shout a happy noise to the Lord,
　　all peoples of the earth!

---

1. The word "song" rather than "psalm" is used here. In Hebrew *shir* means "song" as in *shir ha-david*, "Song of David," or *shir hashirim*, "Song of Songs." *Psalm* is a Greek word meaning "song for a harp."

Worship the Lord with gladness.
  Come before him singing.
Know that the Lord is God!
  It is he who made us and we are his.
We are his people
  and the sheep of his pasture.

Enter his temple gates with thanksgiving,
  and into his courtyards go with praise!
Give thanks to him and bless his name.

For the Lord is good
  and his kindness endures forever
and his faith in us goes on to all generations.

Song 120 (of Ascension)

In my agony I cry out to the Lord
  and he answered me.
I say: Lord, deliver me from lying lips
  and from a devious tongue.

What will be given you and done to you,
  devious tongue?
A warrior's sharp arrows
  and burning coals of the broom tree.

I am in despair, an alien in Meshech,
  and must live among the black tents of Kedar.
I have lived too long among those who hate peace.
  I want peace.
They speak. They are for war.

Song 121 (of Ascension)

I will raise my eyes to the mountains.
  Where will my help come from?
My help comes from the Lord,
  who made the sky and the earth.

He will not let your foot be moved.
  He who keeps you will not slumber.
He who keeps Israel
  will not slumber or sleep.

The Lord is your keeper.
  The Lord is your shade on your right hand.
The sun will not smite you by day
  nor the moon by night.

The Lord will keep you from all evil.
    He will keep your life.
He will guard your going out and your coming in
    from this time on and forevermore.

Song 133 (of Ascension)

Look, how good and pleasant it is
    when brothers and sisters live as one.
It is like precious olive oil on the head,
    running down on the beard,
on the beard of Aaron,
    running down on the collar of his robes.
It is like the dew on high Mount Hermon,
    which falls on the mountain of Zion,
for there the Lord commanded his blessing,
    life forevermore.

Song 137

By the rivers of Babylon, there we sat down and wept
    when we remembered Zion.
On the willow trees we hung our harps,
    for there our captors asked us for songs,
and our tormentors asked us for mirth,
    saying: "Sing us a song of Zion."

How can we sing the Lord's song in a foreign land?

If I forget you, O Jerusalem,
    let my right hand wither.
Let my tongue cling to the roof of my mouth,
    if I do not remember you,
if I do not set Jerusalem above my highest joy.

Remember, O Lord, the ways of Edomites on the day
    Jerusalem fell,
how they shouted, "Tear it down!
    Tear it down to the foundations!"
O daughter of Babylon, you devastator!
Happy will be those who pay you in kind
    for what you have done to us.
Happy will be those who take your little ones
    and smash them against a rock!

Song 139 (David to the Leader)

O Lord, you have searched me and known me.
You know me when I sit down and when I rise up.
    You discern my thought from far away.

You search out my path and my lying down
  and are acquainted with all my ways.
Before a word is in my tongue, O Lord,
  look, you know it altogether.
You hem me in, behind and before,
  and lay your hand upon me.
Such knowledge is too wonderful for me,
  so high I cannot attain it.

Where can I go from your spirit?
  Or where can I flee from your presence?
If I ascend to heaven you are there.
  If I make my bed in Sheol[1] you are there!
If I take the wings of the morning
  and dwell in the uttermost parts of the sea,
even there your hand will lead me
  and your right hand will hold me.
If I say, "Let only darkness cover me
  and the light around me be night,"
even the darkness is not dark to you.
  The night glows like day,
  for darkness is like light to you.

And it was you who formed my inner parts.
  You knitted me together in my mother's womb.
I praise you, for I am fearfully and wonderfully made.
  Wonderful are your works.
You know me altogether.
  My frame was not hidden from you
when I was made in secret,
  intricately woven in the depths of the earth.
Your eyes saw my unformed substance.
  In your book they were written.
Every day was formed for me
  when none of them yet was.
How precious and heavy are your thoughts, O God!
  How vast is the sum of them!
If I try to count them, they are more than sand.
  When I wake, I am still with you.

O that you would slay the wicked, O God,
  and men of blood depart from me
who utter your name with wicked thought.
  and rise up against you for evil.

---

1. Sheol, a pit of darkness, sometimes likened to Hell or the underworld.

Do I not loathe those who loathe you, O Lord?
    and do I not strive against those who offend you?
I loathe them with perfect loathing.
    I count them my enemies.
Search me, O God, and know my heart.
    Try me and know my thoughts.
See if there is any grievous way in me
    and lead me in the way everlasting!

Ecclesiastes, or the Preacher (Revised Standard Version)

Ecclesiastes in Greek means "one of the church" or "preacher," and the title is derived from the Septuagint Greek.[1] The Preacher is called the son of David, meaning King Solomon, and so, like Proverbs and The Song of Songs, Ecclesiastes has traditionally been ascribed to Solomon (tenth century B.C.), but it dates from after the return from Exile (after 538 B.C.), and the affinities with Greek thought suggest a third-century text. The Greek word *ekklesiastes* is a translation of Hebrew *qohelet*, meaning "a skeptical preacher," and skepticism and darkness of death is the theme of much of Ecclesiastes. We have some portion of joy under the sun, which, in our vaporous existence, we should seize, but it will not last into the unknown future, which is vanity, meaning death. The possible suggestion of immortality in 3:21, "Who knows whether the spirit of man goes upward and the spirit of the beast goes down to the earth?" is not an Old Testament but a Greek notion, and, like New Testament John, Ecclesiastes seems to be rhetorically influenced by Greek literary forms and its particular reasoning. The agnostic or skeptical tone prevails, however, as we see in the next verse, which informs us: "Who can bring him to see what will be after him?" (3:22). Ecclesiastes is a short, stunning, universal book. The sadness, wisdom, and cautious hope of Ecclesiastes have entered popular song and world thought.

FURTHER READING: Ecclesiastes. Crenshaw, James L. *The Old Testament Wisdom Literature: An Introduction,* 1981. Kugel, James L. *The Idea of Biblical Poetry,* 1981.

ECCLESIASTES 1:1–19

The words of the Preacher, the son of David, king in Jerusalem.

Vanity of vanities, says the Preacher,
    vanity of vanities! All is vanity.

---

1. *Septuagint* refers to the Septuagint Bible, which was a translation of the Old Testament into Greek in the second century B.C. for the Jews of Alexandria who could no longer read Hebrew. The Septuagint has become the standard Bible for the Greek Orthodox and Russian Orthodox churches of Eastern Europe.

What does man gain by all the toil
>at which he toils under the sun?
A generation goes, and a generation comes,
>but the earth remains for ever.
The sun rises and the sun goes down,
>and hastens to the place where it rises.
The wind blows to the south,
>and goes round to the north;
round and round goes the wind,
>and on its circuits the wind returns.
All streams run to the sea,
>but the sea is not full;
to the place where the streams flow,
>there they flow again.
All things are full of weariness;
>a man cannot utter it;
the eye is not satisfied with seeing,
>nor the ear filled with hearing.
What has been is what will be,
>and what has been done is what will be done;
>and there is nothing new under the sun.
Is there a thing of which it is said,
>"See, this is new"?
It has been already,
>in the ages before us.
There is no remembrance of former things,
>nor will there be any remembrance
of later things yet to happen
>among those who come after.

2:1–26

I said to myself, "Come now, I will make a test of pleasure; enjoy yourself." But behold, this also was vanity. I said of laughter, "It is mad," and of pleasure, "What use is it?"

I searched with my mind how to cheer my body with wine—my mind still guiding me with wisdom—and how to lay hold on folly, till I might see what was good for the sons of men to do under heaven during the few days of their life.

I made great works; I built houses and planted vineyards for myself; I made myself gardens and parks, and planted in them all kinds of fruit trees. I made myself pools from which to water the forest of growing trees.

I bought male and female slaves, and had slaves who were born in my house; I had also great possessions of herds and flocks, more than any who had been before me in Jerusalem.

Then I considered all that my hands had done and the toil I had spent in doing it, and behold, all was vanity and a striving after wind, and there was nothing to be gained under the sun.

So I turned to consider wisdom and madness and folly; for what can the man do who comes after the king? Only what he has already done. Then I saw that wisdom excels folly as light excels darkness. The wise man has his eyes in his head, but the fool walks in darkness; and yet I perceived that one fate comes to all of them.

Then I said to myself, "What befalls the fool will befall me also; why then have I been so very wise?" And I said to myself that this also is vanity. For of the wise man as of the fool there is no enduring remembrance, seeing that in the days to come all will have been long forgotten. How the wise man dies just like the fool!

So I hated life, because what is done under the sun was grievous to me; for all is vanity and a striving after wind.

I hated all my toil in which I had toiled under the sun, seeing that I must leave it to the man who will come after me; and who knows whether he will be a wise man or a fool? Yet he will be master of all for which I toiled and used my wisdom under the sun. This also is vanity.

What has a man from all the toil and strain with which he toils beneath the sun? For all his days are full of pain, and his work is a vexation; even in the night his mind does not rest. This also is vanity.

There is nothing better for a man than that he should eat and drink, and find enjoyment in his toil. This also, I saw, is from the hand of God; for apart from him who can eat or who can have enjoyment? For to the man who pleases him God gives wisdom and knowledge and joy; but to the sinner he gives the work of gathering and heaping, only to give to one who pleases God. This also is vanity and a striving after wind.

3:1–8

For everything there is a season, and a time for every matter under heaven:

> a time to be born, and a time to die;
> a time to plant, and time to pluck up what is planted;
> a time to kill, and a time to heal;
> a time to break down, and a time to build up;
> a time to weep, and a time to laugh;
> a time to mourn, and a time to dance;
> a time to cast away stones, and a time to gather stones together;
> a time to embrace, and a time to refrain from embracing;
> a time to seek, and a time to lose;
> a time to keep, and a time to cast away;
> a time to rend, and a time to sew;
> a time to keep silence, and a time to speak;
> a time to love, and a time to hate;
> a time for war, and a time for peace.

3:14–15

I know that whatever God does endures for ever; nothing can be added to it, nor anything taken from it; God has made it so, in order that men should fear before him. That which is, already has been; that which is to be, already has been; and God seeks what has been driven away.

3:18–21

I said in my heart with regard to the sons of men that God is testing them to show them that they are but beasts. For the fate of the sons of men and the fate of beasts is the same; as one dies, so dies the other. They all have the same breath, and man has no advantage over the beasts; for all is vanity. All go to one place; all are from the dust, and all turn to dust again. Who knows whether the spirit of man goes upward and the spirit of the beast goes down to the earth?

4:1–3

Again I saw all the oppressions that are practiced under the sun. And behold, the tears of the oppressed, and they had no one to comfort them! On the side of their oppressors there was power, and there was no one to comfort them. And I thought the dead who are already dead more fortunate than the living who are still alive; but better than both is he who has not yet been, and has not seen the evil deeds that are done under the sun.

4:9–12

Two are better than one, because they have a good reward for their toil. For if they fall, one will lift up his fellow; but woe to him who is alone when he falls and has not another to lift him up. Again, if two lie together, they are warm; but how can one be warm alone? And though a man might prevail against one who is alone, two will withstand him. A threefold cord is not quickly broken.

5:10–18

He who loves money will not be satisfied with money; nor he who loves wealth, with gain: this also is vanity.

    When goods increase, they increase who eat them; and what gain has their owner but to see them with his eyes?

    Sweet is the sleep of a laborer, whether he eats little or much; but the surfeit of the rich will not let him sleep.

    There is a grievous evil which I have seen under the sun: riches were kept by their owner to his hurt, and those riches were lost in a bad venture; and he is father of a son, but he has nothing in his hand. As he came from his mother's womb he shall go again, naked as he came, and shall take nothing for his toil, which he may carry away in his hand. This also is a grievous evil: just as he came, so shall he go; and what gain has he that he toiled for the wind, and spent all his days in darkness and grief, in much vexation and sickness and resentment?

Behold, what I have seen to be good and to be fitting is to eat and drink and find enjoyment in all the toil with which one toils under the sun the few days of his life which God has given him, for this is his lot.

7:1–3

A good name is better than precious ointment;
    and the day of death, than the day of birth.
It is better to go to the house of mourning
    than to go to the house of feasting;
for this is the end of all men,
    and the living will lay it to heart.
Sorrow is better than laughter,
    for by sadness of countenance the heart is made glad.

7:15–18

In my vain life I have seen everything; there is a righteous man who perishes in his righteousness, and there is a wicked man who prolongs his life in his evil-doing. Be not righteous overmuch, and do not make yourself overwise; why should you destroy yourself? Be not wicked overmuch, neither be a fool; why should you die before your time? It is good that you should take hold of this, and from that withhold not your hand; for he who fears God shall come forth from them all.

7:25–29

I turned my mind to know and to search out and to seek wisdom and the sum of things, and to know the wickedness of folly and the foolishness which is madness. And I found more bitter than death the woman whose heart is snares and nets, and whose hands are fetters; he who pleases God escapes her, but the sinner is taken by her. Behold, this is what I found, says the Preacher, adding one thing to another to find the sum, which my mind has sought repeatedly, but I have not found. One man among a thousand I found, but a woman among all these I have not found.

Behold, this alone I found, that God made man upright, but they have sought out many devices.

8:8–13

No man has power to retain the spirit, or authority over the day of death; there is no discharge from war, nor will wickedness deliver those who are given to it. All this I observed while applying my mind to all that is done under the sun, while man lords it over man to his hurt.

Then I saw the wicked buried; they used to go in and out of the holy place, and were praised in the city where they had done such things. This also is vanity. Because sentence against an evil deed is not executed speedily, the heart of the sons of men is fully set to do evil. Though a sinner does evil a hundred times and prolongs his life, yet I know that it will be well with those who fear God, because they fear before him; but it will not be well with the wicked, neither will he prolong his days like a shadow, because he does not fear before God.

8:16–17

When I applied my mind to know wisdom, and to see the business that is done on earth, how neither day nor night one's eyes see sleep; then I saw all the work of God, that man cannot find out the work that is done under the sun. However much man may toil in seeking, he will not find it out; even though a wise man claims to know, he cannot find it out.

9:9–18

Enjoy life with the wife whom you love, all the days of your vain life which he has given you under the sun, because that is your portion in life and in your toil at which you toil under the sun.

Whatever your hand finds to do, do it with your might; for there is no work or thought or knowledge or wisdom in Sheol, to which you are going.

Again I saw that under the sun the race is not to the swift, nor the battle to the strong, nor bread to the wise, nor riches to the intelligent, nor favor to the men of skill; but time and chance happen to them all. For man does not know his time. Like fish which are taken in an evil net, and like birds which are caught in a snare, so the sons of men are snared at an evil time, when it suddenly falls upon them.

I have also seen this example of wisdom under the sun, and it seemed great to me. There was a little city with few men in it; and a great king came against it and besieged it, building great siegeworks against it. But there was found in it a poor wise man, and he by his wisdom delivered the city. Yet no one remembered that poor man.

But I say that wisdom is better than might, though the poor man's wisdom is despised, and his words are not heeded.

The words of the wise heard in quiet are better than the shouting of a ruler among fools. Wisdom is better than weapons of war, but one sinner destroys much good.

11:1–8

Cast your bread upon the waters,
for you will find it after many days.
Give a portion to seven, or even to eight,
for you know not what evil may happen on earth.

If the clouds are full of rain,
>they empty themselves on the earth;
and if a tree falls to the south or to the north,
>in the place where the tree falls, there it will lie.
He who observes the wind will not sow;
>and he who regards the clouds will not reap.

As you do not know how the spirit comes to the bones in the womb of a woman with child, so you do not know the work of God who makes everything.

In the morning sow your seed, and at evening withhold not your hand; for you do not know which will prosper, this or that, or whether both alike will be good.

Light is sweet, and it is pleasant for the eyes to behold the sun.

For if a man lives many years, let him rejoice in them all; but let him remember that the days of darkness will be many. All that comes is vanity.

12:1–14

Remember also your Creator in the days of your youth, before the evil days come, and the years draw nigh, when you will say, "I have no pleasure in them"; before the sun and the light and the moon and the stars are darkened and the clouds return after the rain; in the day when the keepers of the house tremble, and the strong men are bent, and the grinders cease because they are few, and those that look through the windows are dimmed, and the doors on the street are shut; when the sound of the grinding is low, and one rises up at the voice of a bird, and all the daughters of song are brought low; they are afraid also of what is high, and terrors are in the way; the almond tree blossoms, the grasshopper drags itself along and desire fails; because man goes to his eternal home, and the mourners go about the streets; before the silver cord is snapped, or the golden bowl is broken, or the pitcher is broken at the fountain, or the wheel broken at the cistern, and the dust returns to the earth as it was, and the spirit returns to God who gave it.

Vanity of vanities, says the Preacher; all is vanity.

Epilogue

Besides being wise, the Preacher also taught the people knowledge, weighing and studying and arranging proverbs with great care. The Preacher sought to find pleasing words, and uprightly he wrote words of truth.

The sayings of the wise are like goads, and like nails firmly fixed are the collected sayings which are given by one Shepherd. My son, beware of anything beyond these. Of making many books there is no end, and much study is a weariness of the flesh.

The end of the matter; all has been heard. Fear God, and keep his commandments; for this is the whole duty of man. For God will bring every deed into judgment, with every secret thing, whether good or evil.

The Song of Songs

TRANSLATED BY WILLIS BARNSTONE

There are poems and there is the poem of poems. The Song of Songs, a sequence of Hebrew lyrics from western Asia, has survived for three millennia as the poetic book of books in Israel, Europe, and ultimately everywhere. This biblical poem has been given multiple titles and its speakers diverse names; it has suffered many historical interpretations, and its words have been fiddled with — as has been the fate of all biblical texts — by many redacting fingers. Yet despite centuries of alterations and intentional miscopying (for purposes of creating figures of great name, such as Solomon, or changing sensual passages), the sequence of the Song of Songs persists as the most profound and beautiful book of love poems in the world. It is the song of songs.

The Song of Songs is the quintessential document of love between woman and man, of lovers who search, join in body and spirit, and depart. In the Song are the darkness of solitude, the sensual culmination and joy of union, the despair of abandonment, and the morning landscape of reunion. Love as an emotion and state of being is its own end. Love is better than wine, stronger than death. It justifies human existence. The Song states itself in images and dramatic passion. It is naked and carries its own complexity. The texts as they are, richly impure, reworked by many hungry hands, remain candid, obverse, provocatively obscure, and startlingly wondrous poems of love. Like the greatest poems, they are devoid of certain meaning and continue after the last word, never finished, and demand and invite rereading. In their single yet cumulative sequence, their simplicity grows deep.

The Song of Songs in its present form appears to be a fragmentary love idyll, with a dramatic structure, albeit a confused one. It is the sole book of love poems in the Bible and has been the most influential book of love lyrics in the West. Although the original lyrics have no surface religious meaning, these love poems have been widely interpreted, in both Jewish and Christian traditions, as a spiritual allegory of union with the deity. We read reworkings and interpretations from early Kabbalah to the thirteenth-century *Libre d'amic e Amat (Book of the Friend and the Beloved)* by Ramon Llull, the Catalan Illuminated Doctor. The Song's strong sensual elements are normally allegorized to diminish the perception of physical lovers and to transform eros into a celebration of a mystical marriage of Israel to Yahweh in the Old Testament and of the church to Christ in the New Testament. However, despite the antisexual bias of orthodox Christianity in which original sin and carnal knowledge are equated, through the guise of the mystics and their allegorization of sexuality as a way to union with God, there has always been a place in Western literature for a celebration and candid description of physical love between the sexes. The Spanish poet Saint John of the Cross (1542–1591) wrote magnificent mystico-erotic versions of the Song of Songs in his "Spiritual Canticle" and his "Dark Night of the Soul" in which his voice is of the female lover. Saint John, a Carmelite monk, enters the mist of heresy by ignoring state and church and creating a personal mystical union of a single woman with God.

The Song's title in Hebrew is given as the "Song of Songs which are of Solomon." However, neither the title, which is an editorial superscription, nor the text itself gives us a hint of actual title or authorship. The uncertainty of title and author implies large questions of what the songs are, when they were written, and by whom. Many books of the Bible have been ascribed to great figures—Moses, David, Solomon, Isaiah, Daniel—whose presumed authorship was at one time sufficient to ensure inclusion in the canon. Although tradition ascribes the Song of Songs to Solomon, the tenth-century B.C. king of Israel, the notion is discounted by modern scholars. Some claim the poems to be Hebrew versions of Egyptian popular love songs, and there is certainly an affinity with extant songs surviving from the Late Kingdom period. A common notion is that they are wedding songs, an idea that accommodates religious orthodoxy and is the same assumption of classical scholars well into the twentieth century who asserted that Sappho's passionate poems to other women were actually wedding songs addressed to the bride. In the Song of Songs, woman is primary. Her love is stronger than wine or death or a society that would oppress her. The male figure praises and the female praises, but the woman also longs and suffers. When she searches for her lover, she is stopped and beaten by the city guardians, for whom she has contempt. Their love is in the privacy of their paradise, their enclosed orchards and gardens, and their escape into the countryside and small villages. Lovers are alone, and love is the physical and spiritual god of their huge paradise.

No reliable close dating of the text is possible. It is safe to say that the poems were written between the tenth and third centuries B.C. It is probable that the poems were composed, by various hands, between the fifth and third centuries B.C. and that the variant titles of the collection as well as the names of the main speakers, Solomon and the Shulamite, are contributions of later compilers. Because of the erotic themes, the Song of Songs was not incorporated into the canon of the Hebrew Bible until after the destruction by the Romans of the Second Temple in A.D. 70, and then only over the objections of some rabbis. The extant Hebrew text offers little help as to when a poem begins and ends and who the speakers are. As for the haunting repetition of key passages and choral refrains, we do not know what corresponds to earlier lyrics from which the work was derived and what was contributed by later editors. Whatever the effect of tampering, rewriting, cutting, and fragmentation, the work survives as a perfectly intoxicating poetic sequence.

FURTHER READING: The Song of Songs. Alter, Robert. *The Art of Biblical Poetry*, 1985. Barnstone, Willis. *The Song of Songs: Shir Hashirim*, 1973. Falk, Marcia. *The Song of Songs: A New Translation and Interpretation*, 1990. Fox, Michael. *The Song of Songs and Ancient Egyptian Love Poetry*, 1985. Lady, Francis. *Paradoxes of Paradise: Identity and Difference in the Song of Songs*, 1983.

Your Love Is Better than Wine (1:1–4)

Kiss me with kisses from your mouth.
Your love is better than wine.
Your ointments have a good fragrance!
Your name is spread far like fragrance of oils
poured on the body
and so young women love you.
Take my hand.
We will run together.

You the king took me to your rooms.
I am happy, happy in you,
and say your love at night is better than wine.
It is right for me to love you.

I Am Black (1:5–7)

I am black yet beautiful,
daughters of Jerusalem,
as black as Kedar's tents,
as lovely as Solomon's tapestries.
Don't look at me with scorn
because I am black,
because the sun has scorched me.

My mother's sons hated me.
They made me guardian of the vineyards
yet I failed to guard my own vineyard.
You whom my soul loves, tell me
where you graze your sheep,
where they lie down at noon.

Why should I wander veiled
among the flocks of your companions?

Like My Glowing Mare (1:8–11)

O beautiful one, if you don't know,
go and follow the flocks

and feed your lambs and small goats
by the shepherd's tents.

I compare you to my mare
glowing among the Pharaoh's stallions.
Your cheeks tease me with earrings,
your necks with strings of jewels.
I will make gold loops for your ears,
with studs of silver.

Between My Breasts (1:12–14)

While the king lay on his couch
the spikenard aroma of my body filled the air.
My love is a sachet of myrrh
as he lies at night between my breasts.
My love is a cluster of henna blossoms
in the desert orchard of Ein Gedi.

King and Woman (1:15–17)

You are beautiful, my darling.
You are beautiful,
your eyes are doves.

You are beautiful, my lover.
You are beautiful,
our couch is the fresh grass,
the beams of our house are cedar,
our rafters are the cypress.

Lily (2:1–2)

I am a rose of Sharon,
a lily of the valleys.

A lily among thorns
is my love among women.

In the Rooms (2:3–7)

An apple tree among young men.
I delight in his shadow

and lie before him
and his fruit is sweet to my tongue.

He led me to his drinking room
and his banner over me is love.

Feed me your raisins,
comfort me with apples,

for I am sick with love.
His left hand is under my head,

his right hand caresses my body.
O daughters of Jerusalem,

swear by the gazelles
and the deer of the hills

not to wake us
till after we have merged in love.

My Lover's Voice (2:8–14)

My lover's voice is coming.
Hear him. O hear

him leaping on the mountains,
dancing on the hills!

My love is like a gazelle
or a young stag.

Here is he standing
behind our wall,

gazing in though the window,
peering through the lattice.

My lover answers
and speaks to me:

"Rise, my love, my beauty
and come away.

Winter is past,
the rains are over and gone.

Wild flowers appear on the earth,
the time of the nightingale has come.

The voice of the turtledove
is heard in our land.

The fig tree is grown heavy
with small green figs,

and grapevines are in bloom,
pouring out fragrance.

Rise, my love, my beauty,
and come away.

My dove, you are in the crevices of the rock,
in the recess of the cliffs.

Let me look at your face,
let me hear you.

Your voice is delicious
and your face is clear beauty."

The Foxes (2:15)

We must catch the foxes,
the little foxes,

who are ravaging the grapes.
Our vineyards are in blossom.

In Lilies and Mountains (2:16–17)

My lover is mine
and I am his.

He feeds his sheep
among the lilies.

Till day cools
and shadows tumble,

come stay with me.
Be a gazelle

or a young stag bounding
on jagged mountains.

In My Bed at Night (3:1–5)

In my bed at night
I look for him whom my soul loves
and cannot find him.

I'll rise and wander in the city
through streets and markets,
looking for him whom my soul loves.

Yet I cannot find him.
The watchmen who go about the city
find me. I ask them:

Have you seen him whom my soul loves?
I barely leave them
when I find him whom my soul loves.

I seize him. I won't let him go
until I've taken him to my mother's room
and he is lying in the bed

of her who conceived me.
O daughters of Jerusalem,
swear by the gazelles

and the deer of the hills
not to wake us
till after we have merged in love.

Solomon Is Coming (3:6–11)

Who is coming up from the sand and wilderness
        like a pillar of smoke
from burning myrrh and frankincense
        and all the powders of the merchant?

Look. It is the carriage of Solomon
        and around it sixty brave men,
sixty brave men from Israel.
        They carry swords and are expert in war.

Swords are strapped to their thighs
        against the terror in the night.
King Solomon made a carriage
        from the cedars of Lebanon.

He made the posts of silver, its backs
        of gold, its seat purple
and the interior inlaid with love
        by the daughters of Jerusalem.

Come outdoors, daughters of Zion. Gaze
        on the king with the crown
his mother gave him on his wedding day,
        the day his heart was happy.

Your Lips Are a Thread of Scarlet (4:1–5)

You are beauty, my love,
you are the beautiful.
Your eyes are doves

behind your veil.
Your hair is a flock
of black goats weaving

down the hills of Gilead.
Your teeth are flocks
of lambs newly shorn

fresh from the watering
trough, perfect,
with no flaw in them.

Your lips are a thread
of scarlet and your voice
is cloth of softness.

Your cheeks are halves
of a fresh pomegranate
cut open and gleaming

behind your veil.
Your neck is a straight
tower of David

built with turrets
and a thousand shields,
armor of brave men.

Your breasts are twin
fawns, twins of a gazelle
feeding among the lilies.

Before Twilight (4:6)

Till afternoon is cold
and its shadows blur,

I will climb over
the mountains of myrrh

and wander across a hill
of spices.

Perfection (4:7)

In you is beauty,
my lover, with
no stain in you.

Come Away with Me (4:8)

Come away with me. Let us leave Lebanon.
Let us leave the hills,
my bride.
Come down from the peak of Amana.
Let us descend the peaks of Senir
and Hermon. We will abandon
the dens of lions
and walk down the mountain of leopards.

Love Better than Wine (4:9–11)

You have ravished my heart, my sister, my bride,
you ravished my heart with one of your eyes,

with a single jewel from your necklace.
How tasty are your breasts, my sister, my bride!
How much better is your love than wine.
Your ointments are richer than any spice,
your lips drip like the honeycomb, my bride,
and under your tongue are honey and milk.
Your clothing tastes of Lebanon's meadows.

My Sister, My Bride (4:12–15)

My sister, my bride, you are a garden
enclosed and hidden,

a spring locked up, a fountain sealed.
Your cheeks

are an orchard of pomegranates
with rare fruits,

henna with, spikenard, spikenard and saffron,
calamus and cinnamon

and every tree bearing incense. From you
drip aloes

and all choice spices. You are a fountain
of gardens,

a well of living waters and bubbling springs
from Lebanon.

Winds (4:16)

Awake, north wind and come south wind!
Blow on my garden, let the spices

be tossed about. Let my love come into
his garden and eat his precious fruits.

Gardener (5:1)

My sister and bride, I enter the orchard and gather
        wild herbs and condiments.
I eat my honeycomb with honey, drink wine with milk.

Friends and lovers, imitate me. Drink deep.

My Hair Is Wet with Drops of Night (5:2–8)

I'm sleeping but my heart is awake.
My lover's voice is knocking:
"Open, let me in, my sister and darling, my dove
        and perfect one.
My head is soaked with dew,
my hair is wet with drops of night."

I have taken off my garments.
How can I put them on?
I have washed my feet.
How can I dirty them now?
My lover's hand shows at the door
and in me I burn for him.
I rise to open to my love,
my hands drip with liquid myrrh,
my fingers drench perfume
over the handle of the bolt.
I open to my love
but my love has turned and gone.
He has vanished.
When he spoke my soul vanished.
I look for him and can't find him.
I call. He doesn't answer.
The watchmen who go about the city
find me.
They beat me, they wound me,
they strip me of my mantle,
those guardians of the walls!

I beg you, daughters of Jerusalem,
if you find my love
you will say
that I am sick with love.

Her Companions (5:9)

How is your friend the prince of lovers,
O beautiful woman?
How is your friend the prince of lovers?
Why do you swear us to an oath?

Doves by the Small Rivers (5:10–16)

My love is radiant. He is ruddy,
one in ten thousand.
His head is fine gold,
his locks are palm leaves in the wind,
black like ravens.
His eyes are doves by the small rivers.
They are bathed in milk
and deeply set.
His cheeks are a bed of spices
blowing in fragrance.
His lips are lilies,
moist with tastes.

His arms are rounded gold
inset with beryl.
His belly is luminous ivory
starred with sapphires.
His legs are columns of alabaster
set on bases of gold.
His appearance is the tall city of Lebanon,
excellent with cedars.
His mouth is luscious, made of desire,
all of him is pleasant.
This is my lover and friend,
O daughters of Jerusalem.

Companions (6:1)

Where has your lover gone, beautiful
        woman?
He's disappeared. Where has he turned to?
Tell us. We will help you find him.

Lilies (6:2–3)

My love has gone down to his garden
to the beds of spices,
to feed his sheep in the orchards,
to gather lilies.
I am my lover's and my lover is mine.
He feeds his flock among the lilies.

A City with Banners (6:4–10)

Your beauty is Tirzah
or even Jerusalem
and frightening as

an army with banners.
Look away from me.
You make me tremble.

Your hair is a flock
of black goats weaving
down the hills of Gilead.

Your teeth are flocks
of lambs newly shorn
fresh from the watering

trough, perfect,
with no flaw in them.
Your cheeks are halves

of a fresh pomegranate
cut open and gleaming
behind your veil.

Sixty queens and eighty
concubines and countless
virgins are nothing

like my dove, my perfect
love who is unique. She's
the darling of her mother.

Women look at her and call
her happy. Concubines
and queens praise her.

Who is she? Her gaze
is daybreak, her beauty
the moon, and she is

the transparent sun,
yet frightening as
an army with banners.

Walking Around (6:11–12)

I go down to the orchard of nut trees
to see the green plants of the valley,
to see if the vines are in bud,
whether the pomegranates have blossomed.
Unaware, my soul leads me
into a chariot beside my prince.

Companions (6:13)

Come back, come back, O Shulamite,
and we shall look at you.

Dancer (6:13)

Will you look at the Shulamite
as at a dancer before two armies?

Your Navel a Moon-Hollow Goblet (7:1–7)

Your sandaled feet define grace,
O queenly woman!

Your round thighs are jewels,
handiwork of a cunning craftsman,

your navel a moon-hollow goblet
filled with mixed wines.

Your belly is a bed of wheat
laced with daffodils.

Your two breasts are two fawns,
twins of a gazelle.

Your neck is a tower of ivory,
your eyes are pools in Heshbon

by the gate of Beth-rabbim.
Your nose is a tower of Lebanon

facing the city of Damascus.
Your head is like Carmel,

and purple is your flowing hair
in which a king lies captive.

How calm and beautiful you are,
my happy love.

You are stately like a palm tree
and your breasts a cluster of grapes.

I Will Climb (7:8–9)

I will climb the palm tree
and take hold of the bough.
Let your breasts be the grapes of the vine,
your breath the taste of apples.
Your mouth is choice wine,
and swallowing it smoothly
makes my lips tremble in sleep.

Let Us Go Out into the Fields (7:10–13)

I am my lover's and he desires me.

Come, my darling,
let us go out into the fields
and spend the night in villages.
Let us wake early and go to the vineyards
and see if the vine is in blossom,
if the new grape-bud is open
and the pomegranates are in bloom.

There I will give you my love.
The mandrakes will spray aroma,
and over our door will be precious fruit,

all the new and old
that I have saved for you, my darling.

If You Were My Brother (8:1–4)

Oh, if you were my brother
who sucked my mother's breasts!

When I find you in the streets
or country, unashamed

I will kiss you
and no one will despise me.

I'll take you to my mother's home
and into her room

where she conceived me
and there you'll instruct me.

I'll give you spiced wine to drink,
the juice of my pomegranates.

Your left hand lies under my head,
your right hand caresses my body.

O daughters of Jerusalem,
swear by the deer of the hills

not to wake us
till after we have merged in love.

Companions (8:5)

Who is coming out of the desert wilderness,
leaning on her lover?

Under the Apple Tree (8:5)

Under the apple tree I aroused you
and you woke to me
where your mother was in labor,
where she who bore you was in labor.

A Seal on Your Heart (8:6–7)

Set me as a seal on your heart,
as a seal on your arm,
for love is strong as death.
Jealousy is cruel as the grave.

Its flashes are flashes of fire,
a flame of God.
Many waters cannot quench love,
rivers cannot drown it.
If a man measured love
by all the wealth of his house,
he would be utterly scorned.

The Brothers (7:8–9)

We have a young sister
and she has no breasts.
What will we do for our sister
when they ask for her hand?
If she is a wall
we will build turrets of silver on her.
If she is a door
we will enclose her with boards of cedar.

Her Towers (7:10)

I am a wall
and my breasts are towers,
and in his eyes
I bring peace.

Her Vineyard (7:11–12)

Solomon has a vineyard at Baal-hamon.
He let out the vines to the guardians,
each bringing a thousand pieces of silver
for the good fruit.

My own vineyard is about me.
You may keep the thousand, my king,
and use two hundred to pay off the guardians.

The King Begs (7:13)

You who live in the gardens,
my friends are listening for your voice.
Let me hear it too.

Come, Young Stag (7:14)

Hurry, my darling!
and be like a gazelle
or a young stag
upon my mountain of spices.

Isaiah (Revised Standard Version)

Isaiah, the son of Amos, was a prophet who lived in Jerusalem. He prophesied largely about the city and Judah during the period 740 to 687 B.C. But the book of Isaiah contains the philosophy and writings of at least three distinct figures: Isaiah 1–39, Deutero-Isaiah 40–55 (553–539 B.C.), and Trito-Isaiah 55–66, who was post-Exilic, that is, after the return of the Jews from Babylon in 538 B.C. For the sake of general statements, however, it is convenient as well as traditional to speak of the book and author simply as Isaiah. Isaiah is one of the most powerful and glorious poets in the Bible—especially First and Second Isaiah. First Isaiah is one of the supreme rhetorical and lyrical poets of the Bible; Second Isaiah is sumptuous and sonorous in speech, passionate in his hope of return to Zion. To gain return, he says,

> I will open rivers in high places,
>> and fountains in the midst of the valleys;
> I will make the wilderness a pool of water,
>> and the dry land springs of water. (41:18)

Isaiah has many voices, of wrath and promised punishment, but also one that reveals his hopes for an era of Edenic peace when war will be gone and people and beast all live in harmony. Among his most famous passages are 9:5–7, in which he states "a child is born" who will be called "Wonderful Counselor, Mighty God, Everlasting Father, Prince of Peace." Such messianic prediction is central to the Hebrew Bible. In this context, Isaiah informs us that the Prince's dominion in peace will be to ensure forever the integrity and power of the throne of David, that is, the stability and continuation of the Jewish monarchy in Jerusalem. Standard Christian typological interpretation of this passage informs us that Isaiah is predicting the coming of the later rabbinical messiah, Jesus Christ.

FURTHER READING: Isaiah. Ackroyd, Peter R. *Exile and Restoration,* 1968. Blenkinsopp, Joseph. *A History of Prophecy in Israel,* 1983. Delitzch, F. J. *Biblical Commentary on the 5-Prophesies of Isaiah,* 1980. Fishbane, Michael. *Biblical Interpretation in Ancient Israel,* 1985. Kaiser, Otto. *Isaiah 1–12: A Commentary,* 1983.

The People Who Walked in Darkness

9:2–3

The people who walked in darkness
>have seen a great light;
those who dwelt in a land of deep darkness,
>on them has light shined.
Thou hast multiplied the nation,
>thou hast increased its joy;
they rejoice before thee

as with joy at the harvest,
     as men rejoice when they divide the spoil.

9:6–7

For to us a child is born,
     to us a son is given;
and the government will be upon his shoulder,
     and his name will be called
"Wonderful Counselor, Mighty God,
     Everlasting Father, Prince of Peace."
Of the increase of his government and of peace
     there will be no end,
upon the throne of David, and over his kingdom,
     to establish it, and to uphold it
with justice and with righteousness
     from this time forth and for evermore.
The zeal of the LORD of hosts will do this.

11:1–9

There shall come forth a shoot from the stump of Jesse,
     and a branch shall grow out of his roots.
And the Spirit of the LORD shall rest upon him,
     the spirit of wisdom and understanding,
     the spirit of counsel and might,
     the spirit of knowledge and the fear of the LORD.
And his delight shall be in the fear of the LORD.

He shall not judge by what his eyes see,
     or decide by what his ears hear;
but with righteousness he shall judge the poor,
     and decide with equity for the meek of the earth;
and he shall smite the earth with the rod of his mouth,
     and with the breath of his lips he shall slay the wicked.
Righteousness shall be the girdle of his waist,
     and faithfulness the girdle of his loins.

The wolf shall dwell with the lamb,
     and the leopard shall lie down with the kid,
and the calf and the lion and the fatling together,
     and a little child shall lead them.
The cow and the bear shall feed;
     their young shall lie down together;
     and the lion shall eat straw like the ox.
The sucking child shall play over the hole of the asp,
     and the weaned child shall put his hand on the adder's den.

> They shall not hurt or destroy
>   in all my holy mountain;
> for the earth shall be full of the knowledge of the LORD
>   as the waters cover the sea.

Daniel (Revised Standard Version)

The Daniel of the book that bears his name lived in the days of the last Babylonian kings Nebuchadnezzar and Belteshazzar. The book attributed to him contains stories, parables, dream interpretations, and apocalyptic visions. Earlier figures may be the source of the "wise and just" Daniel, such as Dan'l in the fourteenth-century B.C. Ugaritic epic *Aqhat*. Written in Hebrew and Aramaic, Daniel has been called a diaspora novel. The first half contains six amazing court tales about Daniel and his three friends Hananiah, Mishael, and Azariah (Shadrach, Meshach, and Abednego), who were to be tested by fire. Astoundingly, Daniel has such power through his faith and God's intervention that he can read a Babylonian king's mind and interpret his dream and also survive unharmed in a Persian king's den of lions; as a result, each monarch acknowledges the power and superiority of Daniel's living god. Like Joseph, the interpreter of dreams who succeeds in rising high in the Egyptian court by explaining the Pharaoh's dream, Daniel, also an exile, interprets his monarch's dreams and is similarly favored with high station. Then follows the second section with dreams and visions, which includes the persecution and salvation of Jews in Jerusalem under Antiochus IV Epiphanes in the second century B.C.

Daniel is another book whose authorship and period are steeped in controversy. A sixth-century historian by Jewish designation, and prophet by Christian regard, he speaks in detail about many events in the third and second centuries B.C., such as third-century wars between the Ptolemaic and Selucid empires, and his historical writing extends to the second-century Maccabean revolt. Modern scholarship dates the bulk of Daniel early in the second century B.C. It was anciently common to predate a text and attribute it to an earlier great figure, thereby giving it authority and a possible place in the canon by appearing to predict what historically had actually occurred. So, while the chapters of Daniel concerning Babylon may have been composed by a sixth-century author, that same author could only by miracle have had foreknowledge of events described in the text that took place three and four centuries later. It is probable that there is more than one author to Daniel or that a book, based on earlier texts, was composed much later than that of the traditional Daniel, by one who was willing to suppress his own name for inclusion of his work in the Holy Bible. The huge amount of scriptures from the Judeo-Christian intertestamental period, similarly pseudepigraphical and often of insuperable beauty and imagination, attests to the practice of predating work and authorship for canonical acceptance. The book of Daniel as we have it, which some commentators suggest was written between 167 B.C. and 164 B.C., is a book of divination and a precursor of the apocalyptic vision in Revelation. It also announces the good news of God's triumphant intervention on behalf of his people as earlier he intervened to save Daniel's three friends from the furnace. God, following a timetable of events, will bring those who serve the cause of justice and righteousness the kingdom of Heaven. As the latest book of the Hebrew Bible, Daniel, close to the apocalyptic scriptures of the intertestament period and Revelation itself, is a bridge to the New Testament.

FURTHER READING: Daniel. di Lella, A. A. *Introduction to The Book of Daniel*, 1978.

Nebuchadnezzar's Dream

2:1–19

In the second year of the reign of Nebuchadnezzar, Nebuchadnezzar had dreams; and his spirit was troubled, and his sleep left him. Then the king commanded that the magicians, the enchanters, the sorcerers, and the Chaldeans be summoned, to tell the king his dreams. So they came in and stood before the king.

And the king said to them, "I had a dream, and my spirit is troubled to know the dream."

Then the Chaldeans said to the king, "O king, live for ever! Tell your servants the dream, and we will show the interpretation."

The king answered the Chaldeans, "The word from me is sure: if you do not make known to me the dream and its interpretation, you shall be torn limb from limb, and your houses shall be laid in ruins. But if you show the dream and its interpretation, you shall receive from me gifts and rewards and great honor. Therefore show me the dream and its interpretation."

They answered a second time, "Let the king tell his servants the dream, and we will show its interpretation."

The king answered, "I know with certainty that you are trying to gain time, because you see that the word from me is sure that if you do not make the dream known to me, there is but one sentence for you. You have agreed to speak lying and corrupt words before me till the times change. Therefore tell me the dream, and I shall know that you can show me its interpretation."

The Chaldeans answered the king, "There is not a man on earth who can meet the king's demand; for no great and powerful king has asked such a thing of any magician or enchanter or Chaldean. The thing that the king asks is difficult, and none can show it to the king except the gods, whose dwelling is not with flesh."

Because of this the king was angry and very furious, and commanded that all the wise men of Babylon be destroyed. So the decree went forth that the wise men were to be slain, and they sought Daniel and his companions to slay them.

Then Daniel replied with prudence and discretion to Arioch, the captain of the king's guard, who had gone out to slay the wise men of Babylon; he said to Arioch, the king's captain, "Why is the decree of the king so severe?"

Then Arioch made the matter known to Daniel. And Daniel went in and besought the king to appoint him a time, that he might show to the king the interpretation.

Then Daniel went to his house and made the matter known to Hananiah, Mishael, and Azariah, his companions, and told them to seek mercy of the God of heaven concerning this mystery, so that Daniel and his companions might not perish with the rest of the wise men of Babylon. Then the mystery was revealed to Daniel in a vision of the night. Then Daniel blessed the God of heaven.

2:24–29

Therefore Daniel went in to Arioch, whom the king had appointed to destroy the wise men of Babylon; he went and said thus to him, "Do not destroy the wise men of Babylon; bring me in before the king, and I will show the king the interpretation."

Then Arioch brought in Daniel before the king in haste, and said thus to him: "I have found among the exiles from Judah a man who can make known to the king the interpretation."

The king said to Daniel, whose name was Belteshazzar, "Are you able to make known to me the dream that I have seen and its interpretation?"

Daniel answered the king, "No wise men, enchanters, magicians, or astrologers can show to the king the mystery which the king has asked, but there is a God in heaven who reveals mysteries, and he has made known to King Nebuchadnezzar what will be in the latter days. Your dream and the visions of your head as you lay in bed are these:

"To you, O king, as you lay in bed came thoughts of what would be hereafter, and he who reveals mysteries made known to you what is to be.

2:31–49

"You saw, O king, and behold, a great image. This image, mighty and of exceeding brightness, stood before you, and its appearance was frightening. The head of this image was of fine gold, its breast and arms of silver, its belly and thighs of bronze, its legs of iron, its feet partly of iron and partly of clay.

"As you looked, a stone was cut out by no human hand, and it smote the image on its feet of iron and clay, and broke them in pieces; then the iron, the clay, the bronze, the silver, and the gold, all together were broken in pieces, and became like the chaff of the summer threshing floors; and the wind carried them away, so that not a trace of them could be found. But the stone that struck the image became a great mountain and filled the whole earth.

"This was the dream; now we will tell the king its interpretation. You, O king, the king of kings, to whom the God of heaven has given the kingdom, the power, and the might, and the glory, and into whose hand he has given, wherever they dwell, the sons of men, the beasts of the field, and the birds of the air, making you rule over them all—you are the head of gold. After you shall arise another kingdom inferior to you, and yet a third kingdom of bronze, which shall rule over all the earth. And there shall be a fourth kingdom, strong as iron, because iron breaks to pieces and shatters all things; and like iron which crushes, it shall break and crush all these.

"And as you saw the feet and toes partly of potter's clay and partly of iron, it shall be a divided kingdom; but some of the firmness of iron shall be in it, just as you saw iron mixed with the miry clay. And as the toes of the feet were partly iron and partly clay, so the kingdom shall be partly strong and partly brittle. As you saw the iron mixed with miry clay, so they will mix with one another in marriage, but they will not hold together, just as iron does not mix with clay.

"And in the days of those kings the God of heaven will set up a kingdom which shall never be destroyed, nor shall its sovereignty be left to another people. It shall break in pieces all these kingdoms and bring them to an end, and it shall stand for ever; just as you saw that a stone was cut from a mountain by no human hand, and that it broke in pieces the iron, the bronze, the clay, the silver, and the gold. A great God has made known to the king what shall be hereafter. The dream is certain, and its interpretation sure."

Then King Nebuchadnezzar fell upon his face, and did homage to Daniel, and commanded that an offering and incense be offered up to him.

The king said to Daniel, "Truly, your God is God of gods and Lord of kings, and a revealer of mysteries, for you have been able to reveal this mystery."

Then the king gave Daniel high honors and many great gifts, and made him ruler over the whole province of Babylon, and chief prefect over all the wise men of Babylon. Daniel made request of the king, and he appointed Shadrach, Meshach, and Abednego over the affairs of the province of Babylon; but Daniel remained at the king's court.

The Golden Image and the Fiery Furnace

3:1–2

King Nebuchadnezzar made an image of gold, whose height was sixty cubits and its breadth six cubits. He set it up on the plain of Dura, in the province of Babylon. Then King Nebuchadnezzar sent to assemble the satraps, the prefects, and the governors, the counselors, the treasurers, the justices, the magistrates, and all the officials of the provinces to come to the dedication of the image which King Nebuchadnezzar had set up.

3:4–9

And the herald proclaimed aloud, "You are commanded, O peoples, nations, and languages, that when you hear the sound of the born, pipe, lyre, trigon, harp, bagpipe, and every kind of music, you are to fall down and worship the golden image that King Nebuchadnezzar has set up; and whoever does not fall down and worship shall immediately be cast into a burning fiery furnace."

Therefore, as soon as all the peoples heard the sound of the born, pipe, lyre, trigon, harp, bagpipe, and every kind of music, all the peoples, nations, and languages fell down and worshiped the golden image which King Nebuchadnezzar had set up.

At that time certain Chaldeans came forward and maliciously accused the Jews. They said to King Nebuchadnezzar, "O king, live for ever!

3:12–14

There are certain Jews whom you have appointed over the affairs of the province of Babylon: Shadrach, Meshach, and Abednego. These men, O king, pay no heed to you; they do not serve your gods or worship the golden image which you have set up."

Then Nebuchadnezzar in furious rage commanded that Shadrach, Meshach, and Abednego be brought. Then they brought these men before the king.

Nebuchadnezzar said to them, "Is it true, O Shadrach, Meshach, and Abednego, that you do not serve my gods or worship the golden image which I have set up?"

3:16–19

Shadrach, Meshach, and Abednego answered the king, "O Nebuchadnezzar, we have no need to answer you in this matter. If it be so, our God whom we serve is able to deliver us from the burning fiery furnace; and he will deliver us out of your hand, O king. But if not, be it known to you, O king, that we will not serve your gods or worship the golden image which you have set up."

Then Nebuchadnezzar was full of fury, and the expression of his face was changed against Shadrach, Meshach, and Abednego. He ordered the furnace heated seven times more than it was wont to be heated.

3:21–22

Then these men were bound in their mantles, their tunics, their hats, and their other garments, and they were cast into the burning fiery furnace. Because the king's order was strict and the furnace very hot, the flame of the fire slew those men who took up Shadrach, Meshach, and Abednego.

3:24–30

Then King Nebuchadnezzar was astonished and rose up in haste. He said to his counselors, "Did we not cast three men bound into the fire?"

They answered the king, "True, O king."

He answered, "But I see four men loose, walking in the midst of the fire, and they are not hurt; and the appearance of the fourth is like a son of the gods."

Then Nebuchadnezzar came near to the door of the burning fiery furnace and said, "Shadrach, Meshach, and Abednego, servants of the Most High God, come forth, and come here!"

Then Shadrach, Meshach, and Abednego came out from the fire. And the satraps, the prefects, the governors, and the king's counselors gathered together and saw that the fire had not had any power over the bodies of those men; the hair of their heads was not singed, their mantles were not harmed, and no smell of fire had come upon them.

Nebuchadnezzar said, "Blessed be the God of Shadrach, Meshach, and Abednego, who has sent his angel and delivered his servants, who trusted in him, and set at nought the king's command, and yielded up their bodies rather than serve and worship any god except their own God. Therefore I make a decree: Any people, nation, or language that speaks anything against the God of Shadrach, Meshach, and Abednego shall be torn limb from limb, and their houses laid in ruins; for there is no other god who is able to deliver in this way."

Then the king promoted Shadrach, Meshach, and Abednego in the province of Babylon.

Jewish Apocrypha: Susanna, and Bel and the Dragon (New Revised Standard Version)

The Jewish Apocrypha designates a group of important scriptures that survives only in Greek translation. Because a Hebrew original was not available, their authenticity could not be proved, and, although they were given a place in most Bibles, they were never fully received into the canon. Hence, their origin was "apocryphal," that is, hidden. They were found only in the Septuagint Bible, a translation from the Hebrew made during the second century B.C., for Jews who could no longer read Hebrew, in Alexandria, the greatest center of Jewish life in the Hellenistic world. Since the Septuagint was known to be a translation from the Hebrew Bible, it could be assumed that at least some of the Apocryphya, whose source texts were missing, must have had original Scripture behind them. This view was reinforced with the discovery of the Dead Sea Scrolls at Qumran in 1947. There, scattered among the major Dead Sea Scrolls, were fragments in Hebrew of the standard Apocrypha, such as Sirach (Ecclesiasticus). Along with other earlier discoveries of fragmentary Hebrew manuscripts (the Geniza finds in the Qarite synagogue in Old Cairo between 1896 and 1900), there is ample evidence to believe not only that there was a Hebrew original for some books of the Apocrypha but that certain ones, as in the instance of Susanna, were translations of Hebrew or Aramaic texts that went all the way back to the sixth-century B.C. exile in Babylon.

The Jewish Apocrypha, sometimes called the "deuterocanonical" (secondarily canonical) books, are included as a quasi-canonical supplement in the Bibles read by Jews, Catholics, and Eastern Orthodox, but not by Protestants. Consequently, we do not find the Apocrypha in the King James Version. In the Christian Bibles that include the Apocrypha, they are placed between the Old and New Testaments. Since the Hebrew, Catholic, and Greek Orthodox Bibles accept different books of the Apocrypha, the number of standard Apocrypha varies according to denomination. In the New Revised Standard Version (1989) many books are listed: Additions to Esther, Baruch, Bel and the Dragon, Ecclesiasticus, 1 Edras, 2 Edras, Judith, Letter of Jeremiah, Ecclesiasticus or the Wisdom of Jesus Son of Sirach, 1 Maccabees, 2 Maccabees, 3 Maccabees, 4 Maccabees, Prayer of Azariah, Prayer of Manasseh, Psalm 151, 235, Song of the Three Jews, Susanna, Tobit, and Wisdom of Solomon. In addition to these standard Apocrypha (and 3 and 4 Maccabees have only recently been included among the standard Apocrypha), there is an enormous literature of noncanonical Apocrypha in Hebrew, Greek, Syriac, Latin, and other languages, which constitutes the majority of intertestamental scriptures (books between the Old and New Testaments) and which are usually designated as the pseudepigrapha; among the great intertestamental works are the now-famed Dead Sea Scrolls.

The two Apocrypha included in this volume are Susanna and Bel and the Dragon.

Susanna was a beautiful young woman, married to Joakim, a respected and wealthy Jew in Babylonia during the period of exile (597/586–538/537 B.C.). She had the habit of walking in her garden every afternoon. Two elders of the community entered the garden, hid, and found Susanna (meaning "lily") bathing in her garden. The men desired her. They concocted a plot against her virtue. They rushed out and demanded that she sleep with them or they would accuse her of adultery with a young man. She refused and the elders carried out their threat. She was denounced, tried, and sentenced to death. In the end, she was saved by Daniel's intervention and wisdom, with dire consequences for her accusers. It is a marvelous story, which has been a persistent subject in Christian literature and art. The implications of this sensual tale have led to multiple moral and historic interpretations, and, like good narration, they are mere speculations, meaning that the tale must always be interpreted anew. The origin of the story, as all the tales in which Daniel is a character, is equally uncertain. It may be, as some scholars contend, a standard folk tale, with names changed. In any case, it remains a vivid wisdom tale, replete with symbolism, and one of the great short pieces of world literature.

In Bel and the Dragon, we again find Daniel the detective coming up with solutions to save the good and the faithful. Bel, equivalent to Baal, was a name for Marduk, the high god of Babylon. In Bel and the Dragon, the dragon god Bel and his priests are undone by Daniel, who immediately asserts that there is no god but the God of Daniel. With Houdini skill, Daniel slips out of life-threatening situations to prove, by his own ingenuity and the miraculous journey of God's angel, that the faith of the Jews is unique and right. This brief book, with all its charm and its fascinating, incredible plot, has a distinct ring of national and religious propaganda to it. It is not unusual for religious literature to carry on a polemic against other religions, especially when threatened, as in the Exilic setting of Bel. Despite the story's setting in Babylon of the Exile, it is believed that Bel was actually composed centuries later in the Hellenistic period. The didactic purpose of this tale may have been to set up an allegory between the temptations of Babylon (remember "the whore of Babylon" from Revelation) and the temptations of pagan Hellenism. So this popular fable of Bel and the Dragon may have been intended to counter the strong attraction to the Jews of the prevailing Greek culture.

FURTHER READING: Susanna, and Bel and the Dragon. Metzger, Bruce M., and Michael D. Coogan. *The Oxford Companion to the Bible,* 1993.

Susanna (Chapter 13 of the Greek version of Daniel)

There was a man living in Babylon whose name was Joakim. He married the daughter of Hilkiah, named Susanna, a very beautiful woman and one who feared the Lord. Her parents were righteous, and had trained their daughter according to the law of Moses. Joakim was very rich, and had a fine garden adjoining his house; the Jews used to come to him because he was the most honored of them all.

That year two elders from the people were appointed as judges. Concerning them the Lord had said: "Wickedness came forth from Babylon, from elders who were judges, who were supposed to govern the people." These men were frequently at Joakim's house, and all who had a case to be tried came to them there.

When the people left at noon, Susanna would go into her husband's garden to walk. Every day the two elders used to see her, going in and walking about, and they began to lust for her. They suppressed their consciences and turned away their eyes from looking to Heaven or remembering their duty to administer justice. Both were overwhelmed with passion for her, but they did not tell each other of their distress, for they were ashamed to disclose their lustful desire to seduce her. Day after day they watched eagerly to see her.

One day they said to each other, "Let us go home, for it is time for lunch." So they both left and parted from each other. But turning back, they met again; and when each pressed the other for the reason, they confessed their lust. Then together they arranged for a time when they could find her alone.

Once, while they were watching for an opportune day, she went in as before with only two maids, and wished to bathe in the garden, for it was a hot day. No one was there except the two elders, who had hidden themselves and were watching her. She said to her maids, "Bring me olive oil and ointments, and shut the garden doors so that I can bathe." They did as she told them: they shut the doors of the garden and went out by the side doors to bring what they had been commanded; they did not see the elders, because they were hiding.

When the maids had gone out, the two elders got up and ran to her. They said, "Look, the garden doors are shut, and no one can see us. We are burning with desire for you; so give your consent, and lie with us. If you refuse, we will testify against you that a young man was with you, and this was why you sent your maids away."

Susanna groaned and said, "I am completely trapped. For if I do this, it will mean death for me; if I do not, I cannot escape your hands. I choose not to do it; I will fall into your hands, rather than sin in the sight of the Lord."

Then Susanna cried out with a loud voice, and the two elders shouted against her. And one of them ran and opened the garden doors. When the people in the house heard the shouting in the garden, they rushed in at the side door to see what had happened to her. And when the elders told their story, the servants felt very much ashamed, for nothing like this had ever been said about Susanna.

The next day, when the people gathered at the house of her husband Joakim, the two elders came, full of their wicked plot to have Susanna put to death. In the presence of the people they said, "Send for Susanna daughter of Hilkiah, the wife of Joakim." So they sent for her. And she came with her parents, her children, and all her relatives.

Now Susanna was a woman of great refinement and beautiful in appearance. As she was veiled, the scoundrels ordered her to be unveiled, so that they might feast their eyes on her beauty. Those who were with her and all who saw her were weeping.

Then the two elders stood up before the people and laid their hands on her head. Through her tears she looked up toward Heaven, for her heart trusted in the Lord. The elders said, "While we were walking in the garden alone, this woman came in with two maids, shut the garden doors, and dismissed the maids. Then a young man, who was hiding there, came to her and lay with her. We were in a corner of the garden, and when we saw this wickedness we ran to them. Although we saw them embracing, we could not hold the man, because he was stronger than we, and he opened the doors and got away. We did, however, seize this woman and asked who the young man was, but she would not tell us. These things we testify."

Because they were elders of the people and judges, the assembly believed them and condemned her to death.

Then Susanna cried out with a loud voice, and said, "O eternal God, you know what is secret and are aware of all things before they come to be; you know that these men have given false evidence against me. And now I am to die, though I have done none of the wicked things that they have charged against me!"

The Lord heard her cry. Just as she was being led off to execution, God stirred up the holy spirit of a young lad named Daniel, and he shouted with a loud voice, "I want no part in shedding this woman's blood!"

All the people turned to him and asked, "What is this you are saying?" Taking his stand among them he said, "Are you such fools, O Israelites, as to condemn a daughter of Israel without examination and without learning the facts? Return to court, for these men have given false evidence against her."

So all the people hurried back. And the rest of the elders said to him, "Come, sit among us and inform us, for God has given you the standing of an elder." Daniel said to them, "Separate them far from each other, and I will examine them."

When they were separated from each other, he summoned one of them and said to him, "You old relic of wicked days, your sins have now come home, which you have committed in the past, pronouncing unjust judgments, condemning the innocent and acquitting the guilty, though the Lord said, 'You shall not put an innocent and righteous person to death.' Now then, if you really saw this woman, tell me this: Under what tree did you see them being intimate with each other?" He answered, "Under a mastic tree." And Daniel said, "Very well! This lie has cost you your head, for the angel of God has received the sentence from God and will immediately cut you in two."

Then, putting him to one side, he ordered them to bring the other. And he said to him, "You offspring of Canaan and not of Judah, beauty has beguiled you and lust has perverted your heart.

This is how you have been treating the daughters of Israel, and they were intimate with you through fear; but a daughter of Judah would not tolerate your wickedness. Now then, tell me: Under what tree did you catch them being intimate with each other?" He answered, "Under an evergreen oak." Daniel said to him, "Very well! This lie has cost you also your head, for the angel of God is waiting with his sword to split you in two, so as to destroy you both."

Then the whole assembly raised a great shout and blessed God, who saves those who hope in him. And they took action against the two elders, because out of their own mouths Daniel had convicted them of bearing false witness; they did to them as they had wickedly planned to do to their neighbor. Acting in accordance with the law of Moses, they put them to death. Thus innocent blood was spared that day.

Hilkiah and his wife praised God for their daughter Susanna, and so did her husband Joakim and all her relatives, because she was found innocent of a shameful deed. And from that day onward Daniel had a great reputation among the people.

Bel and the Dragon (Chapter 14 of the Greek version of Daniel)

When King Astyages was laid to rest with his ancestors, Cyrus the Persian succeeded to his kingdom. Daniel was a companion of the king, and was the most honored of all his friends.

Now the Babylonians had an idol called Bel, and every day they provided for it twelve bushels of choice flour and forty sheep and six measures of wine. The king revered it and went every day to worship it. But Daniel worshipped his own God.

So the king said to him, "Why do you not worship Bel?" He answered, "Because I do not revere idols made with hands, but the living God, who created heaven and earth and has dominion over all living creatures."

The king used to say to him, "Do you not think that Bel is a living god? Do you not see how much he eats and drinks every day?" And Daniel laughed, and said, "Do not be deceived, O king, for this thing is only clay inside and bronze outside, and it never ate or drank anything."

Then the king was angry and called the priests of Bel and said to them, "If you do not tell me who is eating these provisions, you shall die. But if you prove that Bel is eating them, Daniel shall die, because he has spoken blasphemy against Bel." Daniel said to the king, "Let it be done as you have said."

Now there were seventy priests of Bel, besides their wives and children. So the king went with Daniel into the temple of Bel. The priests of Bel said, "See, we are now going outside; you yourself, O king, set out the food and prepare the wine, and shut the door and seal it with your signet. When you return in the morning, if you do not find that Bel has eaten it all, we will die; otherwise Daniel will, who is telling lies about us." They were unconcerned, for beneath the table they had made a hidden entrance, through which they used to go in regularly and consume the provisions. After they had gone out, the king set out the food for Bel. Then Daniel ordered his servants to bring ashes, and they scattered them throughout the whole temple in the presence of the king alone. Then they went out, shut the door and sealed it with the king's signet, and departed. During the night the priests came as usual, with their wives and children, and they ate and drank everything.

Early in the morning the king rose and came, and Daniel with him. The king said, "Are the seals unbroken, Daniel?" He answered, "They are unbroken, O king." As soon as the doors were opened, the king looked at the table, and shouted in a loud voice, "You are great, O Bel, and in you there is no deceit at all!"

But Daniel laughed and restrained the king from going in. "Look at the floor," he said, "and notice whose footprints these are." The king said, "I see the footprints of men and women and children."

Then the king was enraged, and he arrested the priests and their wives and children. They showed him the secret doors through which they used to enter to consume what was on the table. Therefore the king put them to death, and gave Bel over to Daniel, who destroyed it and its temple.

Now in that place there was a great dragon, which the Babylonians revered. The king said to Daniel, "You cannot deny that this is a living god; so worship him." Daniel said, "I worship the Lord my God, for he is the living God. But give me permission, O king, and I will kill the dragon without sword or club." The king said, "I give you permission."

Then Daniel took pitch, fat, and hair, and boiled them together and made cakes, which he fed to the dragon. The dragon ate them, and burst open. Then Daniel said, "See what you have been worshiping!"

When the Babylonians heard about it, they were very indignant and conspired against the king, saying, "The king has become a Jew; he has destroyed Bel, and killed the dragon, and slaughtered the priests." Going to the king, they said, "Hand Daniel over to us, or else we will kill you and your household." The king saw that they were pressing him hard, and under compulsion he handed Daniel over to them.

They threw Daniel into the lions' den, and he was there for six days. There were seven lions in the den, and every day they had been given two human bodies and two sheep; but now they were given nothing, so that they would devour Daniel.

Now the prophet Habakkuk was in Judea; he had made a stew and had broken bread into a bowl, and was going into the field to take it to the reapers. But the angel of the Lord said to Habakkuk, "Take the food that you have to Babylon, to Daniel, in the lions' den." Habakkuk said, "Sir, I have never seen Babylon, and I know nothing about the den." Then the angel of the Lord took him by the crown of his head and carried him by his hair; with the speed of the wind he set him down in Babylon, right over the den.

Then Habakkuk shouted, "Daniel, Daniel! Take the food that God has sent you." Daniel said, "You have remembered me, O God, and have not forsaken those who love you." So Daniel got up and ate. And the angel of God immediately returned Habakkuk to his own place.

On the seventh day the king came to mourn for Daniel. When he came to the den he looked in, and there sat Daniel! The king shouted with a loud voice, "You are great, O Lord, the God of Daniel, and there is no other besides you!" Then he pulled Daniel out, and threw into the den those who had attempted his destruction, and they were instantly eaten before his eyes.

■ The New Testament

The New Testament is a collection of gospels, acts (a sequel to the Gospel of Luke), letters, and, like the Hebrew Bible, an anthology of distinct literary genres. Specifically, the New Testament consists of the canonical gospels, the Acts of the Apostles, the Letters, and the Book of Revelation. A gospel (meaning a book of "good news") tells the life, teachings, and death by crucifixion of Jesus Christ and is also an account of Jesus' followers, including his disciples and the crowds that traveled with this itinerant rabbi and healer around the hills of Upper and Lower Galilee, the fields of Judea, and the streets of Jerusalem. Jesus is presented in the New Testament as the Messiah, whose coming was prophesied in the Old Testament. As described in Isaiah and elsewhere in the Old Testament, the Messiah would be a salvific figure, giving his people a vision of life on earth, a special relationship with God, and the possibility of eternal life. Those who believed that Jesus was the Messiah were called Messianists. The Hebrew word *Messiah* (*Mashiah*) in Greek is translated as "Christ." So the followers of Jesus were Messianists or Christians. And Yeshua the Messiah, who was born in Israel, became known by his Greek name *Iesous O Christos,* which in English is Jesus the Christ, or simply Jesus Christ.

Jesus was born in turbulent times of rebellion against the Roman occupiers of Israel in about 3 B.C. to 7 B.C. It may seem strange to say that Christ was born before Christ, but it is now generally accepted among scholars that the date set for Jesus' birth, by Dionysius Exiguus, the creator of the Christian calendar, was off by several years. The punishment for sedition against Rome was crucifixion, and it is probable that Jesus was perceived not as a docile Jew accepting Roman rule but as an opponent. But in the form we have the New Testament, whose earliest gospel was assembled almost four decades after Jesus' death, the gospels exonerate Roman rule and justice, and by implication the later Roman Church. They depict Jesus passively before the Romans at a time when fellow Jews were being killed in great numbers for their opposition. These were not the glorious days of David and Solomon, but a crisis period of despair, with desperate hope for the coming of the Messiah promised in Holy Scripture to deliver the Jews on earth from their terrible foreign masters.

The New Testament does not present a people under oppressive foreign rule. The governor (actually the prefect) Pontius Pilate is depicted with such care that later in the Orthodox Church he will attain sainthood and be called Saint Pilate. In the gospels, he washes his hands innocently of the crucifixion and orders the execution reluctantly, coerced by others but not by his own good will, which is to esteem Jesus. In reality, Pilate was a brutal master, who massacred Samaritans and Jews, and who was eventually called back to Rome because of his excesses. Similarly, the first to recognize

Jesus' divinity after the execution is the centurion, the Roman officer in charge of the execution troops. Such a presentation clearly fits the political and religious agenda of a later time, but not the moment of Jesus' ministry and death.

The earliest texts of the New Testament that we have are written in Greek. Although Paul's Letters were written in Greek, the gospels of Matthew, Mark, Luke, and John are later Greek versions of earlier lost accounts, both oral and written, from Aramaic and probably Hebrew sources. The scriptures of the Christian New Testament concern the lives of Jews who followed Jesus and Paul, who reflected one sect among other revolutionary Jewish sects, which included the Pharisees, Zealots, Essenes, and early Gnostics. The gospels of the New Testament were written by or ascribed to Matthew, Mark, Luke, and John, who are called the Evangelists. They are traditionally thought to be three Jews and a convert to Judaism (Luke), though any knowledge of the Evangelists outside of the texts ascribed to them does not have a scholarly or historical basis. Like the Hebrew Bible, the Greek scriptures of Christianity underwent countless modifications and radical restructuring as they moved from oral history to a fixed place in the canon. As for the extent to which the narration itself has a historical base, again we have essentially no source outside the gospels themselves. We do not know what scribal hands copied, redacted, and fashioned the gospels into their present narration. In a few documents in Tacitus, Philo, and Josephus, it is noted that there was a man named Jesus who was crucified by the Romans.

In the first years after the crucifixion, the Christian Jews (those who followed Jesus) were in contention with other Jews in the synagogues for dominance. Paul wrote letters to the congregations of the synagogues in Rome, Corinth, Thessaloniki, Antioch, and Athens to persuade his co-religionists to follow Christ. By the time of the destruction of Jerusalem by Titus in A.D. 70 and the subsequent diaspora of the inhabitants of the city, the division between Christian Jews and those who did not receive Jesus as Messiah became more decisive; by the second century, the separation between Jew and Christian was irreversible. But the new Christians had no Scripture of their own. The Pauline letters were not then considered holy documents. The Old Testament was the sole Christian Bible, which most of the "primitive Christians" read in the Greek Septuagint version. The New Testament gradually was assembled, but throughout the next centuries its contents were debated fiercely by the church fathers until the end of the fourth century when there was consensus. Athanasius (A.D. 293–373) set the twenty-seven books in the order we have them today. Then, after the councils of Laodicea (A.D. 363), Hippo (A.D. 393), and Carthage (A.D. 397), the Athanasian collection was accepted as canon. With the translation by Jerome (A.D. 347–420) of the Greek New Testament into Latin, and with the Old Latin version of the Old Testament, the Christians who depended on Rome at last had a complete Bible, in Latin, the famous Vulgata.

Matthew (A.D. 80–110) Israel or Syrian Antioch (gospel)

TRANSLATED WILLIS BARNSTONE

The authorship and place and date of composition of the Gospel of Matthew are matters of speculation. In the gospel itself, the writer is identified as Levi the tax collector. "Matthew" apparently is the apostolic name of Levi, given to him by churchmen in the second century A.D. Biblical scholarship describes Matthew as steeped in rabbinical reference and learning and as a Greek-speaking Christian Jew of the second generation. It is increasingly thought that Matthew was composed in the early second century rather than soon after A.D. 70, the year of the destruction of the Temple by Titus, which is alluded to in Matthew and in the other gospels. The allusion to this specific historical event of A.D. 70 is sufficient evidence to place the composition of all the gospels at least after that year. Traditionally, Matthew is placed first in the order of the gospels, but this placement is not chronological, for Matthew derives from Mark and probably from a lost sayings gospel, the so-called Q source. The Gnostic Gospel of Thomas (50–60 B.C.) found at Nag Hammadi, Egypt, in 1945, is a sayings gospel and may have been one of those sayings books of Jesus' aphorisms and parables that fed into the sources from which Matthew derives. Matthew begins with a genealogy (most certainly appended at a later date) and with the birth of Jesus. (Luke also begins with a genealogy and is followed by the famous nativity scene of Jesus' birth in Bethlehem in a feeding trough, the manger, and hence on most grounds there is as much reason for beginning the New Testament with Luke as with Matthew.) That Mark is the earliest of the gospels and a direct source for Matthew and Luke is widely accepted, and in recent years the traditional presentation of the gospels has been changed, placing Mark at the beginning of the New Testament, as in the Richmond Lattimore and the Jesus Seminar translations of the New Testament.

There are more allusions to the Old Testament in this gospel than in the others. Matthew wrote to persuade Jews that Jesus was the foretold Messiah so they might become Christian Jews. Biblical scholarship agrees that passages of extreme anti-Semitism, such as "Let his blood be upon us and upon our children!" (27:25), in which the Jews in the street shout a curse upon themselves now and on their progeny forever, are later interpolations. The agenda of the church of Rome a century after Jesus' death was not to convert Jews to believe that their Messiah had come but to persuade new Christians that neither Jesus nor his followers were really Jews and that Jews rather than Romans had executed the Jewish rabbi.

Matthew may be said to be the most aphoristic and poetic of the gospels and closest to a sayings book. This teaching book does not have the same austere plainness and drama of Mark, which is more uniformly narrative and ends abruptly at a moment of fear and ecstasy in the cave where Jesus' body has disappeared. But Matthew also has a deep pathos and conveys a sense of Jesus as a leader of the poor and the disenfranchised in an epic of hunger and hope. Matthew covers many aspects of Jesus' life and mission, including his discourse dealing with death, resurrection, and immortality (24:1–25:46). Many of the critical moments in the New Testament are fully elaborated in Matthew, including the coming of the Magi, the birth of Jesus, the baptizing mission of John the Baptist, John's arrest and execution, and the passion week scene of Jesus' arrest, crucifixion, and the risen Jesus. Matthew's most extraordinary literary and philosophical contribution is the Sermon on the Mount (5:1–7:29), including the Beatitudes (5:3–12) and the Lord's Prayer (6:9–13). Much of the material in the Sermon on the Mount also appears dispersed through the other synoptic gospels (these are Matthew, Mark, and Luke, but not John), and the Lord's Prayer, in a shorter form, also appears in Luke 11:2–4. Apart from Revelation (Apocalypse), which is the epic poem of the New Testament, the poetry in Matthew takes its place among the great bodies of world poetry.

CHAPTER 1

The Birth of Jesus

*18*The birth of Yeshua the Messiah[1] happened in this way. Miryam[2] his mother was engaged to Yosef[3], yet before they came together she discovered a child in her womb, placed there by the holy spirit. *19*Yosef her husband, a fair man and loath to make her appear scandalous, resolved to divorce her secretly. *20*But as he was making plans, look, an angel of the Lord[4] appeared to him in a dream and said, "Yosef son of David, do not fear to take Miryam as your wife, for what is engendered in her came from the holy spirit. *21*And she will have a son, and you will name him Yeshua, for he will save[5] his people from their sins."

---

1. Jesus Christ.

2. Mary.

3. Joseph.

4. "Angel of the Lord" refers to "the malakh of Yahweh" or "Adonai (Lord)." "Angel" is a Greek word meaning merely a messenger, associated with Hermes, without the divine powers of Yahweh's malakh. However, "angel" has taken on meanings of divinity in biblical Greek and, in its translations, is also a word connoting great beauty and fear. A more accurate rendering would be "Yahweh's malakh" or "Yahweh's messenger."

5. The naming of the infant Messiah as "Jesus" (*Iesous* in Greek) is followed by the phrase "for he will save," which lacks sense, since *Iesous* does not mean "he will save." However, *Iesous* is from Hebrew and Aramaic *Yeshua* (pronounced Yeshua), short for *Yehoshua*, which is appropriate since *Yehoshua* means "Yahweh saves." This passage suggests either an earlier text in Hebrew or Aramaic or that the author of Greek Matthew, or of its source, had in mind Yeshua or Yehoshua for the salvific Lord and expected the readers or listeners to understand the salvific Lord when pronouncing the name Yeshua or Yehoshua.

22All this was done to fulfill the word of God uttered through his prophet Isaiah, saying:

23Listen.

A young woman will have a child in her womb
and give birth to a son,
and his name will be Immanuel,
meaning, 'God is with us.'[6]

24When Yosef woke from his dream, he did what the angel of the Lord told him, and he accepted her as his wife, 25yet did not know her as a wife to sleep with her until after she bore a son. And he named him Yeshua.

CHAPTER 2

Now when Yeshua was born in Bethlehem of the land of Yehuda[7] in the days of King Herod, look, some Magi, astrologer priests from the East, came to Yerushalayim[8] 2and said, "Where is he who was born King of the Jews? We saw his star in the East and we have come to worship him."

3Hearing this, King Herod was troubled as well as all Yerushalayim, 4and calling together all the high priests and the scholars of the people, he asked them where the Messiah was born.

5And they said to him, "In Bethlehem in Yehuda, for so it is written by the prophet Micah":

6And you, Bethlehem, in the land of Yehuda,
you are in no way least among the leaders of Yehuda,
for out of you will come a leader
who will be a shepherd of my people Israel.

7Then Herod secretly called in the Magi astrologers and asked them precisely when the star had appeared, 8and sent them to Bethlehem, saying, "Go and inquire carefully about the child. When you find him, bring me word so that I too may worship him."

9And after hearing the king they set out, and look, the star, which they had seen in the East, went before them until it stood above the place where the child lay. 10When they saw the star, they were marvelously glad. 11And they went into the house and saw the child with Miryam his mother, and fell to the ground and worshiped him. Opening their treasure boxes, they offered him gifts—gold and frankincense and myrrh. 12Then having been

---

6. Matthew cites Isaiah not directly from the Hebrew Bible but from the second-century B.C. Septuagint translation into Greek, which includes the Apocrypha, done for the Jews of Alexandria who could no longer read Hebrew. In the Hebrew Bible, however, Isaiah (Yeshayahu) refers to a "young woman," not a "virgin."

7. *Yehuda* is Judea.

8. *Yerushalayim* is Jerusalem.

warned in a dream not to go back to Herod, they returned to their own country by another road.

*13*When they had gone, an angel appeared to Yosef in a dream, saying, "Awake, and take this child and his mother, and fly into Egypt, and remain there until I tell you. Herod is looking for the child to destroy him." *14*Then he woke and took the child and his mother through the dark of night to Egypt, *15*and stayed there until the death of Herod, thereby fulfilling the word uttered through Hosiah his prophet, saying,

> Out of Egypt I have called my son.

*16*Herod, seeing that he had been outfoxed by the three astrologers, was in a rage and sent his men to kill all the male children in Bethlehem and in all the coastal region, those of two years and under, according to the exact age, based on the time of the star he had ascertained from the Magi. *17*Thereby was fulfilled the word spoken through the prophet Jeremiah, saying,

> *18*A voice was heard in Ramah,
> weeping and grave lamentation,
> Rahel[9] weeping for her children,
> and she would not be comforted,
> because her children are gone.

*19*Now when Herod died, suddenly an angel flew down, appearing in a dream to Yosef in Egypt, *20*saying, "Awake, take the child and his mother, and go to the land of Israel, for those who sought to put out the life of the child are dead."

*21*Yosef awoke, took the child and the mother, and went to the land of Israel. *22*But hearing that Archelaos was now King in Yehuda, replacing his father Herod, he feared to go there. And being warned in a dream, he withdrew to a place in Galilee, where he went *23*and lived in a city called Nazareth. So the prophets' word was fulfilled:

> And he will be called a Nazarene.

CHAPTER 3

John the Baptist

In those days came Yohanan the Baptizer[10] preaching in the desert of Yehuda, *2*saying, "Repent, for the kingdom in the skies is near." *3*He was the one mentioned by the prophet Isaiah, saying:

> A voice of one crying in the desert:

---

9. *Rahel* is Rachel.
10. *Yohanan the Baptizer* is John the Baptist.

Prepare the way of the Lord[11]
and straighten the roads before him.

₄Now Yohanan wore a raiment of camel's hair and a belt of hide
around his waist, and his food was locusts and wild honey. ₅At that time
the people of Yerushalayim came to him and also all of Yehuda and
the whole countryside about Jordan, ₆He baptized them in the river Jordan,
and they confessed their sins. ₇But on seeing many of the Pharisees and
Sadducees coming to baptism, he said to them:

You offspring of vipers, who warned you to flee from
    the coming wrath?
₈Prepare fruit worthy of your repentance.
₉And do not plan to say among yourselves,
'We have Avraham as our father.'
For I say to you that out of these stones
God is able to raise up children to Avraham.

₁₀The axe is also set against the root of the trees,
and every tree that fails to yield good fruit is cut down
    and cast into the fire.

₁₁I baptize you in water for repentance,
but after me will come one stronger than I,
and I am not worthy to carry his sandals.
He will baptize you in the holy spirit and fire.
₁₂His winnowing fork is in his hand,
and he will clear his threshing floor and put his grain
    in the storehouse
but he will burn the chaff in unquenchable fire.

₁₃Then came Yeshua from Galilee to the Jordan and to Yohanan to be
baptized by him.
₁₄Yohanan tried to stop this, saying, "I need to be baptized by you, yet
you come to me?"
₁₅But Yeshua answered, saying to him:

Leave things as they are.
It is right for us to fulfill our whole spirit
of the good.

Then Yohanan consented.
₁₆And when Yeshua was baptized, at once he came out of the water, and
look, the skies opened, and he saw the spirit of God coming down like a
dove, coming down upon him. ₁₇And immediately a voice from the skies
said:

---

11. Lord here might be replaced by *Adonai,* or preferably *Adonenu* meaning *our Lord.*

This is my son whom I love,
in whom I am well pleased.

CHAPTER 4

The Temptation of Jesus

In those days Yeshua was led by the spirit up into the desert to be tempted by the Devil. ₂And he fasted forty days and forty nights, and afterward he hungered. ₃And coming up to him, the tempter said:

If you are the son of God, speak
and make these stones loaves of bread.

₄But he answered, saying,

It is written in Deuteronomy:
"Not by bread alone does a person live
but by every word issuing through the mouth of God."

₅Then the Devil took him to the holy city, and he stood on the pinnacle wing of the temple ₆and said to him,

If you are the son of God,
cast yourself down from the high wing,
for it is written in the Psalms:
'He will put his angels in charge of you,
and with their hands they will hold you up
so you won't smash your foot against a stone.'

₇Yeshua said to him, "Again it is written in Deuteronomy:

You must not tempt the lord, your God."

₈Once more the Devil led him to a very high mountain and showed him all the kingdoms of the world and their glory, ₉and said to him:

All this I will give you
if you will fall down before me and worship me.

₁₀Finally Yeshua said to him, "Go away, Satan, for therein it is also written:

'You will worship God
and you will serve him alone.'"

₁₁Then the Devil left him, and suddenly angels came down and cared for him.

Yeshua's Ministry and Miraculous Healings

*12*On hearing that Yohanan had been arrested, Yeshua withdrew to Galilee, *13*and leaving Nazareth he came to and settled in Kefar-Nahum[12] by the great lake, in the districts of Zevulun and Naftali. *14*He came to fulfill the words spoken through the prophet Isaiah:

*15*Land of Zevulun and Land of Naftali,
the way to the sea beyond the Jordan,
Galilee of Gentiles, of those who are not Jews,
*16*the people who were sitting in darkness
saw a great light,
and for those sitting in the land and shadow of death
the light sprang into dawn.

*17*From that instant Yeshua began to preach his word and said:

Repent, for the kingdom of the skies is near.

*18*And as he was walking by the Sea of Galilee, he saw two brothers, the one called Petros,[13] and his brother Andreas, casting their net into the sea, for they were fishermen. *19*He said to them:

Come, and I will make you fishers of people.

*20*And they immediately dropped their nets and followed him. *21*Going on from there he saw two more brothers, Yaakov the son of Zebedee and Yohanan his brother, in the boat with Zebedee their father, mending their nets. He called out to them. *22*And they left their boat and their father, and followed him.

*23*Yeshua went all over Galilee, teaching in the synagogues, preaching the good message from the kingdom, and healing every sickness and infirmity among the people. *24*His fame spread into all of Syria. And they brought him all who suffered diverse diseases and were seized by pain and those who were possessed by demons, lunatic epileptics and paralytics, and he healed them. *25*Huge crowds followed him around from Galilee and Dekapolis and Yerushalayim, Yehuda and beyond the Jordan.

---

12. *Kefar-Nahum* is Capernaum.

13. *Kefa* or *kef* means *boulder* or *cliff*. *Tzur* also means rock. In English *Kefa* corresponds to the English name "*Peter.*" In Greek *Petros* is a name, from which the English name "*Peter*" comes, and "*stone.*" While it would be perhaps more consistent with the practice of restoring the biblical name to use *Kefa* each time Greek *Petros* occurs in the Greek text, there is nothing (as in the case of going from *Joseph* to *Yosef*) to help the reader understand the biblical name as it goes from *Kefa* to Peter. *Petros* has the advantage of resembling English Peter and also meaning stone. When Peter is called *Simon Peter* or *Simeon Peter*, I do restore Hebrew *Shimon*, which offers little problem for an English reader.

CHAPTER 5

The Sermon on the Mount

And seeing the crowds, he went up the mountain. When he was seated, his disciples came to him. ₂And he opened his mouth and from the mountain gave them his teachings:

> ₃Blessed are the poor in spirit
> for theirs is the kingdom of the skies.[14]
> ₄Blessed are they who mourn the dead
> for they will be comforted.
> ₅Blessed are the gentle
> for they will inherit the earth.
> ₆Blessed are the hungry and thirsty for right justice
> for they will be heartily fed.
> ₇Blessed are they who have pity
> for they will be pitied.
> ₈Blessed are the clean in heart
> for they will see God.
> ₉Blessed are the peacemakers
> for they will be called the children of God.
> ₁₀Blessed are they who are persecuted for the sake of right justice
> for theirs is the kingdom of the skies.
> ₁₁Blessed are you when they revile and persecute
> and speak every cunning evil[15] against you, lying,
> because of me.
> ₁₂Rejoice and be glad, for your reward in the heavens is huge,
> and in this way did they persecute the prophets before you.

> ₁₃You are the salt of the earth.
> But if the salt has lost its taste, how will it recover its salt?
> Its powers are for nothing except to be thrown away and trampled
> underfoot by others.

> ₁₄You are the light of the world.
> A city cannot be hidden when it is set on a mountain.
> ₁₅Nor do they light a lamp and place it under a basket, but on a stand,
> and it glows on everyone in the house.
> ₁₆So let your light glow before people so they may see your good works
> and glorify your father in the skies.

---

14. These 11 blessings are known as "the Beatitudes."

15. *Poneros* in classical Greek had a positive meaning as in "nimble-witted" or "cunning" Odysseus and has retained that specific earthly meaning into modern Greek. So some sense of the shade of cunning is desired in the New Covenant usage, where it is entered as evil.

17Do not think that I have come to destroy the law or the prophets.
I have not come to destroy but to fulfill.
18And yes I say to you, until the sky and the earth are gone,
not one tiny iota or serif will disappear from the law
     until all has been done.
19Whoever breaks even the lightest of the commandments
     and teaches others to do the same
will be esteemed least in the kingdom in the skies.
Whoever performs and teaches them
will be called great in the kingdom in the skies.
20I say to you, if you don't exceed the right justice
     of the scholars and the Pharisees,
you will never enter the kingdom in the skies.

21You have heard our people in ancient times told in Exodus,
     You must not murder.
     and whoever murders will be liable to judgment.
22I say to you, whoever is angry with a companion will be judged
     in court,
and whoever calls a companion a fool will go before the Sanhedrin,
     the highest court,
and whoever calls a companion a scoundrel will taste the fire of
     Gehenna.
23If then you bring your gift to the altar,
and there you remember your companion holds something
     against you,
24leave your gift before the altar,
and go first to be reconciled with your companion
and then come back and present your offering.

25When you see your adversary walking in the street on the way
     to the court,
quickly, be of good will toward him and reconcile
26or your accuser will hand you over to the judge,
     the judge to the baliff
and you will be thrown into prison.
I tell you, there will be no way out
until you have paid back the last penny.

27And you have heard in Exodus the words:
     You must not commit adultery.
28Yet I say, if a man looks at a woman with lust
he has already slept with her in his heart.
29So if your right eye takes you to scandalous sin,
tear it out and cast it away.
It is better to lose a part of your body
than for your whole body to be cast into Gehenna.
30And if your right hand takes you to scandalous sin,

cut it off and cast it away.
It is better to lose a part of your body
than for your whole body to be cast into Gehenna.

31And you have heard in Deuteronomy, if a man sends his wife away,
give her a proper bill of divorce,
32but I also tell you that any man divorcing and sending his wife away,
except for dirty harlotry,
makes her the victim of adultery;
and any man who marries a woman divorced and sent away
is himself an adulterer.

33You have heard our people in ancient times told in Exodus,
"You must not swear false oaths,
but make good your oaths before God."
34But I tell you not to swear at all:
Not by heaven, for heaven is God's throne,
35nor by earth, for earth is God's footstool,
nor by Yerushalayim, for Yerushalayim is the city of the great king.
36Don't swear by your own head,
since you cannot make one hair white or black.
37If your word is yes, say yes.
If your word is no, say no.
To say more is to indulge in evil.

38And you have heard in Exodus, "an eye for an eye"
        and a tooth for a tooth.
39But I tell you not to resist the wicked person,
and if someone strikes you on the right cheek,
turn your other cheek as well.
40If someone wants to sue you for your tunic,
give him your outer cloak as well.
41If someone forces you to go a mile with him,
go a second mile with him.

42Give to who asks you. And don't turn away one
who wants to borrow from you
43You have heard it said in Leviticus,
"You will love your neighbor and hate your enemy."
44I say to you to love your enemies
and pray for those who persecute you
45so you may become the children of your father in the skies.
For he makes the sun rise over the evil and the good,
and he brings the rains to the just and the unjust among us.

46If you love those who love you, what is the good deed in that?
Don't even the tax collectors do the same?
47If you greet only those who are your friends,
how have you done more than others?

_48_Have you done more than the Gentiles—than those who are not
    Jews?
Be perfect as your father the heavenly one is perfect.

CHAPTER 6

Take care not to do your acts of righteousness[16] before other people
so as to be seen by them,
for you will have no reward from your father in the skies.
_2_When you give alms, don't sound a trumpet before you
like the actors in our synagogues and in the streets,
who seek the praise of the onlookers.
I say to you, they have their reward in the street from the onlookers.
_3_Yet when you give alms, do not let the left hand know
    what the right hand is doing
_4_so the alms may be given in secret,
and your father seeing you in secret will repay you.

_5_And when you pray, don't do so like the actors.
They love to stand in our synagogues and in the corners
    of the open squares, praying
so they will be seen by others.
I say to you, they have their rewards.
_6_When you pray, go into your inner room and close the door
and pray to your father who is in secret,
and your father who sees you in secret will repay you.

_7_Yet when you pray, do not babble empty words like the Gentiles, like
    those who are not Jews,
for the Gentiles think by uttering a glut of words they will be heard.
_8_Be as you are, the Jews, and not like the Gentiles,
for your father knows what you need before you ask him.

_9_And pray like this:

    Our father in the heavens,
    may your name be holy.[17]
    _10_May your kingdom come.
    May your will be spread
    on earth as it is in heaven.
    _11_Give us today our daily bread
    _12_and forgive us our debts
    as we forgave our debtors.
    _13_Do not lead us into temptation,
    but rescue us from the evil one.[18]

---

16. The Majority Text reads _eleimosunin_, charitable giving.
17. This prayer poem is known as the "Lord's Prayer."
18. _apo tou ponerou_ is literally "from the evil one," meaning the Devil.

[For yours is the kingdom,
and the power and the glory
for all of time. Amen.]¹⁹

14If you forgive the people who have stumbled and gone astray,
then your heavenly father will forgive you,
15but if you will not forgive those who stumble and fall,
your father will not forgive your failures.

16When you fast do not scowl darkly like actors.
They distort their faces to show others they are fasting.
Yes, they have their reward.
17But when you fast, anoint your head with oil
to make it smooth and wash your face
18so your fasting will be unknown to people
and known only to your father who is not visible.
Your father who sees you in secret will repay you.

19Do not hoard your treasures on earth
where moth and earthworms consume them,
where thieves dig through walls and steal them,
20but store up your treasures in heaven
where neither moth nor earthworms consume
or thieves dig through the walls and steal,
21since your treasure
is there where your heart is.

22The lamp of the body is the eye.
If your eye is clear, your whole body is filled with light,
23but if your eye is clouded, your whole body will inhabit darkness.
And if the light in your whole body is darkness,
how dark it is!

24No one can serve two masters,
for either one will hate one and love the other
or cling to one and despise the other.
You cannot serve God and the mammon of riches.

25So I tell you, do not worry about your life
or say, "What am I to eat? What am I to drink?"
and about the body, "What am I to wear?"
Isn't life more than its food, and your body more than its clothing?

---

19. This famous ending of the Lord's Prayer is in brackets, since it does not appear in the earliest Greek texts. It does appear in the later Majority Greek text, in Tyndale and the authorized
translations. See introduction for further discussion.

26Consider the birds of the sky.
They do not sow or reap or collect for their granaries,
yet your heavenly father feeds them.
Are you not more valuable than they?
Who among you by brooding can add one more hour to your life?

27And why care about clothing?
28Consider the lilies of the field, how they grow.
They do not labor or spin
29but I tell you not even Solomon in all his splendor
was clothed like one of these lilies.
30And if the grass of the field is there today
and tomorrow is cast into the oven
and in these ways God has dressed the earth,
will he not clothe you in a more stunning raiment,
        you who suffer from poor faith.

31Do not brood, mumbling, what is there to eat or drink?
Or what shall we wear?
32All those things the Gentiles, those who are not Jews,
        set their hearts on.
Your heavenly father knows your need for these things.
33But seek first his kingdom and his justice,
and all things will be given to you.
34Do not worry about tomorrow,
for tomorrow will worry about itself.
Each day has enough troubles in it.

CHAPTER 7

Don't pass judgment or you will be judged.
2By your judgment you will be judged
and by your measure you will be measured.
3Why do you gaze at the splinter in your friend's eye
yet not recognize the log in your own eye?
4Or why say to your friend,
"Let me take the splinter out of your eye"
when your own eye carries a log of wood?
5False actor,
first remove the wood from your own vision,
and you will see clearly enough to pluck the sliver
from your friend's eye.

6Don't give the holy to the dogs
or cast your pearls before the pigs.
They will probably trample them underfoot
and turn and tear you to pieces.

7Ask and it will be given to you.
Seek and you will find.
Knock and the door will be opened for you.
8Everyone who asks receives,
and the seeker finds,
and the door will be opened to one who knocks.

9And who among you if your son asks for bread
will give him stone?
10Or if he asks for fish
will give him snake?
11If you, in your evil, know how to give good gifts to your children,
how much more will your father in the skies
give good gifts to those who ask him.

12All things in the world you wish others to do for you,
do for them.
Such is the meaning of the law and the prophets.

13Go in through the narrow gate,
since wide is the gate and spacious the road
that leads to destruction,
and there are many who go in through it.
14But how narrow the gate and cramped the road
that leads to life,
and there are few who find it.

15Beware of the false prophets,
who come to you in sheep's clothing,
but who inside are ravening wolves.
16From their fruit you will know them.
From thorns can you gather grapes
or from thistles pick figs?
17Every good tree gives delicious fruit,
but the diseased tree gives rotting fruit.
18A good tree cannot yield rotting fruit,
nor a diseased tree delicious fruits.
19Every tree incapable of delicious fruit is cut down
and tossed in the fire.
20So from their fruit you will know them.

21Not everyone who says to me, Adonai, Adonai,
will come into the kingdom in the skies,
but one who follows the will of my father,
who is in the heavens.
22On that day of judgment many will say to me,
"Didn't we prophesy in your name
and in your name cast out demons
and in your name take on great powers?"

₂₃And then I will say my word clearly to them:
"I never knew you. Go from me,
you who are working against the law."

₂₄Everyone who hears my words and follows them
will be like the prudent man
who built his house upon the rock.
₂₅The rain fell and the rivers came
and the winds blew and battered that house
and it didn't fall,
because it was founded upon the rock.

₂₆Everyone who hears my words and doesn't follow them
will be like the young fool who built his house upon the sand.
₂₇And the rain fell and the rivers came
and the winds blew and battered that house
and it fell and it was a great fall.

₂₈And it happened that when Yeshua ended these words, the crowds were amazed at his teaching, ₂₉for he taught them as one who has authority and not like one of our scholars.

Mark (after A.D. 70) Israel, Syria, Alexandria, or Rome? (gospel)

TRANSLATED BY WILLIS BARNSTONE

As in the other gospels, there is no internal evidence of the authorship of the book of Mark. An early church figure, Bishop Papias (c. A.D. 130–140), claims that Mark was John Mark, a close associate of Peter, and that the gospel of Mark is essentially an arrangement of Peter's preachings in Rome. The second-century Bishop Iraeneus also places Mark in Rome. Another tradition claims Alexandria as the place of origin. Others assume that because the Marcan gospel is the earliest, it was composed in Israel. Mark was written at least forty years after Jesus' death, and the gospel authors' names were appended to the gospels more than a hundred years after Jesus' death. The traditions that assert authorship of the gospels frequently deny each other and here, as elsewhere, none has a strong historical probability. Authorship in the New Testament remains an enigma.

Like Luke 1:1, Mark 1:1 begins with the presentation of the "good news" about Jesus Christ. Mark stresses Jesus' miracles, his powers of healing, the drama and mystery of his death. The first verses quote the prophet Isaiah to prove that Jesus is the "voice crying out in the wilderness" and that he is therefore God's messenger. But after this initial declaration, Mark plunges directly into the stories of John the Baptist and of Jesus tempted for forty days in the desert by Satan (which parallels Moses' forty years in the desert tempted by Baal). It follows his wanderings through the land of Israel, where he takes on disciples and crowds of followers who accompany him in his ministry. Mark gives us a series of miracles, teachings through parables, and finally the "passion week" of Jesus' arrest, trial, death, burial, and disappearance from the tomb. Here the gospel ends. This so-called "abrupt ending" has bothered theologians and has caused some to speculate that we have a truncated or unfinished gospel. Most disturbing is that there is no mention of Christ risen, and since Mark is the source of Matthew and Luke, the absence of a resurrected Jesus is not desirable. As a probable result of this discomfort with the present ending, two appended endings have been added, the so-called "Shorter Ending of Mark" and the "Longer Ending of Mark." The very short one has Jesus send word of eternal salvation out from east to west. The longer one has Jesus appear resurrected before Mary Magdalene and the disciples and then describes Jesus ascending into heaven. The short ending may have been added in the fourth century, the longer one as early as the second. Both endings are termed *orphans* because they are spurious and do not exist in copies of the earliest manuscripts.

Mark is most often characterized as an author whose Greek is crude and rudimentary in contrast especially to Luke, who is more classical, and John, who is clearly influenced by Greek philosophical and Gnostic models. But Mark is in many ways the greatest stylist among the Evangelists. Mark writes with plain clarity, concision, dramatic power, and minimal and striking diction. The original ending of the Gospel of Mark may be less satisfying as theology, but it is overwhelmingly dramatic and mysterious in its understatement of the sublime terror of Jesus' disappearance from the tomb. When the two Marys enter the tomb and find that Jesus is not there, Mark writes, "So they went out and fled from the tomb, seized by trembling and ecstasy. And they said nothing to anyone. They were afraid" (17:18).

CHAPTER 6

Miracles

30The apostles[1] gathered together around Yeshua[2] and reported to him everything they had done and taught. 31He said to them:

> Come yourselves alone to a deserted place
> and rest a while.

For they were many coming and going and they had no chance even to eat. 32And they went off in a ship to a deserted place by themselves.

33Now many saw them going and knew of them, and from all the towns they ran there on foot and got there ahead of them.

---

1. *oi apostoloi*, the apostles. The word "apostle," "messenger," or "one who is sent" appears in Mark only here and in other manuscripts in 3:14.

2. *Yeshua* is Jesus.

₃₄On coming ashore, Yeshua saw a great crowd and he pitied them, for they were like sheep without a shepherd, and he began to teach them many things.

₃₅When it was already late the disciples came to him, saying, "This is a deserted place and it is already late. ₃₆Send them off so they can go into the surrounding farms and villages and buy themselves something to eat."

₃₇But he answered, saying to them:

You give them something to eat.

They said to him, "Shall we go off and buy two hundred denars worth of loaves and give them that to eat."

₃₈And he said to them:

How many loaves do you have?
Go and see.

When they knew, they said, "Five, and two fish."

₃₉He told them all to sit down in groups on the green grass. ₄₀They sat down in groups of hundreds and fifties. ₄₁He took the five loaves and the two fish, and looking up into the sky he blessed and broke the loaves and gave them to his disciples to set before the people, and the two fish he divided among them all. ₄₂Everyone ate and they were filled. ₄₃And they picked up twelve full baskets of crumbs and fish. ₄₄Those who had eaten were five thousand men.[3]

₄₅Immediately Yeshua had his disciples climb into the ship and go ahead to the far side of Bethsaida, while he dismissed the crowd. ₄₆And after saying goodbye to them he went off to the mountains to pray.

₄₇When dusk came the ship was in the middle of the sea and he was alone on the land. ₄₈Seeing the disciples straining at the oars—the wind was against them—about the fourth watch of the night[4] he came toward them, walking on the sea and he wanted to pass by them. ₄₉But seeing him walking on the sea they thought he was a phantom, and they cried out. ₅₀They saw him and they were terrified.

At once he spoke with them and said:

Take courage. It is I. Don't be afraid.

₅₁Then he climbed into the boat and the wind fell, and deep in themselves they were astonished. ₅₂They had not understood about the loaves and their heart hardened.

₅₃When they crossed over to the land, they came to Gennesaret and anchored. ₅₄They got out of the ship, and immediately recognized him.

---

3. *andres*, men. Here the word is specifically "men" rather than people. It is possible that the multitude consisted entirely or largely of men, and he was observing this, or, as is the habit in most languages "men" meant "people."

4. About three in the morning.

55Wherever he went into villages or cities or into the farmland, in the marketplaces they laid out the sick and begged that they might touch even the hem of his garment. And as many who touched him were healed.

CHAPTER 14

The Last Supper

After two days it would be Pesach,[5] the Feast of the Matzot Cakes,[6] and the high priests and the scholars were looking for a way to arrest him by treachery and to kill him. 2"Not at the festival," they were saying, "for there would be an outcry from the people."

3While he was in Bethany in the house of Shimon[7] the leper, reclining, a woman came with an alabaster jar of pure and costly spikenard ointment. Breaking the alabaster jar she poured it on his head. 4Now some were angry among themselves, "Why was there this waste of ointment?" 5This ointment could have been sold for more than three hundred dinars[8] and the money given to the poor. And they scolded her.

6But Yeshua[9] said:

Let her be. Why do you bother her?
She has done a good thing for me.
7You always have the poor with you
and whenever you want you can
do good for them. But me you do not
always have. 8She did what she could.
She prepared ahead of time to anoint
my body for the burial. 9Amen I say
to you. Wherever in the whole world
the good news is preached, also what
this woman did will tell her memory.

10Yehuda of Kerioth[10] one of the twelve went to the high priests to betray him to them.

11Hearing of this they were happy and promised to give him silver. He was looking for an easy way of betraying him.

---

5. Passover.

6. Unleavened bread.

7. *Shimon* is Simon.

8. Also translated as "denarius." The dinar was an ancient Roman silver coin, the penny of the New Testament.

9. *Yeshua* is Jesus.

10. *Yehuda of Kerioth* is Judas Iscariot. The figure of Judas lacks historical probability, since this story of the betrayer appears to be lifted intact and anachronistically from Midrashic tale. (*Midrash*, meaning "explanation" in Hebrew, is an early collection of tales and rabbinical commentary in Scripture.) The choice of the name Yehuda, signifying "Jew" in Hebrew, was chosen to suggest that Judas alone among the disciples was a Jew, when in fact all the disciples were Jews.

*12*On the first day of the Feast of the Matzoh, when the Pesach lamb was sacrificed, his disciples said to him, "Where do you want us to go for us to arrange for you to eat the Pesach?"

*13*And he sent two of his disciples and said to them:

> Go into the city and you will meet
> a man carrying a clay pot of water.
> Follow him *14*and wherever he goes tell
> the owner of the house, "The teacher asks,
> 'Where is the guest room for me to eat the Pesach?'"
> *15*And he will show you a large upstairs room,
> furnished and ready. There prepare for us.

*16*And the disciples left and came into the city and found things just as they were told and prepared the Pesach lamb....*18*As they were reclining at the table and eating, Yeshua said to them:

> Amen amen I say to you
> one of you will betray me,
> one who is eating with me.

*19*They began to grieve and said to him, one by one, "Surely not I?" *20*He said to them:

> One of the twelve who is dipping in the bowl.[11]
> *21*The Son of People[12] goes just as Isaiah
> has written of him.[13] But oh for that one
> through whom the Son of People was betrayed.[14]
> Better for him never to have been born!

*22*While they were eating he took bread and blessing it he broke it and gave it to them and said:

> Take it. This is my body.

*23*And taking a cup and giving thanks he gave it to them, and everyone drank from it. *24*And he said to them:

---

11. Presumably dipping "bread" in the bowl.

12. Son of Man.

13. The Greek says "just as it is written," meaning, for the informed reader, Isaiah 1–12 in which Isaiah describes the birth, life, and sacrificial death of the coming Messiah in great and moving detail.

14. *ouai* is closer to "oh!" or "ah" than to "woe," which is the traditional translation of this interjection. The strength of his curse is developed in the next sentences, and it is better to follow the strategy in Greek of an undefined "oh" leading up to the explicit punishment.

₂₅This is the blood of the covenant,
which is poured out for many.[15]
Amen amen I say to you,
I will no longer drink the fruit of the wine
until that day when I drink it new in the kingdom
      of God.

₂₆After singing the hymn they went to the Mountain of Olives.
₂₇Then Yeshua said to them:

You will all stumble as Zecharaiah wrote:
    I will strike down the shepherd
        and the sheep will be scattered.
₂₈But after I'm raised up I will find my way
before you in Galilee.

₂₉But Petros[16] said to him, "Even if everyone stumbles, I will not."
₃₀Then Yeshua said to him:

Amen I say to you
this same night before the cock crows twice
you will deny me three times.

₃₁But he said forcefully, "If I must die for you, I will not deny you."
So they all said.

₃₂And they came to a place whose name was Gethsemane and he said to
his disciples:

Sit here while I pray.

₃₃And he took Petros and Yaakov[17] and Yohanan[18] with him and he
began to be shaken and in agony ₃₄and he said to them:

My soul is in sorrow to the point of death.
Stay here and keep awake.

---

15. The word "Eucharist" is derived from the Greek *euharistesas,* "having given thanks," which
appears in this passage of the Pesach supper. The "blood of the covenant" derives from the
covenant between God and Moses at Sinai: "Moses then took the blood, sprinkled it on the
people and said, 'This is the blood of the covenant that the Lord has made with you in accordance with all these words'" (Ex. 24:8). Moses has set up "twelve stone pillars representing the
twelve tribes of Israel." The sacred symbolism of the twelve, representing all the tribes of Israel, is repeated in having Yeshua choose to be followed by twelve disciples.

16. *Petros* is Peter.

17. *Yaakov* is James.

18. *Yohanan* is John.

35And going a little farther he fell on the ground and prayed that if it were possible the hour pass away from him. 36And he said:

> Abba, Father, for you all things are possible.
> Take this cup from me. Yet not what I will
> but what you will.

37And he came and found them sleeping, and said to Petros:

> Shimon,[19] are you sleeping? Did you not have
> the strength to keep awake for an hour?
> 38Stay awake and pray that you are not tested.
> Oh the spirit is ready but the flesh is weak.

39He went away again and prayed, saying the same word.
40And he came again and found them sleeping. Their eyes were very heavy, and they didn't know what to say to him.
41And he came a third time and said to them:

> Sleep what is left of the night and rest.
> Enough! The hour has come. Look,
> the Son of People has been betrayed
> into the hands of those who do wrong.[20]
> 42Get up and let us go. Look, the one
> betraying me is drawing near.

43Immediately while he was still speaking, Yehuda came, one of the twelve, and with him a crowd with swords and clubs from the high priests and the scholars and the elders. 44Now he who betrayed him gave them a signal saying, "The one I kiss is the one. Seize him and take him away under guard."

45When he came, he at once went up to him and said, "Rabbi," and kissed him.

46They got their hands on him and seized him.

47But one standing by drew his sword and struck the slave of the high priest and cut off his ear.

48Then Yeshua spoke out to them:

> As against a thief have you come with swords
> and clubs to arrest me? 49Day after day I was with you

---

19. *Shimon* is Simon as in Simon Peter.

20. *hamartolon*, of the sinners. Here translated as "those who wrong," *Hamartolos* is by tradition translated "sinner," but the notion of missing the mark literally, or failing, or doing wrong persists.

in the Temple, teaching. Then you did not seize me.
Only now so that the scriptures may be fulfilled.

50And leaving him, they all fled.

51And one young man followed him, dressed in linen cloth around his naked body, and they seized him. 52But he left the linen cloth behind and fled.

53They led Yeshua to the high priest. All the high priests and the elders and the scholars were assembled.

54Petros followed him from a distance until he was inside the high priest's courtyard and he sat together with the servants, warming himself near the fire.

55The high priest and the whole Sanhedrin[21] were looking for evidence against him to put him to death, but they didn't find any. 56Many gave false testimony against him, and their testimonies were not the same. 57Some stood up and gave false testimony against him, saying, 58"We heard him say, 'I will tear down this Temple made with hands and after three days I will build another not made with hands.'" 59But their testimony was not identical.

60Then the high priest stood up in their midst and questioned Yeshua, saying, "Won't you answer anything that they have testified against you?"

61But he was silent and gave no answer to anything.

Again the high priest questioned him and said to him, "Are you the Messiah the son of the blessed one?"

62Yeshua said:

I am.
And you will see the Son of People
sitting at the right of the power
and coming with the clouds of the sky.[22]

63The high priest tore his tunic, saying, "What further need do we have of witnesses? 64You heard this blasphemy. How does it look to you?"

They all condemned him as deserving death.

65And some began to spit on him, and to cover his face and struck him, saying to him, "Prophesy!" And the servants pummeled him.

66While Petros was below in the courtyard, one of the maidservants of the high priest came 67and when she saw Petros warming himself she stared at him and said, "You were also with Yeshua from Nazareth."

68But he denied it, saying, "I don't know or understand what you are saying." Then he went outside into the forecourt. [And the cock crowed.][23]

---

21. Court.

22. Lines 1 and 3 of Hebrew Scripture cited are from Daniel 7:13, and line 2 from Psalms 110:1.

23. "And the cock crowed" is omitted in other texts and bracketed in the Nestle-Aland, which is used here.

⁶⁹And the maid seeing him began again to say to the bystanders, "This is one of them."

⁷⁰But again he denied it.

After a short while the bystanders said to Petros, "Surely you must be one of them, since you are a Galilean."

⁷¹He began to curse and to swear, "I don't know this man you're talking about." ⁷²At once the cock crowed a second time. And Petros remembered the word Yeshua said to him:

Before the cock crows twice
you will deny me three times.

And he broke down and wept.

CHAPTER 15

The Crucifixion

As soon as it was morning, the high priests with the elders and scholars held a meeting. And they bound Yeshua, led him away and handed him over to Pilatus.[24]

₂Pilatus asked him, "Are you the king of the Jews?"

Answering him, he said:

You say.[25]

₃The high priests were accusing him of many things.

₄Pilatus again questioned him, saying, "Don't you answer anything? Look how much you are accused of."

₅But Yeshua still answered nothing.

Pilatus was amazed.

₆Now at that festival he released one prisoner to the people, whichever one they asked for. ₇There was a man called Barabbas who was bound along with other revolutionaries, who in the uprising had committed murder.[26]

₈So the crowd came and began to ask Pilatus for what he did for them.

---

24. Pilate.

25. *Su legeis,* You say. Most translations give "You say it," adding "it," or "You say so," adding "so." These conversions are good idiomatic equivalents to the Greek, but it is perhaps stronger to give no more than the Greek (since Greek can also add the "it" or "so" but chooses not to) by simply saying "You say." Until it becomes natural the phrase will jar but may still be more memorable.

26. Nothing is known of Barabbas, but from his revolutionary activities it is assumed that he was a Zealot, a Jewish sect that was rebelling against Roman occupation. Insurrectionists were treated by the Romans as bandits and hence crucified. Only from the gospels do we know that the Romans followed the custom of releasing one prisoner during the Passover.

9But Pilatus answered them, saying, "Do you want me to release the king of the Jews?" 10He knew that the high priests had handed him over to him out of envy.

11But the high priests incited the crowd to release Barabbas instead to them.

12Pilatus again answered, saying to them, "What do you want me to do with the King of the Jews?"

13"Crucify him."[27]

14Pilatus said to them, "What wrong did he do?"

But they cried out louder, "Crucify him."

15So Pilate, wanting to satisfy the crowd, released Barabbas to them, and had Yeshua flogged and handed him over to be crucified.

16The soldiers led him away into the courtyard, which is the praetorium,[28] and assembled the whole cohort. 17And they clothed him in purple and twisted some thorns into a crown, which placed it on his head. 18Then they began to salute him, "Hail, King of the Jews." 19They beat him on the head with a reed club and spat on him, and going down on their knees they worshiped him. 20And after mocking him, they stripped off the purple and put his own clothes on him. Then they led him out to crucify him.

21And a certain Shimon of Cyrene,[29] the father of Alexandros and Rufus, was passing by from the countryside, and they forced him to carry his cross. 22They brought him to the place Golgotha, which translated is the Place of the Skull. 23And they gave him wine mixed with myrrh,[30] but he didn't take it. 24And they crucified him.

---

27. This pivotal but unlikely scene that has the crowd shout "Crucify him," which is to say, "crucify a dissident rabbi," suggests not the voice of a Jewish mob in the street but the voice of Rome enunciated through the Evangelist. The voice of Rome comes through more emphatically in Matthew's elaboration of the same scene, in which Pilate declares both his own innocence and Jesus' innocence and blames the crowd: "When Pilatus saw that he could do nothing and that an uproar was starting, he took water and washed his hands before the crowd, saying, 'I am innocent of the blood of this man. You see to it'" (27:24). To clear himself, and by extension Rome, of responsibility for the crucifixion, Pilate asks the crowd, "What wrong did he do?" By revealing to the crowd—and to the reader—his conviction that Yeshua did no wrong, he places himself squarely on Jesus' side at the very moment of ordering the rabbi to be flogged and crucified. Mark paints Pilate as the helpless tool of a murderous mob; the Eastern Orthodox Church will later elevate the same Roman governor to sainthood. The historical view of Pilate depicts the procurator of Judea, Idumea, and Samaria, A.D. 26–36, as an unusually brutal ruler of peoples under Roman occupation. He was recalled to Rome for the massacre of the Samaritans in A.D. 35. It should also be noted that crucifixion was a Roman means of execution, not one either practiced by Jews or conceivably ordered by Jews against a Jew.

28. The governor's residence.

29. *Cyrene* is modern Libya.

30. In the Talmud, incense is mixed with wine to deaden pain.

and they divided his clothings
and cast lots for them to see
who would take them.[31]

25It was the third hour, nine in the morning, when they crucified him.
26The inscription of the charge against him was written above: The King of
the Jews. 27With him they crucified two thieves, one on the right and one on
the left of him.

29And those passing by blasphemed him, shaking their heads, and saying, "Ha! You who would destroy the Temple and rebuild it in three days,
30save yourself by coming down from the cross." 31Likewise the high priests
mocked him among each other and with the scholars said, "He saved others but he can't save himself. 32The King of Israel, let him now come down
from the cross so we can see and believe." And those who crucified him
taunted him.

33At when it was the sixth hour, at noon, the whole earth become dark
until the ninth hour, at three, 34and at the ninth hour Yeshua called out
words from the Psalms in a loud voice:

Eloi Eloi, lema sabachtani?

which translated is,

My God, my God, why do you abandon me?[32]

35Some of those standing near heard him and said, "See, he's calling
Elijah."[33] 36And someone ran up with a sponge soaked in sour wine, placed
it on a reed stick and gave it to him to drink, saying, "Let him alone. Let us
see if Elijah comes to take him down."

37And Yeshua let out a loud shout and took his last breath.

38The Temple curtain was torn in two from top to bottom.

39A Roman centurion who was near saw him breathe his last and said,
"Truly this man was the son of God."[34]

40And there were women looking on from a distance, among whom
were both Miryam[35] the Magdalene and Miryam mother of Yaakov the

---

31. Ps. 22:18. These near passages contain many citations from Psalms.

32. Ps. 22:1.

33. The bystanders heard mistakenly "Elijas" for "Eloi," "my God."

34. A centurion was a commander of one hundred Roman soldiers. In the story of the crucifixion, after Jesus has been mocked by Jewish bystanders and the high priests, and the curtain
in the Temple has sympathetically torn in two, foretelling the Temple's imminent doom, the
first to recognize that Jesus was the son of God is the commander of the execution squad. This
exoneration of Roman leadership, who now are not only guiltless in Jesus' execution but the
first in Jerusalem to state his divinity, follows the pattern of preparing the move of the authority of Jesus' messiahship to Rome.

   In Hebrew 9:8–10, 12; 10:19–20, Paul tells us that the tearing of the curtain means that
Jesus has entered heaven for us so that we too now may enter God's presence.

35. *Miryam* is Mary.

younger and of Joses, and Salome, *41*who was in Galilee following him and serving him, and there were many other women who had gone up with him to Yerushalayim.[36]

*42*When evening came since it was Friday, Preparation Day for the Sabbath, *43*Yosef of Arimathea,[37] a prominent member of the council, who was also looking for the kingdom of God, boldly went to Pilatus and asked for the body of Yeshua.

*44*Pilatus wondered if he was already dead and called the centurion, and asked him if he was dead yet. *45*Informed by the centurion, he gave the corpse to Yosef.

*46*Then Yosef bought a linen cloth, took him down and wrapped him in the linen cloth and placed him in a tomb which had been cut out of the rock, and he rolled a stone against the entrance to the tomb.

*47*Miryam the Magdalene and Miryam of Joses saw where he was laid.

CHAPTER 16

The Burial

When the Sabbath was over, Miryam the Magdalene and Miryam of Yaakov, and Salome bought aromatic spices so they could come and anoint him. *2*Very early on the first day of the week, they came to the tomb as the sun was rising. *3*They said to each other, "Who will roll away the stone for us from the entrance to the tomb?" *4*They looked up and saw that the stone had been rolled away. And it was huge. *5*Then on going into the tomb they saw a young man sitting on the right, dressed in a white robe, and they were utterly astonished.[38]

*6*He said to them, "Don't be alarmed. You are looking for Yeshua of Nazareth, the one who was crucified. He was raised. He is not here. See the place where they laid him. *7*But go tell his disciples and Petros, 'He is going ahead of you to Galilee. There you will see him, just as he told you.'"

*8*So they went out and fled from the tomb, seized by trembling and ecstasy. And they said nothing to anyone. They were afraid.[39]

---

36. *Yerushalayim* is Jerusalem.

37. *Yosef* is Joseph.

38. Matthew identifies the young man as an angel (28:2).

39. The earliest manuscripts end with the dramatic fear of the women in *ekstasis,* here rendered "ecstasy," which conveys the literal meaning of "being outside themselves" as well as "ecstasy" with its multiple meanings of "amazement" in "being elsewhere" and "beside themselves" with fear. The ending is called abrupt, although not in this translator's opinion. There are three "orphan" supplements, now generally held to be added later, which are said to smooth out the "abrupt" ending. They are now considered to be later additions to make Mark conform to the appearances of the resurrected Messiah as revealed in the other gospels.

Luke (A.D. 80–85?) Place
of composition unknown (gospel)

TRANSLATED BY WILLIS BARNSTONE

There is general agreement among scholars that little is certain about authorship, place, and date with regard to Luke. Although this uncertainty exists for all the gospels, Luke remains a special case. Older scholarship has given us the authorial name Luke and the places of his gospel composition as Rome or cities in the East such as Achaia, Ephesus, or Caesarea in Israel. The name Luke appears to come from Bishop Iraneus (late second century), who claimed that Luke was Paul's "inseparable collaborator" in Antioch. But the depiction of Paul in the Acts, which is also ascribed to Luke, has little to do with the self-portrait of Paul that emerges in the apostle's own letters. There are also traditions, of no more certainty, that speak of Luke as the "beloved physician," as a "convert" to the Christian Jews, and as the Evangelist who wrote for gentile converts. There is no substantial evidence for any of this. It is clear that Luke the author never read or even knew of Paul's letters, and hence all attempts to identify who the author of Luke was, who his associates were, for whom he wrote, and what city or country he wrote in fall apart. Luke was not the companion of Paul. Regardless of unproved speculations about the person of Luke, the gospel of Luke is a splendid achievement.

Luke is the longest of the gospels and, according to most commentators, the most skillfully constructed, composed in an elegant Greek at times approaching classical Hellenistic Greek of the first century. The main example cited by scholars to demonstrate Luke's classical Greek is the brief prologue (1:1–4). This text resembles the prologue to Acts and has been used as proof that Luke is the common author of the Gospel of Luke and the Acts of the Apostles. While it is true that the prologue is a good example of the Hellenistic complexity of rhetoric, this editor finds its convoluted rhetoric polite but also heavy and believes that the prologue, in fact and in spirit, is not by the same author who wrote the rest of the Gospel of Luke. And whether or not the same author wrote Luke and the Acts should not be proven by the similarities of the prologues. Once we go beyond the prologue, the Greek of Luke is different and more inflected, but not decisively removed from Mark and Matthew. Indeed, similarities rather than differences characterize the text.

The Gospel of Luke reads as a fluent late scripture, greatly enlarging the scope of the New Testament. Its immediate sources in the synoptic chain are the unknown Q source, which is presumed to be a sayings gospel, and both Mark and Matthew. Luke expands on both Mark and Matthew, and we cannot explain the source for this additional material. Perhaps the most original and beautiful passages in Luke (for which there are no counterparts in the other gospels) are the annunciation (1:26–38), Mary's visit to Elizabeth, mother of John the Baptist (1:39–56), the nativity scene of the birth of Jesus in the manger (2:1–7), the parable of the good Samaritan (10:29–37), and the parable of the prodigal son (15:11–32). Only the rich treasury of Luke gives us the birth of John the Baptist (1:5–25, 57–80), the angelic announcement and the visit of the shepherds (2:8–20), and the prayers of Simeon and Anna (2:25–38). Among the poetic masterpieces in the New Testament is Mary's song, the Magnificat (1:39–55), beginning "My soul magnifies the Lord."

Much has been written about Luke as the great narrator, which is true, and Luke's means are often contrasted with Mark's more modest style. The comparison is mistaken. *Both* Mark and Luke are master narrators of the New Covenant, and Luke is closer to Mark than is normally acknowledged. The cliches of Mark as a rude populist and Luke as an elegant Henry James are unfounded. In their best moments, especially in the rush and drama of the passion week, the two authors are cut from the same cloth. Although Mark has no resurrection scene and Luke does, the ending of Luke resembles the narrative genius of Mark. Luke speaks of Jesus, who has come back to life and is walking the roads of Israel, startling his disciples and friends, and engaging in the most profound and compelling conversations of the gospels.

The Birth of Jesus Foretold

26In the sixth month the angel Gabriel was sent by God to a city in Galilee called Nazareth, 27to a virgin engaged to a man whose name was Yosef,[1] from the house of David, and the name of the virgin was Miryam.[2] 28And he came near her and said, "Hello, favored one, the Lord is with you."

29Miryam was deeply troubled by his word and pondered what kind of greeting this might be.

30The angel said to her, "Do not fear, Miryam, for you have found favor with God. 31Look, you will conceive in your womb and bear a son and you will name him Yeshua. 32He will be great and be called son of the highest, and the Lord God will give him the throne of his father David, 33and he will rule over the house of Yaakov[3] forever, and his kingdom will have no end."

34But Miryam said to the angel:

How will this be since I do not know a man?

35The angel answered her, "The holy spirit will come to you and the power of the highest will overshadow you. So the one being born will be

---

1. *Yosef* is Joseph.

2. *Miryam* is Mary. Greek word here is *Mariam*.

3. *Yaakov* is James.

called the holy son of God. ₃₆And look, Elizabeth your relative has also conceived a son in her old age and this is the sixth month for her who had been called barren. ₃₇For with God nothing is impossible."[4]

₃₈Miryam said, "Here I am a slave of the Lord. May it happen to me according to your word."

The angel left her.

The Magnificat

₄₆And Mary said:

₄₇My soul magnifies the Lord
>   and my spirit is joyful in God my savior,[5]
₄₈for he looked upon his young slave
>   in her low station.
Look, as of now
>   all generations will call me blessed.
₄₉In his power he did wondrous things for me
>   and his name is holy.
₅₀His mercy goes from generation to generation
>   to those who fear him.
₅₁He showed the strength of his arm
>   and scattered those who were proud in the mind
>   of their heart.
₅₂He toppled monarchs from their thrones
>   and raised the poor.
₅₃He filled the hungry with good foods
>   and sent the rich away empty.
₅₄He helped Israel his servant and child
>   to remember mercy
₅₅as he spoke to our fathers,
>   to Avraham and his seed forever.

CHAPTER 2

The Nativity

It happened in those days that a decree was sent out from Caesar Augustus to enroll the whole world.[6] ₂This was the first census, when Quirinius was governor of Syria. ₃And all went to their own cities to be registered.

---

4. The texts vary on line 1:37, some putting it in doubt.

5. Mary's song, traditionally called the Magnificat, resembles Hannah's song over Samuel's birth (1Sam. 2:1–10).

6. A census presumably in the whole Roman world that could be used for purposes of taxation and military service.

4Now Yosef also went up from Galilee, from the city of Nazareth, to Yehuda,[7] to the city of David which is called Bethlehem, because he was of the house and family of David. 5He went to be enrolled with Miryam, who was engaged to him and who was pregnant.[8] 6And it happened that while they were there, the days were completed for her to give birth, 7and she bore a son, her first-born, and she wrapped him in strips of cloth and laid him in a feeding trough of a stable because there was no place for them in the inn.[9]

8And there were shepherds in the region, living in the fields and keeping guard at night over their flock. 9An angel of the Lord stood before them and glory of the Lord shone around them, and they were terrified.

10The angel said to them:

> Don't be afraid. Look, I tell you good news,
> a great joy for all people.
> 11Because on this day was born to you in the city of David
> a savior who is Messiah the Lord.
> 12Here is your sign. You will find a child wrapped in cloths
> and lying in a feeding trough of a stable.

13And suddenly with the angel there was a multitude of the heavenly army praising God and saying:

> 14Glory to God in the highest
> and on earth peace among people of good will.[10]

15And it happened that after the angels had gone from them into the sky, the shepherds said to one another, "Let us go to Bethlehem and see this thing that has happened, which the Lord made known to us."

16And they left, hurrying, and found Miryam and Yosef, and the baby lying in the feeding trough. 17When they saw this, they made known what had been said to them about the child. 18And all who heard wondered at what the shepherds told them.

19But Miryam took all these words in and pondered them in her heart.

20The shepherds returned, glorifying and praising God over all they had heard and seen, as it had been told them.

---

7. Judea.

8. It was important to establish Jesus' lineage through Joseph, who was of the family of David, as indicated in Luke's genealogy, 3:23–37, but with the reservation "so it was thought." The virgin birth would, it would seem, deprive Jesus of the paternal link back to David, but through Mary there was a blood line.

9. *fatni,* feeding trough. "Manger" is a feeding trough for animals. Though a beautiful and evocative word, "manger" has come, incorrectly, to signify the stable itself rather than the feeding box, which conveys a more extraordinary incident.

10. *eudokias,* of good will or good pleasure, or variously translated "whom he favors."

Parable of the Prodigal Son (15:11–32)

*11*And he said:

There was a man who had two sons.
*12*The younger said to his father, "Father,
give me the share of the property
that will belong to me." So he divided
his resources between them. *13*And not
many days later the younger son
got all his things together and went off
to a far country and there he squandered
his substance by riotous living.
*14*When he had spent everything he had,
there came a severe famine throughout
that country, and he began to be in need.
*15*And he went and hired out to a citizen
of that land, who sent him to his fields
to feed the pigs. *16*He longed to be fed
on the pods the pigs were eating, but no one
gave him anything. *17*He came to himself[11]
and said, "How many of the day laborers
of my father have bread leftover and here
I'm starving and dying. *18*I will rise up
and go to my father and I will say
to him, "'Father, I have sinned against
heaven and before you. *19*I am no longer
worthy to be called your son. Make me
like one of your hired hands.'" *20*And he rose up
and went to his father. While he was still
far off, his father saw him and was filled
with compassion and tears fell on his neck
and he kissed him. *21*And the son said to him,
"Father, I have sinned against heaven
and before you. I am no longer worthy
to be called your son." *22*But his father said
to his slaves, "Quick, bring out the finest robe
and put it on him, and give him a ring
for his hand and sandals for his feet.
*23*And bring the fatted calf, slaughter it,
and let us eat and celebrate, *24*for my son
was dead and he came back to life,
he was lost and he has been found."
And they began to celebrate.

---

11. Meaning, "he came to his senses."

25Now the older son was in the fields
and as he drew near the house he heard
music and dancing. 26And he called over
one of his slaves and asked what was going on.
27He told him, "Your brother is here,
and your father has slaughtered the fatted calf
because he took him back in good health."
28He was angry and did not want to go in,
but his father came out and pleaded with him.
29Yet he answered and said to his father,
"Look, so many years I have served you
and never disobeyed an order of yours,
and for me you never gave a young goat
so I could celebrate with my friends.
30But when this son of yours came, who ate up
your property with prostitutes, for him
you slaughtered the fatted calf." 31And he said
to him, "Child, you are always with me,
and everything that is mine is yours,
32but we had to be happy and celebrate.
Your brother was a dead man and he lived
and he was lost and has been found."

Coming of the Son of People and Parable of the Fig Tree (21:25–38)

25There will be signs in sun and moon and stars,
and on the earth the dismay of foreign nations
in bewilderment at the sound of the sea
and surf. 26People will faint from fear
and foreboding of what is coming upon the world,
for the powers of the skies will be shaken.
27And then they will see the Son of People coming
on a cloud with power and enormous glory.
28When these things happen, stand up straight
and raise your heads, for your redemption is near.

29And he told them a parable:

Look at the fig tree and all the trees.
30When they sprout leaves, you look at them
and know that summer is already near.
31So too when you see these things happening
you know the kingdom of God is near.
32I tell you truth. This generation will not
pass by until all these things take place.

33The sky and the earth will pass away
but my words will not at all pass away.

34Be careful that you do not burden your hearts
with dissipation and drunkenness and worries
of life lest that day suddenly come upon you
35as a trap, for it will rush in on all
who are sitting on the face of all the earth.
36Be alert and pray at all times for strength
to escape all these things that are to happen,
and to stand before the Son of People.

37Now during those days he was in the Temple, teaching, and in the nights he went out and stayed on the mountain, the one called "Of the Olives."[12] 38And all the people rose at dawn to go to the Temple to hear him.

The Resurrection

In the first day of the week at early dawn they came to the tomb bringing the spices which they had prepared. 2And they found the stone had been rolled away from the tomb, 3and when they went inside they did not find the body [of the Lord Yeshua].[13]

4And it happened that while they were at a loss about this, look, two men stood near them in clothing that gleamed like lightning.

5The women were terrified and bowed their faces to the earth but the men said to them:

Why do you look for the living among the dead?
6He is not here, but has risen.
Remember how he spoke to you when you were in Galilee:
7"The Son of People must be delivered into the hands
        of the wrongdoers
and be crucified
and on the third day he shall rise again."

8And they remembered his words.
9When they returned from the tomb they reported all this to the eleven and to the others. 10The women were Miryam the Magdalene and Yohanna and Miryam of Yaakov and the other women with them. They told the apostles these things, 11and to them their words seemed madness. They did not

---

12. The Mountain of Olives.
13. The words in brackets are omitted in some manuscripts.

believe them. *12*[But Petros got up and ran to the tomb and bending over saw only the linen cloth, and he left, wondering what happened.]¹⁴

*13*And look, on the same day, two of them were traveling to a village about seven miles from Yerushalayim,¹⁵ whose name was Emmaous¹⁶ *14*and they were speaking to each other about all that took place. *15*And it happened that during their talk and discussion Yeshua came near and went with them. *16*But their eyes were kept from recognizing him.

*17*He said to them:

What are you saying as you toss words
back and forth?

And they stood still, downcast. *18*One of them whose name was Kleopas answered and said to him, "Are you the only one visiting Yerushalayim who does not know what happened there in these days?"

*19*He said to them:

What things?

And they said to him, "The things about Yeshua the Nazarene, who was a prophet powerful in act and word. Before God and all the people, *20*and how our high priests and leaders handed him over to the judgment of death and they crucified him. *21*We had hoped that he was going to redeem Israel. But now it is already the third day since these things occurred. *22*And more, some women among us amazed us. They went at dawn to the tomb, *23*and did not find the body and came back saying they saw a vision of angels who say that he is alive. *24*Then some of us went back to the tomb and found it as the women said, but did not see him."

*25*And he said to them:

O how mindless and slow of heart you are to believe
        all that the prophets spoke!
*26*Didn't the Messiah
have to suffer all these things to enter
into his glory?

*27*And starting with Moshe¹⁷ and through all the prophets he explained to them all the things in the Torah concerning himself.¹⁸

---

14. The words in brackets are omitted in some manuscripts.

15. *Yerushalayim* is Jerusalem.

16. Emmaus. In Hebrew the word means "warm baths."

17. *Moshe* is Moses.

18. There is an extreme contrast between the routinely didactic lines in verse 27, the imagination of later churchmen, which again converts the Old Testament from Moses on into an unbroken prophesy about Jesus, and the dramatic passage of Jesus through the village with his students, who entreat him to stay with them, not knowing, yet knowing, who he is, and as we will learn, with their hearts on fire because of the presence and speech.

28And as they approached the village they were traveling to, he pretended to be going on further. 29They entreated him, "Stay with us. It is almost evening and the day has fallen."

So he went in to stay with them.

30And it happened that as he reclined at the table with them, he took the bread and blessed it and broke it and gave it to them.

31Then their eyes opened and they recognized him. But he vanished from them.[19]

32They said to each other, "Were our hearts not burning inside us when he talked to us on the road as he revealed the Torah to us?"

33And they rose up in that very hour and returned to Yerushalayim, and found the eleven and those with them.

34They said, "The Lord has truly risen and he appeared to Shimon."

35Then they described the things on the road and how they recognized him in the breaking of the bread.

36While they were saying these things, he stood in their midst [and said to them:

Peace be with you.][20]

37They were startled and full of fear and thought they were looking at a ghost.

38And he said to them:

Why are you shaken and why do doubts rise
in your hearts? 39Look at my hands and my feet
and see I am myself. Touch me and see,
because a ghost does not have flesh and bones
which as you see I have.

40[And when he said this, he showed them his hands and feet.]

41And when in their joy they still could not believe him and wondered, he said to them:

Do you have something to eat?

42They gave him a piece of broiled fish.

43And he took it and in their presence he ate it.

44Then he said to them:

These are my words which I spoke to you
while I was still with you:

---

19. Or "he became unseen to them."

20. The words in brackets are omitted in some texts.

all that was written about me in the law of Moshe
and the prophets and Psalms must be fulfilled.

45Then he opened their minds to an understanding of the Torah, 46and
he said to them:

It is written that the Messiah is to suffer and to rise
from the dead on the third day,
47and in his name you will preach repentance
and forgiveness of sins
to all nations, beginning with Yerushalayim.
48You are witnesses of this.
49And I am sending the promise of my father
to you. So stay in the city
until you are clothed with power from on high.[21]

50And he led them out as far as Bethany, and raised his hands and
blessed them. 51And it happened that while he blessed them, he departed
from them [and was carried up into the sky].[22]

52And they [worshiped him and][23] returned to Yerushalayim with great
joy, 53and they were constantly in the Temple blessing God.

John (between A.D. 80 and A.D. 120) Ephesus? (gospel)

TRANSLATED BY WILLIS BARNSTONE

The prologue of the Gospel of John, "In the beginning was the word,"
imitates the first words of the creation in Genesis, "In the beginning God
created the heavens and the earth." The word in Greek is "logos," and
logos was a familiar philosophical term, already in Greek currency through
its usage by the Presocratic philosopher Heraclitus and by the Stoics. In
John, the usage of the word, the logos, is to convey a specific message. The

---

21. Mark ends abruptly, powerfully, and mysteriously, Matthew and John dramatically end with
great pathos. Here the drama is also intense until these last ecclesiastical instructions to prepare witnesses for the missionary duties of the church. The instructions "to stay in the city /
until you are clothed with power from on high" serve as a perfect afterword to the road and
house scenes, and this last formal message contains hope and a promise of power to be delivered from the father on high to the faithful who will go out from the city to preach the good
news. The dramatic narration of the postcrucifixion gospel ends by verse 44, however, preceding the send off, with the immensely poignant gloom of the followers at the earthly loss of the
Messiah, their joy at the recognition on the road and at the breaking of the bread, the plain
reality and immediacy of his instructions to look at his mutilations of hand and feet—"Touch
me and see"—and his last human act, which is to ask for food and then, in the presence of the
intimates, to eat the cooked fish.

22. The words in brackets are omitted in some texts.

23. The words in brackets are omitted in some texts.

word is the divine savior, who comes into the world to bring hope and eternal life. The "word become flesh" is Jesus, God's emissary incarnated in the world. In contrast to the synoptic gospels (Matthew, Mark, and Luke), in which Jesus' divinity is always there and is not there and is elusive, John suggests decisively that Jesus is the Messiah, that the Messiah is divine, and he is the Son of God. The prologue also emphasizes light and darkness, truth and lies, which seems to be directly related to these dichotomies found in the Dead Sea Scrolls of the Essene community. There is a profound influence of Essene thought on John. And finally, in this perhaps richest of all passages in the New Testament, with the discovery of the Gnostic Gospel of Thomas at Nag Hammadi, Egypt, a similarly strongly Gnostic element should now be observed in John. In short, John is a mirror to a time of diverse beliefs and philosophies, and key terms and concepts, from the Neoplatonist Jew Philo of Alexandria to the scrolls of the Essenes and the Gnostics, flash in and out of his text with unusual intensity.

The authorship of John is a complex puzzle for which there is no solution. Traditionally, the author is John, son of Zebedee, one of Jesus' disciples and apostles. For many reasons, including the probable dating of the work, this view is not generally accepted today. We do not know the name of the author. Some scholars suggest that the author of the prologue may not be the author of the rest of the gospel, or that it may even be the work of a Johannine community (those who follow John's ideas).

John is distinct from the synoptic gospels in many ways. There is no Sermon on the Mount. Jesus tells no parables and does not heal lepers. Demons are not exorcized; there is no Lord's Prayer or Last Supper; and the notion of religious instruction and moral teachings found in the synoptics is absent. As in the other gospels, the book of John does use miracles as "signs" to prove the powers of the Messiah and God. However, in contrast, Jesus is a more abstracted figure, and the presentation of his crucifixion, in contrast with that of the other gospels, is not of an especially suffering man, tortured and dying for human sin, but of a controlled, even aloof figure, following his own divine purpose without fear. There are similarities to the language of Revelation, which is also ascribed, probably falsely, to John. In both texts, Jesus is the Word and the "Lamb of God." But it should be emphasized that the apocalyptic nature of Revelation, the epic vision of heaven and hell, the phantasmagoric images, are wholly apart from anything found in the Gospel of John and may discredit the traditional notion of common authorship.

There is a special problem with regard to the Jews who did not accept Christ as the promised Messiah. Like Matthew, John is a deeply Jewish gospel, steeped in Old Testament thought and allusion. But more than Matthew, the reference to Jews as the opponents is fierce and constant, while at the same time the gospel presents Jesus as a Jew and rabbi. One explanation for John's presentation of this intramural struggle between Jews lies in the politics of his own later time. If, as many scholars believe, John dates from early in the second century, anywhere from A.D. 80 to possibly

A.D. 120, then it is probable that he is addressing the increasingly tense struggle in many parts of the diaspora world, especially in Asia Minor, between Christian Jews and non-Christian Jews for their place in the synagogues.

Above all, John is a literary document of the Bible. The prologue is magic for believers or nonbelievers, surely one of the summit moments in world literature. As Mark is the most poignant and dramatic, Matthew perhaps the most poetic, Luke the most literarily accomplished in its telling of the Nativity and the parables, John is the most spiritual, philosophical, and independent of the gospels.

CHAPTER 1

The Word Become Flesh

In the beginning was the word
and the word was with God,
and God was the word.

2The word in the beginning was with God.
3Through God everything was born
and without the word nothing was born.

What was born 4through the word was life
and life was the light of all people
5and the light in the darkness shines
and the darkness could not apprehend the light.

6There was a man sent from God.
His name was Yohanan.[1] 7He was a witness
to testify about the light
so all might believe through him.
8He was not the light,
but came to testify about the light.
9He was the true light
which illuminates every person
who comes into the world.

10He was in the world
and through him the world was born,
and the world did not know him.
11He went to his own
and his own did not take him in.

12To all who took him in
he gave power to become the children of God,

---

1. John.

to those who believed in his name,
*13*who were not from blood
or from the will of the flesh
or from the will of a man,
but were born from God.

*14*And the word became flesh
and lived among us.

And we saw his glory,
the glory of the only son born of the father,
who is filled with grace and truth.

*15*Yohanan testifies about him,
he who was the baptizer cried out,
yes, he cried out, saying:
"One who will come after me was before me,
because before me he was."

*16*From his bounty all of us have received grace
    and more grace,
*17*and as the law was given through Moshe,[2]
grace and truth have come through Yeshua the Messiah.
*18*No one has ever seen God.
Only the one who was born of God
and who lies in the bosom of his father,
he has made him known.

CHAPTER 4

Jesus and the Samaritan Woman

Now when Yeshua learned that the Pharisees heard that Yeshua was making and baptizing more disciples than Yohanan[3]—*2*though Yeshua himself didn't baptize but his disciples did—*3*he left Yehuda[4] and went again into Galilee. *4*But it was necessary to pass through Samaria. *5*He came to a town in Samaria called Sychar near the piece of land that Yaakov[5] gave his son Yosef.[6] *6*There was a well of Yaakov there. Yeshua was tired from the trip and sat down by the well. It was near noon.

*7*A Samaritan woman came to draw water.

Yeshua said to her, "Give me a drink." *8*His disciples had gone off to the town to buy food.

---

2. Moses.

3. *Yohanan* is John the Baptist.

4. *Yehuda* is Judea.

5. *Yaakov* is James.

6. *Yosef* is Joseph.

*9*The Samaritan woman said to him, "How can you a Jew ask to be given a drink by me, a Samaritan? Jews do not mingle with Samaritans."[7]

*10*Yeshua said to her:

If you knew the gift of God
and who is saying to you "Give me a drink,"
you would have asked and he would have given you
living water.

*11*She said to him:

Sir, you have no bucket and the well is deep.
Where do you have this living water?
You are not greater than our father Yaakov
*12*who gave us the well and who himself drank
and whose sons and cattle drank?

*13*Yeshua answered her:

Everyone who drinks this water will be thirsty again.
*14*But whoever drinks the water I give them
will not be thirsty forevermore.
The water I give them will become in them
a fountain of water springing into eternal life.

*15*The woman said to him, "Sir, give me this water so I won't be thirsty or come here to draw it up."

16"Go and call your husband and come back here," he said to her.

17"I have no husband," she answered him.

"You're right to say, 'I have no husband.' *18*You had five husbands and the one you have now is not your husband. What you said is true."

19"Sir, I see that you are a prophet," she tells him. *20*"Our parents[8] worshiped on this mountain and you say Yerushalayim[9] is the place where we must worship."

*21*Yeshua said to her:

Believe me, woman,
the hour is coming when not on this mountain

---

7. "Jews don't mingle with Samaritans" in other editions is put in brackets, parentheses, or a bottom-of-page note, which in effect acknowledges a later scribal commentary. It could be either way, and here I think it goes better without being set off as spurious. This notable identification of Yeshua as a Jew by an "outsider" Samaritan contradicts the prevalent dejudaising of Yeshua and his circle and the repeated use of Jew as the deadly opponent. Revealed once again is the disturbed, schizoid nature of the Scripture, as we have it from multiple hands, which in contingent passages esteems and scourges the Jew.

8. *our parents* is literally our fathers. *Fathers* means ancestors, with male preference intended. Rather than use ancestors, which loses the metaphor of the single for the whole, I use parents. In most contemporary European languages, our fathers (as in Spanish *nuestros padres* or French *nos pères*) is the common word for parents, and by extension ancestors, or to keep up the male-preferred forefathers.

9. *Yerushalayim* is Jerusalem.

or in Yerushalayim will you worship the father.
22You worship what you do not know.
We worship what we know
since salvation is from the Jews.

23The hour is coming and it is now
when the true worshipers will worship the father
in spirit and truth,
for the father seeks such people to worship him.
24God is spirit
and those worshiping must worship him
in spirit and truth.

25The woman said to him:

I know a Messiah is coming,
who is called the Anointed.
When he comes he will declare all things to us.

26Yeshua said to her:

I am he,
talking to you.

27At this his disciples came and were amazed that he was talking with a woman, but no one said, "What are you looking for?" or "Why are you talking with her?"

28Then the woman left her water jar and went back into the town and said to the people, 29"Come see a man who told me everything I ever did. Can he be the Messiah?"

30They went out of the town and came toward him.
31Meanwhile the disciples were saying "Rabbi, eat."
32But he said to them:

I have a meat[10] to eat which you don't know.

33Then the disciples said to each other, "Could someone have brought him something to eat?"
34Yeshua said to them:

My meat is to do the will of him
who sent me and to complete his work.
35Don't you say, "Four more months and then comes harvest?"

---

10. *brosis* also means "food."

Look, I say, lift up your eyes
and you will see the fields are white for harvest.
36Already the reaper is taking his pay
and gathering its fruit for the eternal life
so sower and reaper alike may be happy.
37The words of Job and Micah are true
that one sows and another reaps.
38I sent you to reap what you didn't labor.
Others worked and you entered their work.

39And many Samaritans from the city believed in him, because of what
the woman said when she testified, "He told me everything I ever did." 40So
when they came near him, the Samaritans asked him to stay with them.

He stayed there two days.

41And many more believed because of his word, 42and they said to the
woman, "It's no longer because of your talk that we believe. We ourselves
have heard and we know that he is truly the savior of the world."

CHAPTER 19

The Crucifixion and Burial (19:17–42)

They took Yeshua. 17Carrying the cross himself, he went to what was called
the Place of the Skull, which in Hebrew is Golgotha, 18where they crucified
him and with him two others on this side and that, and in the middle
Yeshua.

19And Pilatus wrote a placard and put it on the cross. It read, "Yeshua
the Nazarene the King of the Jews."

20Many Jews read the placard because the place where Yeshua was crucified was near the city. And it was written in Hebrew, Latin, and Greek. 21So
the high priests of the Jews said to Pilatus, "Do not write, 'The King of the
Jews,' but that this man said 'I am king of the Jews.'"

22Pilatus answered, "What I've written I've written."

23The soldiers when they crucified Yeshua took his clothes and divided
them in four parts, one part for each soldier. And took his tunic too. Now
his tunic shirt was seamless, woven in one piece from the top straight down.
24So they said to each other, "Let's not tear it, but casts lots for it to see
whose it will be." This was to fulfill the words written in the Psalms saying:

They divided my clothes among them
and for my clothes they cast lots.

The soldiers did those things.

25But near the cross of Yeshua stood Miryam his mother and his mother's sister Miryam of Klopas and Miryam the Magdalene.

26Then Yeshua seeing his mother and the disciple he loved standing
near said to his mother:

Woman, here is your son.[11]

27Then he said to the disciple:

Here is your mother.

And from that hour the disciple took her into his home.[12]

28After this Yeshua, knowing that all had been done to fulfill the words of the Psalms, he said:

I am thirsty.

29A jar filled with sour wine[13] was lying there. So they put a sponge soaked with the sour wine on a hyssop and held it to his mouth.

30Then when Yeshua had taken the wine, he said:

It is ended.

Bowing his head he gave up the spirit.

31Since it was Friday the Preparation Day, the Jews asked Pilatus that their legs be broken and they be taken away so that the bodies would not remain on the cross on the Sabbath. 32The soldiers came and broke the bones of the first man and then of the other one crucified with him. 33But when they came to Yeshua and saw that he was already dead, they did not break his legs. 34But one of the soldiers stabbed his side with his spear, and at once blood and water came out.

35And the one who saw this has testified to it, and the testimony is true, and he knows he is speaking the truth so that you may also believe. 36These things happened so the Psalms be fulfilled, "No bone of his will be broken." 37And in Zechariah it says, "They will look at him whom they stabbed."

38After these things Yosef of Arimathea, being a disciple of Yeshua, but a secret one for fear of the Jews, asked Pilatus if he could take away Yeshua's body.

Pilatus allowed it.

Then he came and took the body.

39Nikodemos came too, the one who first came to him during the night, and he brought a mixture of myrrh and aloes, about a hundred pounds. 40So they took the body of Yeshua and wrapped it in aromatic spices in linen cloths, as is the Jewish custom.[14]

41Now in the place where he was crucified there was a garden, and in the garden a new tomb in which no one had been placed. 42So because it

---

11. Literally, "Woman, look, your son," which is followed by "Look, your mother."

12. Although *home* or *care* may be the implied translation, it says no more than "He took her into his *own.* "

13. *sour wine,* literally "vinegar," meaning a cheap sour wine.

14. In Mathew and Luke, there is also a shroud, a large sheet.

was Friday the Preparation Day of the Jews, and the tomb was near, in it they placed Yeshua.

CHAPTER 20

Mary Magdalene and Jesus

On Sunday the first day of the week, Miryam the Magdalene came to the tomb early while it was still dark and saw that the stone had been removed from the tomb. ₂So she ran and came to Shimon Petros and to the other disciple whom Yeshua loved and said to them, "They took the Lord from the tomb, and we don't know where they put him."

₃Then Petros and the other disciple came out and went to the tomb. ₄The two ran together, but the disciple ran faster than Petros and reached the tomb first. ₅And he stooped down and saw the linen cloths lying there, but didn't go in. ₆Then Shimon Petros[15] came, following him, and he went into the tomb, and saw the linen cloths lying there, ₇but the kerchief which had been on his head was not lying next to the cloths but apart folded up in one place. ₈And the other disciple, who had come first to the tomb, saw and believed. ₉They didn't yet know the scripture that he must rise from the dead.

₁₀Then the disciples went off to their own places.

₁₁But Miryam stood by the tomb, weeping. Then as she was weeping, she stooped into the tomb ₁₂and saw two angels in white sitting there, one at the head and one at the feet where the body of Yeshua was lain.

₁₃And they said to her, "Woman, why are you weeping?"

She said to them, "They have taken my Lord away, and I don't know where they put him."

₁₄Saying this she turned around and saw Yeshua standing there and didn't know it was Yeshua.

₁₅Yeshua said to her, "Woman, why are you weeping? Whom are you looking for?"

Thinking he was the gardener, she said to him, "Sir, if you took him away, tell me where you put him, and I will take him."

₁₆Yeshua said to her, "Miryam!"

She turned and said to him in Hebrew, "Rabboni!" (which means teacher).

₁₇Yeshua said to her, "Don't hold me, since I have not yet gone up to the father. But go to my brothers and tell them, "I am ascending to my father and your father and my God and your God."

---

15. *Shimon Petros* is Simon Peter.

*18*Miryam the Magdalene went and announced to the disciples, "I have seen the Lord." And she told them that he had said these things to her.

Paul (A.D. 5 to A.D. mid-60s) Tarsus/Jerusalem (letter) (New Revised Standard Version)

After considering the gospels and their unknown authors, we must speak of Paul (born Saul), a Greek-speaking Jew from the diaspora, whose literary qualities are equal to the finest passages of the Hebrew Bible and the gospels and whose ideas and mission were fundamental in defining and promoting Christianity. Paul was born in Tarsus, present-day southern Turkey, and was educated at the synagogue in Tarsus and later in Jerusalem, where under the tutelage of Rabbi Gamaliel, the grandson of the ethical leader Hillel, he became an eminent Pharisee. The Pharisees formed a popular movement and, like the Essenes, saw themselves as democratic regionalists, upholding traditional meditation and biblical Law, opposing the strong Hellenizing ways in Jerusalem, and enthusiastically supporting the successful Maccabean independence war against the Syrian ruler Antiochus IV. New Testament writers inaccurately painted the Pharisees as hypocrites and conformists, yet they were to provide the rank and file of the Christian Jews (Jews who followed Jesus and Paul and initiated Christianity) because of their belief in messianism, Judgment Day, the resurrection, and life after death. In contrast to earlier Jewish belief, in which God's reward for a good life was received on earth, in these dark times of uncertainty and foreign rule, the radical and revolutionary Pharisees believed in a future in which reward and punishment would take place, after the resurrection, in an eternal afterlife. It was natural for the Pharisees, like Paul, to be immediate adherents to the communal and apocalyptic persuasions of their first fellow Christians.

Paul's conversion took place three years after the crucifixion (he did not know Jesus), but his letters, which he wrote as letters, not Scripture, were canonized and are the earliest written documents of the New Testament. The writing down of the first of the Christian gospels was at least thirty-five years after Paul's conversion. Before his conversion, he had approvingly attended the stoning-to-death of the first Christian-Jewish martyr, Stephen, who was to be canonized as Saint Stephen. Paul was chasing Christian Jews to Damascus in Syria when he saw a blinding light and heard Jesus ask why he had been persecuting him. After being led to Damascus blind, he regained his sight, was baptized, and immediately set out to preach in synagogues and market places in Judah, Greece, and Rome.

Paul spoke to Jews and Gentiles and, as the father of Christology, he initiated the new sect of the Christian Jews. As recounted in Acts 15 and Galatians 2, around A.D. 50 in a decisive debate at a council of apostles in Jerusalem, Paul's arguments persuaded the apostles to decide that converts to Christ need not already be or become circumcised, which was tantamount to declaring that thereafter Christianity was not to be an exclusively Jewish sect. For the next two centuries, Christian-Jewish noncanonical writings contained all gradations and mixtures of Jewish and Christian thought (see following section of Intertestamental Scriptures). With the canonization of the New Testament at the end of the fourth century A.D., distinctions between Jew and Christian, in person and texts, were clearer, though they would still remain forever confused for several reasons: Jew and Christian accepted the Hebrew Bible; Jesus himself had been a traditional Jewish rabbi; and late Jewish messianic thought of resurrection and afterlife, as embodied in the Pharisees' beliefs, was to link the theological convictions of Jews and early Christians. There were Jews in all the synagogues where Paul preached conversion. Paul himself never ceased to believe that the Old Testament was inspired Scripture, that God had chosen the Jews to be his people, and that he Paul was one of them. In his own eyes, he was not an apostate but a reformer and expander of Judaism. In Philippians 3:4–6, he argues passionately that he is a circumcised member of the tribe of Benjamin, a Jew born of Jews, a zealous Pharisee, and blameless under the law. Since there was no Christian sect as such when his mission began, he was himself one of the many radical and revolutionary thinkers and changers that this period spawned.

In his letters, Paul introduced new doctrines and organized old ones. Of the fourteen letters attributed to Paul, seven are considered genuine; Romans, 1 and 2 Corinthians, Galatians, Philippians, 1 Thessalonians, and Philemon; pseudonomous and disputed are 2 Thessalonians, Colossians, Ephesians, Hebrews, 1 and 2 Timothy, and Titus. Although Paul scarcely refers to Jesus' teachings, there are four references (Rom. 14:14; 1 Cor. 7:10, 9:14, 11:23–26) centered on Jesus' crucifixion and resurrection and Jesus as Lord. Jesus is the Son of Man, the Messiah (in Hebrew *mashiah*, "the annointed," in Greek *christos,* the "Christ"), and the church is the mystical body of Christ. In Isaiah and Ezekiel, the Messiah was to be a leader, from the Davidian monarchy, who would save and redeem Jerusalem and the Jews on earth.

Like the Quakers, the Jews were ethically earthbound, heaven was less than a dream, and hell (*Gehenna*) a stinking, smoking garbage pit outside Jerusalem. However, by the intertestamental period, Jewish thinking, influenced by Greek Neoplatonic notions of the immortality of the soul, was no longer limited to the earth and a meaningless death. Jews eagerly awaited the savior to come at the end of the world to save and redeem. Paul focuses all these yearnings for a salvational Messiah and some form of life after death into his scriptorial mission. Although his degradation of women — who should be subservient to their husbands, silent in church, silent as teachers or preachers, and veiled — excludes women from professional ambitions, equality, and most aspects of human love, he also has sublime words about love for people and Christ as a high principle. Apart from proselytizing labors, Paul, as thinker and writer, made love, faith, hope, and immortality of the soul the core of the developing religion. While the later gospels report the teachings of Jesus (which are always ambiguous with regard to immortality and his own divinity), for Paul, Jesus is the Son of Man, is God, and is God's earthly incarnation, and the promises of Paul's ideas were to reside in the heart of Christianity.

FURTHER READING: Paul. Doty, W. G. *Letters in Primitive Christianity,* 1973. Hanson, A. T. *Studies in Paul's Technique and Theology,* 1974. Meeks, Wayne A. *The First Urban Christians: The Social World of the Apostle Paul,* 1979.

from First Letter to the Corinthians (1 Cor.)

CHASTITY AND SEXUAL IMMORALITY (5:1–6:20)

It is actually reported that there is sexual immorality among you, and of a kind that is not found even among pagans; for a man is living with his father's wife. And you are arrogant! Should you not rather have mourned, so that he who has done this would have been removed from among you?

For though absent in body, I am present in spirit; and as if present I have already pronounced judgment in the name of the Lord Jesus on the man who has done such a thing. When you are assembled, and my spirit is present with the power of our Lord Jesus, you are to hand this man over to Satan for the destruction of the flesh, so that his spirit may be saved in the day of the Lord.

Your boasting is not a good thing. Do you not know that a little yeast leavens the whole batch of dough? Clean out the old yeast so that you may be a new batch, as you really are unleavened. For our paschal lamb, Christ, has been sacrificed. Therefore, let us celebrate the festival, not with the old yeast, the yeast of malice and evil, but with the unleavened bread of sincerity and truth.

I wrote to you in my letter not to associate with sexually immoral persons—not at all meaning the immoral of this world, or the greedy and robbers, or idolaters, since you would then need to go out of the world. But now I am writing to you not to associate with anyone who bears the name of brother or sister who is sexually immoral or greedy, or is an idolater, reviler, drunkard, or robber. Do not even eat with such a one. For what have I to do with judging those outside? Is it not those who are inside that you are to judge? God will judge those outside. "Drive out the wicked person from among you."

When any of you has a grievance against another, do you dare to take it to court before the unrighteous, instead of taking it before the saints? Do you not know that the saints will judge the world? And if the world is to be judged by you, are you incompetent to try trivial cases? Do you not know that we are to judge angels—to say nothing of ordinary matters? If you have ordinary cases, then, do you appoint as judges those who have no standing in the church? I say this to your shame. Can it be that there is no one among you wise enough to decide between one believer and another, but a believer goes to court against a believer—and before unbelievers at that?

In fact, to have lawsuits at all with one another is already a defeat for you. Why not rather be wronged? Why not rather be defrauded? But you yourselves wrong and defraud—and believers at that.

Do you not know that wrongdoers will not inherit the kingdom of God? Do not be deceived! Fornicators, idolaters, adulterers, male prostitutes, sodomites, thieves, the greedy, drunkards, revilers, robbers—none of these will inherit the kingdom of God. And this is what some of you used to be. But you were washed, you were sanctified, you were justified in the name of the Lord Jesus Christ and in the Spirit of our God.

"All things are lawful for me," but not all things are beneficial. "All things are lawful for me," but I will not be dominated by anything. "Food is meant for the stomach and the stomach for food," and God will destroy both one and the other. The body is meant not for fornication but for the Lord, and the Lord for the body. And God raised the Lord and will also raise us by his power. Do you not know that your bodies are members of Christ? Should I therefore take the members of Christ and make them members of a prostitute? Never! Do you not know that whoever is united to a prostitute becomes one body with her? For it is said, "The two shall be one flesh." But anyone united to the Lord becomes one spirit with him. Shun fornication! Every sin that a person commits is outside the body; but the fornicator sins against the body itself. Or do you not know that your body is a temple of the Holy Spirit within you, which you have from God, and that you are not your own? For you were bought with a price; therefore glorify God in your body.

CHASTITY AND MARRIAGE (7:1–24)

Now concerning the matters about which you wrote: "It is well for a man not to touch a woman." But because of cases of sexual immorality, each man should have his own wife and each woman her own husband. The husband should give to his wife her conjugal rights, and likewise the wife to her husband. For the wife does not have authority over her own body, but the husband does; likewise the husband does not have authority over his own body, but the wife does. Do not deprive one another except perhaps by agreement for a set time, to devote yourselves to prayer, and then come together again, so that Satan may not tempt you because of your lack of self-control. This I say by way of concession, not of command. I wish that all were as I myself am. But each has a particular gift from God, one having one kind and another a different kind.

To the unmarried and the widows I say that it is well for them to remain unmarried as I am. But if they are not practicing self-control, they should marry. For it is better to marry than to be aflame with passion.

To the married I give this command—not I but the Lord—that the wife should not separate from her husband (but if she does separate, let her remain unmarried or else be reconciled to her husband), and that the husband should not divorce his wife.

To the rest I say—I and not the Lord—that if any believer has a wife who is an unbeliever, and she consents to live with him, he should not divorce her. And if any woman has a husband who is an unbeliever, and he consents to live with her, she should not divorce him. For the unbelieving husband is made holy through his wife, and the unbelieving wife is made holy through her husband. Otherwise, your children would be unclean, but as it is, they are holy. But if the unbelieving partner separates, let it be so; in such a case the brother or sister is not bound. It is to peace that God has called you. Wife, for all you know, you might save your husband. Husband, for all you know, you might save your wife.

However that may be, let each of you lead the life that the Lord has assigned, to which God called you. This is my rule in all the churches. Was anyone at the time of his call already circumcised? Let him not seek to remove the marks of circumcision. Was anyone at the time of his call uncircumcised? Let him not seek circumcision. Circumcision is nothing, and uncircumcision is nothing; but obeying the commandments of God is everything. Let each of you remain in the condition in which you were called.

Were you a slave when called? Do not be concerned about it. Even if you can gain your freedom, make use of your present condition now more than ever. For whoever was called in the Lord as a slave is a freed person belonging to the Lord, just as whoever was free when called is a slave of Christ. You were bought with a price; do not become slaves of human masters. In whatever condition you were called, brothers and sisters, there remain with God.

CONCERNING VIRGINS (7:25–40)

Now concerning virgins, I have no command of the Lord, but I give my opinion as one who by the Lord's mercy is trustworthy. I think that, in view of the impending crisis, it is well for you to remain as you are. Are you bound to a wife? Do not seek to be free. Are you free from a wife? Do not seek a wife. But if you marry, you do not sin, and if a virgin marries, she does not sin. Yet those who marry will experience distress in this life, and I would spare you that. I mean, brothers and sisters, the appointed time has grown short; from now on, let even those who have wives be as though they had none, and those who mourn as though they were not mourning, and those who rejoice as though they were not rejoicing, and those who buy as though they had no possessions, and those who deal with the world as though they had no dealings with it. For the present form of this world is passing away.

I want you to be free from anxieties. The unmarried man is, anxious about the affairs of the Lord, how to please the Lord; but the married man is anxious about the affairs of the world, how to please his wife, and his interests are divided. And the unmarried woman and the virgin are anxious about the affairs of the Lord, so that they may be holy in body and spirit; but the married woman is anxious about the affairs of the world, how to please her husband. I say this for your own benefit, not to put any restraint upon you, but to promote good order and unhindered devotion to the Lord.

If anyone thinks that he is not behaving properly toward his fiancée, if his passions are strong, and so it has to be, let him marry as he wishes; it is no sin. Let them marry. But if someone stands firm in his resolve, being under no necessity but having his own desire under control, and has determined in his own mind to keep her as his fiancée, he will do well. So then, he who marries his fiancée does well; and he who refrains from marriage will do better.

A wife is bound as long as her husband lives. But if the husband dies, she is free to marry anyone she wishes, only in the Lord. But in my judgment she is more blessed if she remains as she is. And I think that I too have the Spirit of God.

VEILING OF WOMEN (11:2–16)

I commend you because you remember me in everything and maintain the traditions just as I handed them on to you. But I want you to understand that Christ is the head of every man, and the husband is the head of his wife, and God is the head of Christ. Any man who prays or prophesies with something on his head disgraces his head, but any woman who prays or prophesies with her head unveiled disgraces her head—it is one and the same thing as having her head shaved. For if a woman will not veil herself, then she should cut off her hair; but if it is disgraceful for a woman to have her hair cut off or to be shaved, she should wear a veil. For a man ought not to have his head veiled, since he is the image and reflection of God; but woman is the reflection of man. Indeed, man was not made from woman, but woman from man. Neither was man created for the sake of woman, but woman for the sake of man. For this reason a woman ought to have a symbol of authority on her head, because of the angels. Nevertheless, in the Lord woman is not independent of man or man independent of woman. For just as woman came from man, so man comes through woman; but all things come from God. Judge for yourselves: is it proper for a woman to pray to God with her head unveiled? Does not nature itself teach you that if a man wears long hair, it is degrading to him, but if a woman has long hair, it is her glory? For her hair is given to her for a covering. But if anyone is disposed to be contentious—we have no such custom, nor do the churches of God.

Obedience to the Church (12:1–28)

Now concerning spiritual gifts, brothers and sisters, I do not want you to be uninformed. You know that when you were pagans, you were enticed and led astray to idols that could not speak. Therefore I want you to understand that no one speaking by the Spirit of God ever says "Let Jesus be cursed!" and no one can say "Jesus is Lord" except by the Holy Spirit.

Now there are varieties of gifts, but the same Spirit; and there are varieties of services, but the same Lord; and there are varieties of activities, but it is the same God who activates all of them in everyone. To each is given the manifestation of the Spirit for the common good. To one is given through the Spirit the utterance of wisdom, and to another the utterance of knowledge according to the same Spirit, to another faith by the same Spirit, to another gifts of healing by the one Spirit, to another the working of miracles, to another prophecy, to another the discernment of spirits, to another various kinds of tongues, to another the interpretation of tongues. All these are activated by one and the same Spirit, who allots to each one individually just as the Spirit chooses.

For just as the body is one and has many members, and all the members of the body, though many, are one body, so it is with Christ. For in the one Spirit we were all baptized into one body—Jews or Greeks, slaves or free—and we were all made to drink of one Spirit.

Indeed, the body does not consist of one member but of many. If the foot would say, "Because I am not a hand, I do not belong to the body," that would not make it any less a part of the body. And if the ear would say, "Because I am not an eye, I do not belong to the body," that would not make it any less a part of the body. If the whole body were an eye, where would the hearing be? If the whole body were hearing, where would the sense of smell be? But as it is, God arranged the members in the body, each one of them, as he chose. If all were a single member, where would the body be? As it is, there are many members, yet one body. The eye cannot say to the hand, "I have no need of you," nor again the head to the feet, "I have no need of you." On the contrary, the members of the body that seem to be weaker are indispensable, and those members of the body that we think less honorable we clothe with greater honor, and our less respectable members are treated with greater respect; whereas our more respectable members do not need this. But God has so arranged the body, giving the greater honor to the inferior member, that there may be no dissension within the body, but the members may have the same care for one another. If one member suffers, all suffer together with it; if one member is honored, all rejoice together with it.

Now you are the body of Christ and individually members of it. And God has appointed in the church first apostles, second prophets, third teachers; then deeds of power, then gifts of healing, forms of assistance, forms of leadership, various kinds of tongues.

LOVE IS PATIENT; LOVE IS KIND (13:1–13)

If I speak in the tongues of mortals and of angels, but do not have love, I am a noisy gong or a clanging cymbal. And if I have prophetic powers, and understand all mysteries and all knowledge and if I have all faith, so as to remove mountains, but do not have love, I am nothing. If I give away all my possessions, and if I hand over my body so that I may boast, but do not have love, I gain nothing.

Love is patient; love is kind; love is not envious or boastful or arrogant or rude. It does not insist on its own way; it is not irritable or resentful; it does not rejoice in wrongdoing, but rejoices in the truth. It bears all things, believes all things, hopes all things, endures all things.

Love never ends. But as for prophecies, they will come to an end; as for tongues, they will cease; as for knowledge, it will come to an end. For we know only in part, and we prophesy only in part; but when the complete comes, the partial will come to an end. When I was a child, I spoke like a child, I thought like a child, I reasoned like a child; when I became an adult, I put an end to childish ways. For now we see in a mirror, dimly, but then we will see face to face. Now I know only in part; then I will know fully, even as I have been fully known. And now faith, hope, and love abide, these three; and the greatest of these is love.

SPEAKING IN TONGUES (14:1–40)

Pursue love and strive for the spiritual gifts, and especially that you may prophesy. For those who speak in a tongue do not speak to other people but to God; for nobody understands them, since they are speaking mysteries in the Spirit. On the other hand, those who prophesy speak to other people for their upbuilding and encouragement and consolation. Those who speak in a tongue build up themselves, but those who prophesy build up the church. Now I would like all of you to speak in tongues, but even more to prophesy. One who prophesies is greater than one who speaks in tongues, unless someone interprets, so that the church may be built up.

Now, brothers and sisters, if I come to you speaking in tongues, how will I benefit you unless I speak to you in some revelation or knowledge or prophecy or teaching? It is the same way with lifeless instruments that produce sound, such as the flute or the harp. If they do not give distinct notes, how will anyone know what is being played? And if the bugle gives an indistinct sound, who will get ready for battle? So with yourselves; if in a tongue you utter speech that is not intelligible, how will anyone know what is being said? For you will be speaking into the air. There are doubtless many different kinds of sounds in the world, and nothing is without sound. If then I do not know the meaning of a sound, I will be a foreigner to the speaker and the speaker a foreigner to me. So with yourselves; since you are eager for spiritual gifts, strive to excel in them for building up the church.

Therefore, one who speaks in a tongue should pray for the power to interpret. For if I pray in a tongue, my spirit prays but my mind is unproductive. What should I do then? I will pray with the spirit, but I will pray with the mind also; I will sing praise with the spirit, but I will sing praise with the mind also. Otherwise, if you say a blessing with the spirit, how can anyone in the position of an outsider say the "Amen" to your thanksgiving, since the outsider does not know what you are saying? For you may give thanks well enough, but the other person is not built up. I thank God that I speak in tongues more than all of you; nevertheless, in church I would rather speak five words with my mind, in order to instruct others also, than ten thousand words in a tongue.

Brothers and sisters, do not be children in your thinking; rather, be infants in evil, but in thinking be adults. In the law it is written,

> "By people of strange tongues
>   and by the lips of foreigners
> I will speak to this people;
>   yet even then they will not
>   listen to me."[1]

says the Lord. Tongues, then, are a sign not for believers but for unbelievers, while prophecy is not for unbelievers but for believers. If, therefore, the whole church comes together and all speak in tongues, and outsiders or unbelievers enter, will they not say that you are out of your mind? But if all prophesy, an unbeliever or outsider who enters is reproved by all and called to account by all. After the secrets of the unbeliever's heart are disclosed, that person will bow down before God and worship him, declaring, "God is really among you."

What should be done then, my friends? When you come together, each one has a hymn, a lesson, a revelation, a tongue, or an interpretation. Let all things be done for building up. If anyone speaks in a tongue, let there be only two or at most three, and each in turn; and let one interpret. But if there is no one to interpret, let them be silent in church and speak to themselves and to God. Let two or three prophets speak, and let the others weigh what is said. If a revelation is made to someone else sitting nearby, let the first person be silent. For you can all prophesy one by one, so that all

---

1. Isaiah 28:11–12.

may learn and all be encouraged. And the spirits of prophets are subject to the prophets, for God is a God not of disorder but of peace.

WOMEN MUST BE SUBORDINATE AND NOT SPEAK IN CHURCH (14:33–40)

(As in all the churches of the saints, women should be silent in the churches. For they are not permitted to speak, but should be subordinate, as the law also says. If there is anything they desire to know, let them ask their husbands at home. For it is shameful for a woman to speak in church. Or did the word of God originate with you? Or are you the only ones it has reached?)

Anyone who claims to be a prophet, or to have spiritual powers, must acknowledge that what I am writing to you is a command of the Lord. Anyone who does not recognize this is not to be recognized. So, my friends, be eager to prophesy, and do not forbid speaking in tongues; but all things should be done decently and in order.

RESURRECTION OF CHRIST (15:1–34)

Now I would remind you brothers and sisters, of the good news that I proclaimed to you, which you in turn received, in which also you stand, through which also you are being saved, if you hold firmly to the message that I proclaimed to you—unless you have come to believe in vain.

For I handed on to you as of first importance what I in turn had received: that Christ died for our sins in accordance with the scriptures, and that he was buried, and that he was raised on the third day in accordance with the scriptures, and that he appeared to Cephas, then to the twelve. Then he appeared to more than five hundred brothers and sisters at one time, most of whom are still alive, though some have died. Then he appeared to James, then to all the apostles. Last of all, as to one untimely born, he appeared also to me. For I am the least of the apostles, unfit to be called an apostle, because I persecuted the church of God. But by the grace of God I am what I am, and his grace toward me has not been in vain. On the contrary, I worked harder than any of them—though it was not I, but the grace of God that is with me. Whether then it was I or they, so we proclaim and so you have come to believe.

Now if Christ is proclaimed as raised from the dead, how can some of you say there is no resurrection of the dead? If there is no resurrection of the dead, then Christ has not been raised; and if Christ has not been raised, then our proclamation has been in vain and your faith has been in vain. We are even found to be misrepresenting God, because we testified of God that he raised Christ—whom he did not raise if it is true that the dead are not raised. For if the dead are not raised, then Christ has not been raised. If Christ has not been raised, your faith is futile and you are still in your sins.

Then those also who have died in Christ have perished. If for this life only we have hoped in Christ, we are of all people most to be pitied.

But in fact Christ has been raised from the dead, the first fruits of those who have died. For since death came through a human being, the resurrection of the dead has also come through a human being; for as all die in Adam, so all will be made alive in Christ. But each in his own order; Christ the first fruits, then at his coming those who belong to Christ. Then comes the end, when he hands over the kingdom to God the Father, after he has destroyed every ruler and every authority and power. For he must reign until he has put all his enemies under his feet. The last enemy to be destroyed is death. For "God has put all things in subjection under his feet." But when it says, "All things are put in subjection," it is plain that this does not include the one who put all things in subjection under him. When all things are subjected to him, then the Son himself will also be subjected to the one who put all things in subjection under him, so that God may be all in all.

Otherwise, what will those people do who receive baptism on behalf of the dead? If the dead are not raised at all, why are people baptized on their behalf?

And why are we putting ourselves in danger every hour? I die every day! That is as certain, brothers and sisters, as my boasting of you—a boast that I make in Christ Jesus our Lord. If with merely human hopes I fought with wild animals at Ephesus, what would I have gained by it? If the dead are not raised.

> "Let us eat and drink,
>   for tomorrow we die."
> Do not be deceived:
>   "Bad company ruins good morals."

Come to a sober and right mind, and sin no more; for some people have no knowledge of God. I say this to your shame.

RESURRECTION OF THE DEAD (15:35–58)

But someone will ask, "How are the dead raised? With what kind of body do they come?" Fool! What you sow does not come to life unless it dies. And as for what you sow, you do not sow the body that is to be, but a bare seed, perhaps of wheat or of some other grain. But God gives it a body as he has chosen, and to each kind of seed its own body. Not all flesh is alike, but there is one flesh for human beings, another for animals, another for birds, and another for fish. There are both heavenly bodies and earthly bodies, but the glory of the heavenly is one thing, and that of the earthly is another. There is one glory of the sun, and another glory of the moon, and another glory of the stars; indeed, star differs from star in glory.

So it is with the resurrection of the dead. What is sown is perishable, what is raised is imperishable. It is sown in dishonor, it is raised in glory. It is sown in weakness, it is raised in power. It is sown a physical body, it is raised a spiritual body. If there is a physical body, there is also a spiritual body. Thus it is written, "The first man, Adam, became a living being"; the last Adam became a life-giving spirit. But it is not the spiritual that is first, but the physical, and then the spiritual. The first man was from the earth, a man of dust; the second man is from heaven. As was the man of dust, so are those who are of the dust; and as is the man of heaven, so are those who are of heaven. Just as we have borne the image of the man of dust, we will also bear the image of the man of heaven.

What I am saying, brothers and sisters, is this: flesh and blood cannot inherit the kingdom of God, nor does the perishable inherit the imperishable. Listen, I will tell you a mystery! We will not all die, but we will all be changed, in a moment, in the twinkling of an eye, at the last trumpet. For the trumpet will sound, and the dead will be raised imperishable, and we will be changed. For this perishable body must put on imperishability, and this mortal body must put on immortality. When this perishable body puts on imperishability, and this mortal body puts on immortality, then the saying that is written will be fulfilled:

"Death has been swallowed up in
    victory."
"Where, O death, is your
    victory?
Where, O death, is your
    sting?"

The sting of death is sin, and the power of sin is the law. But thanks be to God, who gives us the victory through our Lord Jesus Christ.

Therefore, my beloved, be steadfast, immovable, always excelling in the work of the Lord, because you know that in the Lord your labor is not in vain.

Revelation (Apocalypse) (100?) Ephesus or Patmos?

TRANSLATED BY WILLIS BARNSTONE

Apocalypse is the alternative title of Revelation and in 1.1 the Greek word *apokalypsis* appears, meaning "revelation," which describes the visionary nature of the book. Visionary writing is common in the Hebrew Bible, found in Isaiah, Ezekiel, and Jeremiah and in the Book of Daniel, which contains four formal apocalypses. The apocalyptic form is found in virtually all religions of the world, be it as murals in a Tibetan monastery or in the Egyptian Book of the Dead. These allegorical works, usually prompted by some historical conflict, have enormous spatial dimensions. In Revelation, characters float between earth, heaven, and hell, and, with Christ's help, the good on defeating the wicked enter the fulfillment of a New Age. God declares himself the Alpha and the Omega, and he appears with the mystery of the seven stars in his hand. The four Horsemen of the Apocalypse ride by. A woman gives birth in midair. The angel Michael fights the dragons. Christ and his army throw the beasts of evil into a lake of fire, whereupon a heavenly Jerusalem descends to replace the earthly city, and the millennium arrives.

In the second century, Bishop Iraneus ascribed the Book of Revelation to the evangelist John, son of Zebedee, one of the twelve apostles, who is also credited with writing the Gospel of John and the three Letters of John. Modern scholars, however, find the style, language, thought, and historic circumstance of Revelation so different from the Gospel of John as to obviate the notion of single authorship. John does identify himself as "John" in 1:9, "I Yohanan your brother and companion in suffering," and there is good reason to suppose that the author was a Christian Jew named Yohanan, which is anglicized as John. On the basis of the Greek style, which has elements of Hebrew syntax and vision, it is speculated that the author was a native of Israel who emigrated to Asia Minor, perhaps in the diaspora after the Jewish revolt against Rome (A.D. 66–73) when many had to flee Jerusalem. Although the John who presumably wrote Revelation is almost certainly not the author of the Gospel of John, until recently they were generally held to be the same author. It should be remembered that books of the Old Testament and New Testament as well as scripture of the Intertestamental period were regularly ascribed to major figures in order that such scriptures might be taken into the canon. So we have works attributed to Enoch and Moses well into the first and second centuries A.D. in order to give those religious texts major significance. Seven of the fourteen letters ascribed to Paul are not by Paul. Similarly, the attachment of the Evangelist's name John to Revelation gave great authority to the book and surely helped it find its way into the canon.

There is a crypt in a monastery on Patmos, the Greek island to which John was exiled for two years; and in a small cave room at the edge of this crypt, John is said to have composed Revelation. Since the speaker in the book says that the risen Christ appeared to him on the island of Patmos, then part of a Roman province, and ordered him to write the book, there is good reason to suppose that Revelation might have been written there. Ephesus is given as an alternative place of composition. The date is uncertain. Because of the scarcely disguised anger against the Romans who were persecuting Jews and Christians, some suggest that the book was composed during the rule of the Roman emperor Nero (A.D. 54–68), who massacred both Christian Jews and Christian Gentiles, or during the rule of Domitian (A.D. 81–96).

During the Intertestament period when Revelation was written, the apocalypse form was a common, indeed a popular, form, and there are significant extant examples, such as The Book of Enoch (Jewish), The Apocalypse of Peter (Christian), and The Apocalypse of Thomas (Christian). To the apocalyptic mind, a visionary experience yields a revelation of the future, of a holy city of redemption, or a terrible hell of punishment. Revelation is peopled by angels, monsters, or four-headed beasts that may represent Satan or a Roman emperor; a woman clothed with the sun, representing the faithful people of God; or the great whore of Babylon, representing nefarious Rome. God in his glorious city of gold and precious stones remains the blessing in wait for the pious reader. Though bestial and chaotic creatures of evil battle against heavenly forces, the heavens will triumph through the intervention of Christ as the Christian message will triumph over the hostility of Rome.

The book of Revelation opens with the Seven Letters to the Seven Churches, warning against lawlessness and deceit (1–3). In chapters four to seven, the Seven Seals on a heavenly scroll are opened, telling of war, plague, famine, and the birthpangs of the new age. In six to eight appear the White Horse, the Red Horse, the Black Horse, the Pale Horse, the Souls under the Altar, the Great Earthquake, the Sealing of the 144,000, and the Silence in Heaven. These visions are followed by seven trumpets (8–11), victory in heaven and disaster for earth as Anti-Christ and false prophet rage. In chapters fifteen to twenty-two the Seven bowls of God's wrath overflow and final battles take place: the whore of Babylon is destroyed as well as the beast's worshipers. Christ returns with the millennium, bringing a last judgment. Finally the bride, New Jerusalem, descends as Babylon falls and we have a description of New Heaven, New Earth, and New Jerusalem (21:1–22:5). These visionary pictures have led fundamentalists, those who take the Bible literally, to see Revelation as the end of the world, the battle of Armageddon (16:12–16). For those who take the Bible as parable and allegory, the struggle between the forces of Satan and Christ are taken as a warning against idolatry and an inducement to save one's soul, and also the church, through faith.

The Apocalypse is an epic poem and takes its place with *Gilgamesh* (Babylonian c. 2000 B.C.), John Milton's *Paradise Lost* (1667), and William Blake's *Jerusalem* (1824) as one of the world's critical visionary poems. As a single, unified work, Revelation may be seen as the literary masterpiece of the New Testament. The symbolism is complex and obscure, a vision blindingly fearful and beautiful. Although Revelation is an intensely luminous book, it suggests more mysteries than it unravels. For that reason, the book is unfinished, as great books are, and its open ending permits the reader endless meditation. There is a circular phenomenon in the fact that Revelation, composed probably on a pagan Greek island, stands as the last work in the Asian New Testament, which returns, as no other volume in Christian Scripture, to the speech, vision, and hopes of salvation of Old Testament visionaries.

FURTHER READING: Revelation and Apocalypses. Barnstone, Willis, ed. *The Other Bible*, 1984. Charlesworth, James H., ed. *Apocalyptic Literature and Testaments*. Vol. 1 of *The Old Testament Pseudepigrapha*, 1983. McGinn, Bernard. "Revelation." In Alter, Robert, and Frank Kermode, *The Literary Guide to the Bible*, 1987. Barnstone, Willis, tr. The Apocalypse, John of Patmos, 1999.

CHAPTER 1

The Alpha and the Omega

₈The Lord God says:

> I am the Alpha and the Omega,[1]
> and who is and who was and who is coming.
> I am the Pantocrator.[2]

> ₉I Yohanan your brother and companion in suffering
> and kingdom and endurance through Yeshua
> was on the island called Patmos for the word
> of God and testimony of Yeshua.
> ₁₀I was fixed in the spirit on the Lord's Day
> and I heard behind me a great voice like a trumpet
> ₁₁saying: "What you have seen, write in a book
>   and send it off to the seven churches,
> to Ephesos, Smyrna, Pergamon and Thyatria,
> to Sardis and Philadelphia and Laodicea."

> ₁₂And I turned to see the voice speaking to me,
> and when I turned I saw seven gold lamps
> ₁₃and in the midst of the lamps was one like
> the Son of People clothed in a robe down to his feet
> and girt around his breasts with a gold belt.
> ₁₄His head and his hair were white like white wool
> like snow and his eyes like a flame of fire,
> ₁₅his feet like fine bronze as if fired in a furnace
> and his voice like the sound of many waters.
> ₁₆And in his right hand he held seven stars
> and from his mouth came a sharp two-edged sword
> and his face was like the sun shining in its power.
> ₁₇When I saw him I fell at his feet like a dead man
> and he placed his right hand on me and said:
> ₁₈"Don't be afraid. I am the first and last
> and the living one, and I have been dead,
> and look, I am alive forevermore

---

1. *alpha and the omega* in Greek. As with the gospels, the dates and names are unknown. If like the gospels, the text represents a Greek version of a lost earlier version, written or oral, going back to Aramaic or Hebrew, then to represent the first and last letters of the alphabet, as the beginning and the end, we would have *alef and the tav* rather than *alpha and the omega*.

2. *the Pantocrator,* "the Almighty." In the Greek Orthodox Church "Pantocrator," meaning "all powerful," from *pan,* "all," and *kratos,* "strong," is regularly used in the Greek liturgy to signify "Almighty," and chosen to reflect the Greek usage, although since these first two verses come directly from Isaiah 6:3, "Almighty" better reflects the tradition of translation from the Hebrew Bible.

and I have the keys of Death and of Hell.
19So write what you have seen and what you see
and after this what is about to happen.
20The mystery of the seven stars you saw
in my right hand, and seven golden lamps.
Seven stars are angels for seven churches
and seven golden lamps are seven churches."

CHAPTER 6

The Seven Seals

And I saw the lamb open one of the seals
and I head one of the four animals saying
in a voice that seemed like thunder, "Come!"
2and I saw, and look, a white horse
and its rider had a bow and was given a crown
and he went out conquering and to conquer.

3And when the lamb opened the second seal,
I heard the second animal saying, "Come!"
4Another horse of fire red came out.
Its rider was ordered to take peace away
from earth so men might kill each other,
and he was given a great sword.

5And when the lamb opened the third seal,
I heard the third animal saying, "Come!"
And I saw, and look, a black horse,
and its rider held a pair of scales in his hand.
6And I heard what seemed to be a voice
in the midst of the four animals, saying,
"A measure of wheat for a denarius
and three measures of barley for a denarius,
and do not damage the olive oil with wine."

7And when the lamb opened the fourth seal,
I heard the voice of the fourth animal saying,
"Come!" 8and I saw, and look, a pale green horse,
and the name of his rider was Death, and Hell
was following him. Power was given them
over a quarter of the globe to kill
by sword and by hunger and by death
and by the wild beasts of the earth.

9And when the lamb opened the fifth seal,
I saw under the altar the souls of those
who were slaughtered for the word of God
and the testimony which they held.

*10*And they cried out in a great voice saying,
"How long, O absolute ruler, holy and true,
will you wait to judge and avenge our blood
from those who live upon the earth?"
*11*They were each given a white robe and told
to rest a little time until the number was filled
of their fellow slaves, brothers and sisters
who are to be killed as they were killed.

*12*When the lamb opened the sixth seal I looked
and there took place a great earthquake
and the sun became black like sackcloth of hair
and the full moon became like blood.
*13*and the stairs of the sky fell to the earth
as the fig tree drops its unripe fruit
shaken by a great wind. *14*And the sky
vanished like a scroll rolling up
and every mountain and island of the earth
was torn up from its place and moved.
*15*And the kings of the earth and the great men
and commanders of thousands and every slave
and the free hid in caves and mountain rocks,
*16*and said to the mountains and rocks, "Fall on us
and hide us from the face of him who is sitting
on the throne and from the anger of the lamb,
*17*because the great day of his anger has come,
and before him who has the force to stand?"

CHAPTER 12

A Great Portent in the Sky

Then there was a great portent in the sky,
a woman clothed in the sun, and moon
under her feet and on her head a crown
of seven stars. *2*In her womb she had a child
and screamed in labor pains, aching to give birth.
*3*And another portent was seen in the sky,
look, a great fire-red dragon with seven heads
and ten horns, and on his heads seven diadems.
*4*His tail dragged a third of the stars of heaven
and hurled them to the earth. The dragon stood
before the woman about to give birth
so when she bore her child he might devour it.
*5*She bore a son, a male, who will shepherd
all nations with a rod of iron,
and her child was snatched away to God

and to his throne. 6And the woman fled
into the desert where she has a place
made ready by God that they might nourish
her one thousand two hundred sixty days.

7And in the sky were Mikhael[3] and his angels
battling with the dragon. 8The dragon and his angels
fought back, but they were not strong enough.
No longer was there place for them in the sky.
9The great dragon, the ancient snake, who is called
Devil and Satan, the deceiver of the whole
inhabited world, was flung down to earth.
and his angels were flung down with him.
10And I heard a great voice in the sky, saying,
"Now has come the salvation and the power
and the kingdom of our God and the authority
of his Messiah, for the accuser of our brothers
and sisters has been cast down, and the accuser
abused them day and night before our God.
11They defeated him through the blood of the lamb
and by the word to which they testified
and did not cling to life while facing death.
12Be happy, skies, and those who set their tents
on you. Earth and sky, you will know grief,
because the Devil has come down to you
in great rage, knowing he has little time."

13When the dragon saw that he had been cast
down on the earth, he pursued the woman
who had borne the male child. 14And she was given
two wings of the great eagle that she might fly
into the desert to her place where she is nourished
for a time, and times, and half a time away
from the face of the snake. 15But from his mouth
the snake cast water, a flood behind the woman,
so he might sweep her away on the river.
16But the earth helped the woman, and the earth
opened its mouth and swallowed the river
which the dragon had cast out of his mouth.
17The dragon was angry at the woman and left
to battle against her remaining seed,
those who keep the commandments of God
and keep the testimony of Yeshua.

18Then the dragon stood on the sand of the sea.

---

3. *Mikhael,* Hebrew for Michael.

CHAPTER 13

A Beast Coming Up from the Sea

Then I saw a beast coming up from the sea,
with ten horns and seven heads and on his horns
ten diadems, and on his heads were the names
of blasphemy. ₂The beast I saw was like a leopard,
his feet like a bear and his mouth like the mouth
of a lion. And the dragon gave him his power
and his throne and fierce power of dominion.
₃One of his heads seemed to be stricken to death
but the wound causing his death was healed
and the whole world marveled after the beast.
₄They worshiped the dragon since he had given
dominion to the beast, and they worshiped the beast,
saying, "Who is like the beast and can battle him?"
₅He was given a mouth to speak great things
and blasphemies. And he was given dominion
to act for forty-two months. ₆Then he opened
his mouth to utter blasphemies against God,
blaspheming his name and his tenting place,
and those who have set their tent in the sky.
₇He was given powers to battle the saints
and to overcome them, and was given powers
over every tribe and people and tongue and nation.
₈All who dwell on the earth will worship him,
each one whose name has not been written since
the foundation of the world in the book of life
of the slaughtered lamb. ₉Who has an ear, hear
Jeremiah:

> ₁₀He who leads into captivity goes into captivity.
> He who kills with the sword will be killed
> by the sword.[4]

Such is the endurance and faith of the saints.

₁₁Then I saw another beast rising from the earth
and he had two horns like a lamb and he spoke
like a dragon. ₁₂He exercises all the dominion
of the first beast before him, and makes the earth
and its inhabitants worship the first beast,
whose wound of death was healed. ₁₃He does great portents,
even making a fire plunge from the sky
down to the earth in the sight of the people.

---

4. Jeremiah 15:2, 14:11.

14He fools the inhabitants on the earth
by means of the portents he contrives to make
on behalf of the beast, creating an image
to show the beast as wounded by the sword
yet comes out alive. 15And he had the power
to give breath[5] to the image of the beast
and the image of the beast could even speak
and cause all who will not worship the beast
to be killed. 16He causes all, the small and great,
the rich and poor, the free and the slaves,
to be marked on the hand and the forehead
so that no one can buy or sell without the mark,
the name of the beast or number of his name.
17Here is wisdom. Who has a mind, calculate
the number of the beast, which is the number
for a human. And the number is 666.

CHAPTER 15

A Sea of Glass

And I saw another great portent in the sky,
great and wonderful, seven angels with seven plagues,
the last ones, since the anger of God is fulfilled
in them. 2I saw what seemed a sea of glass
mingled with fire, and victors over the beast
and his image and the number of his name,
standing on the sea of glass, holding harps of God.
3They sang the song of Moses the slave of God
and the song of the lamb:

> Great and wonderful are your works,
>> Lord God the Pantocrator.
> Just and true are your ways,
>> O king of nations!
> 4Who will not fear you, Lord,
>> and glorify your name?
> Because you alone are holy,
>> because all nations come
>> and worship before you,
> because your judgments are revealed.

5After this I looked. The temple of the tent[6]
of testimony was opened in the sky,
6and the seven angels with the seven plagues

---

5. *pneuma* means breath or spirit and sometimes both.

6. *skenes,* "tent" or "pavilion."

came out of the temple. They were robed in linen
clean and bright and gold belts girding their breasts.
7One of the four animals gave the seven angels
seven gold bowls filled with the anger of God
who lives forevermore. 8The temple was filled
with smoke from the glory of God and from
his power, and none could enter the temple until
the seven plagues of the seven angels were done.

CHAPTER 21

A New Haven

And I saw a new sky and a new earth,
for the first sky and the first earth were gone
and the sea is no more. 2I saw the holy
city, the new Yerushalayim, coming down
out of the sky from God who prepared her
like a bride adorned for her groom. 3And then
I heard a great voice from the throne, saying:
"Look, now the tent of God is with the people,
and he will spread his tent over them,
and he God himself will be with them,
4and he will wipe away each tear from their eyes
and death will be no more. And grief and crying
and pain will be no more. The past has perished."

5And he who sat upon the throne said, "Look,
I made all new." And he said, "Write, because
these words are true and faithful." 6And he said
to me, "It's done. I am the Alpha and the Omega,
the beginning and the end. And to the thirsty
I will give a gift from the spring of the water
of life. 7The victor will inherit these things
and I will be his God and he will be
a son. 8But to the cowards and unbelieving
and abominable and murderers and copulators
and sorcerers and all who are false, their fate
will be the lake burning with fire and sulfur,
which is the second death."

9One of the angels came with the seven bowls
full of the seven last plagues, and he spoke
with me, saying, "Come, I will show you the bride,
the wife of the lamb." 10And he took me away
in spirit onto a mountain great and high,
and showed me the city of holy Yerushalayim
coming down out of the sky from God,

11wearing the glory of God, and her radiance
like a precious stone, like a jasper stone
and crystal clear. 12She has a great and high wall
with twelve gates and at the gates twelve angels,
their names inscribed on them, the twelve tribes
who are the sons and daughters of Israel.
13On the east three gates and on the north three gates,
on the south three gates and on the west three gates.
14The walls of the city have twelve foundations,
and on them twelve names, the twelve apostles of
        the lamb.
15The angel speaking to me had a gold
measuring reed[7] to gage the city and her gates
and walls. 16The city lies foursquare, its length
and width the same. He gaged the city with
the reed, twelve thousand furlongs in length,[8]
her length and width and height the same. 17He gaged
her wall a hundred forty-four cubits,[9]
by human measurement the same as angels'.

18The wall is built of jasper and the city
clear gold like clear glass. 19The foundations of
the city are adorned with precious stones,
the first foundation jasper, the second sapphire,
third of agate, fourth of emerald, 20fifth of onyx,
the sixth carnelian, the seventh chysolite,
the eighth beryl, ninth of topaz, tenth of chysopase,
eleventh hyacinth and the twelfth amethyst.
21The twelve gates pearl, each gate a single pearl.
The great square in the city is clear gold
like a diaphanous glass.

22I saw no temple in her, for the temple
is Lord God the Pantocrator and the lamb.
23The city has no need of sun or moon
to shine on her, for the glory of God
illumined her and her lamp is the lamb.
24The Gentile nations will walk around
through her light, and the kings of the earth
bring glory into her. 25Her gates will never
be shut by day, and night will not be there.

---

7. *kalamos*, "reed." A "reed" was a basis for measuring; hence a measuring "rod."
8. About fifteen hundred miles.
9. Almost seventy-five yards.

*26*Her people will bring the glory and honor
of nations into her. *27*But no common thing[10]
will enter her, or anyone who stoops
to abominations and lies, but only those
written in the book of life of the lamb.

CHAPTER 22

The Throne of God and of the Lamb

The angel showed me a river of water
of life shining like crystal and issuing
from the throne of God and of the lamb.
*2*Between the great plaza and the river
and on either side stands the tree of life
with her twelve fruits, yielding a special fruit
for every month, and the leaves of the tree
are for healing the nations. *3*Every curse
will no longer exist. The throne of God
and of the lamb will be in her. His slaves
will serve him *4*and will see his face. His name
will be on their foreheads. *5*And night will not
be there and they'll need no light of a lamp
or light of sun, for the Lord God will glow
on them, and they will reign forevermore.

*6*Then he said to me, "These words are faithful
and true, and the Lord God of the spirits of
the prophets sent his angel to show his slaves
those things which soon must take place. *7*Look,
I'm coming quickly. Blessed is the one
who keeps the words of this book's prophecy."

*8*I Yohanan am the one who heard and saw
these things. And when I heard and saw I fell
and worshiped before the feet of the angel
showing me these things. *9*And he said to me,
"You must not do that! I am your fellow slave
and of your brothers the prophets and those
who keep the words of this book. Worship God."
*10*And he tells me, "Do not seal the words
of prophecy of this book. The time is near.

---

10. *koinon,* "common." Here this word, as many common words in New Covenant lexicons, is given a religious boost by translating it as "profane," which means "in contrast to the sacred." But its sense of "common" or "plain" contrasts specifically and only with the shining magnificence of the city in the sky, which is lost when the dominant meaning "common" is not rendered.

_11_Let the unjust still be unjust, the filthy
still be filthy, the righteous still do right,
and the holy one be holy still. _12_Look,
I'm coming soon, and my reward is with me
to give to each according to your work.
_13_I am the Alpha and the Omega, the first
and the last, the beginning and the end.
_14_Blessed are they who are washing their robes
so they will have the right to the tree of life
and can enter the city through the gates.
_15_Outside will be the dogs and sorcerers
and copulators and murderers and idolaters
and everyone who loves to practice lies.

_16_I Yeshua sent my angel to you
to witness these things to you for the churches.
I am the root and the offspring of David
the bright star of morning. _17_And the spirit
and bride say, 'Come.' Let you who hear say, 'Come.'
Let you who thirst come, and let you who wish
take the water of life, which is a gift."

_18_I give my testimony to all who hear
these words of the prophecy of this book.
If anyone adds to these, then God will add
to them the plagues recorded in this book.
_19_If anyone takes away from the words
of this book's prophecy, God will cut off
their share of the tree of life and the holy
city, those things recorded in this book.
_20_And he who witnesses all these things says,
"Yes, I am coming soon."
　　Amen, come, Lord Yeshua.
_21_May the grace of the Lord Yeshua be with all.

■ Intertestament: Jewish Pseudepigrapha, Dead Sea Scrolls, Jewish-Christian Odes, Gnostic Scriptures (Second Century B.C.–Third Century A.D.)

Between the closing of the Hebrew Bible in the second century and the canonization of the New Testament in A.D. 363, there is a huge literature of holy scriptures, the Intertestamental texts, that did not find a place in either Testament. These texts, including the Dead Sea Scrolls, Noncanonical

Apocrypha, Jewish and Christian Apocalypses, Gospels and Infancy Gospels, Acts, Kabbalah, Psalms, and Gnostic Scriptures, many of which were unavailable until early twentieth-century archeological discoveries, are important as literature, and they also radically change our picture of the development of the Judeo-Christian tradition.

After the closing of the Old Testament and during the first centuries A.D., inspired authors continued to write sacred scriptures. They were written by Jews, Christians, Gnostics, and pagans. Many of these texts were of amazing beauty and religious importance and competed with books within the canon. The Jewish texts are in large part called pseudepigrapha (falsely ascribed texts), and include the Dead Sea Scrolls; the Christian texts are called Christian Apocrypha; the Gnostic scriptures, today so fascinating and even modish, were called by their orthodox rivals heretical. Had events been otherwise and certain of these inspired texts incorporated in our Bible, our understanding of the tradition of religious thought would have been radically altered. Today, free of doctrinal strictures, we can read the "greater bible" of the Judeo-Christian world.

The holy texts that were not included in the Old or New Testaments include creation and Eden myths, psalms and romances, gospels and epistles, prophecies and apocalypses, histories and mystical documents. Every genre of the Bible is represented.

Why did the specifically Jewish and Christian texts fail to find a place in the Bible? Was it a question of divine authority, period, or doctrine? These errant scriptures are often aesthetically and religiously the equal of books in the canon and offer vital information, such as Infancy Gospels on Jesus' childhood, as well as alternative versions of major biblical stories. In a Manichaean version of Genesis, it is Eve who gives life to Adam, and the serpent, the Luminous Jesus, is a liberating figure urging the first couple to take the first step toward salvation by eating from the Tree of Gnosis. The exclusion of many texts was often as arbitrary and dubious as was the inclusion of such magnificent and dangerous books as Ecclesiastes and the Song of Songs.

At times, the cause of exclusion was fierce political and religious rivalry between sects; between factions; between Jew, Christian, and Gnostic. The antiquity of a book was a primary factor influencing inclusion, and for this reason many competing texts were attributed to great figures of the Bible—to Enoch, Isaiah, Thomas, Paul—to give them both age and authority. For similar reasons, pseudonymous books of the Bible—the Song of Songs, the Psalms, and certain Epistles—assumed the names of Solomon, David, and John in their titles. As for the abundant Gnostic scriptures, these were excluded precisely because of their Gnosticizing tendencies. Indeed, it is said that the early Gnostic Marcion of Sinope so angered the followers of the new religion of Jesus Christ that he provoked the Christian Fathers into establishing a New Testament canon.

The Gnostics were serious rivals of orthodox Christians. The most systematized and organized Gnostic cult was Manichaeism, which spread from Mesopotamia through Asia Minor to North Africa and the European territories of the Roman Empire. It extended to eastern Iran and into Chinese Turkestan, where it became the state religion of the Uigur Empire. Western China remained Manichaean until the thirteenth century. In the West it rose here and there as various medieval sects, such as the Bogomils and Cathari, and the Albigensians in southern France. Today in Iran and southwest Iraq, the Mandaeans, a Gnostic offshoot of heterodox Jewish sects originally from eastern Syria and Palestine, continue in the Gnostic faith.

The most serious conflict between Christians and Gnostics was in the first four centuries A.D. In the second century, Valentinus, a major Gnostic thinker, sought election as Pope of Rome. Surely the fixation of the New Testament in Carthage in 397 would have been drastically different had Valentinus succeeded; and what would have been the views of that former Gnostic, Saint Augustine, whose words so affected the conciliar decisions at Carthage? Leaving aside speculations, we can say categorically that the Bible, with the absence of sacred texts from the entire Intertestamental period, with its acceptance of a small and repetitious canon for the New Testament, with the exclusion of all later Christian Apocrypha, and the total rejection of Gnostic scriptures, has given us a highly censored and distorted version of ancient religious literature.

Deprived of all scriptures between the Testaments, the common reader is left with the impression that somehow Christianity sprang self-generated like a divine entity, with no past, into its historical setting. Yet a reading of the texts between the Testaments shows how major eschatological themes of the New Testament—the appearance of the Son of Man, the imminence of the End, the apocalyptic vision in the Book of Revelation, the notion of salvation through the Messiah—are all the preoccupation of Intertestamental literature.

In regard to the New Testament, the Epistles and the Book of Revelation could be increased, if not replaced, by other works in these genres. Noncanonical Christian Apocrypha conveys a lucid picture of the life and ideals of early Christendom. We see the wanderings of the apostles in Asia Minor and India, and note their legendary adventures, the sermons of chastity, the bloody accounts of much-desired martyrdom. The Apocrypha is particularly rich in apocalypses, which immediately informs the reader that the canonical Apocalypse is not really an odd and obscure text but, rather, one that is perfectly consistent with noncanonical Jewish and Christian scriptures. In these wondrous texts, we witness visionary journeys to Heaven and Hell, which feed stock images into the tradition that Dante followed in the Commedia when he himself became a figure in Hell, Purgatory, and Heaven.

As for the Gnostics, their scriptures were anathema to orthodox Christians, for they reversed fundamental notions of Christian theology—although they thought themselves the true and uncorrupted Christians.

As a result of conflict between these two major sects of primitive Christianity and the victory of the orthodox, the Gnostic texts disappeared; they were destroyed or left uncopied, achieving the same end. Until a few years ago, the loss appeared so complete that we relied for information largely on the works of early Christian Fathers, such as Irenaeus, Hippolytus, Clement of Alexandria, and Augustine, who wrote refutations of the Gnostics. Then, in 1945, extensive Gnostic treatises were discovered in earthenware jars buried in a field at Nag Hammadi in Egypt. The fifty-two scriptures were in Coptic, translated from Greek. Just as the discovery of the Dead Sea Scrolls at Qumran in 1947 gave us for the first time Essene scriptures, so the startling appearance of these Egyptian documents gave us at last the actual words of the Gnostics. The books are rich in cosmogonies and anthropogonies. They contain apocalyptic visions and secret scrolls of Jesus' life and sayings. The magnificent Gospel of Truth and Gospel of Thomas add greatly to the information provided by the New Testament.

Hermes Trismegistus (more likely a tradition than a person) is included because the Hermetic theology and lexicon reveal Jewish, Christian, and Gnostic parallels and exemplify in extraordinary texts the syncretic nature of religious traditions in the first centuries A.D. Plotinus, a thoroughly Hellenized Egyptian Neoplatonist, gives us the vocabulary and system of mystical introspection and ascension to God.

As we move into the first centuries A.D., we encounter a mixture of several traditions, often in the same Scripture. The Gospel of John, an excellent example of such syncretic tendencies, begins with the haunting logic of "In the beginning was the Word, and the Word was with God, and the Word was God." The Word or logos in the Fourth Gospel comes from Philo of Alexandria (c. 20 B.C.–A.D. 40), who linked the Stoic logos with the Platonic world of ideas, making logos the means of knowing the transcendent God. So in one famous Christian passage, we see clear currents of Greek Platonism through the intermediary of a Hellenized Alexandrian Jew who, among other contributions, invented allegorical exegesis of the Bible, which Christian apologists soon adopted.

Many of the Christian Apocrypha are Jewish scriptures with a Christian overlay. So the Son of Man, a common messianic term in Jewish pseudepigrapha, obviously becomes in Christian recension Jesus the Messiah. Often the Apocrypha have a Gnostic dimension, as do passages of the gospels. The Odes of Solomon, a Syriac text discovered in 1909, is a Jewish hymnbook, in Christian redaction, subjected to Gnostic interpolations. The original text was almost certainly composed in Greek.

The Intertestamental scriptures reveal the great diversity of ancient thought. Each view, it seems, is contradicted by a second and a third. The reader has several perspectives to aid in interpretations and judgments. In contrast to Old Testament concern with the historical destiny of a people, the scriptures between the Testaments emphasize salvation, eternity, and otherworldly *topoi*. We may find three conflict-ing views of a single event. Thus after Jesus Christ is crucified, the Jews think him another man and go on seeking the Messiah; the Christians proclaim the crucified Jesus both man and God, and the Gnostics take the Docetic view that Jesus was only a simulacrum on the cross, for God is always God. In fact, in the Gnostic works *The Second Treatise of the Great Seth* and *The Apocalypse of Peter,* Jesus the Savior stands above the cross, laughing at the ignorance of his would-be executioners who think that men can kill God.

Whereas the New Testament speaks of a Jesus who rewards the faithful with salvation and condemns the "men of little faith" to eternal damnation, the Apocrypha depict a much more compelling picture of these rewards: we find Jesus on his throne of glory in seventh heaven or descending into Hell to torture sinners with his breath of fire. Whereas the Christian mystic searched through the dark night of ignorance, the Gnostic replaced faith and ignorance with gnosis, that is, knowledge and inner illumination. Whereas the Judeo-Christian view held that our Fall occurred when Eve and Adam ate from the Tree of Knowledge, the Gnostics held that the Fall occurred earlier and Adam and Eve were innocent of wrongdoing. The great error took place when the Creator God himself (as opposed to the alien God) fell into sin by creating the world, by trapping divine sparks of spirit in the darkness, in the material prison of the human body.

The Book of Jubilees (Second Century B.C.)
Israel/Alexandria (anonymous Jewish Genesis)

TRANSLATED BY R. H. CHARLES, ADAPTED BY WILLIS BARNSTONE

The Book of Jubilees is an extensive retelling of Genesis and Exodus in which the author's emphasis on *Halakhah* (the teachings and ordinances of biblical law) suggests both opposition to the Hellenizing spirit in Israel and an affinity with the Qumran community, the so-called Essenes of the Dead Sea Scrolls. The emphasis on *halakhic* commentary is seen in references to "commandments written down on heavenly tablets."

In this "Little Genesis"—an alternate title to a book longer than Gene-sis as well as any book of the pseudepigrapha—God secretly reveals to Moses on Mount Sinai the history of the Jews from the creation of the world to the passage through the Red Sea. God's agent is the "angel of the presence," who orders Moses to write down God's exact words. Events in the book follow a solar calendar, and dates and numbers are specific and emphatic. For example, the regulations governing the uncleanness of a woman after the birth of a son or daughter specify the number of days of the mother's separation from the sanctuary, and God gives this information to Adam directly on his arrival in Eden from the land of his creation. The emphasis on the prohibition of nakedness, on Adam and Eve's shame and God's gift of clothing to them, reflects an attempt to protect Israel from the Greek *gymnasion* (where athletes trained naked), which were popular in Jerusalem and even among its Maccabean rulers. A notable richness in the book is its angelology—angels of the winds and of the waters—which is referred to in Matthew, Acts, and Revelation. In the final section (not given here), the righteous live a mythical existence and enjoy a prediluvian longevity of a thousand years or more. Their souls will enjoy immortality.

The date of composition is uncertain, but most scholars indicate the middle of the Jubilees was written in Hebrew, then translated into Greek, and from Greek into Ethiopic. The complete text exists in Ethiopic today, edited by R. H. Charles. Fragments of a Latin translation are also extant.

The Creation of the World[1]

On the first day[2] he created the tall heavens and the earth and waters and all the spirits who served him: the angels of the presence, the angels of sanctification, the angels of the spirit of fire, the angels of the spirit of the winds, of the clouds, of darkness, of snow, hail, and hoarfrost, the angels of the voices of thunder and lightning, the angels of the spirits of cold and heat, of winter, spring, autumn, and summer, and of all spirits of his creatures in Heaven and on the earth. He created the abysses and darkness, twilight and night, and light, dawn, and day, and he prepared them in the knowledge of his heart. Thereupon we saw his works, and praised him.

He created seven great works on the first day. On the second day he created the firmament in the midst of the waters, and on that day the waters were divided, half of them going above, half below, the firmament hanging over the face of the entire earth. This was God's only work on the second day. On the third day he commanded the waters to roll off the face of the earth, to gather in one place, and for dry land to appear. The waters did as he commanded and rolled off the face of the earth, and in a single place the dry land appeared. On that day he created all the seas according

---

1. Chapter 2. This selection is a modern revision by Willis Barnstone of R. H. Charles, *The Book of Jubilees* (Oxford: Clarendon Press, 1902), 40–43, 46–51.

2. The Book of Jubilees is presented as a secret revelation given to Moses by God's angel on Mount Sinai. The first line of chapter 2 omitted in the above text, introduces the retelling of the Genesis creation: "And the angel of the presence spoke to Moses according to the word of the Lord, saying: 'Write the complete history of the creation, how in six days the Lord God finished all his works and all that he created, and kept Sabbath on the seventh day and hallowed it for all ages, and appointed it as a sign for all his works.'"

to their separate gathering places, all rivers, waters in the mountains and along the earth, the lakes and dew, seed which is sown, and all sprouting things, fruit trees, trees of the forest, and the Garden of Eden. In Eden he formed every manner of plant. These were his great works on the third day.

And on the fourth day he created the sun and moon and stars, and placed them in the firmament of heaven to give light on earth, to rule over day and night, to separate light from darkness. And God appointed the sun to be a great sign on the earth for days and for sabbaths and for months, for feasts, years, sabbaths of years, for jubilees, and every season of the years. The sun divided light from darkness so that all things may prosper which shoot and grow in the earth. These three things he made on the fourth day.

And on the fifth day he created great sea monsters in the depths of the waters—these were the first things of flesh created by his hands—the fish and everything that moves in the waters, and everything that flies—all the birds. The sun rose above them to enrich all his creations—plants shooting on the earth, trees, and flesh. These three things he created on the fifth day.

And on the sixth day he created all the animals of the earth, cattle, and all moving things. And after all this he created man, a man and woman, and he gave him dominion over all on the earth, in the seas, in the air, over beasts and cattle he gave him dominion. And these four species he created on the sixth day. There were altogether twenty-two kinds. He finished his work on the sixth day—in Heaven and earth, in the waters and abysses, in light and darkness. And he gave us a great sign, the Sabbath: that we should work six days but on the Sabbath, the seventh day, we should keep from all work.

Adam, Eve, and Paradise[1]

During six days of the second week, according to God's word, he brought Adam all beasts, cattle, all birds and things creeping on the earth and moving in the water. Beasts were on day one, cattle on day two, birds on day three, all that creeps on the earth on day four, all that moves in the water on day five. And Adam named them. As he called them so was their name. And during these five days Adam saw that each species had male and female, but he was alone. He had no helpmate. The Lord said to us: "It is not good for the man to be alone. I will make him a helpmate." Our God caused a deep sleep to fall on him, and while he slept God took one of his ribs as a woman. This was the origin of woman. And he built up the flesh on it. He constructed woman. And he woke Adam from his sleep, and on this sixth day he brought her to the rising Adam, and Adam knew her and said,

---

1. Chapter 3.

"She is now bone of my bones and flesh of my flesh. She will be called my wife because she was taken from her husband." So man and wife will be one, so a man will leave his father and mother and cleave to his wife, and they will be one flesh.

Adam was created in the first week, and his wife, his rib, in the second week. God showed her to him, and so the commandment was given for a male to keep in his defilement for seven days and for a female twice seven days.

After Adam had completed forty days in the land where he was created, he was brought into the Garden of Eden to till and to keep it. His wife was brought in on the eightieth day. For that reason the commandment is written on the heavenly tablets in regard to the mother: "She who bears a male shall remain in her uncleanness seven days, and thirty-three days in the blood of purification. She shall not touch any hallowed things, nor enter in the sanctuary until the days for the male or female child are accomplished." This is law and testimony written down for Israel.

In the first week of the first jubilee, Adam and his wife were in the Garden of Eden for seven years tilling and reaping. He was given work and instructed how to farm correctly. He tilled the Garden and was naked, but he did not know it, and was not ashamed. He protected the Garden from birds and beasts and cattle, and gathered fruit and food, which he stored for himself and his wife. After exactly seven years, in the seventeenth day of the second month, the serpent came and said to the woman, "Did God command you not to eat of any tree in the Garden?" She said, "God told us to eat fruit from all trees in the Garden, except for the fruit of the tree in the middle of the Garden. God said to us: 'You must not eat from it, nor touch it, or you will die.'"

And the serpent said to the woman, "You will surely not die. For God knows that on the day you eat of that tree your eyes will be opened. You will be like gods and know good from evil." And the woman looked at the tree, which was pleasant to her eye, and its fruit good for food, and she picked a fruit and ate. She covered her shame with a fig leaf and gave Adam what she had taken from the tree. He ate, and his eyes were opened and he saw that he was naked. He took fig leaves, sewed them together, made an apron for himself, and covered his shame.

Then God cursed the serpent and was forever angry with it. He was angry with the woman, for she had listened to the serpent and had eaten. He said to her: "I will greatly multiply your sorrows and your pains. In sorrow you will bring forth children. You will return to your husband, who will rule over you." To Adam he said: "Because you listened to your wife's voice and ate from the tree I commanded you not to touch, let the ground be cursed under you. Thorns and thistles will grow in it, and you will eat your bread in the sweat of your face until you return to the earth from which you were taken. You are earth and to earth you will return." He made them coats out of skins, clothed them, and sent them out of the Garden of Eden.

On the day Adam left the Garden, he made an offering of sweet-smelling frankincense, galbanum, and stacte, and spices of the morning. And on that day was closed the mouth of all beasts, of cattle, birds, whatever walks and crawls, so that they could not speak. They had all spoken to each other with one lip and one tongue. He sent out of the Garden all flesh that was there, and all flesh was scattered according to its kinds in the places created for them. He gave only Adam the means of covering his shame not any of the beasts and cattle. And so those who know the judgment of law prescribed on the heavenly tablets know to cover their shame. They should not uncover themselves as the Gentiles do.[2]

On the new moon of the fourth month Adam and his wife left the Garden of Eden and dwelled in the land of Elda, in the land of their creation. Adam called his wife Eve. They had no son till the first jubilee, and after this he knew her. Now he farmed the land as he had been instructed to in the Garden of Eden.

The Thanksgiving Psalms (Dead Sea Scrolls) (First Century A.D.) Israel

TRANSLATED BY WILLIS BARNSTONE

The book of psalms contained in one of the scrolls found by the Dead Sea consists of at least twenty-five separate poems. These psalms (or hymns) offer thanksgiving to the Lord who has given the community the secrets of salvation. They were probably learned and sung by initiates when they entered the brotherhood. The majority of scholars believe that many of the psalms are in the voice of the Teacher of Righteousness, and perhaps written by him. Theodor H. Gaster belittles this notion as restrictive and unsubstantiated. He compares their passion and conceits to the work of the great English metaphysical poets John Donne, George Herbert, and Henry Vaughan and stresses their mystical component.[1]

The French scholar A. Dupont-Sommer, who views the scrolls as a harbinger of primitive Christianity, sees in the psalms not only their biblical source but ideas connected with the adjacent worlds of the Zoroastrians and the Gnostics. He writes:

But however close their bond with ancient Jewish piety, the Hymns of Qumran constantly betray new ideas which are obviously connected with the religious

---

2. This passage suggests opposition to stripping by Greeks (as well as Jews) for athletic games. In a larger sense it suggests opposition to Hellenizing Jews and Hellenization in Palestine.

---

1. Theodor H. Gaster, *The Dead Sea Scrolls* (New York: Doubleday Anchor, 1956), 112.

world of Zoroastrianism and Hellenistic Gnosis. The psalmist is a "man who knows," a Gnostic; knowledge that is the principle of his salvation and the source of his joy.[2]

Whatever the source, whoever the speaker in the psalms, commentators agree that the poems are the literary jewel of the Dead Sea Scrolls. Indeed, they are equal to the very best psalms of the Old Testament. Their magnificent language, their flow and universal passion, their sweeping images of Heaven, Hell, lions, humanity, and clay frequently render them overwhelming.

Psalm 1[1]

These things I know from your wisdom,
and you have freed my ears to hear wondrous mysteries.
I am a thing
formed of clay and kneaded with water,
the earth of nakedness and well of pollution,
a furnace of iniquity and fabric of sin,
My perverted spirit strays into error,
fearing good judgment.
What can I say that you do not know beforehand?
All things are graven before you with a pen of remembrance,
for all times, for the years of eternity.
From you nothing is absent or obscure.

Psalm 10

I am striken dumb like a ewe lamb,
my arm is wrenched from its socket,
my foot sinks in filth,
my eyes blur from seeing evil,
my ears are closed from hearing the cry of bloodshed,
my heart is appalled at the thought of evil
when human baseness is revealed.
Then my foundations shudder
and my bones are out of joint.
My entrails heave like a ship in a slamming storm from the East.
My heart is utterly sore,

---

2. A. Dupont-Sommer, ed., G. Vermes, tr., *The Essene Writings from Qumran* (Oxford: Basil Blackwell, 1961), 200

---

1. Versions of Psalms 1 and 10 by Willis Barnstone are based on earlier translations by Theodor H. Gaster, Millar Burrows, and G. Vermes.

and in the havoc of transgression
a whirlwind swallows me up.

Gnosticism

Before considering the Gospel of Thomas and other Gnostic scriptures it is best to consider the nature of Gnosticism itself. The term Gnosticism designates a religious movement made up of many sects, which by the second century A.D. was widespread in Europe, the Middle East, and even extended to western China where in the city of Turfan and the area of Chinese Turkestan it was dominant until well into the thirteenth century.

The Gnostics believed in a radical dualism in which forces of light contend with forces of darkness, knowledge contends with ignorance, truth contends with error (rather than sin), and spirit contends with body and the physical universe. An essential characteristic of all Gnostic systems is a shift from a God-oriented to a self-oriented religion. Gnosticism is based on *gnosis*, Greek for knowledge, and is a personal religion or philosophy based on knowing oneself, as a means to discovering the divinity within oneself. As such, the Gnostic sects, with the exception of the Manichaeans, did not rely on clergy and organization but on self-knowledge, and in this they resembled the personalization and internalization of religion that accompanied the Protestant Reformation many centuries later. We find an especial coincidence of tenets between Gnosticism and the Protestant Quakers, who similarly believe in personal knowledge of "an inner light," which can be found without priest or rites. "Faith" among the Gnostics was not necessarily a virtue, for faith implied surrendering power to the clergy and church. So self-knowledge—rather than a faith in church officials' knowledge— leads to salvation. The Gnostics rejected this world and considered the body a prison from which the soul or, more important, the divine spark, longs to escape in order to return to the unknown, alien, true God, who is androgynous in nature.

The theologian Robert M. Grant suggests that Gnosticism arose among ex-Jews because of the "failure of Jewish apocalyptic hopes."[1] The people were waiting for the Messiah, for divine intervention, during years when the Romans burned the Temple (A.D. 70) and drove the populace into exile. The failure of their expectations provoked a turn away from apocalyptic Judaism, and a turn toward inward speculation. Hence the Jewish Gnostic speculation.

The fulfillment of Jewish apocalyptic hope however, was realized in Christianity, which proclaimed Jesus the Messiah, thereby redeeming the

---

1. Robert M. Grant, *Gnosticism and Early Christianity* (London: Oxford University Press, 1959), 36.

dream that had obsessed Essenes and Zealots and other groups who despaired of contemporary religious and political realities. But then some Christians sensed a failure in Christian *apokalypsis* (revelation); rejected Yahweh, church, and traditional faith; and turned inward—hence the Christian Gnostic speculation. Because the Christian Gnostics violently altered orthodox doctrine, they sought justification of their systems through biblical exegesis. As Philo of Alexandria (15 B.C.– A.D. 50) had earlier allegorized the Old Testament, the Gnostics, and particularly the Valentinians, became exegetes of both New and Old Testaments. In addition, they rewrote many of the main books of the Bible; for example, in The Origin of the World, they retell the Creation and Adam and Eve in the garden. The Gnostics reversed many traditional Judeo-Christian beliefs. Eve creates Adam, and Eve is good, rather than sinful and disobedient, for she gave humanity knowledge. Whereas traditional Christians considered sex a proper part of marriage if its purpose was procreation, the Gnostics held that sex was proper and more valuable when it did not lead to procreation and trapping more spirits in the flesh. There developed two views: the sects of Caprocrates and Ophites who practiced extreme eroticism and the Valentinians who inspired extreme asceticism. All sects held the common belief that through meditation on and knowledge of the divine spark, salvation is attained. Salvation is complete when the divine spark returns to union with the alien God.

The Gospel of Thomas (c. A.D. 200) Syria, Palestine, or Mesopotamia (prophecies, proverbs, and parables of Jesus)

TRANSLATED BY HELMET KOESTER

The Gospel of Thomas is a collection of traditional sayings, prophecies, proverbs, and parables of Jesus. The Coptic Gospel of Thomas was translated from the Greek; in fact, several fragments of this Greek version have been preserved and can be dated to about A.D. 200. Thus the Greek (or even Syriac or Aramaic) collection was composed in the period before A.D. 200, possibly as early as the second half of the first century, in Syria, Palestine, or Mesopotamia. The authorship of the Gospel of Thomas is attributed to Didymos Judas Thomas, that is, Judas "the Twin," who was identified particularly within the Syrian Church as the apostle and twin brother of Jesus.

The relationship of the Gospel of Thomas to the New Testament gospels has been a matter of special interest: many of the sayings of the Gospel of Thomas have parallels in the synoptic gospels (Matthew, Mark, and Luke). A comparison of the sayings in the Gospel of Thomas with their parallels in the synoptic gospels suggests that the sayings in the Gospel of

Thomas either are present in a more primitive form or are developments of a more primitive form of such sayings. Indeed, the Gospel of Thomas resembles the synoptic sayings source, often called "Q" (from the German word *Quelle*, "source"), which was the common source of sayings used by Matthew and Luke. Hence the Gospel of Thomas and its sources are collections of sayings and parables that are closely related to the sources of the New Testament gospels.

The influence of Gnostic theology is clearly present in the Gospel of Thomas, though it is not possible to ascribe the work to any particular school or sect. The collected sayings are designated as the "secret sayings which the living Jesus spoke." Thus the collection intends to be esoteric: the key to understanding is the interpretation or secret meaning of the sayings, for "whoever finds the interpretation of these sayings will not experience death." According to the Gospel of Thomas, the basic religious experience is not only the recognition of one's divine identity, but more specifically the recognition of one's origin (the light) and destiny (the repose). In order to return to one's origin, the disciple is to become separate from the world by "stripping off" the fleshly garment and "passing by" the present corruptible existence; then the disciple can experience the new world, the kingdom of light, peace, and life.

The numeration of 114 sayings is not in the manuscript but is followed by most scholars today.

These are the secret sayings which the living Jesus spoke and which Didymos Judas Thomas wrote down.

(1) And he said, "Whoever finds the interpretation of these sayings will not experience death."

(2) Jesus said, "Let him who seeks continue seeking until he finds. When he finds, he will become troubled. When he becomes troubled, he will be astonished, and he will rule over the All."

(3) Jesus said, "If those who lead you say to you, 'See, the Kingdom is in the sky,' then the birds of the sky will precede you. If they say to you, 'It is in the sea,' then the fish will precede you. Rather, the Kingdom is inside of you, and it is outside of you. When you come to know yourselves, then you will become known, and you will realize that it is you who are the sons of the living Father. But if you will not know yourselves, you dwell in poverty and it is you who are that poverty."

(4) Jesus said, "The man old in days will not hesitate to ask a small child seven days old about the place of life, and he will live. For many who are first will become last, and they will become one and the same."

(5) Jesus said, "Recognize what is in your sight, and that which is hidden from you will become plain to you. For there is nothing hidden which will not become manifest."

(6) His disciples questioned him and said to him, "Do you want us to fast? How shall we pray? Shall we give alms? What diet shall we observe?"

Jesus said, "Do not tell lies, and do not do what you hate, for all things are plain in the sight of Heaven. For nothing hidden will not become manifest, and nothing covered will remain without being uncovered."

(7) Jesus said, "Blessed is the lion which becomes man when consumed by man; and cursed is the man whom the lion consumes, and the lion becomes man."

(8) And he said, "The man is like a wise fisherman who cast his net into the sea and drew it up from the sea full of small fish. Among them the wise fisherman found a fine large fish. He threw all the small fish back into the sea and chose the large fish without difficulty. Whoever has ears to hear, let him hear."

(9) Jesus said, "Now the sower went out, took a handful of seeds, and scattered them. Some fell on the road; the birds came and gathered them up. Others fell on rock, did not take root in the soil, and did not produce ears. And others fell on thorns; they choked the seeds and worms ate them. And others fell on the good soil and produced good fruit: it bore sixty per measure and a hundred and twenty per measure."

(10) Jesus said, "I have cast fire upon the world, and see, I am guarding it until it blazes."

(11) Jesus said, "This heaven will pass away, and the one above it will pass away. The dead are not alive, and the living will not die. In the days when you consumed what is dead, you made it what is alive. When you come to dwell in the light, what will you do? On the day when you were one you became two. But when you become two, what will you do?"

(12) The disciples said to Jesus, "We know that you will depart from us. Who is to be our leader?"

Jesus said to them, "Wherever you are, you are to go to James the righteous, for whose sake heaven and earth came into being."

(13) Jesus said to his disciples, "Compare me to someone and tell me whom I am like."

Simon Peter said to him, "You are like a righteous angel."

Matthew said to him, "You are like a wise philosopher."

Thomas said to him, "Master, my mouth is wholly incapable of saying whom you are like."

Jesus said, "I am not your master. Because you have drunk, you have become intoxicated from the bubbling spring which I have measured out."

And he took him and withdrew and told him three things. When Thomas returned to his companions, they asked him, "What did Jesus say to you?"

Thomas said to them, "If I tell you one of the things which he told me, you will pick up stones and throw them at me; a fire will come out of the stones and burn you up."

(14) Jesus said to them, "If you fast, you will give rise to sin for yourselves; and if you pray, you will be condemned; and if you give alms, you will do harm to your spirits. When you go into any land and walk about in the

districts, if they receive you, eat what they will set before you, and heal the sick among them. For what goes into your mouth will not defile you, but that which issues from your mouth—it is that which will defile you."

(15) Jesus said, "When you see one who was not born of woman, prostrate yourselves on your faces and worship him. That one is your Father."

(16) Jesus said, "Men think, perhaps, that it is peace which I have come to cast upon the world. They do not know that it is dissension which I have come to cast upon the earth: fire, sword, and war. For there will be five in a house: three will be against two, and two against three, the father against the son, and the son against the father. And they will stand solitary."

(17) Jesus said, "I shall give you what no eye has seen and what no ear has heard and what no hand has touched and what has never occurred to the human mind."

(18) The disciples said to Jesus, "Tell us how our end will be."

Jesus said, "Have you discovered, then, the beginning, that you look for the end? For where the beginning is, there will the end be. Blessed is he who will take his place in the beginning; he will know the end and will not experience death."

(19) Jesus said, "Blessed is he who came into being before he came into being. If you become my disciples and listen to my words, these stones will minister to you. For there are five trees for you in Paradise which remain undisturbed summer and winter and whose leaves do not fall. Whoever becomes acquainted with them will not experience death."

The Odes of Solomon (Second Century) Syria

TRANSLATED BY WILLIS BARNSTONE

The *Pistis Sophia,* a Gnostic text preserved in Coptic, contains five odes from *The Odes of Solomon,* and these were all we had of that very important hymnbook until J. Rendel Harris's discovery in 1909 of a four-hundred-year-old Syriac text of the collection. The original language of the odes was probably Greek, although some scholars argue for a Syriac original. Harris conjectured a Jewish-Christian origin from the first century A.D. Others suggest a Jewish original with a Christian redaction. W. Bauer offers a third possibility: "But more and more the view became established that we have to do with a Gnostic hymn-book from the 2nd century."[1] Whatever the origin, in their present form it is clear that they are based on Jewish hymnal tradition, that many of them have been subjected to a Christian overlay,

---

1. Edgar Hennecke and Wilhelm Schneemelcher, eds., *New Testament Apocrypha,* Vol. 2 (Philadelphia: Westminster Press, 1964), 809.

and that there are also Gnostic references, which are more significant than their mere inclusion in the *Pistis Sophia*. Harris also points out many quotations of the odes in the works of the early Church Fathers. The odes were of particular interest because of their Christology, that is, the use of Christ as a speaker. Frequently, the structure of an ode consists of a prologue on the part of the odist, then an oracular statement *ex ore Christi*, and finally a doxology for the congregation to participate in.

Many of the odes are hauntingly beautiful. The images soar. The diction is rich with surprising references, such as "milk from the Lord," which apologists explain away as odd symbolism. Actually, the odes are as poetic, profound, and astonishing as the most compelling psalms of the Old Testament. So we read "The dew of the Lord rinsed me with silence/ and a cloud of peace rose over my head" (Ode 35); or, with typical chariot imagery of Jewish mysticism: "I went up to the light of truth as into a chariot/ and truth took me/ across canyons and ravines" (Ode 38). The words are graceful in "My heart was cloven and there appeared a flower,/ and grace spang up" (Ode 11), and the thought of three prevailing traditions, Jewish, Christian, and Gnostic, is suggested in Ode 7:

> The father of knowledge
> is the word of knowledge.
>
> He who created wisdom
> is wiser than his works.

The Odes of Solomon are one of the great poetic and wisdom documents of antiquity.

Ode 15

> As the sun is joy to those who seek daybreak,
> so my joy is the Lord.
>
> He is my sun and his rays have lifted me up
> and chased all darkness from my face.
>
> In him I have acquired eyes
> and seen his sacred day.
>
> I have acquired eyes
> and heard his truth.
>
> I have acquired knowledge
> and been made happy by him.
>
> I left the way of error and went to him
> and was saved.
>
> According to his bounty he gave me,
> according to his beauty he made me.

I found purity through his name,
I shed corruption through his grace.

Death has died before my countenance,
hell is abolished by my word.

A deathless life appears in the land of the Lord,
is known to those with faith,
and is given to those with faith, unceasingly.

Ode 19

A cup of milk I was offered
and I drank its sweetness as the delight of the Lord.

The Son is the cup
and he who was milked is the Father
and he who milked him is the Holy Ghost.

His breast were full
and his milk should not drip out wastefully.

The Holy Ghost opened the Father's raiment
and mingled the milk from the Father's two breast

and gave that mingling to the world, which was unknowing.
Those who drink it are near his right hand.

The Spirit opened the Virgin's womb
and she received the milk.

The Virgin became a mother of great mercy;
she labored, but not in pain, and bore a Son.
No midwife came.

She bore him as if she were a man,
openly, with dignity, with kindness.
She loved him, and swaddled him, and revealed his majesty.

Ode 21

I raised my arms high
to the grace of the Lord,

for he had cast off my bonds.
My helper had lifted me to his grace and salvation.

I discarded darkness
and clothed myself in light.

My soul acquired a body
free from sorrow,
affliction or pain.

The thought of the Lord restored me.
I fed on his incorruptible fellowship.

And I was raised in the light
and went to him,
near him,
praising and proclaiming him.

He made my heart flood into my mouth,
made it shine on my lips.

On my face the exultation of the Lord increased,
and his praise.

Ode 30

Drink deeply from the living fountain of the Lord.
It is yours.

Come, all who are thirsty, and drink,
and rest by the fountain of the Lord.

How beautiful and pure.
It rests the soul.

That water is sweeter than honey.
The combs of bees are nothing beside it.

It flows from the lips of the Lord.
Its name is from the Lord's heart.

It is invisible but has no borders
and was unknown until it was set in our midst.

They who drink are blessed
and they rest.

Ode 34

The simple heart finds no hard way,
good thought finds no wounds.
Deep in the illuminated mind is no storm.

Surrounded on every side by the beauty of the open country,
one is free of doubt.

Below
is like above.

Everything is above.
Below is nothing, but the ignorant think they see.

Now you know grace. It is for your salvation.
Believe and live and be saved.

Ode 35

The dew of the Lord rinsed me with silence
and a cloud of peace rose over my head,

guarding me.
It became my salvation.

Everybody quivered in horror.
They issued smoke and a judgment,

but I was silent, near my Lord,
who was more than shadow, more than foundation.

He carried me like a child by its mother.
He gave me milk, his dew,

and I grew in his bounty,
rested in his perfection.

I spread my hands out as my soul pointed to the firmament
and I slipped upward to him
who redeemed me.

Ode 38

I went up to the light of truth as into a chariot
and truth took me

across canyons and ravines,
and preserved me against waves smashing the cliffs.

It was my haven and salvation
and put me in the arms of immortal life.

It went with me, soothed me, kept me from error,
since it was and is truth . . .

The Hymn of the Pearl (Second or Third Century) Syria? (narrative poem)

TRANSLATED BY WILLIS BARNSTONE

"The Hymn of the Pearl" is a fabulous narrative poem concerning the adventurous quest for a pearl. Although the tale was probably pre-Gnostic and pre-Christian, in its present form it has been furnished with details that clearly make it Manichaean and, as Günther Bornkamm argues, the young prince and savior is depicted as Mani himself, the founder of

Manichaeism.[1] It is a beautiful poem, one of the most attractive documents in Gnostic literature.

On the surface the poem is simply an adventure. But everywhere in it are clues of other meanings. After all, serpents who sleep with pearls in their possession cannot but have an allegorical dimension. "The Hymn of the Pearl" would be impoverished were one not to decode its symbols, which seem to be determined by their usage in earlier Mandaean traditional tales as well as in such Gnostic works as the *Pistis Sophia*. By consensus of most scholars, the main figures—the Father, Mother, and Prince—form a Gnostic trinity, equivalent to the Christian trinitarian formula. They represent the Father of Truth, the Mother of Wisdom, and the Son. The Son, who is redeemer and savior, is not Christ, however, or at least not primarily Christ. Hans Jonas identifies him with the Manichaean precosmic Primal Man. Curiously, he has a double or twin role, for he appears to be both savior and the soul that he saves; he saves and must himself be saved. So too the Pearl, which at first appears to be a symbol of the soul, is also the deity who saves the soul. So, as Jonas points out, "The interchangeability of the subject and object of the mission, of savior and soul, of Prince and Pearl, is the key to the true meaning of the poem, and to the gnostic eschatology in general."[2] Other symbols in the poem are more obvious, although the notion of the double, so typically Gnostic, continues. The Prince's garment of glory, which he has taken off in order to assume the unclean robe of the world—obviously the unclean human body—represents his heavenly glory, which he has left behind, yet this garment of glory also operates as an independent being. So too the letter, on which is written the call of redemption, flies down as an eagle from heaven and becomes a messenger of light. As for Egypt, it stands traditionally for the body, for material things, for darkness and error. It is the kingdom of death. Likewise, the serpent is the realm of darkness and ignorance. For the Gnostics, who tend to reverse Judeo-Christian values, ignorance is equivalent to Judeo-Christian sin and evil; gnosis (brought about through eating the apple from the Tree of Gnosis, and which Christians speak of as original sin) is good and brings redemption. Thus the food that the Prince carries with him is his gnosis, which the soul needs to find itself and return to its heavenly journey. The Father and Mother's home in the east is, of course, Heaven.

As in many Gnostic tales, the woman has an equal or important role in the divine strategy. In key roles such as the creator of Adam's soul, she is not reduced to the nondeity role of mother and housewife as in the family

1. Günther Bornkamm, ed., R. McL. Wilson, tr., *The Acts of Thomas*. In Edgar Hennecke and Wilhelm Schneemelcher, eds., *New Testament Apocrypha*, Vol. 2 (Philadelphia: Westminster Press, 1965), 434–435.

2. Hans Jonas, *The Gnostic Religion*, 2d ed., rev. (1958; reprint, Boston: Beacon Press, 1963),127.

of Jesus or troublemaker during Adam's sojourn in Eden. In "The Hymn of the Pearl," reference is not simply to the "Father," but to the "parents." The Mother is called the "Mistress of the East," that is, the "Mistress of Heaven."

"The Hymn of the Pearl," sometimes called "The Hymn of the Soul," is a fable of redemption. Unlike the traditional Christian myth, here the savior himself must be saved. For a while he forgets who he is and falls into the sleep of earthly things. But the Father of Truth and the Mother of Wisdom (Mother Sophia) do not forget him and send messages. He wakes from the prison of earthly things, steals the pearl, and returns to his true parents.

The hymn exists in an early Syriac text and a somewhat later Greek version. It is attached to the Apocryphal Acts of Thomas, which deal with the deeds of the Apostle Judas Thomas.

When I was a little child[1]
living in my kingdom, in my father's house
happy in the glories and riches
of my family that nurtured me,
my parents gave me provisions   5
and sent me forth from our home in the east.
From their treasure house
they made up a bundle for me.
It was big though light
so I might carry it alone,   10
and it held gold from the House of the Highest Ones
and silver of Gazzak the Great
and rubies of India
and opals from the land of Kushan,
and they girded me with adamant   15
which can crush iron.
And they took off my bright robe of glory,
which they had made for me out of love,
and took away my purple toga,
which was woven to fit my stature.   20
They made a covenant with me
and wrote it in my heart so I would not forget:
"When you go down into Egypt
and bring back the One Pearl
which lies in the middle of the sea   25
and is guarded by the snorting serpent,

---

1. Version by Willis Barnstone, derived from earlier translations. Reliable translations appear in Edgar Hennecke and Wilhelm Schneemelcher, eds., *New Testament Apocrypha,* Vol. 2 (Philadelphia: Westminster Press, 1965), 498–504; and in Robert M. Grant, *Gnosticism* (New York: Harper & Brothers, 1961), 116–122.

you will again put on your robe of glory
and your toga over it,
and with your brother, our next in rank,
you will be heir in our kingdom."   30
I left the east and went down
with my two royal envoys,
since the way was dangerous and harsh
and I was very young to walk alone.
I crossed the borders of Maishan,   35
the gathering place of merchants of the east,
and came into the land of Babel
and entered the walls of Sarbug.
I went down into Egypt
and my companions left me.   40
I went straight to the serpent
and settled in close by his inn,
waiting for him to sleep
so I could take my pearl from him.
Since I was all alone   45
I was a stranger to others in the inn,
Yet I saw one of my own people there,
a nobleman from the east,
young, handsome, lovable,
a son of kings—an anointed one,   50
and he came and was close to me.
And I made him my confidante
with whom I shared my mission.
I warned him against the Egyptians
and of contact with the unclean ones.   55
Then I put on a robe like theirs
lest they suspect me as an outsider
who had come to steal the pearl;
lest they arouse the serpent against me.
But somehow they learned   60
I was not their countryman,
and they dealt with me cunningly
and gave me their food to eat.
I forgot that I was a son of kings,
and served their king.   65
I forgot the pearl
for which my parents had sent me.
Through the heaviness of their food
I fell into a deep sleep.
But when all these things happened   70
my parents knew and grieved for me.

It was proclaimed in our kingdom
that all should come to our gate.
And the kings and princes of Parthia
and all the nobles of the east   *75*
wove a plan on my behalf
so I would not be left in Egypt.
And they wrote me a letter
and every noble signed it with his name.
"From your father, the King of Kings,   *80*
and your mother, the Mistress of the East,
and from your brother, our next in rank,
to you, our son in Egypt, greetings:
Awake and rise from your sleep
and hear the words of our letter!   *85*
Remember that you are a son of Kings
and see the slavery of your life.
Remember the pearl
for which you went into Egypt!
Remember your robe of glory   *90*
and your splendid mantle
which you may wear
when your name is named in the book of life,
is read in the book of heroes,
when you and your brother inherit   *95*
our kingdom."
And serving as messenger
the letter was a letter
sealed by the king with his right hand
against the evil ones, the children of Babel   *100*
and the savage demons of Sarbug.
It rose up in the form of an eagle,
the king of all winged fowl;
it flew and alighted beside me,
and became speech.   *105*
At its voice and the sound of its rustling
I awoke and rose from my sleep.
I took it, kissed it,
broke its seal and read.
And the words written on my heart   *110*
were in the letter for me to read.
I remembered that I was a son of Kings
and my free soul longed for its own kind.
I remembered the pearl
for which I was sent down into Egypt,   *115*
and I began to enchant

the terrible and snorting serpent.
I charmed him into sleep
by naming the name of my Father over him,
and the name of the next in rank, 120
and of my Mother, the queen of the east.
I seized the pearl
and turned to carry it to my Father.
Their filthy and impure garment
I stripped off, leaving it in the fields, 125
and directed my way
into the light of our homeland, the east.
On my way the letter that awakened me
was lying on the road.
And as it had awakened me with its voice 130
so it guided me with its light;
it was written on Chinese silk,
and shone before me in its own form.
Its voice soothed my fear
and its love urged me on. 135
I hurried past Sarbug,
and Babel on the left,
and came to Maishan,
the haven of merchants,
perched next to the sea. 140
My robe of glory which I had taken off
and the toga over it
were sent by my parents
from the heights of Hyrcania.
They were in the hands of treasurers 145
to whom they were committed
because of their faith,
and I had forgotten the robe's splendor
for as a child I had left it
in my Father's house. 150
As I gazed on it
suddenly the garment seemed to be a mirror
of myself. I saw it in my whole self,
and in it I saw myself apart,
for we were two entities 155
yet one form.
The treasurers brought me one robe:
they were two of the same shape
with one kingly seal.
They gave me wealth, 160
and the bright embroidered robe

was colored with gold and beryls,
with rubies and opals,
and sardonyxes of many colors
were fastened to it in its high home.   *165*
All its seams were fastened
with stones of adamant;
and the image of the King of Kings
was embroidered on it,
and it glowed with sapphires   *170*
of many colors.
I saw it quiver all over
with the movements of gnosis,
and as it prepared to speak
it moved toward me,   *175*
murmuring the sound of its songs
as it descended:
"I am the one who acted for him
for whom I was brought up in my Father's house.
I saw myself growing in stature   *180*
according to his labors."
With regal movements
it was spreading toward me,
urging me to take it,
and love urged me   *185*
to receive it,
and I stretched forth and received it
and put on the beauty of its colors.
I cast my toga of brilliant colors
all around me.   *190*
Therein I clothed myself and ascended
to the Gate of Salutation and Adoration.
I bowed my head and adored
the majesty of my Father who had sent it to me.
I had fulfilled his commandments   *195*
and he had fulfilled what he promised,
and at the gate of his princes
I mingled with his nobles.
He rejoiced in me and received me
and I was with him in his kingdom,   *200*
and all his servants praised him
with resounding voices.
He promised me that I would journey quickly
with him to the Gate of the King of Kings,
and with my gifts and my pearl   *205*
I would appear with him before our King.

On the Origin of the World (Third Century) Greek/Coptic Egypt (Gnostic genesis)

TRANSLATED BY HANS-GEBHARD BETHGE AND ORVAL S. WINTERMUTE

The modern title *On the Origin of the World* is used to name a tractate that has been transmitted without a title but discusses what this hypothetical title suggests. *On the Origin of the World* is a compendium of essential Gnostic ideas, a work written in the form of an apologetic essay offering to the public an explanation of the Gnostic worldview. Although the treatise does not represent any known Gnostic system, there are reminiscences of Sethian, Valentinian, and Manichaean themes; the author obviously draws upon a variety of traditions and sources. For example, some sort of connection with the *Hypostasis of the Archons* (Codex II, 4) is clear, though the precise nature of this relationship is uncertain. *On the Origin of the World* was probably composed in Alexandria at the end of the third century A.D. or the beginning of the fourth. The place and date of composition are suggested by the juxtaposition of various sorts of materials: the varieties of Jewish thought, Manichaean motifs, Christian ideas, Greek or Hellenistic philosophical and mythological concepts, magical and astrological themes, and elements of Egyptian lore together suggest that Alexandria may have been the place where the original Greek text was composed.

After opening with a reference to the philosophical controversy regarding the origin of Chaos, *On the Origin of the World* proceeds to a detailed portrayal of primeval history. The Genesis story of the creation of the world, the place of the arrogant demiurge Ialdabaoth, and the climactic creation and enlightened transgression of Adam and Eve are described from a Gnostic viewpoint. In addition, important salvific roles are played by Wisdom (Pistis Sophia and Sophia Zoë), the little blessed spirits, and Jesus the logos and Savior. Finally, in a victorious blaze of destruction, light triumphs over darkness, and life over death.

The treatise *On the Origin of the World* is an important Gnostic work in several respects. This text provides insight into the thought, methodology, and argumentation of a Gnostic author presenting to the public at large certain information on the origin and end of the world and of man. Furthermore, the tractate also shows the freedom and skill with which such a writer could utilize various materials of a diverse character, all in the service of Gnostic proclamation. *On the Origin of the World* illustrates how the Gnostic worldview can assert itself in dialogue with other spiritual movements and in part even replace them.

The Raising of Adam from the Mud by Eve (Zoë-Life)

Then the authorities received knowledge necessary to create man. Sophia Zoë, who is beside Sabaoth, anticipated them, and laughed at their decision because they were blind—in ignorance they created him against them-selves—and they do not know what they will do. Because of this she antici-pated them. She created her man first in order to inform their molded body of how he would condemn them. And in this way he will save them.

Now the birth of the instructor occurred in this way. When Sophia cast a drop of light, it floated on the water. Immediately the man appeared, being androgynous. That drop first patterned the water as a female body. Afterward it patterned itself within the body of the likeness of the mother who appeared, and it fulfilled itself in twelve months. An androgynous man was begotten, one whom the Greeks call "Hermaphrodites." But the He-brews call his mother "Eve of Life," i.e., "the instructor of life." Her son is the begotten one who is lord. Afterward, the Authorities called him "the beast" in order to lead their molded bodies astray. The interpretation of the "beast" is "the instructor"; he was found to be wiser than all of them. Moreover, Eve is the first virgin, not having a husband. When she gave birth, she is the one who healed herself. On account of this it is said con-cerning her that she said,

> "I am the portion of my mother,
>> and I am the mother,
> I am the woman,
>> and I am the virgin.
> I am the pregnant one.   5
>> I am the physician.
>> I am the midwife.
> My husband is the one who begot me,
>> and I am his mother,
> and he is my father and my lord.   10
> He is my potency.
> That which he desires he speaks with reason.
> I am still in a nascent state,
>> but I have borne a lordly man."

Now these things were revealed by the will of Sabaoth and his Christ to the souls who will come to the molded bodies of the Authorities; and con-cerning these, the holy voice said, "Multiply and flourish to rule over all the creatures." And these are the ones who are taken captive by the First Father according to lot and thus they were shut up in the prisons of the molded bodies until the consummation of the Aeon. And then at that time, the First Father gave those who were with him a false intention concerning the man. Then each one of them cast his seed on the midst of the navel of the earth. Since that day, the seven Rulers have formed the man: his body is like their body, his likeness is like the man who appeared to them. His mold-ed body came into being according to a portion of each one of them. Their chief created his head and the marrow. Afterward he appeared like the one who was before him. He became a living man, and he who is the father was called "Adam," according to the name of the one who was before him.

Now after Adam was completed, he left him in a vessel since he had taken form like the miscarriages, having no spirit in him. Because of this deed, when the chief ruler remembered the word of Pistis, he was afraid lest perhaps the man come into his molded body and rule over it. Because of this, he left his molded body forty days without soul. And he withdrew and left him.

But on the fortieth day Sophia Zoë sent her breath into Adam, who was without soul. He began to move upon the earth. And he was not able to rise. Now when the seven Rulers came and saw him, they were very much disturbed. They walked up to him and seized him, and Ialdabaoth said to the breath which was in him, "Who are you? And from whence have you come hither?" He answered and said, "I came through the power of the Light-man because of the destruction of your work." When they heard, they glorified him because he gave them rest from their fear and concern. Then they called that day "the rest," because they rested themselves from their troubles. And when they saw that Adam was not able to rise, they rejoiced. They took him and left him in Paradise, and withdrew up to their heavens.

After the day of rest, Sophia sent Zoë, her daughter, who is called "Eve [of Life]," as an instructor to raise up Adam, in whom there was no soul, so that those whom he would beget might become vessels of the light. When Eve saw her co-likeness cast down, she pitied him, and she said, "Adam, live! Rise up on the earth!" Immediately her word became a deed. For when Adam rose up, immediately he opened his eyes. When he saw her, he said, "You will be called 'the mother of the living' because you are the one who gave me life."

The Rape of Eve by the Prime Ruler (God) and by His Angels

Then the Authorities were informed that their molded body was alive, and had arisen. They were very much disturbed. They sent seven archangels to see what had happened. They came to Adam. When they saw Eve speaking with him, they said to one another, "What is this female light-being? For truly she is like the likeness which appeared to us in the light. Now come, let us seize her and let us cast our seed on her, so that when she is polluted she will not be able to ascend to her light, but those whom she will beget will serve us. But let us not tell Adam that she is not derived from us, but let us bring a stupor upon him, and let us teach him in his sleep as though she came into being from his rib so that the woman will serve and he will rule over her."

Then Eve, since she existed as a power, laughed at their false intention. She darkened their eyes and left her likeness there stealthily beside Adam. She entered the Tree of Knowledge, and remained there. But they tried to follow her. She revealed to them that she had entered the tree and became tree. And when the blind ones fell into a great fear, they ran away.

Afterward, when they sobered up from the stupor, they came to Adam. And when they saw the likeness of that woman with him, they were troubled, thinking that this was the true Eve. And they acted recklessly, and came to her and seized her and cast their seed upon her. They did it with a lot of tricks, not only defiling her naturally but abominably, defiling the seal of her first voice, which before spoke with them, saying, "What is it that exists before you?" But it is impossible that they might defile those who say that they are begotten in the consummation by the true man by means of the word. And they were deceived, not knowing that they had defiled their own body. It was the likeness which the Authorities and their angels defiled in every form.

She conceived Abel first from the Prime Ruler; and she bore the rest of the sons from the seven Authorities and their angels. Now all this came to pass according to the foresight of the First Father, so that the first mother might beget within herself every mixed seed which is joined together with the fate of the world and its schemata and fate's justice. A dispensation came into being because of Eve so that the molded body of the Authorities might become a hedge for the light. Then it will condemn them through their molded bodies.

Moreover, the first Adam of the light is spiritual. He appeared on the first day. The second Adam is soul-endowed. He appeared on the sixth day, and is called "Hermaphrodite." The third Adam is earthy, i.e., "man of law," who appeared on the eighth day after "the rest of poverty," which is called "Sunday." Now the progeny of the earthy Adam multiplied and completed the earth. They produced by themselves every knowledge of the soul-endowed Adam. But as for the All, he was in ignorance of it. Afterwards, let me continue, when the Rulers saw him and the woman who was with him, erring in ignorance like the beasts, they rejoiced greatly. When they knew that the deathless man would not only pass by them, but that they would also fear the woman who became a tree, they were troubled and said, "Is perhaps this one, who blinded us and taught us about this defiled woman who is like him, the true man, in order that we might be conquered by her?"

Then the seven took counsel. They came to Adam and Eve timidly. They said to him, "Every tree which is in Paradise, whose fruit may be eaten, was created for you. But beware! Don't eat from the Tree of Knowledge. If you do eat, you will die." After they gave them a great fright, they withdrew up to their Authorities.

Then the one who is wiser than all of them, this one who was called "the beast," came. And when he saw the likeness of their mother, Eve, he said to her, "What is it that God said to you? 'Don't eat from the Tree of Knowledge'?" She said, "He not only said 'Don't eat from it,' but 'Don't touch it lest you die.'" He said to her, "Don't be afraid! You certainly shall not die. For he knows that when you eat from it your mind will be sobered and you will become like God, knowing the distinctions which exist between evil and good men. For he said this to you, lest you eat from it, since he is jealous."

Now Eve believed the words of the instructor. She looked at the tree. And she saw that it was beautiful and magnificent, and she desired it. She took some of its fruit and ate, and she gave to her husband also, and he ate too. Then their mind opened. For when they ate, the light of knowledge shone for them. When they put on shame, they knew that they were naked with regard to knowledge. When they sobered up, they saw that they were naked, and they became enamored of one another. When they saw their makers, they loathed them since they were beastly forms. They understood very much.

■ Neoplatonism

Plotinus (205–270) Alexandria, Egypt (Neoplatonic philosophy)

TRANSLATED BY A. H. ARMSTRONG

Plotinus was born in upper Egypt, probably in Lykopolis in A.D. 205. He is thought to have been a Hellenized Egyptian rather than a Greek. He had an adventurous early life, joining an army that was to invade Persia where he wished to go in order to steep himself in Persian and Indian wisdom. Most of his life was spent in Rome, where he founded a school of philosophy. The *Enneads* (six books containing nine treatises each) were written in the last sixteen years of his life and arranged in their present form by his pupil Porphyry. Porphyry recounts that Plotinus was almost ashamed of existing in a human body since the whole material world was created by the soul and has no real existence in itself. When a painter asked permission to paint his portrait, Plotinus said, "Why paint an illusion of an illusion?" He died outside of Rome, probably of leprosy in 270.

According to Plotinus, the supreme source of the world is the One. It is the highest principle, a pure unity entirely undifferentiated, that is, without multiplicity. Plotinus states that the One is without cognition, ignorant even of itself, for self-cognition presupposes the duality of subject and object. The One can no more know itself than can the soul, upon ascending to the One, know the One, for at that point the soul is the One, subject and object are the same. One cannot see the sun when one is the sun; the seer cannot see the seen because the seer is the seen. And using other metaphors (the mystics always resort to metaphors), Plotinus states, explaining the monistic union and its ineffable nature:

> In this state the seer does not see or distinguish or imagine two things; he becomes another, he ceases to be himself and to belong to himself. He belongs to him and is one with him, like two concentric circles; they are one when they coincide, and two only when they are separated. It is only in this sense that the Soul is other than God. Therefore this vision is hard to describe. For how can

one describe, as other than oneself, that which, when one saw it, seemed to be one with oneself? (*Enneads*, 6.9.11)

In Plotinus, the One causes the world. But it does not "create" the world as a separate entity, with an independent existence, as in Judaism, Christianity, and Islam. In the theistic religions of the West, there is always a dualism of God and his creations. In Plotinus, the world is an emanation or manifestation of the One, or rather a series of descending emanations. Since the cosmos descends from the One, it is not independent of it. God is pantheistically the world. The first emanation from the One is described as *nous*, Intelligence; and from Intelligence emanates the Soul. The final emanation that proceeds from the Soul is matter, the farthest from the sun and therefore the darkest. Utter darkness is pure nonbeing. If we use the same image of the sun to represent the One, the return to the One is the ascent of the soul to its mystical union.

The ascent to God in Plotinus occurs in three stages of perfection. These levels were already anticipated in Philo (20 B.C.–A.D. 40), who, through his stages of purgation, illumination, and union, provided a chart of the mystical way. Both Philo and Plotinus speak of the knowledge of God as ineffable (a term not used in Greek philosophy prior to Philo); yet knowledge in itself, as in all Hellenic thought, is good, and the way to God is not to follow the mandate of ignorance of the Creator God but to follow reason as far as it will take us. Therein the Gnostics—who reversed the notion of the serpent by making the serpent provide us with virtuous knowledge in order for us to waken from the illusion of the world—are once more aligned with Plotinus, the author of polemical attacks on the Gnostics. In common is their mutual purpose of seeking self-knowledge in order to rise from the world of illusion to the God of total light.

Plotinus goes much further than Plato in recording human consciousness (the soul) and tracing its union with a larger consciousness, which is the universe, call it God, the One, the Alone, the Sun. Plotinus offers a specific method of mystical identification. In his method and quest, he seems to unite monastic visions from eastern Asian Buddhism to Spinoza's pantheistic philosophy in the West. An Egyptian, immersed in the Hellenism of Alexandria and Rome, he is Africa's greatest philosopher, whose word is as eloquently literary as Plato's allegories and as elevating as the poems of the Spanish mystic Saint John of the Cross.

FURTHER READING: Armstrong, A. H., ed. *Plotinus,* 1953.

from *The Enneads*

THE ASCENT TO UNION WITH THE ONE

Here the greatest, the ultimate contest is set before our souls; all our toil and trouble is for this, not to be left without a share in the best of visions. The man who attains this is blessed in seeing that blessed sight, and he who fails to attain it has failed utterly. A man has not failed if he fails to win beauty of colors or bodies, or power or office or kingship even, but if he fails to win this and only this. For this he should give up the attainment of kingship and rule over all earth and sea and sky, if only by leaving and over-looking them he can turn to that and see.

But how shall we find the way? What method can we devise? How can one see the inconceivable beauty which stays within the holy sanctuary and does not come out where the profane may see it? Let him who can follow and come within, and leave outside the sight of his eyes and not turn back to the bodily splendors which he saw before. When he sees the beauty in bodies he must not run after them; we must know that they are images, traces, shadows, and hurry away to that which they image. For if a man runs to the image and wants to seize it as if it was the reality (like a beautiful re-flection playing on the water, which some story somewhere, I think, said riddlingly a man wanted to catch and sank down into the stream and disap-peared) then this man who clings to beautiful bodies and will not let them go, will, like the man in the story, but in soul, not in body, sink down into the dark depths where *nous* has no delight, and stay blind in Hades, con-sorting with shadows there and here. This would be truer advice, "Let us fly to our dear country." Where then is our way of escape? How shall we put out to sea? (Odysseus, I think, speaks symbolically when he says he must fly from the witch Circe, or Calypso, and is not content to stay though he has delights of the eyes and lives among much beauty of sense.) Our country from which we came is there, our Father is there. How shall we travel to it, where is our way of escape? We cannot get there on foot: for our feet only carry us everywhere in this world, from one country to another. You must not get ready a carriage, either, or a boat. Let all these things go, and do not look. Shut your eyes and change to and wake another way of seeing, which everyone has but few use.

The discursive reason, if it wishes to say anything, must seize first one element of the truth and then another; such are the conditions of discur-sive thought. But how can discursive thought apprehend the absolutely simple? It is enough to apprehend it by a kind of spiritual intuition. But in this act of apprehension we have neither the power nor the time to say any-thing about it; afterwards we can reason about it. We may believe that we have really seen, when a sudden light illumines the Soul; for this light comes from the One and is the One. And we may think that the One is pre-sent, when, like another god, he illumines the house of him who calls upon him; for there would be no light without his presence. Even so the soul is dark that does not behold him: but when illumined by him, it has what it desired, and this is the true end and aim of the soul, to apprehend that light, and to behold it by that light itself, which is no other than the light by which it sees. For that which we seek to behold is that which gives us light, even as we can only see the sun by the light of the sun. How then can this come to us? Strip yourself of everything.

We must not be surprised that that which excites the keenest of long-ings is without any form, even spiritual form, since the Soul itself, when in-flamed with love for it, puts off all the form which it had, even that which belongs to the spiritual world. For it is not possible to see it, or to be in har-mony with it, while one is occupied with anything else. The soul must re-move from itself good and evil and everything else, that it may receive the One alone, as the One is alone. When the soul is so blessed, and is come to it, or rather when it manifests its presence, when the soul turns away from visible things and makes itself as beautiful as possible and becomes like the One; (the manner of preparation and adornment is known to those who practice it;) and seeing the One suddenly appearing in itself, for there is nothing between, nor are they any longer two, but one; for you cannot dis-tinguish between them, while the vision lasts; it is that union of which the union of earthly lovers, who wish to blend their being with each other, is a copy. The soul is no longer conscious of the body, and cannot tell whether it is a man or a living being or anything real at all; for the contemplation of such things would seem unworthy, and it has no leisure for them; but when, after having sought the One, it finds itself in its presence, it goes to meet it and contemplates it instead of itself. What itself is when it gazes, it has no leisure to see. When in this state the soul would exchange its present con-dition for nothing, no, not for the very Heaven of Heavens; for there is nothing better, nothing more blessed than this. For it can mount no high-er; all other things are below it, however exalted they be. It is then that it judges rightly and knows that it has what it desired, and that there is noth-ing higher. For there is no deception there; where could one find anything truer than the true? What it says, that it is, and it speaks afterwards, and speaks in silence, and is happy, and is not deceived in its happiness. Its hap-piness is no titillation of the bodily senses; it is that the soul has become again what it was formerly, when it was blessed. All the things which once pleased it, power, wealth, beauty, science, it declares that it despises; it could not say this if it had not met with something better than these. It fears no evil, while it is with the One, or even while it sees him; though all else perish around it, it is content, if it can only be with him; so happy is it.

The soul is so exalted that it thinks lightly even of that spiritual intu-ition which it formerly treasured. For spiritual perception involves move-ment, and the soul now does not wish to move. It does not call the object of its vision spirit, although it has itself been transformed into spirit before the vision and lifted up into the abode of spirits. When the soul arrives at the intuition of the One, it leaves the mode of spiritual perception. Even so a traveler, entering into a palace, admires at first the various beauties which adorn it; but when the master appears, he alone is the object of attention. By continually contemplating the object before him, the spectator sees it no more. The vision is confounded with the object seen, and that which was before object becomes to him the state of seeing, and he forgets all else. The spirit has two powers. By one of them it has a spiritual perception of what is within itself, the other is the receptive intuition by which it perceives what is above itself. The former is the vision of the thinking spirit, the latter is the spirit in love. For when the spirit is inebriated with the nectar, it falls in love, in simple contentment and satisfaction; and it is better for it to be so intoxicated than to be too proud for such intoxication.

If you are perplexed because the One is none of those things which you know, apply yourself to them first, and look forth out of them; but so look, as not to direct your intellect to externals. For it does not lie in one place and not in another, but it is present everywhere to him who can touch it, and not to him who cannot. As in other matters one cannot think of two things at once, and must add nothing extraneous to the object of thought, if one wishes to identify oneself with it, so here we may be sure that it is impossible for one who has in his soul any extraneous image to conceive of the One while that image distracts his attention. Just as we said that matter must be without qualities of its own, if it is to receive the forms of all things, so *a fortiori* must the soul be formless if it is to receive the fullness and illumination of the first principle. If so, the soul must forsake all that is external, and turn itself wholly to that which is within; it will not allow itself to be distracted by anything external, but will ignore them all, as at first by not attending to them, so now last by not seeing them; it will not even know itself; and so it will come to the vision of the One and will be united with it; and then, after a sufficient converse with it, it will return and bring word, if it be possible, to others of its heavenly intercourse. Such probably was the converse which Minos was fabled to have had with Zeus, remembering which he made the laws which were the image of that converse, being inspired to be a law-giver by the divine touch. Perhaps, however, a Soul which has seen much of the heavenly world may think politics unworthy of itself and may prefer to remain above. God, as Plato says, is not far from every one of us; he is present with all, though they know him not. Men flee away from him, or rather from themselves. They cannot grasp him from whom they have fled, nor when they have lost themselves can they find another, any more than a child who is mad and out of his mind can know his father. But he who has learnt to know himself will know also whence he is.

If a soul has known itself throughout its course, it is aware that its natural motion has not been in a straight line (except during some deflection from the normal) but rather in a circle round a center; and that this center is itself in motion round that from which it proceeds. On this center the soul depends, and attaches itself thereto, as all Souls ought to do, but only the Souls of gods do so always. It is this that makes them gods. For a god is closely attached to this center; those further from it are average men, and animals. Is then this center of the soul the object of our search? Or must we think of something else, some point at which all centers as it were coincide? We must remember that our "circles" and "centers" are only metaphors. The Soul is no "circle" like the geometrical figure; we call it a circle because the archetypal nature is in it and around it, and because it is derived from this first principle, and all the more because the souls as wholes are separated from the body. But now, since part of us is held down by the body (as if a man were to have his feet under water), we touch the center of all things with our own center—that part which is not submerged—as the centers of the greatest circles coincide with the center of the enveloping sphere, and then rest. If these circles were corporeal and not psychic, the coincidence of their centers would be spatial, and they would lie around a center somewhere in space; but since the souls belong to the spiritual world, and the One is above even spirit, we must consider that their contact is through other powers—those which connect subject and object in the world of spirit, and further, that the perceiving spirit is present in virtue of its likeness and identity, and unites with its like without hindrance. For bodies cannot have this close association with each other, but incorporeal things are not kept apart by bodies; they are separated from each other not by distance, but by unlikeness and difference. Where there is no unlikeness, they are united with each other. The One, which has no unlikeness, is always present; we are so only when we have no unlikeness. The One does not strive to encircle us, but we strive to encircle it. We always move round the One, but we do not always fix our gaze upon it: we are like a choir of singers who stand round the conductor, but do not always sing in time because their attention is diverted to some external object; when they look at the conductor they sing well and are really with him. So we always move round the One; if we did not, we should be dissolved and no longer exist; but we do not always look towards the One. When we do, we attain the end of our existence, and our repose, and we no longer sing out of tune, but form in very truth a divine chorus round the One.

In this choral dance the soul sees the fountain of life and the fountain of Spirit, the source of being, the cause of good, the root of soul. These do not flow out of the One in such a way as to diminish it; for we are not dealing with material quantities, else the products of the One would be perishable, whereas they are eternal, because their source remains not divided among them, but constant. Therefore the products too are permanent, as the light remains while the sun remains. For we are not cut off from our source nor separated from it, even though the bodily nature intervenes and draws us toward itself, but we breathe and maintain our being in our source, which does not first give itself and then withdraw, but is always supplying us, as long as it is what it is. But we are more truly alive when we turn towards it, and in this lies our well-being. To be far from it is isolation and diminution. In it our soul rests, out of reach of evil: it has ascended to a region which is pure from all evil; there it has spiritual vision, and is exempt from passion and suffering; there it truly lives. For our present life, without God, is a mere shadow and mimicry of the true life. But life yonder is an activity of the spirit, and by its peaceful activity it engenders gods also, through its contact with the One, and beauty, and righteousness, and virtue. For these are the offspring of a soul which is filled with God, and this is its beginning and end—its beginning because from this it had its origin, its end because the Good is there, and when it comes there it becomes what it was. For our life in this world is but a falling away, an exile, and a loss of the Soul's wings. The natural love which the Soul feels proves that the Good is there; this is why paintings and myths make Psyche the bride of Cupid. Because the Soul is different from God, and yet springs from him, she loves him of necessity; when she is yonder she has the heavenly love, when she is here below, the vulgar. For yonder dwells the heavenly Aphrodite, but here she is vulgarized and corrupted, and every soul is Aphrodite. This is figured in the allegory of the birthday of Aphrodite, and Love who was born with her. Hence it is natural for the soul to love God and to desire union with him, as the daughter of a noble father feels a noble love. But when, descending to generation, the soul, deceived by the false promises of a lover, exchanges its divine love for a mortal love, it is separated from its father and submits to indignities; but afterwards it is ashamed of these disorders and purifies itself and returns to its father and is happy. Let him who has not had this experience consider how blessed a thing it is in earthly love to obtain that which one most desires, although the objects of earthly loves are mortal and injurious and loves of shadows, which change and pass; since these are not the things which we truly love, nor are they our good, nor what we seek. But yonder is the true object of our love, which it is possible to grasp and to live with and truly to possess, since no envelope of flesh separates us from it. He who has seen it knows what I say, that the soul then has another life, when it comes to God and having come possesses him, and knows, when in that state, that it is in the presence of the dispenser of the true life, and that it needs nothing further. On the contrary, it must put off all else, and stand in God alone, which can only be when we have pruned away all else that surrounds us. We must then hasten to depart hence, to detach ourselves as much as we can from the body to which we are unhappily bound, to endeavor to embrace God with all our being, and to leave no part of ourselves which is not in contact with him. Then we can see him and ourselves, as far as is permitted: we see ourselves glorified, full of spiritual light, or rather we see ourselves as pure, subtle, ethereal, light: we become divine, or rather we know ourselves to be divine. Then indeed is the flame of life kindled, that flame which, when we sink back to earth, sinks with us.

Why then does not the soul abide yonder? Because it has not wholly left its earthly abode. But the time will come when it will enjoy the vision without interruption, no longer troubled with the hindrances of the body. The part of the soul which is troubled is not the part which sees, but the other part, when the part which sees is idle, though it ceases not from that knowledge which comes of demonstrations, conjectures, and the dialectic. But in the vision that which sees is not reason, but something greater than and prior to reason, something presupposed by reason, as is the object of vision. He who then sees himself, when he sees will see himself as a simple being, will be united to himself as such, will feel himself become such. We ought not even to say that he will see, but he will be that which he sees, if indeed it is possible any longer to distinguish seer and seen, and not boldly to affirm that the two are one. In this state the seer does not see or distinguish or imagine two things; he becomes another, he ceases to be himself and to belong to himself. He belongs to him and is one with him, like two concentric circles; they are one when they coincide, and two only when they are separated. It is only in this sense that the soul is other than God. Therefore this vision is hard to describe. For how can one describe, as other than oneself, that which, when one saw it, seemed to be one with oneself?

This is no doubt why in the mysteries we are forbidden to reveal them to the uninitiated. That which is divine is ineffable, and cannot be shown to those who have not had the happiness to see it. Since in the vision there were not two things, but seer and seen were one (for the seeing was no seeing but a merging), if a man could preserve the memory of what he was when he was mingled with the divine, he would have in himself an image of him. For he was then one with him, and retained no difference, either in relation to himself or to others. Nothing stirred within him, neither anger nor concupiscence nor even reason or spiritual perception or his own personality, if we may say so. Caught up in an ecstasy, tranquil and God-possessed, he enjoyed an imperturbable calm; shut up in his proper essence he inclined not to either side, he turned not even to himself; he was in a state of perfect stability; he had become stability itself. The soul then occupies itself no more even with beautiful things; it is exalted above the beautiful, it passes the choir of the virtues. Even as when a man who enters the sanctuary of a temple leaves behind him the statues in the temple, they are the objects which he will see first when he leaves the sanctuary after he has seen what is within, and entered there into communion, not with statues and images, but with the deity itself. Perhaps we ought not to speak of vision; it is rather another mode of seeing, an ecstasy and simplification, an abandonment of oneself, a desire for immediate contact, a stability, a deep intention to unite oneself with what is to be seen in the sanctuary. He who seeks to see God in any other manner, will find nothing. These are but figures, by which the wise prophets indicate how we may see this God. But the wise priest, understanding the symbol, may enter the sanctuary and make the vision real. If he has not yet got so far, he at least conceives that what is within the sanctuary is something invisible to mortal eyes, that it is the source and principle of all; he knows that it is by the first principle that we see the first principle, and unites himself with it and perceives like by like, leaving behind nothing that is divine, so far as the soul can reach. And before the vision, the soul desires that which remains for it to see. But for him who has ascended above all things, that which remains to see is that which is before all things. For the nature of the soul will never pass to absolute not-being: when it falls, it will come to evil, and so to not-being, but not to absolute not-being. But if it moves in the opposite direction, it will arrive not at something else, but at itself, and so, being in nothing else, it is only in itself alone; but that which is in itself alone and not in the world of being is in the absolute. It ceases to be being; it is above being, while in communion with the One. If then a man sees himself become one with the One, he has in himself a likeness of the One, and if he passes out of himself, as an image to its archetype, he has reached the end of his journey. And when he comes down from his vision, he can again awaken the virtue that is in him, and seeing himself fitly adorned in every part he can again mount upward through virtue to Spirit, and through wisdom to the One itself. Such is the life of gods and of godlike and blessed men; a liberation from all earthly bonds, a life that takes no pleasure in earthly things, a flight of the alone to the Alone.

SECTION

3

Early Arabic Literature

■

INTRODUCTION

The Semitic tribes that inhabited the Arabian peninsula consisted of two Arab peoples, the nomadic Bedouin tribes, who subsisted through a wandering sheepherding and goatherding existence, and the settled Hejazis, who were farmers and traders, living in settlements and cities. Hejazi caravans traveled across the Middle East, allowing many merchants to accumulate great wealth, and were often raided by the warlike Bedouins. Arabian tribal groups cohered loosely through the election of a sheik, the leader of the tribe; through animistic religion that maintained no assertion of life after death; through tribal rituals; and through an ethic of bravery, pride, family loyalty, and revenge.

From the fourth to the seventh centuries A.D., a large body of oral Arabic poetry developed, though most of it was transcribed later—in the eighth and ninth centuries—by editors who may have altered, regulated, and edited some of the original works. This is considered the golden age of Arabic poetry. The *qasida*, the basic prosodic form of classical Arabic poetry, was established in this period. These poems survive in anthologies, notably the *Muallaqat*, in which the desert life of brave warriors, the mourning of the fallen, and boasts of erotic conquests are recorded in beautiful, metrically challenging, richly complex, and sustained odes.

Life in the Arabian peninsula was wholly transformed in the seventh century with the development of a new religion with roots in Judaism and Christianity—Islam. This religion originated in the teachings of a middle-aged merchant from Mecca named Muhammad (570–632). Very little is known of the historical Muhammad, but legends about his life, recorded about a century after his death, assert that he was orphaned at an early age, and that he became a merchant in the markets of Mecca. He traveled with the caravans and may have been exposed to Judaism and Christianity in Palestine. When he was forty, Muhammad experienced a vision while praying in a cave outside of Mecca, in which the angel Gabriel appeared to him and commanded him to preach the word of Allah (the supreme God). From this time on, Muhammad preached to the polytheistic Arabs a monotheistic faith. The Meccans, however, were slow to convert and Muhammad fled with his followers north to Medina in 622.

Muslims believe Muhammad to have been the last prophet, equal to Jesus and Moses, but not himself divine. Under Muhammad's Islamic teachings, Arabs are required to pray five times a day, to pray and fast from dawn through dusk during the holy month of Ramadan, to make a pilgrimage to Mecca once during their lives, and to give alms to the poor. Muhammad also attempted to eliminate the blood feuds, drinking, sexual exploits, and gambling that were so much a part of the pre-Islamic Arabic life portrayed in Golden Age poetry. His teachings were recorded sporadically by his followers during his life and collected and arranged after his death into a volume of verse chapters called the Quran.

During his Medinan exile, Muhammad's preachings took root. He became the theocratic ruler of a new state, which he expanded through conquest, and by the time of his death ten years after his flight from Mecca in 622, he had united all of the Bedouin tribes and conquered his enemies in Mecca, as well as the rest of the Arabian peninsula. Islam, carried by holy warfare *(jihad)* and a faith that those who died fighting to spread the religion would be rewarded in Heaven, spread within a hundred years as far as India in the east, across North Africa, and into southern Europe in the west. The definition of an "Arab" became more expansive after the spread of Islam. It became possible to consider oneself an Arab if one spoke Arabic and believed in Islam, despite geography and ethnic origin. Because of the injunction against translating the Quran into other languages, Muslims had to learn Arabic to worship. Classical Arabic thus became a great language unifying cultures across the world, and Arabic literature came to be written by authors of diverse backgrounds for whom Arabic was the formal language of literature and religion.

With the death of Muhammad in 632, the Islamic state fell into crisis, for he had no son to succeed him as ruler. The question of succession was resolved through the development of the institution of the caliphate. The first four Caliphs were elected theocratic rulers. Although the institution maintained, stabilized, and expanded the empire, it was a fragile system; and it failed to ensure orderly succession: three of the four Caliphs were murdered.

In 656, the assassination of the third Caliph, Uthman, and the assumption of the caliphate by Ali (Muhammad's cousin and son-in-law) catalyzed a schism in Islam. Civil war ensued, and eventually Ali was himself assassinated and succeeded by Uthman's cousin Muawiya, who belonged to the family of the Umayyads. Muawiya converted the caliphate to a hereditary institution and moved the capital from Medina to the Syrian city of Damascus. The Umayyad caliphs ruled from 661 to 750. However, the schism between the supporters of Ali (who were called the Shiite Muslims) and the supporters of the Umayyads (who were called the Sunni Muslims) remained, and in fact the Shiite and Sunni split persists today as a major dividing principle within and between Arab nations. In 750, the Umayyads were overthrown by a rebellion supported by the Shiites and others and replaced by a new succession of caliphs, the Abbasids. The Abbasid caliphs ruled from 750 to 1258, and once again moved the capital, this time to the newly founded city of Baghdad in Iraq.

Arabic literature, which had declined as the Quran dominated the written culture, enjoyed a resurgence in the eighth and ninth centuries in Baghdad, where the Abbasid empire had established its capital in 762 under Caliph Mansur. Under Caliph Harun al-Rashid (c. 763–809), Baghdad became a brilliant center of artistry, poetry, and scholarship, and the location of many of the tales of the monumental Arabic prose romance, *The Thousand and One Nights*. Abu Nuwas, one of the major poets of this time, is the star of some of these tales. Arabic poetry in the "new style" of the Abbasids became more complex metrically, more sophisticated in its use of figurative language, and more varied as to subject matter. Prose was slower in developing, but with the decline of the Abbasids from the tenth through the thirteenth centuries, there was a great flowering of Arabic narrative, from autobiography to travel literature to storytelling. A mystical sect of Islam called Sufism had developed in the seventh century; and later in the Abbasid period, the Sufis, who were often persecuted by mainstream Islam, were responsible for some of the greatest literature of the Middle East, at first largely written in Arabic, and later in Persian.

Although the reign of the Abbasids, particularly that of Harun al-Rashid, is considered the Golden Age of Islam, a time of extraordinary advances in medicine, philosophy, literature, and mathematics, it was also a period marked increasingly by a fragmentation of the empire as province after province seceded. As the empire continued to splinter, the true power in Baghdad shifted to the Persian aristocrats who helped the Arabs rule and became, by the middle of the tenth century, the real power behind the throne; to the Turkish military guard; and later to invaders, the Seljuk Turks and the Mongols, each of whom converted to, and helped to spread, Islam. Spain, at the western edge of the Arabic empire, was one of the anticaliphates that maintained an Islamic rule independent of Baghdad; the other anticaliphate was governed by the Shiite Fatimids, who ruled Egypt and its surrounding areas from their center in Cairo from 909 to 1171. Arabic Spain was ruled by the line of an Umayyad prince who had escaped the bloody slaughter of his family by the first Abbasid ruler. The magnificent city of Córdoba in

Andalusia challenged Baghdad in architecture, scholarship, and literature. In addition to extraordinarily beautiful lyric poetry, Córdoba was home to the great twelfth century philosophers Averröes (1126–1198), an Arab, and Maimonides (1135–1204), a Jew who wrote in Arabic. In the nearly thirteen centuries since the birth of Islam, Arabic literature has ceased to be synonymous with the literature of the Arabian peninsula. In the wake of that great religious and cultural diaspora, it has become a literature of the world.

—Ayame Fukuda and the editors

◾ Al-Khansa (575–646) *Arabia* (poems)

TRANSLATED BY WILLIS BARNSTONE

Al-Khansa, whose full name was Tumadir bint Amr ib al Harith ibn al Sharid, was born in Mecca or in Medina and is considered the finest elegiac poet of Arabia, and the best of the women poets whose poetry paralleled their social role of mourning the dead. Al-Khansa came from the Sulaym tribe and much of her work consists of elegies for its fallen warriors—her two brothers, Sakhr and Muqwiya numbered among them, along with four of her sons, who died at the Battle of al-Qadisiyya. The Arabic dirge tends to follow a pattern of expressing endless grief, praising the fallen man's bravery and generosity, questioning who can fulfill his role as protector and benefactor, and, if the death was violent, expressing a need for bloody revenge. Her poems utilize the simple elements of the desert—rain, swords, camels, dust, and mountains topped with fire—to create fierce, passionate, and desperately simple poems of loss. Her *diwan,* or collection of poems, survives. With the coming of Islam, Al-Khansa seems to have converted, and she lived in Medina at the end of her life, near the prophet Muhammad.

Elegy for Her Brother Sakhr

Cry out for Sakhr when a dove with necklaces
mourns gray in the valley.

When warriors put on light woven armor,
swords are the color of smooth salt

and bows groan and wail,   5
and bending spears are wet.

Giving, not weak,
brave like the predatory wood lion

of Bisha, he battles for friends
and kinsmen, who are like the lion,   *10*

whom he defends whether of the village
or wanderers on the desert.

When the wind howled his people were happy
as a wind of dust blew under a freezing cloud.

Sleepless

I was sleepless, I was awake all night
as if my eyes exuded pus.

I watched the stars, though I was not their shepherd,
and veiled my body in ragged cloth,

for I heard—it was black news—   *5*
the messenger's report:

"Sakhr is in the earth,
between wood and stones."

Go, may Allah receive you, as a man
of justice and revenge.   *10*

Your heart was free,
its roots were not weak.

Like a spearhead your shape shines in the night,
strong, firm, the son of free men.

I lament our tribe's hero. Death took you   *15*
and the others.

As long as the ringdove cries, I'll mourn you,
as stars light the midnight traveler.

I'll not make peace with the enemy
till their food kettles turn white . . .   *20*

They washed the shame from you,
your blood's sweat poured out purified,

and war rode a humpbacked herd,
bareback.

Defender in battle,   *25*
you ripped the spearmen, tooth and nail,

until thousands saw you
blind to fear. They were amazed

as your stomach burst, punctured above the nipples,
spurting the foam of your heart's blood.   *30*

■ Muallaqat (Sixth to Early Seventh Centuries) *Arabia* (poems)

TRANSLATED BY TONY BARNSTONE AND BEATRICE GRUENDLER

The *Muallaqat* is the name of an Arabic anthology compiled by Hammad al Rawiya (c. 775) that consists of seven (sometimes nine or ten) *qasida*, or long odes of the pre-Islamic period. They are the high moment of Arabic poetry and a rare window onto Bedouin life. Though these were poems of an oral tradition, they were preserved through a class of poem reciters, called Rawis, who accompanied the poets, learned the poems by heart, and kept the tradition alive. Krishna Chaitanya writes of the role of the poet in this tribal society:

> In the centuries before Muhammad came to unite them into a nation, the Arabs were living as separate tribes, and in the condition of tribal life the poet enjoyed a high status. He was considered as gifted with supernatural powers and thus he became the oracle of the tribe, their guide in peace, and their champion in war.[1]

Eleventh-century scholar Ibn Rashiq of Qairouan writes of the respect in which these ancient poets were held:

> Whenever a poet emerged in an Arab tribe, the other tribes would come and congratulate it. Feasts would be prepared and the women would gather together, playing on lutes, as people do at weddings. For the poet was a defence to their honor, a protection for their good repute. He immortalized their deeds of glory and published their eternal fame.[2]

The tribes would have a great contest at the Uzak fair each year, competing each day for a month. *Muallaqat* is said to mean "suspended poems" due to a myth that these were poems that won prizes at this competition and were inscribed in gold on Egyptian silk and suspended in the holy Kaba shrine in Mecca.

The ode (the *qasida*) is a long lyric poem, in varying meters, with a single end rhyme. In Arabia, where the *qasida* flourished before and after the founding of Islam in A.D. 622, the poem is written with narrative elements that must, nonetheless, be considered antinarrative. The events of the poem occur generally in four parts, which are prescribed by tradition, and

---

1. Krishna Chaitanya, *A History of Arabic Literature* (New Delhi: Manohar, 1983), 31.
2. Ibid.

the poet's task is to execute a virtuoso performance within these strictures. The poet first halts, distraught in a desolate place, and remembers a great personal loss, like Tarafa mourning the absence of his lover Khaula, "on the sand and stone plain of Thahmad." In the next section, the speaker describes a great journey, perhaps spurred by an impulse to escape such emptiness. Other elements that may make up a part of the *qasida* include extended, anecdotal boasts, erotic or military.

What we know of the life of Tarafa, the first poet excerpted here, is a mixture of fact and legend and what can be gleaned from his poems. He died at a young age—between twenty and twenty-six—and seems to have lived the dissolute life his poem records, letting his family's camels get stolen while he wrote poems, wasting his money until, driven out of the tribe, he was separated from Khaula, his lover. He went to live with his cousin Abd Amar, minister to the king of Hira, but could not refrain from writing satirical poems about his cousin and even about the king. The legend of Tarafa's death is well known. He was said to have been sent by the king of Hira to carry a letter to a district governor, but his companion, suspicious of the king's intent, read the letter, finding that it contained instructions to put them both to death! Tarafa, though, was too noble to break his promise to the king—he delivered the letter and was killed for his efforts.

Imru al-Qays, the second poet excerpted here, is considered the finest of the pre-Islamic poets. His family ruled Kinda, a region in Yemen, as vassal kings of Yemen's Himyarite rulers. Imru was the son of Hujr, ruler of the Banu Asad tribe's home region. His father grew angry with him for writing poems and in the end banished him, and for some time he led a dissolute wandering life in the desert. After the tribesmen revolted against his father's harsh rule and killed him in his tent, Imru al-Qays sought revenge on the Banu Asad tribe, allying himself with Emperor Justinian and going to Constantinope. He was made the vassal ruler of Palestine and promised an army, but it is said that he seduced Justinians's daughter, boasted about it, and was murdered with a poisoned cloak. He died in Ankara in 540. He is among the finest erotic Arabic poets.

FURTHER READING: Arberry, A. J. *The Seven Odes,* 1957. Cantarino, Vicente. *Arabic Poetics in the Golden Age: Selections of Texts Accompanied by a Preliminary Study,* 1975. Nicholson, R. A. *A Literary History of the Arabs,* 1930. Sells, Michael A., tr. *Desert Tracings: Six Classic Arabian Odes,* 1989. Zwettler, Michael. *The Oral Tradition of Classical Arabic Poetry: Its Character and Implications,* 1978.

from The Ode of Tarafa

> Like old tattoos on the back of the hand, traces remain of Khaula,
> my lover, on the sand and stone plain of Thahmad.

My friends rein in their camels next to me and say
    "Bear it like a man, don't let this pain kill you."
The morning she leaves, Malikan camels bear litters
    in the valleys of Dad like the great ships
of Adaula or the vessels of Ibn-i Yamen
    that sailors guide straight on, or swing from the course.
Their bows slice through the rippling back of the sea   5
    like a boy's hand plowing furrows in the sand.

There is a young gazelle in the tribe, dark-lipped, shaking fruit
    from her tree, who flaunts a double strand of pearls and
        emeralds.
Holding aloof as she grazes with the herd in a lush thicket
    she nibbles fruit of the *arak* tree, clothes herself in its leaves.
When her deep lips laugh open, her teeth are a camomile flower
    blooming on a moist sand dune in a virgin plain.
Sun rays water her teeth but not her collyrium-stained gums;
    she chews carefully to keep their bright color.
She smiles and her face is the bright cloak of the sun,   10
    so pure and so unwrinkled.

As for me, I put off my grief and race away on a camel bent
    as she dashes through night and the day;
this camel has bones like the solid planks of a strongbox, she won't
    stumble as I spur her down a road broad and rutted like a
        striped cloak,
strong as a male camel, she sprints like an ostrich running
    from a featherless, rutting male; the color of ash,
she rivals the swift purebred camels; on the beaten path
    her back feet light in her forefeet's tracks.

✳ ✳ ✳

I ride a beast this fine when my companion calls out "O I wish   15
    I could ransom us from the journey's burden."
Fear palpitates his chest and he jumps as if sliced by weapons
    when no weapons strike and no ambush waits.
But when people say "Who is that brave young man" I think they
    speak of me; I am no slack fool when faced with danger.
I ply my whip and she races off as mirages shimmer
    on the flaming sands,
swaying gracefully like a dancing girl who shows her master
    the skirts of her long white gown.

If you seek my protection I am not one who will run   20
    into the hills to hide.
Look for me among the people and you'll find me in that circle,
    hunt for me in the taverns and I will be there,

and when you come to me I'll pass you a brimming cup
      and if you don't want it, well, that's that.
And if all the tribes gather you'll find me there,
      a noble of the finest house, to which the people flock.
My companions are white-skinned, like stars, and a dancing girl
      comes to us at night in a striped gown or saffron robe,
undoing her collar and giving her soft and delicate flesh   *25*
      to the hands of my friends.
When we say "Sing for us" she sings smoothly, in a low voice,
      with a lowered head,
and on the sorrowful tremolo you'd think she was a mother
      keening over her dead firstborn.
I drink and seek joy and squander my inheritance
      and everything I earn and don't stop
till the people avoid me, all of them, and I am alone
      like a mangey camel whose hide is painted with tar.
Yet the lowly sons of the dust don't deny the one who gave them alms   *30*
      and the great ones in the leather tents admire me too.

You who reproach me for going to war, for giving gifts,
      can you make me live forever if I give up these pleasures?
If you can't stop death, then let me welcome him
      with the coins still in my hand.
Three things alone give a young man joy and only for them
      would I keep my deathbed visitors away:
first, to swig down red wine that foams when cut with water
      in the morning before my critics come;
second—like a wolf startled from a thorny bush as he seeks water—   *35*
      to streak to the aid of a scared fugitive on a full-shanked horse;
and third, to cut short a cloud-darkened day, though I love the
      darkness of lingering with a lush girl in her pole-propped tent,
one whose anklets and bracelets hang from limbs straight
      and pliant as a gum tree's unpruned branches or castor plant's
        twigs.
Generous men quench their thirst alive;
      if we die tomorrow you'll see which one is dry.
To me the grave of a miser who counts his change
      is the same as that of an idler who wastes his goods—
just two heaps of dust is what you'll see,   *40*
      and deaf granite stones stacked in a cairn.
I see that death will choose the generous and take
      the prize from the miser's hoard;
life itself is a treasure that leaks away from us each night
      and the days erode and time perishes.
I swear by your life that death, though he misses a strong man now,
      is like a loosened lasso held ready to throw.

* * *

When I die, keen for me, O daughter of Ma'bad, tear the collar
    of your gown and sing the praises I deserve;
don't make me out a man with less zeal than I've shown,   *45*
    unskilled and new to battle,
who held back when great affairs occurred, was despised,
    foul-mouthed, scurrying under men's fists —
if I were such a coward my enemies, solitary or with
    friends, would have harmed me soon enough,
but I stood up to them bravely, honest,
    showing noble birth, and sent them flying.
On your life I swear sorrows didn't cloud my days
    nor were my nights anxious and without end.
Many days I stood, spirit firm, in the press of battle,   *50*
    defending the weak and facing the enemy;
where brave men quake in their boots and the shoulders
    of warriors clench with fear I took my stand,
and in gambling I often gave my lucky arrow, yellow and
    smoke blackened, to an unlucky friend and sat out the game.

You will hear the news from the man you gave nothing to
    when time reveals its mysteries to you.

from *The Ode of Imru al-Qays*

How many fine times I've had with women!
    I remember in particular a day at Dara Juljul,
when I slaughtered my riding camel for the virgins to eat.
    My God, how fine it was, and what a load divided among their
      camels.
Then the virgins tossed the cut flesh about
    and the loose fat like white fringes of twisted silk.
On another day I entered Unaiza's litter
    and she cried "You are making me go on foot!"
And she said while the canopy swayed with us,   *5*
    "You are killing my camel, Imru al-Qays, so dismount!"
But I replied "Ride on, just loosen the reins,
    and don't keep me from your succulent fruit;
the camel's young, let it carry us both,
    and now let me eat you like a luscious apple.
For I've been with many women beautiful like you, Unaiza;
    even a nursing mother receives me at night and forgets her infant

for me, and when he whimpers behind us, she gives him half
    her body, but meets me with the other half."

* * *

How many gorgeous veiled woman have I enjoyed at length   *10*
    in tents no other would dare approach?
I slid past sentries on watch and a tribe thirsty
    for my blood, whose every man dreams of bragging of my death,
and the Pleiades were gemstones in the sky,
    spaced like pearls in a jeweled belt.
She was standing by the tent-flap when I slipped in,
    already stripped to a sheer nightgown
and she said "I swear by God there's no escape from you.
    You wild fool, you'll never give up this appetite!"
But she came out with me, trailing an embroidered gown   *15*
    to erase our tracks
and when we'd crossed the tribe's courtyard
    we found the twisting dune of a parched riverbed;
I pulled her to me by her hair and she leaned in
    and her waist was slender and her ankles full.
Small waist, white skin, she had no fat
    and her breasts shone like polished mirrors.
Her complexion like an oyster's first pearl was yellow-white,
    her unmixed blood has nourished her like pure water.
She turned away and I saw her soft cheek, and she warded me off   *20*
    with a wild animal glance, like a deer protecting her young.
And she showed me her white deer neck, elegant
    and hung with jewelry
and from her perfect head the hair fell loose down her back
    thick as a date-cluster on a fruit-laden tree.
Her single and double plaits were lost in strands of loose, wild hair
    taken up against her head.
She pressed her waist against me, slender as the leather nose ring
    of a camel, and her thighs were palm trees bent with fruit.
In the morning she slept late and woke up smelling of musk   *25*
    and not bothering to fasten her gown.
She gives with her fingers, which are slender as Zabi desert worms,
    or toothpicks made of ishil wood,
and she is what brightens the evening dark, like a monk's tower
    with a window lit to guide the traveller in.
Not so tall she wears a long dress, not so short she wears a skirt,
    a wise man will gaze hungrily at such perfection.
Let other men give up love after their youth.
    My heart is not that free.

■ The Quran (Seventh Century) *Arabia* (religious text)

TRANSLATED BY N. K. DAWOOD

The Quran (Koran) is the holy text of Islam, the source and divine example of Arabic literature, and is thought to be the revealed word of Allah. Muslims believe that Muhammad (570–632) was a prophet who was the vehicle for God's words, inscribed on a tablet in Heaven, which were revealed to him by the angel Gabriel. Muhammad, therefore, was not the author of the Quran, but its facilitator. The Quran is a collection of Muhammad's preachings that were collected by his followers, written on parchment, leaves, or bone, whatever was at hand, or committed to memory by professional memorizers. From 651 to 652, several decades after Muhammad's death, these utterances were collected under the orders of Caliph Uthman and formed into the text we know today. Unlike the Old and New Testaments, the Quran did not undergo a process of revision and editing, which makes its chapters seem somewhat less unified and rather more repetitive than these earlier texts; such revision of God's revealed words would have been blasphemous. The Quran is written in rhymed, assonant prose, which makes its oral recitation beautiful and rhythmic, and it is best understood as an oral literature confined to text. In fact, the term *quran* means recitation, text to be recited, and orthodox Muslims recite from the Quran daily. The organizational structure of the Quran is arbitrary, having to do with neither thematic unity nor chronology: it is arranged in general according to the length of the chapters—longer chapters first, shorter chapters at the end. There are 114 chapters *(suras),* divided into verses *(ayas),* with wildly varying numbers of verses per chapter and of words per verse. Each chapter begins with the phrase "In the name of Allah, the compassionate, the merciful," except chapter nine.

Islam is a monotheistic religion that was influenced both by Judaism and Christianity; in fact, Moses is considered a prophet like Muhammad, as is Jesus. The divinity of Jesus is rejected as fiercely as Muhammad rejected the idea that he was himself divine. Much of the Quran paraphrases the Bible, though quoting it rarely, notably the chapter "Joseph," which recounts with some alteration the Old Testament story of Joseph. Muhammad was born in Mecca in 570, at a time when the supreme god Allah was the highest among a number of divinities in Arabian religion. Influenced by Judaism, Muhammad began preaching the doctrine of one God, and many of the early, short Meccan chapters focus on the idea of one God, the creator, merciful, but ready to punish. These chapters are among the most rewarding in literary terms, with their Arabized visions of Heaven, with fruit, running water, and virgin *houris* (heavenly courtesans who reward the faithful), and their equally powerfully imagined visions of endless hellfire for the unbelievers. In later Meccan chapters, these themes remain strong, the compositions are longer, and there are frequent warnings that unbelievers will suffer the dire fates of ancient disbelievers in Arab and Jewish prophets. Though he railed against both Jews and Christians, particularly when frustrated at failing to convert them, Muhammad also considered them "people of the Book" and incorporated aspects of Jewish law and ritual, such as the prohibition against eating pork.

The latest chapters in the Quran derive from the Medinan period, when Muhammad and his followers, persecuted and unsuccessful in Mecca, fled to Yathrib, where the people accepted them, and where Muhammad became the ruler of a theocratic state (Yathrib was renamed Medina, or "City of the Prophet"). These later chapters are legalistic in nature, the basis of Islamic law, and have the least literary value. The year 622, the date of the emigration to Medina, or the "Hegira," became the date chosen to commence the Islamic era (as opposed to, for example, the date of Muhammad's birth). During his Medinan years, Muhammad expanded his empire through holy warfare (*jihad*) and was lawgiver, ruler, and prophet; in 631, he finally captured Mecca by force, and a few months later died in the arms of his favorite wife. Holy warfare and prosletyzing soon carried the Quran across the world, from Europe to Central Asia, starting the process of growth that has not ceased to this day. Although it is a commonplace to state that no translation can capture the oral magic of the original Arabic Quran, and although it is prohibited to translate these revealed divine words into other languages, the Quran has in fact been translated into almost all languages, and Islam today is a multilingual and multiethnic religion.

FURTHER READING: Ali, Abdullah Yusuf, tr. *The Holy Quran: Text, Translation, and Commentary*, 1983. Arberry, A. J., tr. *The Koran Interpreted*, 2 vols., 1955. Bell, Richard, tr. *The Quran. Translated, with a Critical Rearrangement of the Surahs*, 2 vols., 1937–1939. Palmer, Edward H., tr. *The Quran*, 1980. Pickthall, M. M., tr. *The Meaning of the Glorious Koran: An Explanatory Translation*, 1930. Rodwell, J. M., tr. The *Koran*, 1861. Sale, George, tr. *The Koran with Notes and a Preliminary Discourse*, 1734.

The Exordium

In the Name of Allah,
The Compassionate,
The Merciful

Praise be to Allah, Lord of the Creation,
The Compassionate, the Merciful,
King of Judgment Day!
You alone we worship, and to You alone
we pray for help.
Guide us to the straight path,

5

The path of those whom You have favored,   *10*
Not of those who have incurred Your wrath,
Nor of those who have gone astray.

from **Sura 3 The Imrans**

And remember the angel's words to Mary. He said: 'Allah has chosen you. He has made you pure and exalted you above all women. Mary, be obedient to your Lord; bow down and worship with the worshippers.'

This is an account of what is hidden. We reveal it to you.[1] You were not present when they cast lots to see which of them should have charge of Mary; nor were you present when they argued about her.

The angels said to Mary: 'Allah bids you rejoice in a Word from Him. His name is the Messiah, Jesus the son of Mary. He shall be noble in this world and in the next, and shall be favoured by Allah. He shall preach to men in his cradle and in the prime of manhood, and shall lead a righteous life.'

'Lord,' she said, 'how can I bear a child when no man has touched me?'

He replied: 'Such is the will of Allah. He creates whom He will. When He decrees a thing He need only say: "Be," and it is. He will instruct him in the Scriptures and in wisdom, in the Torah and in the Gospel, and send him forth as an apostle to the Israelites. He will say: "I bring you a sign from your Lord. From clay I will make for you the likeness of a bird. I shall breathe into it and, by Allah's leave, it shall become a living bird. By Allah's leave I shall give sight to the blind man, heal the leper, and raise the dead to life. I shall tell you what to eat and what to store up in your houses. Surely that will be a sign for you, if you are true believers. I come to confirm the Torah that has already been revealed and to make lawful to you some of the things you are forbidden. I bring you a sign from your Lord: therefore fear Him and obey Me. Allah is my God and your God: therefore serve Him. That is the straight path." '

When Jesus observed that they had no faith, he said: 'Who will help me in the cause of Allah?'

The disciples replied: 'We are the helpers of Allah. We believe in Him. Bear witness that we have surrendered ourselves to Him. Lord, we believe in Your revelations and follow your apostle. Count us among Your witnesses.'

They plotted, and Allah plotted. Allah is the supreme Plotter. He said: 'I am about to cause you to die and lift you up to Me. I shall take you away

---

1. Muhammad.

from the unbelievers and exalt your followers above them till the Day of Resurrection. Then to Me you shall all return and I shall judge your disputes. The unbelievers shall be sternly punished in this world and in the world to come: there shall be none to help them. As for those that have faith and do good works, they shall be given their reward in full. Allah does not love the evil-doers.'

This revelation, and this wise admonition, We recite to you. Jesus is like Adam in the sight of Allah. He created him of dust and then said to him: 'Be,' and he was.

This is the truth from your Lord: therefore do not doubt it. To those that dispute with you concerning Jesus after the knowledge you have received, say: 'Come, let us gather our sons and your sons, our wives and your wives, our people and your people. We will pray together and call down the curse of Allah on every liar.'

This is the whole truth. There is no god but Allah. It is Allah who is the Mighty, the Wise One!

If they give no heed to you, Allah knows the evil-doers.

Say: 'People of the Book, let us come to an agreement: that we will worship none but Allah, that we will associate none with Him, and that none of us shall set up mortals as gods besides Him.'

from *Sura 5 The Table*

One day Allah will gather all the apostles and ask them: 'How were you received?' They will reply: 'We do not know. You alone have knowledge of what is hidden.' Allah will say: 'Jesus, son of Mary, remember the favour I have bestowed on you and on your mother: how I strengthened you with the Holy Spirit, so that you preached to men in your cradle and in the prime of manhood; how I instructed you in the Scriptures and in wisdom, in the Torah and in the Gospel; how by My leave you fashioned from clay the likeness of a bird and breathed into it so that, by My leave, it became a living bird; how, by My leave, you healed the blind man and the leper, and by My leave restored the dead to life; how I protected you from the Israelites when you brought them veritable signs: when the unbelievers among them said: "This is nothing but plain magic"; how when I enjoined the disciples to believe in Me and in My apostle they replied: "We believe; bear witness that we submit to You utterly." '

'Jesus, son of Mary,' said the disciples, 'can Allah send down to us from heaven a table spread with food?'

He replied: 'Have fear of Allah, if you are true believers.'

'We wish to eat of it,' they said, 'so that we may reassure our hearts and know that what you said to us is true, and that we may be witnesses of it.'

'Lord,' said Jesus, the son of Mary, 'send to us from heaven a table spread with food, that it may mark a feast for us and for those that will come after us: a sign from You. Give us our sustenance; You are the best Giver.'

Allah replied: 'I am sending one to you. But whoever of you disbelieves hereafter shall be punished as no man has ever been punished.'

Then Allah will say: 'Jesus, son of Mary, did you ever say to mankind: "Worship me and my mother as gods beside Allah?"'

'Glory to You,' he will answer, 'how could I say that to which I have no right? If I had ever said so, You would have surely known it. You know what is in my mind, but I cannot tell what is in Yours. You alone know what is hidden. I spoke to them of nothing except what You bade me. I said: "Serve Allah, my Lord and your Lord." I watched over them whilst living in their midst, and ever since You took me to You, You Yourself have been watching over them. You are the witness of all things. They are your own bondsmen: it is for You to punish or to forgive them. You are the Mighty, the Wise One.'

from *Sura 7 The Heights*

We created you and gave you form. Then We said to the angels: 'Prostrate yourselves before Adam.' They all prostrated themselves except Satan, who refused.

'Why did you not prostrate yourself?' Allah asked.

'I am nobler than Adam,' he replied. 'You created me of fire and him of clay.'

He said: 'Begone from Paradise! This is no place for your contemptuous pride. Away with you! Henceforth you shall be humble.'

Satan replied: 'Reprieve me till the Day of Resurrection.'

'You are reprieved,' said He.

'Because You have led me into sin,' said Satan, 'I will way-lay Your servants as they walk on Your straight path, and spring upon them from the front and from the rear, from their right and from their left. Then you shall find the greater part of them ungrateful.'

'Begone!' said Allah. 'A despicable outcast you shall henceforth be. With those that follow you I shall fill the pit of Hell.'

To Adam He said: 'Dwell with your wife in Paradise, and eat of any fruit you please; but never approach this tree or you shall both become transgressors.'

But Satan tempted them, so that he might reveal to them their nakedness, which they had never seen before. He said: 'Your Lord has forbidden you to approach this tree only to prevent you from becoming angels or immortals.' Then he swore to them that he would give them friendly counsel.

Thus he cunningly seduced them. And when they had eaten of the tree, their shame became visible to them, and they both covered themselves with the leaves of the garden.

Their Lord called out to them, saying: 'Did I not forbid you to approach that tree, and did I not warn you that Satan was your sworn enemy?'

They replied: 'Lord, we have wronged our souls. Pardon us and have mercy on us, or we shall surely be among the lost.'

He said: 'Go hence, and may your descendants be enemies to each other. The earth will for a while provide your sustenance and dwelling-place. There you shall live and there you shall die, and thence you shall be raised to life.'

Children of Adam! We have given you clothing with which to cover your nakedness, and garments pleasing to the eye; but the finest of all these is the robe of piety.

That is one of Allah's revelations. Perchance they will take heed.

Children of Adam! Let Satan not deceive you, as he deceived your parents out of Paradise. He stripped them of their garments to reveal to them their nakedness. He and his minions see you whence you cannot see them. We have made the devils guardians over the unbelievers.

from *Sura 8 The Spoils*

Let the unbelievers not think that they will escape Us. They have not the power so to do. Muster against them all the men and cavalry at your disposal, so that you may strike terror into the enemies of Allah and the faithful, and others besides them who may be unknown to you, though Allah knows them. All that you give for the cause of Allah shall be repaid you. You shall not be wronged.

If they incline to peace, make peace with them, and put your trust in Allah. He hears all and knows all. Should they seek to deceive you, Allah is all-sufficient for you. He has made you strong with His help and rallied the faithful round you, making their hearts one. If you had given away all the riches of the earth, you could not have so united them: but Allah has united them. He is mighty and wise.

Prophet, Allah is your strength, and the faithful who follow you.

Prophet, rouse the faithful to arms. If there are twenty steadfast men among you, they shall vanquish two hundred; and if there are a hundred, they shall rout a thousand unbelievers, for they are devoid of understanding.

Allah has now lightened your burden, for He knows that you are weak. If there are a hundred steadfast men among you, they shall vanquish two hundred; and if there are a thousand, they shall, by Allah's will, defeat two thousand. Allah is with those that are steadfast.

A prophet may not take captives until he has fought and triumphed in his land. You[1] seek the chance gain of this world, but Allah desires for you the world to come. He is mighty and wise. Had there not been a previous sanction from Allah, you would have been sternly punished for what you have taken. Enjoy, therefore, the good and lawful things which you have gained in war, and fear Allah. He is forgiving and merciful.

from **Sura 11 Houd**

Long ago We sent forth Noah to his people. He said: 'I have come to warn you plainly. Serve none but Allah. Beware of the torment of a woeful day.'

The unbelieving elders of his people replied: 'We regard you as a mortal like ourselves. Nor can we find any among your followers but men of hasty judgement, the lowliest of our tribe. We see no virtue in you: indeed we know that you are lying.'

He said: 'Think, my people! If my Lord has revealed to me His will and bestowed on me His grace, though it be hidden from you, can we compel you to accept it against your will? I seek of you no recompense for this, my people; for none can reward me but Allah. Nor will I drive away the faithful, for they will surely meet their Lord. But I can see that you are ignorant men. Were I to drive them away, my people, who would protect me from Allah? Will you not take heed?

'I do not say that I possess Allah's treasures, or that I know what is hidden. I do not claim to be an angel, nor do I say to those whom you disdain that Allah will not be bountiful to them — He knows best what is in their hearts — for then I should become a wrongdoer.'

'Noah,' they replied, 'you have argued too long with us. Bring down the scourge with which you threaten us, if what you say be true!'

He said: 'Allah will visit His scourge upon you when He pleases: you shall not escape it. Nor will my counsel profit you if Allah seeks to mislead you, willing though I am to guide you. He is your Lord, and to Him you shall return.'

If they declare: 'He has invented it himself,' say: 'If I have indeed invented it, then may I be punished for my sin! I am innocent of your crimes.'

Allah's will was revealed to Noah, saying: 'None of your people will believe in you save those who have already believed. Do not grieve at their misdeeds. Build an ark under Our watchful eyes, according to Our bidding. Do not plead with Me for the wrongdoers: they shall all be drowned.'

So he built the Ark. And whenever the elders of his people passed by him they jeered at him. He said: 'Mock if you will. Just as you now mock us,

---

1. Muhammad's followers.

so we shall mock you. You shall know who will be punished and put to shame, and who will be afflicted by an everlasting scourge.'

And when Our will was done and water welled out from the Oven. We said to Noah: 'Take into the Ark a pair from every species, your tribe (except those already doomed), and all the true believers.' But none save a few believed with him.

Noah said: 'Embark in it. It will set sail in the name of Allah, and in the name of Allah it will cast anchor. My Lord is forgiving and merciful.'

And as the Ark moved on with them amidst the mountainous waves, Noah cried out to his son, who stood apart. 'Embark with us, my child,' he said. 'Do not stay with the unbelievers!'

He replied: 'I shall seek refuge in a mountain, which will protect me from the flood.'

Noah cried: 'None shall be secure this day from Allah's judgment, except those to whom He will show mercy!' And thereupon the billows rolled between them, and Noah's son was drowned.

A voice cried out: 'Earth, swallow up your waters. Heaven, cease your rain!' The floods abated and Allah's will was done. The Ark came to rest upon Al-Judi, and there was heard a voice, saying: 'Gone are the evil-doers.'

Noah called out to his Lord, saying: 'Lord, my son was my own flesh and blood. Your promise was surely true. You are the most just of judges.'

'Noah,' He replied, 'he was no kinsman of yours: he was an evil-doer. Do not question Me about things you know nothing of. I admonish you lest you become an ignorant man.'

'Forgive me, Lord, for my presumption,' said Noah. 'Pardon me and have mercy on me, or I shall surely be lost.'

'Noah,' He replied, 'go ashore in peace. Our blessings are upon you and on some of the descendants of those that are with you. As for the others, We will suffer them to take their ease in this world and then visit upon them a woeful scourge.'

That which We have now revealed to you is secret history: it was unknown to you and to your people. Have patience; the righteous shall have a joyful end.

Sura 12 Joseph

In the Name of Allah, the Compassionate, the Merciful

Alif lam ra. These are the verses of the Glorious Book. We have revealed the Koran in the Arabic tongue so that you may understand it.

In revealing this Koran We will recount to you the best of histories, though before We revealed it you were heedless of Our signs.

Joseph said to his father: 'Father, I dreamt that eleven stars and the sun and the moon were prostrating themselves before me.'

'My son,' he replied, 'say nothing of this dream to your brothers, lest they should plot evil against you: Satan is the sworn enemy of man. You shall be chosen by your Lord. He will teach you to interpret visions and will perfect His favour to you and to the house of Jacob, as He perfected it to your forefathers Abraham and Isaac before you. Your Lord is wise and all-knowing.'

Surely in the tale of Joseph and his brothers there are signs for doubting men.

They said to each other: 'Joseph and his brother are dearer to our father than ourselves, though we are many. Truly, our father is much mistaken. Let us kill Joseph, or cast him away in some far-off land, so that we may have no rivals in our father's love, and after that be honourable men.'

One of them said: 'Do not kill Joseph. If you must get rid of him, cast him into a dark pit. Some caravan will take him up.'

They said to their father: 'Why do you not trust us with Joseph? Surely we are his friends. Send him with us tomorrow, that he may play and enjoy himself. We will take good care of him.'

He replied: 'It would much grieve me to let him go with you; for I fear lest the wolf should eat him when you are off your guard.'

They said: 'If the wolf could eat him despite our numbers, then we should surely be lost!'

And when they took Joseph with them, they decided to cast him into a dark pit. We addressed him, saying: 'You shall tell them of all this when they will not know you.'

At nightfall they returned weeping to their father. They said: 'We went racing and left Joseph with our goods. The wolf devoured him. But you will not believe us, though we speak the truth.' And they showed him their brother's shirt, stained with false blood.

'No!' he cried. 'Your souls have tempted you to evil. But I will be patient: Allah alone can help me to bear the misfortune of which you speak.'

And a caravan passed by, who sent their waterman to the pit. And when he had let down his pail, he cried: 'Rejoice! A boy!'

They took Joseph and concealed him among their goods. But Allah knew what they did. They sold him for a trifling price, for a few pieces of silver. They cared nothing for him.

The Egyptian who bought him said to his wife: 'Use him kindly. He may prove useful to us, or we may adopt him as our son.'

Thus We found in that land a home for Joseph, and taught him to interpret mysteries. Allah has power over all things, though most men may not know it. And when he reached maturity We bestowed on him wisdom and knowledge. Thus We reward the righteous.

His master's wife sought to seduce him. She bolted the doors and said: 'Come!'

'Allah forbid!' he replied. 'My lord has treated me with kindness. Wrongdoers never prosper.'

She made for him, and he himself would have yielded to her had he not been shown a veritable sign by his Lord. Thus We warded off from him indecency and evil, for he was one of Our faithful servants.

He raced her to the door, but as she clung to him she tore his shirt from behind. And at the door they met her husband.

She cried: 'Shall not the man who sought to violate your wife be thrown into prison or sternly punished?'

Joseph said: 'It was she who sought to seduce me.'

'If his shirt is torn from the front,' said one of her people, 'she is speaking the truth and he is lying. If it is torn from behind, then he is speaking the truth and she is lying.'

And when her husband saw Joseph's shirt rent from behind, he said to her: 'This is one of your tricks. Your cunning is great indeed! Joseph, say no more about this. Woman, ask pardon for your sin. You have done wrong.'

In the city women were saying: 'The Prince's wife has sought to seduce her servant. She has conceived a passion for him. It is clear that she has gone astray.'

When she heard of their intrigues, she invited them to a banquet at her house. To each she gave a knife, and ordered Joseph to present himself before them. When they saw him, they were amazed at him and cut their hands, exclaiming: 'Allah preserve us! This is no mortal, but a gracious angel.'

'This is the man,' she said, 'on whose account you reproached me. I sought to seduce him, but he was unyielding. If he declines to do my bidding, he shall be thrown into prison and held in scorn.'

'Lord,' said Joseph, 'sooner would I go to prison than give in to their advances. Shield me from their cunning, or I shall yield to them and lapse into folly.'

His Lord heard his prayer and warded off their wiles from him. He hears all and knows all.

Yet despite the evidence they had seen, the Egyptians thought it right to jail him for a time.

Two young men went to prison with him. One of them said: 'I dreamt that I was pressing grapes.' And the other said: 'I dreamt that I was carrying a loaf upon my head, and that the birds came and ate of it. Tell us the meaning of these dreams, for we can see you are a man of learning.'

Joseph replied: 'I can interpret them long before they are fulfilled. This knowledge my Lord has given me, for I have left the faith of those that disbelieve in Allah and deny the life to come. I follow the faith of my forefathers, Abraham, Isaac, and Jacob. We must never serve idols besides Allah. Such is the gift which Allah has bestowed upon us and all mankind. Yet most men do not give thanks.

'Fellow-prisoners! Are numerous gods better than Allah, the One, the Almighty? Those whom you serve besides Him are names which you and your fathers have invented and for which Allah has revealed no sanction.

Judgement rests with Allah only. He has commanded you to worship none but Him. That is the true faith: yet most men do not know it.

'Fellow-prisoners, one of you will serve his king with wine. The other will be crucified, and the birds will peck at his head. That is the meaning of your dreams.'

And Joseph said to the prisoner who he knew would be freed: 'Remember me in the presence of your king.'

But Satan made him forget to mention Joseph to his king, so that he stayed in prison for several years.

Now it so chanced that one day the king said: 'I saw seven fatted cows which seven lean ones devoured; also seven green ears of corn and seven others dry. Tell me the meaning of this vision, my nobles, if you can interpret visions.'

They replied: 'It is but an idle dream; nor can we interpret dreams.'

Thereupon the man who had been freed remembered Joseph after all those years. He said: 'I shall tell you what it means. Give me leave to go.'

He said to Joseph: 'Tell us, man of truth, of the seven fatted cows which seven lean ones devoured; also of the seven green ears of corn and the other seven which were dry: for I would inform my masters.'

Joseph replied: 'You shall sow for seven consecutive years. Leave in the ear the corn you reap, except a little which you may eat. Then there shall follow seven hungry years which will consume all but little of that which you have stored for them. Then there will come a year of abundant rain, in which the people will press the grape.'

The king said: 'Bring this man before me.'

But when the king's envoy came to him, Joseph said: 'Go back to your master and ask him about the women who cut their hands. My master knows their cunning.'

The king questioned the women, saying: 'Why did you seek to entice Joseph?'

'Allah forbid!' they replied. 'We know no evil of him.'

'Now the truth must come to light,' said the Prince's wife. 'It was I who sought to seduce him. He has told the truth.'

'From this,' said Joseph, 'my lord will know that I did not betray him in his absence, and that Allah does not guide the work of the treacherous. Not that I am free from sin: man's soul is prone to evil, except his to whom Allah has shown mercy. My Lord is forgiving and merciful.'

The king said: 'Bring him before me. I will make him my personal servant.'

And when he had spoken with him, the king said: 'You shall henceforth dwell with us, honoured and trusted.'

Joseph said: 'Give me charge of the granaries of the realm. I shall husband them wisely.'

Thus We gave power to Joseph, and he dwelt at his ease in that land. We bestow Our mercy on whom We will, and never deny the righteous their reward. Better is the reward of the life to come for those who believe in Allah and keep from evil.

Joseph's brothers came and presented themselves before him. He recognized them, but they knew him not. And when he had given them their provisions, he said: 'Bring me your other brother from your father. Do you not see that I give just measure and am the best of hosts? If you do not bring him, you shall have no corn, nor shall you come near me again.'

They replied: 'We will request his father to let him come with us. This we will surely do.'

Joseph said to his servants: 'Put their money into their packs, so that they may find it when they return to their people. Perchance they will come back.'

When they returned to their father, they said: 'Father, corn is henceforth denied us. Send our brother with us and we shall have our measure. We will take good care of him.'

He replied: 'Am I to trust you with him as I once trusted you with his brother? But Allah is the best of guardians: of all those that show mercy He is the most merciful.'

When they opened their packs, they found that their money had been returned to them. 'Father,' they said, 'what more can we desire? Here is our money untouched. We will buy provisions for our people and take good care of our brother. We shall receive an extra camel-load; that should not be hard to get.'

He replied: 'I shall not let him go with you until you swear in Allah's name to bring him back to me, unless you are prevented.'

And when they had given him their pledge, he said: 'Allah is the witness of your oath. My sons, enter the town by different gates. If you do wrong, I cannot ward off from you the wrath of Allah: judgement is His alone. In Him I have put my trust. In Him alone let the faithful put their trust.'

And when they entered as their father had advised them, his counsel availed them nothing against the decree of Allah. It was but a wish in Jacob's soul which he had thus fulfilled. He was possessed of knowledge which We had given him, though most men were unaware of it.

When they presented themselves before him, Joseph embraced his brother, and said: 'I am your brother. Do not grieve at what they did.'

And when he had given them their provisions, he hid a drinking-cup in his brother's pack.

Then a crier called out after them: 'Travellers, you are thieves!'

They turned back and asked: 'What have you lost?'

'The king's drinking-cup,' he replied. 'He that restores it shall have a camel-load of corn. I pledge my word for it.'

'By Allah,' they cried, 'you know we did not come to do evil in this land. We are no thieves.'

The Egyptians said: 'What penalty shall we inflict on him that stole it, if you prove to be lying?'

They replied: 'He in whose pack the cup is found shall be your bondsman. Thus we punish the wrongdoers.'

Joseph searched their bags before his brother's, and then took out the cup from his brother's bag.

Thus We directed Joseph. By the king's law he had no right to seize his brother: but Allah willed otherwise. We exalt in knowledge whom We will: but above those that have knowledge there is One more knowing.

They said: 'If he has stolen — know then that a brother of his has committed a theft before him.'[1]

But Joseph kept his secret and did not reveal it to them. He thought: 'Your crime was worse. Allah well knows that you are lying.'

They said: 'Noble prince, this boy has an aged father. Take one of us, instead of him. We can see you are a generous man.'

He replied: 'Allah forbid that we should seize any but the man with whom our property was found: for then we should be unjust.'

When they despaired of him, they went aside to confer together. The eldest said: 'Have you forgotten that you gave your father a solemn pledge, and that you broke your faith before this concerning Joseph? I shall not stir from this land until my father gives me leave or Allah makes known to me His judgement: He is the best of judges. Return to your father and say to him: "Your son has committed a theft. We testify only to what we know. How could we guard against the unforeseen? Ask the townsfolk with whom we stayed and the caravan in which we travelled. We speak the truth." '

'No!' cried their father. 'Your souls have tempted you to evil. But I will be patient. Allah may bring them all to me. He alone is wise and all-knowing.' And he turned away from them, crying: 'Alas for Joseph!' His eyes went white with grief and he was oppressed with silent sorrow.

His sons exclaimed: 'By Allah, will you not cease to think of Joseph until you ruin your health and die?'

He replied: 'I complain to Allah of my sorrow and sadness. He has made known to me things beyond your knowledge. Go, my sons, and seek news of Joseph and his brother. Do not despair of Allah's spirit; none but unbelievers despair of Allah's spirit.'

And when they presented themselves before Joseph, they said: 'Noble prince, we and our people are scourged with famine. We have brought but little money. Give us some corn, and be charitable to us: Allah rewards the charitable.'

'Do you know,' he replied, 'what you did to Joseph and his brother in your ignorance?'

They cried: 'Can you indeed be Joseph?'

---

1. Commentators say that Joseph had stolen an idol of his maternal grandfather's and broken it, so that he might not worship it.

'I am Joseph,' he answered, 'and this is my brother. Allah has been gracious to us. Those that keep from evil and endure with fortitude, Allah will not deny them their reward.'

'By the Lord,' they said, 'Allah has exalted you above us all. We have indeed been guilty.'

He replied: 'None shall reproach you this day. May Allah forgive you: He is most merciful. Take this shirt of mine and throw it over my father's face: he will recover his sight. Then return to me with all your people.'

When the caravan departed their father said: 'I feel the breath of Joseph, though you will not believe me.'

'By Allah,' said those who heard him, 'this is but your old illusion.'

And when the bearer of good news arrived, he threw Joseph's shirt over the old man's face, and his sight came back to him. He said: 'Did I not tell you that Allah has made known to me things beyond your knowledge?'

His sons said: 'Father, implore forgiveness for our sins. We have indeed been sinners.'

He replied: 'I shall implore my Lord to forgive you. He is forgiving and merciful.'

And when they presented themselves before Joseph he embraced his parents and said: 'Welcome to Egypt, safe, if Allah wills!'

He helped his parents to a couch, and they all fell on their knees and prostrated themselves before him.

'This,' said Joseph to his father, 'is the meaning of my old vision: my Lord has fulfilled it. He has been gracious to me. He has released me from prison and brought you out of the desert after Satan had stirred up strife between me and my brothers. My lord is gracious to whom He will. He alone is wise and all-knowing.

'Lord, You have given me power and taught me to interpret mysteries. You are the Creator of the heavens and the earth, my Guardian in this world and in the next. Let me die in submission and join the righteous.'

That which We have now revealed to you[2] is secret history. You were not present when Joseph's brothers conceived their plans and schemed against him. Yet strive as you may, most men will not believe.

You shall demand of them no recompense for this. It[3] is an admonition to all mankind.

Many are the marvels of the heavens and the earth; yet they pass them by and pay no heed to them. The greater part of them believe in Allah only if they can worship other gods besides Him.

Are they confident that Allah's scourge will not fall upon them, or that the Hour of Doom will not overtake them unawares, without warning?

---

2. Muhammad.

3. The Koran.

Say: 'This is my path. With sure knowledge I call on you to have faith in Allah, I and all my followers. Glory be to Him! I am no idolater.'

Nor were the apostles whom We sent before you other than mortals inspired by Our will and chosen from among their people.

Have they not travelled in the land and seen what was the end of those who disbelieved before them? Better is the world to come for those that keep from evil. Can you not understand?

And when at length Our apostles despaired and thought that none would believe in them, Our help came down to them, delivering whom We pleased. The evil-doers did not escape Our scourge. Their history is a lesson to men of understanding.

This is no invented tale, but a confirmation of previous scriptures, an explanation of all things, a guide and a blessing to true believers.

from *Sura 13 Thunder*

In the Name of Allah, the Compassionate, the Merciful

Alif lam mim ra. These are the verses of the Book. That which is revealed to you from your Lord is the truth, yet men have no faith.

It was Allah who raised the heavens without visible pillars. He ascended His throne and forced the sun and the moon into His service, each pursuing an appointed course. He ordains all things. He makes plain His revelations so that you may firmly believe in meeting your Lord.

It was He who spread out the earth and placed upon it rivers and immovable mountains. He gave all plants their male and female parts and drew the veil of night over the day. Surely in these there are signs for thinking men.

And in the land there are adjoining plots: vineyards and cornfields and groves of palm, the single and the clustered. Their fruits are nourished by the same water: yet We give each a different taste. Surely in this there are signs for men of understanding.

If anything could make you marvel, then you should surely marvel at those who say: 'When we are dust, shall we be raised to life again?'

Such are those who deny their Lord. Their necks shall be bound with chains and in the fire of Hell they shall abide for ever.

* * *

Say: 'Allah is the Creator of all things. He is the One, the Almighty.'

He sends down water from the sky which fills the riverbeds to overflowing, so that their torrents bear a swelling foam, akin to that which rises from smelted ore when men make ornaments and tools. Thus Allah depicts truth and falsehood. The scum is cast away, but that which is of use to man remains behind. Thus Allah coins His parables.

from *Sura 14 Abraham*

Do you not see how Allah compares a good word to a good tree? Its root is firm and its branches are in the sky; it yields its fruit in every season by Allah's leave. Allah gives parables to men so that they may take heed. But an evil word is like an evil tree torn out of the earth and shorn of all its roots.

from *Sura 18 The Cave*

In the Name of Allah, the Compassionate, the Merciful

Praise be to Allah who has revealed the Book to His servant shorn of falsehood and unswerving from the truth, so that he may give warning of a dire scourge from Him, proclaim to the faithful who do good works that a rich and everlasting reward awaits them, and admonish those who say that Allah has begotten a son. Surely of this they could have no knowledge, neither they nor their fathers: a monstrous blasphemy is that which they utter. They preach nothing but falsehoods.

* * *

Give them this parable. Once there were two men, to one of whom We gave two vineyards set about with palm-trees and watered by a running stream, with a cornfield lying in between. Each of the vineyards yielded an abundant crop, and when their owner had gathered in the harvest, he said to his companion while conversing with him: 'I am richer than you, and my clan is mightier than yours.'

And when, having thus wronged his soul, he entered his vineyard, he said: 'Surely this will never perish! Nor do I believe that the Hour of Doom will ever come. Even if I returned to my Lord, I should surely find a better place than this.'

His companion replied: 'Have you no faith in Him who created you from dust, from a little germ, and fashioned you into a man? As for myself, Allah is my Lord. I will associate none with Him. When you entered your garden, why did you not say: "That which Allah has ordained must surely come to pass: there is no strength save in Allah"? Though you see me poorer than yourself and blessed with fewer children, yet my Lord may give me a garden better than yours, and send down thunderbolts from heaven upon your vineyard, turning it into a barren waste, or drain its water deep into the earth so that you can find it no more.'

His vineyards were destroyed, and he began to wring his hands with grief at all that he had spent on them: for the vines had tumbled down upon their trellises. 'Would that I had served no other gods besides my Lord!' he cried. He had none to help him besides Allah, nor was he able to defend himself.

In such ordeals protection comes only from Allah, the true God. No reward is better than His reward, and no recompense more generous than His.

Coin for them a simile about this life. It is like the green herbs that flourish when watered by the rain, soon turning into stubble which the wind scatters abroad. Allah has power over all things.

Wealth and children are the ornament of this life. But deeds of lasting merit are better rewarded by your Lord and hold for you a greater hope of salvation.

Tell of the day when We shall blot out the mountains and make the earth a barren waste; when We shall gather all mankind together, leaving not a soul behind.

They shall be ranged before your Lord, who will say to them: 'You have returned to Us as We created you at first. Yet you thought Our promise was not to be fulfilled.'

Their book will be set down before them, and you shall see the sinners dismayed at that which is inscribed in it. They shall say: 'Woe to us! What can this book mean? It omits nothing small or great: all are noted down!' and they shall find their deeds recorded there. Your Lord will wrong none.

When We said to the angels: 'Prostrate yourselves before Adam,' all prostrated themselves except Satan, who was a *jinnee* disobedient to his Lord. Would you then serve him and his offspring as your masters rather than Myself, despite their enmity towards you? A sad substitute the wrongdoers have chosen!

I did not call them to witness at the creation of the heavens and the earth, nor at their own creation; nor was I to seek the aid of those who were to lead mankind astray.

On that day Allah will say to them: 'Call on the idols which you supposed divine.' They will invoke them, but shall receive no answer; for We shall place a deadly gulf between them. And when the sinners behold the fire of Hell they will know it is there they shall be slung. They shall find no escape from it.

In this Koran We have set forth for men all manner of parables. But man is exceedingly contentious.

* * *

Your Lord is forgiving and merciful. Had it been His will to scourge them for their sins, He would have hastened their punishment; but He has set for them an appointed hour, which they shall never escape.

And all those nations! We destroyed them when they did wrong; yet of their imminent destruction We gave them warning.

Moses said to his servant: 'I will journey on until I reach the land where the two seas meet, though I may march for ages.'

But when at last they came to the land where the two seas met, they forgot their fish, which made its way into the water, swimming at will.

And when they had journeyed farther on, Moses said to his servant: 'Bring us some food; we are worn out with travelling.'

'Know,' replied the other, 'that I forgot the fish when we were resting on the rock. Thanks to Satan, I forgot to mention this. The fish made its way into the sea in a miraculous fashion.'

'This is what we have been seeking,' said Moses. They went back by the way they came and found one of Our servants to whom We had vouchsafed Our mercy and whom We had endowed with knowledge of Our own. Moses said to him: 'May I follow you so that you may guide me by that which you have been taught?'

'You will not bear with me,' replied the other. 'For how can you bear with that which is beyond your knowledge?'

Moses said: 'If Allah wills, you shall find me patient; I shall not in anything disobey you.'

He said: 'If you are bent on following me, you must ask no question about anything till I myself speak to you concerning it.'

The two set forth, but as soon as they embarked, Moses' companion bored a hole in the bottom of the ship.

'A strange thing you have done!' exclaimed Moses. 'Is it to drown her passengers that you have bored a hole in her?'

'Did I not tell you,' he replied, 'that you would not bear with me?'

'Pardon my forgetfulness,' said Moses. 'Do not be angry with me on account of this.'

They journeyed on until they fell in with a certain youth. Moses' companion slew him, and Moses said: 'You have killed an innocent man who has done no harm. Surely you have committed a wicked crime.'

'Did I not tell you,' he replied, 'that you would not bear with me?'

Moses said: 'If ever I question you again, abandon me; for then I should deserve it.'

They travelled on until they came to a certain city. They asked the people for some food, but they declined to receive them as their guests. There they found a wall on the point of falling down. His companion restored it, and Moses said: 'Had you wished, you could have demanded payment for your labours.'

'Now has the time arrived when we must part,' said the other. 'But first I will explain to you those acts of mine which you could not bear to watch with patience.

'Know that the ship belonged to some poor fishermen. I damaged it because in their rear there was a king who was taking every ship by force.

'As for the youth, his parents both are true believers, and we feared lest he should plague them with his wickedness and unbelief. It was our wish that their Lord should grant them another in his place, a son more righteous and more filial.

'As for the wall, it belonged to two orphan boys in the city whose father was an honest man. Beneath it their treasure is buried. Your Lord decreed in His mercy that they should dig out their treasure when they grew to manhood. What I did was not done by my will.

'That is the meaning of what you could not bear to watch with patience.'

∗ ∗ ∗

Say: 'If the waters of the sea were ink with which to write the words of my Lord, the sea would surely be consumed before His words were finished, though we brought another sea to replenish it.'

Say: 'I am a mortal like yourselves. It is revealed to me that your Lord is one God. Let him that hopes to meet his Lord do what is right and worship none besides Him.'

from *Sura 19 Mary*

And you shall recount in the Book the story of Mary: how she left her people and betook herself to a solitary place to the east.

We sent to her Our spirit in the semblance of a full-grown man. And when she saw him she said: 'May the Merciful defend me from you! If you fear the Lord, leave me and go your way.'

'I am the messenger of your Lord,' he replied, 'and have come to give you a holy son.'

'How shall I bear a child,' she answered, 'when I am a virgin, untouched by man?'

'Such is the will of your Lord,' he replied. 'That is no difficult thing for Him. "He shall be a sign to mankind," says the Lord, "and a blessing from Ourself. That is Our decree."'

Thereupon she conceived, and retired to a far-off place. And when she felt the throes of childbirth she lay down by the trunk of a palm-tree, crying: 'Oh, would that I had died and passed into oblivion!'

But a voice from below cried out to her: 'Do not despair. Your Lord has provided a brook that runs at your feet, and if you shake the trunk of this palm-tree it will drop fresh ripe dates in your lap. Therefore rejoice. Eat and drink, and should you meet any mortal say to him: "I have vowed a fast to the Merciful and will not speak with any man today."'

Then she took the child to her people, who said to her: 'This is indeed a strange thing! Sister of Aaron,[1] your father was never a whoremonger, nor was your mother a harlot.'

She made a sign to them, pointing to the child. But they replied: 'How can we speak with a babe in the cradle?'

---

1. I.e., virtuous woman—Aaron being held in the Koran as a 'prophet' and a saintly man. Such idiomatic expressions are common in Arabic. Muslim commentators deny the charge, often made by Western scholars and based solely on this text, that Muhammad confused Miriam, Aaron's sister, with Maryam (Mary), mother of Jesus.

Whereupon he spoke and said: 'I am the servant of Allah. He has given me the Gospel and ordained me a prophet. His blessing is upon me wherever I go, and He has commanded me to be steadfast in prayer and to give alms to the poor as long as I shall live. He has exhorted me to honour my mother and has purged me of vanity and wickedness. I was blessed on the day I was born, and blessed I shall be on the day of my death; and may peace be upon me on the day when I shall be raised to life.'

Such was Jesus, the son of Mary. That is the whole truth, which they are unwilling to accept. Allah forbid that He Himself should beget a son! When He decrees a thing He need only say: 'Be,' and it is.

Allah is my Lord and your Lord: therefore serve Him. That is the right path.

Yet the Sects are divided concerning Jesus. But when the fateful day arrives, woe to the unbelievers! Their sight and hearing shall be sharpened on the day when they appear before Us. Truly, the unbelievers are in the grossest error.

Forewarn them of that woeful day, when Our decrees shall be fulfilled whilst they heedlessly persist in unbelief. For We shall inherit the earth and all who dwell upon it. To Us they shall return.

from Sura 22 Pilgrimage

In the Name of Allah, the Compassionate, the Merciful

Men, have fear of your Lord. The catastrophe of the Hour of Doom shall be terrible indeed.

When that day comes, every suckling mother shall forsake her infant, every pregnant female shall cast her burden, and you shall see mankind reeling like drunkards although not drunk: such shall be the horror of Allah's vengeance.

Yet there are some who in their ignorance dispute about Allah and serve rebellious devils, though these are doomed to seduce their followers and lead them into the fire of Hell.

Men, if you doubt the Resurrection remember that We first created you from dust, then from a living germ, then from a clot of blood, and then from a half-formed lump of flesh, so that We might manifest to you Our power.

We cause to remain in the womb whatever We please for an appointed term, and then We bring you forth as infants, that you may grow up and reach your prime. Some die young, and some live on to abject old age when all that they once knew they know no more.

You sometimes see the earth dry and barren: but no sooner do We send down rain upon it than it begins to stir and swell, putting forth every kind of radiant bloom. That is because Allah is Truth: He gives life to the dead and has power over all things.

The Hour of Doom is sure to come—in this there is no doubt. Those who are in the grave Allah will raise to life.

* * *

Do you not see how all who dwell in heaven and earth do homage to Allah? The sun and the moon and the stars, the mountains and the trees, the beasts, and countless men—all prostrate themselves before Him. Yet many have deserved His scourge. He who is humbled by Allah has none to honour him. Allah's will is ever done.

The faithful and the unbelievers contend about their Lord. Garments of fire have been prepared for the unbelievers. Scalding water shall be poured upon their heads, melting their skins and that which is in their bellies. They shall be lashed with rods of iron.

Whenever, in their anguish, they try to escape from Hell, the angels will drag them back, saying: 'Taste the torment of Hell-fire!'

As for those that have faith and do good works, Allah will admit them to gardens watered by running streams. They shall be decked with pearls and bracelets of gold, and arrayed in garments of silk. For they have been shown the noblest of words and guided to the path of the Glorious Lord.

The unbelievers who debar others from the path of Allah and from the Sacred Mosque which We gave to all mankind, natives and strangers alike, and those who commit evil within its walls, shall be sternly punished.

When We prepared for Abraham the site of the Sacred Mosque We said: 'Worship none besides Me. Keep My House clean for those who walk around it and those who stand upright or kneel in worship.'

Exhort all men to make the pilgrimage. They will come to you on foot and on the backs of swift camels from every distant quarter; they will come to avail themselves of many a benefit and to pronounce on the appointed days the name of Allah over the beasts which He has given them. Eat of their flesh yourselves, and feed the poor and the unfortunate.

Then let the pilgrims spruce themselves, make their vows, and circle the Ancient House. Such is Allah's commandment. He that reveres the sacred rites of Allah shall fare better in the sight of his Lord.

* * *

Permission to take up arms is hereby given to those who are attacked, because they have been wronged. Allah has power to grant them victory: those who have been unjustly driven from their homes, only because they said: 'Our Lord is Allah.' Had Allah not defended some men by the might of others, the monasteries and churches, the synagogues and mosques in which His praise is daily celebrated, would have been utterly destroyed. But whoever helps Allah shall be helped by Him. Allah is powerful and mighty: He will assuredly help those who, once made masters in the land, will attend to their prayers and pay the alms-tax, enjoin justice and forbid evil. Allah controls the destiny of all things.

If they deny you, remember that before them the peoples of Noah, Abraham and Lot, the tribes of Thamoud and Aad, and the dwellers of

Midian had denied their apostles: Moses himself was charged with imposture. I bore long with the unbelievers and in the end My scourge overtook them. And how terrible was My vengeance!

How many sinful nations We have destroyed! Their cities lie in ruin: desolate are their lofty palaces, and abandoned their wells.

Have they never journeyed through the land? Have they no hearts to reason with, or ears to hear with? It is their hearts, and not their eyes, that are blind.

from *Sura 24 Light*

Allah is the light of the heavens and the earth. His light may be compared to a niche that enshrines a lamp, the lamp within a crystal of star-like brilliance. It is lit from a blessed olive tree neither eastern nor western. Its very oil would almost shine forth, though no fire touched it. Light upon light; Allah guides to His light whom He will.

Allah coins metaphors for men. He has knowledge of all things.

His light is found in temples which Allah has sanctioned to be built for the remembrance of His name. In them morning and evening His praise is sung by men whom neither trade nor profit can divert from remembering Him, from offering prayers, or from giving alms; who dread the day when men's hearts and eyes shall writhe with anguish; who hope that Allah will requite them for their noblest deeds and lavish His grace upon them. Allah gives without measure to whom He will.

As for the unbelievers, their works are like a mirage in a desert. The thirsty traveller thinks it is water, but when he comes near he finds that it is nothing. He finds Allah there, who pays him back in full. Swift is Allah's reckoning.

Or like darkness on a bottomless ocean spread with clashing billows and overcast with clouds: darkness upon darkness. If he stretches out his hand he can scarcely see it. Indeed, the man from whom Allah withholds His light shall find no light at all.

Do you not see how Allah is praised by those in heaven and earth? The very birds praise Him as they wing their flight. He notes the prayers and praises of all His creatures, and has knowledge of all their actions.

To Allah belongs the kingdom of the heavens and the earth. To Him shall all things return.

Do you not see how Allah drives the clouds, then gathers them and piles them up in masses which pour down torrents of rain? From heaven's mountains He sends down hail, pelting with it whom He will and turning it away from whom He pleases. The flash of His lightning almost snatches off men's eyes.

He makes the night succeed the day: surely in this there is a lesson for clear-sighted men.

Allah created every beast from water. Some creep upon their bellies, others walk on two legs, and others on four. Allah creates what He pleases. He has power over all things.

We have sent down revelations showing the truth. Allah guides whom He will to a straight path.

from Sura 29 The Spider

The false gods which the idolaters serve besides Allah may be compared to the spider's cobweb. Surely the spider's is the frailest of all dwellings, if they but knew it. Allah knows what they invoke besides Him; He is the Mighty, the Wise One.

We coin these similes for the instruction of men; but none will grasp their meaning except the wise.

Sura 55 The Merciful[1]

In the Name of Allah, the Compassionate, the Merciful

It is the Merciful who has taught you the Koran.

He created man and taught him articulate speech. The sun and the moon pursue their ordered course. The plants and the trees bow down in adoration.

He raised the heaven on high and set the balance of all things, that you might not transgress it. Give just weight and full measure.

He laid the earth for His creatures, with all its fruits and blossom-bearing palm, chaff-covered grain and scented herbs. Which of your Lord's blessings would you[2] deny?

He created man from potter's clay and the jinn from smokeless fire. Which of your Lord's blessings would you deny?

The Lord of the two easts[3] is He, and the Lord of the two wests. Which of your Lord's blessings would you deny?

He has let loose the two oceans:[4] they meet one another. Yet between them stands a barrier which they cannot overrun. Which of your Lord's blessings would you deny?

Pearls and corals come from both. Which of your Lord's blessings would you deny?

---

1. Compare this chapter with Psalm 136 of the Old Testament.

2. The pronoun is in the dual number, the words being addressed to mankind and the jinn. This refrain is repeated no less than 31 times.

3. The points at which the sun rises in summer and winter.

4. Salt water and fresh water.

His are the ships that sail like banners[5] upon the ocean. Which of your Lord's blessings would you deny?

All who live on earth are doomed to die. But the face of your Lord will abide for ever, in all its majesty and glory. Which of your Lord's blessings would you deny?

All who dwell in heaven and earth beseech Him. Each day some new task employs Him. Which of your Lord's blessings would you deny?

Mankind and jinn, We shall surely find the time to judge you! Which of your Lord's blessings would you deny?

Mankind and *jinn*, if you have power to penetrate the confines of heaven and earth, then penetrate them! But this you shall not do except with Our own authority. Which of your Lord's blessings would you deny?

Flames of fire shall be lashed at you, and molten brass. There shall be none to help you. Which of your Lord's blessings would you deny?

When the sky splits asunder and reddens like a rose or stained leather (which of your Lord's blessings would you deny?), on that day neither man nor jinnee shall be asked about his sins. Which of your Lord's blessings would you deny?

The wrongdoers shall be known by their looks; they shall be seized by their forelocks and their feet. Which of your Lord's blessings would you deny?

That is the Hell which the sinners deny. They shall wander between fire and water fiercely seething. Which of your Lord's blessings would you deny?

But for those that fear the majesty of their Lord there are two gardens (which of your Lord's blessings would you deny?) planted with shady trees. Which of your Lord's blessings would you deny?

Each is watered by a flowing spring. Which of your Lord's blessings would you deny?

Each bears every kind of fruit in pairs. Which of your Lord's blessings would you deny?

They shall recline on couches lined with thick brocade, and within their reach will hang the fruits of both gardens. Which of your Lord's blessings would you deny?

They shall dwell with bashful virgins whom neither man nor jinnee will have touched before. Which of your Lord's blessings would you deny?

Virgins as fair as corals and rubies. Which of your Lord's blessings would you deny?

Shall the reward of goodness be anything but good? Which of your Lord's blessings would you deny?

And beside these there shall be two other gardens (which of your Lord's blessings would you deny?) of darkest green. Which of your Lord's blessings would you deny?

---

5. Or mountains.

A gushing fountain shall flow in each. Which of your Lord's blessings would you deny?

Each planted with fruit-trees, the palm and the pomegranate. Which of your Lord's blessings would you deny?

In each there shall be virgins chaste and fair. Which of your Lord's blessings would you deny?

Dark-eyed virgins sheltered in their tents (which of your Lord's blessings would you deny?) whom neither man nor jinnee will have touched before. Which of your Lord's blessings would you deny?

They shall recline on green cushions and rich carpets. Which of your Lord's blessings would you deny?

Blessed be the name of your Lord, the Lord of majesty and glory!

Sura 56 That Which Is Coming

In the Name of Allah, the Compassionate, the Merciful

When that which is coming comes—and no soul shall them deny its coming—some shall be abased and others exalted.

When the earth shakes and quivers and the mountains crumble away and scatter abroad into fine dust, you shall be divided into three multitudes: those on the right (blessed shall be those on the right!); those on the left (damned shall be those on the left!); and those to the fore (foremost shall be those!). Such are they that shall be brought near to their Lord in the gardens of delight: a whole multitude from the men of old, but only a few from the later generations.

They shall recline on jewelled couches face to face, and there shall wait on them immortal youths with bowls and ewers and a cup of purest wine (that will neither pain their heads nor take away their reason); with fruits of their own choice and flesh of fowls that they relish. And theirs shall be the dark-eyed houris, chaste as hidden pearls: a guerdon for their deeds.

There they shall hear no idle talk, no sinful speech, but only the greeting, 'Peace! Peace!'

Those on the right hand—happy shall be those on the right hand! They shall recline on couches raised on high in the shade of thornless sidrahs and clusters of talh;[1] amidst gushing waters and abundant fruits, unforbidden, never-ending.

We created the houris and made them virgins, loving companions for those on the right hand: a multitude from the men of old, and a multitude from the later generations.

---

1. Probably the banana fruit.

As for those on the left hand (wretched shall be those on the left hand!) they shall dwell amidst scorching winds and seething water: in the shade of pitch-black smoke, neither cool nor refreshing. For they have lived in comfort and persisted in the heinous sin,[2] saying: 'When we are once dead and turned to dust and bones, shall we, with all our forefathers, be raised to life?'

Say: 'This present generation, as well as the generations that passed before it, shall be brought together on an appointed day. As for you sinners who deny the truth, you shall eat the fruit of the Zaqqum-tree and fill your bellies with it. You shall drink boiling water: yet you shall drink it as the thirsty camel drinks.'

Such shall be their fare on the Day of Reckoning.

We created you: will you not believe then in Our power?

Behold the semen you discharge: did you create it, or We?

It was We that ordained death among you. Nothing can hinder Us from replacing you by others like yourselves or transforming you into beings you know nothing of.

You surely know of the first creation. Why, then, do you not reflect? Consider the seeds you sow. Is it you that give them growth or We? If We pleased We could turn your harvest into chaff, so that, filled with wonderment, you would exclaim: 'We are laden with debts! Surely we have been robbed!'

Consider the water which you drink. Was it you that poured it from the cloud or We? If We pleased We could turn it bitter. Why then do you not give thanks?

Observe the fire which you light. Is it you that create its wood, or We? We have made it a reminder for man, and for the traveller a comfort.

Praise then the name of your Lord, the Supreme One.

I swear by the shelters of the stars (a mighty oath, if you but knew it) that this is a glorious Koran, inscribed in a hidden book which none may touch except the purified; a revelation from the Lord of all creatures.

Would you scorn a scripture such as this and make it your daily task to deny it?

When under your very eyes a man's soul is about to leave him (We are nearer to him than you, although you cannot see Us), why do you not restore it, if you will not be judged hereafter? Answer this, if what you say be true!

Thus, if he is favoured, his lot will be repose and plenty and a garden of delights. If he is one of those on the right hand he will be greeted with, 'Peace be to you!' by those on the right hand.

But if he is an erring disbeliever his welcome will be scalding water and he will burn in Hell.

This is the indubitable truth. Praise then the name of your Lord, the Supreme One.

---

2. Idolatry.

from *Sura 57 Iron*

In the Name of Allah, the Compassionate, the Merciful

All that is in heaven and earth gives glory to Allah. He is the Mighty, the Wise One.

His is the kingdom of the heavens and the earth. He ordains life and death and has power over all things.

He is the first and the last, the visible and the unseen. He has knowledge of all things.

He created the heavens and the earth in six days and then mounted His throne. He knows all that goes into the earth and all that emerges from it, all that comes down from heaven and all that ascends to it. He is with you wherever you are. Allah is cognizant of all your actions.

His is the kingdom of the heavens and the earth. To Him shall all things return. He causes the night to pass into the day and the day into the night. He has knowledge of the inmost thoughts of men.

Have faith in Allah and His apostle and give in alms of that which He has made your inheritance; for whoever of you believes and gives in alms shall be richly rewarded.

* * *

Know that the life of this world is but a sport and a pastime, a show and an empty vaunt among you, a quest for greater riches and more children. It is like the plants that flourish after rain: the husbandman rejoices to see them grow; but then they wither and turn yellow, soon becoming worthless stubble. In the life to come a woeful punishment awaits you—or the forgiveness of Allah and His pleasure. The life of this world is but a vain provision.

Therefore strive emulously for the pardon of your Lord, and for a Paradise as vast as heaven and earth, prepared for those who believe in Allah and His apostles. Such is the grace of Allah: He bestows it on whom He will. His grace is infinite.

Sura 81 The Cessation

In the Name of Allah, the Compassionate, the Merciful

When the sun ceases to shine; when the stars fall down and the mountains are blown away; when camels big with young are left untended and the wild beasts are brought together; when the seas are set alight and men's souls are reunited; when the infant girl,[1] buried alive, is asked for what crime she was thus slain; when the records of men's deeds are laid open and the

---

1. An allusion to the pre-Islamic custom of burying unwanted newborn girls.

heaven is stripped bare; when Hell burns fiercely and Paradise is brought near: then each soul shall know what it has done.

I swear by the turning planets and by the stars that rise and set; by the fall of night and the first breath of morning: this is the word of a gracious and mighty messenger, held in honour by the Lord of the Throne, obeyed in heaven, faithful to his trust.

No, your compatriot[2] is not mad. He saw him[3] on the clear horizon. He does not grudge the secrets of the unseen; nor is this the utterance of an accursed devil.

Whither then are you going?

This is an admonition to all men: to those among you that have the will to be upright. Yet you cannot will, except by the will of Allah, Lord of the Creation.

Sura 104 The Slanderer

In the Name of Allah, the Compassionate, the Merciful

Woe to all back-biting slanderers who amass riches and sedulously hoard them, thinking their treasures will render them immortal!

By no means! They shall be flung to the Destroying Flame.

Would that you knew what the Destroying Flame is like!

It is Allah's own kindled fire, which will rise up to the hearts of men. It will close upon them from every side, in towering columns.

■ Rabia the Mystic (c. 712–801) *Iraq* (poems and miracle story)

Rabia al-Adawiyya was born in Basra (now in Iraq) and is considered an important Sufi saint, and many of the miracle tales about her that survive were recorded by another major Sufi writer, Farid ad-Din Attar. We know that Rabia was born poor and that her family life was tragic: famine killed her parents, and she and her sisters were scattered—she to be sold as a slave. Her master eventually gave her her freedom. This story is told about her master's change of heart:

In her life as a slave, Rabia found time for her worship of God by doing without sleep. She fasted and prayed. One night her master awoke, looked down from the window of his house into the courtyard, and saw Rabia in

---

2. Muhammad.
3. Gabriel.

prayer. As he was watching her he was amazed to see a lamp appear above her head suspended in mid-air; the light from this miraculous lamp lit up the whole house. Terrified and astonished, he went back to bed, and sat wondering until dawn. Then he called Rabia to him, confessed what he had seen, and gave her her freedom.[1]

She might have made the pilgrimage to Mecca; she came to be recognized as a saint of great renown who refused worldly offers (fear of falling away from spirituality into the trap of the world is a major theme in her poems); and she is said to have lived a celibate life in humble circumstances. It is hard to know whether these poems were actually written by her or by others, but the singular and/or plural author(s) have inscribed the psychology of at least a ghost-Rabia into these poems, the harshness and depth of whose life experience seems to have translated into a particularly fervent and unyielding asceticism.

FURTHER READING: Nurbakhsh, Dr. Javad. *Sufi Women.* Translated by Leonard Lewisohn, 1983. Sakkakini, Widad El. *First among Sufis: The Life and Thought of Rabi'a al-Adawiyya.* Translated by Dr. Nabil Safwat, 1982. Smith, Margaret. *Rabi'a the Mystic and Her Fellow Saints in Islam,* 1928, 1977. Upton, Charles. *Doorkeeper of the Heart: Versions of Rabi'a,* 1988.

O My Lord, the Stars Glitter and the Eyes of Men Are Closed

O my Lord, the stars glitter and eyes of men are closed,
kings have shut their doors
and each lover is alone with his love.
Here, I am alone with you.

TRANSLATED BY WILLIS BARNSTONE

Miracle Story

One day Rabi'a and her serving-girl were getting ready to break a fast of several days. The serving-girl needed an onion and was about to go next door and borrow one, but Rabi'a said: "Forty years ago I vowed never to ask for anything from anyone but God — we can do without onions."

Just then a bird flew over, and dropped an onion into Rabi'a's frying pan, peeled and ready to fry.

---

1. Charles Upton, *Doorkeeper of the Heart: Versions of Rabi'a* (Putney, VT: Threshold Books, 1988), 9–10.

"Interesting but not convincing," she said. "Am I supposed to believe that God is an onion-vender? I mean, really."

That day they fried their bread without onions.

TRANSLATED BY CHARLES UPTON

How Long Will You Keep Pounding

How long will you keep pounding on an open door
Begging for someone to open it?

TRANSLATED BY CHARLES UPTON

■ Abu Nuwas (b. between 747–762, d. between 813–815) *Baghdad/Abbasid Empire* (poem)

TRANSLATED BY RICHARD SERRANO

Abu Nuwas was among the best writers of the Abbasid school of poetry. His mother was Persian, but he wrote in Arabic, and after studying in Basra and Kufa was a court poet writing panegyrics in Baghdad. A resolute rake, he lived a life of debauched pleasure, and his poems reflect this in their emphasis on drinking songs, love poems (usually about young men, sometimes about women), and obscene poems; his wanton poetry even goes to the point of attacking Islam. His poetry is not all of this nature, though; he also wrote satires, didactic verse, panegyrics, and ascetic verse. He became a folk hero, and stories about his exploits at the court of Caliph Harun al-Rashid appear in *The Thousand and One Nights*. A collection of his poems survives.

Drunkenness after Drunkenness

So pour wine for me and say it is wine;
Don't pour in secret what can be public.

No good life without drunkenness after drunkenness;
If its duration is long then time will be short.

There is no crime but your seeing me sober, no advantage
But in my drunken shakes and stammers.

5

Reveal the name of whom you love without allusion;
There is no good in veiled pleasures,

Nor good in depravity without scandal,
Nor in scandal not followed by unbelief.   *10*

With all my brothers in depravity,
Their brows as crescent moons surrounded by stars,

I woke a taverness from her nap,
Once Gemini had set and Aquila had risen.

She said, "Who knocks?" We answered, "A gang   *15*
Lightened of medicine, wine entices them,

They must fornicate." She said, "In exchange
Take one bright as a dinar, languor in his glance."

"Hand him over. The likes of us are impatient
To ransom our families for the likes of him."   *20*

She brought him out like a moon at full term;
Enchanting, he was no mere enchantment.

So we went to him one by one,
Breaking the fast of our exile.

So we passed the night, God watching a gang   *25*
Let trail the robes of depravity—and this no boast.

■ The Thousand and One Nights (c. Ninth to Fourteenth Centuries) *Persia/Arabia* (stories)

TRANSLATED BY RICHARD BURTON, ADAPTED BY EMMA VARESIO

The Thousand and One Nights, also known as *The Arabian Nights,* is a collection of stories in the form of fables, jokes, anecdotes, didactic tales, parables, fairy tales, and legends, whose sources are Arabic, Persian, and Indian oral and written tales. These stories circulated for hundreds of years before being transcribed between the ninth and fourteenth centuries. The immediate basis for the collection was a Persian book entitled *A Thousand Tales,* which was translated into Arabic around the ninth century. This latter compendium was the model for the framing narrative of *The Thousand*

and One Nights, in which King Shahryar is driven mad with jealousy after discovering his queen in the arms of a slave. He goes in search of anyone who has suffered as much as he. On encountering the wife of a genie, who has been locked in a casket within a chest with seven padlocks, deposited at the bottom of the sea, and yet has cuckolded her husband 570 times, he is convinced that all women are unfaithful. So he kills his queen and takes a new wife every night for three years, murdering her in the morning to ensure her fidelity. Scheherazade, his vizier's daughter, marries the king to try to stop the slaughter of women. To save her own life, she tells a story each night through dawn. Leaving the tale unfinished when morning comes, she keeps the king fascinated: "By Allah," he says, each day, "I won't slay her until I hear the rest of her tale, for it is truly wondrous." By the end of telling, several years later, Scheherazade has borne the king three sons and through her skills and grace has domesticated the mad monarch.

The *Nights* was introduced to the West by Antoine Galland in the early eighteenth century, and since then there have been innumerable translations into the languages of the world, notably that of Sir Richard Burton (1821–1890), whose sixteen-volume unexpurgated and annotated version is the classic and most esteemed version in English. The present selection, which retains Burton's bawdy and energetically elaborate prose style, has been modernized by Emma Varesio. The text, which is erotic, outrageous, and wise, has often been bowdlerized and sanitized in English translation, rendering this adult masterpiece into a collection of children's tales. This Eastern collection has deeply affected the Western literary imagination from Robert Louis Stevenson's *New Arabian Nights* to the labyrinthine narratives of Jorge Luis Borges. Hollywood has frequently adapted the *Nights* into magical, adventurous, or humorous films that deviate wildly from the original. However, since the notion of an authoritative original of a collection with so many recensions is itself questionable, perhaps these film retellings are in the spirit of essential works that are constantly reinvented to fit a new cultural environment. The American writer John Barth recently has adapted the tales of *Sinbad the Sailor* into his fascinating novel *The Last Voyage of Somebody the Sailor,* and the common Modernist technique of the tale within a tale must owe something to the multilayered narrative of the *Nights.* The selection presented here, "The Tale of the Fisherman and the Genie," is a famous sequence of stories that mirrors the collection's framing technique. Like Scheherazade, the fisherman tells story within story and must outwit his fate—in this case an angry genie.

FURTHER READING: Burton, Richard, tr. *The Book of the Thousand Nights and a Night: A Plain and Literal Translation of the Arabian Nights Entertainment,* 10 vols., 1885–1886; tr. *Supplemental Nights to the Book of the Thousand Nights and a Night, with Notes Anthropological and Explanatory,* 6 vols., 1886–1888. Lane, Edward William, tr. *A New Translation of the Tales of A Thousand and One Nights: Known in England as The Arabian Nights' Entertainments,* 1838–1840. Zipes, Jack, tr. *Arabian Nights: The Marvels and Wonders of the Thousand and One Nights,* 1991.

The Tale of the Fisherman and the Genie

I have heard, Oh worthy King, that there was once a poor, old Fisherman who had a wife and three children to support. Each day, it was his custom to cast his fishing-net into the ocean exactly four times, and no more. One day, at about noon, he went towards the seashore, where he set his basket down in the sand. Tucking up his shirt and plunging into the water, he cast his net and waited until it settled to the bottom of the sea. Then, he gathered the cords of the net together, and tried to haul it away. But its heaviness overpowered him, and no matter how hard he tried, he could not pull it up. So he carried the ends of the cords to the shore, drove a stake into the sand, and bound the cords tightly to the stake. Then he stripped his clothes from his body and dove into the water, working hard until he finally raised the net from the sea.

Rejoicing, he put his clothes back on and went to examine the net and found a dead jackass inside of it, which had torn all the net's meshes. As he saw this, the Fisherman sadly exclaimed, "There is no majesty, and there is no might except Allah the glorious, the great! But, well, this is a strange sort of daily bread." He paused, considering, and then murmured to himself, "Well, up and at it! I'll finish my fishing now, for I'm very sure of Allah's goodness."

So the Fisherman gazed at the dead ass for a moment, and then pulled it free from the netting. He wrung out the net, and spread it over the sand. Calling out "In Allah's name!" he plunged back into the sea. He cast the net a second time, and when he tried to pull it out, it grew even heavier and settled down more firmly than before. Now, he thought, there were certainly fish in it this time. Quickly, he tied the cords to the stake again, pulled off his clothes, and dove into the water, hauling the net until it reached the shore. Inside the net lay a large earthen pitcher, clogged full of sand and mud.

As he saw this the Fisherman became very disheartened, and so he prayed for Allah's pardon. After throwing away the pitcher, he wrung out his net, cleaned it, and cast into the sea for the third time. Again, he waited until it sunk to the bottom, and then pulled it up. This time, he found shards of pottery and broken glass inside the net. Raising his eyes toward heaven, he cried out, "Oh Allah! You know that I cast my net into the sea four times every day. I've cast it three times, and so far, You have granted me nothing! I beseech You, my God, this time give me my daily bread!"

Then, calling on Allah's name, he threw his net into the sea again, waiting for it to sink and settle at the bottom. Again, he tugged at it, but it was tangled in the sea bottom. Frustrated, he shouted, "There is no majesty and there is no might but in Allah!" Then he shed his clothes again, dove down to the net, and patiently untangled it, bit by bit, until it rose and he could drag it to shore. He opened the meshes, and in its folds, he found a cucumber-shaped copper jar, brimming with something mysterious. The mouth of the jar was sealed with lead, and stamped with the seal of our Lord Solomon, David's son, Allah praise them! Seeing this the Fisherman rejoiced and said, "If I sell this in the brass bazaar, I could get ten golden dinars for it!" He shook the jar, and finding it heavy, murmured, "I wish I knew what was in it. I feel as if I must find out—so I'll open it and look inside, and then I'll store it in my bag, to sell at the brass market. Taking out a knife, he pried the lead until he had loosened it from the jar. He set the seal on the ground, and turned the vase upside-down, shaking it and trying to pour out whatever could be inside. Surprisingly, nothing emerged, and the fisherman stood in wonder.

But suddenly, a spiral of smoke burst from the jar, rising toward the heavens. The fisherman marvelled as it was drawn into the air, ascending far above him. As it reached its full height, the thick, vaporous smoke condensed and formed a Genie, so huge that his head brushed the sky, and his feet touched the ground. The Genie's head curved as large as a dome; his hands dangled, big as pitchforks. His legs were long as masts, his mouth as wide as a cave, his teeth like large stones, and his nostril flared like pitchers' spouts. His eyes shone like two lamps, and his face proved fierce and threatening.

Now, when the Fisherman saw the Genie, his muscles quivered, his teeth chattered, and his throat grew too dry to swallow. Paralyzed, clenched with fear, he could do nothing.

The Genie looked at him and cried, "There is no god but *the* God, and Solomon is the prophet of God." He added, "Oh Apostle of Allah, do not slay me. Never again will I oppose you or sin against you."

The Fisherman replied, "Oh Genie, did you say, 'Solomon the Apostle of Allah?' Solomon has been dead for nearly eighteen hundred years, and now we're in the last days of the world! Where have you come from? What's happened to you? Why have you been in that jar?"

When the Evil Spirit heard the Fisherman's words, he answered, "There is no god but *the* God. Be happy, Fisherman!"

"Why should I be happy?" asked the Fisherman.

"Because," replied the Genie, "you must die a terrible death this very hour."

"You deserve heaven's abandonment for your good tidings!" cried the Fisherman. "For what reason should you kill me? What have I done to deserve death? I, who freed you from the jar, dragged you from the depths of the sea, and brought you up to dry land?"

"Ask me only in which way you will die, how I will slaughter you," said the Genie.

"What's my crime?" the Fisherman persisted. "Why such retribution?"

"Hear my story, Oh Fisherman!" cried the Genie.

The Fisherman swiftly answered, "Tell it, but tell it briefly. My heart is in my mouth."

And so, the Genie began his tale. "I am one of the heretical Genie," he explained. "I, along with the famous Sakhr al Jinni, sinned against Solomon, David's son. After this, the Prophet Solomon sent his minister, Asaf son of Barkhiya, to seize me. This minister bound me and took me against my will, bringing me to stand before the Prophet Solomon like a supplicant. When Solomon saw me, he appealed to Allah, and demanded that I embrace the True Faith and obey Allah's commands. I refused; and so he sent for this jar and imprisoned me in it, sealing it with lead and stamping it with the Most High Name. He ordered another spirit to carry me off, and cast me into the center of the ocean. I lived there for a hundred years, and during this time I said in my heart, 'I'll forever reward whoever releases me with the greatest of riches.' But an entire century passed, and when no one set me free, I began the second century saying, 'I'll reveal the secret treasures of the earth to whoever will release me.' Still, no one set me free, and soon four hundred years passed. Then I said, 'I'll grant three wishes to whoever will release me.' Yet again, no one set me free. Then I became angry, so furious, I said to myself, 'From now on, I'll kill whoever releases me, and I'll let him choose what type of death he will die.' And now, as you're the one who's released me, I give you the choice of your death."

The Fisherman, hearing the words of the Genie, exclaimed, "Oh Allah! How could it be that I didn't come to free him before this? Spare my life, Genie, and Allah will spare yours; don't kill me, and Allah will never send anyone to kill you!"

"There is no help for you. You must die," the Genie obstinately explained.

"Grant me a release from death, as a generous reward for having released you!" said the Fisherman.

"But it's because you released me that I *must* kill you," insisted the Genie.

"Oh chief of Genies," said the Fisherman. "I've done you something good, and you return my good action with evil!"

"No more of this talk," said the Genie, as he heard the Fisherman's words. "I must kill you!"

As the Genie spoke, the Fisherman said to himself, "This is a Genie, but I'm a man to whom Allah has given a cunning wit. So now, as he uses his malice to destroy me, I'll use my intelligence and cunning to stop *him*." He turned to the Genie and said, "Have you really resolved to kill me?"

"Of course."

"Even so," exclaimed the Fisherman, "if I ask you a question about a certain matter, will you swear by the Most Great Name, engraved on the seal-ring of Solomon, Son of David, that you'll answer it truthfully?"

The Genie trembled as he heard the Fisherman mention the Most Great Name. "Yes," he promised the Fisherman, though his mind grew troubled. "Yes, ask, but be brief."

The Fisherman said, "How did you fit into this bottle, which doesn't even look big enough to hold your hand, or even your foot? How could it have been big enough to contain all of you?"

"What!" replied the Genie. "You don't believe my whole body was in there?"

"No!" cried the Fisherman. "I'll never believe it until I see all of you inside of it, with my own eyes."

And then Shahrazad saw that dawn crept over the edge of the horizon, and so she stopped telling her story. But the next day, when the fourth night came, her sister said to her, "Please finish the story. None of us are sleepy." And so, Shahrazad resumed her storytelling. . . .

It has reached me, Oh worthy King, that after the Fisherman said to the Genie, "I'll never believe you, until I see all of you inside the jar, with my own eyes," then the Evil Spirit instantly shook, transforming himself into a vapor. The vapor condensed, slowly snaking into the jar, until all of him was buried inside of it. Quickly, the Fisherman grabbed the lead cap with the seal, stopping the mouth of the jar with it. He called to the Genie, "Now ask me which way *you* will die! I'll grant you your choice of death! By Allah, I'll throw you into the sea, and right here I'll build a lodge, to warn whoever comes here not to go fishing. I'll say: A Genie lives in these waters, one who grants the person who saves him their choice of death!"

As the Genie heard the Fisherman, he pressed against the jar, trying to escape—but he was prevented by Solomon's seal. He realized the Fisherman had outwitted him, and that his freedom was in peril. And so he became submissive and humble, crying out, "I was only joking with you!"

"That's a lie, you vile Genie!" exclaimed the Fisherman. "It's a mean, filthy lie from the meanest, filthiest Genie!" The Fisherman pushed the jar towards the sea, as the Genie screamed, "No! Stop, no!" and the Fisherman yelled, "Yes, yes!"

As they neared the water, the Genie softened his voice, saying smoothly, "What are you going to do to me, Fisherman?"

"I'm going to throw you back into the sea," the Fisherman answered. "You lived there for eighteen hundred years, and now you'll live there until Judgment Day. Didn't I tell you, if you spared my life, Allah would spare yours? And, if you killed me, Allah would kill you? Even though I did say that, you spurned my speech. You only wanted to treat me terribly. But Allah threw you into my hands, and I'm more cunning than you are!"

The Genie slyly said, "Open the bottle, and I'll bring you wealth."

"You lie," said the Fisherman. "For this is just like it was for the Vizier of King Yunan, and the Sage Duban."

"Who were the Vizier and this Sage Duban?" asked the Genie. "What was their story?"

And so the Fisherman began to tell him. . . .

The Tale of the Vizier and the Sage Duban

You should know, Genie, that in past years, a King named Yunan reigned over the cities of Persia in the Roman land. King Yunan was a powerful ruler, and quite wealthy. He had armies and guards and was allied with all nations. But he was afflicted with leprosy, and all the doctors in the world couldn't heal him. He drank potions, swallowed powders, and used lotions, but nothing would help; nobody could find him a cure.

Eventually, a mighty healer came to his city, called the Sage Duban. This aged wise man knew the works of the Greeks, Persians, Romans, Arabs, and Syrians; he had also studied astronomy and leechcraft. He knew everything, in theory and in practice, that could heal or harm a body. He knew the healing properties of every plant, grass, and herb, and he under-stood philosophy as well as medical science.

Now, this doctor Duban had only been in the city for a couple of days before he heard of the King's illness and suffering, with which Allah had af-flicted him. Duban heard how all the doctors and wise men had failed to heal this King. And so, he sat up all during the night, deep in thought, until dawn broke through and the sun again greeted the world. Then Duban put on his best clothes, and went to see King Yunan. He kissed the ground be-fore him, and prayed for the King's honor and life to prosper.

"Oh King," he said, "I've heard of your illness, and of how many doc-tors have failed to cure it. I can cure you, oh King, without having you drink another drop of medicine, and without having you use another drop of ointment!"

Surprised, King Yunan exclaimed, "But how will you do this? By Allah, if you do heal me, I'll give riches to you and all your sons. I'll give you lavish gifts—whatever you wish will be yours, and you'll be my closest compan-ion." Then the King put a robe of honor on him, asking him graciously, "Can you really cure me of this illness without drug or ointment?"

"Yes," replied the Sage. "I'll heal you without the pains of medicines."

The King marvelled, and said, "Doctor, when should we start, and where, and how soon? Can it be soon?"

"Of course," answered Duban. "The cure will begin tomorrow."

Duban then left the palace, and rented a house nearby, arranging his books, scrolls, medicines and aromatic roots there. Then he set to work, choosing the best drugs and ointments. He carved two long sticks, making them hollow inside, and each one tapering into a flat handle, that could hit a ball. The next day, he would present both of these to the King. And so, after greeting the King and kissing the floor before him, Duban invited him to come play polo on the parade grounds.

The King came, accompanied by his Emirs, Chamberlains, Viziers, and Lords. Before he sat down, the Sage Duban approached him, handing him the stick and saying, "Take this stick and grip it like this." He guided the King's fingers around the instrument. "Good," Duban continued, as the King rested his hands on the polo stick. Then he explained, "Next, lean over your horse and drive the ball with all your strength, until your palm is sweaty and your whole body perspires. Then the medicine will penetrate through your palm and into your body. When you're done playing and you feel the effects of the medicine, return to your palace and make an ablution in the Hamman-bath. Lay down to sleep, and then peace will come upon you, and you'll be healed."

So King Yunan took the polo stick from Sage Duban and grasped it firmly. Mounting his horse, he drove the ball before him, galloping after it until he reached it. Once he came close to it, he struck it again with all his strength, his palm gripping the polo stick the whole time. He didn't stop playing until his palm was sweaty, and his whole body perspiring, so that he imbibed the medicines from the wood. In this way, the Sage Duban knew that the drugs had penetrated his body, and so he told the King to return to the palace and enter the Hamman-bath immediately. So King Yunan returned right away, and ordered that the bath be prepared for him. His subjects hurriedly spread the carpets, and brought the King a change of clothes. The King entered the bath, and made the ablution thoroughly. When he finished, he put on his clothes, lay down, and slept.

Meanwhile, the Sage Duban returned to his house, slept until morning, and then went to the palace to talk with the King. The King admitted him, and the Sage bowed down before him. As Duban rose, the King came towards him, embracing him. King Yunan ordered that Duban be clothed in luxurious robes—for after the King left the Hamman-bath, all traces of leprosy had vanished from his body. His skin was clean as pure silver. The King had never rejoiced more.

Later in the day, the King entered his audience-hall and seated himself on his throne. Chamberlains and Grandees came to see him, bringing the Sage Duban with them. The King rose to greet him, and seated him by his side; he ordered platters of food to be brought, spilling over with the daintiest morsels. The two men did not leave each other's side all day. At night, the King gave Duban two thousand gold pieces, as well as gifts and robes of honor, and sent him home on his own horse.

After Sage Duban left, the King exclaimed, "This man healed my body without even any ointments! By Allah, surely there's no one else with this skill! I'm bound to honor such a man with rewards and distinction, and to make him my companion and friend until the end of my days." And so King Yunan passed the night in joy and gladness, for his body had been made whole, without a trace of this horrible malady.

In the morning, the King sat on his throne again, with the Lords of Estate standing around him, and the Emirs and Viziers sitting at his right and left. He requested that the Sage Duban come. After he was brought, Duban again kissed the ground before the King. King Yunan rose to greet him, sat by his side, ate with him, and wished him a long life. Moreover, he gave Sage Duban more gifts, rich robes, and did not stop speaking with him until night approached. Then the King offered him a salary of one thousand dinars and five robes of honor. Sage Duban returned to his own house, full of gratitude to the King.

As the next morning dawned, the King went to his throne, again surrounded by Lords and Nobles, Chamberlains and Ministers. Now, the King had a Vizier among his nobles, who was spiteful, envious, and devoid of all generosity. His physical features were just as unpleasant, extremely unattractive to anyone's sight. When this Vizier saw the King place the healer Duban near him and give him all these gifts, his jealous nature consumed him. The Vizier instantly plotted to do harm to this Sage.

So the Vizier came before the King, kissing the ground before him and saying, "Oh King of this age and of all time, you who have helped me grow into manhood, I have advice to offer you. I can't withhold this information from you, or else I'd be a coward. If you permit me, I'll tell it to you."

The King grew troubled as he listened to his minister's words. "What is this advice?" he asked.

"Oh glorious monarch," the Vizier said, "wise men have said, 'Whoever does not regard the end is not Fortune's friend.' Indeed, lately I've seen the King taking the wrong path, for he bestows lavish gifts on his enemy—on one whose purpose is to destroy your reign! He shows this man ultimate favor, honoring him with every honor, and making him an intimate friend. For this reason, I fear for the King's life."

The color drained from the King's face, and the Vizier could see how intensely troubled he was. "Whom do you suspect?" he breathed.

"Oh King!" exclaimed the Vizier. "If you've been asleep, you must wake up! I mean the healer, Sage Duban."

"Cursed minister!" cried the King. "Duban is a true friend. I've favored him above all men, because he cured me with something I held in my hand. He healed my leprosy, which baffled all doctors! There's no one else in the whole world like him—from the far east to the far west! How could you accuse such a man? Today, I even granted him a salary and a gift—every month, one thousand gold pieces. And even if I shared my kingdom with him, it wouldn't matter to me! I think that it's your envy and jealousy that accuse him, just like that which accused King Sinbad."

> *And Shahrazad again realized that dawn rose, and stopped her story. Dunyazad said, "Oh my sister, your tale is so beautiful, so pleasant!"*
>
> *Shahrazad replied, "But this is nothing compared with what I could tell you tomorrow night, if the King would spare my life."*
>
> *The King thought to himself, "By Allah, I won't kill her until I hear the rest of her tale, for she's a wonderful storyteller." So they all rested until dawn, and then the King went to his audience-hall, and the Vizier and the troops came in. The audience-hall thronged with people, and the King was busy giving orders, judgments, and appointments the rest of the day. Finally, after the long day, King Shahryar returned to his palace. And as this fifth night approached, Dunyazad said to her sister, "Shahrazad, if you're not sleepy, will you finish the story for us?" And so, she continued her tale. . . .*

The Tale of King Sinbad and His Falcon

It is said that there was once a King of Persia who was especially fond of hunting. The King had raised a falcon, of which he was so fond that he carried it all night on his fist. Whenever he went hunting, he took the bird with him. He constructed a tiny gold cup for it, and hung it around its neck so the falcon could drink whenever it wanted.

One day, as the King sat quietly in his palace, the high falconer of his household suddenly said to him, "Oh King, this day is perfect for hunting."

And so the King gave orders accordingly and set out with the falcon on his fist. The hunting group all went along happily, reaching a ravine where they laid a circle of nets to trap their game. Suddenly, a gazelle came into sight, and the King cried out, "I'll kill whoever lets that gazelle jump over their head and escape!"

The huntsmen narrowed the nets around the gazelle as she drew near the place where the King crouched. As she approached, she sat on her hindquarters, and crossed her forehand over her breast, as if she were about to kiss the earth before the King! The gazelle was so reverent that the King also inclined his own head towards her, bowing in acknowledgement of her unique character. But just as he did, she bounced high over his head, vanishing into the forest.

The King's troops winked and pointed at him. Troubled, he turned to his Vizier. "What are my men saying?" he asked.

The Vizier answered, "They remind you that you did proclaim that any man who let the gazelle escape by jumping over his head should be put to death."

"Now, by the life of my head!" exclaimed the King. "I'll chase that gazelle until I bring her back!" So he set off, galloping on the gazelle's trail and tracking her until he reached the rambling foothills of a mountain chain, where he glimpsed her racing into a cave. The King released the falcon, watching it swoop down towards the gazelle and drive its talons into her eyes, bewildering and blinding her. Then the King drew his club, killing her with one blow. He dismounted, cut the gazelle's throat, and flayed the body, hanging it on the pommel of his saddle.

Now it reached the hottest part of the day, the time for afternoon siesta. No water could be found anywhere around the parched, dry land where the King stood. The King and his horse both grew extremely thirsty, and so he walked around searching for something to drink, until he found a tree whose branches dripped with a water so golden and promising it looked like melted butter. So the King, who wore a leather glove to protect his skin from poison, took the cup from the falcon's neck and filled it with some of the water. But as he set the cup before the falcon, the bird struck it with its talons, spilling it. Again, the King filled the cup with some water, thinking that the falcon must surely be thirsty; but a second time, the falcon upset the cup. Then the King became angry; he filled the cup again and offered it to the horse, instead. But for a third time, the falcon overturned the cup!

"By Allah, you're a horrible, unlucky bird!" cried the King. "You're keeping everyone from drinking, including yourself." He angrily struck the falcon with his sword, cutting off its wing. But the falcon raised his head, motioning for the King to look at the tree more closely.

The King lifted his eyebrows accordingly, and caught sight of a brood of vipers, whose poison-drops he had mistaken for water. As soon as he saw this, he repented having chopped off the falcon's wing. Mounting his horse, he moved on with the dead gazelle until he reached his camp, his starting-place. He threw the gazelle's body to the cook. "Take it, and broil it," he told him, as he sat down in his chair. He still carried the wounded falcon on his fist. But suddenly, the bird gasped, dying, and the King cried out in sorrow and remorse for having slain the very falcon that saved his life.

"Now this is what happened to King Sinbad; and I am certain, Vizier," said the King, "that if I were to do as you wish to Sage Duban, I should repent even more than the man who killed his parrot."

"And what happened to him?" asked the Vizier.

And so the King began to tell. . . .

The Tale of the Husband and the Parrot

Once, a certain merchant had a beautiful, graceful, extraordinarily pretty wife. He was so suspicious and jealous of her that he wouldn't even leave the house to go on business trips. But one day, a certain business situation compelled him to leave her. Before going away, he went to the bird market, and bought a parrot for one hundred gold pieces. He took the parrot to his house to act as his wife's chaperon, expecting that when he returned, the bird would tell him everything that happened while he was away. The parrot, thought the husband, was cunning and never forgot what he saw or heard.

Now, this beautiful wife had fallen in love with a young Turkish man, who visited her as soon as her husband left. She gave him food all day, and lay in bed with him all night. When her husband came home, he asked for the parrot, and questioned it concerning his wife's behavior while he'd been away in foreign countries.

"Your wife had a male friend, who spent every night here with her during your absence," the parrot told him.

In a violent rage, the husband raced toward his wife, beating her until she nearly died. The woman suspected that one of the slave-girls had tattled to her husband, so she called them all together, to interrogate them. All of them swore they had kept her secret—but that the parrot had not. "We heard him with our own ears," the girls told her.

And so, the next night, the wife commanded one of the girls to grind a hand-mill underneath the parrot's cage. She ordered another girl to sprinkle water through the cage's roof, and a third girl to run around the cage, flashing a bright steel mirror all during the night.

The next morning, when the husband returned home after spending the night with friends, he began to talk with the parrot, asking what had happened while he was away.

"Pardon me, oh master," said the bird, "I couldn't see or hear anything last night, because of all that terrible lightning and thunder crashing through the murky night."

"But it's the middle of July!" the master cried, surprised. "There aren't any thunderstorms now."

"By Allah," declared the bird, "I saw it with my own eyes, just as I've told you."

The husband became extremely angry, not suspecting his wife's ploy. Instead, he started to think that he'd wrongly accused his wife. So he pulled the parrot from his cage, thrusting it upon the ground so furiously that he killed it on the spot.

Several days later, one of the slave-girls told him the whole story, but he still wouldn't believe it until he saw the young Turk, his wife's lover, coming out of her bedroom. As the Turk walked out, the husband drew his sword, killing him with a blow on the back of his neck. His wife rushed out of her room, and he instantly murdered her in the same way. The two of them, laden with mortal sin, went straight to the Eternal Fires of Hell.

So the merchant knew that the parrot had told him the truth all along. Though he mourned the bird, all his grief could not bring the parrot back.

The Vizier, hearing these words of King Yunan, said, "Oh Monarch, high in dignity, you must realize that I'm not contriving this man's execution. No, I'm only saying all this to be of service to you, for I do not think that if you accept my advice, you'll be saved—but if you reject it, you'll be destroyed just like that young Prince who was betrayed by the treacherous Vizier."

"What happened to them?" inquired the King.

And so, the minister began. . . .

The Tale of the Prince and the Ogress

Once there was a King whose son enjoyed hunting so much that the King ordered one of his Viziers to accompany his son wherever he went. One day, the Prince and the Vizier went hunting, and as they paced through the fields together, a gigantic wild beast came in sight.

"Let's kill that beast!" cried the Vizier.

The Prince raced after the animal, soon disappearing out of everyone's sight. The beast disappeared from the Prince's own sight too, vanishing into the woods. The Prince, now lost in the forest, couldn't find his way out. He didn't even know which way to turn. Suddenly, a beautiful maiden appeared out of nowhere, her face streaming with tears.

"Who are you?" asked the Prince.

"I'm the daughter of a King among the Kings of the Hind," she said. "I was travelling with a caravan in the desert, when drowsiness suddenly spread through my body. As I fell asleep, I inadvertently fell from my horse. Now I can't find any of my people, and I'm so confused!"

The Prince pitied this unhappy girl, and helped her onto his horse. They travelled until they passed a ruined temple, where the maiden said, "Oh master, I need to obey a call of nature." So the Prince set her down, but she took so long that he thought she was wasting time. He crept towards her direction, and saw her—but she was transformed! She was not a fair damsel, but Ghulah, the wicked Ogress, telling her brood, "Oh my children, today I've got a fine, fat youth for dinner!"

"Bring him to us, mother!" they cried. "We can't wait to fill our stomachs with him!"

The Prince heard this whole conversation, and was sure he would die. All the muscles in his body quivered with fear. He turned around and was about to run, when Ghulah came out, seeing him trembling and afraid. "Why are you scared?" she asked.

"I've discovered a terrible enemy, whom I greatly fear," he replied.

"Aren't you a King's son?" asked the Ogress.

"I am."

"Then why don't you give him some money?" suggested Ghulah. "That would satisfy him."

"This enemy doesn't want my money," said the Prince, "only my life. That's why I dread him so much."

"If you're that distressed," said Ghulah, "ask Allah for protection. Surely Allah would protect you from the evils of this enemy."

So the Prince raised his eyes toward the heavens, calling, "Oh God who helps those in need—Oh God who dispels distress! Let me triumph over my enemy, and let him leave me. Protect me with your might, for you are strong above all else!"

When Ghulah heard this earnest prayer, she turned away from him, and let the Prince leave. The Prince then returned home to his father, and told him how the Vizier had left him lost in the woods while they were on the hunt. So the King summoned the Vizier, and executed him on the spot.

"Similarly, King," spoke the Vizier, "if you continue to trust this doctor, you'll die the worst sort of death. This Sage Duban that you've so admired and become intimate with, he'll bring about your destruction! You've seen how he healed your disease simply by something you grasped in your hand. He'll destroy you with something held in the same manner."

"You've spoken the truth, my Vizier," answered King Yunan thoughtfully. "It may indeed be as you've said. Perhaps this sage has come as a spy, figuring out the best way to kill me. For assuredly, if he cured me by something held in my hand, he can kill me by something given to me to smell. Vizier, what should I do with him?"

"Summon him here this very instant," replied the Vizier. "When he comes, have him beheaded; in this way, you'll be rid of him before he can harm you any more. Deceive him before he can deceive you!"

"You've again spoken the truth, Vizier," responded the King. He sent for the Sage Duban, who came joyfully to him, for he didn't know what the

King intended. Duban praised and thanked the King for his compassion and generosity.

"Do you know why I've summoned you?" replied the King, coldly.

"Only Allah knows," said the Sage.

"I summoned you so that I could take your life, and destroy you," the King told him.

"Oh King," said Sage Duban wonderingly, his breath gasping in astonishment. "Why would you kill me? What harm have I done to you?"

"Men tell me that you're a spy, sent here to murder me," explained the King. "But I'll kill you before you kill me." He called to his executioner and said, "Behead this traitor and deliver us from his evil practices."

"If you spare my life, Allah will spare yours," Sage Duban replied. "If you don't kill me, Allah won't kill you."

The Fisherman paused in his story, and glanced towards the bottled Genie. "Yes, Genie, he repeated these very words that I said to you. You wouldn't let me go, you were so bent on killing me. Likewise, King Yunan did the same. . . ."

King Yunan only replied to Duban, "I won't be safe unless I kill you. For just as you healed me by something in my hand, you could kill me by something you give me to smell or to drink."

"You're returning evil for good," answered the Sage. "This is your reward?"

The King replied, "Nothing can help you now. You must die, without delay."

Now, when Sage Duban was certain that the King would kill him right away, he wept and regretted all the good he had done to such a bad man. The executioner stepped forward, tied a blindfold over the Sage Duban's eyes, and drew his sword. Turning to the King, he said, "Do I have your permission?"

Sage Duban wept and cried, "Spare me, that Allah might spare your own life. Don't kill me, or Allah will kill you! Is this the reward I deserve from you? It's nothing but crocodile-boon."

"What's this tale of the crocodile-boon?" inquired the King.

"It's impossible for me to tell it in this state right now," explained the doctor Duban. "May Allah bless you and spare your life if you spare mine."

He wept, tears streaming down his face until one of the King's favorite men stood up and said, "Oh King! Kill me, and not this Sage, for we've never seen him harm you. We've never seen him do anything but heal you from a disease that baffled every other scientist and doctor here."

"You don't know why I'm really putting him to death," explained the King. "If I spare his life, I'm condemning myself to his means of death. For the one who healed me of such a terrifying illness by something I held in my hand can surely kill me by something he holds to my nose. He may be killing me for a certain price. I fear that he might even be a spy, whose only purpose was to come here and plot my destruction. So there's no way out; he must die. Only then can I be sure that my own life is safe."

Again, Sage Duban cried, "Spare me and Allah will spare you! Kill me, and Allah will kill you." But this was all in vain.

"Now, Genie," interjected the Fisherman. "When the doctor Duban knew for certain that the King would kill him, he anxiously began to reason to him. . . ."

"Oh King," said Sage Duban. "If there is no help for me, if I indeed must die, let me just go to my house, release myself from my obligations, and tell my friends and neighbors where to bury me and how to distribute my medical books. Among these books there is one, extremely rare, which I would like to give you to keep as a treasure in your vaults."

"What's in this book?" asked the King.

"Things beyond your wildest dreams," said the Sage. "Astonishing secrets and mysteries—the best of which is, that after you behead me, you can open this book to the third page and read three lines from it, and then my head will speak to you and answer any question you wish."

The King shivered as Duban spoke, and delighted at such a novelty, exclaimed, "Oh Sage, do you really think that your head will speak to me after I cut it off?"

"Yes, King!" cried Duban.

"This is indeed a strange matter," mused the King. And so he sent Sage Duban, closely guarded, to his house; and there Duban settled all of his obligations. The next day, he went to the King's audience-hall, where Emirs and Viziers, Chamberlains and Nabobs, Grandees and Lords of Estate were gathered together, their robes making the room as colorful as a flower garden.

Sage Duban came up and stood before the King, holding a worn old volume of medical practices, and a little tin full of something resembling kohl, a dark powder for the eyes. He sat down, and requested a tray; then he poured the strange black powder onto it, spreading it around. "Oh King," he said, "take this book, but don't open it until my head falls; then, set my head on this tray, press it down upon the powder, and the blood will stop flowing. That is your cue to open the book."

So the King took the book and gave the sign to the executioner. The swordsman rose, striking off the doctor's head, placing it on the middle of the tray, and pressing it down on the powder. The blood stopped flowing, and Sage Duban opened his eyes, saying, "Now, oh King, open the book!"

The King opened the book, finding the pages stuck together; so he put his fingers to his mouth, moistening them so as to turn over the pages. He flipped through six pages, but found nothing written on them. "Oh doctor, there's no writing here!" said King Yunan.

"Turn over a few more pages," replied Duban faintly. And so, the King moistened his fingers again and turned over a few more pages in the same way. But the book was poisoned; and quickly, the deadly venom penetrated the King's body. He convulsed, crying out, "The poison has done its work!"

Duban's head ceased to speak as the King, too, rolled over dead.

"Now I would have you know, Genie," spoke the Fisherman, "that if the King Yunan had spared the Sage Duban, Allah would have spared him; but he refused to do so, and so Allah slew him. If you had spared me, Genie," said the Fisherman, "Allah would have spared you, too."

Now Shahrazad saw the dim lights of dawn creeping into the room once more, and so she stopped her story. But Dunyazad again exclaimed, "Oh my sister, your tale is so beautiful, so pleasant!"

And again, Shahrazad responded, "But that was nothing compared to what I could tell you tomorrow night, if the King spares my life."

The King thought to himself, as he had during the past nights, "By Allah, I won't kill her until I hear the rest of her story, for it's truly wonderful!" And so they all slept until morning, when the King went to his audience-hall crowded with Viziers and troops. Again, the King gave orders and appointments and judgements all day long. When his duties were finally done, King Shahryar went back to his palace. The sixth night fell, and Dunyazad told Shahrazad, "Please finish your story!"

"I will, if the King lets me," she replied.

"Go on with your tale," said the King. And so, she continued. . . .

It has reached me, Oh worthy King, that after the Fisherman told the Genie, "If you had spared my life, I would have spared yours—but you were so intent on killing me, I'm going to throw your jar into the sea," then the Genie shouted, "By Allah, Fisherman, don't do it! Spare me, and pardon my past actions. Return my tyrannical deeds with generous ones—for it's said, 'If one returns good for evil, then the evildoer will stop his evil deeds.' Don't deal with me as Umamah did to Atikah."

"What's their story?" asked the Fisherman.

"I don't have time for story-telling in this prison," said the Genie. "But if you set me free, I'll tell you my tale."

"Do be quiet," snapped the Fisherman. "There's no help left for you. I'm going to throw you so far into the sea that you'll never escape. When I humbled myself before you, weeping, you still only wanted to kill me. I'd never harmed you, never done any evil act against you. I only did you good when I released you from that jar. But now I know your truly evil nature; and so when I cast you back into the sea, I'll warn whoever catches you of what happened to me, and tell him to cast you back into the water again. You'll be trapped in this ocean until the End of Time!"

"No, set me free!" cried the Genie. "This is a perfect time to display your generosity. I swear to you, I'll never hurt you again in any way. In fact, I'll even help put an end to your poverty!"

The Fisherman considered the Genie's words, and accepted his promise—with the conditions that the Genie would never harm him, and would also go into his service, making him wealthy. After making the Genie swear a solemn oath by Allah the Most High, the Fisherman opened the lead seal to the jar. The pillar of smoke again snaked out from it, spiraling into the air. When all the smoke had trickled out, it condensed, once more forming the hideous presence of the Genie—who immediately kicked the bottle and sent it flying into the sea.

The Fisherman piddled in his pants as he saw how the Genie treated the bottle, certain that his own death would come next. "This does not seem to bode well for me," he murmured. But then he strengthened himself, shouting to the Genie, "Allah has said, keep your promises, for the performance of these things shall matter when you are judged! You've made a vow to me. You've sworn an oath not to deceive me, and if you don't follow this oath, then Allah will deceive you. For truly, He is a jealous God, who may give respite to sinners, but He doesn't let them ever actually escape. I say to you just as the Sage Duban said to King Yunan, 'Spare me so that Allah will spare you!'"

The Genie burst into laughter and stalked away, calling to the Fisherman, "Follow me." So the Fisherman followed at a safe distance, in case he needed to escape along the way. The Genie led him past the suburbs of the city, and deep into the wilderness. As they hiked through the uncultivated lands, they came to a still, cool mountain lake. Its steep, rocky banks sloped sharply downward, and tufts of willowy grass poked out from the calm, crystal pool. The Genie waded into the middle of its waters, again calling to the Fisherman, "Follow me."

As the Fisherman and the Genie both stood in the middle of the lake, the Genie told the Fisherman to cast his net and catch some fish. As the Fisherman looked into the water, astonishment rushed over him, for he saw the pond spilling over with multi-colored fish—white, red, blue, and yellow. He cast his net, and as he hauled it in he saw that it had trapped four fish, one of each color. He rejoiced when he saw these beautiful creatures, and became even happier as the Genie told him, "Carry these fish to the King and set them in his presence. When he sees them, he'll give you enough riches to make you a wealthy man. Now, please excuse me, for since I've lain in the sea for eighteen hundred years, I don't known any other way of helping you right now. Oh, but remember to only fish here once a day." The Genie departed, calling to the Fisherman, "May Allah be with you." Then the Genie struck the earth with one foot, cleaving the earth into two parts, so that it swallowed him whole.

The Fisherman marvelled at all that had happened with the Genie, and then he gathered the fish and walked back towards the city. As soon as he reached his home, he filled an earthen bowl with water and threw the struggling, writhing fish into it. He placed the bowl on his head, carrying it to the King's palace, just as the Genie had instructed him to do. Once the King welcomed him, the Fisherman laid the fish before the King.

As soon as the King saw these creatures, amazement and wonder swept over him, for he'd never seen any fish like these before. "Give these fish to the slave-girl, and have her cook them for me," he ordered. Now, the slave-girl who fixed the fish had been sent to the King only three days earlier, and had not learned much about cooking, or about the King's favorite dishes. As the Vizier handed these fish to her, he instructed her to fry them. Then he gently mentioned to her, "This dish is apparently a rare one, a present to the King. Hopefully he'll approve of your delicate handiwork and savory cooking."

After the Vizier had carefully prompted her, he returned to the King, who commanded the Vizier to give four hundred dinars to the Fisherman. After the Fisherman received these he ran home, stumbling and falling in excitement, imagining that the whole thing must be a dream. But it was all true, and as he burst indoors he rushed to his wife, full of joy since he'd thought he wouldn't see her again. Then he bought his family anything they wanted.

Meanwhile, the King's cook, the slave-girl, cleaned and fried the fish, basting them with oil. As she flipped them over in their pan, to baste their other side, the kitchen walls split open! A slender, gracefully beautiful young woman appeared from the rift in the wall, her eyes lined with heavy, black kohl. Large hoops dangled from her ears, and bracelets circled her wrists. Her blue, silk dress draped itself around her whole body, and her kerchief was edged with blue tassels. Thick rings, studded with expensive gems, rested on each finger; and in her hand, she held a long rattan cane, which she thrust into the frying pan saying, "Oh fish! Oh fish! Are you keeping your promise?"

The slave-girl fainted as she saw this apparition. The beautiful woman repeated her words several times, and finally the fish raised their heads from the pan, answering, "Yes! Yes!" And so the woman left the kitchen as she had entered, disappearing into the walls and letting them close in upon her. When the young girl woke up, she discovered the four fish charred black as charcoal, each one yelling, "His staff broke in his first bout," and so she immediately fainted again.

The Vizier came to gather the plate of fish, and seeing the young cook lying on the ground, nudged her with his foot and said, "Bring the fish to the King!"

She woke once again from her daze, weeping and informing the Vizier of all that had happened. Astonished, the Vizier exclaimed, "This is indeed a very strange matter." So he sent for the Fisherman, telling him, "You must catch four fish exactly like those you brought before." So the Fisherman returned to the lake the next day, cast his net, and brought up four fish exactly like the others. He gave them to the Vizier, who brought them to the cooking-girl, saying, "Fry these fish right here in my presence, so that I can see this apparition for myself."

So the girl rose and cleaned the fish, and set them in a frying pan over the fire. Only minutes later, the walls cleaved open and the woman appeared. Again, she shoved her cane into the pan, crying out, "Oh fish! Have you really kept your promise?"

"Yes! Yes!" replied the fish, lifting their heads from the pan.

And Shahrazad realized that dawn had risen, and so she stopped her story until the seventh night; then she continued. . . .

It has reached me, O worthy King, that when these fish spoke, and the woman upset the frying pan with her rod and disappeared into the wall, the Vizier cried out, "This matter can't be kept secret from the King."

So the Vizier went and told the King what had happened, and the King replied, "I must see this with my own eyes." So he sent for the Fisherman, and commanded him to bring four more fish exactly like the first. He also sent three men with the Fisherman, as witnesses. The Fisherman immediately brought the fish, and the King repaid him with four hundred gold pieces. Then the King turned to the Vizier and ordered, "Fry these fish right here before me!"

"To hear is to obey," the minister replied, cleaning the fish and throwing them into the frying pan. Instantly, the walls split in half, and a black slave burst forth, carrying a green branch in each hand.

"Oh fish," he intoned, his terrifying voice rising through the palace, "Have you indeed kept your ancient pledge?"

"Yes! Yes!" cried the fish, lifting their heads from the frying pan. Then the man turned over the pan, and disappeared once more into the walls.

As he vanished, the King inspected the fish, finding them charred black as charcoal. Bewildered, he told the Vizier, "Truly, this matter can't be kept a secret any longer. Surely there's something marvelous connected to these fish." He turned to the Fisherman, demanding, "Where did these fish come from?"

"From a nearby mountain lake," he replied.

"How many day's journey from here?"

"Oh King, our Lord, only about half-an-hour's walk," answered the Fisherman.

Confused about the fish, and desperately hoping to unravel this mystery, the King ordered his troops to journey to the lake immediately. The Fisherman guided them, cursing the Genie under his breath. He led the troops over the mountain and through the desert valley, none of which the King's men had ever seen in their lives. The King and his troops rode in amazement, marvelling at the wildly beautiful, uncultivated nature surrounding them. Finally they reached the lake and its multi-colored fish of blue, red, yellow, and white. The King stood rooted to one spot near the edge of the water, asking everyone nearby, "Has anybody here ever seen this lake before?"

"Never, King," each one replied. Even the oldest men there had never heard of such a lake.

"Then, by Allah," declared the King, "I'm not going to return to my palace or sit on my throne until I learn the truth about the fish and this lake." So he ordered all his troops to dismount, and to set up camp near the mountains. After this, he summoned the Vizier, whom he regarded as an experienced, wise, and perceptive minister. "I must tell you about something," the King hurriedly informed him. "My heart is telling me to go forth alone tonight, to seek and uncover the mystery of this lake and its fish. You must help me by sitting at my tent-door and telling all the Emirs and Nabobs and Chamberlains that 'the King is ill, and you must not come in.' Be careful not to let anyone else know my plan."

The Vizier couldn't oppose the King, and so the King proceeded to change his clothes, sling his sword over his shoulder, and hike up a twisting mountain path, out of sight. The King hiked until dawn, and then well into the next day, despite the blazing heat. After only a short rest, he continued hiking through the second night until dawn, when he glimpsed a black point far in the distance. "Maybe there's somebody here who can tell me about the lake and the fish," the King said happily.

As he came closer to the dark object, he realized it was a stone palace, plated with iron. One side of the gate lay open, though the other was shut. The King's spirits rose as he stood before the gate, lightly rapping to be let inside. He knocked twice, then three times, and then a fourth time quite loudly, but nobody seemed to be home. "It must be empty," he thought to himself, and so he mustered up the courage to walk through the gates and into the main hall. "Hello, people of the palace," he called, his voice echoing through the room. "I'm a stranger, a traveller, in need of food. Is anybody here?" He repeated his words, but there was still no response. So he decided to explore the palace, and stalked through the hallways to its central rooms. Even there, he found no one. Still, even though nobody was present, the rooms were lavishly furnished with tapestries, and decorated with silken materials patterned with gold stars. In the middle of these rooms a spacious courtyard was laid out, with four open halls on each side. Canopies shaded the courtyard, and in the center stood a flowing fountain with four reddish-gold figures of lions. The water rushing from the fountain poured as clear as pearls, glittering like translucent gems. Birds flew freely around the palace, held inside by a net of golden wire. Really, thought the King, there was everything imaginable in this palace but human beings.

The King grew amazed at all this, but also became disappointed that there was nobody to explain the mystery of the lake and the fish—or to reveal the mystery of the palace itself. He sat between the palace doors, deep in thought, when he suddenly heard a mournful voice murmuring through the walls. The King sprang to his feet, following the sound to one chamber. Lifting the curtain over its door, he found a handsome young man there, sitting on a couch about three feet off the ground. His rosy cheeks shone brightly, and his forehead was white as a flower; on one cheek rested a tiny grey mole.

Rejoicing, the King greeted him, but the young man remained seated on his silken caftan, lined with Egyptian gold. The King could see that beneath his gem-studded crown, the young man's face was lined with sorrow.

The man returned the King's salute, and said, "Oh my lord, your dignity demands that I rise to greet you, and I beg your pardon for not doing this."

"Certainly you have my pardon," replied the King. "Think of me as a guest who's here on a special mission. Please, tell me about this mysterious mountain lake and the fish there, and also about this lonely palace and why you're so unhappy."

When the young man heard the King's words, he wept so much his whole body became drenched with tears. This astounded the King, and he asked, "Why do you weep like this, young man?"

"How could I not weep, when I'm in this situation!" cried the man. Then he lifted the skirts of his garment, showing the King that his lower body, from his navel to his feet, had turned into stone, while the rest of his body remained human flesh. This moved the King to compassion, and he grieved for the lonely boy. "You heap sorrow upon my sorrow," the King explained. "I was going to ask you only about the mystery of the fish, but now I'm as interested in your story as in theirs." The King focused on the young man. "There is no majesty, no might, except Allah, the glorious and the great! Now, tell me your whole story."

"Lend me your ears, your sight, and your intuition," said the boy.

"All are at your service," replied the King.

"My situation is almost beyond imagination," began the young man. "It's as amazing as the fish themselves. I wish it could be engraved somewhere, warning all who see it."

"Why is that?" inquired the King.

And so the young man began to tell. . . .

The Tale of the Enchanted Prince

My lord, you should know that my father was King Mahmud, ruler of this city and Lord of the Black Islands, as well as the owner of these four mountains. He ruled for seventy years before his death, and then I was appointed Sultan in his place. I married my cousin, the daughter of my paternal uncle; and her love for me was so abounding that she wouldn't eat or drink while I was away. We lived together for five years, until one day when she went to the Hamman-bath. I'd told the cook to prepare dinner for us, and then I came to lie on this bed and sleep, asking two servants to fan me as I waited for my wife to return. But I was restless and troubled because of her absence, and couldn't sleep. Even though my eyes were closed, my thoughts raced wildly in my head and kept me awake.

Suddenly, I heard the slave-girl fanning my head say to the other one, "Our poor master really must be miserable! His youth is wasted, and I pity that our mistress has betrayed him, that cursed whore!"

"Yes, indeed," the other replied. "May Allah curse all faithless, adulterous women. Our handsome, worthy master deserves someone better than this harlot who sleeps with other men every single night."

"Why is our master so foolish?" the first girl wondered. "I wish he would question her."

"Our master isn't foolish, don't say such a thing!" reprimanded the other girl. "He doesn't know what she's doing, so he doesn't have a choice whether to question her or not. What's more, she drugs his drink every night before he sleeps, so that he won't know where she goes or what she does. Only *we* know that after giving him that drugged wine, she slips into her richest clothes, puts on perfume, and leaves until daybreak. When she comes back, she burns a poultice under his nose, so that he'll finally wake up from that deathlike sleep."

Now, when I heard the slave-girls' words, I fumed with rage, anxiously waiting for night to fall. I thought it would never come. When my wife came home from the baths, we had dinner and drank some wine, as was our habit. She called for the particular wine I used to drink before sleeping, and poured me a cup. But instead of drinking it, that night I poured the contents down my shirt. I feigned sleep, waiting. Eventually she cried, "Sleep out the night, and never wake up! By Allah, I despise you and I loathe your whole body. My soul is disgusted every time I sleep with you, and I can't wait for the day when Allah ends your life!" Then she rose, putting on her prettiest dress, and perfume, and slinging my sword over her shoulder. Opening the palace gates, she went on her evil way.

I rose, following her out of the palace, and walking behind her as she threaded through the streets until she came to the city gate. There, she spoke some words I couldn't understand, and the padlocks to the gates dropped by themselves, as if they were broken. The gates actually swung open before her! I pursued her without her noticing, finally stopping when she reached the garbage-heaps. There was a reed fence built there around a mud-brick, round-roofed hut. As she entered the hut's door, I climbed on its roof to spy inside. And there I saw my wife, gone inside to an ugly black slave! He was also a leper and a paralytic, lying upon some matted, rotting sugar-cane and wrapped in tattered, ragged blankets. My wife kissed the ground before him, and he raised his head to see her saying, "Woe to you! Why have you been gone all this time? Some friends were here with me for a while, drinking wine with their young ladies, but I couldn't drink, because you were gone."

"Oh, my lord," she murmured. "My heart's love, don't you know that I'm married to my cousin, whose very looks I hate? I even despise my own self when I'm near him. If I wasn't afraid for your sake, I wouldn't let a single night pass before I turned this whole city into rubble—so that the ravens would croak, the owls hoot, and the jackals and wolves run around wildly! Indeed, I'd remove every stone of the city and throw it behind Mt. Caucasus!"

"You're lying, damn you!" cried the slave. "Now I'll swear an oath, by the honor of black men—and don't think our manliness is like the poor manliness of white men—that from this day forth, if you stay away from me for this length of time again, I'll reject you completely. I won't glue my body to yours again! Do you think you can play fast and loose with us, that we satisfy your dirty lusts, you stinking bitch? Vilest of the vile whites!"

As I heard his words, and saw with my own eyes what was happening between them, everything around me darkened, and my soul no longer knew where it was. My wife stood humbly before the slave, weeping and begging, "Oh my beloved, fruit of my heart, there is nobody who makes me happy like you. If you reject me, who will love me?" She didn't stop crying until he accepted her once more. When they reconciled, she became joyful again, slipping off her clothes and asking, "Oh my master, what is there for your handmaiden to eat?"

"Uncover that pot," he grumbled, "and at the bottom, you'll find some broiled bones of the rats we dined on. Pick at them, and then go to the slop-pot, where you'll find some leftover beer that you can drink."

So she ate and drank this, and washed her hands. Then she lay down beside the slave, stripping naked and creeping inside his foul, dirty blankets and rags. When I saw my wife, my cousin, the daughter of my uncle do this deed, I lost all my senses. Climbing down from the roof, I entered the hut and grabbed the sword she'd taken with her. I drew it, determined to kill both of them. I struck the slave's neck first, and thinking he'd died. . . .

> *And Shahrazad saw that dawn crept into the room, and stopped her tale; on the eighth night, she continued. . . .*

It has reached me, Oh worthy King, that the young enchanted Prince said to the King: When I struck the slave, intending to chop off his head, I thought I'd killed him—for he'd uttered a loud, hissing groan. But really, I'd only cut his flesh and two arteries! His moans woke up my wife, so I sheathed the sword and hurried back inside the city. Entering the palace, I slept in my bed until morning. Later, my wife woke me up, and I saw that she'd cut off all her hair, and put on mourning garments.

"Oh son of my uncle," she said to me. "Don't blame me for this, for I've just heard that my mother is dead, my father's been killed in a holy war, one of my brothers has lost his life due to snake-sting, and another by falling off a cliff. I can do nothing but mourn for them."

When I heard her words, I didn't reproach her, but only said, "Do as you must. I won't stop you."

She continued grieving, weeping, and wailing for one whole year, and when this was done, she said to me, "I'd like to build a tomb with a cupola in your palace, which I'll set apart for mourning, and name the House of Lamentations."

"Do as you must," I told her again.

So she built this tomb where she could mourn, with a dome in its center, over the place where the body should rest. She carried the slave here, housing him. But due to his wound, he was exceedingly weak, and unable to make love to her. He could only drink wine, and since the day of his injury he hadn't spoken a single word. But he continued to live, because his appointed hour of death had not yet come. My wife tended to him every day, bringing him wines and strong soups, and weeping over him incessantly. She kept doing this for well over one more year. I patiently accepted it, not paying any attention to her.

However, one I day I approached her without her noticing, and I found her crying and slapping her face, hysterically shrieking, "Why are you absent from me, my heart's delight? Speak to me, my life! Talk to me, my love!"

When she paused in her tears and her weeping, I told her, "My cousin, stop this mourning. Your grief isn't going to change anything."

"Don't stop me," she demanded. "I have to do this, and if you stop me, I'll kill myself!"

So I kept my peace and let her go her own way, and she cried and indulged her affliction for a third year. At the end of this third year, I grew incredibly tired of all this mourning. One day—after already being annoyed and frustrated at something else—I passed near the tomb, hearing my wife say, "Oh my lord, I never hear you speak a single word to me! Why don't you answer me, my master?"

Rage tumbled through my body as I heard her, and I shrieked, "How long must this sorrow of yours last?"

When she heard my words, she sprang to her feet, screaming, "You wretched, foul cur! This is all your fault! You've wounded my heart's darling one, and wasted his youth. You've made him lie here for three years! He's lying here more dead than alive because of you! It's because of you that I've grieved all this time!"

"Foul harlot! Filthiest whore, hired to sleep with slaves!" I cried, my body rising with wrathful anger. "Yes, indeed, I'm the one who did this good deed to your heart's darling!" And without speaking another word, I snatched my sword, drawing it to cut her down.

But she laughed as I drew the blade, scornfully shouting, "Heel, you hound! Oh, yes, I grieve for the past that can't ever come back to life, and for the fact that nobody can raise the dead. But now Allah has placed into my hands the person who did this vile thing—this action that burned my heart with an undying fire, with a flame that will never be quenched!" She stood up, pronouncing some unintelligible words. Then she said, "By virtue of my magic you'll become half stone, half man."

And so I became what you see now: unable to rise or sit, neither dead nor alive. Moreover, she enchanted the whole city, every street and field, using her sorcery to transform the four islands into four mountains around the lake about which you've asked me. The citizens, who were of four different faiths—Muslim, Christian, Jewish, and Magian—she transformed into fish: Muslims as white fish; Christians as blue; Jews as yellow; and Magians as red. And every day she tortures me with one hundred lashes, each one cutting me so deeply it draws floods of blood, and scars my skin. Then she covers my upper body with a haircloth, and throws these robes over it.

As the Prince finished his story, shedding some tears, the King was moved by his situation. He turned toward the unfortunate Prince, saying,

"You've removed one of my concerns, only to add another. Tell me, where is she? And where's the mausoleum with this wounded slave?"

"The slave's under that dome there," the Prince told him. "And my wife, she's sitting in that room across from the door. Every day at sunrise she comes in here. First she strips me naked, and then she beats me one hundred times with a leather whip. I shriek, I cry, but my body won't let me run away from her. After she finishes tormenting me she visits the slave, bringing him wine and boiled meat. Early tomorrow morning she'll be here."

"By Allah, young Prince," the King proclaimed, "I'll undoubtedly come then, and do you a good deed that the world won't ever forget. It'll be so daring, people will write about it long after I'm dead and gone." Then the King sat beside the young Prince, talking with him until night fell.

The King slept until the first lights of dawn began to gleam in the horizon. He hurriedly awakened, threw on his shirt and unsheathed his sword, hastening to the palace where the slave lay. He slipped quickly past the lighted candles and lamps, and followed scents of incense and ointments that led him to the slave. As the woman's lover lay in the tomb, the King struck him dead with one blow. Then he slung him over his shoulder, carrying him to a well in the palace and tossing him to the bottom. The King then moved back towards the tomb, putting on the slave's clothes and lying down in the mausoleum, with his sword drawn and ready at his side.

After an hour or so, the accursed, conniving wife arrived. First, she went to her husband, whipping him cruelly as he cried out, "Enough! Stop, and take pity on me, my cousin!"

"Did you ever take pity on me? Did you spare the life of my true love?" the woman replied. She drew the haircloth over his raw, bleeding skin and tossed the robe over his shoulders. Then she approached the slave with a goblet of wine and a bowl of meat-broth in her hands. She entered the dome weeping and wailing, "Oh my lord, my master! Speak just one word to me, talk just awhile with me!"

The King lowered his voice, twisted his tongue, and spoke in the slave's voice, saying, "There is no majesty, no might except Allah, the glorious, the great!"

As she heard these words, the wife shouted in joy and fainted, dropping to the floor. As her senses returned, she asked, "Oh my lord, is it true that you've regained the power of speech?"

"Cursed one," the King whispered in a small, faint voice. "Do you deserve me talking to you?"

"Why?" cried the wife worriedly.

"All day long you torment your husband," the King replied. "He keeps calling on heaven to help him so much that I can't sleep from evening to morning. He prays and curses both of us so much, and I'm truly disturbed by it! If this had been different, I would've become healthy long ago; I would've answered you and spoken with you long before."

"With your permission," replied the wife, "I'll release him from the spell I cast upon him."

"Release him, and let's have some rest," declared the King.

"To hear is to obey," the woman said, slipping out into the palace. She took a metal bowl, filling it with water and saying some words over it so that it started to bubble and boil, as if it were a cauldron on a fire. She sprinkled her husband with its waters, saying, "Because of the dreadful words I spoke, you became half-stone under my spells. Come forth from that form into your own original being."

Suddenly, the young Prince violently trembled, slowly rising to his feet. Still shaking, and rejoicing at his transformation, he shouted, "I testify that there is no God but *the* God, and Muhammad is His true apostle, Allah bless Him!"

The wife turned toward him, demanding, "Get out and don't come back. If you do return, I'll kill you."

So the Prince walked out from the palace, and the wife returned to the tomb, saying, "Oh lord, come to me so that I can look at you and your beauty!"

"Why?" answered the King faintly. "You've only gotten rid of the branch of my problems, but not the root."

"Oh my darling," she cried, "tell me the root."

"Cursed soul!" the King replied. "The people of this city, and the people of the four islands that you've turned into fish, all torment me. They lift their heads from the lake every night, crying out to heaven to come down in anger upon us. I can hear their cries of distress, and this is the reason why my body won't heal. Set them free at once. Then come to me, take my hand, and raise me up, for I have a little strength back within me."

When she heard the King's words, still supposing that he was the slave, she joyfully exclaimed, "Oh my master, every word you say is my command!" So she sprang to her feet, giddy with happiness, and ran down to the magical mountain lake. She cupped a bit of water in her hand. . . .

And Shahrazad saw the gleaming lights of dawn pouring into the room, so she stopped her story. On the ninth night, she continued. . . .

It has reached me, Oh worthy King, that when this young woman, the sorceress, cupped some water in her hand, she spoke more unintelligible words over it. Soon, the fish lifted their heads, stood up, and their bodies reshaped into human forms. The spell on all the people of the city was removed. The lake became a crowded city; the bazaars thronged with buyers and sellers; the four mountains again became islands; and each citizen became busy once more, as they had before the spell.

The young woman returned to the palace, approaching the King, whom she still thought was the slave. "Oh my love!" she murmured to him. "Stretch forth your honored hand, so I can help you to rise."

"Come nearer to me," the King urged.

She came close enough to embrace him, when he suddenly grasped the sword lying by his side, and stabbed her between the breasts, so that the sword's tip shone gleaming through her back. He struck her a second time, cutting her in two, and casting her halves on the ground.

He went outside the palace, finding the young Prince happily waiting for him. The Prince kissed the King's hand as the King told him what happened, and the Prince offered abundant thanks.

"Would you like to dwell here in this city, or come with me to my capital?" asked the King.

"How far is it between your capital and this city?" the Prince asked.

"Two-and-a-half days," answered the King.

Surprised, the Prince cried, "Oh, King, no! It must be at least a year's march. You must have only got here in two-and-a-half days because the city was under an enchanted spell. But, my King, I'll never part from you, not even for the twinkling of an eye!"

The King rejoiced as he heard these words, and cried, "Thanks be to Allah, who has brought us together. From this moment on, you're my son, my only son, for until now I've never been blessed with children." The two men embraced, full of gladness.

As they reached the palace, the Prince told his Lords and Grandees that he would go on a pilgrimage, and directed them to make everything ready for this. The preparations lasted ten days, and after this, he set out with the King.

The King's heart yearned to see the city from which he'd been separated for one whole year. An escort of servants carried all sorts of precious, rare gifts as they journeyed twelve months to reach the capital. As they reached the city, the Vizier and the whole army came to meet them. They rejoiced to see the King back safely, for they had all given up any hope of seeing him again. The troops kissed the ground before him, and the ministers led him to his throne. When everyone learned of what had happened to the young Prince, they congratulated the two men on their narrow escape.

After restoring order throughout his lands, the King gave gifts to numerous people, and then said to the Vizier, "Bring us the Fisherman who brought us those fish!"

So the Vizier sent for the man who had been the first cause of the citizens' release from enchantment. As the Fisherman came into the King's presence, he was bestowed a robe of honor, and asked if he had any children. The Fisherman replied that he had two daughters and a son. So the King sent for them, and took one of the daughters as his wife, and had the other daughter marry the young Prince. He made the Fisherman's son the country's head treasurer, and then he appointed his Vizier as Sultan of the City of the Black Islands, the Prince's previous home. He dispatched the Vizier with an escort of fifty armed slaves carrying robes of honor for all the nobles of that city.

The Vizier kissed the King's hands and went forth on his journey; and the King and the Prince dwelled at home, in solace and delight, content with their lives. The Fisherman became the richest man of his time, and his daughters lived as the kings' wives, until death came to them.

> *"And yet, Oh King!" continued Shahrazad, immediately after finishing this tale, "This is not more wondrous than the story of the Porter, and the Three Ladies of Baghdad. . . ."*

■ Usamah ibn Munqidh (1095–1188) *Syria* (memoir)

TRANSLATED BY PHILLIP K. HITTI

Usamah ibn Munqidh's *The Book of Reflections* is a fascinating inversion of the Westerner's gaze at the Middle East. This book of memoirs was written (or dictated) when he was more than ninety years old and "too feeble to carry a pen," though his hand "had been strong enough to break a lance in a lion's breast." It describes a life begun at the start of the Crusades and has many passages that describe the Franks, Frankish medicine, and aspects of Frankish behavior that strike him as strange and outlandish. Usamah was born in 1095 to the family of a Syrian prince, in Shayzar, northern Syria. His family were lords of the Castle of Shayzar, a place of key strategic importance, located in the valley of the Orontes River. Invading armies from the north and south had to contend with it and with another key castle (Apamea), and so his life proved to be one of ongoing warfare with the Franks, the Ismailites, and other enemies. He was raised a gentleman and a warrior, with a literary and religious education, and the life he records in these memoirs is filled with dangerous encounters with lions, hyenas, and leopards, with stories of extraordinary bravery and remarkable cowardice, anecdotes of marvelous swordthrusts, trusty servants, captivity, redemption, holy men, and witches. His father was a deeply religious man who abdicated the sultanate in favor of his brother and led a life dedicated to hunting animals and to copying the Quran. Usamah was doted upon by his uncle, the Sultan, until the Sultan had his own sons, and jealousies developed that caused Usamah to leave the family castle. Usamah's son Murhaf was a friend and fellow-warrior to Saladin, the Kurdish warrior who founded a dynasty in Egypt, conquered much of the Middle East, and defeated the invading Crusaders. When Usamah was in his eighties, Saladin became his patron and established him first as governor of Beirut and then in Damascus, where he was a lecturer and the center of a literary salon.

He lived a life of close contact with the Frankish invaders, on the battlefield and in the town, and his stories of their peculiar medicine, strange attitudes, and system of justice are a valuable window onto a period otherwise scantily recorded. Throughout, they are replete with human interest and zest of narrative. The book is really a collection of anecdotes that are linked primarily by association, contrast, or whim. It is an old man's remembrances, and he is impatient with his longevity that "has left me no energy," and he bemoans (in a poem) that though "I have always been the firebrand of battle," now "I have become like an idle maid who lies / On stuffed cushions behind screens and curtains. / I have almost become rotten from lying still so long, just as / The sword of Indian steel becomes rusty when kept long in its sheath." A lusty, grumbling, rambling storyteller, famed as a chivalric warrior, literary raconteur, and avid hunter, his personality is writ large in this book. As Phillip K. Hitti notes, "More delectable stories can be had nowhere else in Arabic literature."

FURTHER READING: Hitti, Phillip K., tr. *An Arab-Syrian Gentleman and Warrior in the Period of the Crusades: Memoirs of Usamah ibn-Munqidh (Kitab al-I'ti-bar),* 1929.

from *The Book of Reflections*

A KURD CARRIES HIS BROTHER'S HEAD AS A TROPHY

One of the amazing things that happened in connection with the Franks in the course of that combat was the following: In the army of Ḥamāh were two Kurdish brothers, one named Badr and the other 'Annāz. The latter, 'Annāz, was feeble of sight. When the Franks were overpowered and massacred, their heads were cut off and tied to the belts of the horses. 'Annāz cut off one head and tied it to the belt of his horse. Seeing him, the army of Ḥamāh said to him, "O 'Annāz, what is this head with thee?" He replied, "Worthy of admiration is Allah because of what happened between me and him which resulted in my killing him!" They said to him, "Man, this is the head of thy brother, Badr!" 'Annāz looked at the head and investigated it, and behold! it was the head of his brother. He was so ashamed of himself before the men that he left Ḥamāh and we do not know where he went. In fact, we never heard a word about him since. It was, however, the Franks who killed his brother, Badr, in that battle.

PREFERS TO BE A FRANKISH SHOEMAKER'S WIFE TO LIFE IN A MOSLEM CASTLE

A number of maids taken captive from the Franks were brought into the home of my father, may Allah's mercy rest upon his soul! The Franks (may

Allah's curse be upon them!) are an accursed race, the members of which do not assimilate except with their own kin. My father saw among them a pretty maid who was in the prime of youth, and said to his housekeeper, "Introduce this woman into the bath, repair her clothing and prepare her for a journey." This she did. He then delivered the maid to a servant of his and sent her to al-Amīr Shihāb-al-Dīn Mālik ibn-Sālim, the lord of the Castle of Ja'bar, who was a friend of his. He also wrote him a letter, saying, "We have won some booty from the Franks, from which I am sending thee a share." The maid suited Shihāb-al-Dīn, and he was pleased with her. He took her to himself and she bore him a boy, whom he called Badrān.[1] [So] Badrān's father named him his heir apparent, and he became of age. On his father's death, Badrān became the governor of the town and its people, his mother being the real power. She entered into conspiracy with a band of men and let herself down from the castle by a rope. The band took her to Saruj,[2] which belonged at that time to the Franks. There she married a Frankish shoemaker, while her son was the lord of the Castle of Ja'bar.

THEIR CURIOUS MEDICATION

A case illustrating [the Franks'] curious medicine is the following:

The lord of al-Munay{t}irah[1] wrote to my uncle asking him to dispatch a physician to treat certain sick persons among his people. My uncle sent him a Christian physician named Thābit. Thābit was absent but ten days when he returned. So we said to him, "How quickly hast thou healed thy patients!" He said:

> *They brought before me a knight in whose leg an abscess had grown; and a woman afflicted with imbecility.[2] To the knight I applied a small poultice until the abscess opened and became well; and the woman I put on diet and made her humor wet. Then a Frankish physician came to them and said, "This man knows nothing about treating them." He then said to the knight, "Which wouldst thou prefer, living with one leg or dying with two?" The latter replied, "Living with one leg." The physician said, "Bring me a strong knight and a sharp ax." A knight came with the ax. And I was standing by. Then the physician laid the leg of the patient on a block of wood and bade the knight strike his leg with the ax and chop it off at one blow. Accordingly he struck it—while I was looking on—one blow, but the leg was not severed. He dealt another blow, upon which the marrow of the leg flowed out and the patient died on the spot. He then*

---

1. Mentioned later by Kamāl-al-Dīn in *Recueil: historiens orientaux,* vol. III, p. 728.

2. In Mesopotamia, southwest of Edessa. Cf. ibn-al-Athīrin *Recueil: historiens orientaux,* vol. I, p. 207.

---

1. In Lebanon near Afqah, the source of Nahr-Ibrāhīm, i.e., ancient Adonis.

2. Ar. *nashāf;* "dryness," is not used as a name of a disease. I take the word therefore to be Persian *nishāf* = "imbecility."

examined the woman and said, "This is a woman in whose head there is a devil which has possessed her. Shave off her hair." Accordingly they shaved it off and the woman began once more to eat their ordinary diet—garlic and mustard. Her imbecility took a turn for the worse. The physician then said, "The devil has penetrated through her head." He therefore took a razor, made a deep cruciform incision on it, peeled off the skin at the middle of the incision until the bone of the skull was exposed and rubbed it with salt. The woman also expired instantly. Thereupon I asked them whether my services were needed any longer, and when they replied in the negative I returned home, having learned of their medicine what I knew not before.

I have, however, witnessed a case of their medicine which was quite different from that.

The king of the Franks[3] had for treasurer a knight named Bernard [*barnād*], who (may Allah's curse be upon him!) was one of the most accursed and wicked among the Franks. A horse kicked him in the leg, which was subsequently infected and which opened in fourteen different places. Every time one of these cuts would close in one place, another would open in another place. All this happened while I was praying for his perdition. Then came to him a Frankish physician and removed from the leg all the ointments which were on it and began to wash it with very strong vinegar. By this treatment all the cuts were healed and the man became well again. He was up again like a devil.

NEWLY ARRIVED FRANKS ARE ESPECIALLY ROUGH: ONE INSISTS THAT USAMAH SHOULD PRAY EASTWARD

Everyone who is a fresh emigrant from the Frankish lands is ruder in character than those who have become acclimatized and have held long association with the Moslems. Here is an illustration of their rude character.

Whenever I visited Jerusalem I always entered the Aq{s}a Mosque, beside which stood a small mosque which the Franks had converted into a church. When I used to enter the Aq{s}a Mosque, which was occupied by the Templars [*al-dāwiyyah*], who were my friends, the Templars would evacuate the little adjoining mosque so that I might pray in it. One day[1] I entered this mosque, repeated the first formula, "Allah is great," and stood up in the act of praying, upon which one of the Franks rushed on me, got hold of me and turned my face eastward saying, "This is the way thou shouldst pray!" A group of Templars hastened to him, seized him and repelled him from me. I resumed my prayer. The same man, while the others were otherwise busy, rushed once more on me and turned my face eastward, saying, "This is the way thou shouldst pray!" The Templars again came in to him and expelled him. They apologized to me, saying, "This is a stranger who

---

3. Fulk of Anjou, king of Jerusalem.

---

1. About 1140.

has only recently arrived from the land of the Franks and he has never before seen anyone praying except eastward." Thereupon I said to myself, "I have had enough prayer." So I went out and have ever been surprised at the conduct of this devil of a man, at the change in the color of his face, his trembling and his sentiment at the sight of one praying towards the *qiblah*.[2]

FRANKS LACK JEALOUSY IN SEX AFFAIRS

The Franks are void of all zeal and jealousy. One of them may be walking along with his wife. He meets another man who takes the wife by the hand and steps aside to converse with her while the husband is standing on one side waiting for his wife to conclude the conversation. If she lingers too long for him, he leaves her alone with the conversant and goes away.

Here is an illustration which I myself witnessed:

When I used to visit Nāblus,[1] I always took lodging with a man named Mu'izz, whose home was a lodging house for the Moslems. The house had windows which opened to the road, and there stood opposite to it on the other side of the road a house belonging to a Frank who sold wine for the merchants. He would take some wine in a bottle and go around announcing it by shouting, "So and so, the merchant, has just opened a cask full of this wine. He who wants to buy some of it will find it in such and such a place." The Frank's pay for the announcement made would be the wine in that bottle. One day this Frank went home and found a man with his wife in the same bed. He asked him, "What could have made thee enter into my wife's room?" The man replied, "I was tired, so I went in to rest." "But how," asked he, "didst thou get into my bed?" The other replied, "I found a bed that was spread, so I slept in it." "But," said he, "my wife was sleeping together with thee!" The other replied, "Well, the bed is hers. How could I therefore have prevented her from using her own bed?"

"By the truth of my religion," said the husband, "if thou shouldst do it again, thou and I would have a quarrel." Such was for the Frank the entire expression of his disapproval and the limit of his jealousy.

Another illustration:

We had with us a bath-keeper named Sālim, originally an inhabitant of al-Ma'arrah,[2] who had charge of the bath of my father (may Allah's mercy rest upon his soul!). This man related the following story:

> I once opened a bath in al-Ma'arrah in order to earn my living. To this bath there came a Frankish knight. The Franks disapprove of girding a cover around one's waist while in the bath. So this Frank stretched out his arm and pulled off my cover from my waist and threw it away. He looked and saw that I had recently shaved off my pubes. So he shouted, "Sālim!" As I drew near him he

2. The direction of the Ka'bah in the holy city, Mecca.

1. Neapolis, ancient Shechem.
2. Ma'arrah-al-Nu'mān, between Ḥamāh and Aleppo.

stretched his hand over my pubes and said, "Sālim, good! By the truth of my re-
ligion, do the same for me." Saying this, he lay on his back and I found that in
that place the hair was like his beard. So I shaved it off. Then he passed his
hand over the place and, finding it smooth, he said, "Sālim, by the truth of my
religion, do the same to madame [al-dāma]" (al-dāma in their language
means the lady), referring to his wife. He then said to a servant of his, "Tell
madame to come here." Accordingly the servant went and brought her and made
her enter the bath. She also lay on her back. The knight repeated, "Do what thou
hast done to me." So I shaved all that hair while her husband was sitting look-
ing at me. At last he thanked me and handed me the pay for my service.

Consider now this great contradiction! They have neither jealousy nor
zeal but they have great courage, although courage is nothing but the
product of zeal and of ambition to be above ill repute.

ORDEAL BY WATER

I once went in the company of al-Amīr Mu'īn-al-Dīn (may Allah's mercy rest
upon his soul!) to Jerusalem. We stopped at Nāblus. There a blind man, a
Moslem, who was still young and was well dressed, presented himself before
Al-Amīr carrying fruits for him and asked permission to be admitted into his
service in Damascus. The amir consented. I inquired about this man and was
informed that his mother had been married to a Frank whom she had killed.
Her son used to practice ruses against the Frankish pilgrims and coöperate
with his mother in assassinating them. They finally brought charges against
him and tried his case according to the Frankish way of procedure.

They installed a huge cask and filled it with water. Across it they set a
board of wood. They then bound the arms of the man charged with the act,
tied a rope around his shoulders and dropped him into the cask, their idea
being that in case he was innocent, he would sink in the water and they
would then lift him up with the rope so that he might not die in the water;
and in case he was guilty, he would not sink in the water. This man did his
best to sink when they dropped him into the water, but he could not do it.
So he had to submit to their sentence against him—may Allah's curse be
upon them: They pierced his eyeballs with red-hot awls.

Later this same man arrived in Damascus. Al-Amīr Mu'īn-al-Dīn (may
Allah's mercy rest upon his soul!) assigned him a stipend large enough to
meet all his needs and said to a slave of his, "Conduct him to Burhān-al-Dīn
al-Balkhi (may Allah's mercy rest upon his soul!) and ask him on my behalf
to order somebody to teach this man the Koran and something of Moslem
jurisprudence." Hearing that, the blind man remarked. "May triumph and
victory be thine! But this was never my thought." "What didst thou think I
was going to do for thee?" asked Mu'īn-al-Dīn. The blind man replied, "I
thought thou wouldst give me a horse, a mule and a suit of armor and
make me a knight." Mu'īn-al-Dīn then said, "I never thought that a blind
man could become a knight."

STRONG SPIRITS: A NEGRO SAWS HIS OWN LEG

Now for a contrary case.

Among our men of the banu-Kinānah was a black man named 'Ali ibn-Farah,[1] in whose foot appeared a pustule. The pustule turned malignant. His toes fell off, and the whole leg began to rot. The surgeon said to him, "There is nothing to do for thy leg but amputation. Otherwise thou art lost." The man procured a saw and sawed his leg[2] until the flow of blood made him faint. On coming back to consciousness he would start sawing it again. This continued until he amputated it at the middle of the leg. After some treatment, it was cured.

This 'Ali' (may Allah's mercy rest upon his soul!) was one of the most enduring and powerful of all men. He used to sit his saddle using one stirrup and putting his knee in a strap on the other side, and in this condition take part in combat and exchange lance thrusts with the Franks. I used to see him myself (may Allah's mercy rest upon his soul!): no man was able to stand a finger contest or come to grips with him. With all his strength and courage, he was a jovial and light-hearted fellow.

---

1. Possibly "Faraj."

2. The pronouns and their antecedents are a little confused in this narrative and may be taken to mean that the surgeon did the sawing.

4

Poems of Arab Andalusia

■

INTRODUCTION (711–1492)[1]

In 711, Arab and Berber armies invaded Spain, and until 1492, the date of the Spanish reconquest, much of Spain was a multicultural, polyglot nation of Muslims, Christians, and Jews. The invasion occurred when most of Europe was living in darkness, between the fall of the Roman Empire and the high Middle Ages. The Arab world of the Middle East, Africa, and Spain was flourishing culturally. Aristotle, Plato and Neoplatonism, and Greek science and philosophy were preserved in Persian and Arabic translations and slowly made their way into Europe. Only in the eastern section of Europe was there an equivalent high culture: the empire of Byzantine Greece, with its magnificent capital of Constantinople. The cultural heritage of the Arab world, its law, academic disciplines, mathematics, medicine, architecture, and poetry, was transferred to Spain and especially to the great cities of the southern province of Andalusia—Granada, Córdoba, and Sevilla—as well

---

1. Poems of Arab Andalusia are from Arabic unless specifically noted to be from Hebrew. Frequently, little or nothing is known of the author's life. Hence, only a brief headnote appears when information is available.

as to Toledo, which eventually, under the Christian monarch Alfonso the Wise, with its school of translators, became the main crossroads for Spain and Europe of the diverse learning of the Iberian Peninsula. For at least four centuries after the conquest, Arabic civilization in this Spanish Eden was resplendent. Great libraries, mosques, and palaces made Andalusia as significant as Baghdad or Damascus. The royal courts in the cities attracted poets and scholars. Then, as the Christians began the reconquest of most of northern Spain and part of the south, in 1086, the ruler of Sevilla invited the fierce troops of the Amoravids to fight against the Christian armies. This fundamentalist militant sect of Muslim Berbers, strong in northwest Africa, fought well but disdained the arts and cared little about Arabic-language culture, since Berber, not Arabic, was their tongue. In 1145, the Almohads replaced the Amoravids and Arabic culture once again flourished. However, city after city fell to the Christians until in 1492 Granada, the last Muslim enclave, was overcome by the Catholic monarchs Fernando and Isabela.

Many arts and sciences claimed precedence in Andalusia. The thirteenth-century Córdoban Neoplatonic philosopher Averroës, in Arabic Ibn Rushd (1126–1198), was a renowned commentator on Aristotle when Aristotle was little more than a name in Western Europe. His erudition conquered not only Christian Spain and its philosophers, such as the Catalan mystic Ramon Llull, but also Christian theologians in Paris, which was at one time divided between its Averroists and its anti-Averroist factions. Eventually Averroës's radical notions of the immortality of matter as well as the personal soul and his contention that truth is derived from reason, not faith, were condemned by Aquinas and the Catholic Church. Moses Maimonides, the greatest Jewish philosopher of the Middle Ages, practiced medicine in Córdoba, where he wrote his famous *Guide for the Perplexed* (1190). The city of Granada was graced with the gardens of the Alhambra Palace; Córdoba was a marvel of beautiful mosques and synagogues; and the whitewashed city of Sevilla, known as the poet's paradise, was then, as now, a city of architectural beauty, including its Alcazar tower.

Just as al-Andalus (Arab Andalusia) is still remembered as the Arab world's lost Garden of Eden, the poems of Andalusia are a rare fruit of Arabic poetry, sharing the qualities of the Arabic poem of the Middle East and North Africa. These poems—and poetry was always an eminent Arab art—contain all the classical poems, such as the mono-rhyming ode *(qasida)*, the *rajaz* epic, and, most typical of Islamic Spain, the *muwashshaha*, a postclassical poem, which had a refrain called the *kharja* (*jarcha* in Spanish) composed in Spanish, though transliterated into Arabic script. The Jews of Arab Andalusia similarly wrote poems in Hebrew and composed the *jarcha* in Spanish transliterated into Hebrew script. The earliest examples of literature in the Spanish language, preceding the epic *Poem of the Cid* (1100–1140) by at least a century, are the *jarchas* written by Arabs and Jews in al-Andalus. Since the refrain is spoken in Spanish in a woman's colloquial voice and the main body of the *muwashshaha* is spoken in Arabic in a male voice, we find within the Arabic *muwashshaha* a dynamic dialogic scene of male and female, Arabic and Spanish, conveying essential oppositions in life and language in Islamic Spain. The most important volume of Arabic Andalusian writers was compiled by Ibn Said al-Maghribi (1213–1286) from Alcalá de Real, outside Granada.

■ Ibn Shuhayd (992–1034) *Córdoba*

Ibn Shuhayd, born in Córdoba, was an aristocratic poet and close friend of the famous poet Ibn Hazm.

After the Orgy

When he was completely drunk
and asleep and the eyes
of the watchmen also closed,

I came timidly toward her
like a friend staking out a secret   5
meeting on the sly, as if nothing

happened. I crawled toward her
inperceptibly as in dream. I rose
toward her softly like a breath.

I kissed the white brilliance   10
of her neck, drank her mouth's
eager redness.

I spent a delicious night with her
until darkness smiled,
revealing the dawn's white teeth.   15

TRANSLATED BY WILLIS BARNSTONE

■ Ibn Hazm (994–1064) *Córdoba*

Ibn Hazm of Córdoba is the outstanding poet of Islamic Spain. He wrote a long treatise on love, *The Ring of the Dove,* comparable to *The Book of Good Love* by Juan Ruiz, the Archpriest of Hita, who is medieval Spain's

Chaucer. Ibn Hazm was also a philosopher, jurist, and vizier to the ruler of Córdoba.

My Love Comes

You came to me just before
the Christians rang their bells,

when the half moon
was surging into the sky

like an old man's eyebrow   5
covered almost wholly with white hairs

or like the delicate curve
of an instep.

Though it was still night,
when you came God's   10

rainbow gleamed
on the horizon,

decked in all colors
like a peacock's tail.

TRANSLATED BY WILLIS BARNSTONE

■ Solomon ben Gabirol (1021/22–c. 1055) *Málaga* (Hebrew)

Born in Málaga, Solomon ben Gabirol ben Judah, poet and philosopher, spent most of his life in Saragossa. He died in Valencia. Orphaned as a child, his life was harsh. Gabirol seems to have suffered from angry rivals, and he may have been murdered. A poet from very young, he wrote secular poems about love and nature and also religious poems. He wrote in Hebrew, but, as other Jewish poets from Arab Spain, he followed the conventions of Hispano-Arabic poetry. His best-known work is a long philosophical poem called "The Kingly Crown" in which he reveals his knowledge of Neoplatonic thought, the mysticism of the Midrash, and Islamic astronomy. He wrote his major prose work, *The Well of Life*, in Arabic and signed it Avicebron (an Arabic version of Gabirol); this treatise also was an extension of his strong Neoplatonic thought. Its Latin translation, *Fons vitae* (Fountain of Life), strongly influenced later Christian thought. His work is incorporated in Jewish liturgy.

Dawn Storm

Fat clouds low like oxen.
Winter is annoyed and suddenly the sky

races like masts in a squall. A captain
grabs his horn and madly screams alarm.

Then the firmament is black mist 5
and morning stars babble with tiny light.

Sun carries the clouds on its wings
around the earth.

They burst and the earth bursts.
They were still, now eagles. 10

Wind blows rain into the abysses.
An infantry of clouds flattens out the earth,

cutting strange ridges for the sowing.
The harvest hides, is known

to only one. All winter the clouds 15
weep until the dead trees wake.

TRANSLATED BY WILLIS BARNSTONE

Ibn Ammar (1030–1083) *Sevilla*

Ibn Ammar was born in Sevilla and lived his life in Sevilla and Córdoba. He was well known and a friend of the king, al-Mutamid. It is said that Ibn Ammar betrayed the king, and, consequently, the king killed him with his own hand.

Reading

My pupil ransoms what the pages traps:
the white white and the black black.

TRANSLATED BY WILLIS BARNSTONE

■ Ibn Burd (d. 1053) *Córdoba*

Moon

The moon is a mirror
whose metal is stained
by sighs of virgins.

Night clothes itself
with light from its lamp   5

as black ink
dresses up in white paper.

TRANSLATED BY WILLIS BARNSTONE

■ Judah Halevi (c. 1075–1141) *Tudela* (Hebrew)

Judah ben Samuel Halevi was a philosopher, poet, and rabbi from Muslim Tudela, in Spain. He traveled and studied in the Jewish centers of learning in Andalusia but settled in Toledo, another great city of learning under Alfonso VI and then the capital of Castile. There, he practiced medicine and was apparently the king's doctor. But many of his compatriots, including his spiritual master, Solomon ben Ferrizuel, were murdered, and he moved to Muslim Spain, to Córdoba, also the city of the great Jewish philosopher Maimonides (who wrote in Arabic). Halevi wrote a famous book in Arabic, *The Book of Argument and Proof in Defence of the Despised Faith*. It was later translated into Hebrew and other languages. It became known as *The Book of the Kuzari* and contains a dialogue between a Jewish scholar and the king of the Khazars, an eighth-century convert to Judaism. This book continues to have a powerful effect on authors from Jorge Luis Borges to Umberto Eco. Finally, Halevi left Spain, which he loved, for Zion, for which he longed. As he wrote, his heart was in the East. After a difficult sea voyage, he reached Alexandria, where he was much appreciated, and where he continued writing at a great pace. He died six months later. He is the great Hebrew poet of the diaspora. The modern Spanish poet Rafael Alberti has a wonderful poem about Halevi in his *Book of Returns,* which he titles "Judah Halevi, first poet of Spain."

My Heart Is in the East

My heart is in the East, and I live at the edge of the West.
I eat. I taste nothing. How can I enjoy it?

How can I fulfil my word to leave
while Zion is locked up in red Edom
and I stand in the ropes of Arabia?
Easily I could give up
all the good wonders of Spain.
Glory would be to see the dust of the Temple,
our ravaged shrine.

5

TRANSLATED BY WILLIS BARNSTONE

Abu l-Hasan al-Husr (d. 1095)
Eastern Andalusia

Mourning in Andalusia[1]

If white is the proper color
of mourning in Andalusia,
why not look at me?
I dress in white hair,
in mourning for my youth.

5

TRANSLATED BY WILLIS BARNSTONE

Ibn Abi l-Haytham (uncertain period)

Sun

Look at the beautiful sun.
Rising it shows one gold eyebrow,
plays the miser with the other,

---

1. This poem alludes to a poem by the famous Persian poet Rudaki (d. 940). Rudaki's poem (translated by Tony Barnstone) reads:
   I dye my hair black
   not to look young
   and act wild again.
   Black clothes are worn
   to mourn;
   I dyed my hair
   to mourn my youth.

but we know it won't be
stingy. Soon it will splash its veil   *5*
of beauty everywhere.

A mirror of wonder
out of the East
hides again in dusk.

The horizon   *10*
is desolate at its escape
and puts on mourning robes.

Falling stars
are tears
of iron.   *15*

TRANSLATED BY WILLIS BARNSTONE

▪ Ibn Iyad (1083–1149) *Central Andalusia*

Grainfield

Ripe wheat
is bending in the wind.

Horsemen flee defeated,
bleeding from
red wounds of the poppies.   *5*

TRANSLATED BY TONY BARNSTONE AND WILLIS BARNSTONE

▪ Abu l-Hasan ibn al-Qabturnuh (d. 1134) *Badajoz*

Born in Badajoz, Abu l-Hasan ibn al-Qabturnuh wrote in the late
eleventh and twelfth centuries. He was secretary to the king.

During the Battle

I remembered Sulayma
when the heat of battle

was like my body's fury
the night I left her.

I saw her slim waist   5
among the spears
and as they bent toward me
I embraced them.

TRANSLATED BY WILLIS BARNSTONE

Candle Light

The more you hurt me
the more I am patient.
When you cut its wick
the candle glows brighter.

TRANSLATED BY WILLIS BARNSTONE

■ Abu l-Qasim al-Manisi (Twelfth Century)
Sevilla

Rain over the River

The wind's hand
belongs to a silversmith who hammers
the river
into a thousand metal wrinkles.

The water is a delicate coat   5
of mail. When rain comes
the scales are riveted together
with tiny nails.

TRANSLATED BY TONY BARNSTONE AND WILLIS BARNSTONE

5

Persian Literature

■

INTRODUCTION

Around 1000 B.C., a nomadic Indo-European–speaking people related to the Aryans (who themselves migrated to India) left southern Russia and central Europe and joined with the prehistoric village cultures of Iran to become the Persians of the south and a related people of the north, the Medes. The Persians were conquered by the Medes in the eighth century B.C.; the Medes then proceeded in 612 B.C. to ally themselves with the Babylonians and conquer their common enemy, the brutal and warlike Assyrian Empire. The Medes in turn were overthrown by the first Persian empire, which emerged under the reign of Cyrus the Persian (550–530 B.C.), and his two successors, Cambyses II (r. 529–522 B.C.) and Darius I (522–486 B.C.). By 500 B.C., Achaemenid Persia, named in honor of an ancestor of Cyrus, had for the first time unified the greater Middle East under one imperial rule, which spanned from Egypt in the south to Greek Macedonia in the north and as far east over the Indus River as northwestern India. The Persian empire encompassed a wide range of conquered states and peoples—the Egyptians, Babylonians, Lydians, Greeks, Persians, Medes, Scythians, Parthians, and the Hindu Kush—and under the leadership of Darius I (also called Darius the Great) was organized into twenty-four provinces, each governed by an appointed satrap, creating a considerable administrative order. Darius resourcefully adapted the technological and governmental methods of his conquered subjects for the advancement and unification of his empire. He created a uniform legal system modeled upon the Mesopotamian legal code developed by the Babylonian king Hammurabi, adopted the practice of minting coins that was used in Lydia (modern-day Turkey), and borrowed from Egypt a common calendar. Darius unified his empire further with a series of royal roads that linked one end of Persia to the other and used horses for speedy communication and transportation across the empire. The empire was also linked through the ruling-class religion of Zoroastrianism (though both Cyrus and Darius allowed conquered peoples to maintain their original faiths). In fact it was this tolerance, cosmopolitan attitude, and the peace assured by the protection of the powerful Persian empire that led many of its conquered peoples to accept its rule without significant dissent.

The literature of Persia begins with the writings of the Zoroastrian tradition, particularly the poems of the *Avesta,* said to be the words of the prophet Zoroaster (c. 628 B.C.–c. 551 B.C.), whose religion celebrated Ahura Mazda, the god of light and creator of all things. As Zoroastrianism developed, it incorporated a host of lesser beneficial deities, and also an antagonist deity, Ahriman, the god of darkness, and his host of evil spirits. The universe was the battleground for these opposing deities. Each person had to choose whether to be aligned with good or with evil. Humans were to be judged after their death and rewarded with an afterlife of everlasting bliss joined with Ahura Mazda or of everlasting punishment. Darius converted to Zoroastrianism, and the religion quickly spread through Persia. Though it has largely died out today, its concepts were a powerful contributor to Jewish thought and especially to the later Jewish thought that was to evolve into Christianity.

The Persians had periodic conflicts with the Ancient Greeks, culminating in the Persian wars of 500 B.C. to 449 B.C. Darius and his successor Xerxes were unsuccessful in conquering the Greek city-states, and about a hundred years later, in the fourth century B.C., Alexander the Great unified Greece and quickly conquered Persia. Although Alexander's empire fragmented after his death, Seleucus I, one of his successors, maintained control over much of Persia, and during his rule and that of his successors, the Seleucids, Persia was deeply Hellenized. The Greek occupation was replaced by Parthian occupation, and the Parthians were overthrown in A.D. 224 by the Sassanid dynasty. Although the Persian empire never regained the sweeping extent or glory of the Achaemenids, the Sassanids restored native rule for Persia and maintained it as a great empire during the Roman era.

The Sassanids were conquered around A.D. 640 by Arabic armies in a continuation of the holy war to spread Islam that Muhammad had initiated in the last years of his life. Persian administrators soon became essential to the effective management of the sprawling new empire, and Persian and Arabic culture became deeply intertwined. Arabic and Persian literatures were fused into an uneasy whole by the common religious tradition of

Islam. The injunction against translating the Quran (though, in practice, generally ignored) caused Arabic to become the holy language of Islam, much as Latin was to Christianity until the Reformation. Therefore, educated Persians were pervasively influenced by the Arabic literary example, by an Arabic vocabulary that migrated into the Persian language, and by the position of the Quran as the supreme Muslim literary exemplar. Many great Arabic writers were in fact ethnic Persians who had adopted the conqueror's tongue. However, later Persian writers are celebrated in part because they strove to eliminate Arabic linguistic elements and to found a truly Persian national literature. Ferdowsi (c. 940–1020) is one such author, a major figure in the golden age of Persian literature, which began in the eleventh century in the court of Mahmud of Ghazna. Ferdowsi was the author of the Persian national epic *The Epic of the Kings*. Many of the great writers of the mystical literary tradition of Sufism were Persian, including such major figures as Attar (c. 1120–c. 1220), Rumi (1207–1273), Sadi (1184–1292), and Hafiz (c. 1320–1390). These great writers lived under the rule of the successors to the Arabs, the Seljuk Turk invaders, who had converted to Islam, and later of Genghis Khan's Mongols, who conquered Persia in the 1350s and ruled for a century. Surprisingly, Persian literature declined after native Persian rule was restored in 1500 under the Safavids, but great literature continued to be written in Persian and in Persian literary forms far from Baghdad—in India at the courts of the Islamic Mughal kings.

—Ayame Fukuda and the editors

■ Ferdowsi (Abul Qasim Hasan Ferdowsi) (c. 940–1020) *Persia* (epic poem)

TRANSLATED BY REUBEN LEVY, REVISED BY AMIN BANANI

The Epic of the Kings has always been the Persian national poem, and even today parts of it are recited on holidays in Iran, and it is taught to school children as are the Greek classics in parts of the West. It tells the history of Iran from the creation to the seventh century (when Iran was subjugated by Muslim Arabs) in a work of more than sixty-thousand couplets. Ferdowsi himself was born in Tus, in the province of Khorasan, to a moderately wealthy landowning family, and he spent twenty-five years composing the poem, dying, according to legend, poor and embittered. The original thousand lines of the poem were written by a young man named Daqiqi, who was murdered by his Turkish slave in 980; at this point,

Ferdowsi continued the epic, incorporating Daqiqi's lines. The heroic tales, lyrics, and fairy tales that make up this history were drawn from a large oral tradition and from earlier written sources. Like most epics, *The Epic of the Kings* engages in exaggeration and repetition and portrays characters in ideal types, and the poetry reflects the ornamentation, hyperbole, and repetitive tropes that tend to characterize epic language. The sheer size of the work, and the fact that Ferdowsi attempted to write a purely Persian poem with as few words of Arabic as possible, had a decisive effect in establishing a separate Persian language and literature.

The great hero of the saga is Rustam, and the epic became widely known in the West after Matthew Arnold reworked into English poetry the episode in which Rustam kills his son Suhrab. The episodes presented here come before Rustam's introduction to the epic. They consist of an archetypal battle between good and evil, in which Eblis (the Devil) tempts a young prince, Zahhak, into murdering his father and ruling through witchcraft, until a young avenger named Kava rises among the people to set them free. Kava creates a banner that becomes the royal banner of Iranian kings, whereas Zahhak is of Arabic blood, so that the ethnic disputes of Ferdowsi's day, disputes that are still active today, take on mythic dimensions in his poem.

FURTHER READING: Banani, Amin. "Ferdowsi and the Art of Tragic Epic" in *Persian Literature*. Edited by Ehsan Yarshater, 1988. Davis, Dick, tr. *Ferdowsi: The Legend of Sevavash*, 1992. Levy, Reuben, tr. *The Epic of the Kings: Shah-Nama, the National Epic of Persia by Ferdowsi*. Revised by Amin Banani, 1990.

from **The Epic of the Kings (Shah-Nama)**

The Reign of Jamshid

[After Hushang came his son Tahmuras, who subjugated the demons and earned the title of 'Demon-binder' and reigned for thirty years. He was followed by his son Jamshid.]

For a time Jamshid had respite from war, since all the demons, birds and peris were subject to his command. 'I am,' he declared, 'endowed with the divine *Farr*[1] and at the same time both king and priest. I shall stay the hand of the evil-doers from evil, and I shall guide the soul towards light.' He first devoted himself to the making of weapons of war, which he gave to valiant heroes eager for renown. By virtue of his kingly *Farr* he was able to mould

---

1. A certain refulgence or 'nimbus,' symbolizing Divine favour, and reserved for kings and other royal personages. It had almost a physical character, being as it were a palladium, talisman or mascot, which was recognizable by beholders and implied infallible greatness and good fortune as long as its possessor held the favour of the Divine Powers.

iron into such equipment as helmets, chain-mail, and laminated armour as well as missile-proof vests, to swords and horse-armour, all of which he invented by his perspicuous intellect. He spent fifty years at this task, part of the time being devoted to the accumulation of stores.

For the next fifty years he gave his mind to the subject of apparel and such matters as the dress appropriate to feasting or to battle. Hence he contrived materials of linen, silk, wool and floss as well as rich brocades and satins. He taught men how to spin and weave and how to interlace the warp with the weft; then, when the weaving was completed, they learnt from him how to wash the materials and how to sew.

When that task was completed he turned to another employ, which was the bringing together of all the men engaged in each craft. Over that he spent fifty years. The class of men known as 'Katuzi,' regarded as being specially charged with the rites of worship, was set apart from the common herd of mankind. As for the priests, the mountains were allotted to them as temples, where they were to devote themselves to worship and to supplication of their divine Master.

In contrast to them he established the caste whom men call 'Neysari.' They are lion-hearted warriors who shed lustre over the army and the whole land and because of whom the king sits securely on the throne. Through them the term 'manliness' was established.

The third group claiming recognition was that of the 'Nasudi' caste. They give homage to no man; tilling, sowing and themselves reaping. They heed no person's censure when the time comes for eating. Their heads refuse to bow to command; they are men of independence although clad in rags, and their ears are deaf to abuse. By them the earth is kept under cultivation and clear of strife and discord.

The fourth class is named 'Ahnukhwashi,' who industriously spend themselves in all crafts. Their work is consummately skilled and their minds teem with ideas.

Over that task Jamshid consumed another fifty years, distributing benefits generously in every region. Thus he assigned to every living creature the right rank or station [proper to it] and directed [it on] its path, so that each might be aware of its place and understand the measure of it. Upon the demons he laid the duty of mingling earth with water, and when they understood what could be produced with clay they quickly fashioned moulds for bricks. With stone and mortar they built walls, upon which they were the first to erect works of masonry such as baths and lofty arches and castles which could provide refuge against attack.

For a length of time the king sought for gems amongst the rocks and by experiment discovered their lustre. Precious minerals of various kinds came into his hands. They included jacinth, yellow amber, silver and gold, which he extracted from the rock by magic art, the key to unloosening any bond of conglomeration. He also distilled sweet perfumes in whose fragrance men delight; essences like balsam, camphor, pure musk, aloes, ambergris and limpid rose-water. These are drugs and restoratives for those who suffer disease, and they are of use in health as well as during illness. All these hidden things he brought to light, there being no equal to him as a discoverer in the whole universe.

After that he went over the water in a ship, voyaging swiftly from one clime to another. In that way he spent another fifty years. And then he set foot even beyond greatness. With the aid of the royal *Farr*, he fashioned a marvellous throne, which at his bidding was lifted by demons into the air. He sat upon that throne like the sun in the firmament. To celebrate, that day was called a new day—the festival of Now-Ruz—the first day of the new year.

Thus another three hundred years went by and men never saw death, remaining unacquainted even with toil and hardship, for the demons waited ever ready to serve. All men were obedient to the king's command and the world was pervaded by the pleasant sounds of music. And so years went by until the royal *Farr* was wrested from him. The reason for it was that the king, who had always paid homage to God, now became filled with vanity and turned away from Him in forgetfulness of the gratitude he owed Him. He summoned those of his followers who were held in highest esteem and in these words addressed his nobles of long experience,

'I recognize no lord but myself. It was through me that skills appeared on earth, and no throne however famed has ever beheld a monarch like me. It was I who adorned the world with beauty and it is by my will that the earth has become what it now is. Sunshine, sleep and repose all come through me, and even your clothing and what enters your mouths originate from me. Power, crown and kingship are my prerogative. Who can claim that anyone but I am king? By means of drugs and other medicaments the world has been brought to such a level of health that sickness and death befall no one. Who but I have banished death from amongst mankind, although many kings have been upon the earth? It is because of me that you have minds and souls in your bodies. And now that you are aware that all this was accomplished by me, it is your duty to entitle me Creator of the World.'

The priests to a man remained with heads bowed low, none daring to ask 'Why?' or 'How?'. But as soon as he had made his speech the Farr departed from him and the world became full of discord. Men deserted his court and no one desiring repute would remain in his service, for when pride combines with power of action it brings ruin in its train and converts good fortune into bad. Jamshid's destiny was overcast with gloom and his world-illumining splendour disappeared.

(i) The Story of Zahhak

In those days there lived a man who came from the deserts where men rode horses and brandished spears. He was a person much honoured for his generosity and one who in his fear of the Lord trembled as though shaken by a gale. The name of this noble man was Merdas. This true believer and prince had a son, whom he loved with a love beyond measure and who was called Zahhak, a youth of high courage, swift in action and bold. Of each day and night he spent two parts out of three in the saddle on noble enterprises, never for any unlawful purpose.

Now one day Eblis [the Devil] arrived on pretence of being a visitor who wished to pay him homage. The visitor's speeches fell agreeably on his ear, for he had no inkling of his character, and he surrendered to him with his whole mind, heart and pure soul, and humbled himself before him. Eblis, feeling that the prince had been completely won over by him, rejoiced beyond measure at his own cunning and said,

'I have many things to impart to you which no one knows but me.'

'Tell me then,' replied the youth, 'and hold nothing back. You are the man to give good advice. Instruct me.'

'First,' said he, 'I require an oath of you, and then I shall reveal such matters as I have to impart.'

The youth was innocent of heart. He gave his word, swearing an oath in which Eblis demanded that he would never disclose any part of his secret to anyone and would obey his every word. Eblis then said,

'Within this palace, my noble lord, what need for a being other than yourself? Why is a father necessary when a son like you exists? Listen to counsel. Over this aged nobleman long years have passed; he lingers on while you endure in wretchedness. Seize upon these riches and this palace; the high rank which he enjoys in the world is well suited to you. If you will have trust in what I say, you will be the only ruler in the world.'

As he heard this Zahhak became pensive, but his heart filled with pain at the thought of taking his father's life. 'It would conflict with all justice,' said he to Eblis. 'Suggest some other plan, for that is something which I cannot do.'

'If you fail in carrying out my advice,' replied Eblis, 'you will dishonour your pledge and the oath which you swore to me; that oath and your bond will lie heavily upon you. Moreover you will linger on as a person disregarded by all, while your father continues to command reverence.'

The head of the Arab Zahhak fell into the net and he was cowed into submission to the other's will. He asked what scheme he advised and declared he would not reject the slightest detail.

Now within the palace bounds the king had a garden which rejoiced his heart, and into it every night he went to prepare himself in privacy for the rites of worship by washing his head and body. The servants who accompanied him carried no lanterns, and on the path leading into the garden the vile demon, in pursuance of his evil plan, dug a deep pit, and covered it with straw. Night fell and the Arab chief [the king], that noble lord ever zealous for his good repute, arose to enter the garden. As he approached the abysmal pit, the royal fortunes sank heavily; down into it he fell and lay there broken. So departed that benevolent and God-fearing man.

Zahhak, despicable malefactor, seizing his opportunity, usurped his father's place and set on his head the crown of the Arabs, amongst whom he became the giver of good and evil.

Once Eblis understood that he had brought this matter to an end with success, he began to elaborate a further scheme. He said to Zahhak,

'When you turned to me for aid, you won all that you desired. If you will make another such compact with me, leaving nothing undone that I suggest and obeying my commands, the sovereignty of the whole world will be yours. Every living animal wild or tame, together with the birds and the fishes, shall be in submission to you.'

So saying he departed to further this scheme and to devise another strange artifice.

(ii) Eblis Turns Cook

Having tricked himself out as a young man, glib-tongued, active and clean-limbed, Eblis found his way into the presence of Zahhak, whom he addressed in the language of flattery and said,

'If I am agreeable to your Majesty, I am myself a renowned and perfectly-trained cook.'

Zahhak accepted this with approval. He had a place got ready for him where he could prepare his viands, entrusted him with the key of the royal kitchens and gave him full oversight of all. In those days flocks were not plentiful, and living creatures were rarely killed for eating. Except for herbs men had nought to eat and it was the ground that produced all, until Ahriman, the Evil-doer, conceived and lodged in the minds of men the thought of killing animals. Out of every genus both of birds and quadrupeds he contrived eatables, making use of all. With their blood he fed Zahhak, as though it were milk, in order to make him stout of heart. And Zahhak obeyed every word that Eblis uttered, giving his mind in pledge to his command.

First Eblis gave Zahhak the yolk of an egg to eat and for a time kept his body in good health with it. Zahhak ate and, finding it agreeable to his palate, gave praise to Eblis. One day Eblis said to him,

'Proud monarch, may you live for ever! Tomorrow I will prepare a dish that will give you the perfection of sustenance.' Then he went to rest and all night long his mind was occupied with the thought of the wondrous dishes his cook would concoct on the morrow. Next day, when the azure vault [of heaven] raised aloft and displayed the yellow jacinth [of the sun], Eblis cooked a dish of partridge and white pheasant and brought it in with his mind full of expectation, and as the Arab king stretched out his hand to the tray of food, his foolish head betrayed him into a partiality for Eblis.

On the following day the tray was decked by Eblis with chicken and lamb as well as with other viands. On the next day again when he set his tray before the king, he had prepared a saddle of veal enriched with saffron and rose-water as well as with old wine and clarified musk. When Zahhak partook of this delicacy and savoured it, he was filled with admiration at the man's skill and said to him,

'Consider what you would most desire and then ask me for it.'

The cook replied.

'May your Majesty live happily for ever, endowed with all-powerful command! My heart is wholly devoted to love for you and from your countenance comes all that sustains my spirit. I have one petition to make of your Majesty, although I am not of the degree to aspire to it. It is, if your Majesty command, that I may be permitted to kiss your shoulders and rub them with my eyes and face.'

Zahhak heard the words and, little suspecting what lay behind all the doings of Eblis, replied,

'I grant your desire. Mayhap your fame will get advancement from it.'

And so he let him have his wish, as though he were his dearest friend, to kiss him on his shoulders. This Eblis did, and immediately vanished into the ground—a marvel such as no man in the world has ever seen.

From Zahhak's shoulders now two black serpents thrust their heads out, filling him with terror. On every hand he sought for a remedy and at last had recourse to cutting them off. But, just as branches sprout anew from trees, so those two black serpents grew again from the royal shoulders. Learned physicians crowded about him, each in turn advising what should be done; and every kind of wizardry was tried. Yet no remedy was found for the affliction.

And then Eblis appeared again, this time in the guise of a physician. Presenting himself gravely before Zahhak, he said,

'This is an occurrence predestined by fate. Leave all alone. Since they are there, you must not cut them off; rather let food be prepared and given them to eat so that they can be propitiated. That is the only proper expedient. For food let them have nothing but human brains, and it may be that given that kind of nurture they will die.' [And in this his secret intent was to empty the world of people.]

(iii) Jamshid's Fortunes Decline

Days passed, and then, [God having withdrawn His favour from Jamshid] a mighty discontent arose throughout Iran. On every hand strife and turmoil erupted and glorious bright day was turned to darkness. Jamshid's allies broke away from him, his divine *Farr* became tarnished and he took to crooked paths and folly. On every hand new kings sprang up, on every frontier men sought a way to power. They gathered armies and made war, their hearts having been emptied of all affection for Jamshid. By ones and twos a host of men forsook Iran and went along the roads towards the Arabs, in whose land, they had heard, was an awe-inspiring king with a dragon's body.

Iranian knights, in search of a new king, turned their glances in unison towards Zahhak and, saluting him as sovereign, they proclaimed him king of Iran.

Swift as the wind the dragon-king journeyed to Iran, where he assumed the crown. In Iran and from amongst the Arabs he chose an army composed of the champions of every region. Then when fortune had withdrawn its face from Jamshid, the new king hemmed him in closely until he came and surrendered throne and crown, his high rank vanishing with his diadem, treasure and retinue. The world grew black in his sight, so that he hid himself away and no one saw him again for a hundred years. At last he, prince of besmirched faith, appeared in the sea of China. There Zahhak had him seized and, without granting him a moment's respite, had his body sawn in two, thus cleansing the world and ridding it of all fear of him.

After Zahhak had enthroned himself as emperor, a thousand years accumulated over him, an era during which the ways of rational men disappeared and the wishes of the devil-possessed everywhere prevailed. Virtue was humiliated and wizardry esteemed; truth hid itself and evil flourished openly. Now it became the practice that each night two young men, either humbly born or sons of noble families, were carried away to the royal palace by a cook, who out of them provided something for the solace of the king. He killed them and then drew out their brains, from which he made a dish with which to feed the dragon.

Faridun

(i) The Birth of Faridun

[Zahhak dreamt one night that a hero named Faridun would appear to dethrone and slay him.]

A long time went by, spent in anxiety by Zahhak, and then Faridun, blessed by fortune, came into the world. He grew up as beautiful as a slender cypress, and the royal *Farr* radiated from him. It had been inherited from Jamshid and he was refulgent as the sun that shines in the heavens, and as needful to the world as rain to the earth and as appropriate as knowledge to the mind. Over his head in affection for him the skies revolved in benignity.

[To discover Faridun's dwelling-place] Zahhak filled the world with hue and cry, hunting for him and searching in every direction. Faridun's father, Abtin, when the world narrowed about him, fled away in despair of his life but unsuspectingly fell into the lion's toils, for vile guards found him and carried him, bound like a tiger, into the presence of Zahhak, who put an end to his life.

[Faranak, the hero's prudent mother, at that took flight with her child and after a number of adventures settled in a hiding place in the Alborz mountains.]

(ii) Zahhak and Kava the Blacksmith

Day and night the thoughts of Zahhak were occupied with Faridun, of whom he was constantly speaking. Fear of him caused his upright stature to become bowed and because of him his heart was ever pervaded with dread. One day, seated on his ivory throne and with his turquoise crown placed on his head, he summoned the princes charged with ruling over his provinces in order to secure from them their affirmation of his sovereignty. He then addressed his ministers, to whom he said,

'My revered and talented counsellors, I have a hidden enemy; a fact which is patent to men of understanding like yourselves. And, however despicable an enemy may be, I do not hold him in contempt, for I am ever doubtful of the malice of fate. I therefore stand in need of a large army, in which demons and peris shall be enrolled along with men, and such an army I am about to raise. Since I am unable to support the burden of it alone, you must ally yourselves with me in the project. And now I desire you to subscribe to a proclamation on my behalf that as commander in chief I have sown no seed but that of uprightness, that I have never spoken anything but the truth and that I would never fail to maintain justice.'

Being in awe of the monarch, those upright men allied themselves with him in his scheme and, old and young, willingly or unwillingly, wrote on the dragon's proclamation the assurance he desired. Just then an unexpected petitioner for justice entered the king's palace. He was a man who had been grievously wronged and, being summoned into the royal presence, was given a seat before those famous men. With an anxious countenance the monarch said to him,

'Tell me at whose hands it is that you have suffered wrong.'

Striking his head with his hand at seeing the king himself, the man cried out,

'Your Majesty, I am Kava, seeking for justice. Grant me justice! I have come here running and I implore you with grief in my soul. If you are active in doing justice, then the esteem in which you are held will be heightened to the extreme. Most of the wrong done to me comes from yourself. It is you who constantly thrust the lancet into my heart. If as you say you would not suffer an outrage upon me, why then do you inflict harm on my children? I had eighteen alive in the world, and now only one remains. Spare me this one child, or my spirit will everlastingly be tortured. My king, what crime have I committed? Tell me. If I am innocent, do not seek pretexts against me. Misfortune has bowed me down, as you see; it has left my heart devoid of hope and my mind full of misery. My youth is gone, and without children I will have no ties left in the world. There is a middle and a limit to injustice; even then it must have a pretext. If you have an accusation against me, present it, for you plan my destruction.

'I am a simple blacksmith, doing no wrong; yet fire descends on my head from your Majesty. Although you have a dragon's form, you are the king and it's your duty to let me have justice in this thing. You have sovereignty over the seven [planet-ruled] climes; why should the fate allotted to me be all grief and misery? You and I must come to a reckoning, and then the world will stand in amazement. Perhaps the reckoning with you will make clear how my last son's turn has come, how it was that from amongst all the people it was my son's brains which had to be sacrificed to your Majesty.'

The monarch at this speech opened his eyes wide and he was overcome with astonishment at the words. The man's son was restored to him and an effort was made with kindly treatment to win his support for the king. However, when the king commanded Kava to add his testimony to what was contained in the proclamation, Kava perused the document from end to end and then, turning swiftly to the elders of the land, he cried out,

'Henchmen of the Devil, you have cut off your hearts from fear of the Lord. All of you have turned your faces towards Hell and surrendered your hearts to obedience of the Devil. I will not lend my testimony to this proclamation, nor will I ever stand in awe of the king.'

With a cry he sprang up trembling, tore the proclamation into pieces, which he trampled underfoot. Out of the palace he went thundering into the street, his son ahead of him.

[In the audience-hall] the nobles made sycophantic speeches to the king.

'Most famous king of the world,' they said, 'even the cool winds of heaven do not venture to pass over your head on the day of battle. How then dare this crude-spoken Kava address you in anger as though he were your equal? He has destroyed our proclamation containing the covenant made with you and rejects your authority. His heart and head are swollen with wrath and he has gone as though to make common cause with Faridun. Never have we beheld viler conduct; we stand outraged by his actions.'

'Listen to a strange thing that has happened,' said the king in speedy reply. 'When Kava appeared in the audience-hall, as soon as my ears heard the sound of his voice there immediately arose between him and me in the chamber what seemed a mountain of iron, and then, when he struck his head with his hand, the thing fell, shattered in pieces. I do not know what will emerge from this portent; nobody knows Heaven's secrets.'

Meantime, when Kava came out after leaving the king's presence, the people crowded about him in the market-place. He called out, summoning men to come to his aid and urging the world to demand justice. On to the end of a spear he fastened a piece of leather, of the kind which blacksmiths wear in front of their legs when using their hammers, and as out of the market-place the dust rose high, with the spear held aloft he began to march, crying out as he went,

'Noble worshippers of God, let all who side with Faridun liberate their heads from the yoke of Zahhak! Let us go to Faridun and find refuge in the shelter of his *Farr*. Let us proclaim that this present king is Ahriman [the Maker of Evil], who is at heart the enemy of the Creator. By means of that leather, worth nothing and costing nothing, the voice of the enemy was distinguished from that of the friend.'

As the stout-hearted man marched onwards, an army of no small size rallied about him. He knew where Faridun lay and went directly towards the place, and as they at last approached the castle of the young prince they greeted him with a shout when they espied him in the distance. His eye caught the piece of leather attached to the spearhead and he beheld in it the foundation of prosperity to come. The leather he decorated with Greek brocade and as background to it had a golden figure outlined with jewels sewn on it. Ribands of red, yellow, and violet cloth were hung from it and it was given the title of 'The Kaviani Banner.' Since those days anyone who has assumed kingly rank and placed the crown of royalty on his head has added fresh jewels to that trifling thing of blacksmith's leather.

With him as his constant companions Faridun had two brothers, both older than himself, and to them he opened his heart, declaring that the skies revolved only to a benevolent purpose and the diadem of greatness would inevitably come to him.

'Get me cunning smiths to fashion me a heavy mace,' he bade them, and outlined in the dust a figure portraying the likeness of a buffalo's head.

(iii) Faridun Makes War on Zahhak

Proudly Faridun raised his head sun-high and girt himself tightly to exact vengeance for his father's death. On an appointed day he eagerly began his undertaking beneath a happy star and with omens that brightened his day. At his palace, whose pinnacles reached the skies, troops massed about him with massive elephants, and buffaloes laden with the army's provender. In the forefront of the troops rode Kava, head on high, moving spiritedly from the halting-place and bearing aloft the the Kaviani Banner, regal emblem of majesty.

Faridun set his face towards the Arvand river as a man determined to find a crown. (If you are ignorant of the Pahlavi tongue, you call the Arvand by its Arabic name of Dijla [i.e. the Tigris].) When he reached the stream he sent salutations to its wardens and commanded them quickly to launch ships and other vessels.

'Ferry me and my soldiers across to the other bank,' he said, 'and leave no man behind on this side.'

The chief river-guard however, ignoring Faridun's command, brought no ships, but said in answer to him,

'The King of the World [Zahhak] secretly ordered me to launch no ship unless I had first obtained a permit from him, attested by his seal.'

Faridun was stirred to wrath by these words. Without fear of the deep flood, he fastened his royal girth tightly, sprang upon his lion-hearted steed and, with his mind sharply intent on vengeance and battle, spurred his rose-coloured horse into the torrent. His comrades, similarly girt for action, charged into the river with him, sinking on their swift-footed mounts as deep as the saddle. Coming to dry land on the opposite side they continued on their way to Jerusalem, which is now in Arabic called 'The Immaculate Abode,' where Zahhak, you must know, had erected his palace.

From across the desert the warriors approached the city in high hopes of storming it. At the distance of a league Faridun observed it, and what caught his eye in the royal city was a palace whose pillared hall appeared to rise higher than the planet Saturn, so that you could have imagined it sweeping the stars out of the sky. There it shone against the heavens like Jupiter, as though it might be the abode of joy, peace and love. But he knew that it was the lair of the dragon and the seat of his power, a place filled with treasure. He said to his comrades,

'I am afraid that one who on the dark earth can build up so mighty an edifice, raising it out of the bowels of the ground, is in a conspiracy with the earth. Our best course in this campaign is to attack at once and permit no delay.'

With the words Faridun stretched out his hand to grasp his [bull-headed] mace and gave the rein to his swift-galloping courser. You would have said that fire burst forth of its own free will as he charged the men on guard. He raised his heavy club above the saddle, and, as the earth seemed to crash together in folds, he rode into the great palace—a youth inexperienced in the world, but stout of heart. Not a man of the sentinels had remained at the gates, and Faridun gave blessings to the Creator of the world.

(iv) Faridun and the Deputy of Zahhak

At such times as the land was unoccupied by Zahhak's presence, there remained in his stead a certain worthy dignitary who occupied the throne, the treasury and the palace, since his master had great admiration of his trustiness. He was named 'Kondrow' ['Slow-mover'], because he walked with deliberate pace when in the presence of his tyrannical master. This Kondrow now came at a run into the palace and in the pillared hall saw a young man of princely stature at his ease in the place of honour, looking as beautiful as a tall cypress topped by the sphere of the moon. The citadel swarmed with his troops, every man ready for action, while others were arrayed in the portals. Kondrow showed no trepidation nor did he inquire the reason for this enigmatical occurrence, but approached uttering salutations and with blessings on his lips.

Faridun invited him to come forward and disclose to him the inner purpose of his arrival, then commanded them to set out the appurtenances of a royal banquet.

'Bring wine,' he bade, 'and call the musicians. Fill cups and let platters be decked. Let all who are able to provide me with music come to the feast and enliven my spirits. And invite to my dais such company as shall be in harmony with my good fortune.'

As he drank his wine and made his choice of music Faridun celebrated a night of feasting that accorded with his circumstances. At dawn, however, Kondrow swiftly withdrew from his new master and, mounted on a willing beast, rode off in search of Zahhak. When he had entered the royal presence he told of what he had seen and heard.

'King of the mighty,' he said, 'signs have appeared that your fortunes are in decline. Three great men with troops have arrived from a foreign land. The one that stands between the other two is the youngest, but he has the stature of a cypress and the visage of a king. Although he is youngest he is superior in dignity and it is he who stands forth amongst them. He wields a mace like a fragment of mountain and in any assembly he shines out. He rode on horseback into your Majesty's palace with those two mighty warriors, one on either side, and when he arrived at your Majesty's throne he sat on it, making nothing of your interceptors and your magic talisman. As for those stationed in your pillared hall, whether human beings or your own demons, he cut off all their heads as he sat on his horse, and mingled their brains with their blood.'

'Let him stay,' replied Zahhak, 'Perhaps he is a guest, and must be entertained.'

'A guest?' queried his steward. 'A person who boldly seats himself in the place where you yourself rest, who expunges your name from your crown and girdle and converts unfaithful creatures to his malpractices? If you wish to acknowledge such a one as your guest, do so!'

'Do not protest so loudly,' bade him Zahhak. 'An arrogant guest is an omen of the happiest kind.'

'I hear you,' retorted Kondrow. 'Now listen to what I have to say. If this renowned warrior is your guest, what business has he in your women's quarters? There he sits with Jamshid's sisters, discussing every kind of topic with them, with one hand fondling the cheeks of Shahrnaz, with the other the red lips of Arnavaz. When the night grows dark his conduct is even worse. Under his head he lays a pillow of musk, which is nothing other than the tresses of your two beauteous ones, who were ever your favourites.'

Zahhak was roused to fury like a wolf. At hearing this speech he cried aloud for death. With foul obloquy he raged in savage tones against the unfortunate steward.

'Never again,' said he, 'will you be my warden.' To that the steward replied,

'I believe now, my king, that you no longer enjoy fortune's favour. How then will you be able ever again to give me charge of the city? Since you are to be deprived of your office as ruler, how will you entrust to me the task of acting in your stead? You have been torn from the place of majesty as a hair is plucked out of dough. Now, my lord, make your plans and look to what needs to be done, for this is an occasion that has had no precedent.'

(v) Faridun Takes Zahhak Prisoner

Zahhak boiled with rage at this exchange of talk and determined on speedy action. He commanded that his horse, swift of foot and of the keenest sight, should be saddled and at a breath-taking gallop he set off with a great army entirely composed of male demons inured to war. Moving by a devious way he reached the palace, whose gates and roof he occupied, with no thought in his head but that of exacting vengeance. Faridun's army received news of this and made by untrodden paths for the same goal, where, leaping in a spate from their war-horses, they attacked the closely guarded palace. On every roof and in every doorway stood the men of the city who had any strength to fight. But all sided with Faridun, for their hearts were sore at Zahhak's oppression, and although missiles rained down—bricks from the walls, stones from the roofs and, in the streets, javelins and poplar-wood arrows—in the city the youths, like their battle-hardened elders, deserted to Faridun's army in order to escape the wizardry of Zahhak.

He, meanwhile, cast about for a means of sating his venom. Leaving his troops he entered the palace clad in iron armour from head to foot in order to avoid recognition. In his hand he carried a lasso sixty cubits long, by the aid of which he quickly climbed to the top of the lofty building. From there he beheld that dark-eyed Shahrnaz, full of enchantment, in dalliance with Faridun, her cheeks bright as day and her tresses like night. He opened his mouth with curses, understanding that this was God's will and that he could not evade the clutch of evil. With the fires of jealousy searing his brain he flung the end of his lasso down into the portico and, reckless of throne and precious life, he climbed down from the palace roof. From its sheath he plucked his sharp dagger and, without a word that would reveal his secret, without calling on any name, and holding the tempered steel weapon in his clutch, he came forward athirst for the blood of the peri-cheeked woman. No sooner, however, had he set foot on the ground than Faridun advanced upon him with the speed of a storm-wind and dealt him a blow from his bull-headed mace that shattered his helmet. But at that instant an angel approached at speed and said,

'Do not strike him down; his time has not yet come. He is wounded; bind him firmly as a rock and carry him up to where two mountains close together will come in sight. Tie him securely inside one of them, where neither his kinsfolk nor his associates can have access to him.'

Faridun heard the words and with little hesitation carried out the behest. He got ready a noose of lion-skin and with it tied Zahhak's hands and waist so tightly together that a raging elephant could not have loosened the bond. Afterwards he seated himself on Zahhak's golden throne and cast down the symbols of his wicked rule, while at the palace gates a proclamation was by his command uttered in these words,

'You noble men of worth and good sense, it is not fitting that you should remain burdened with the weapons of war and be forced to seek fame and repute in this fashion. That soldiers and workmen should both win merit in one and the same way is not right; some are craftsmen, others wield the mace, and each man's occupation displays its worth in its own fashion. When, therefore, one group seeks to perform the other's task, the whole world becomes confused. That fellow who was so vile is now in fetters—that creature who kept the world in terror. As for you, may you live long and remain ever happy. Now depart to your tasks with song.'

In accordance with the advice which he had been given, Faridun, blessed by fortune, drove the tightly-bound Zahhak towards Shirkhan and into the mountains. There he would have stricken off the demon's head, but the benevolent angel appeared once again and gently spoke a quiet word in his ear, telling him to take the captive at the same good pace as before to Mount Damavand. No escort was to accompany them but one composed of men whose services were indispensable and who could be of assistance at a difficult moment. Accordingly, swift as a rumour, he brought Zahhak to Mount Damavand, where he left him in fetters. There he remained hanging, his heart's blood pouring down on to the earth.

■ Omar Khayyam (c. 1048–1131)
Persia (poems)

TRANSLATED BY PETER AVERY AND JOHN HEATH-STUBBS

The fact that the astronomer and mathematician Omar Khayyam, a minor poet, has become the best known of all Persian poets in the West (though challenged in recent years by Rumi) is testimony to the lasting power of the fantastically altered version of his *Rubaiyat* rendered into English by Edward FitzGerald in 1859. His own biographers speak only of his achievements in science and seem unaware that he ever wrote poetry, as in fact were the majority of Khayyam's countrymen prior to FitzGerald's translation. The form of the poem is that of the *rubai*, or epigrammatic quatrain, many of which FitzGerald linked together with the work of other poets into a long connected poem, though in fact each should be understood as standing alone. The *rubai* is not a major form, and thus it is no surprise that one who only wrote in this form should not be considered a poet, at least professionally. But there is a wit, a pithiness, and a hard-edged materialism to the poems that seem to have been characteristic of Khayyam, the scientist, that make his work come across particularly well today. Seen as a whole, his *rubais* add up to a meditation on life and mortality (of the sort that FitzGerald intuited) as the same tropes return again and again. In this sense, his work is a constellation of isolate stars, the lines between which the reader is free to imagine.

Khayyam was an astronomer in the service of the Seljuk king of Malekshah, for whom he constructed an observatory and compiled astronomical tables to construct a revised calendar that was many centuries ahead of anything of which Europe could boast. We also know that he wrote a pioneering work about algebra and in his forties went on an extensive journey to Mecca, Baghdad, and other places. He spent his last years in his hometown of Nishapur, teaching, and he died there in 1131, at around eighty-three years of age. Though there are those who say that Khayyam was a Sufi, there is more historical evidence that he was an early Persian scientific empiricist, a profound pessimist, doubting the afterlife, complaining about human helplessness in the hands of fate, and turning to a sensual *carpe diem* as consolation. In fact, he is chided for his materialism in a poem by mystical poet Farid ad-Din Attar, who presents Omar Khayyam in heaven, full of knowledge that does him no good when he is rejected by God.

FURTHER READING: Arberry, A. J. *Omar Khayyam: A New Version Based Upon Recent Discoveries*, 1952. Avery, Peter, and John Heath-Stubbs, trs. *The Ruba'iyat of Omar Khayyam*, 1981. Elwell-Sutton, L. P. "Omar Khayyam" in *Persian Literature*. Edited by Ehsan Yarshater, 1988, pp. 147–160. FitzGerald, Edward. *Rubaiyat of Omar Khayyam*, undated.

from *The Rubaiyat*

1

Although I have a handsome face and colour,
Cheek like the tulips, form like the cypress,
It is not clear why the Eternal Painter
Thus tricked me out for the dusty show-booth of earth.

4

Oh heart you will not arrive at the solving of the riddle,
You will not reach the goal the wise in their subtlety seek;
Make do here with wine and the cup of bliss,
For you may and you may not arrive at bliss hereafter.

33

The firmament secretly whispered in my heart,
'Do you know what sentence fate laid on me?
If my revolving were in my control,
I would release myself from this circling.'

34

The good and evil that are in man's heart,
The joy and sorrow that are our fortune and destiny,
Do not impute them to the wheel of heaven because, in the light of
    reason,
The wheel is a thousand times more helpless than you.

41

There was a water-drop, it joined the sea,
A speck of dust, it was fused with earth;
What of your entering and leaving this world?
A fly appeared, and disappeared.

42

You asked, 'What is this transient pattern?'
If we tell the truth of it, it will be a long story;
It is a pattern that came up out of an ocean
And in a moment returned to that ocean's depth.

43

It is a bowl the Creative Reason casts,
Pressing in tenderness a hundred kisses on its brim;
This cosmic potter makes such a rare bowl,
Then throws it back again to the ground.

44

The parts of a cup which are joined together
The drunkard does not hold it lawful to break:
So many delicate heads, legs, hands,
Through whose love were they joined, by whose hatred smashed?

50

We are the puppets and the firmament is the puppet-master,
In actual fact and not as a metaphor;
For a time we acted on this stage,
We went back one by one into the box of oblivion.

51

Oh what a long time we shall not be and the world will endure,
Neither name nor sign of us will exist;
Before this we were not and there was no deficiency,
After this, when we are not it will be the same as before.

58

Every particle of dust on a patch of earth
Was a sun-cheek or brow of the morning star;
Shake the dust off your sleeve carefully—
That too was a delicate, fair face.

65

I saw a man working on a building site,
He was stamping down the clay;
The clay protested,
'Stop it, you like me will be stamped on by many a foot.'

66

Oh heart-seeker raise the cup and the jug,
Go back to the meadows on the stream's verge:
This wheel has made many a radiant-cheeked, idol-form
Over and over again into cups and jugs.

71

I watched a potter in his work-place,
Saw the master, his foot on the wheel's treddle;
Unabashed, he was making a jug's lid and handle
From a king's head and a beggar's hand.

72

This jug was love-sick like me,
Tangled in a fair girl's locks;
This handle you now see on its neck
Was his hand on the neck of the girl.

80

I drink so much wine, its aroma
Will rise from the dust when I'm under it;
Should a toper come upon my dust,
The fragrance from my corpse will make him roaring drunk.

98

I need a jug of wine and a book of poetry,
Half a loaf for a bite to eat,
Then you and I, seated in a deserted spot,
Will have more wealth than a Sultan's realm.

104

I saw a waster sitting on a patch of ground,
Heedless of belief and unbelief, the world and the faith—
No God, no Truth, no Divine Law, no Certitude:
Who in either of the worlds has the courage of this man?

110

Nobody has known anything better than sparkling wine
Since the morning star and the moon graced the sky:
Wine-sellers astonish me because
What can they buy better than what they sell?

140

Khayyam, if you are drunk on wine, enjoy it,
If you are with the tulip-cheeked, enjoy her:
Since the world's business ends in nothing,
Think that you are not and, while you are, enjoy it.

213

Every now and then someone comes along saying, 'It is I.'
He arrives with favours, silver and gold, saying, 'It is I.'
When his little affair is sorted out for a day,
Death suddenly jumps out of ambush saying, 'It is I.'

216

Oh eye you are not blind, see the grave
And see this world full of distraction and bitterness;
Kings, heads and princes are under the clay,
See moon-bright faces in the jaws of ants.

234

If chance supplied a loaf of white bread,
Two casks of wine and a leg of mutton,
In the corner of a garden with a tulip-cheeked girl
There'd be enjoyment no Sultan could outdo.

Attar (Farid ad-Din Attar) (c. 1120–c. 1220) *Persia* (poems)

TRANSLATED BY AFKHAM DARBANDI AND DICK DAVIS

The Persian mystical poet Farid ad-Din Attar was born at Neishapour (located in northeast Iran) sometime during the twelfth century. There is considerable debate about when he was born, and estimates run from 1120 to 1157. He was educated at a religious school at the shrine of Imam Reza at Mashad and was said to have traveled to Rey, Egypt, Damascus, Mecca, Turkestan, and India in search of knowledge. Apparently, he was also seeking stories about the Islamic saints, which he collected and published in his prose work *Memorials of the Saints.* Attar's name suggests his profession, which seems to have been that of a perfume and drug seller, perhaps even that of a doctor, a profession he took up upon ending his travels and settling once again in Neishapour. The great Persian mystical poet Rumi was said to have played on Attar's knee, though this may be apocryphal. At some point in his life, Attar was tried and convicted of heresy, was banished, and was deprived of his property. He died sometime between 1193 and 1235.

Though he also wrote other important works, such as *The Book of the Divine, The Book of Secrets,* and *The Book of Affliction, The Conference of the Birds,* written in 1177, was his major effort. This epic collection of poems is a loosely bound depiction of the stages of religious experience as the Sufi seeks unity with God. Riddling teaching tales are set like gems within a framing narrative in which the hoopoe convinces the birds of the world to embark on a mystical Way to seek the ideal, spiritual king, the Simorgh. They must overcome their own weaknesses and attachments to the world, passing through the seven valleys (the Valleys of the Quest of Love, of Insight into Mystery, of Detachment and Serenity, of Unity, of Awe, of Bewilderment, and of Poverty and Nothingness). They lose many questers on the way until a bedraggled group of thirty persevering birds finally meets the king. As translator Dick Davis notes, the birds at last find "that the Simorgh they have sought is none other than themselves. The moment depends on a pun—only thirty (*si*) birds (*morgh*) are left at the end of the Way, and the *si morgh* meet the Simorgh, the goal of their quest." The Sufism that the poem expounds often celebrates an ecstatic self-annihilation, in addition to celebrations of passionate love. Often this love causes its victims to break conventions, as beggars love kings, princesses love slaves, and men love men; the passionate commitment to the religious Way also demands that the mystic listen to the demands of spiritual love and ignore the world's judgment. In this poem we see that to the Sufi, the "world's bright surfaces" are illusion, a hall of mirrors hiding the supreme truth, a truth in which all disparate experiences are revealed to be the same when the mirror is broken: "The lovely forms and colours are undone, / And what

seemed many things is only one. / All things are one—there isn't any two;
It isn't me who speaks; it isn't you." As Rumi says, "I thought I knew who I
was, but I was you."

In this version, Dick Davis and Afkham Darbandi translate the rhyming
end-stopped *masnavi* form into an equivalent English form, heroic couplets, with remarkable grace and fluidity—a difficult task at best. For the
most part, the chosen selections are from the self-contained teaching
poems; the framing narrative that they illustrate has been eliminated, since
these smaller jewels lend themselves more readily to excerption.

FURTHER READING: Attar, Farid ad-Din. *The Conference of the Birds.* Translated by A.
Darbandi and D. Davis, 1984; *The Ilahi-Nama; or, Book of God of Farid al-Din 'Attar.*
Translated by John A. Boyle, 1976; *Muslim Saints and Mystics: Episodes from the Tad-
hikirat Al-Auliya ("Memorial of the Saints")*. Translated by A. J. Arberry, 1966; reprint,
1976. Rice, Cyprian. *The Persian Sufis,* 1964. Schimmel, Annemarie. *As through a Veil:
Mystical Poetry in Islam,* 1982.

from The Conference of the Birds

How Sheikh Abou Bakr's Self-satisfaction Was Reproved

Sheikh Abou Bakr of Neishapour one day
Led his disciples through a weary way.
His donkey carried him, aloof, apart—
And then the beast let out a monstrous fart!
The sheikh began to tear his clothes and cry   *5*
Till one of his disciples asked him why.
The sheikh said: "When I looked I saw a sea
Of my disciples sworn to follow me;
They filled the roads and in my mind there slid
The thought: 'By God, I equal Bayazid!'[1]   *10*
So many praise me, can I doubt this sign
That heaven's boundless glories will be mine?'
Then as I triumphed in my inmost heart,
My donkey answered me—and with a fart;
My pompous, self-deceiving soul awoke,   *15*
And this is why I weep and tear my cloak."
How far away the truth remains while you
Are lost in praise for all you say and do—
Destroy your arrogance, and feed the fire

1. Bistami or Bayazid (Bistam, which was about halfway Rey and Neishapour, was his birthplace) was a famous ascetic associated with the "ecstatic" rather than the "sober" Sufi path. He
died in 874 in Bistam.

With that vain Self you foolishly admire.   20
You change your face each moment, but deep down
You are a Pharaoh and you wear his crown,
Whilst one small atom of this "you" survives
Hypocrisy enjoys a hundred lives.
If you put all your trust in "I" and "me"   25
You've chosen both worlds as your enemy—
But if you kill the Self, the darkest night
Will be illuminated with your light.
If you would flee from evil and its pain
Swear never to repeat this "I" again!   30

A Drunkard Accuses a Drunkard

A sot became extremely drunk—his legs
And head sank listless, weighed by wine's thick dregs.
A sober neighbour put him in a sack
And took him homewards hoisted on his back.
Another drunk went stumbling by the first,   5
Who woke and stuck his head outside and cursed.
"Hey, you, you lousy dipsomaniac,"
He yelled as he was borne off in the sack,
"If you'd had fewer drinks, just two or three,
You would be walking now as well as me."   10
He saw the other's state but not his own,
And in this blindness he is not alone;
You cannot love, and this is why you seek
To find men vicious, or depraved, or weak—
If you could search for love and persevere   15
The sins of other men would disappear.

The Valley of Detachment

Next comes the Valley of Detachment; here
All claims, all lust for meaning disappear.
A wintry tempest blows with boisterous haste;
It scours the land and lays the valley waste—
The seven planets seem a fading spark,   5
The seven seas a pool, and heaven's arc
Is more like dust and death than paradise;
The seven burning hells freeze cold as ice.
More wonderful than this, a tiny ant
Is here far stronger than an elephant;   10
And, while a raven feeds, a caravan

Of countless souls will perish to a man.
A hundred thousand angels wept when light
Shone out in Adam and dispelled the night;
A hundred thousand drowning creatures died   15
When Noah's ark rode out the rising tide;
For Abraham, as many gnats were sent
To humble Nimrod's vicious government;
As many children perished by the sword
Till Moses' sight was cleansed before the Lord;   20
As many walked in wilful heresy
When Jesus saw Truth's hidden mystery;
As many souls endured their wretched fate
Before Mohammad rose to heaven's gate.
Here neither old nor new attempts prevail,   25
And resolution is of no avail.
If you should see the world consumed in flame,
It is a dream compared to this, a game;
If thousands were to die here, they would be
One drop of dew absorbed within the sea;   30
A hundred thousand fools would be as one
Brief atom's shadow in the blazing sun;
If all the stars and heavens came to grief,
They'd be the shedding of one withered leaf;
If all the worlds were swept away to hell,   35
They'd be a crawling ant trapped down a well;
If earth and heaven were to pass away,
One grain of gravel would have gone astray;
If men and fiends were never seen again,
They'd vanish like a tiny splash of rain;   40
And should they perish, broken by despair,
Think that some beast has lost a single hair;
If part and whole are wrecked and seen no more,
Think that the earth has lost a single straw;
And if the nine revolving heavens stop,   45
Think that the sea has lost a single drop.

The Moths and the Flame

Moths gathered in a fluttering throng one night
To learn the truth about the candle's light,
And they decided one of them should go
To gather news of the elusive glow.
One flew till in the distance he discerned   5
A palace window where a candle burned—

And went no nearer; back again he flew
To tell the others what he thought he knew.
The mentor of the moths dismissed his claim,
Remarking: "He knows nothing of the flame."   *10*
A moth more eager than the one before
Set out and passed beyond the palace door.
He hovered in the aura of the fire,
A trembling blur of timorous desire,
Then headed back to say how far he'd been,   *15*
And how much he had undergone and seen.
The mentor said: "You do not bear the signs
Of one who's fathomed how the candle shines."
Another moth flew out—his dizzy flight
Turned to an ardent wooing of the light;   *20*
He dipped and soared, and in his frenzied trance
Both Self and fire were mingled by his dance—
The flame engulfed his wing-tips, body, head;
His being glowed a fierce translucent red;
And when the mentor saw that sudden blaze,   *25*
The moth's form lost within the glowing rays,
He said: "He knows, he knows the truth we seek,
That hidden truth of which we cannot speak."
To go beyond all knowledge is to find
That comprehension which eludes the mind,   *30*
And you can never gain the longed-for goal
Until you first outsoar both flesh and soul;
But should one part remain, a single hair
Will drag you back and plunge you in despair—
No creature's Self can be admitted here,   *35*
Where all identity must disappear.

■ Rumi (Jalal ad-Din Rumi) (1207–1273)
Persia/Turkey (poems)

The *Mathnavi*, Rumi's epic-length verse collection of mystical stories, has been called the Quran of the Persians. His poetry was an inspiration for Johann Goethe, Mahatma Gandhi recited his poems, and Georg Hegel, who esteemed his poetry, also admired him as a major thinker. He was the founder of the Sufi sect called the Mavlavis, who are known as the Whirling Dervishes because of their ritual of ecstatic dance. Rumi's *Mathnavi* is the mystical Bible of the Sufis, which is itself the mystical branch of Islam. Sufism derives its name from *suf*, meaning wool, a material from which the robes of these mystics were woven. After Rabia the Mystic preached a doctrine of pure love, Sufism became a belief of transcendence in which stages of mysticism were delineated, and, through music, chanting, and dances, the subject sought self-abolition and an ecstatic union with God.

Jalal ad-Din Rumi was born in 1207 in Balkh in the Persian province of Khorasan, the son of a mystical theologian. His family was forced to flee during the Mongol invasion of central and western Asia and, after a decade of wandering through Persia, Iraq, Arabia, and Syria, settled in Anatolia, in Konya, the capital of the Seljuk empire. The region of Asia Minor, conquered from the Byzantines, was called Rum (Rome) in Turkish and Persian, and hence Jalal ad-Din became known as Rumi (literally, "the Roman"). "Jalal ad-Din" is an honorific meaning "majesty of religion." While in Konya, he married, took over his father's professorship, and became associated with a Sufi community. He became a sheik, or elder, and was given the title "Mevlana," meaning "our master," a name by which he is also known throughout the Middle East and India. It is also the etymological source of his sect, the Mavlavis.

In 1244, Rumi's life was changed when he met Shams ad-Din of Tabriz, who was destined to be the physical incarnation of his spiritual love and the specific source of much of his mystico-erotic poetry. After fifteen months, Shams disappeared and Rumi, heartbroken, wrote poems of desolate loss and abandonment by his God. Rumi traveled to Tabriz and Damascus, searching for his Sun (the meaning of Shams), but in vain. At last Rumi's son and Rumi's disciples went to Damascus and retrieved Shams, despite their disapproval of his master's attachment to him. A few months later, Shams disappeared again and was rumored to have been murdered, perhaps by Rumi's jealous disciples. Later, Rumi found mystical love for another man, a goldsmith named Salahoddin Zarkub, and his last lover was Hosamoddin Chelebi, who was his successor as leader of his Sufi sect. In addition to the *Mathnavi*, an epic of twenty-six thousand couplets, Rumi wrote a collection of lyrics entitled the *Divan of Shams of Tabriz*, containing about thirty thousand verses. Certainly, Rumi is one the world's major spiritual poets, a brother to the Spaniard Saint John of the Cross, the Indians Mirabai and Kabir, the Japanese Saigyo, and the Chinese Wang Wei. His poems wake us to a concealed union with each other and with God and, to use his words, open "a window . . . from one mind to another." At once ascetic and carnal, he celebrates drunkenness, erotic amazement, and disappearance into the mystical lover.

FURTHER READING: Arberry, A. J., tr. *Discourses of Rumi*, 1975; *More Tales from Masnavi*, 1963; *Mystical Poems of Rumi; First Selection, Poems 1–200*, 1968. Barks, Coleman, tr. *Delicious Laughter: Rambunctious Teaching Stories from the Mathnawi*, 1990. Barks, Coleman, and John Moyne, trs. *Open Secret: Versions of Rumi*, 1984; *This Longing: Poetry, Teaching Stories, and Selected Letters*, 1988. Bly, Robert, tr. *When Grapes Turn to Wine: Versions of Rumi*, 1986. Iqbal, Afzal. *The Life and Work of Muhammad Jalal-ud-Din Rumi*, 1974. Nicholson, Reynold A., tr. *Rumi, Poet and Mystic*, 1978; Chittick, William C., tr. *The Sufi Path of Love: The Spiritual Teachings of Rumi*, 1983.

Love's Body

The moon and a batallion of stars came
and the sun, a lonely horseman, dissolved.

The moon lives beyond the night, beyond the day.
What eye can see him?

The sightless eye is a minaret.   5
How can it make out the bird on the minaret?

Sometimes the cloud in our heart is tight
because we love the moon.

Sometimes it falls away.
When you began to love your passion died   10

and though you had a thousand things to do,
you did nothing,

but since one day granite becomes a ruby,
it isn't lazy.

If in the market of love you see decapitated heads   15
hanging from butcher hooks,

don't run off. Come in. Look closely.
The dead are alive again.

TRANSLATED BY TONY BARNSTONE, WILLIS BARNSTONE,
AND REZA BARAHENI

A New Promise

Last night I swore
my eyes
wouldn't leave your face
and I won't leave
though you hack me into chunks of meat   5
    with a sword.
No one else can cure me. I'm sick. You're gone.
Toss me into a bonfire.
If I let out one yelp I'm not a man.
I am dust. You raise me when you come.
When you've gone down the road, I collapse   10
    again into dust.

TRANSLATED BY TONY BARNSTONE, WILLIS BARNSTONE,
AND REZA BARAHENI

Caring for My Lover

Friends, last night I carefully watched my love
sleeping by a spring circled with eglantine.
The houris of paradise stood around him,
      their hands cupped together
between a tulip field and jasmines.
Wind tugged softly in his hair.   5
His curls smelled of musk and ambergris.
Wind turned mad and tore the hair right off
      his face
like a flaming oil lamp in a gale.
From the beginning of this dream I told myself
      go slowly, wait
for the break into consciousness. Don't breathe.   10

TRANSLATED BY TONY BARNSTONE, WILLIS BARNSTONE,
AND REZA BARAHENI

The New Rule

It's the old rule that drunks have to argue
and get into fights.
The lover is just as bad: He falls into a hole.
But down in that hole he finds something shining,
worth more than any amount of money or power.   5

Last night the moon came dropping its clothes in the street.
I took it as a sign to start singing,
falling up into the bowl of sky.
The bowl breaks. Everywhere is falling everywhere.
Nothing else to do.   10

Here's the new rule: Break the wineglass,
and fall toward the glassblower's breath.

TRANSLATED BY JOHN MOYNE AND COLEMAN BARKS

The Clear Bead at the Center

The clear bead at the center changes everything.
There are no edges to my loving now.

I've heard it said there's a window that opens
from one mind to another,

but if there's no wall, there's no need   5
for fitting the window, or the latch.

TRANSLATED BY JOHN MOYNE AND COLEMAN BARKS

Someone Who Goes with Half a Loaf of Bread

Someone who goes with half a loaf of bread
to a small place that fits like a nest around him,
someone who wants no more, who's not himself
longed for by anyone else,

He is a letter to everyone. You open it.   5
It says, *Live.*

TRANSLATED BY JOHN MOYNE AND COLEMAN BARKS

Who Says Words with My Mouth

All day I think about it, then at night I say it.
Where did I come from, and what am I supposed to be doing?
I have no idea.
My soul is from elsewhere, I'm sure of that,
and I intend to end up there.   5

This drunkenness began in some other tavern.
When I get back around to that place,
I'll be completely sober. Meanwhile,
I'm like a bird from another continent, sitting in this aviary.
The day is coming when I fly off,   10
but who is it now in my ear, who hears my voice?
Who says words with my mouth?

Who looks out with my eyes? What is the soul?
I cannot stop asking.
If I could taste one sip of an answer,   15
I could break out of this prison for drunks.
I didn't come here of my own accord, and I can't leave that way.
Whoever brought me here will have to take me back.

This poetry. I never know what I'm going to say.
I don't plan it.   20

When I'm outside the saying of it,
I get very quiet and rarely speak at all.

TRANSLATED BY JOHN MOYNE AND COLEMAN BARKS

■ Sadi (1184–1292) *Persia* (prose and poems)

TRANSLATED BY EDWARD REHATSEK

Sadi was born in Shiraz in 1184 and fled the Mongol invaders to Baghdad, where he studied at the Nizamiya college. After leaving college, he lived the life of a dervish, roving throughout the Middle East and making several pilgrimages to Mecca. In 1256, he returned to Shiraz and devoted himself to a literary life, achieving great fame in his own lifetime. He wrote many lyric *ghazals* and longer, laudatory *qasidas,* but he is best known for his *mathnavi* verse epic the *Bustan* or *The Scented Garden* and the mixed prose and poetry *Gulistan* or *The Rose Garden,* parts of which are presented here. He also wrote absurd and obscene verses, or *hazaliyat.* The moral lessons of his delightful teaching tales make him a "philosopher of common sense" whose work treats questions of overeating and flatulence, homosexual and heterosexual love, puberty, spitefulness, and ways to divide your enemies to conquer them. Yet, despite his profane subject matter, his work is infused with a deeper Islamic mysticism that teaches how to live and love in the world as an ethical person. His *Gulistan* has been translated into many languages, including Turkish as early as the fourteenth century, and it is the first book read in Persian classes throughout the Middle East. Ralph Waldo Emerson considered the *Gulistan* one of the world's bibles, and it has won the admiration of François-Marie Voltaire, Benjamin Franklin, and Matthew Arnold, among other Western luminaries. In fact, Franklin successfully passed off one of its parables as a missing chapter of Genesis as a practical joke.

FURTHER READING: Arberry, A. J., tr. *Kings and Beggars: The First Two Chapters of Sa'di's Gulistan,* 1945. Clarke, H. Wilberforce, tr. *The Bustan by Shaikh Muslihu-d-din Sa'di Shirazi: Translated for the First Time into Prose,* 1985. Levy, Reuben. *An Introduction to Persian Literature,* 1969. Nakosteen, Mehdi, tr. *The Maxims of Sa'di: Selected Translations,* 2nd ed., 1977. Rehatsek, Edward, tr. *The Gulistan, or Rose Garden, of Sa'di,* 1965. Wickens, G. M., tr. *Morals Pointed and Tales Adorned: The Bustan of Sa'di,* 1974.

The Rose Garden

Chapter I: The Manners of Kings

STORY 2

One of the Kings of Khorasan, in Afghanistan, saw in a dream a vision of the Sultan Mahmud, one hundred years dead. Though his body had dissolved and become dust, the eyes still rotated in their sockets and gazed around him. None of the sultan's sages could interpret this vision, with the exception of one dervish, who bowed and stated, "His eyes still gaze about in amazement, to see his kingdom in the hands of others."

> Many famous kings are beneath the soil.
> Above ground, no trace of them remains.
> An old corpse given to earth
> is so eaten by soil that not even a bone is left.
> But the glorious name of Nushirvan survives untarnished
> though he's been dead so long.
> Do only good since life's a gift
> that will cease like a shout leaving the throat.

STORY 7

Once a king and a Persian slave were seated in the same ship. The slave had never before seen the sea, nor experienced the troubles of sailing, and soon began to moan and weep and to tremble from head to foot. No one could calm him. The king was becoming increasingly irate at this disturbance, but no one could figure out what to do to bring the slave to his senses. There was, though, a philosopher on board who claimed to have the solution. The king responded, "I would consider it a great favor." The philosopher ordered the slave tossed into the salt sea, where he floundered and swallowed great mouthfuls of water. Then a crewmember grabbed him by the hair and dragged him back to the ship, whereupon the slave grabbed hold of the rudder and clung there until they pulled him aboard again. Once back in the ship, the slave sat meekly in a corner and stayed absolutely quiet. The king was amazed by the success of this experiment, and asked "What was the secret behind this thing?" The philosopher responded, "Before tasting the agony of being drowned, he didn't know the safety of the ship. In the same way, a man does not appreciate the value of freedom from misfortune until calamity hits."

> If you're gorged, you scorn barley bread;
> she who you think is ugly is my lover!
> To the houris of paradise, purgatory seems Hell;
> but those in hell would think purgatory Heaven.

> How different is the man who holds his lover
> from the one whose eyes rest expectantly on the door.

from STORY 12

A cruel king asked a religious man what the best form of devotion would be. He replied, "For you to sleep till noon so you don't harm your people for a while."

STORY 31

The viziers of Nushirvan were debating a matter of state, and each one gave his opinion based on what he knew. The king also gave his opinion, and Barzachumihr adopted the same point of view. Taking him aside in private, the viziers asked him "What did you discover in the king's opinion to judge it superior to that of so many sage men?" Barzachumihr replied, "Because the outcome of this affair remains unknown, and since it depends upon God's will whether our opinions will turn out to be right or wrong, it was better to conform to the king's opinion. That way, even if it turns out he is wrong, he cannot blame us without blaming himself!"

> Disagree with a king
> and you wash your hands in your own blood.
> Should he say in daylight, "It is night"
> you must shout "I can see the moon and the Pleiades!"

Chapter II: The Morals of Dervishes

from STORY 8

> To the world I appear beautiful
> but my inner sins bow my head with shame;
> people praise the peacock for his magnificent colors
> while he is ashamed of his ugly feet.

from STORY 19

> When rust has bitten into steel
> no polishing will remove it.
> Don't bother preaching to the corrupt;
> an iron nail can't pierce a stone.

STORY 31

There was a man who, afflicted by a powerful tempest in his belly, and lacking the strength to restrain it, allowed it to escape. He exclaimed, "O friends, forgive me! I had no choice in what has happened, and so no fault should fall upon me. Besides, I feel much better now."

> Wind rustles in the dungeon of the belly
> but no sage can keep the wind chained.
> If wind whirls in your belly, let it free
> because a storm in the belly afflicts the heart.

Chapter III: The Fruits of Contentment

STORY 6

It is said that King Ardeshir Babekan, first king of the Persian Sasanian dynasty (reigned A.D. 226–240), once asked an Arabic physician how much food he should eat each day. The physician answered, "A hundred dirhams of food would be enough." The king asked, "And what strength of body will this amount give me?" The doctor retorted, "This is enough to carry you, and if you eat any more you will have to carry it!"

> We eat to live so we may praise God,
> but you think we live to eat!

Chapter IV: The Advantages of Holding Your Tongue

from STORY 14

A fellow with an annoying voice was reading the Quran one day in a braying loud tone. A holy man passed by and inquired of him what his monthly wage happened to be for reading. The man replied, "Nothing at all." "Why, then," continued the sage, "do you take the trouble?" He replied, "I am reading for the sake of God." The holy man returned, "For God's sake, stop reading!"

Chapter V: Love and Youth

STORY 10

In the fire of my youth I had a lover with a sweet voice and a body beautiful as the moon just rising on the horizon.

> To see his new beard is to live forever,
> to see his sugar lips is to eat candy.

However, one day I found something unnatural in how he behaved, and we had a fight. Now disapproving of my lover, I took my gown away from him and abandoned the chess game of our friendship. I said to him:

> Go do what you want.
> You're not in my heart, so follow your own.

As he left me I heard him sing out,

> If the bat doesn't want to join with the sun
> the sun is no less beautiful.

After he left I fell into a deep despair.

> The time of our union is gone, I knew nothing
> of its value and delight until it had departed.

> Come back! Kill me! Even to die with you
> is better than living without you.

God is great, and through his mercy my lover came back to me after some time. Now, however, my lover's sweet voice had gone harsh, his beauty which had rivaled that of Joseph had dissipated, there was dust on the apple of his skin, and all of his marvelous grace had abandoned him. He came up to me to take me in his arms and I let him, saying,

> When you had your first wonderful growth of beard
> you drove out of sight the one who lusted for that sight.
> Today you are here to reconcile with him
> but your beard shows straight I's and coiled S's,
> you have turned yellow, and your fresh spring is exhausted.
> Put away that kettle! There's no fire between us.
> You strut about proudly
> thinking of joys that have died.
> Leave me! Go to someone who will buy your body,
> flirt with someone who desires you.

> It's said that green in a garden is pleasant
> and I know this as I say these words
> since the fresh grass of a moustache
> mesmerizes lovers' hearts without end.
> But your garden is a bed of weeds,
> and the more you weed it, the more it grows.

> You can pluck your beard all you want
> but your happy youth is over.
> If my life were as strong as your beard
> I wouldn't die till resurrection day.
> I asked, "What's happened to your beautiful face?
> Ants are crawling on its moon."
> He responded with a smile, "I don't know exactly.
> Maybe it wears black to mourn my dead beauty."

Chapter VI: Weakness and Decrepitude

from STORY 2

> When a woman rises frustrated from bed
> she'll raise no end of trouble.
> An old man can't arise without a stick,
> so how can his stick arise?

> Though you're quick tempered and beat me
> I'll do anything for your beauty;

I'd rather be with you in Hell
than in a Heaven of old men.

Chapter VII: Education

It is written in the compositions of the philosophers that scorpions are not
born like other animals, but that they devour the entrails of their mothers,
eat through the belly, and scatter into the desert. The skins that can be found
in scorpion holes are the vestiges of this process. I told this story to a great
man, who responded, "My heart can bear witness to the truth of this tale, for
it couldn't be any other way: since they behave this way to their parents in infancy, they are loved and respected in the same way when they grow old."

Chapter VIII: Society and Duty

MAXIM 80

What can an old whore do but give up sex, and a fired policeman do but
give up oppression?

> A young man who sits in the corner in prayer is a hero,
> because an old man cannot even rise from his corner.

> In youth it's difficult to squelch desire,
> but when old it's more difficult to make your tool rise.

from The Conclusion to the Book

> All praise to God by whose grace this book is ended
> before my own life has reached its conclusion.

■ Hafiz (Khajeh Shamsoddin Mohammad Hafez-e Shirazi) (c. 1320–1390) *Persia* (poems)

Hafiz is considered the finest lyric poet of the Persian language. He was
born in great poverty in Shiraz around A.D. 1320. His pen name, Hafiz, is
the epithet given to one who has learned the Quran by heart. He seems to
have been familiar with the science of his day as well. Though he stayed in
his native Shiraz, he became famous throughout Persia, the Middle East,
and India, and the Sultan of Baghdad and the Sultan of Bengal invited him
to their courts. He specialized in the *ghazal*, or lyric ode, consisting of

around six to fifteen rhymed couplets; in the final couplet, the poet usually addresses himself by name, in the third person.

After the death of his father, a merchant of moderate means from Isfahan, when Hafiz was young, the family seems to have lived a penurious existence. Until his poems won him fame and patronage, Hafiz lived as a scribe, a teacher, and perhaps a baker's apprentice. He was patronized by several shahs and wrote religious commentaries, but his poetry celebrates wine, women, and young men as much as mysticism. For some reason, he seems to have been banished from Shiraz for six years (1368–1374). Perhaps the Shah Shoja, who was his drinking companion, became jealous of Hafiz's superior poetry; perhaps the priesthood plotted against him as a famous freethinker and sensualist. While in exile, he met Dordane, the woman he celebrates in his poems, though no historical record of her remains. It is important to note, however, that the beloved in his poems is often male, the conventional figure of Beauty as a beautiful youth. Often the gender gets switched in the process of translation.

Hafiz's highly romantic, mystical poetry attracted an appreciative Western audience from the seventeenth century through the early twentieth century. He was a favorite of Goethe's and was translated into Latin, French, English, German, and Greek. However, he has been relatively ignored in the West for the past several decades. Emerson said of Hafiz, "He sees too far; he sees throughout; such is the only man I wish to see or be." Goethe wrote, "Hafiz has no peer!" He was called the "Tongue of the Hidden," suggesting that his work gives vent to hidden mystical concepts, perhaps in hidden ways, but there is conflict between those who interpret his poems as Sufi mysticism, in which the Beloved stands for God, and those who see his work as sensual in nature, in which case the Beloved is a human lover. Perhaps, like William Blake, Hafiz discovered a marriage of these two opposites (Goethe has suggested as much). It is true that one critic believes him to have been part of the Malamatiyye Sufi sect, whose members behaved like beggars and drunkards. Certainly the Sufi trope of the worshiper annihilating him- or herself in God like a moth into a flame appears again and again in his verse. There is also evidence, in poems such as "The Body's Cup," that the drinking of wine is to be seen as a mystical intoxication, and that the tavern becomes a kind of temple. Peter Avery and John Heath-Stubbs suggest that the imbibing of wine in Hafiz's poetry is to be understood as drinking from the magical cup of Jamshid, a hero of Ferdowsi's *Shahnama*, in which "His cup reflects the whole world in its depths, and confers all knowledge on him who drinks of it."[1]

FURTHER READING: Aryanpur, A., tr. *Poetical Horoscope or Odes*, 1965. Avery, Peter, and John Heath-Stubbs, trs. *Hafiz of Shiraz: Thirty Poems Translated*, 1952. Bell, G., tr. *Poems from the Divan*, 1928. Smith, Paul, tr. *Toyve of the Midden: Poems from the Divan*, 1986. Street, C. K., tr. *Hafiz in Quatrains*, 1946.

---

1. Peter Avery, and John Heath-Stubbs. *Hafiz of Shiraz: Thirty Poems Translated* (London: Jon Murray, 1952), 7.

The Body's Cup

Last night I saw angels knocking at the tavern door;
they shaped and cast a winecup from Adam's clay,

and I was drunk with potent wine poured
by ascetic angels who dwell behind the sacred veil.

The sky couldn't bear that burden of love alone,   5
so they cast the dice and my poor name came up.

Seventy-two sects bicker over fairy tales;
forgive them, they don't know the truth.

Thank you God for making peace with me;
the Sufis dance and raise their cups to you.   10

The candle laughs flame, but the true fire
harvests bodies of countless ecstatic moths.

The brides of poetry have combed my hair.
Only Hafiz has ripped the veil from wisdom's face.

TRANSLATED BY TONY BARNSTONE

The Sickle

I see the new moon's sickle slicing
through the sky's green field
and think of what I've sown
and of the coming harvest.
"Fortune, you've overslept," I say,   5
"the sun is already high."
But he replies "Don't worry
about the past;
if like the Messiah you rise
pure and bodiless into the sky,   10
your light will illuminate the sun.
Don't rely on that night thief the moon,
he stole Kay Kaus's crown and Kay Khusrau's belt;
though gold and rubies
hang from your ear,   15
hear this advice
before your beauty passes.
May the evil eye
not gaze on your beauty mark,
for that mole like a pawn   20

on heaven's chessboard
holds sun and moon in check.
Let the sky not boast
of its beautiful harvest
for a lover would trade the halo   25
of the moon for a barleycorn
and all the Pleiades for two.
As to the harvest of religion,
hypocrisy scorches it like wildfire.
So Hafiz, toss on your woolen cloak   30
and leave this place."

TRANSLATED BY TONY BARNSTONE

Love's Journey

Boy, bring me a cup of wine and make it quick;
love seemed easy at first but trouble followed.
I can still smell his musky hair twisting
on the wind; it clots my heart.

In this caravansary I can't rest long;   5
the trader's bells are always calling me to move on.
Listen to the wise man even if he says to stain
           your prayer mat with wine;
that adept traveler understands the way.

My life is whirlpools, waves and tarry night;   10
what do people on shore know of me? Nothing.
Yet my selfish lust has made me infamous;
my secrets are the latest juicy gossip.

Hafiz, don't renounce your lover's bed;
love him and forget the world instead.   15

TRANSLATED BY TONY BARNSTONE

6

Modern Arabic, Hebrew, Turkish, Alexandrian Greek, and Persian Literatures

INTRODUCTION

The modern period in the Middle East and North Africa has been marked by European imperialism, the resistance to colonial power, revolutionary movements, and ethnic and religious conflicts within and between nations. At the turn of the nineteenth century, the French moved into Egypt, where they stayed until the British forced them out in the 1880s. Britain and Russia fought over Iran and Afghanistan, as the British strove to attain a secure land route to their colonial possessions in India. The French extended their economic influence into Lebanon and Syria, and the Germans created close economic and military ties with the Turkish Ottoman Empire. North Africa largely lost its independence in the imperialist frenzy of the

late nineteenth century. Conflict between the European colonial powers over their African and Middle Eastern holdings helped set the stage for World War I. The soldiers of the massive Ottoman Empire fought on the side of Germany against the British, who were aided by Arabic forces marshaled by Lawrence of Arabia. After World War I, anticolonial movements, nationalism, and at times armed resistance to European imperialism developed in North Africa, fueled by a widespread resurgence of Islamic culture and ideals, and by resistance to Christianity, which had become associated with the imperialist conquerors. Much of the Middle East had been under the dominion of the Ottoman Empire, which had spread rapidly from the fourteenth to the sixteenth centuries over Egypt, Persia, Mesopotamia, Arabia, Byzantium, Syria, Palestine, parts of North Africa, and large parts of southeastern Europe. After the late seventeenth century, however, the empire began to collapse in on itself and by the nineteenth century it was known as the "Sick Man of Europe." Its demise as an empire took place at the conclusion of World War I. The history of the modern Middle East and North Africa is in great part the history of the dissolution of the Ottoman Empire and the creation of newly independent states. The demise of the remnants of European colonial empires in the Middle East and North Africa took place in the years following World War II.

Egypt has been a marker of many of the essential political changes that the Middle East area has seen in our time. A brief look at its modern history will reflect a larger picture of the Middle East and North Africa, the foreign occupations and humiliations, the revolutions and birth of new states. After dealing with French, Turkish, and British occupiers, an autonomous Egypt under Khedive Ismail Pasha built the Suez Canal. However, by 1875, in severe debt from overspending, the Egyptian leader was forced to sell the canal to the British and accept the establishment of a French-English Debt Commission. In 1881, Ismail's son rebelled against English interference, which prompted the landing of British troops and the country became a British protectorate. Egypt won back much of her independence from Britain in 1923, except for the Suez Canal, which remained in British hands. The Egyptians also were compelled to share with the British the Sudan, which had been a booty from an earlier Egyptian imperial conquest. In addition, Britain retained extraterritorial rights to station troops in parts of Egypt, a privilege that lasted until 1949.

In the years following World War II, there was a substantial influx to Palestine of Jewish survivors of the Holocaust in Europe, which was a continuation of earlier immigration in the 1930s, with the purpose of realizing the late-nineteenth-century Zionist movement to establish a Jewish homeland in the area. The Arabic population resisted this movement, leading to widespread violence and instability in the region. Concern over this conflict, and international sentiment over the massacre of approximately six million Jews by the Nazis, helped to catalyze a compromise settlement by the United Nations. In this 1947 settlement, the United Nations partitioned Palestine into a Jewish state, Israel (inhabited both by Jews and

Arabs), and an Arabic state, Palestine, and ended the British mandate over the territory. Although there had always been a Jewish presence in the area (descendents from ancient communities in Israel, Iraq, Iran, Egypt, Yemen, and Libya), the Arab states did not accept what they saw as another European intrusion. As the British withdrew from the region in 1948, war broke out, and Israel was invaded by a coalition of surrounding Arab nations. As a result of the war, many Arabs were forced to leave Israel, and Jews were expelled from their homes in Arab nations. The Arab nations were defeated in the 1948 war, and the nascent Arab state of Palestine disappeared when Jordan (which had not recognized the validity of either Israel or Palestine) annexed East Jerusalem and the West Bank, and Egypt occupied the Gaza Strip. Israel also expanded as a result of the war, and it grew even more as a consequence of the later 1967 war. This history of frequent warfare (there have been several wars between Israel and its neighbors since Israel's founding), of dispute over territory, and of the dual diaspora of Arabs and Jews, has been the source of continuing embittered contention to this day. However, in 1977, Anwar Sadat, the president of Egypt, surprised the world with a peace initiative, and in 1979, Egypt and Israel formalized a peace treaty. Though for a while the region was somewhat quiet with further rapprochement between Israel and the Arab nations, and difficult negotiations between Israel and the Palestine Liberation Organization over the establishment of a Palestinian state, as of this writing, struggle in the area continues and the outcome is by no means certain.

Earlier in Egypt, under the military governments of General Muhammad Naguib, the monarchy was overthrown and abolished in 1953 and, under pressure from President Gamal Abdel Nasser, the English evacuated Suez in 1956. Egypt was finally free of foreign rule. That same year the huge Sudan announced its independence from Egyptian and British rule. Soon after, northern Muslim Sudan began an intermittent war with southern Christian Sudan, a terrible religious and ethnic battle that continues to this day.

Now, the process of overturning monarchies, which had begun in Turkey in the 1920s, spread and soon the monarchs and their retinues fled from Iraq, Iran, and Libya. In Saudi Arabia, Jordan, Morocco, and in small oil sheikdoms of the Arabian peninsula, they remained. After a devastating war of independence by Algerians against the French, Algeria achieved independence in 1962. The last of the imperialists went home, and colonial rule formally disappeared from this huge basis of ancient and modern civilization.

The political history of these regions has necessarily permeated the cultural life of each country. While Kemal Attaturk (1881–1938) was abolishing the Turkish sultanate (1922) and religious caliphate (1924), turning Turkey into a secular republic, social poets arose to add their word about further reform. The greatest poet of Turkey was Nazim Hikmet (1902–1963), a man who spent most of his adult life in prison as a Communist critic to each regime and a magnificent poet of solitude, prison, love, and everyday miseries and glories. In recent years, Turkey has produced many novelists and poets who are entering the world scene.

In Egypt are two great writers, the poet Constantine Cavafy (1873–1933), who wrote in Modern Greek, the language of his native Alexandria, and the novelist Naguib Mahfouz (1911–), who has emerged as the foremost fiction writer in the Arabic language. In Syria, Iraq, Palestine, Jordan, Egypt, and Algeria, there have been remarkable new talents in poetry as well as the novel, and Israel has likewise seen a flourishing in the arts, including the fiction of Nobel Prize–winning novelist S. Y. Agnon. Other important modern writers of the Middle East area include Yashar Kemal (1922–) in Turkey, and the extraordinary feminist poet Forugh Farrokhzad (1935–1967) of Iran, who, like Sylvia Plath, died in her thirty-second year. After 1200 in Spain and 1300 in the East, there was a decline in Arabic writing, but in the nineteenth and twentieth centuries, there has been a resurgence of Arabic literatures exemplified by outstanding poets, such as Adunis (1930–) and Mahmud Darwish (1942–), and novelists such as Naguib Mahfouz, winner of the 1988 Nobel Prize for Literature.

Similarly, Hebrew literature of the Bridge area—except for a flowering in Muslim Spain in poetry, philosophy, and mystical Kabbalah—was largely dormant after the biblical period. The diaspora Jews, spread around the world, usually wrote in the languages spoken in their adopted nations, and their work was assimilated into the literatures of their habitation. The Spanish-Portuguese philosopher Spinoza, living in Holland in safe exile from the Spanish Inquisition, wrote in Latin. Moses Mendelssohn, Karl Marx, Heinrich Heine, and Franz Kafka wrote in German, Primo Levi in Italian. Osip Mandelstam, Boris Pasternak, and Isaac Babel wrote in Russian. Sholom Aleichem and Isaac Bashevis Singer wrote in Yiddish, and Benjamin Disraeli, Saul Bellow, and many others wrote in English. But Hebrew took on new life as the diaspora Jews in Israel once again adopted biblical Hebrew as their literary language. Major Israeli writers include the poets Yehuda Amichai (1924–2000) and Dan Pagis (1930–1986) and many outstanding novelists, who have been translated into the world's languages.

The English and French were the main colonial powers of the Middle East and North Africa. By the second decade after World War II, Europe had withdrawn its political hegemony over the region, and so the English were gone from Iraq, Palestine, Jordan, Israel, the Arabian Peninsula, Egypt, and the Suez Canal, and the French from Lebanon, Tunisia, Libya, Algeria, and Morocco. But in many countries, English and French have remained not only as a *lingua franca* for purposes of commerce and travel, but also as the literary language of writers in Lebanon and especially in Algeria. There, despite the intense war of independence against the French, many of the leading novelists have chosen to write in French in order to reach a global audience. But apart from the Algerians, Lebanese, and a few Egyptians who write in English or French, the writers of Asia Minor and North Africa largely continue to use their ancient tongues, Persian, Arabic,

Turkish, Berber, and Hebrew, as the vehicle for verbal expression. They write in languages that still have an ancient memory and a modern historical vitality.

These modern writers often confront and absorb colonial experience and Western influence, as well as their own ancient traditions. The West itself, which owes so much of its philosophy, religion, and literature to western Asia and North Africa, has usually been an unacknowledging child, but our parents and their enormous surviving work continue to be read. With the increasing availability of fine translations, we are persuaded both to return to our historic and cultural progenitors and to hear the new voices that echo deeply today.

■ Traditional Song (from uncertain period) *Algeria*

TRANSLATED BY WILLIS BARNSTONE

The old *haufi* traditional women's songs of Algeria were recorded in our century by Mostefa Lacheraf. They deal with many themes, including love, desert and garden landscapes of Algeria, and in this instance family social criticism, which is handled through the comic insult poem.

FURTHER READING: Lacheraf, Mostefa. *Écrits didactiques sur la culture, l'histoire et la societé en Algerie,* 1988.

Be Happy

Be happy for me, girls,
my mother-in-law is dead!
In the morning I found her
stiff, her mouth shut.
Yet I won't believe it
till I see the grass
waving over her tomb.

5

■ Constantine Cavafy (1863–1933) *Alexandria, Egypt* (poems)

Constantine Cavafy was born in Alexandria, Egypt, to a family originally from Constantinople. From the age of nine to age sixteen, Cavafy was in England with his family, where he acquired English and a love for English literature. From 1882 to 1885, he lived in Constantinople and, thereafter, remained in Alexandria, where for thirty years he worked as a clerk and ultimately as assistant director in the irrigation section of the Ministry of Public Works. Alexandria, founded by Alexander the Great in 332 B.C., was a cosmopolitan city of Greek-speaking and Arabic-speaking inhabitants. Except for a few trips to Athens, Cavafy stayed in Alexandria, writing his poems, ordering them in an intended final canon, publishing a few of them privately, and gathering a secret major reputation in continental Greece and abroad. E. M. Forster was a great believer and carrier of his word.

Although Cavafy is considered the greatest modern poet in the Greek language—a language that has given us, among other poets, two Nobel Prize laureates, George Seferis and Odysseus Elytis—Cavafy did not formally publish a book during his lifetime. Rather, he had pamphlets printed, containing a few poems. Forster, who lived in Alexandria for five years, proclaimed Cavafy's originality and quality in England, where T. S. Eliot published "Ithaka" in his magazine *Criterion.* Eschewing turn-of-the-century sentimentality, Cavafy was, before others, a modernist, whose work is characterized by a straightforwardness about homosexual themes, and by a deep interest in classical mythology. Cavafy's myth, in which his personal obsessions and ideals were realized, was Alexandria, the city of Neoplatonists and mystery religions, of geometers and grammarians—the diverse Hellenic world bound together by the Mouseion, an extraordinary library-university. His myth also included Roman settlements and Byzantine Greece of Asia Minor, as well as the color, shadows, intrigues, and antihistory of high and low life, of patriarchs and emperors and their jealous plotting relatives in Constantinople. When he wrote of everyday life in the Alexandria of his own period, it was of illicit, erotic encounters and their splendors, memories, and regrets; sordid and cheap rooms, where one heard voices from the workers playing cards in the suspect tavern downstairs, where in his plain bed he was drunk with love; of how a pencil sketch of a sensitive friend done on a ship evokes an afternoon on a ship, long ago, "out of time, out of time," that his soul brings back to him. The pessimism, idealism, realism, historical recreations, and allegories in "Waiting for the Barbarians," "The City," "The God Abandons Antony," and "Ithaka" place these poems permanently in the world canon of literature. The South African novelist J. M. Coetzee chose "Waiting for the Barbarians" as the title for his great novel and effectively translated the poem into the mood and lesson of his entire work.

T. S. Eliot and Ezra Pound radically changed modern literature by their ventures into antiquity, and it is increasingly clear that their model was Cavafy. Yet, while Eliot and Pound explored history and myth through literature and anthropology and recreated a past that remained exotically remote, Cavafy was a participant in his histories and myths and created ancient history indistinguishable from the present—as would later Greek poets George Seferis and Yannis Ritsos in their distinguished imitations of his work. For Cavafy, Greece is all times, and he lives in them through his personal participatory creations. Cavafy, Pablo Neruda, and Rainer Maria Rilke are today probably the most translated poets in all languages. The obscure Alexandrian, a word-of-mouth myth during his lifetime, has become an icon for our century.

FURTHER READING: Bien, Peter. *Constantine Cavafy*, 1964. Cavafy, Constantine. *Collected Poems*. Translated by Edmund Keeley and Philip Sherrard, 1975; *The Complete Poems of Cavafy*. Translated by Rae Dalven, 1961. Keeley, Edmund. *Cavafy's Alexandria: A Study of Myth in Progress*, 1976.

The Windows

In these shadowy rooms where I spend
boring days, I walk up down and around
to find the windows. When a window opens
it will be a consolation.
But the windows are unfindable or I can't   5
find them. And perhaps it is better not to find them.
Perhaps the light will be a new tyranny.
Who knows what new things it will disclose?

TRANSLATED BY ALIKI BARNSTONE AND WILLIS BARNSTONE

An Old Man

Back in a corner, alone in the clatter and babble
An old man sits with his head bent over a table
And his newspaper in front of him, in the cafe.

Sour with old age, he ponders a dreary truth—
How little he enjoyed the years when he had youth,   5
Good looks and strength and clever things to say.

He knows he's quite old now: he feels it, he sees it,
And yet the time when he was young seems—was it?
Yesterday. How quickly, how quickly it slipped away.

Now he sees how Discretion has betrayed him,   10
And how stupidly he let the liar persuade him
With phrases: *Tomorrow. There's plenty of time. Some day.*

He recalls the pull of impulses he suppressed,
The joy he sacrificed. Every chance he lost
Ridicules his brainless prudence a different way.   15

But all these thoughts and memories have made
The old man dizzy. He falls asleep, his head
Resting on the table in the noisy cafe.

TRANSLATED BY ROBERT PINSKY

Walls

Without concern or pity or shame,
they have built wide and tall walls around me,

and now I sit here and despair,
thinking of nothing else. This fate eats me up.

I had so much to do outside.   5
When they were putting up the walls, how could I
      have been blind!

I never heard the noise. No sound of builders.
Imperceptibly they closed me off from the world.

TRANSLATED BY TONY BARNSTONE AND WILLIS BARNSTONE

He Swears

He swears now and then to start a better life.
But when life comes with its own counsel,
its own compromises and promises,
when night comes with its own compulsion
of the body that wants and demands,   5
he returns, lost, to the same fatal joy.

TRANSLATED BY WILLIS BARNSTONE

Desires

Like beautiful bodies that haven't aged
and were locked, with tears, in a brilliant mausoleum,
with roses at the head and jasmine at the feet,
that is what desires look like when they pass by
without having been fulfilled, without even   5
a single night of passion, or a moon at dawn.

TRANSLATED BY ALIKI BARNSTONE AND WILLIS BARNSTONE

The City

You said, "I will go to another city, go to another sea,
find another city better than this one.
Whatever I try to do is fated to go wrong
and my heart lies buried as if it were dead.
How long will my mind linger in this marasma?   5
Wherever my eye wanders, wherever I look,
I see black ruins of my life, here
where I've spent so many years and wasted them
and destroyed them."

You won't find a new country, won't find another sea.   10
The city will pursue you. You will walk
the same streets. In the same neighborhood you will grow old
and in the same houses you'll turn gray.
You will always end up in the city.
Don't hope for things elsewhere.   15
There is no ship for you, there is no road.
As you have wasted your life here
in this small corner, you have destroyed it all over the earth.

TRANSLATED BY WILLIS BARNSTONE

The Afternoon Sun

This room, how well I know it.
Now they're renting it and the one next door
as business offices. The whole house has become
an office building for agents, merchants, companies.

This room, how familiar it is.   5

Here near the door was the couch,
and a Turkish carpet in front of it.
Close by, the shelf with two yellow vases.
To the right—no, opposite—a wardrobe with a mirror.
In the middle the table where he wrote,   10
and the three big wicker chairs.
Next to the window was the bed
where we made love so many times.

They must still be around somewhere, those other things.

Beside the window was the bed;   15
the afternoon sun fell half across it.

One afternoon at four o'clock we separated
for only a week . . . And then
that week became forever.

TRANSLATED BY WILLIS BARNSTONE

Morning Sea

Let me stop here. Let me too look at nature awhile.
The glowing blue of the morning sea
and cloudless sky and yellow shore, all
beautiful and brightly lighted.

Let me stop here. Let me pretend I see this   5
(I really did see it for a second when I first stopped)
and not the usual daydreams here too,
my memories, the images of the body's pleasure.

TRANSLATED BY WILLIS BARNSTONE

Manuel Komminós

One melancholy day in September
Emperor Manuel Komminós
felt his death was near. The astronomers
(paid off, of course) went on babbling
about how many years he still had to live.   5
But while they were talking, he
remembered an old religious custom
and ordered ecclesiastical vestments
to be brought from a monastery,
and he wore them, pleased to assume   10
the modest image of a priest or monk.

Happy are all those who believe,
and like Emperor Manuel leave this world
dressed modestly in their faith.

TRANSLATED BY WILLIS BARNSTONE

Since Nine O'Clock

Half past twelve. Time has gone by quickly
from nine o'clock when I lit the lamp,
and sat down here. I've been sitting without reading
without speaking. Whom could I talk to
all alone in this house?   5

Since nine when I lit the lamp
the image of my young body
came and took me and reminded me
of closed aromatic rooms
and past sensual pleasure—what daring pleasure!   10
And it also brought back to my eyes
streets now unrecognizable,
bustling crowded night clubs closed down,
and theaters and cafes that once were.

The image of my young body   15
came and brought me the sad things too:
family grief, separations,
feelings of my own people, feelings
of the dead so little acknowledged.

Half past twelve. How time has gone by.   20
Half past twelve. How the years have gone by.

TRANSLATED BY WILLIS BARNSTONE

Waiting for the Barbarians

What are we waiting for, assembled in the forum?

   The barbarians are coming today.

Why is nothing happening in the senate?
Why are senators sitting there without making laws?

   Because the barbarians are coming today.   5
   What laws can the senators make now?
   When the barbarians come, they make the laws.

Why did our emperor get up so early
and sit at the city's main gate,
on his throne, in state, wearing his crown?   10

   Because the barbarians are coming today
   and the emperor is waiting to receive

their leader. Yes, he is preparing
to give him a pergamon scroll. He has
inscribed it with many titles and names.   *15*

Why have our two consuls and praetors come out
today in red robes, in embroidered togas?
Why have they put on bracelets with so many amethysts,
and rings glittering with magnificent emeralds?

Why today are they carrying elegant canes   *20*
exquisitely worked in silver and gold?

    Because the barbarians are coming today
    and such things dazzle the barbarians.

Why don't our distinguished orators come as usual
and whip out their speeches, and say their piece?   *25*

    Because the barbarians are coming today
    and they are fed up with rhetoric and public speaking.

Why are there these sudden signs of worry
and confusion? (How grave the faces have become.)
Why are the streets and squares quickly emptying   *30*
and everyone going home so lost in thought?

    Because it is night and the barbarians haven't come.
    And some have arrived from the borders
    and said there are no barbarians any longer.

And now what will happen without barbarians?   *35*
Those people were a kind of solution.

TRANSLATED BY WILLIS BARNSTONE

Nero's Deadline

Nero wasn't troubled when he heard
the utterance of the Delphic oracle.
"Beware of the seventy-third year."
Plenty of time left for enjoyment.
He's thirty. The deadline the god   *5*
gave him is long enough
to confront his future dangers.

Now he'll go back to Rome, a little tired,
but wonderfully tired from that journey
whose days all devoted to pleasure—   *10*
the theaters, the gardens, friends, the stadiums,

evenings in the cities of Achaia,
and naked bodies and sweet lusts, especially . . .

So much for Nero. And in Spain Galba
secretly musters and drills his army, 15
the old general in his seventy-third year.

TRANSLATED BY WILLIS BARNSTONE

Ithaka[1]

When you set out on your journey to Ithaka,
pray that the road be long,
full of adventures, full of knowledge.
Don't be afraid of the Laistrygonians,
the Cyclops and angry Poseidon. 5
You'll never find such things on your way
if your thoughts remain high, if a rare
excitement touches your spirit and your body,
You will not encounter the Laistrygonians,
the Cyclops and angry Poseidon 10
if you do not harbor them inside your soul,
if your soul does not raise them up before you.

Pray that the road be long,
that there be many summer mornings
when with pleasure and joy 15
you enter ports seen for the first time;
may you stop at Phoenician market places
to buy fine merchandise,
mother of pearl and coral, amber and ebony,
sensual perfume of every kind, 20
as many sensual perfumes as you can;
may you walk through many Egyptian cities
to learn and to learn from their scholars.

Always keep Ithaka in your mind.
To arrive there is your destined vision. 25
But do not hurry the journey at all.
Better for it to last for years,
for you to be old when you reach the island,

---

1. In Homer's *Odyssey*, the protagonist Odysseus takes ten years to find his way back to Ithaka, his home island where he was king. The Cyclops and Laistrygonians are monster obstacles on his path.

rich with all you have gained on the way,
not expecting Ithaka to make you rich.   *30*

Ithaka gave you the beautiful voyage.
Without her you would not have taken the road.
But she has nothing else to give you.
And if you find her poor, Ithaka didn't fool you.
Wise as you've become, with so much experience,   *35*
but now you'll understand what Ithakas mean.

TRANSLATED BY WILLIS BARNSTONE

The God Abandons Antony[2]

When suddenly at the hour of midnight
you hear the invisible troupe passing by
with beautiful music, with voices—
don't futilely mourn your luck giving out, your work
collapsing, the designs of your life   *5*
that have all proved to be illusions.
As if long time prepared, as if full of courage,
say goodbye to her, the Alexandria who is leaving.
Above all don't fool yourself, don't say how it was
a dream, how your ears tricked you.   *10*
Don't stoop to such empty hopes.
As if long time prepared, as if full of courage,
as is right for you who are worthy of such a city,
go and stand tall by the window
and listen with emotion, but not   *15*
with the pleas and whining of a coward,
hear the voices—your last pleasure—
the exquisite instruments of that secret troupe,
and say goodbye to her, the Alexandria you are losing.

TRANSLATED BY ALIKI BARNSTONE AND WILLIS BARNSTONE

---

2. The title is a quotation from Plutarch's *Life of Antony*. In Cavafy's version the poet recounts that the night before Antony will fight and lose to Augustus Caesar for control of Alexandria, he hears a mysterious musical troupe passing through the streets under his window. He is urged to enjoy this last esthetic moment and also to confront, courageously, that this will be his last pleasure before defeat and death on the next day. In Plutarch this passing bacchanalia is interpreted as a sign that Bacchus, Antony's protector, had abandoned him, for the troupe is heading for the gates of the city nearest the enemy.

One Night

The room was cheap and sordid,
hidden above the suspect tavern.
From the window you could see the alley
filthy and narrow. From below
came the voices of some workers   5
who were playing cards, having a good time.

And there on the plain, ordinary bed
I had love's body, I had the lips,
voluptuous and rosy lips of drunken ecstasy—
rosy lips of such ecstasy that now   10
as I write, after so many years
in my lonely house, I am drunk again.

TRANSLATED BY WILLIS BARNSTONE

September, 1903

At least let me fool myself with illusions
so as not to feel the emptiness of my life.

And I came so close so many times.
And how paralyzed I was, and how cowardly;
Why did I keep my lips sealed   5
while the emptiness of my life wept inside me,
and my desires put on black clothes?

To have been so close so many times
to the eyes, to the voluptuous lips,
to the body I dreamed of, I loved.   10
To have been so close so many times.

TRANSLATED BY WILLIS BARNSTONE

Of the Jews (A.D. 50)

Painter and poet, runner and discus thrower,
beautiful as Endymion: Ianthis, son of Antony,
from a family close to the synagogue.

"My noblest days are those
when I give up the search for sensation,   5

when I desert the bright and stark Hellenism,
with its masterly fixation
on perfectly shaped and perishable white limbs.
And become the man I would always
want to be: A son of the Jews, of the holy Jews." *10*

His declaration was very fiery. "Be always
of the Jews, the holy Jews."

But he didn't stay that way at all.
The Hedonism and the Art of Alexandria
possessed him as their child. *15*

TRANSLATED BY WILLIS BARNSTONE

On the Ship

Of course it looks like him,
this little pencil drawing.

Quickly drawn on the deck of the ship,
on a magic afternoon, *5*
the Ionian Sea around us.
It looks like him. But I remember him as handsomer.
He was sensitive to the point of suffering
and it illumined his expression.
He appears to me handsomer *10*
now as my soul calls him back, out of Time.

Out of Time. All these things are very old—
the sketch, and the ship, and the afternoon.

TRANSLATED BY WILLIS BARNSTONE

The Bandaged Shoulder

He said he'd banged into a wall or had fallen down.
But probably there was another reason
for the wounded and bandaged shoulder.

With a rather violent movement
as he was reaching for a shelf to take down *5*
some photographs he wanted to look at closely,
the bandage came loose and a little blood oozed out.

I did it up again, slowly, taking my time
with the binding. He wasn't in pain
and I liked looking at the blood. It was   *10*
a thing of my love, that blood.

When he left I found in front of his chair
a bloody rag, from the dressing,
a rag to be thrown immediately into the garbage.

And I put it to my lips,   *15*
and kissed it a long time—
the blood of love against my lips.

TRANSLATED BY WILLIS BARNSTONE

Hidden

From all I did and all I said,
let no one try to find out who I was.
An obstacle was there and it transformed
the actions and manner of my life.
An obstacle was there, and often it stopped me   *5*
when I was about to speak.
From my most unobserved actions
and my most veiled writing—
from these alone I will be understood.
But maybe it isn't worth going through   *10*
so much care and effort to discover who I am.
Later, in a more perfect society,
someone else made like me
is certain to appear and act freely.

TRANSLATED BY WILLIS BARNSTONE

■ S. Y. Agnon (1888–1970) *Israel* (story)

TRANSLATED BY ROBERT ALTER

Shmuel Yosef Agnon was born Samuel Josef Czaczkes in Buczacz, Galicia, at that time a part of the Austro-Hungarian Empire, now part of southern Poland. He adopted the pen name Agnon from the title of one of his stories, "Agunot" ("Deserted Wives"), after settling in Palestine in 1907. Often considered Israel's premier fiction writer, in 1966 he shared the Nobel Prize for Literature with the poet Nelly Sachs. He began writing in

Yiddish when he was sixteen, and later on wrote prolifically in Hebrew, helping to form the modern language as a superbly rich vehicle for evoking modern and ancient Jewish traditions, from the biblical Song of Songs to the mystical Kabbalah to life in the East European Pale and Jerusalem. On one of his stays in Germany, early in the century, he collaborated with Martin Buber to co-edit a collection of Hasidic folklore. Some of his deepest, most ironic, and mysterious tales are dreamlike Kafkaesque allegories of men and women caught between ancient beliefs and modern despair. "The Doctor's Divorce," on the other hand, is a masterful psychological exploration of an obsessive personality destroyed by jealousy, set in Vienna, the city of Sigmund Freud.

FURTHER READING: Agnon, S. Y. *Forever More,* 1961; *Twenty-one Stories,* 1970; *Guest for the Night,* 1968; *Two Tales: Betrothed, & Edo and Enam,* 1966; *Tehilla and Other Israeli Tales,* 1956.

The Doctor's Divorce

1

When I joined the staff of the hospital, I discovered there a blonde nurse who was loved by everyone and whose praise was on the lips of all the patients. As soon as they heard her footsteps, they would sit up in bed and stretch their arms out toward her as an only son reaches for his mother, and each one of them would call, "Nurse, nurse, come to me." Even the ill-tempered kind who find all the world provoking—as soon as she appeared, the frown-lines in their faces faded, their anger dissolved, and they were ready to do whatever she ordered. Not that it was her way to give orders: the smile that illuminated her face was enough to make patients obey her. In addition to her smile, there were her eyes, a kind of blue-black; everyone she looked at felt as if he were the most important thing in the world. Once I asked myself where such power comes from. From the moment I saw her eyes, I was just like the rest of the patients. And she had no special intentions toward me, nor toward anybody in particular. That smile on her lips, however, and that blue-black in her eyes had the further distinction of doing on their own more than their mistress intended.

One indication of the degree of affection in which she was generally held was the fact that even her fellow nurses liked her and were friendly toward her. And the head nurse, a woman of about forty, well born, thin and wan as vinegar, who hated everyone, patients and doctors alike, with the possible exception of black coffee and salted cakes and her lap dog—even she was favorably disposed in this case. Such a woman, who couldn't look at a girl without imagining her half wasted away, showed special kindness to this nurse. And one hardly need mention my fellow doctors. Every doctor with whom she happened to work thanked his stars. Even our professor, accustomed as he was to concern himself less with the suffering of the sick than with the orderliness of their beds, made no fuss if he found her sitting on a patient's bed. This old man, the master of so many disciples and the discoverer of cures for several diseases, died in a concentration camp where a Nazi trooper tormented him daily by forcing him to go through exercises. One day the trooper ordered him to lie flat on his belly with arms and legs outstretched, and as soon as he was down, he was commanded to get up. As he was not quick about it, the trooper trampled him with his cleated boots until the old man's thumbnails were mutilated. He contracted blood poisoning and died.

What more can I say? I took a liking to this girl just as everyone else did. But I can add that she also took a liking to me. And though any man could say as much, others did not dare while I dared, and so I married her.

2

This is how it came about. One afternoon, as I was leaving the dining hall, I ran into Dinah. I said to her, "Are you busy, nurse?"

"No, I'm not busy."

"What makes today so special?"

"Today is my day off from the hospital."

"And how are you celebrating your day off?"

"I haven't yet considered the matter."

"Would you allow me to give you some advice?"

"Please do, doctor."

"But only if I am paid for the advice. Nowadays you don't get something for nothing."

She looked at me and laughed. I continued, "I have one good piece of advice which is actually two—that we go to the Prater[1] and that we go to the opera. And if we hurry, we can stop first at a cafe. Do you agree, nurse?" She nodded yes good-humoredly.

"When shall we go?" I asked.

"Whenever the doctor wants."

"I'll take care of what I have to as soon as possible and I'll be right over."

"Whenever you come, you'll find me ready."

She went to her room and I to my responsibilities. A little while later, when I arrived to pick her up, I discovered that she had changed clothes. All at once she seemed a new person to me, and with the metamorphosis her charm was doubled, for she had both the charm I felt in her when she was in uniform and that which was lent her by the new clothes. I sat in her

---

1. Prater is a park in Vienna [Editor].

room and looked at the flowers on the table and by the bed, and after asking her whether she knew their names, I recited the name of each flower, in German and in Latin. But I quickly became apprehensive that a serious patient might be brought in and I would be paged. I got up from my seat and urged that we leave at once. I saw she was disturbed.

"Is something bothering you?" I asked.

"I thought you'd have something to eat."

"Right now, let's go, and if you are still so kindly disposed toward me, I'll come back to enjoy everything you give me, and I'll even ask for more."

"May I count on that?"

"I've already given you my word. Not only that, but, as I said, I'll ask for more."

As we left the hospital court, I said to the doorman, "You see this nurse? I'm taking her away from here." The doorman looked at us benevolently and said, "More power to you, doctor. More power to you, nurse."

We walked to the trolley stop. A trolley came along, but turned out to be full. The next one that arrived we thought we would be able to take. Dinah got onto the car. When I tried to climb up after her, the conductor called out, "No more room." She came down and waited with me for another car. At that point I commented to myself, Some people say that one shouldn't worry about a trolley or a girl that has gone because others will soon come along. But those who think that are fools. As far as the girl is concerned, can one find another girl like Dinah? And as to the trolley, I regretted every delay.

Along came a suburban trolley. Since its cars were new and spacious and empty of passengers, we got on. Suddenly (or, according to the clock, after a while), the trolley reached the end of the line and we found ourselves standing in a lovely place filled with gardens, where the houses were few.

We crossed the street talking about the hospital and the patients and the head nurse and the professor, who had instituted a fast once a week for all patients with kidney ailments because someone with kidney pains had fasted on the Day of Atonement and afterward there was no albumen in his urine. Then we mentioned all the cripples the war had produced, and we were pleased by the setting for our walk because there were no cripples around. I threw up my arms suddenly and said, "Let's forget about the hospital and cripples and speak about more pleasant things." She agreed with me, even though from her expression one could tell she was concerned that we might not find any other subject for conversation.

Children were playing. They saw us and began to whisper to each other. "Do you know, Fräulein," I asked Dinah, "what the children are talking about? They are talking about us."—"Perhaps." "Do you know what they're saying?" I went on. "They're saying, 'The two of them are bride and groom.'" Her face reddened as she answered, "Perhaps that's what they are saying."

"You mean you don't object to it?"

"To what?"

"To what the children are saying."

"Why should I care?"

"And if it were true, what would you say?"

"If what were true?"

I summoned my courage and answered, "If what the children say were true, I mean, that you and I belong together." She laughed and looked at me. I took her hand and said, "Give me the other one, too." She gave me her hand. I bent over and kissed both her hands, then looked at her. Her face became still redder. "There is a proverb," I told her, "that truth is with children and fools. We've already heard what the children say, and now listen to what a fool has to say, I mean, myself, for I have been touched with wisdom."

I stuttered and went on, "Listen, Dinah . . . " I had hardly begun to say all that was in my heart before I found myself a man more fortunate than all others.

3

Never was there a better time in my life than the period of our engagement. If it had been my opinion that marriage exists only because a man needs a woman and a woman a man, I now came to realize that there is no higher need than that one. At the same time, I began to understand why the poets felt it necessary to write love poems, despite the fact that I would have no part of them or their poems, because they wrote about other women and not about Dinah. Often I would sit and wonder, How many nurses there are in the hospital; how many women in the world; and I am concerned with one girl alone, who absorbs all my thoughts. As soon as I saw her again, I would say to myself, The doctor must have lost his wits to put her in the same category as other women. And my feelings toward her were reciprocated. But that blue-black in her eyes darkened like a cloud about to burst.

Once I asked her. She fixed her eyes on me without answering. I repeated my question. She pressed against me and said, "You don't know how precious you are to me and how much I love you." And a smile spread across her melancholy lips, that smile which drove me wild with its sweetness and its sorrow.

I asked myself, If she loves me, what reason could there be for this sadness? Perhaps her family is poor. But she said they were well-to-do. Perhaps she had promised to marry someone else. But she told me she was completely free. I began to pester her about it. She showed me still more affection, and she remained silent.

Nevertheless, I began to investigate her relatives. Perhaps they were rich but had been impoverished and she felt bad about them. I discovered that some of them were industrialists and some were people of distinction in other fields, and they all made comfortable livings.

I grew proud. I, a poor boy, the son of a lowly tinsmith, became fastidious about my dress, even though she paid no attention to clothes, unless I asked her to look at them. My love for her grew still greater. This was beyond all logic, for, to begin with, I had given her all my love. And she, too, gave me all her love. But her love had a touch of sadness in it which injected into my happiness a drop of gall.

This drop worked its way into all my limbs. I would ponder, What is this sadness? Is that what love is supposed to be like? I continued to beleaguer her with questions. She promised an answer but persisted in her evasiveness. When I reminded her of her promise, she took my hand in hers and said, "Let's be happy, darling, let's be happy and not disturb our happiness." And she sighed in a way that broke my heart. I asked her, "Dinah, what are you sighing about?" She smiled and answered through her tears, "Please, darling, don't say anything more." I was silent and asked no more questions. But my mind was not at ease. And I still awaited the time when she would agree to tell me what it was all about.

4

One afternoon I stopped in to see her. At that hour she was free from her work with the patients and she was sitting in her room sewing a new dress. I took the dress by the hem and let my hand glide over it. Then I lifted my eyes toward her. She looked straight into my eyes and said, "I was once involved with somebody else." She saw that I didn't realize what she meant, so she made her meaning more explicit. A chill ran through me and I went weak inside. I sat without saying a word. After a few moments I told her, "Such a thing would have never even occurred to me." Once I had spoken, I sat wondering and amazed, wondering over my own calmness and amazed at her for having done a thing so much beneath her. Nevertheless, I treated her just as before, as though she had in no way fallen in esteem. And, in fact, at that moment she had not fallen in my esteem and was as dear to me as always. Once she saw that, a smile appeared on her lips again. But her eyes were veiled, like someone moving out of one darkness into another.

I asked her, "Who was this fellow who left you without marrying you?" She evaded the question. "Don't you see, Dinah," I pursued, "that I bear no ill feeling toward you. It's only curiosity that leads me to ask such a question. So tell me, darling, who was he?" "What difference does it make to you what his name is?" Dinah asked. "Even so," I persisted, "I would like to know." She told me his name. "Is he a lecturer or a professor?" I asked. Dinah said, "He is an official." I reflected silently that important officials worked for her relatives, men of knowledge and scholars and inventors. Undoubtedly it was to the most important of them that she gave her heart. Actually, it made no difference who the man was to whom this woman more dear to me than all the world gave her love, but to delude myself I imagined that he was a great man, superior to all his fellows. "He's an official?" I said to her. "What is his job?" Dinah answered. "He is a clerk in the legislature." "I'm amazed at you, Dinah," I told her, "that a minor official, a clerk, was able to sweep you off your feet like that. And, besides, he left you, which goes to show that he wasn't good enough for you in the first place." She lowered her eyes and was silent.

From then on I did not remind her of her past, just as I would not have reminded her what dress she had worn the day before. And if I thought of it, I banished the thought from my mind. And so we were married.

5

Our wedding was like most weddings in these times, private, without pomp and ceremony. For I had no family, with the possible exception of the relative who once hit my father in the eye. And Dinah, ever since she became close to me, had grown away from her relatives. During that period, moreover, it was not customary to have parties and public rejoicing. Governments came and governments went, and between one and the next there was panic and confusion, turmoil and dismay. People who one day were rulers the next day were chained in prisons or hiding in exile.

And so our wedding took place with neither relatives nor invited guests, except for a bare quorum summoned by the beadle, miserable creatures who an hour or two ago were called for a funeral and now were summoned for my wedding. How pitiful were their borrowed clothes, how comic their towering high hats, how audacious their greedy eyes that looked forward to the conclusion of the ceremony when they could go into a bar with the money they had gotten through my wedding. I was in high spirits, and as strange as the thing seemed to me, my joy was not diminished. Let others be led under the bridal canopy by renowned and wealthy wedding guests. I would be married in the presence of poor people who, with what they would earn for their trouble, could buy bread. The children we would have wouldn't ask me, "Father, who was at your wedding?" just as I never asked my father who was at his wedding.

I put my hand in my pocket and pulled out several shillings which I handed to the beadle to give to the men over and above the agreed price. The beadle took the money and said nothing. I was afraid they would overwhelm me with thanks and praise, and I prepared myself to demur modestly. But not one of them came up to me. Instead, one fellow bent over, leaning on his cane, another stretched himself in order to appear tall, and a third looked at the bride in a way that was not decent. I asked the beadle about him. "That one," the beadle replied, and he bore down emphatically on the "th"-sound, "that one was an official who got fired." I nodded and said, "Well, well," as though with two well's I had concluded all the fellow's affairs. Meanwhile, the beadle chose four of his quorum, put a pole in the hand of each of the four, stretched a canopy over the poles,[2] and, in doing that, pushed one man who bent forward and thus brought the canopy tumbling down.

Afterward, while standing under the bridal canopy, I recalled the story of a man whose mistress forced him to marry her. He went and gathered for the ceremony all her lovers who had lived with her before her marriage, both to remind her of her shame and to punish himself for agreeing to marry such a woman. What a contemptible fellow and what a contemptible act! Yet I found that man to my liking, and I thought well of what he had done. And when the rabbi stood and read the marriage contract, I looked at the wedding guests and tried to imagine what the woman was like and what her lovers were like at that moment. And in the same way, just before, when my wife put out her finger for the wedding ring and I said to her, "Behold thou art consecrated unto me," I knew without anyone's telling me what that man was like at that moment.

6

After the wedding we left for a certain village to spend our honeymoon. I won't tell you everything that happened to us on the way and in the station and on the train; and, accordingly, I won't describe every mountain and hill we saw, nor the brooks and springs in the valleys and mountains, as tellers of tales are accustomed to do when they set about describing the trip of a bride and groom. Undoubtedly there were mountains and hills and springs and brooks, and several things did happen to us on the way, but everything else has escaped me and been forgotten because of one incident which occurred on the first night. If you're not tired yet, I'll tell you about it.

We arrived at the village and registered at a little hotel situated among gardens and surrounded by mountains and rivers. We had supper and went up to the room that the hotel had set aside for us, for I had telegraphed our reservation before the wedding. Examining the room, my wife let her eyes dwell on the red roses that had been put there. "Who was so nice," I said jokingly, "to send us these lovely roses?" "Who?" asked my wife with genuine wonder, as though she thought there were someone here beside the hotel people who knew about us. "In any case," I said, "I'm taking them away, because their fragrance will make it hard to sleep. Or perhaps we should leave

2. The bride, groom, their parents, and the Rabbi stand below this canopy in traditional Jewish weddings [Editor].

them in honor of the occasion." "Oh yes," my wife answered after me in the voice of a person who speaks without hearing his own words. I said to her, "And don't you want to smell them?"—"Oh, yes, I want to." But she forgot to smell them. This forgetfulness was strange for Dinah, who loved flowers so much. I reminded her that she hadn't yet smelled the flowers. She bent her head over them. "Why are you bending down," I asked her, "when you can hold them up to you?" She looked at me as though she had just heard something novel. The blue-black in her eyes darkened, and she said, "You are very observant, my darling." I gave her a long kiss; then with closed eyes I said to her, "Now, Dinah, we are alone."

She stood up and took off her clothes with great deliberation, and began to fix her hair. As she was doing that, she sat down, bending her head over the table. I leaned over to see why she was taking so long, and I saw that she was reading a little pamphlet of the kind one finds in Catholic villages. The title was "Wait for Your Lord in Every Hour That He May Come."

I took her chin in my hand and said to her, "You don't have to wait, your lord has already come," and I pressed my mouth against hers. She lifted her eyes sadly and laid the pamphlet aside. I took her in my arms, put her in bed, and turned the lamp-wick down.

The flowers gave off their fragrance and sweet stillness surrounded me. Suddenly I heard the sound of footsteps in the room next to ours. I forced the sound out of my mind and refused to pay attention to it, for what difference did it make to me whether or not there was someone there. I didn't know him and he didn't know us. And if he did know us, we had a wedding and were properly married. I embraced my wife with great love and was happy beyond limit with her, for I knew she was entirely mine.

With Dinah still in my arms, I strained attentively to make out whether that fellow's footsteps had stopped, but I heard him still pacing back and forth. His footsteps drove me to distraction: a strange idea now occurred to me, that this was the clerk my wife had known before her marriage. I was horror-stricken at the thought, and I had to bite my lip to prevent myself from cursing out loud. My wife took notice.

"What's wrong, sweetheart?"

"Nothing, nothing."

"I see something's troubling you."

"I've already told you nothing is."

"Then I must have been mistaken."

I lost my head and said to her, "You were not mistaken."

"What is it, then?"

I told her.

She began to sob.

"Why are you crying?" I said.

She swallowed her tears and answered, "Open the door and the windows and tell the whole world of my depravity."

I was ashamed of what I had said, and I tried to mollify her. She listened to me and we made peace.

7

From then on that man was never out of my sight, whether my wife was present or not. If I sat by myself, I thought about him, and if I talked with my wife, I mentioned him. If I saw a flower, I was reminded of the red roses, and if I saw a red rose, I was reminded of him, suspecting that was the kind he used to give my wife. This, then, was the reason she refused to smell the roses on the first night, because she was ashamed in her husband's presence to smell the same kind of flowers that her lover used to bring her. When she cried, I would console her. But in the kiss of reconciliation I heard the echo of another kiss which someone else had given her. We are enlightened individuals, modern people, we seek freedom for ourselves and for all humanity, and in point of fact we are worse than the most diehard reactionaries.

Thus passed the first year. When I wanted to be happy with my wife, I would remember the one who had spoiled my happiness, and I would sink into gloom. If she was happy, I told myself, What makes her so happy? She must be thinking of that louse. As soon as I mentioned him to her, she would burst into tears. "What are you crying for?" I would say. "Is it so difficult for you to hear me talk against that louse?"

I knew that she had long since put all thought of him out of her mind, and if she thought of him at all, it was only negatively, for she had never really loved him. It was only his supreme audacity together with a transient moment of weakness in her that had led her to lose control and listen to his demands. But my understanding of the matter brought me no equanimity. I wanted to grasp his nature, what it was in him that had attracted this modest girl raised in a good family.

I began to search through her books in the hope of finding some sort of letter from him, for Dinah was in the habit of using her letters as bookmarks. I found nothing, however. Perhaps, I thought, she has deliberately hidden them somewhere else, inasmuch as I have already searched all her books and found nothing. I could not bring myself to examine her private things. And that made me still angrier, for I was pretending to be decent while my thoughts were contemptible. Since I had spoken with no one else about her past, I sought counsel in books and began to read love stories in order to understand the nature of women and their lovers. But the novels bored me, so I took to reading criminal documents. My friends noticed and jokingly asked me if I were planning to join the detective squad.

The second year brought no mitigation or relief. If a day passed without my mentioning him, I spoke about him twice as much on the following day. From all the anguish I caused her, my wife fell sick. I healed her with medicines and battered her heart with words. I would tell her, "All your illness comes to you only because of the man who ruined your life. Right now he's playing around with other women, and me he has left with an invalid wife to take care of." A thousand kinds of remorse would sting me for every single word, and a thousand times I repeated those words.

At that time I began visiting my wife's relatives together with her. And here a strange thing occurred. I've already mentioned that Dinah came of good family and that her relatives were distinguished people. In consequence, they and their homes gratified me, and I began to show favor to my wife because of her relatives. These people, the grandchildren of ghetto[3] dwellers, had achieved wealth and honor: their wealth was an ornament to their honor and their honor an ornament to their wealth. For even during the war, when the great figures of the nation made money out of people's hunger, they kept their hands clean of all money coming from an evil source, and, accordingly, they refused to stuff themselves with food and accepted only their legitimate rations. Among their number were the kind of imposing men we used to imagine but never really saw with our own eyes. And then there were the women. You don't know Vienna, and if you know it, you know the sort of Jewish women the gentiles wag their tongues over. If they could only see the women I saw, they would stop up their own mouths. Not that I care what the non-Jewish peoples say about us, for there is no hope that we'll ever please them, but inasmuch as I have mentioned their censure of us, I also mention their praise, because there is no higher praise for a brother than that which he receives from his sisters, through whom he is commended and extolled.

Before long I thought of my wife's relatives without connecting them with her, as though I and not she were their relation. I would think to myself, If they only knew how miserable I make her. And I was just about ready to unlock my lips and to open my heart to them. When I realized that my heart was urging me to talk, I stayed away from them, and they quite naturally stayed away from me. It's a big city and people are busy. If someone avoids his friends, they don't go hunting after him.

The third year my wife adopted a new mode of behavior. If I mentioned him, she ignored what I said, and if I connected his name with hers, she kept silent and didn't answer me, as though I weren't speaking about her. Infuriated, I would comment to myself, What a miserable woman not to take notice!

8

One summer day at twilight she and I were sitting at supper. It hadn't rained for a number of days, and the city was seething with heat. The water

---

3. The city area where the Jews lived [Editor].

of the Danube[4] showed green, and a dull odor floated over the city. The windows in our glass-enclosed porch gave off a sultry heat that exhausted body and soul. Since the day before, my shoulders had been aching, and now the pain was more intense. My head was heavy, my hair was dry. I ran my hand over my head and said to myself, I need a haircut. I looked across at my wife and saw that she was letting her hair grow long. Yet ever since women adopted men's haircuts, she always wore her hair close-cropped. I said to myself, My own head can't bear the weight of the little hair it has, and she's growing herself plumes like a peacock without even asking me if it looks nice that way. As a matter of fact, her hair looked lovely, but there was nothing lovely about my state of mind. I shoved my chair back from the table as though it were pushing against my stomach, and I ripped a piece of bread from the middle of the loaf and chewed it. It had been several days since I last mentioned him to her, and I hardly have to say that she made no mention of him to me. At that time, I was accustomed to saying very little to her, and when I did speak to her, I spoke without anger.

All at once I said to her, "There's something I've been thinking about."

She nodded her head. "Oh, yes," she said, "I feel the same way."

"So you know what is in the secret corners of my heart. Then, go ahead, tell me what I was thinking of."

In a whisper, she said, "Divorce."

As she spoke, she lifted her face to me and looked at me sadly. My heart was torn from its moorings, and I felt weak inside. I thought to myself, What a pitiful creature you are to treat your wife this way and cause her such pain. I lowered my voice and asked, "How do you know what is in my heart?"

"And what do you think I do with all my time? I sit and think about you, my dear."

The words leaped out of my mouth: I said to her, "Then you agree?"

She lifted her eyes to me. "You mean the divorce?"

I lowered my eyes and nodded in affirmation.

"Whether I want to or not," she said, "I agree to do whatever you ask, if it will only relieve your suffering."

"Even a divorce?"

"Even a divorce."

I was aware of all that I was losing. But the statement had already been made, and the desire to turn my wrath against myself drove me beyond reason. I clenched both hands and said angrily, "Well and good."

Several days passed, and I mentioned to her neither the divorce nor the one who had brought down ruin upon us. I told myself, Three years have passed since she became my wife. Perhaps the time has come to wipe out the memory of that affair. If she had been a widow or a divorcee when I

---

4. River in Vienna [Editor].

married her, would there be anything I could have held against her? As things are, then, let me consider her as though she were a widow or a divorcee when I took her to be my wife.

And having reached this conclusion, I upbraided myself for every single day I had tormented her, and I resolved to be good to my wife. During that period I became a completely new person, and I began to feel an awakening of love as on the day I first met her. I was soon ready to conclude that everything is the result of man's will and desire: if he so wills it, he can introduce anger and hatred into his heart; if he wills it, he can live in peace with everyone. If this is so, I reasoned, what cause is there to stir up anger and bring evil upon ourselves when we are capable of doing good for ourselves and being happy? So I reasoned, that is, until something happened to me which set things back right where they were before.

9

What happened was this. One day a patient was brought to the hospital. I examined him and left him with the nurses to be washed and put to bed. In the evening I entered the ward to make my rounds. When I came to his bed, I saw his name on the card over his head, and I realized who he was.

What could I do? I'm a doctor, and I treated him. As a matter of fact, I gave him an extraordinary amount of care, so that all the other patients grew jealous of him and called him doctor's pet. And he really deserved the name, for whether he needed it or not, I treated him. I told the nurses that I had discovered in him a disease which hadn't been adequately studied yet, and that I wanted to investigate it myself. I left instructions for them to give him good food, and sometimes to add a glass of wine, so that he would get a little enjoyment out of his hospital stay. Further, I asked the nurses not to be too strict with him if he took certain liberties and didn't follow all the hospital regulations.

He lay in his hospital bed eating and drinking and enjoying all sorts of luxuries. And I came in to visit him and examine him again and again, asking him if he had a good night's sleep and if he was given all the food he wanted. I would order medication for him and praise his body to him, telling him that it would in all probability last to a ripe old age. He on his part listened with enjoyment and basked in pleasure before me like a worm. I told him, "If you're used to smoking, go ahead and smoke. I myself don't smoke, and if you ask me whether smoking is a good thing, I'll tell you it's bad and harmful to the body. But if you're used to smoking, I won't stop you." And in this way I gave him various special privileges, just so he would feel completely comfortable. At the same time I reflected, Over a man for whom I wouldn't waste so much as a word I am going to all this trouble, and it's all because of that business which is difficult to speak of and difficult to forget. Not only that, but I watch him and study him as though I could learn what rubbed off on him from Dinah and what rubbed off on her from him—and from devoting so much attention to him, I was acquiring some of his gestures.

At first I kept the whole matter secret from my wife. But it burst forth when I tried to suppress it, and it told itself. My wife listened without the slightest sign of interest. On the surface, one would have thought that this was just what I wanted, but I was not satisfied, even though I realized that if she had responded differently I would certainly not have been pleased.

After some while he was cured and had recuperated, and it was high time for him to leave the hospital. I kept him day after day and ordered the nurses to give him the best of treatment, so that he would not be anxious to leave. And that was the period right after the war, when it was hard to get provisions for the sick, not to speak of the convalescent, and certainly not to speak of the healthy, so I gave him from my own food which the farmers used to bring me. He sat in the hospital eating and drinking and gladdening his heart, reading newspapers and strolling in the garden, playing with the patients and laughing with the nurses. He put on some weight and was healthier than the people who took care of him, so that it became impossible to keep him any longer in the hospital. I gave instructions that a proper final dinner be prepared for him, and I discharged him.

After the dinner, he came to say goodbye to me. I looked at the double chin he had developed. His eyes were embedded in fat, like those of a woman who has given up everything for the sake of eating and drinking. I stood by my desk rummaging through the papers on it as though I were looking for something I had lost. Then I took a stethoscope to examine him. As I was trying to appear busy, two nurses came in, one to ask me something and one to say goodbye to the doctor's pet. I pulled my head back suddenly, as though I had been reminded that someone was waiting for me, and I let out a brief exclamation of surprise, the way Dinah does when she sees that someone has been waiting for her. As I did that, I looked at the healthy patient with his double chin and I said to myself, You don't know who I am, but I know who you are. You are the man who brought ruin down on me and wrecked my wife's life. Anger surged within me, and I became so furious that my eyes ached.

He extended his hand to me in special deference and began to stutter words of thanks about my saving him from death and restoring him to life. I offered him my fingertips to shake, in an impolite and deprecatory manner, and immediately I wiped them on my white coat, as though I had touched a dead reptile. Then I turned my face away from him as from some disgusting thing, and I walked away. I sensed that the nurses were looking at me and knew the reason for my behavior, even though there were no grounds for such apprehension.

After a little while I went back to work, but my head and heart were not with me. I went up to the doctors' lounge and looked for a friend to take my place. I told him that I had been summoned to court to give testimony about a certain criminal, and that it was impossible to postpone the case. A nurse came and asked whether she should order a cab. "Certainly, nurse, certainly," I answered. While she went to the switchboard to telephone, I ran out of the hospital like someone who had gone berserk.

I passed by a bar and considered going in to drown my sorrows in drink, as embittered men are accustomed to say. I grew a bit calmer and told myself, Troubles come and go, your troubles will also pass. But I had only grown calm temporarily, and only to lose control again. I began walking. After an hour or so, I stopped and saw that I had gone all around myself and completed a circle around the same spot.

10

I came home and told my wife. She listened and said nothing. I was infuriated that she should sit there in silence, as if she had heard nothing of significance. I bowed my head over my chest the way he did when he stood before me to thank me, and, imitating his voice, I said, "I wish to thank you, doctor, for saving me from death and restoring me to life." And I told my wife, "That's the way his voice sounds and that's the way he stands," in order to show her how low he was, what a pitiful creature was the man whom she had preferred to me and to whom she had given her love before she knew me. My wife looked up at me as though the whole thing were not worth her while to care about. Rising, I scrutinized her face in the hope of finding some indication of joy over that good-for-nothing's recovery, but just as I had seen no signs of sorrow when I told her he was sick, I saw now not the slightest sign of joy over his recovery.

After two or three days, the experience lost its sting and no longer disturbed me. I treated patients, talked much with the nurses, and immediately after work went home to my wife. Sometimes I would ask her to read to me from one of her books, and she would agree. She read while I sat looking at her, thinking, This is the face that had the power to drive away the frowns and dissipate the anger of whoever saw it. And I would run my hand over my face in gratification as I continued to look at her. Sometimes we had a friend over for coffee or for supper. And once again we talked about everything people talk about, and once again I realized that there were things in the world other than woman-trouble. Often now I climbed into bed at night with a feeling of contentment and gratification.

One night this fellow came to me in a dream: his face was sickly and yet just a little — just a little — likable. I was ashamed of myself for thinking evil of him, and I resolved to put an end to my anger against him. He bent down and said, "What do you want from me? Is the fact that she raped me any reason for you to have it in for me?"

The next night we had as dinner guests two of our friends, a married couple, whom we both particularly liked — him because of his admirable qualities, her because of her blue eyes filled with radiance, and because of her high forehead which deceived the eye into thinking that she was unusually intelligent, and because of the golden curls trembling on her head, and also because of her voice, the voice of a woman who suppresses her longings within her. We sat together some three hours without being aware of the time. He discussed the questions of the day, and she helped him with the radiance from her eyes.

After they left, I said to my wife, "Let me tell you a dream."

"A dream?" cried my wife in surprise, and fixed her eyes on me sorrowfully and repeated in a whisper, "A dream." For it was not my way to tell dreams, and it seems to me that all those years I had not dreamed at all.

"I had a dream," I told her. And as I said it, my heart suddenly quaked.

My wife sat down and looked into my face intently. I proceeded to tell her my dream. Her shoulders shook and her body began to tremble. She stretched out her arms all of a sudden and, placing them around my neck, she embraced me. I returned her embrace and we stood clinging together in love and affection and pity, while all that time, this fellow never left my sight, and I could hear him saying, "Is the fact that she raped me any reason for you to have it in for me?"

I pushed my wife's arms away from my neck, and a terrible sadness welled up within me. I got into bed and thought over the whole affair quietly and calmly until I fell asleep.

The next day we got up and ate breakfast together. I looked over at my wife and saw that her face was the same as always. I thanked her in my heart for bearing no grudge against me over the night before. At that moment, I recalled all the trouble and suffering I had caused her since the day she married me, how time after time I drained her lifeblood and insulted her in every possible way, while she took everything in silence. My heart swelled with love and tenderness for this miserable soul whom I had tortured so much, and I resolved to be good to her. And so I was for one day, for two days, for three days.

11

And I was quite prepared to conclude that everything was being set right. In point of fact, nothing had been set right. From the very day I made peace with myself, that peace was robbed from me through another means. My wife treated me as though I had become a stranger to her. Yet all the efforts I was making with her were for her sake. How this woman failed to take notice! But she did notice.

One day she said to me, "What a good thing it would be if I were dead!"

"Why do you say that?"

"Why, you ask?" And in the wrinkles around her lips there was visible a sort of smile which made my heart jump.

"Don't be a fool," I scolded her.

She sighed. "Ah, my dear, I am not a fool."

"Then I am a fool."

"No, you're not a fool either."

I raised my voice and challenged her. "Then what do you want from me?"

"What do I want?" she answered. "I want the same thing you want."

I brushed one palm off with the other and said, "There's nothing at all I want."

She looked into my face intently. "There's nothing at all you want. Then everything must be all right."

"All right?" I laughed scornfully.

"You see, my dear," she said, "that laugh does not sit well with me."

"What am I supposed to do, then?"

"Do what you've been wanting to do."

"Namely?"

"Namely, why should I repeat something you yourself know?"

"I'm afraid I don't know what that something is. But since you know, you can tell me."

She pronounced in a whisper, "Divorce."

I raised my voice as I answered. "You want to force me into giving you a divorce."

She nodded. "If you think it's proper for you to put it that way and say that I want to force you, then I agree."

"Meaning what?" I asked.

"Why do we have to repeat things when there's no call for it? Let us do what is written for us above."

In anger, I mocked her. "Even Heaven is an open book for you, as you know what's written there. I am a doctor and I can only go by what my eyes see, while you, madam, you know what is written on high. Where did you pick up such knowledge, maybe from that louse?"

"Be still!" Dinah cried. "Please, be still!"

"You don't have to get so angry," I told her. "After all, what did I say?"

She rose, went to her room, and locked the door behind her.

I came to the door and asked her to open it for me, but she refused. "Look, I'm leaving," I said to her. "The whole house is yours, and you don't have to lock the door." When she still did not answer, I began to be afraid that she had taken sleeping pills and, God forbid, committed suicide. I began to beg and plead for her to open the door, but still she did not open. I peeked through the keyhole, my heart pounding me blow after blow, as though I were a murderer. Thus I stood before the locked door until evening came on and the walls darkened.

With darkness, she came out of her room, pale as a corpse. When I took her hands in mine, a deathly chill flowed out of them that made my own hands cold. She made no effort to pull her hands away from me, as though she had no feeling left in them.

I laid her down on her bed and calmed her with sedatives, nor did I move from her until she had dozed off. I looked at her face, a face innocent of any flaw, without the slightest blemish, and I said to myself, What a lovely world in which such a woman exists, and what difficult lives we have to live! I bent down in order to kiss her. She turned her head in sign of refusal. "Did you say something?" I asked. "No," she said, and I couldn't tell whether she was conscious of me or simply was talking in her sleep. Thoroughly disconcerted, I kept my distance from her. But I sat there all night long.

The next day I went to work and came back at noon. Whether out of prudence or for some other reason, I made no mention to her of what had happened the day before. She on her part did not speak of it either. So it was on the second day, so again on the third day. I was ready to conclude that matters were returning to their previous state. Yet I knew that though I might try to forget, she would not forget.

During that period her appearance became more vigorous and she changed some of her habits. Where she was accustomed to greet me as I came in the door, she no longer greeted me. Sometimes she would leave me and go off somewhere, and there were times when I came home and did not find her.

The anniversary of our engagement fell at that time. I said to her, "Let's celebrate and take a trip to the place we went to when we were first married."

"That's impossible."

"Why?"

"Because I have to go somewhere else."

"Pardon me, but where is it you are going?"

"There's a patient I'm taking care of."

"Why this all of a sudden?"

"Not everything a person does is all of a sudden. For a long time now I've felt that I ought to work and do something."

"And isn't it enough for you that I am working and doing something?"

"Once that was enough for me. Now it's not enough."

"Why not?"

"Why not? If you yourself don't know, I can't explain it to you."

"Is it such a complicated issue that it's difficult to explain?"

"It's not hard to explain, but I doubt if you would want to understand."

"Why are you doing it?"

"Because I want to earn my own living."

"Do you think you're not supported adequately in your own home, that you have to go look for a living elsewhere."

"Right now I'm being supported. Who knows what will be tomorrow?"

"Why all of a sudden such ideas?"

"I already told you that nothing happens all of a sudden."

"I don't know what you're talking about."

"You understand, all right, but you prefer to say, 'I don't understand.'"

I nodded my head in despair and said, "That's how it is, then."

"Really, that's how it is."

"This whole dialectic is beyond me."

"It's beyond you, and it's not particularly close to me. So it would be better if we kept still. You do what you have to do, and I'll do what I have to."

"What I do, I know. But I have no idea what it is you want to do."

"If you don't know now, you'll soon find out."

But her efforts did not succeed. And however they may have succeeded, she failed to make a penny out of them. She was caring for a paralyzed girl, the daughter of a poor widow, and she received no payment for her work. On the contrary, she helped the widow financially, and she even brought her flowers. At that time Dinah's strength drained from her as though she were sick, and she herself needed someone to take care of her instead of her caring for others. Once I asked her, "How long are you going to continue working with that sick girl?" She fixed her eyes on me and said, "Are you asking me as a doctor?"

"What difference does it make whether I ask as a doctor or as your husband?"

"If you ask as a doctor, I don't know what to tell you, and if you ask for other reasons, I see no need to answer."

I tried to act as if she were joking with me, so I laughed. She averted her face from me, and, leaving me where I was, went off. The laughter immediately died on my lips, nor has it yet returned.

It's just a mood, I told myself, and I can put up with it. Yet I knew that all my optimism was completely baseless. I recalled the first time she spoke to me about a divorce, and I remembered what she said: "Whether I want it or not, I am prepared to do whatever you ask, if only it will relieve your suffering—even a divorce." Now I thought, However you look at it, there's no way out for us except a divorce. As soon as this idea occurred to me, I dismissed it, as a man will dismiss something painful from his thoughts. But Dinah was right when she said we had to do what was written for us above. Before long I saw with my own eyes and I grasped with my own understanding what at first I had not seen and I had not grasped. At once I decided that I would grant Dinah the divorce. We had no children, for I had been apprehensive about begetting children for fear they would look like him. I arranged our affairs and gave her the divorce.

And so we parted from one another, the way people will part outwardly. But in my heart, my friend, the smile on her lips is still locked up, and that blue-black in her eyes, as on the day I first saw her. Sometimes at night

I sit up in bed like those patients she used to take care of, and I stretch out both hands and call, "Nurse, nurse, come to me."

▪ Nazim Hikmet (1902–1963) *Turkey* (poem)

TRANSLATED BY RANDY BLASING AND MUTLU KONUK

Nazim Hikmet was born in Salonica, Greece, in 1902, when it was part of the Ottoman Empire. He was the grandson of Nazim Pasha, a poet and critic who introduced him to the Turkish literary heritage; his mother introduced him to the music and literature of the West. He studied at Istanbul's Heybeli Naval Academy in 1917 but was expelled for participating in a student strike. He went into hiding and became a Communist, moving to Moscow, where he studied at the University of the East (in 1922). On his return to Turkey, he quickly found himself in jail, serving a fifteen-year sentence for his political poetry. He was released early, but in 1937 he was sentenced to 28 years in jail for writing an anti-Fascist tract. International pressure brought about his release in 1951, and he emigrated to the Soviet Union, living in a number of socialist countries before taking Polish citizenship. His work celebrated the poor people of Anatolia, who became his heroes, and moved more and more toward simple melodic poetry based on folk songs. He also wrote plays and novels. He died in Moscow in 1963.

FURTHER READING: Hikmet, Nazim. *The Day before Tomorrow: Poems.* Translated by Taner Baybars, 1972; *The Epic of Sheik Bedreddin and Other Poems.* Translated by Randy Blasing and Mutlu Konuk, 1977; *Landscapes.* Translated by Randy Blasing and Mutlu Konuk, 1982; *The Moscow Symphony and Other Poems.* Translated by Taner Baybars, 1970; *Poems.* Translated by Ali Yunus, 1954; *Poems of Nazim Hikmet.* Translated from the Turkish by Randy Blasing and Mutlu Konuk, 1994; *A Sad State of Freedom.* Translated by Taner Baybars and Richard McKane, 1990; *Things I Didn't Know I Loved: Selected Poems of Nazim Hikmet.* Translated by Randy Blasing and Mutlu Konuk, 1975.

Since I Was Thrown Inside

Since I was thrown inside
     the earth has gone around the sun ten times.
If you ask it:
     "Not worth mentioning—
     a microscopic span."
If you ask me:
     "Ten years of my life."

5

I had a pencil
  the year I was thrown inside.
It was used up after a week of writing.   *10*
If you ask it:
  "A whole lifetime."
If you ask me:
  "What's a week."

Since I've been inside,   *15*
  Osman, who was in for murder,
    did his seven-and-a-half and left,
    knocked around on the outside for a while,
    then landed back inside for smuggling,
    served six months and was out again; *20*
    yesterday we got a letter—he's married,
    with a kid coming in the spring.

They're ten-years-old now,
  the children who were conceived
    the year I was thrown inside.   *25*
And that year's foals—shaky on their long, spindly legs—
  have been wide-rumped, contented mares for some time
  now.

But the olive seedlings are still saplings,
  still children.   *30*
New squares have opened in my faraway city
  since I was thrown inside.
And my family now lives
  on a street I don't know,
    in a house I haven't seen.   *35*

Bread was like cotton—soft and white—
  the year I was thrown inside.
Then it was rationed,
and here inside people killed each other
  over a black loaf the size of a fist.   *40*
Now it's free again,
but it's dark and has no taste.

The year I was thrown inside
  the SECOND hadn't started yet.
The ovens at Dachau hadn't been lit,   *45*
the atom bomb hadn't been dropped on Hiroshima.

Time flowed like blood from the slit throat of a child.
Then that chapter was officially closed—
now the American dollar is talking of a THIRD.

But in spite of everything the day has gotten lighter   *50*
     since I was thrown inside.
And "at the edge of darkness,
     pushing against the earth with their heavy hands.
       THEY've risen up" halfway.

Since I was thrown inside   *55*
     the earth has gone around the sun ten times.
And I repeat once more with the same passion
     what I wrote about Them
     the year I was thrown inside:
"They who are numberless like ants in the earth.   *60*
     fish in the sea,
       birds in the air,
who are cowardly, brave,
     ignorant, wise,
       and childlike,   *65*
and who destroy
     and create, they—

our songs tell only of their adventures."
     And anything else,
       such as my ten years here,   *70*
       is just so much talk.

■ Naguib Mahfouz (1911–) *Egypt* (story)

TRANSLATED BY DENYS JOHNSON-DAVIES

In October 1988, the world learned that an Egyptian novelist, Naguib Mahfouz (also transliterated as Najib Mahfuz), highly esteemed in his country, but a secret beyond the borders of Arabic letters, had won the Nobel Prize for Literature. Mahfouz, an author concerned with family generations, had been read by millions in the Arab world, and his short stories and novels were also known through film and television adaptations. More than any writer, he had established a demotic Arabic literary speech, which made the language of Egypt the standard. With his greater recognition, the readers of many nations would soon, by way of multiple translations, follow the generations of ordinary middle-class life in Egypt as it changed with the social and political climates of our century.

Mahfouz was born in Cairo on December 12, 1911. His father was a civil servant, and he was one of seven children. After attending public schools, he went to the University of Cairo in 1934 and four years later received a degree in philosophy. He grew up in a turbulent period that saw

England alter its occupation of Egypt into a protectorate in 1914. A constitutional monarchy was established in 1923. The momentous year of 1952 saw Gamal Abdel Nasser overthrow the monarchy and institute a republic. At first optimistic, later disappointed with the promised reforms, Mahfouz became an open critic of the Nasser regime. After graduation from the university, Mahfouz began to publish short stories, including his first book *Whispers of Madness* (1938). To earn a living, he wrote for magazines and the newspaper *Al-Ahram*. He also worked for the Ministry of Culture, adapted fiction for film and television, and became director of the government Cinema Organization, where he worked until his retirement in the early 1970s. Although Mahfouz has rarely traveled abroad—once to Yemen and once to Yugoslavia—and even sent his two daughters to receive his Nobel honors in Stockholm, he learned the craft of the novel from the European and American masters, including Leo Tolstoy, Anton Chekhov, Honoré de Balzac, Thomas Mann, Ernest Hemingway, and William Faulkner. Because of his frequent focus on everyday reality in generations of merchant families, he has been called, perhaps too simply, the Balzac of the Arab world. Whether it was Balzac, Émile Zola, or, as he claims, their disciples who helped him find his way, the thematic sources of his early novels were ancient and contemporary Egypt. He is obsessed with time, with glamorous dancing girls and their shattered ambitions, with life in the coffee houses and tyranny in the home as fathers enslave, with those around him, and, especially, with women. His masterpiece is usually said to be his Cairo trilogy (1956–1957), *Palace Walk*, *Palace of Desire*, and *Sugar Street*, which traces generations of a Cairo merchant family. The fierce patriarch reflects the desires, aspirations, debauchery, and social ills of the period between 1917 and 1944. Mahfouz brings into his fiction an almost journalistic, and sometimes surreal, view of love, death, and despair, in his depictions of picaresque Cairo types and political prisoners and men and women with broken dreams. He has stood alone, unafraid to criticize and praise, and has spread his gaze from extreme left to extreme right, from kind to cruel, from idealists to the corrupt. Independent of his awards, he is generally esteemed as the leading author in the Arabic language.

FURTHER READING: Mahfouz, Naguib. *Children of Gebelawi*, 1981; *Autumn Quail*, 1985; *Wedding Song*, 1984; *Thief and the Dogs*, 1984; *Beggar*, 1986; *Day the Leader Was Killed*, 1989; *Palace Walk*, 1989; *The Time and the Place and Other Stories*, 1991; *Palace of Desire*, 1991; *Sugar Street: The Cairo Trilogy*, 1992; *Adrift on the Nile*, 1993.

Zaabalawi

Finally I became convinced that I had to find Sheikh Zaabalawi.

The first time I had heard his name had been in a song:

Oh what's become of the world, Zaabalawi?
They've turned it upside down and taken away its taste.

It had been a popular song in my childhood, and one day it had occurred to me to demand of my father, in the way children have of asking
endless questions:
"Who is Zaabalawi?"
He had looked at me hesitantly as though doubting my ability to understand the answer. However, he had replied, "May his blessing descend
upon you, he's a true saint of God, a remover of worries and troubles. Were
it not for him I would have died miserably—"
In the years that followed, I heard my father many a time sing the praises of this good saint and speak of the miracles he performed. The days
passed and brought with them many illnesses, for each one of which I was
able, without too much trouble and at a cost I could afford, to find a cure,
until I became afflicted with that illness for which no one possesses a remedy. When I had tried everything in vain and was overcome by despair, I remembered by chance what I had heard in my childhood: Why, I asked
myself, should I not seek out Sheikh Zaabalawi? I recollected my father saying that he had made his acquaintance in Khan Gaafar at the house of
Sheikh Qamar, one of those sheikhs who practiced law in the religious
courts, and so I took myself off to his house. Wishing to make sure that he
was still living there, I made inquiries of a vendor of beans whom I found in
the lower part of the house.
"Sheikh Qamar!" he said, looking at me in amazement. "He left the
quarter ages ago. They say he's now living in Garden City and has his office
in al-Azhar Square."
I looked up the office address in the telephone book and immediately
set off to the Chamber of Commerce Building, where it was located. On
asking to see Sheikh Qamar, I was ushered into a room just as a beautiful
woman with a most intoxicating perfume was leaving it. The man received
me with a smile and motioned me toward a fine leather-upholstered chair.
Despite the thick soles of my shoes, my feet were conscious of the lushness
of the costly carpet. The man wore a lounge suit and was smoking a cigar;
his manner of sitting was that of someone well satisfied both with himself
and with his worldly possessions. The look of warm welcome he gave me
left no doubt in my mind that he thought me a prospective client, and I felt
acutely embarrassed at encroaching upon his valuable time.
"Welcome!" he said, prompting me to speak.
"I am the son of your old friend Sheikh Ali al-Tatawi," I answered so as
to put an end to my equivocal position.
A certain languor was apparent in the glance he cast at me; the languor
was not total in that he had not as yet lost all hope in me.
"God rest his soul," he said. "He was a fine man."
The very pain that had driven me to go there now prevailed upon me
to stay.

"He told me," I continued, "of a devout saint named Zaabalawi whom he met at Your Honor's. I am in need of him, sir, if he be still in the land of the living."

The languor became firmly entrenched in his eyes, and it would have come as no surprise if he had shown the door to both me and my father's memory.

"That," he said in the tone of one who has made up his mind to terminate the conversation, "was a very long time ago and I scarcely recall him now."

Rising to my feet so as to put his mind at rest regarding my intention of going, I asked, "Was he really a saint?"

"We used to regard him as a man of miracles."

"And where could I find him today?" I asked, making another move toward the door.

"To the best of my knowledge he was living in the Birgawi Residence in al-Azhar," and he applied himself to some papers on his desk with a resolute movement that indicated he would not open his mouth again. I bowed my head in thanks, apologized several times for disturbing him, and left the office, my head so buzzing with embarrassment that I was oblivious to all sounds around me.

I went to the Birgawi Residence, which was situated in a thickly populated quarter. I found that time had so eaten away at the building that nothing was left of it save an antiquated façade and a courtyard that, despite being supposedly in the charge of a caretaker, was being used as a rubbish dump. A small, insignificant fellow, a mere prologue to a man, was using the covered entrance as a place for the sale of old books on theology and mysticism.

When I asked him about Zaabalawi, he peered at me through narrow, inflamed eyes and said in amazement, "Zaabalawi! Good heavens, what a time ago that was! Certainly he used to live in this house when it was habitable. Many were the times he would sit with me talking of bygone days, and I would be blessed by his holy presence. Where, though, is Zaabalawi today?"

He shrugged his shoulders sorrowfully and soon left me, to attend to an approaching customer. I proceeded to make inquiries of many shopkeepers in the district. While I found that a large number of them had never even heard of Zaabalawi, some, though recalling nostalgically the pleasant times they had spent with him, were ignorant of his present whereabouts, while others openly made fun of him, labeled him a charlatan, and advised me to put myself in the hands of a doctor—as though I had not already done so. I therefore had no alternative but to return disconsolately home.

With the passing of days like motes in the air, my pains grew so severe that I was sure I would not be able to hold out much longer. Once again I fell to wondering about Zaabalawi and clutching at the hope his venerable name stirred within me. Then it occurred to me to seek the help of the local sheikh of the district; in fact, I was surprised I had not thought of this to begin with. His office was in the nature of a small shop, except that it contained a desk and a telephone, and I found him sitting at his desk, wearing a jacket over his striped galabeya. As he did not interrupt his conversation with a man sitting beside him, I stood waiting till the man had gone. The sheikh then looked up at me coldly. I told myself that I should win him over by the usual methods, and it was not long before I had him cheerfully inviting me to sit down.

"I'm in need of Sheikh Zaabalawi," I answered his inquiry as to the purpose of my visit.

He gazed at me with the same astonishment as that shown by those I had previously encountered.

"At least," he said, giving me a smile that revealed his gold teeth, "he is still alive. The devil of it is, though, he has no fixed abode. You might well bump into him as you go out of here, on the other hand you might spend days and months in fruitless searching."

"Even you can't find him!"

"Even I! He's a baffling man, but I thank the Lord that he's still alive!"

He gazed at me intently, and murmured, "It seems your condition is serious."

"Very."

"May God come to your aid! But why don't you go about it systematically?" He spread out a sheet of paper on the desk and drew on it with unexpected speed and skill until he had made a full plan of the district, showing all the various quarters, lanes, alleyways, and squares. He looked at it admiringly and said, "These are dwelling-houses, here is the Quarter of the Perfumers, here the Quarter of the Coppersmiths, the Mouski, the police and fire stations. The drawing is your best guide. Look carefully in the cafés, the places where the dervishes perform their rites, the mosques and prayer-rooms, and the Green Gate, for he may well be concealed among the beggars and be indistinguishable from them. Actually, I myself haven't seen him for years, having been somewhat preoccupied with the cares of the world, and was only brought back by your inquiry to those most exquisite times of my youth."

I gazed at the map in bewilderment. The telephone rang, and he took up the receiver.

"Take it," he told me, generously. "We're at your service."

Folding up the map, I left and wandered off through the quarter, from square to street to alleyway, making inquiries of everyone I felt was familiar with the place. At last the owner of a small establishment for ironing clothes told me, "Go to the calligrapher Hassanein in Umm al-Ghulam—they were friends."

I went to Umm al-Ghulam, where I found old Hassanein working in a deep, narrow shop full of signboards and jars of color. A strange smell, a mixture of glue and perfume, permeated its every corner. Old Hassanein was squatting on a sheepskin rug in front of a board propped against the wall; in the middle of it he had inscribed the word "Allah" in silver lettering. He was engrossed in embellishing the letters with prodigious care. I stood behind him, fearful of disturbing him or breaking the inspiration that flowed to his masterly hand. When my concern at not interrupting him had lasted some time, he suddenly inquired with unaffected gentleness, "Yes?"

Realizing that he was aware of my presence, I introduced myself. "I've been told that Sheikh Zaabalawi is your friend; I'm looking for him," I said.

His hand came to a stop. He scrutinized me in astonishment. "Zaabalawi! God be praised!" he said with a sigh.

"He *is* a friend of yours, isn't he?" I asked eagerly.

"He was, once upon a time. A real man of mystery: he'd visit you so often that people would imagine he was your nearest and dearest, then would disappear as though he'd never existed. Yet saints are not to be blamed."

The spark of hope went out with the suddenness of a lamp snuffed by a power-cut.

"He was so constantly with me," said the man, "that I felt him to be a part of everything I drew. But where is he today?"

"Perhaps he is still alive?"

"He's alive, without a doubt. . . . He had impeccable taste, and it was due to him that I made my most beautiful drawings."

"God knows," I said, in a voice almost stifled by the dead ashes of hope, "how dire my need for him is, and no one knows better than you of the ailments in respect to which he is sought."

"Yes, yes. May God restore you to health. He is in truth, as is said of him, a man, and more . . . ."

Smiling broadly, he added, "And his face possesses an unforgettable beauty. But where is he?"

Reluctantly I rose to my feet, shook hands, and left. I continued wandering eastward and westward through the quarter, inquiring about Zaabalawi from everyone who, by reason of age or experience, I felt might be likely to help me. Eventually I was informed by a vendor of lupine that he had met him a short while ago at the house of Sheikh Gad, the well-known composer. I went to the musician's house in Tabakshiyya, where I found him in a room tastefully furnished in the old style, its walls redolent with history. He was seated on a divan, his famous lute beside him, concealing within itself the most beautiful melodies of our age, while somewhere from within the house came the sound of pestle and mortar and the clamor of children. I immediately greeted him and introduced myself, and was put at my ease by the unaffected way in which he received me. He did not ask, either in words or gesture, what had brought me, and I did not feel that he even harbored any such curiosity. Amazed at his understanding and kindness, which boded well, I said, "O Sheikh Gad, I am an admirer of yours, having long been enchanted by the renderings of your songs."

"Thank you," he said with a smile.

"Please excuse my disturbing you," I continued timidly, "but I was told that Zaabalawi was your friend, and I am in urgent need of him."

"Zaabalawi!" he said, frowning in concentration. "You need him? God be with you, for who knows, O Zaabalawi, where you are."

"Doesn't he visit you?" I asked eagerly.

"He visited me some time ago. He might well come right now; on the other hand I mightn't see him till death!"

I gave an audible sigh and asked, "What made him like that?"

The musician took up his lute. "Such are saints or they would not be saints," he said, laughing.

"Do those who need him suffer as I do?"

"Such suffering is part of the cure!"

He took up the plectrum and began plucking soft strains from the strings. Lost in thought, I followed his movements. Then, as though addressing myself, I said, "So my visit has been in vain."

He smiled, laying his cheek against the side of the lute. "God forgive you," he said, "for saying such a thing of a visit that has caused me to know you and you me!"

I was much embarrassed and said apologetically, "Please forgive me; my feelings of defeat made me forget my manners."

"Do not give in to defeat. This extraordinary man brings fatigue to all who seek him. It was easy enough with him in the old days, when his place of abode was known. Today, though, the world has changed, and after having enjoyed a position attained only by potentates, he is now pursued by the police on a charge of false pretenses. It is therefore no longer an easy matter to reach him, but have patience and be sure that you will do so."

He raised his head from the lute and skillfully fingered the opening bars of a melody. Then he sang:

"I make lavish mention, even though I blame myself, of those I love,
For the stories of the beloved are my wine."

With a heart that was weary and listless, I followed the beauty of the melody and the singing.

"I composed the music to this poem in a single night," he told me when he had finished. "I remember that it was the eve of the Lesser Bairam. Zaabalawi was my guest for the whole of that night, and the poem was of his choosing. He would sit for a while just where you are, then would get up and play with my children as though he were one of them. Whenever I was overcome by weariness or my inspiration failed me, he would punch me playfully in the chest and joke with me, and I would bubble over with melodies, and thus I continued working till I finished the most beautiful piece I have ever composed."

"Does he know anything about music?"

"He is the epitome of things musical. He has an extremely beautiful speaking voice, and you have only to hear him to want to burst into song and to be inspired to creativity. . . ."

"How was it that he cured those diseases before which men are powerless?"

"That is his secret. Maybe you will learn it when you meet him."

But when would that meeting occur? We relapsed into silence, and the hubbub of children once more filled the room.

Again the sheikh began to sing. He went on repeating the words "and I have a memory of her" in different and beautiful variations until the very walls danced in ecstasy. I expressed my wholehearted admiration, and he gave me a smile of thanks. I then got up and asked permission to leave, and he accompanied me to the front door. As I shook him by the hand, he said, "I hear that nowadays he frequents the house of Hagg Wanas al-Damanhouri. Do you know him?"

I shook my head, though a modicum of renewed hope crept into my heart.

"He is a man of private means," the sheikh told me, "who from time to time visits Cairo, putting up at some hotel or other. Every evening, though, he spends at the Negma Bar in Alfi Street."

I waited for nightfall and went to the Negma Bar. I asked a waiter about Hagg Wanas, and he pointed to a corner that was semisecluded because of its position behind a large pillar with mirrors on all four sides. There I saw a man seated alone at a table with two bottles in front of him, one empty, the other two-thirds empty. There were no snacks or food to be seen, and I was sure that I was in the presence of a hardened drinker. He was wearing a loosely flowing silk galabeya and a carefully wound turban; his legs were stretched out toward the base of the pillar, and as he gazed into the mirror in rapt contentment, the sides of his face, rounded and handsome despite the fact that he was approaching old age, were flushed with wine. I approached quietly till I stood but a few feet away from him. He did not turn toward me or give any indication that he was aware of my presence.

"Good evening, Mr. Wanas," I greeted him cordially.

He turned toward me abruptly, as though my voice had roused him from slumber, and glared at me in disapproval. I was about to explain what had brought me when he interrupted in an almost imperative tone of voice that was nonetheless not devoid of an extraordinary gentleness, "First, please sit down, and second, please get drunk!"

I opened my mouth to make my excuses, but, stopping up his ears with his fingers, he said, "Not a word till you do what I say."

I realized I was in the presence of a capricious drunkard and told myself that I should at least humor him a bit. "Would you permit me to ask one question?" I said with a smile, sitting down.

Without removing his hands from his ears he indicated the bottle. "When engaged in a drinking bout like this, I do not allow any conversation between myself and another unless, like me, he is drunk, otherwise all propriety is lost and mutual comprehension is rendered impossible."

I made a sign indicating that I did not drink.

"That's your lookout," he said offhandedly. "And that's my condition!"

He filled me a glass, which I meekly took and drank. No sooner had the wine settled in my stomach than it seemed to ignite. I waited patiently till I had grown used to its ferocity, and said, "It's very strong, and I think the time has come for me to ask you about—"

Once again, however, he put his fingers in his ears. "I shan't listen to you until you're drunk!"

He filled up my glass for the second time. I glanced at it in trepidation; then, overcoming my inherent objection, I drank it down at a gulp. No sooner had the wine come to rest inside me than I lost all willpower. With the third glass, I lost my memory, and with the fourth the future vanished. The world turned round about me, and I forgot why I had gone there. The man leaned toward me attentively, but I saw him—saw everything—as a mere meaningless series of colored planes. I don't know how long it was before my head sank down onto the arm of the chair and I plunged into deep sleep. During it, I had a beautiful dream the like of which I had never experienced. I dreamed that I was in an immense garden surrounded on all sides by luxuriant trees, and the sky was nothing but stars seen between the entwined branches, all enfolded in an atmosphere like that of sunset or a sky overcast with cloud. I was lying on a small hummock of jasmine petals, more of which fell upon me like rain, while the lucent spray of a fountain unceasingly sprinkled the crown of my head and my temples. I was in a state of deep contentedness, of ecstatic serenity. An orchestra of warbling and cooing played in my ear. There was an extraordinary sense of harmony between me and my inner self, and between the two of us and the world, everything being in its rightful place, without discord or distortion. In the whole world there was no single reason for speech or movement, for the universe moved in a rapture of ecstasy. This lasted but a short while. When I opened my eyes, consciousness struck at me like a policeman's fist, and I saw Wanas al-Damanhouri peering at me with concern. Only a few drowsy customers were left in the bar.

"You have slept deeply," said my companion. "You were obviously hungry for sleep."

I rested my heavy head in the palms of my hands. When I took them away in astonishment and looked down at them, I found that they glistened with drops of water.

"My head's wet," I protested.

"Yes, my friend tried to rouse you," he answered quietly.

"Somebody saw me in this state?"

"Don't worry, he is a good man. Have you not heard of Sheikh Zaabalawi?"

"Zaabalawi!" I exclaimed, jumping to my feet.

"Yes," he answered in surprise. "What's wrong?"

"Where is he?"

"I don't know where he is now. He was here and then he left."

I was about to run off in pursuit but found I was more exhausted than I had imagined. Collapsed over the table, I cried out in despair, "My sole reason for coming to you was to meet him! Help me to catch up with him or send someone after him."

The man called a vendor of prawns and asked him to seek out the sheikh and bring him back. Then he turned to me. "I didn't realize you were afflicted. I'm very sorry. . . ."

"You wouldn't let me speak," I said irritably.

"What a pity! He was sitting on this chair beside you the whole time. He was playing with a string of jasmine petals he had around his neck, a gift from one of his admirers, then, taking pity on you, he began to sprinkle some water on your head to bring you around."

"Does he meet you here every night?" I asked, my eyes not leaving the doorway through which the vendor of prawns had left.

"He was with me tonight, last night, and the night before that, but before that I hadn't seen him for a month."

"Perhaps he will come tomorrow," I answered with a sigh.

"Perhaps."

"I am willing to give him any money he wants."

Wanas answered sympathetically, "The strange thing is that he is not open to such temptations, yet he will cure you if you meet him."

"Without charge?"

"Merely on sensing that you love him."

The vendor of prawns returned, having failed in his mission.

I recovered some of my energy and left the bar, albeit unsteadily. At every street corner I called out "Zaabalawi!" in the vague hope that I would be rewarded with an answering shout. The street boys turned contemptuous eyes on me till I sought refuge in the first available taxi.

The following evening I stayed up with Wanas al-Damanhouri till dawn, but the sheikh did not put in an appearance. Wanas informed me that he would be going away to the country and would not be returning to Cairo until he had sold the cotton crop.

I must wait, I told myself; I must train myself to be patient. Let me content myself with having made certain of the existence of Zaabalawi, and even of his affection for me, which encourages me to think that he will be prepared to cure me if a meeting takes place between us.

Sometimes, however, the long delay wearied me. I would become beset by despair and would try to persuade myself to dismiss him from my mind completely. How many weary people in this life know him not or regard him as a mere myth! Why, then, should I torture myself about him in this way?

No sooner, however, did my pains force themselves upon me than I would again begin to think about him, asking myself when I would be fortunate enough to meet him. The fact that I ceased to have any news of Wanas and was told he had gone to live abroad did not deflect me from my purpose; the truth of the matter was that I had become fully convinced that I had to find Zaabalawi.

Yes, I have to find Zaabalawi.

▪ Mririda Naït Attik (1919–) *Morocco* (Berber) (poems)

TRANSLATED BY DANIEL HALPERN AND PAULA PALEY

Little is known of the life of Mririda except that she was a courtesan of the *souk* (the market) of Azilal in the Atlas Mountains of Morocco and sang her poems in Tachelhait, a Berber dialect. The poem songs were rescued from anonymity by René Euloge, a French soldier, who translated them into French and published them. Although the poems have a defiant individualism, they also partake of an oral tradition. Her clients, French soldiers or local truck drivers and merchants, evidently paid no attention to her songs, but this did not dissuade her from composing or singing them. Euloge describes her voice as "a bouquet of thistles and wild oats, not a sumptuous carnation with a sweet perfume."[1] As a creative courtesan, she reflects a universal role, found in small and great civilizations, from the educated and high-class *hetaerae* (companions) of Greece to the *geishas* of Japan and the Tang and Song dynasty concubine poets of China. These women, literate in societies in which few men and fewer women could read and write, often came from the educated entertainment and companion class. Mririda's poems were translated from their French translation by two gifted American poets, Daniel Halpern and Paula Paley.

FURTHER READING: Attik, Mririda n'Aït. *Songs of Mririda: Courtesan of the High Atlas.* Translated from the French of René Euloge by Daniel Halpern and Paula Paley, 1974.

Mririda

They nicknamed me Mririda.
Mririda, nimble tree-frog of the meadow.
I don't have her gold eyes,
I don't have her white throat
Or green tunic.   5
But what I have, like Mririda,
Is my *zezarit*, my call
That carries up to the sheepfolds—
The whole valley
And the other side of the mountain   10
Speak of it. . . .
My call, which brings astonishment and envy.

---

1. Mririda n'Aït Attik, *Songs of Mririda:Courtesan of the High Atlas*. Translated from the French at René Euloge by Daniel Halpern and Paula Paley (Greensboro, NC: Unicorn Press, 1924), 10.

They named me Mririda
Because the first time I walked in the fields
I gently took a tree-frog,   *15*
Afraid and trembling in my hands,
And pressed her white throat
To my lips of a child,
And then of a girl.

And so I was given the *baraka,*   *20*
The magic that gives them their song
Which fills the summer nights,
A song clear as glass,
Sharp as the sound of an anvil
In the vibrating air before rain. . . .   *25*
Because of this gift
They call me Mririda,
And he who will come for me
Will feel my heart beat in his hand
As I have felt the racing hearts of frogs   *30*
Beneath my fingertips.

In the nights bathed in moonlight
He will call me, *Mririda, Mririda,*
Sweet nickname that I love,
And for him I will release my piercing call,   *35*
Shrill and drawn-out,
Bringing wonder from men
And jealousy from women,
Nothing like it ever heard in this valley.

The Bad Lover

Leave me, soldier without sense or manners!
I can see that you are full of contempt,
Your hand raised, insults on your lips,
Now that you've had what you want from me.
And you leave, calling me a dog!   *5*
Sated with my pleasures,
You'd have me blush for my trade,
But you, were you ashamed
When you pushed gently at my door,
Up like a bull?   *10*
Were you coming to play cards?
You turned yourself into something humble,
Agreeing right off to my demands,

To losing all your pay in advance.
And the more your eyes undressed me, 15
The more your rough desire put you in my power.

When you finally took off my clothes
I could have had your soul for the asking!
I could have cursed your mother
And your father, and their ancestors! 20
Toward what paradise were you flying?

But now that you've calmed down,
You're back on earth,
Arrogant, rough and coarse as your *djellaba*.

Guest of mine for the moment, my slave, 25
Don't you feel my disgust and hate?
One of these days
The memory of tonight will bring you back to me
Conquered and submissive again.
You'll leave your pride at the door 30
And I'll laugh at your glances and your wishes.
But you'll have to pay three times the price next time!
This will be the cost of your insults and pride.

I'll no more notice your clutching
Than the river notices a drop of rain. 35

■ Yashar Kemal (1922–)
Turkey (story)

TRANSLATED BY THILDA KEMAL

Yashar Kemal is Turkey's finest living writer, a candidate for the Nobel Prize in Literature. He was born Yashar Kemal Gokceli in 1922 in Hemite, a small village in Southern Anatolia, to a family that blended his father's line of feudal lords with his mother's line of thieves. When he was five, his father was murdered before his eyes in a mosque, and he developed a stammer from the shock that left him only when he sang. He walked long distances to a secondary school to learn to read and write, but after several years had to go to work in the cotton fields and later as a factory worker. He was a tireless defender of the poor workers and peasants, which cost him jobs and eventually led to his arrest in 1950 on allegations, later disproved, of involvement with Communist propaganda. He worked as a public letter writer and later as a reporter in Istanbul, where he dropped his surname. He published his first book of short stories in 1952. His novel *Ince Memed* appeared in 1955 and was translated into English in two parts as *Memed My*

Hawk (1961) and *They Burn the Thistles* (1977). He was a member of the Central Committee of the Turkish Worker's Party until it was banned. Other books available in English are *Anatolian Tales, Wind from the Plain, The Legend of Ararat, The Legend of the Thousand Bulls, The Undying Grass, The Lords of Akchasaz, Murder in the Ironsmiths,* and *Iron Earth, Copper Sky.*

A Dirty Story

The three of them were sitting on the damp earth, their backs against the dung-daubed brush wall and their knees drawn up to their chests, when another man walked up and crouched beside them.

"Have you heard?" said one of them excitedly. "Broken-Nose Jabbar's done it again! You know Jabbar, the fellow who brings all those women from the mountain villages and sells them in the plain? Well, this time he's come down with a couple of real beauties. The lads of Misdik have got together and bought one of them on the spot, and now they're having fun and making her dance and all that . . . It's unbelievable! Where does the fellow find so many women? How does he get them to come with him? He's the devil's own son, he is . . ."

"Well, that's how he makes a living," commented one of the men. "Ever since I can remember, this Jabbar's been peddling women for the villagers of the Chukurova plain. Allah provides for all and sundry . . ."

"He's still got the other one," said the newcomer, "and he's ready to give her away for a hundred liras."

"He'll find a customer soon enough," put in another man whose head was hunched between his shoulders. "A good woman's worth more than a team of oxen, at least, in the Chukurova plain she is. You can always put her to the plow and, come summer, she'll bind and carry the sheaves, hoe, do anything. What's a hundred liras? Why, a woman brings in that much in one single summer. In the fields, at home, in bed. There's nothing like a woman. What's a hundred liras?"

Just then, Hollow Osman came up mumbling to himself and flopped down beside them without a word of greeting. He was a tall, broad-shouldered man with a rather shapeless potbellied body. His lips drooped foolishly and his eyes had an odd squintlike gaze.

"Hey, Osman," the man who had been talking addressed him. "Broken-Nose Jabbar's got a woman for sale again. Only a hundred liras. Tell Mistress Huru to buy her for you and have done with living alone and sleeping in barns like a dog."

Osman shrugged his shoulders doubtfully.

"Look here, man," pursued the other, "this is a chance in a million. What's a hundred liras? You've been slaving for that Huru since you dropped out of your mother's womb and she's never paid you a lira. She owes you this. And anyway she'll get back her money's worth in just one summer. A woman's good for everything, in the house, in the fields, in bed . . ."

Osman rose abruptly.

"I'll ask the Mistress," he said. "How should I know? . . ."

A couple of days later, a short, broad-hipped girl with blue beads strung into her plaited hair was seen at the door of Huru's barn in which Hollow Osman always slept. She was staring out with huge wondering eyes.

A month passed. Two months . . . And passersby grew familiar with the sight of the strange wide-eyed girl at the barn door.

One day, a small dark boy with a face the size of a hand was seen pelting through the village. He rushed up to his mother where she sat on the threshold of her hut gossiping with Seedy Doneh.

"Mother," he screeched, "I've seen them! It's the truth, I swear it is. Uncle Osman's wife with . . . May my eyes drop out right here if I'm telling a lie."

Seedy Doneh turned to him sharply.

"What?" she cried. "Say it again. What's that about Fadik?"

"She was with the Agha's son. I saw them with my own eyes. He went into the barn with her. They couldn't see me where I was hiding. Then he took off his boots, you know the shiny yellow boots he wears . . . And then they lay down and . . . Let my two eyes drop out if . . ."

"I knew it!" crowed Seedy Doneh. "I knew it would turn out this way."

"Hollow Osman never had any manhood in him anyway," said the child's mother. "Always under that viper-tongued Huru's petticoats . . ."

"Didn't I tell you, Ansha, the very first day she came here that this would happen?" said Doneh. "I said this girl's ready to play around. Pretending she was too bashful to speak to anyone. Ah, still waters run deep . . ."

She rose quickly and hurried off to spread the news.

"Have you heard? Just as I foretold . . . Still waters . . . The Agha's son . . . Fadik . . ."

In a trice all the neighboring women had crowded at Ansha's door, trying to squeeze the last drop of information out of the child.

"Come on, tell us," urged one of the women for perhaps the hundredth time. "How did you see them?"

"Let my two eyes drop out right here if I'm lying," the child repeated again and again with unabated excitement. "The Agha's son came in, and then they lay down, both of them, and did things . . . I was watching through a chink in the wall. Uncle Osman's wife, you know, was crying. I can't do it, she was saying, and she was sobbing away all the time. Then the Agha's son pulled off those shiny yellow boots of his . . . Then I ran right here to tell Mother."

The news spread through the village like wildfire. People could talk about nothing else. Seedy Doneh, for one, seemed to have made it her job to leave no man or woman uninformed. As she scoured the village for new listeners, she chanced upon Osman himself.

"Haven't you heard what's come upon you?" she said, drawing him aside behind the wall of a hut. "You're disgraced, you jackass. The Agha's son has got his fingers up your wife's skirt. Try and clear your good name now if you can!"

Osman did not seem to understand.

"I don't know . . ." he murmured, shrugging his shoulders. "I'll have to ask the Mistress. What would the Agha's son want with my wife?"

Doneh was incensed.

"What would he want with her, blockhead?" she screamed. "Damn you, your wife's become a whore, that's what! She's turned your home into a brothel. Anyone can come in and have her." She flounced off still screaming. "I spit on you! I spit on your manhood . . ."

Osman was upset.

"What are you shouting for, woman?" he called after her. "People will think something's wrong. I have to ask the Mistress. She knows everything. How should I know?"

He started walking home, his long arms dangling at his sides as though they had been hitched to his shoulders as an afterthought, his fingers sticking out wide apart as was his habit. This time he was waylaid by their next-door neighbor, Zeynep, who planted herself before him and tackled him at the top of her voice.

"Ah Osman! You'd be better off dead! Why don't you go and bury yourself! The whole village knows about it. Your wife . . . The Agha's son . . . Ah Osman, how could you have brought such a woman into your home? Where's your honor now? Disgraced . . . Ah Osman!"

He stared at her in bewilderment.

"How should I know?" he stammered, his huge hands opening out like pitchforks. "The Mistress knows all about such things. I'll go and ask her."

Zeynep turned her back on him in exasperation, her large skirt ballooning about her legs.

"Go bury yourself, Osman! I hope I see you dead after this."

A group of children were playing tipcat nearby. Suddenly one of them broke into a chant.

"Go bury yourself, Osman . . . See you dead, Osman . . ."

The other children joined in mechanically without interrupting their game.

Osman stared at them and turned away.

"How should I know?" he muttered. "I must go to the Mistress."

He found Huru sitting at her spinning wheel. Fadik was there too, squatting near the hearth and listlessly chewing mastic gum.

"Mistress," said Osman, "have you heard what Seedy Doneh's saying? She's saying I'm disgraced . . ."

Huru stepped on the pedal forcefully and brought the wheel to a stop.

"What's that?" she said. "What about Seedy Doneh?"

"I don't know . . . She said Fadik . . ."

"Look here," said Huru, "you mustn't believe those lying bitches. You've got a good wife. Where would you find such a woman?"

"I don't know. Go bury yourself, they said. The children too . . ."

"Shut up," cried Huru, annoyed. "People always gossip about a beautiful woman. They go looking for the mote in their neighbor's eye without seeing the beam in their own. They'd better hold their peace because I've got a tongue in my head too . . ."

Osman smiled with relief.

"How could I know?" he said.

Down in the villages of the Chukurova plain, a sure sign of oncoming spring is when the women are seen with their heads on one another's lap, picking the lice out of one another's hair. So it was, on one of the first warm days of the year. A balmy sun shone caressingly down on the fields and village, and not a leaf stirred. A group of women were sitting before their huts on the dusty ground, busy with the lice and wagging their tongues for all they were worth. An acrid odor of sweat hung about the group. Seedy Doneh was rummaging in the hair of a large woman who was stretched full length on the ground. She decided that she had been silent long enough.

"No," she declared suddenly, "it's not as you say, sister! He didn't force her or any such thing. She simply fell for him the minute she saw those shiny yellow boots. If you're going to believe Huru! . . . She's got to deny it, of course."

"That Huru was born with a silver spoon in her mouth," said white-haired, toothless old Zala, wiping her bloodstained fingers on her ragged skirt. "Hollow Osman's been slaving for her like twenty men ever since she took him in, a kid the size of your hand! And all for a mere pittance of food. And now there's the woman too. Tell me, what's there left for Huru to do?"

"Ah," sighed another woman, "fortune has smiled on Huru, she has indeed! She's got two people serving her now."

"And both for nothing," old Zala reminded her.

"What it amounts to," said Seedy Doneh spitefully, "is that Huru used to have one wife and now she's got two. Osman was always a woman, and as for Fadik she's a real woman. He-he!"

"That she is, a real woman!" the others agreed.

"Huru says the Agha's son took her by force," pursued Doneh. "All right, but what about the others? What about those lining up at her door all through the night, eh? She never says no to any one of them, does she? She takes in everyone, young and old."

"The Lady Bountiful, that's what she is," said Elif. "And do you know something? Now that Fadik's here, the young men are leaving Omarja's yellow bitch in peace . . ."

"They've got somewhere better to go!" cackled the others.

Omarja's dumpy wife jumped up from where she was sitting on the edge of the group.

"Now look here, Elif!" she cried. "What's all this about our yellow dog? Stop blackening people's characters, will you?"

"Well, it's no lie, is it?" Doneh challenged her. "When was that bitch ever at your door where she should be all night? No, instead, there she came trotting up a-mornings with a rope dangling from her neck!"

"Don't go slandering our dog," protested Omarja's wife. "Why, if Omarja hears this, he'll kill the poor creature. Upon my word he will!"

"Go on!" said Doneh derisively. "Don't you come telling me that Omarja doesn't know his yellow bitch is the paramour of all the village youths! What about that time when Stumpy Veli caught some of them down by the river, all taking it in turns over her? Is there anyone in this village who didn't hear of that? It's no use trying to whitewash your bitch to us!"

Omarja's wife was alarmed.

"Don't, sister," she pleaded. "Omarja'll shoot the dog, that's sure . . ."

"Well, I'm not to blame for that, sister," retorted Doneh tartly. "Anyway, the bitch'll be all right now that Fadik's around. And so will Kurdish Velo's donkey . . ."

Kurdish Velo's wife began to fidget nervously.

"Not our fault," she blurted out in her broken Turkish. "We lock our donkey in, but they come and break the door! Velo furious. Velo say people round here savage. He say, with an animal deadly sin! He say he kill someone. Then he complain to the Headman. Velo going sell this donkey."

"You know what I think?" interposed Seedy Doneh. "They're going to make it hot for her in this village. Yes, they'll do what they did to Esheh."

"Poor Esheh," sighed old Zala. "What a woman she was before her man got thrown into prison! She would never have come to that, but she had no one to protect her. May they rot in hell, those that forced her into it! But she is dead and gone, poor thing."

"Eh!" said Doneh. "How could she be otherwise after the youths of five villages had done with her?" She straightened up. "Look here, sister," she said to the woman whose head was on her lap, "I couldn't get through your lice in days! They say the Government's invented some medicine for lice which they call Dee-Dee. Ah, if only we had a spoonful of that . . . Do you know, women, that Huru keeps watch over Fadik at night? She tells the youths when to come in and then drives them out with a stick. Ha-ha, and she wants us to believe in Fadik's virtue . . ."

"That's because it suits her. Where will she find people who'll work for nothing like those two?"

"Well, the lads are well provided for this year," snickered Doneh. "Who knows but that Huru may hop in and help Fadik out!"

Just then, Huru loomed up from behind a hut. She was a large woman with a sharp chin and a wrinkled face. Her graying hair was always carefully dyed with henna.

"Whores!" she shouted at the top of her voice, as she bore down upon them with arms akimbo. "City trollops! You get hold of a poor fellow's wife and let your tongues go wagging away. Tell me, are you any better than she? What do you want of this harmless mountain girl?" She pounced on Doneh who cringed back. "As for you, you filthy shitty-assed bitch, you'll shut your mouth or I'll start telling the truth about you and that husband of yours who pretends he's a man. You know me, don't you?"

Doneh blenched.

"Me, sister?" she stammered. "Me? I never . . . Other people's good name . . ."

The women were dispersing hastily. Only Kurdish Velo's wife, unaware of what was going on, continued picking lice out of her companion's hair.

"Velo says in our country women like this burnt alive. He says there no virtue in this Chukurova. No honor . . ."

The eastern sky had only just begun to pale as, with a great hullabaloo and calls and cries, the women and children drove the cattle out to pasture. Before their houses, red-aproned matrons were busy at the churns beating yogurt. The damp air smelled of spring.

Osman had long ago yoked the oxen and was waiting at Huru's door.

She appeared in the doorway.

"Osman, my lion," she said, "you're not to come back until you've plowed through the whole field. The girl Aysheh will look after your food and get you some bedding. Mind you do the sowing properly, my child. Husneh's hard pressed this year. And there's your wife to feed too now . . ."

Husneh was Huru's only child, whom in a moment of aberration she had given in marriage to Ali Efendi, a low-salaried tax collector. All the product of her land, everything Huru had, was for this daughter.

Osman did not move or say a word. He stood there in the half-light, a large black shadow near the yoked oxen whose tails were flapping their legs in slow rhythm.

Huru stepped up to him.

"What's the matter with you, Osman, my child," she said anxiously. "Is anything wrong?"

"Mistress," whispered Osman, "it's what Seedy Doneh's saying. And Zeynep too . . . That my house . . . I don't know . . ."

Huru flared up.

"Shut up, you spineless dolt," she cried. "Don't you come babbling to me about the filthy inventions of those city trollops. I paid that broken-nosed thief a hundred good bank notes for the girl, didn't I? Did I ask you for as much as a lira? You listen to me. You can find fault with pure gold, but not with Fadik. Don't let me hear such nonsense from you again!"

Osman hesitated.

"I don't know . . ." he murmured, as he turned at last and drove the oxen off before him.

It was midmorning. A bright sun glowed over the sparkling fields.

Osman was struggling with the lean, emaciated oxen, which after plowing through only one acre had stretched themselves on the ground and simply refused to budge. Flushed and breathless, he let himself drop onto a mound and took his head in his hands. After a while, he rose and tried pulling the animals up by the tail.

"Accursed beasts," he muttered. "The Mistress says Husneh's in need this year. Get up this minute, accursed beasts!"

He pushed and heaved, but to no avail. Suddenly in a burst of fury, he flung himself on the black ox, dug his teeth into its nose, and shook it with all his might. Then he straightened up and looked about him sheepishly.

"If anyone saw me . . ." He swore as he spat out blood. "What can I do? Husneh's in need and there's Fadik to feed too. And now these heathen beasts . . . I don't know."

It was in this state of perplexity that Stumpy Veli found him when he strolled over from a neighboring field.

"So the team's collapsed eh?" he commented. "Well, it was to be expected. Look at how their ribs are sticking out. You won't be able to get anything out of them."

"I don't know," muttered Osman faintly. "Husneh's in a bad way and I got married . . ."

"And a fine mess that's landed you in," burst out Veli angrily. "You'd have been better off dead!"

"I don't know," said Osman. "The Mistress paid a hundred liras for her . . ."

Stumpy Veli took hold of his arm and made him sit down.

"Look, Osman," he said, "the villagers told me to talk to you. They say you're giving the village a bad name. Ever since the Agha's son took up with your wife, all the other youths have followed suit and your house is just like a brothel now. The villagers say you've got to repudiate her. If you don't, they'll drive you both out. The honor of the whole village is at stake, and you know honor doesn't grow on trees . . ."

Osman, his head hanging down, was as still as a statue. A stray ant had caught his eye.

What's this ant doing around here at this time of day, he wondered to himself. Where can its nest be?

Veli nudged him sharply.

"Damn you, man!" he cried. "Think what'll happen if the police get wind of this. She hasn't got any papers. Why, if the gendarmes once lay their hands on her, you know how it'll be. They'll play around with her for months, poor creature."

Osman started as though an electric current had been sent through his large frame.

"I haven't got any papers either," he whispered.

Veli drew nearer. Their shoulders touched. Osman's were trembling fitfully.

"Papers are the business of the Government," Veli said. "You and me, we can't understand such things. If we did, then what would we need a Government for? Now, listen to me. If the gendarmes get hold of her, we'll be the laughingstock of villages for miles around. We'll never be able to hold up our heads again in the Chukurova. You mustn't trifle with the honor of the whole village. Get rid of her before she drags you into more trouble."

"But where will I be without her?" protested Osman. "I'll die, that's all. Who'll do my washing? Who'll cook bulgur pilaf for me? I'll starve to death if I have to eat gruel again every day. I just can't do without her."

"The villagers will buy you another woman," said Veli. "We'll collect the money among us. A better woman, an honorable one, and beautiful too . . . I'll go up into the mountain villages and pick one for you myself. Just you pack this one off quickly . . ."

"I don't know," said Osman. "It's the Mistress knows about these things."

Veli was exasperated.

"Damn the Mistress!" he shouted. "It's up to you, you idiot!"

Then he softened. He tried persuasion again. He talked and talked. He talked himself hoarse, but Osman sat there immovable as a rock, his mouth clamped tight. Finally Veli spat in his face and stalked off.

It was well on in the afternoon when it occurred to Osman to unyoke the team. He had not stirred since Veli's departure. As for the oxen, they had just lain there placidly chewing the cud. He managed to get them to their feet and let them wander about the field, while he walked back to the village. He made straight for the Agha's house and waited in the yard, not speaking to anyone, until he saw the Agha's son riding in, the bridle of his horse lathered with sweat.

The Agha's son was taken aback. He dismounted quickly, but Osman waylaid him.

"Listen," he pleaded, "you're the son of our all-powerful Agha. What do you want with my wife?"

The Agha's son became the color of his famous boots. He hastily pulled a five-lira note out of his pocket and thrust it into Osman's hand.

"Take this," he mumbled and hurried away.

"But you're a great big Agha's son!" cried Osman after him. "Why do you want to drive her away? What harm has she done you? You're a great big . . ."

He was crushed. He stumbled away towards Huru's house, the five-lira note still in his hand.

At the sight of Osman, Huru blew her top.

"What are you doing here, you feebleminded ass?" she shouted. "Didn't I tell you not to come back until you'd finished all the plowing? Do you want to ruin me, you idiot?"

"Wait, Mistress," stammered Osman. "Listen . . ."

"Listen, he says! Damn the fool!"

"Mistress," he pleaded, "let me explain . . ."

Huru glared at him.

"Mistress, you haven't heard. You don't know what the villagers are going to do to me. They're going to throw me out of this village. Stumpy Veli said so. He said the police . . . He said papers . . . We haven't got any papers. Fadik hasn't and I haven't either. He said the gendarmes would carry Fadik away and do things to her. He said I must repudiate her because my house is a brothel. That's what he said. I said the Mistress knows these things . . . She paid the hundred liras . . ."

Huru was dancing with fury. She rushed out into the village square and began howling at the top of her voice.

"Bastards! So she's a thorn in your flesh, this poor fellow's wife! If you want to drive whores out of this village why don't you start with your own wives and daughters? You'd better look for whores in your own homes, pimps that you are, all of you! And tell your sons to leave poor folks' women alone . . ."

Then she turned to Osman and gave him a push.

"Off you go! To the fields! No one's going to do anything to your wife. Not while I'm alive."

The villagers had gathered in the square and had heard Huru out in profound silence. As soon as she was gone, though, they started muttering among themselves.

"Who does that bitch think she is, abusing the whole village like that? . . ."

The Agha, Wolf Mahmut, had heard her too.

"You just wait, Huru," he said grinding his teeth. "If you think you're going to get away with this . . ."

The night was dark, a thick damp darkness that seemed to cling to the face and hands. Huru had been waiting for some time now, concealed in the blackest shadow of the barn, when suddenly she perceived a stirring in the darkness, and a voice was calling softly at the door.

"Fadik! Open up, girl. It's me . . ."

The door creaked open and a shadow glided in. An uncontrollable trembling seized Huru. She gripped her stick and flung herself on the door. It was unbolted and went crashing back against the wall. As she stood there trying to pierce the darkness, a few vague figures hustled by and made their escape. Taken by surprise, she hurled out a vitriolic oath and started groping about until she discovered Fadik crouching in a corner. She seized her by the hair and began to beat her with the stick.

"Bitch!" she hissed. "To think I was standing up for you Grades 7–8:"

Fadik did not utter a sound as the blows rained down on her. At last Huru, exhausted, let go of her.

"Get up," she ordered, "and light some kindling."

Fadik raked out the dying embers and with much puffing and blowing managed to light a stick of torchwood. A pale honeyed light fell dimly over the stacked hay. There was an old pallet in one corner and a few kitchen utensils, but nothing else to show that the place was lived in.

Huru took Fadik's hand and looked at her sternly.

"Didn't you promise me, girl, that you'd never do it again?"

Fadik's head hung low.

"Do you know, you bitch," continued Huru, "what the villagers are going to do? They're going to kick you out of the village. Do you hear me?"

Fadik stirred a little. "Mistress, I swear I didn't go after them! They just came in spite of everything."

"Listen to me, girl," said Huru. "Do you know what happened to Esheh? That's what you'll come to if you're not careful. They're like ravening wolves, these men. If you fall into their clutches, they'll tear you to shreds. To shreds, I tell you!"

"But Mistress, I swear I never did anything to—"

"You must bolt your door because they'll be after you whether you do anything or not, and their pimps of fathers will put the blame on me. It's my hundred liras they can't swallow. They're dying to see it go to pot . . . Just like Esheh you'll be. They had no one in the world, she and her man, and when Ali was thrown into jail she was left all alone. He'd lifted a sheep from the Agha's flock and bought clothes and shoes for their son. A lovely child he was, three years old . . . Ali doted on him. But there he was in jail, and that yellow-booted good-for-nothing was soon after Esheh like the plague. She kept him at arm's length for as long as she could, poor Esheh, but he got what he wanted in the end. Then he turned her over to those ravening wolves . . . They dragged her about from village to village, from mountain to mountain. Twenty, thirty good-for-nothings . . . Her child was left among strangers, the little boy she had loved so. He died . . . Those who saw her said she was like a consumptive, thin and gray, but still they wouldn't let her go, those scoundrels. Then one day the village dogs came in all smeared with blood, and an eagle was circling over the plain. So the men went to look, and they found Esheh, her body half devoured by the dogs . . . They'd made her dance naked for them . . . They'd done all sorts of things to her. Yes, they as good as killed her. That's what the police said when they came up from the town. And when Ali heard of it, he died of grief in jail. Yes, my girl, you've got Esheh's fate before you. It isn't my hundred liras that I care for, it's you. As for Osman, I can always find another woman for him. Now I've warned you. Just call me if they come again. Esheh was all alone in the world. You've got me, at least. Do you swear to do as I'm telling you?"

"I swear it, Mistress," said Fadik.

Huru was suddenly very tired.

"Well, I'm going. You'll call me, won't you?"

As soon as she was gone, the youths crept out of the darkness and sneaked into the barn again.

"Hey, Fadik," they whispered. "Huru was lying to you, girl. Esheh just killed herself . . ."

There was a stretch of grass in front of the Agha's house, and on one side of it dung had been heaped to the size of a small hillock. The dung steamed in the early morning sun and not a breath stirred the warm air. A cock climbed to the top of the heap. It scraped the dung, stretched its neck, and crowed triumphantly, flapping its wings.

The group of villagers squatting about on the grass silently eyed the angry Agha. Wolf Mahmut was a huge man whose shadow when he was sitting was as large as that of an average man standing up. He was never seen without a frayed, checked overcoat, the only one in the village, that he had been wearing for years now.

He was toying irritably with his metal-framed glasses when Stumpy Veli, who had been sent for a while ago, made his appearance. The Agha glared at him.

"Is this the way you get things done, you fraud?" he expostulated. "So you'd have Hollow Osman eating out of your hand in no time, eh?"

Stumpy Veli seemed to shrink to half his size.

"Agha," he said, "I tried everything. I talked and talked. I told him the villagers would drive them both out. I warned him of the gendarmes. All right, he said, I'll send her away. And then he didn't . . . If you ask me, Huru's at the bottom of it all."

The others stirred. "That she is!" they agreed.

Mahmut Agha jumped up. "I'll get even with her," he growled.

"That, you will, Agha," they assented. "But . . ."

"We've put up with that old whore long enough," continued the Agha, sitting down again.

"Yes, Agha," said Stumpy Veli, "but, you see, she relies on her son-in-law Ali, the tax collector. They'd better stop treading on my toes, she said, or I'll have Ali strip this village bare . . ."

"He can't do anything," said the Agha. "I don't owe the Government a bean."

"But we do, Agha," interposed one of the men. "He can come here and take away our blankets and rugs, whatever we have . . ."

"It's because of Huru that he hasn't fleeced this village up to now," said another. "We owe a lot of money, Agha."

"Well, what are we to do then?" cried Mahmut Agha angrily. "All our youths have left the plow and the fields and are after the woman night and day like rutting bulls. At this rate, the whole village'll starve this year."

An old man spoke up in a tremulous voice. "I'm dead, for one," he wailed. "That woman's ruined my hearth. High morning it is already. Go to the plow, my son, I beg the boy. We'll starve if you don't plow. But he won't listen. He's always after that woman. I've lost my son because of that whore. I'm too old to plow any more. I'll starve this year. I'll go and throw myself at Huru's feet. There's nothing else to do . . ."

The Agha rose abruptly. "That Huru!" He gritted his teeth. "I'll settle her account."

He strode away.

The villagers looked up hopefully. "Mahmut Agha'll settle her account," they muttered. "He'll find a way . . ."

The Agha heard them and swelled with pride. "Yes, Mahmut Agha'll settle her account," he repeated grimly to himself.

He stopped before a hut and called out.

"Hatije Woman! Hatije!"

A middle-aged woman rushed out wiping her hands on her apron.

"Mahmut Agha!" she cried. "Welcome to our home. You never visit us these days." Then she whirled back. "Get up, you damned lazybones," she shouted angrily. "It's high morning, and look who's here."

Mahmut Agha followed her inside.

"Look, Agha," she complained, pointing to her son, "it's high morning and Halil still abed!"

Startled at the sight of the Agha, Halil sprang up and drew on his black shalvar trousers shamefacedly, while his mother continued with her lamentations.

"Ah, Mahmut Agha, you don't know what's befallen us! You don't know, may I kiss your feet, my Agha, or you wouldn't have us on your land any longer . . . Ah, Mahmut Agha! This accursed son of mine . . . I would have seen him dead and buried, yes, buried in this black earth before . . ."

"What are you cursing the lad for?" Mahmut Agha interrupted her. "Wait, just tell me first."

"Ah, Agha, if you knew! It was full day when he came home this night. And it's the same every night, the same ever since Hollow Osman's woman came to the village. He lies abed all through the livelong day. Who'll do the plowing, I ask you? We'll starve this year. Ah, Mahmut Agha, do something! Please do something . . ."

"You go outside a little, will you, Hatije," said the Agha. Then he turned to Halil, stretching out his long, wrinkled neck which had become as red as a turkey's. "Listen to me, my boy, this has got to end. You must get this whore out of our village and give her to the youths of another village, any village. She's got to go and you'll do it. It's an order. Do you hear me?"

"Why, Agha!" Halil said ingratiatingly. "Is that what's worrying you? I'll get hold of her this very night and turn her over to Jelil from Ortakli village. You can count on me."

The Agha's spirits rose.

"Hatije," he called out, "come in here. See how I'm getting you out of this mess? And all the village too . . . Let that Huru know who she's dealing with in the future. They call me Wolf Mahmut and I know how to put her nose out of joint."

Long before dawn, piercing shrieks startled the echoes in the village.

"Bastards! Pimps!" Huru was howling. "You won't get away with this, not on your life you won't. My hundred liras were too much for you to swallow, eh, you fiends? You were jealous of this poor fellow's wife, eh? But you just wait and see, Wolf Mahmut! I'll set the tax collector after you all in no time. I'll get even with you if I have to spend my last penny! I'll bribe the Mudir, the Kaymakam, all the officials. I'll send telegrams to Ankara, to Ismet Pasha, to the head of the Democrats. I'll have you all dragged into court, rotting away in police stations. I'll get my own back on you for Fadik's sake."

She paused to get her breath and was off again even louder than before.

Fadik had disappeared, that was the long and the short of it. Huru soon found out that someone else was missing too. Huseyin's half-witted son, The Tick.

"Impossible," she said. "The Tick ravishing women? Not to save his life, he couldn't! This is just another trick of those good-for-nothings . . ."

"But really, Huru," the villagers tried to persuade her, "he was after her all the time. Don't you know he gathered white snails in the hills, threaded them into a necklace, and offered it to Fadik, and she hung it up on her wall as a keepsake? That's the plain truth, Huru."

"I don't believe it," Huru said stubbornly. "I wouldn't even if I saw them together with my own eyes . . ."

The next day it started raining, that sheer, plumb-line torrent which sets in over the Chukurova for days. The minute the bad news had reached him, Osman had abandoned his plow and had rushed back to the village. He was standing now motionless at Huru's door, the peak of his cap droop-ing over his eyes. His wet clothes clung to his flesh, glistening darkly, and his rawhide boots were clogged with mud.

"Come in out of the rain, Osman, do!" Huru kept urging him.

"I can't. I don't know . . ." was all he could say.

"Now, look here, Osman," said Huru. "She's gone, so what? Let them have that bitch. I'll find you a good woman, my Osman. Never mind the money. I'll spend twice as much on a new wife for you. Just you come in out of the rain."

Osman never moved.

"Listen, Osman. I've sent word to Ali. Come and levy the taxes at once, I said. Have no mercy on these ungrateful wretches. If you don't fleece them to their last rag, I said, you needn't count on me as a mother again. You'll see what I'm going to do to them, my Osman. You just come in-side . . ."

The rain poured down straight and thick as the warp in a loom, and Osman still stood there, his chin resting on his staff, like a thick tree whose branches have been lopped off.

Huru appealed to the neighbors. Two men came and pulled and pushed, but he seemed nailed to the ground. It was well in the afternoon when he stirred and began to pace the village from one end to the other, his head sunk between his shoulders and the rain streaming down his body.

"Poor fellow, he's gone mad," opined the villagers.

A few strong men finally carried him home. They undressed him and put him to bed.

Huru sat down beside him. "Look, Osman, I'll get you a new woman even if it costs me a thousand liras. You mustn't distress yourself so. Just for a woman . . ."

The next morning he was more his normal self, but no amount of reasoning or pleading from Huru could induce him to go back to the field. He left the house and resumed his pacing up and down.

The villagers had really begun to feel sorry for him now.

"Alas, poor Osman!" they murmured as he passed between the huts.

Osman heard them and heaved deep, heartrending sighs. And still he roamed aimlessly round and round.

Wolf Mahmut should have known better. Why, the whole village saw with half an eye what a rascal Halil was! How could he be trusted to give up a woman once he had got her into his hands? He had indeed got Fadik out of the way, but what he had done was to shut her up in one of the empty sheep pens in the hills beyond the village, and there he had posted The Tick to guard her.

"Play around with her if you like," he had told him contemptuously. "But if you let her give you the slip—" and he had seized The Tick's wrist and squeezed it until it hurt—"you're as good as dead."

Though twenty years old, The Tick was so scraggy and undersized that at first glance people would take him to be only ten. His arms and legs were as thin as matchsticks and he walked sideways like a crab. He had always had a way of clinging tenaciously to people or objects he took a fancy to, which even as a child had earned him his nickname. No one had ever called him by his real name and it looked as though his own mother had forgotten it too . . .

Halil would come every evening bringing food for Fadik and The Tick, and he would leave again just before dawn. But it was not three days before the village youths found out what was going on. After that there was a long queue every night outside the sheep pen. They would take it in turns, heedless of Fadik's tears and howls, and at daybreak, singing and firing their guns as though in a wedding procession, they would make their way back to the village.

Night was falling and Fadik began to tremble like a leaf. They would not be long now. They would come again and torture her. She was weak with fear and exhaustion. For the past two days, her gorge had risen at the very sight of food, and she lay there on the dirt floor, hardly able to move, her whole body covered with bruises and wounds.

The Tick was dozing away near the door of the pen.

Fadik tried to plead with him. "Let me go, brother," she begged. "I'll die if I have to bear another night of this."

The Tick half-opened his eyes. "I can't," he replied.

"But if I die, it'll be your fault. Before God it will . . . Please let me go."

"Why should it be my fault?" said The Tick. "I didn't bring you here, did I?"

"They'll never know. You'll say you fell asleep. I'll go off and hide some-where. I'll go back to my mother . . ."

"I can't," said The Tick. "Halil would kill me if I let you go."

"But I want to go to my mother," she cried desperately. "You must let me go. Please let me go . . ."

It was dark now and the sound of singing drifted up from the village.

Fadik was seized with a violent fit of trembling. "They're coming," she said. "Let me get away now, brother. Save me! If you save me, I'll be your woman. I'll do anything . . ."

But The Tick had not been nicknamed for nothing.

"They'd kill me," he said. "Why should I die because of you? And Halil's promised to buy me a pair of shoes, too. I'm not going to go without shoes because of you."

Fadik broke into wild sobbing. There was no hope now.

"Oh, God," she wept, "what shall I do now? Oh, Mother, why was I ever born?"

They lined up as usual at the entrance to the pen. The first one went in and a nerve-racking scream rose from Fadik, a scream that would have moved the most hardened of hearts. But the youths were deaf to every-thing. In they went, one after the other, and soon Fadik's screams died down. Not even a moan came out of her.

There were traces of blood on the ground at the back of the sheep pen. Halil and the Agha's son had had a fight the night before and the Agha's son had split open Halil's head.

"The woman's mine," Halil had insisted. "I've a right to go in first."

"No, you haven't," the Agha's son had contended. "I'm going to be the first."

The other youths had taken sides and joined the fray which had lasted most of the night, and it was a bedraggled band that wended back to the vil-lage that night.

Bowed down with grief, Hatije Woman came weeping to the Muhtar.

"My son is dying," she cried. "He's at his last gasp, my poor Halil, and it's the Agha's son who did it, all because of that whore of Huru's. Ah, Muhtar, if my son dies what's to become of me? There he lies struggling for life, the only hope of my hearth. But I won't let the Agha get away with this. I'll go to the Government. An old woman's only prop, I'll say . . ."

The Muhtar had great difficulty in talking Hatije out of her purpose.

"You go back home, Hatije Woman," he said when she had calmed down a little, "and don't worry. I'll deal with this business."

He summoned the Agha and the elders, and a long discussion ensued. It would not do to hand over the woman to the police station. These rapa-cious gendarmes! . . . The honor of the whole village was at stake. And if they passed her on to the youths of another village, Huru was sure to find out and bring her back. She would not rest until she did.

After long deliberation, they came to a decision at last. The woman would be returned to Osman, but on one condition. He would take himself off with her to some distant place and never appear in the village again. They had no doubt that Osman, grateful to have Fadik back to himself, would accept. And that would cook Huru's goose too. She would lose both the woman and Osman. It would teach her to insult a whole village!

A couple of men went to find Osman and brought him back with them to the Muhtar's house.

"Sit down," they urged him, but he just stood there grasping his staff, staring about him with bloodshot eyes. His clothes hung down torn and crumpled and stained yellow from his lying all wet on the hay. His hair was a tangled, clotted mass and bits of straw clung to the stubble on his chin.

Wolf Mahmut took off his glasses and fidgeted with them.

"Osman, my lad," he remonstrated, "what's this state you're in? And all for a woman! Does a man let himself break down like this just for a woman? You'll die if you go on like this . . ."

"I don't know," said Osman. "I'll die . . ."

"See here, Osman," said the Agha. "We're here to help you. We'll get your woman back for you from out of those rascals' hands. Then you'll take her and go. You'll both get away from here, as far as possible. But you're not to tell Huru. She mustn't know where you are."

"You see, Osman," said Stumpy Veli, "how good the Agha's being to you. Your own father wouldn't have done more."

"But you're not to tell Huru," the Agha insisted. "If you do, she'll never let you go away. And then the youths will come and take your woman away from you again. And how will you ever get yourself another woman?"

"And who'll wash your clothes then?" added Stumpy Veli. "Who'll cook your bulgur pilaf for you? You mustn't breathe a word to Huru. Just take Fadik and go off to the villages around Antep. Once there, you'll be sure to get a job on a farm. You'll be much better off than you ever were with Huru, and you'll have your woman with you too . . ."

"But how can I do that?" protested Osman. "The Mistress paid a hundred liras for Fadik."

"We'll collect that much among us," the Agha assured him. "Don't you worry about that. We'll see that Huru gets her money back. You just take the woman and go."

"I don't know," said Osman. His eyes filled with tears and he swallowed. "The Mistress has always been so good to me . . . How can I . . . Just for a woman . . ."

"If you tell Huru, you're lost," said the Agha. "Is Huru the only mistress in the world? Aren't there other villages in this country? Take the woman and go. You'll never find another woman like Fadik. Listen, Veli'll tell you where she is and tomorrow you'll take her and go."

Osman bowed his head. He thought for a long time. Then he looked up at them.

"I won't tell her," he said at last. "Why should I want to stay here? There are other villages . . ."

Before dawn the next day, he set out for the sheep pen which Stumpy Veli had indicated.

"I don't know . . ." he hesitated at the door. "I don't know . . ." Then he called out softly, "Fadik? Fadik, girl . . ."

There was no answer. Trembling with hope and fear, he stepped in, then stopped aghast. Fadik was lying there on the dirt floor with only a few tatters left to cover her naked body. Her huge eyes were fixed vacantly on the branches that roofed the pen.

He stood frozen, his eyes filling with tears. Then he bent his large body over her.

"Fadik," he whispered, "are you all right?"

Her answering moan shook him to the core. He slipped off his shirt and helped her into it. Then he noticed The Tick who had shrunk back into a corner, trying to make himself invisible. Osman moved on him threateningly.

"Uncle Osman," cried The Tick shaking with fear, "I didn't do it. It was Halil. He said he'd buy me a pair of shoes . . . And Fadik would have died if I hadn't been here . . ."

Osman turned away, heaved Fadik onto his back swiftly, and threw himself out of the pen.

The mountain peaks were pale and the sun was about to rise. A few white clouds floated in the sky and a cool breeze caressed his face. The earth was wet with dew.

The Tick was scurrying off towards the village.

"Brother," Osman called after him, "go to the Mistress and tell her I thank her for all she's done for me, but I have to go. Tell her to forgive me . . ."

He set out in the opposite direction with Fadik on his back. He walked without a break until the sun was up the height of two minarets. Then he lowered Fadik to the ground and sat down opposite her. They looked at each other for a long while without speaking.

"Tell me," said Osman. "Where shall we go now? I don't know . . ."

Fadik moaned.

The air smelled of spring and the earth steamed under the sun.

■ Nizar Qabbani (1923–1998) *Syria* (poem)

TRANSLATED BY BEN BENNANI

Syrian poet Nizar Qabbani studied law at Syrian University, graduating in 1945, and embarked on a career in the Syrian diplomatic corps, which has taken him to China, Europe, and across the Arab world. His early work tended to be about women and his later work focused more on social and political questions. He published his first of twenty-five collections of poetry at age nineteen and is considered the most popular living Arab poet. When the poem "Bread, Hashish, and Moon" appeared, Qabbani was threatened with prosecution for its anti-Arab and Muslim sentiments, but he left Syria before the government acted and settled in Beirut, where he started his own publishing firm.

FURTHER READING: Al-Udhari, Abdullah, tr. and ed. *Modern Poetry of the Arab World*, 1986. Bennani, Ben, ed. and tr. *Bread, Hashish, and Moon: Four Modern Arab Poets*, 1982. Khouri, Mounhah A., and Hamid Algar, eds. and trs. *An Anthology of Modern Arabic Poetry*, 1974.

Bread, Hashish, and Moon

When the moon rises in the East
The white roofs fall asleep
Beneath a heap of flowers
And people leave their shops and walk in groups
To meet the moon   5
Carrying bread, hashish, and phonographs to mountain tops
To sell and buy delusions
To die so the moon may live.

What does a disc of light do
To my country?   10
To a country of prophets
A country of simple people
Tobacco chewers and dope peddlers?
What does the moon do to us
To make us lose pride   15
And spend our lives imploring heaven?
What does heaven have
For the stuporous and weak
Who choose to die so the moon may live
Who shake the tombs of saints   20
Begging for rice and children
Who spread out carpets of delicate embroideries
And flirt with a drug we call fate
And divine decree?

In my country, in the country of simple people   25
What weakness and decay
Overcome us when light flows everywhere

And carpets and thousands of baskets
Teacups and children take the hills?
In my country   30
Where people live without eyes
Where the innocent weep
And pray
And fornicate
And live on fatalism   35
(they have always lived on fatalism)
Calling to the moon:

O, moon!
Spring of diamonds
Hashish and slumber   40
O, suspended marble god
You are unbelievable!
Live for the East
A cluster of diamonds!
Live for the millions who are senseless . . .   45

At night in the East when
The moon is full
The East strips off all dignity
And resistance
The millions who run off without shoes   50
And who believe in four wives
And the Day of Judgment,
The millions who never find bread
Except in dreams
Who spend their nights in houses   55
Made of coughs
Never having medicine to take
Become corpses under the moonlight
In my country
Where the imbeciles weep   60
And die weeping
Whenever the moon's face rises over them
And go on weeping
Whenever a tender lute moves them to amorous chants
That death we call in the East   65
Layali,[1] and to songs
In my country
In the country of simple people
Where we regurgitate Andalusian chants
A disease that ravishes the East   70

---

1. Layali [sing, layl, night] are equivalent to evening concerts in the West.

The long *tawashih*[2]
Our East that regurgitates its history
Lazy dreams
And ancient superstitions
Our East that seeks all kinds of heroism   75
In Abu-Zayd al-Hilali.[3]

■ Yehuda Amichai (1924–2000) *Israel* (poems)

TRANSLATED BY CHANA BLOCH

Yehuda Amichai was the leading poet in Israel and had gained widespread international fame. He was born in Würzburg, Germany, in 1924, and he immigrated to Palestine in 1936. During World War II, he fought in the British army and later in the Israeli army during the War of Independence and two later wars. He went to Hebrew University and gained fame as a poet and as a novelist and short story writer. He also won first prize for a radio script in a national competition. He lived in Israel and until recently was a teacher and a sergeant-major in the Israeli army. Among his fiction publications are *The World Is a Room and Other Stories* (a collection of short stories) and *Not of This Time, Not of This Place* (a novel); *Selected Poetry of Yehuda Amichai* and *Travels* (a long autobiographical poem) both appeared in English in 1986. Earlier collections in English translation include *Selected Poems* (1969), *Poems* (1971), and *Songs of Jerusalem and Myself* (1973). He was a poet who had experienced a lifetime of war and who wrote of searching for the possibility of love and peace (as in his poem "Wildpeace"). Bombs and shrapnel and a lush, elegiac humanism inform the work of this self-ironic dreamer, and his words open doors to the Bible and to hidden rooms of consciousness.

The Sweet Breakdowns of Abigail

Everyone whacks her with tiny blows
the way you peel an egg.

With desperate bursts of perfume
she strikes back at the world.

---

2. *Tawashih* [sing, *muwashshah*] are stanzaic and lyrical poems dealing exclusively with love and nature, invented and perfected by the Arabs in the 11th century.

3. Abu Zayd al-Hilali is a fictional character supposedly endowed with supernatural and heroic qualities.

With sharp giggles she gets even   5
for all the sadness,

and with quick little fallings-in-love,
like burps and hiccups of feeling.

A terrorist of sweetness,
she stuffs bombshells with despair and cinnamon,   10
with cloves, with shrapnel of love.

At night when she tears off her jewelry,
there's a danger she won't know when to stop
and will go on tearing and slashing away at her whole life.

The Diameter of the Bomb

The diameter of the bomb was thirty centimeters
and the diameter of its effective range about seven meters,
with four dead and eleven wounded.
And around these, in a larger circle
of pain and time, two hospitals are scattered   5
and one graveyard. But the young woman
who was buried in the city she came from,
at a distance of more than a hundred kilometers,
enlarges the circle considerably,
and the solitary man mourning her death   10
at the distant shores of a country far across the sea
includes the entire world in the circle.
And I won't even mention the crying of orphans
that reaches up to the throne of God and
beyond, making   15
a circle with no end and no God.

When I Banged My Head on the Door

When I banged my head on the door, I screamed,
"My head, my head," and I screamed, "Door, door,"
and I didn't scream "Mama" and I didn't scream "God."
And I didn't prophesy a world at the End of Days
where there will be no more heads and doors.   5

When you stroked my head, I whispered,
"My head, my head," and I whispered, "Your hand, your hand,"
and I didn't whisper "Mama" or "God."
And I didn't have miraculous visions

of hands stroking heads in the heavens 10
as they split wide open.
Whatever I scream or say or whisper is only
to console myself: My head, my head.
Door, door. Your hand, your hand.

You Carry the Weight of Heavy Buttocks

You carry the weight of heavy buttocks,
but your eyes are clear.
Around your waist a wide belt that won't protect you.

You're made of the kind of materials that slow down
the process of joy 5
and its pain.

I've already taught my penis
to say your name
like a trained parakeet.

And you're not even impressed. As if 10
you didn't hear.
What else should I have done for you?

All I have left now is your name,
completely independent,
like an animal: 15

it eats out of my hand
and lies down at night
curled up in my dark brain.

Wildpeace

Not that of a cease-fire,
let alone the vision
of the wolf and the lamb,
but rather
as in the heart after a surge of emotion: 5
to speak only about a great weariness.
I know that I know how
to kill: that's why I'm an adult.
And my son plays with a toy gun that knows
how to open and close its eyes and say Mama. 10
A peace
without the big noise of beating swords into plowshares,

without words, without
the heavy thud of the rubber stamp; I want it
gentle over us, like lazy white foam.   *15*
A little rest for the wounds—
who speaks of healing?
(And the orphans' outcry is passed from one generation
to the next, as in a relay race:
the baton never falls.)   *20*

I want it to come
like wildflowers,
suddenly, because the field
needs it: wildpeace.

■ Badr Shakir al-Sayyab (1926–1964) *Iraq* (poem)

TRANSLATED BY LENA JAYYUSI AND CHRISTOPHER MIDDLETON

Badr Shakir al-Sayyab was born in southern Iraq in 1926 in the village of Jaikur and was educated in Basra and later at the Teachers Training College of Baghdad. He was a schoolteacher, a journalist, and a civil servant. Early on he was a Communist, but then he moved toward mainstream Arab nationalism, rejecting the Communists for not supporting Palestinian autonomy. Ironically, he was persecuted both by Arab nationalists and by the Communists and died destitute and in shattered health. He was influenced in his work by English-language poets, first the Romantics, Percy Bysshe Shelley and John Keats, and later T. S. Eliot, and he was one of the innovators who introduced free verse to Arabic. His books of poems include *Faded Flowers* (1947), *Legends* (1950), *Song of Rain* (1960), *The Drowned Shrine* (1962), *The House of Slaves* (1963), *The Oriel Window of the Nobleman's Daughter* (1964), and *Iqbal* (1965).

Song in August

Tammuz dies on the skyline,[1]
His blood seeps away with twilight
In the dim cavern. Darkness

---

1. Tammuz was an ancient Babylonian nature god, a god of agriculture. He was the lover of the fertility goddess Ishtar, who, according to one legend, killed him and then restored his life for part of the year. When he lived, spring came; when he died, it was winter. His Sumerian name was Dumuzi [Editor].

Is a black ambulance,
Night a flock of women: 5
Kohl, black cloaks.
Night, an enormous tent.
Night, a blocked day.

I called to my negro maid:
"Murjana, it's dark now,   10
Switch the light on. You know what? I'm hungry.
There's a song, I forgot, some sort of a song.
What's this chatter on the radio?
From London, Murjana, a
Jazz concert so   15
Find it, I'm happy, jazz,
Blood rhythm."

Tammuz dies and Murjana
Crouches cold like the forest.
She says, breathless: 20
"The night, wild pig,
How miserable the night is."
"Murjana, was that the doorbell?"
So she says, breathless:
"There are women at the door."   25
And Murjana makes the coffee.

Fur over white shoulders:
Wolf covers woman.
On her breasts a whole sheen of tiger skin
Filling the forest, stealing from the trees.   30
Night stretches,
Distraction, night
An earth-oven, radiant from ghosts,
Bread inhaling the night fires,
And the visitor eats, famished.   35
Murjana crouches
Cold like the forest.

The visitor laughs, she says: "Su'ad's boyfriend,
Been giving her a bad time, broke the engagement,
The dog disowned the bitch . . ."   40
Tammuz dies, never to return.
Coldness drips from the moon,
The visitor huddles at the fire gossiping, sharp-tongued.
Night has extinguished the coasts,
The visitor crouches, cold, robed   45
With wolf fur.

The fire she lit with bloody talk
Goes out.

Night and ice,
Across them a sound falls, clank of iron   *50*
Muffled by wolf howls.
Distant sound,
The visitor, like me, is cold.
So come on over and share my cold,
Come by God,   *55*
Husband, I'm alone here,
The visitor is cold as I am—
So come on over,
Only with you can I talk about everyone.
And there are so many people to be talked about.   *60*
The dark is a hearse, the driver blind
And your heart is a burial ground.

■ Yusuf Idris (1927–1990)
Egypt (story)

TRANSLATED BY DENYS JOHNSON-DAVIES

Yusuf Idris was born in a village in Egypt in 1927. He was trained as a physician and worked for a period as a government health inspector. Like other great doctor writers, such as Anton Chekov and William Carlos Williams, Idris's fiction shows a great interest in the common people his profession brought him in contact with. And like the lush lines of "The Ode to a Nightingale" by John Keats (a surgeon by profession) —

I cannot see what flowers are at my feet,
Nor what soft incense hangs upon the boughs,
But, in embalmèd darkness, guess each sweet,

—Idris's story "House of Flesh" hinges upon a sensual encounter in blind darkness. Idris published novels, plays, and short story collections and was considered among the finest short fiction masters in the Arab world. His work has been translated into Russian and other East European tongues, and it is available in several good English-language editions.

FURTHER READING: Idris, Yusuf. *In the Eye of the Beholder: Tales of Egyptian Life from the Writings of Yusuf Idris,* 1978; *The Cheapest Nights: Short Stories.* Translated by Wadida Wassef, 1991; *Rings of Burnished Brass and Other Stories.* Translated by Catherine Cobham, 1992.

House of Flesh

The ring is beside the lamp. Silence reigns and ears are blinded. In the silence the finger slides along and slips on the ring. In silence too, the lamp is put out. Darkness is all around. In the darkness eyes too are blinded.

The widow and her three daughters. The house is a room. The beginning is silence.

* * *

The widow is tall, fair-skinned, slender, thirty-five years of age. Her daughters too are tall and full of life. They never take off their flowing clothes which, whether they be in or out of mourning, are black. The youngest is sixteen, the eldest twenty. They are ugly, having inherited their father's dark-skinned body, full of bulges and curves wrongly disposed; from their mother they have taken hardly anything but her height.

Despite its small size, the room is large enough for them during the daytime; despite the poverty of it, it is neat and tidy, homely with the touches given to it by four females. At night their bodies are scattered about like large heaps of warm, living flesh, some on the bed, some around it, their breathing rising up warm and restless, sometimes deeply drawn.

Silence has reigned ever since the man died. Two years ago the man died after a long illness. Mourning ended but the habits of the mourners stayed on, and of these silence was the most marked, a silence long and interminable, for it was in truth the silence of waiting. The girls grew up and for long they waited expectantly, but the bridegrooms did not come. What madman will knock at the door of the poor and the ugly, particularly if they happen to be orphans? But hope, of course, is present, for—as the proverb says—even a rotten bean finds some blind person to weigh it out, and every girl can find her better half. Be there poverty, there is always someone who is poorer; be there ugliness, there is always someone uglier. Hopes come true, sometimes come true, with patience.

A silence broken only by the sound of reciting from the Koran; the sound rises up, with dull, unimpassioned monotony. It is being given by a Koranic reciter and the reciter is blind. It is for the soul of the deceased and the appointed time for it never changes: Friday afternoons he comes, raps at the door with his stick, gives himself over to the hand stretched out to him, and squats down on the mat. When he finishes he feels around for his sandals, gives a greeting which no one troubles to answer, and takes himself off. By habit he recites, by habit he takes himself off, and so no one is aware of him.

The silence is permanent. Even the breaking of it by the Friday afternoon recital has become like silence broken by silence. It is permanent like the waiting, like hope, a hope that is meager yet permanent, which is at least hope. However little a thing may be, there is always something less, and they are not on the look-out for anything more; never do they do so.

Silence goes on till something happens. Friday afternoon comes and the reciter does not come, for to every agreement however long it may last there is an end—and the agreement has come to an end.

Only now the widow and her daughters realize what has occurred: it was not merely that his was the only voice that broke the silence but that he was the only man, be it only once a week, who knocked at the door. Other things too they realized: while it was true that he was poor like them, his clothes were always clean, his sandals always polished, his turban always wound with a precision of which people with sound eyesight were incapable, while his voice was strong, deep and resonant.

The suggestion is broached: Why not renew the agreement, right away? Why not send for him this very moment? If he's busy, so what—waiting's nothing new? Towards sunset he comes and recites, and it is as if he recites for the first time. The suggestion evolves: Why doesn't one of us marry a man who fills the house for us with his voice? He is a bachelor, has never married, has sprouted a sparse moustache and is still young. One word leads to another—after all he too is no doubt looking for some nice girl to marry.

The girls make suggestions and the mother looks into their faces so as to determine to whose lot he shall fall, but the faces turn away, suggesting, merely suggesting, saying things without being explicit. Shall we fast and break that fast with a blind man? They are still dreaming of bridegrooms— and normally bridegrooms are men endowed with sight. Poor things, they do not yet know the world of men; it is impossible for them to understand that eyes do not make a man.

"You marry him, Mother. You marry him,"

"I? Shame on you! And what will people say?"

"Let them say what they like. Whatever they say is better than a house in which there is not the sound of men's voices."

"Marry before you do? Impossible."

"Is it not better that you marry before us so that men's feet may know the way to our house and that we may marry after you. Marry him. Marry him, Mother."

She married him. Their number increased by one and their income increased slightly—and a bigger problem came into being.

It is true that the first night passed with the two of them in their bed, but they did not dare, even accidentally, to draw close to one another. The three girls were asleep but from each one of them was focused a pair of searchlights, aimed unerringly across the space between them; searchlights made up of eyes, of ears, of senses. The girls are grown up; they know; they are aware of things, and by their wakeful presence it is as if the room has been changed into broad daylight. During the day, however, there is no reason for them to stay there, and one after the other they sneak out and do not return till around sunset. They return shy and hesitant, moving a step forward, a step back, until, coming closer, they are amazed, thrown into confusion, are made to hasten their steps by the laughter and guffaws of a man interspersed by the giggling of a woman. It must be their mother who is laughing, also laughing is the man whom previously they had always heard behaving so correctly, so properly. Still laughing, she met them with open arms, her head bared, her hair wet and combed out, and still laughing. Her face, which they had instinctively perceived as nothing but a dead lantern where spiders, like wrinkles, had made their nest, had suddenly filled with light; there it was in front of them as bright as an electric bulb. Her eyes were sparkling; they had come forth and shown themselves, bright with tears of laughter; eyes that had previously sought shelter deep down in their sockets.

The silence vanished, completely disappeared. During dinner, before dinner, and after dinner, there are plenty of jokes and stories, also singing, for he has a beautiful voice when he sings and imitates Umm Kulthoum and Abdul Wahhab; his voice is loud and booming, raucous with happiness.

You have done well, Mother. Tomorrow the laughter will attract men, for men are bait for men.

Yes, daughters. Tomorrow men will come, bridegrooms will make their appearance. Yet the fact is that what most occupied her was not men or bridegrooms but that young man—albeit he was blind, for how often are we blind to people just because they are blind—that strong young man full of robust health and life who had made up for her the years of sickness and failure and premature old age.

The silence vanished as though never to return and the clamour of life pervaded the place. The husband was hers, her legitimate right in accordance with the law of God and His Prophet. What, then, was there to be ashamed about when everything he does is lawful? No longer does she even worry about hiding her secrets or being discreet, and even as night comes and they are all together and bodies and souls are set loose, even as the girls are scattered far apart about the room, knowing and understanding, as though nailed to where they are sleeping, all sounds and breathing aquiver, controlling movements and coughs, suddenly deep sighs issue forth and are themselves stifled by more sighs.

She spent her day doing the washing at the houses of the rich, he his day reciting the Koran at the houses of the poor. At first he did not make it a practice to return to the house at midday, but when the nights grew longer and his hours of sleep less, he began to return at midday to rest his body for a while from the toil of the night that had passed and to prepare himself for the night to come. Once, after they had had their fill of the night, he suddenly asked her what had been the matter with her at midday; why was she talking unrestrainedly now and had maintained such complete silence then, why was she now wearing the ring that was so dear to him, it being the only thing by way of bridal money and gifts the marriage had cost him, while she had not been wearing it then?

She could have risen up in horror and screamed, could have gone mad. He could be killed for this, for what he is saying has only one meaning—and what a strange and repulsive meaning.

A choking lump in the throat stifled all this, stifled her very breathing. She kept silent. With ears that had turned into nostrils, tactile sense and eyes, she began listening, her sole concern being to discover the culprit. For some reason she is sure it is the middle one: in her eyes there is a boldness that even bullets cannot kill. She listens. The breathing of the three girls rises up, deep and warm as if fevered; it groans with yearning, hesitates, is broken, as sinful dreams interrupt it. The disturbed breathing changes to a hissing sound, a hissing like the scorching heat that is spat out by thirsty earth. The lump in the throat sinks down deeper, becomes stuck. What she hears is the breathing of the famished. However much she sharpens her senses she is unable to distinguish between one warm, muffled heap of living flesh and another. All are famished; all scream and groan, and the moaning breathes not with breathing but perhaps with shouts for help, perhaps with entreaties, perhaps with something that is even more.

She immersed herself in her second legitimate pursuit and forgot her first, her daughters. Patience became bitter-tasting, even the mirage of bridegrooms no longer made its appearance. Like someone awakened in terror to some mysterious call, she is suddenly stung into attention: the girls are famished. It is true that food is sinful, but hunger is even more so. There is nothing more sinful than hunger. She knows it. Hunger had known her, had dried up her soul, had sucked at her bones; she knows it, and however sated she is, it is impossible for her to forget its taste.

They are famished, and it was she who used to take the piece of food out of her own mouth in order to feed them; she, the mother, whose sole concern it was to feed them even if she herself went hungry. Has she forgotten?

Despite his pressing her to speak, the feeling of choking turned into silence. The mother kept silent and from that moment silence was ever with her.

At breakfast, exactly as she had expected, the middle one was silent—and continued in her silence.

Dinner-time came with the young man happy and blind and enjoying himself, still joking and singing and laughing, and with no one sharing his laughter but the youngest and the eldest.

Patience is protracted, its bitter taste turns to sickness—and still no one shows up.

One day, the eldest one looks at her mother's ring on her finger, expresses her delight in it. The mother's heart beats fast—and beats yet faster as she asks her if she might wear it for a day, just for one single day. In silence she draws it off her finger; in silence the eldest puts it on her own same finger.

At the next dinner-time the eldest one is silent, refuses to utter.

The blind youth is noisy; he sings and he laughs, and only the youngest one joins in with him.

But the youngest one, through patience, through worry, through lack of luck, grows older and begins asking about when her turn will come in the ring game. In silence she achieves her turn.

The ring lies beside the lamp. Silence descends and ears are blinded. In silence the finger whose turn it is stealthily slips on the ring. The lamp is put out: darkness is all-embracing and in the darkness eyes are blinded.

No one remains who is noisy, who tells jokes, who sings, except for the blind young man.

Behind his noisy boisterousness there lurks a desire that almost makes him rebel against the silence and break it to pieces. He too wants to know, wants to know for certain. At first he used to tell himself that it was the nature of women to refuse to stay the same, sometimes radiantly fresh as drops of dew, at other times spent and stale as water in a puddle; sometimes as soft as the touch of rose petals, at other times rough as cactus plants. True, the ring was always there, but it was as if the finger wearing it were a different finger. He all but knows, while they all know for certain, so why does the silence not speak, why does it not utter?

One dinner-time the question sneaks in upon him unawares: What if the silence should utter? What if it should talk?

The mere posing of the question halted the morsel of food in his throat.

From that moment onwards he sought refuge in silence and refused to relinquish it.

In fact it was he who became frightened that sometime by ill chance the silence might be scratched; maybe a word might slip out and the whole edifice of silence come tumbling down—and woe to him should the edifice of silence tumble down!

The strange, different silence in which they all sought refuge.

Intentional silence this time, of which neither poverty nor ugliness nor patient waiting nor despair is the cause.

It is, though, the deepest form of silence, for it is silence agreed upon by the strongest form of agreement—that which is concluded without any agreement.

✳ ✳ ✳

The widow and her three daughters.

And the house is a room.

And the new silence.

And the Koran reciter who brought that silence with him, and who with silence set about assuring for himself that she who shared his bed was always his wife, all proper and legitimate, the wearer of his ring. Sometimes she grows younger or older, she is softskinned or rough, slender or fat—it is solely her concern, the concern of those with sight, it is their responsibility alone in that they possess the boon of knowing things for certain; it is they who are capable of distinguishing while the most he can do is to doubt, a doubt which cannot become certainty without the boon of sight and so long as he is deprived of it just so long will he remain deprived of certainty, for he is blind and no moral responsibility attaches to a blind man.

Or does it?

■ **Joyce Mansour (1928–1988)**
Egypt/England/France (poems)

TRANSLATED BY MOLLY BENDALL

Of Egyptian origin, Joyce Mansour was born in Bowden, England, in 1928. She was educated in Egypt, England, and Switzerland. Her work, imbued with imagery of diverse backgrounds — the Egypt of the pharaonic mummies and desert landscape blended with her adopted Paris cityscape — she was early championed by André Breton, the leader of the French surreal movement. Mansour's first collection, _Cris_ (_Cries_), was published by Seghers in 1953, and it brought her instant recognition. Subsequently, she published numerous collections of poetry and prose. She died in Paris in 1988. Her poems are filled with an unabashed sexuality and provocative wit. Egypt, eroticism, and French surrealism come together in her book _Phallus and Mummies_ (1969). Like Derek Walcott (Saint Lucia), Khaled Mattawa (Libya), and Bharati Mukherjee (India), she is a writer who has crossed borders and language, yet carries the wealth of her background language and culture, which she infuses into the intensely personal, erotic poetry of her adopted France. Her collected works were published posthumously, _Prose & Poésie: Oeuvre Complète_ (1991). Her poems have been superbly rendered into English by Molly Bendall.

FURTHER READING: Mansour, Joyce. _Cris_ (_Cries_), 1953; _Les Gisants satisfaits_, 1958; _Rapaces_, 1960; _Carré Blanc_, 1965; _Phallus et momies_, 1969; _Faire signe au machiniste_, 1977; _Ça_, 1970; _Prose & Poésie: Oeuvre Complète_, 1991.

In the Gloom on the Left

Why my legs
Around your neck
Tight neck-tie puffed dark blue
Same old entrance of the laughing crack
White olives of Christianity

5

Why should I wait in front of the closed door
Shy and beseeching passionate cello
Have children
Soak your gums with rare vinegars
The most delicate white is tainted with black   *10*
Your cock is smoother
Than a virgin's complexion
More provoking than pity
Feathered tool of incredible hubbub
Goodbye see you again it's done adieu   *15*
The longing for abundant blossoms is exhausted
Will come back
More vivid more violent
These mauve bonbons with their devoted swoons
Anxious and tetanus-like   *20*
The fervid nightmares of afternoon
Without you

A Mango

I long for a mango
I detest men who don't know how to eat
Without bestowing their wisdom in quick sputters
You cry
Alone wounded and healed by my friendly lip   *5*
Do you see a phallus eaten by the hand
I'm hungry for dust
There's no accommodation spacious enough
Not a century nor beach empty enough for my taste
The sleepy vigil by Caesar's descendents   *10*
I lose my hair without a shudder too sad to resist
My heart needs a mango
It's not necessary to kill anyone
Today someone says be careful
The eyes of love are dry   *15*
Oil stains replace the Corn Festival on our walls
The heavy carts of dawn
Pass interminably
Behind the teddy bear
The intoxicated look of the serpent   *20*
And my mother who dreams in English far far
Far the mango and its odor of night

■ Adunis (Ali Ahmed Said) (1930–)
Syria/Lebanon (poem)

TRANSLATED BY ABDULLAH AL-UDHARI

Best known by his pen name "Adunis" or "Adonis," Ali Ahmed Said was born in the Syrian village of Qassabin and attended Damascus University, where he studied philosophy and literature. Later he earned a doctorate from St. Joseph's University in Beirut. Because his work questioned Syrian society and political organization, he found himself imprisoned and later exiled to Beirut in 1956. That same year, he became a citizen of Lebanon, where he settled. He founded and edited first *Shi'r* magazine and then, in 1968, the journal of experimental poetry *Mawagif.* He is considered the foremost poet of the Arab world and is a critic, philosopher, and translator as well. He works as a literary journalist. In addition to many books of poetry, he has published several books of literary criticism and a three-volume anthology of classical Arabic poetry.

FURTHER READING: Al-Udhari, Abdullah, ed. and tr. *Modern Poetry of the Arab World,* 1986. Bennani, Ben, ed. and tr. *Bread, Hashish, and Moon: Four Modern Arab Poets,* 1982. Khouri, Mounhah A., and Hamid Algar, eds. and trs. *An Anthology of Modern Arabic Poetry,* 1974.

from *The Desert*

The Diary of Beirut under Siege, 1982

The cities break up
The land is a train of dust
Only poetry knows how to marry this space.

* * *

No road to his house — the siege.
And the streets are graveyards:
    Far away a stunned moon
    Hangs on threads of dust
    Over his house.

        5

* * *

I said: This street leads to our house. He said: No.
    You won't pass. And pointed his bullets at me.

Fine, in every street
    I have homes and friends.

* * *

They found people in sacks:
    One without a head
    One without a tongue or hands
    One strangled
    The rest without shape or names.   5
Have you gone mad? Please,
        Don't write about these things.

* * *

In a page of a book
Bombs see themselves,
Prophetic sayings and ancient wisdom see themselves,
Niches see themselves.
The thread of carpet words   5
Go through memory's needle
Over the city's face.

* * *

From the palm wine to the calmness of the desert . . . etc.
From the morning that smuggles its stomach and sleeps on the
    corpses of the refugees . . . etc.
From the streets, army vehicles, concentration of troops . . . etc.
From the shadows, men, women . . . etc.
From the bombs stuffed with the prayers of Muslims and infidels . . .   5
    etc.
From the flesh of iron that bleeds and sweats pus . . . etc.
From the fields that long for the wheat, the green and the workers . . .
    etc.
From the castles walling our bodies and bombarding us with darkness
    . . . etc.
From the myths of the dead which speak of life, express life . . . etc.
From the speech which is the slaughter, the slaughtered and the   10
    slaughterers . . . etc.
From the dark dark dark
I breathe, feel my body, search for you and him, myself and others.
And hang my death
Between my face and these bleeding words . . . etc.

* * *

Seeds are scattered in our land.
So keep the secret of this blood,
Fields that nourish our myths —

I'm talking about the zest of the seasons
About the lightning in space.   5

* * *

My era tells me bluntly:
You do not belong.
I answer bluntly:
I do not belong,
I try to understand you   5
Now I am a shadow
Lost in the desert
And shelter in the tent of a skull.

* * *

The door of my house is closed.
Darkness is a blanket:
    A pale moon comes with
    A handful of light
    My words fail   5
    To convey my gratitude.

* * *

He shuts the door
Not to trap his joy
. . . But to free his grief.

* * *

The night descends (these are the papers he gave to the ink—
    morning's ink that never came)
The night descends on the bed (the bed of the lover who never came)
The night descends/not a sound (clouds, smoke)
The night descends (someone has in his hands rabbits? Ants?)   5
The night descends (the wall of the building shakes. All the curtains
    are transparent)
The night descends, listens (the stars as the night knows are dumb,
    and the last trees at the end of the wall remember nothing of
    what the air said to their branches)
The night descends (the wind whispers to the windows)
The night descends (the light penetrates. A neighbour lies in his
    nakedness)
The night descends (two people. A dress holding a dress—and the
    windows are transparent)   10
The night descends (this is a whim: the moon complains to its
    trousers about what the lovers have always complained of)
The night descends (he relaxes in a pitcher filled with wine. No friends
    just one man turning in his glass)

The night descends (carries a few spiders, feels at ease with insects
      which are a pest only to houses/signs of light: an angel coming,
      missiles or invitations? Our women neighbours have gone on
      pilgrimage/come back less slim and more coquettish)
The night descends (he enters between the breasts of the days/our
      women neighbours are my days)
The night descends (that sofa/that pillow: this is an alleyway, this is a
      place)
The night descends (what shall we prepare? Wine? Meat, soup and   15
      bread? The night hides from us its appetite)
The night descends (he plays for a short while with his snails, with
      strange doves which came from an unknown land, and with the
      insects not mentioned in the chapters of the book about
      reproduction among different animal species)
The night descends (thunder—or is it the noise of angels coming on
      their horses?)
The night descends (he mumbles, turning in his glass . . .)

                  ✳ ✳ ✳

The flower
      That tempted the wind to carry its perfume
Died yesterday.

                  ✳ ✳ ✳

A bat
      Claims the light is dark.
      And the sun a road to the grave.
Then babbles on.
      The bat didn't fall,   5
Only the child asleep in dawn's lap fell off.

                  ✳ ✳ ✳

A creator devoured by his creatures, a country
      Hiding in the blood running from his remains.
This is the beginning of a new era.

                  ✳ ✳ ✳

Whenever I say: my country is within reach
      And bears fruit in a reachable language
Another language kicks me
To another language.

                  ✳ ✳ ✳

Trees bow to say goodbye
Flowers open, glow, lower their leaves to say goodbye,
Reads like pauses between the breathing and the words say goodbye,

A body wears sand, falls in a wilderness to say goodbye.
The papers that love ink.   5
   The alphabet, the poets say goodbye.
And the poem says goodbye.

* * *

All the certainty I have lived slips away
All the torches of my desire slip away
All that was between the faces that lit my exile and me slips away
I have to start from the beginning
To teach my limbs to reach the future.   5
To talk, to climb, to descend from the beginning
In the sky of beginnings, in the abyss of the alphabet.

* * *

They are falling, the land is a thread of smoke
   Time a train
   Travelling along a track of smoke . . .
My obsession is here now, loss.
My concern is the end   5
   Is not over.
They are falling, I am not looking for a new beginning.

■ Dan Pagis (1930–1986)
Israel (poems)

TRANSLATED BY STEPHEN MITCHELL

Dan Pagis was born in Bukovina, now a part of Russia, though it had formerly been part of Austria, and then Romania. During World War II, he survived three years in a Nazi concentration camp and moved to Israel in 1946, where he learned Hebrew and taught in a kibbutz. In 1956, he moved to Jerusalem, where he received a doctorate from Hebrew University and was a professor of Medieval Hebrew literature. He wrote his poems in Hebrew, and though he was not limited to poems about the Holocaust, his poems on that subject are among the most powerful written anywhere. He died on July 29, 1986. His books of poems are *The Shadow Dial* (1959), *Late Leisure* (1964), *Transformation* (1970), *Brain* (1975, 1977), *Twelve Faces* (1981), *Double Exposure* (1983), and *Last Poems* (1987). He also wrote a number of scholarly books.

FURTHER READING: Mitchell, Stephen, tr. *Variable Directions: The Selected Poetry of Dan Pagis,* 1989.

End of the Questionnaire

Housing conditions: number of galaxy and star,
number of grave.
Are you alone or not.
What grass grows on top of you,
and from where (e.g., from your stomach, eyes, mouth, etc.).   5

You have the right to appeal.

In the blank space below, state
how long you have been awake and why you are surprised.

Written in Pencil in the Sealed Railway-Car

here in this carload
i am eve
with abel my son
if you see my other son
cain son of man   5
tell him that i

■ Nawal al-Saadawi (1931–) *Egypt* (story, memoir)

TRANSLATED BY J. RYDER

Born in Egypt in 1931, Nawal al-Saadawi is a prominent feminist, physi-cian, and prolific writer, publishing in many genres, including short stories, essays, and novels. Receiving her medical degree in 1955, al-Saadawi has practiced psychiatry, surgery, family medicine, and gynecology. In the field of gynecology, she has strongly criticized the conservative Islamic practice of clitoridectomy and the general suppression of female sexuality. Much of her writing examines femaleness—both femininity and being a female— in Arab cultures. Her experience as a doctor has given her special access and insight into a society she wishes to comment on and explore. Over the years, she has traveled extensively and is a familiar and passionate speaker at international literary and political forums. She has also taught at various universities, including Duke University, where she was a visiting professor. Her *Memoirs of a Female Physician* has been superbly rendered into English by Fedwa Malti-Douglas. Nawal al-Saadawi is one of the most forceful and accomplished writers in Arabic, and her influential books have been trans-lated into the languages of the world.

FURTHER READING: al-Saadawi, Nawal. *A Daughter of Isis: An Autobiography.* Translated by Sherif Hetata, 1999; *The Hidden Face of Eve: Women in the Arab World.* Translated and edited by Sherif Hetata, 1980; *Memoirs from the Women's Prison.* Translated by Marilyn Booth, 1986; *Memoirs of a Woman Doctor: A Novel.* Translated by Catherine Cobham, 1988; *The Well of Life and the Thread: Two Short Novels.* Translated by Sherif Hetata, 1993; *Woman at Point Zero.* Translated by Sherif Hetata, 1983.

The Thirst

The fierce heat of the noonday sun made the cement pavement soft under her feet, burning her like a piece of molten iron. She jumped here and there, stumbling about like a little moth that collides unawares with the walls of a burning lamp. She could have turned toward the shade at the roadside and sat awhile on the moist ground, but the vegetable basket was hanging on her arm and her right hand was closed upon a ragged 50-piaster note as she repeated to herself the things she would buy at the market so that she'd remember them . . . ½ a kilo of meat for 35 piasters, a kilo of zucchini for 5 piasters, a kilo of tomatoes for 7 piasters, and 3 piasters change; ½ a kilo of meat for 35 piasters, a kilo of zucchini for 5 piasters, a kilo of tomatoes for 7 piasters, and 3 piasters change; ½ a kilo of meat for . . .

She could have continued the enumeration as she did every day until reaching the market, but her eyes suddenly spotted something strange, something she never would have dreamed of, and her surprise prevailed over the heat of the ground and she stopped and stared, her eyes wide and her mouth open; there was Hamida, in the flesh, standing before the kiosk with a bottle of ice-cold soda-pop in her hand, lifting it up to her mouth and drinking from it.

For the first instant she wasn't aware that it was Hamida; she saw her from behind as she stood in front of the kiosk, but it didn't occur to her that it was Hamida. It might have been one of the girls she used to see every day in front of the kiosk drinking soda-pop . . . the middle-class girls like Suad and Muna and Amal and Mirvat, all her young mistress Sahir's friends.

She had thought it was one of those girls, and she was going to continue along her way, but she spotted the vegetable basket; she spotted it hanging from her arm as she stood in front of the kiosk, and she couldn't believe her eyes, so she looked closer and saw her curly locks of hair hanging down upon the nape of her neck from under a white scarf. This was Hamida's head scarf, and this was her arm on which the vegetable basket hung, but was it possible that this was, in fact, Hamida?

She began to examine her closely from behind, and she saw her cracked heels protruding from her green plastic slippers; these were Hamida's green slippers and her heels. But in spite of all that, she couldn't believe it, and she began to scrutinize her from every angle—from the left

and from the right—and every time, she saw something that could only belong to the Hamida she knew: the yellow linen galabiyya with a little split on
the side above her left thigh, the rusted earring in her right ear, and the old
deep wound on her right temple. It was Hamida before her eyes, in the
flesh, and not under any circumstances another girl, and she stood looking
at her even more closely.

Hamida was standing in front of the kiosk and in her right hand was a
soda-pop bottle with those transparent watery drops on its outer surface.
She wasn't drinking quickly like the other girls; she drank with extreme
slowness, moving her fingers down around the bottle and feeling its coldness with delight. She continued to hold the bottle for a moment, then she
lifted it slowly to her mouth and touched the edge of her lips to the bottle
mouth and licked it, gathering up all the droplets around it with her
tongue; then she raised her arm a bit higher to tilt the bottle up to her
mouth slightly, only allowing herself a single sip of the rosy, ice-cold liquid.
Here she closed her lips with great control, keeping the sip in her mouth
for a while without swallowing it all at once; she swallowed it slowly until the
last drop of it disappeared from her mouth, enjoying herself tremendously,
tossing her head back a bit, her back muscles going limp, leaning in relaxation against the wooden wall of the kiosk.

Now she couldn't resist, for bit by bit she had drawn closer to the kiosk
without noticing, and she stood seeking shelter from the sun in its shade.
She sat upon the ground and put the vegetable basket down beside her, her
eyes riveted, observing the passionate meeting between Hamida's lips and
the bottle mouth, then the sip and the slow sucking process and the enjoyment and relaxation which followed it. The ground was hot and burned
her lean buttocks through her threadbare calico galabiyya, but she paid it
no heed; all that interested her was to continue watching, to continue following Hamida's movements one by one with her eyes and her limbs. She
inclined her head backwards whenever Hamida bent her head backwards,
and she opened her lips whenever Hamida opened her lips, and she moved
her tongue around inside her mouth whenever Hamida moved her
tongue. But her throat was dry, without so much as a single drop of saliva,
and her tongue was stiff, moving back and forth and striking the walls of
her mouth like a wooden stick. The dryness stretched from her palate to
her throat and even plunged down into her stomach . . . a strange, horrible
dryness she hadn't felt before, as if the water had suddenly evaporated
from every cell in her body . . . from her eyes and her nose and from the
skin that covered every part of her. The dryness reached her veins and the
blood which flowed in them, and it dried up too. She felt burning pains inside, and she ran her hand over her skin and it felt thick, dry and wrinkled,
like the skin of a dried sardine. She noticed a salty taste in her mouth, bitter like colocynth, acrid, burning, and she tried to search for the saliva to
moisten her salty lips, but the tip of her tongue caught fire without stumbling upon so much as a single drop, and all the while Hamida remained
before her, encircling the icy bottle mouth with her lips, the cells of her

body sucking in the soda-pop one cell at a time. Hamida carried a vegetable basket, like hers, on her arm, and she had slippers, like hers, on her feet, and she had a cheap, torn galabiyya, like hers, on her body, and she worked, as she did, in houses.

The muscles of her fingers which clasped the dirty 50-piaster note twitched slightly, and she returned to the litany she was memorizing . . . ½ a kilo of meat for 35 piasters, a kilo of zucchini for 5 piasters, a kilo of tomatoes for 7 piasters, and 3 piasters change, and the price of a bottle of soda-pop is 3 piasters. Very expensive! It was only 1½ piasters last year. If this had happened last year it would have been possible to consider buying a bottle. One and a half piasters wasn't cheap, but it might be possible to sort things out. Sometimes zucchini cost 5½ and tomatoes 7½; as for the meat, it couldn't possibly cost more than ½ a piaster extra because it had a fixed price, and her mistress knew the prices by heart, and nothing could possibly escape her. Even as regarded the vegetables, whose price changed every day, going up or down by ½ a piaster, she knew of the increase or decrease day by day as well, as if she dreamt of the price list every night. And supposing that she were able to cheat her out of ½ a piaster on the zucchini and ½ a piaster on the tomatoes, where would she get the third ½ a piaster? It wouldn't be easy to claim that she had lost them, for that was a ploy which her honest mistress with the hard slaps wouldn't believe, even if she were to resort to lying for all this. Lying was akin to stealing, and as her mother had told her: "Beware, Fatima, of stretching out your hands for a piaster; theft, my daughter, is forbidden, and our Lord will burn you in hell."

She was afraid of hell; how could the fire burn in her hair and her head and her body? The sting of a matchstick caused her pain, but hellfire consuming her entire body was inconceivable. She couldn't imagine this fire; she neither knew it nor felt it. What she did feel was this other fire which burned inside her . . . the fire of dryness and thirst, a fire which nothing other than some sips from a bottle of soda-pop would extinguish. She could touch the walls of the kiosk beside her with the palm of her hand, and Hamida was in front of her, drinking a bottle of soda-pop . . . but how would she get the 3 piasters? The easiest thing would be for her to allot it equally to the meat and the zucchini and tomatoes, to add a piaster to all of them. Her mother's words had no meaning now. She didn't know the hell her mother threatened her with; she didn't see anyone burning in it before her. Perhaps this hell didn't exist. If it did exist it was very far away from her, far away after death. She didn't know when she would die, but she didn't imagine that she would die today.

She got up from where she was sitting and shook the dust off her galabiyya and stood staring at Hamida as she emptied the last mouthful of soda-pop into her mouth and closed her lips around the bottle mouth, not wanting to part with it. But the man grabbed the bottle from her hand and she left the mark of a long good-bye kiss upon it before removing it forever from between her lips. Then she opened her left hand in desire and counted 3 whole piasters . . .

She trembled a bit as she stood before the kiosk in the very place where Hamida had stood. A cool breeze bearing the aroma of soda-pop drifted out of the kiosk. Let what happens happen'after this . . . the hard slaps could no longer cause her pain, for she had become used to them, and the hellfire that burned could no longer frighten her because it was far away, and the world with all its pains and fears was not equal to a single sip of an ice-cold soda-pop.

◼ Forugh Farrokhzad (1935–1967) *Iran* (poems)

TRANSLATED BY LEORA BAUDE AND ALI SHASHAANI

Forugh Farrokhzad was born in Tehran and educated in the public schools, though she did not graduate from high school. She was a prodigy, composing *ghazals* (short lyrics) by age thirteen. At sixteen, she married Parviz Shapur, and she published her first book of poems, *The Captive*, in 1952, a volume that created a great controversy because of its sexual candor. She had a son in 1953, but in the divorce that soon followed she lost custody of him. Her other books of poems include *The Wall* (1956), *Rebellion* (1957), *Rebirth* (1961), and a book of selected poems published in 1964. She was a filmmaker, and she studied film production in England in 1959. Both Bernardo Bertolucci and UNESCO produced film biographies about her in 1965. At the peak of her mature creativity, she died tragically, in 1967, in an automobile accident. Farrokhzad's poems move from an early formalism to free verse and are characterized by fierce passion, melancholy, ironic belligerence, and a modern original diction. Her stark and simple poems of love shift easily into a surreal nightmare of modern existence suffused with Quranic apocalypse. Her fearless intelligence and disdain for the inferior role dictated socially for Iranian women and the sheer brilliance of her poems make her a sister of Sylvia Plath — to whom she is often compared. She was the leading poet of Iran and one of Asia's outstanding twentieth-century poets.

Window

a window for seeing
a window for hearing
like a well shaft reaches to the core
of the earth and turns its eye
to a landscape of kindness

5

blue, the color of water
a window filled each night
with mercy and the fragrance of stars
by the little hands of loneliness
and there you could invite the sun   *10*
to join the red geraniums
in exile

one window is enough for me

I come from toyland
from under the shade of cardboard trees   *15*
from a storybook garden
I come from drought stricken fields of love
the dust bowl of innocence
from desks at the tuberculosis school
where alphabet letters grow wan with age   *20*
from that moment when children first print "stone" on the board
and a flock of starlings quit their ancient tree
I come from the roots of flesh eating plants
and my brain is braced
for the butterfly's scream   *25*
of anguish, pinned to a page
a textbook crucifixion

when my faith was hanging
by fraying righteousness
my lamp smashed   *30*
and scattered city wide
when the infant eyes of my love
were gouged by justice
and my temples
spewed blood   *35*
when my life made no noise
but tick tock tick tock tick tock
I learned I must love
insanely

one window is enough for me   *40*
one window for seeing for knowing
for silence
look, the walnut sapling
now is grown so big
it teaches its leaves   *45*
the meaning of "wall"
ask for the name
the savior's name
isn't the earth that has rotted under your feet
lonelier than you?   *50*

prophets handed down to us
the tablets of destruction
do the poisonous clouds
the unceasing explosions
shine in the holy mirrors?   55
my friend, my brother, flesh of my flesh
when you take the moon, remember
and record the genocide of flowers

all dreams die
thrown from the peak of their folly   60
four leaf clovers root
and suck up sap
through the mounded grave of meaning
is it me
the woman wrapped in the winding sheet   65
of chastity?
will I ever climb again
on the steps of curiosity
to meet god on the roof
I sense the time has passed   70
I sense my day is torn from the calendar
I sense a distance the width of a table
between my hair and these sad, strange hands
Say something to me
Say something to me   75
What do I ask when I offer you my body
but to know I am alive?
Say something to me
Say something to me
I am safe at my window   80
I am coupled with the sun

The Windup Doll

More than this—yes,
you can be more still than this

You can stare long hours
with a look of the dead, still
stare, eyes trapped by your cigarette's smoke   5
stare into the vortex of a teacup
a blanched flower, a faded rug
a possible crack in the plaster
You can pull aside the curtain

with your dried up paw   *10*
to see in the street sheets of rain
slamming down
A child and its colorful kites
take shelter in an archway
as an old cart rolls from the unpeopled square   *15*
raucous and fast

You can stay put
behind the curtain
but blind
but deaf   *20*

You can cry
estranged, the liar's strident cry:
I love—
You can seem fine, unblemished stuff
in his strapping arms   *25*
your skin a leather table cloth
topped by two big cones
your breasts
You can lie
in sheets clean as love   *30*
with a slobbering drunk
an idiot, a tramp
You can make fun of
any puzzle without answers
You can work a crossword   *35*
all by yourself
You can make up
an answer all by yourself
an answer in five or six letters

You can kneel and nod   *40*
at a mausoleum
You can see God
in an unmarked grave
You can find faith
in a collection plate   *45*
You can rot
with the pious
in a mosque

You can cipher like zero
a constant sum   *50*
You can pop your eye
from its petulant lid
replace it with a button

from an antique boot
You can dry up   *55*
and vacate your gutter

You can hide the moment
in a box, with shame;
an awkward shot from a photo booth
You can hang   *60*
in the empty frame of your day
an icon of the damned one, defeated one
the crucified
You can cover the cracks with faces
and other such vacant designs   *65*

You can be a windup doll
with two glass eyes to see your sphere
You can sleep and sleep in your cloth lined box
sleep in your tulle and confetti
your body stuffed with straw   *70*
For every squeeze, every groping hand
you can scream and mechanically say:
Oh yes I am so happy!

■ Reza Baraheni (1935–) *Iran* (poem)

Reza Baraheni, born in Tabriz, a Turkish-speaking city in Iran, is an Iranian Turk who writes in Persian, the national language. The author of some forty-five volumes in Persian, he is a leading novelist, essayist, and poet in Iran. In the 1960s he was a professor of American and English literature at the University of Tehran and was also a visiting professor at the universities of Maryland and Indiana and at Bard College. Under the Shah he was tortured and imprisoned. After the Shah's fall, he returned to Iran, resumed his position at the university, and frequently broadcast news and commentary for NPR's "All Things Considered." With the rise of the Islamic Republic he was fired from his university post and again imprisoned. Under the mullahs he has managed to publish many novels, which have been immediate best-sellers, censored and withdrawn from circulation, followed by legal appeals for republication. In his introduction to Baraheni's *The Crowned Cannibals* (1971), E. L. Doctorow called him "the chronicler of his nation's torture industry." For thirty-five years Reza Baraheni has been in the forefront of the struggle for democracy and human rights in Iran. Once more in exile, he lives in Toronto, Canada.

FURTHER READING: Baraheni, Reza. *God's Shadow: Prison Poems,* 1976; *The Crowned Cannibal.* Introduction by E. L. Doctorow, 1977.

Autumn in Tehran

At first   A strange whisper   Began in the wind
    and the leaves
then carefree kids of the street came down
    with colds that sent them to bed
defining how such people use their eyes suits only
    minds in love with music
when the wind blew it whirled tears deep within
    weary eyes of retired men in the parks
as if an eternal grief had rained on their cheeks   5
the women hurried   The queue grew restless   they
    were shivering
in the wind the leaves on the surface young and
    green watched them   eyeless and wet
in fragments they consoled the women in love
    leaned their shoulders against their lovers' chests
—I'm cold! It suddenly got cold! Aren't you cold?
—no, perhaps from your kisses I still feel warm   still   10
then a blatant crow flew in the horizon   drew
    its dagger at the swallows   with the convex
    dagger of its beak the crow savaged the air
the crow screamed: here comes the season of sphere
    in flames   I'm your emperor!
The looting of the branches began in the evening
as though there was no end to it
it poured down in the sparkling of rain and wind   15
    in the street lights
millions of small, wet, and coloured balancing
    scales landed from the sky
men with bare heads, having no umbrellas, walked
    with newspapers over their heads
the night drove freshets from the bright north
    down in the dark south
and the next day   The world's streets were full
and the fresh perfume of the season's opium came   20
    from the piles of leaves
a strange siesta took hold of the world and bore it
    away
in the dull hour   the haggard autumn man thrust
    his wooden spear into death's leafy food

▨ Dahlia Ravikovitch (1936–)
Israel (poem)

TRANSLATED BY CHANA BLOCH AND ARIEL BLOCH

Dahlia Ravikovitch is Israel's finest woman poet. She was born in 1936 in Ramat Gan, a suburb of Tel Aviv. She studied at Jerusalem's Hebrew University and has worked as a journalist and a teacher. In addition to her poems, she has written two books of children's verse, a book of short stories, and many television reviews. She has won Israel's top literary awards. Her poetry has moved from rhyming high diction, archaic and biblical, to unrhymed colloquial free verse. After the Israeli invasion of Lebanon in June 1982, she joined other Israeli antiwar intellectuals, writing protest poems about the waste of life. Her ironic poem "Clockwork Doll," like Forugh Farrokhzad's "The Windup Doll," portrays a woman as an automaton valued for her graceful exterior and programmed interior. The poems often treat the roles, the powers, and the oppressions of women. In a *New Republic* review, Irving Howe noted that her poetry

> deals overwhelmingly with extreme states of personal life: desolation, loss, estrangement, breakdown. . . . Landscape, history, the Bible, and best of all a caustic mother wit: all figure behind the shaken self. . . . To read these poems is to see the whole world pressed into one imperiled being, and then, through the calming maneuvers of imagination, to watch that being glide past its own squalor and smallness.

Her five volumes of poetry are *The Love of an Orange, A Hard Winter, The Third Book, Deep Calleth unto Deep,* and *Real Love.* Her book of selected poems is entitled *All Thy Breakers and Waves.*

FURTHER READING: Ravikovitch, Dahlia. *The Window: Poems by Dahlia Ravikovitch.* Translated by Chana Bloch and Ariel Bloch, 1989.

Clockwork Doll

That night, I was a clockwork doll
and I whirled around, this way and that,
and I fell on my face and shattered to bits
and they tried to fix me with all their skill.

Then I was a proper doll once again
and I did what they told me, poised and polite.
But I was a doll of a different sort,
an injured twig that dangles from a stem.

5

And then I went to dance at the ball,
but they left me alone with the dogs and cats   *10*
though my steps were measured and rhythmical.

And I had blue eyes and golden hair
and a dress all the colors of garden flowers,
and a trimming of cherries on my straw hat.

■ Haydar Haydar (1936–)
Syria (story)

TRANSLATED BY MICHAEL G. AZRAK, REVISED BY M. J. L. YOUNG

Haydar Haydar was born in Tartous in 1936. He worked in Algeria for
many years and was employed as a schoolteacher until 1962. In addition to
short stories, he published a novel (*Savage Time*) in 1974.

The Ants and the Qat

As the first ant crawled over the toe of Mahmud ibn Abdullah al-Zubayri as
he lay beneath the tree, he gazed at it for a moment; an idle chuckle over-
came him as he watched the diminutive creature climb over his giant body.
In a sweetly languorous state he chewed a mouthful of qat,[1] moving it about
in his mouth with relish, like a man caressing a woman's breast.

Mahmud ibn Abdullah al-Zubayri said to himself: "What a pity these
poor mites are deprived of this pleasure!"

The sunlight, piercing through the leaves of the tree, combined with
the delicious taste of the qat to produce a refreshing torpor in the body of
the man, lying half in the sun and half in the shade. From a nearby cafe
wafted the voice of an eastern singer, bearing him away to an ineffable tran-
quility.

Just as he was sucking the morsel of qat and greedily squeezing the last
drop from it, another ant, followed by a companion, began to scale the toes
of his supine body. The ascent of the third ant tickled him. Then the ant
nipped him with its tiny jaws, and it felt as though a small thorn had
pricked him. Mahmud ibn Abdullah said, "How stupid ants are!" and with
a drowsy movement stirred his toes to shake the ant off or crush it. The ant,
however, was more deft than this movement: it abandoned his toe and descended to the sole of his foot.

---

1. A shrub native to Arabia, the leaves of which are chewed to produce a pleasant state of
drugged elation.

Torpor oozed into every cell of the man's recumbent body. He gave himself up to the sun, the qat, and the sweet soothing voice of the Star of the East.[2] The sleepy daze gave rise to visions and variegated daydreams, like a rainbow. He saw himself flying above the fields and mountains until he had reached the stars in their courses. As he looked on the stars they changed to flowers. He plucked them and put them in his buttonhole, proudly displaying himself like a peacock. Then he noticed that the stars had been transformed into golden globes. He took them to sell in the market place, and with the money bought guns and horses and falcons and hunting dogs.

When he was weary of the stars and the gold and the guns and the falcons, he dreamed of white-skinned women the color of snow, their hair like ears of corn, and their eyes the color of the sea.

Then he imagined himself a knight riding into the wind, with a sword and a lance in his hand, and he was the unchallenged monarch of the world; and lo! Here was the world at his feet, with him issuing commands as he pleased, while around him serfs, slave-girls and soldiers obeyed his every whim. He married several wives, and allotted a palace and a night to each one.

At length, when his rule was firmly established, he considered it a good idea to eliminate his enemies—beginning with his neighbor of long standing, she of the sharp tongue, whom he had desired, but who had rebuffed him. He summoned her and condemned her, ordering her to kneel naked at his feet and to acknowledge that he was a king without peer in manliness and courage. Then he ordered his executioner to cut out her tongue, and passed her over to his slaves, for each of them to have, one after the other.

The happy king Mahmud ibn Abdullah al-Zubayri then commanded that a certain man should be brought to him who had once comprehensively described him as impotent, an ignoramus and a fool. He ordered his two hangmen to flog him until the blood flowed. Then they emasculated him and threw the remains to the dogs in front of the assembled people.

Then Mahmud ibn Abdullah al-Zubayri, recumbent upon his throne, began to avenge himself upon his enemies one after another, while the tiny insignificant ants climbed over the body swimming in its dreamy stupor. Now they were slowly making their way in throngs over it, attacking it with confidence.

The man's eyelids began to grow heavy; the visions and the fantasies began to dance, and jump from mountaintop to mountaintop, from city to city, as he was borne aloft on a gentle breeze and one imaginary voice melted into another, from star to star, from the sweet-voiced eastern songstress. The overpowering qat coursed through his thirsty veins.

---

2. Umm Kulthum, the famous Arab woman singer.

Mahmud ibn Abdullah al-Zubayri slept as the sun began to decline toward the horizon. Deep sleep carried him to remote islands filled with mermaids and buried treasures: treasures of rubies, diamonds and qat. Then he noticed that all these islands with all their treasures and rocks and trees had become a forest of qat trees. He embraced it with open arms and went on chewing with savage ecstasy.

The ants had now become armies. They swarmed from all directions, invading the body of the dreaming man; they pried all over him without let or hindrance. When the ants with their formic instinct had made sure that the man was beyond the sphere of consciousness and that the chewing had ceased, they peered at the fixed wide stupid smile, and began their relentless work on their prey, which had now become transformed into a corpse.

■ Mohamed el-Bisatie (1938–) *Egypt* (story)

TRANSLATED BY DENYS JOHNSON-DAVIES

Mohamed el-Bisatie was born in Egypt and has worked as an Egyptian government official. His well-received volumes of short stories describe quotidian Egyptian society with deep compassion. In "A Conversation from the Third Floor," el-Bisatie illustrates the complicated interactions of a woman visiting her prisoner husband, the lewd chorus of fellow prisoners, and the stoic and mutely sympathetic policeman. His lucid prose records every tiny perception and event, sketching out with cinematic patience the scorched prison landscape and the slightest motion of shadow and emotion. El-Bisatie has also published a novel that has yet to be translated from Arabic.

A Conversation from the Third Floor

She came to the place for the second time. The policeman stared down at her from his horse.

The time was afternoon. The yellow-coloured wall stretched right along the road. Inside the wall was a large rectangular three-storey building; its small identical windows looked more like dark apertures. The woman stood a few paces away from the horse. The policeman looked behind him at the windows, then at the woman. He placed both hands on the pommel of the saddle and closed his eyes. After a while the horse moved. It was standing halfway down the street. Then, a moment later, it made a half-turn and once again stood itself at the top of the street.

The woman came two steps forward. The horse bent one of its forelegs, then gently lowered it.

'Sergeant, please, just let me say two words to him.'

His eyes remained closed, his hands motionless on the pommel.

Above the wall stretched a fencing of barbed wire at the end of which was a wooden tower. Inside there stood an armed soldier.

The woman took another step forward.

'You see, he's been transferred. . . .'

The sun had passed beyond the central point in the sky. Despite this the weather was still hot. A narrow patch of shade lay at the bottom of the wall.

The woman transferred the child to her shoulder.

When she again looked at the policeman's face, she noticed thin lines of sweat on his forehead.

Quietly she moved away from in front of the horse and walked beside the wall. About halfway along it she sat down on a heap of stones opposite the building.

The prisoners' washing, hung by the arms and legs, could be seen outside the bars of the windows. Mostly it was completely motionless, even with the breeze that blew from time to time.

The woman whispered to herself: 'They must be wet.'

She placed the child in her lap. For a moment her eyes fastened on a djellaba that gently swayed to the movement of the wind. She stretched out her leg and gazed at her toes and the dried mud that clung to them. She rubbed her feet together, then gazed at them once again.

Putting back her head, she looked up at the windows of the third floor with half-closed eyes.

The soldier in the tower took a step forward. He rested his against the edge of the wooden wall.

He looked at the sky, at the roofs of the houses, at the street, then at the head of the white horse.

Suddenly a shout broke the silence. The woman quickly drew back her leg. She caught sight of a bare arm waving from between the bars of a window on the third floor.

'Aziza! Aziza! It's Ashour.'

She moved a step nearer to the wall and stared in silence at the window.

'It's Ashour, Aziza. Ashour.'

She saw his other arm stretching out through the window. She searched with her eyes for something between the two arms and succeeded in making out a face pressed between the two bars. Other faces could be seen above and alongside him.

'Aziza, I've been transferred. Did you get my letter? In four days I'll be transferred. Did you prune the two date palms? Where are Hamid and Saniyya? Why didn't you bring them with you? I'm being transferred. Where's Hamid?'

He turned round suddenly, shouting:

'Stop it, you bastards!'

She heard him shouting and saw the faces disappear from the window. After a while his face was again looking out through the bars, then the other faces looked out above his.

'Aziza!'

She looked at the policeman on the horse, then at the soldier in the tower.

'Who are you holding? Shakir? Aziza!' She shook her head twice.

'Lift him up. Lift him up high.'

She took the child between her hands and lifted him above her head.

She noticed his arms suddenly being withdrawn inside and his hands gripping the iron bars of the window. Then his face disappeared from view. For a while she searched for him among the faces that looked down. She lowered her arms a little and heard shouts of laughter from the window. She spotted his arm once again stretching outwards, then his face appeared clearly in the middle.

'Up, Aziza. Up. Face him towards the sun so I can see him.' She lowered her arms for a moment, then raised him up again, turning his face towards the sun. The child closed his eyes and burst out crying.

'He's crying.'

He turned round, laughing.

'The boy's crying! The little so-and-so! Aziza, woman, keep him crying!'

He cupped his hand round his mouth and shouted: 'Let him cry!'

Again he laughed. A few shouts went up around him. She heard their words and shoutings. Then she saw his large nose poking out through the bars.

'Woman! Don't be silly, that's enough! Cover the boy—he'll get sunstroke!'

She hugged the child to her chest and saw the soldier withdrawing inside the tower.

'Did you prune the two date palms?'

She shook her head.

'Why not? Why don't you talk? I'm being transferred. Pass by Abu Ismail and tell him I send him my best wishes—he'll do it as a favour and prune the trees, then you can bring along a few dates. Did you bring the cigarettes?'

She made a sign with her hand.

'Talk. What are you saying?'

'You've got 'em.'

'Louder, woman.'

'You've got 'em, I sent them to you.'

'When?'

'Just now.'

'Just now? Here, hang on—don't move.'

He disappeared suddenly. Two faces remained at the window. One of them stretched out his arm; he made an obscene movement in the air with his hand. She lowered her eyes, then went back to the pile of stones.

'Aziza!'

Though she did not recognise the voice, she looked up at the window. She saw the man was smiling, his arm still moving about. The second man was kneeling, having raised his djellaba above his thighs. She heard him call out:

'Aziza, look!'

She smiled. The policeman was still sitting on his horse as though asleep. From the side window of the tower she had a partial view of the soldier's head. He had taken off his helmet.

She heard several voices calling her. She listened attentively, concentrating her gaze on the soldier's head as he moved within the opening of the window. The calls were repeated, interspersed with abuse. The soldier put on his helmet, but remained inside the tower.

Suddenly the voices were silent and some moments later there came to her the breathless voice of her husband:

'Aziza? I said five — didn't I tell you five packets?' She stared up towards him in silence.

'Woman, what's the use of three packets?' She gestured to him with her hand.

'What are you saying?'

'Five — I sent five.'

'Five?' he shouted fiercely. 'The bastards!'

He disappeared suddenly, then leant out again shouting:

'Wait! Don't go!'

She turned her face towards the window of the tower. He was away for a while, then he returned.

'It's all right, Aziza. Never mind. Five — yes, there were five. Never mind, a couple got taken, it doesn't matter. Listen — what was I going to say?' Silence. She saw him staring out in silence from the window. She shook out her black djellaba and walked forward towards the wall. He smiled.

'Aziza, I was thinking of saying something to you.'

Again there was silence. She turned away her head so that part of her face was against the sun. She shifted her head-veil slightly from her head.

'They took a couple of packets. Never mind, Aziza. Never mind.'

He laughed. His voice had become calm. The other faces disappeared from above him, only a single face remaining alongside his.

'Did you build the wall?'

'Not yet.'

'Why not?'

'When Uncle Ahmed lights the furnace, I'll get some bricks from him.'

'All right. Be careful on the tram. Look after the boy.'

She remained standing.

'Anything you want?'

'No.'

She gazed at his face, his large nose, his bare arms. She smiled. The face next to his smiled back.

Suddenly he shouted. 'Did you get the letter? I'm being transferred.'

'Where to?'

'I don't know.'

'When?'

'You see, they're pulling down the prison.'

'Where will you go?'

'God knows—anywhere. No one knows.'

'When?'

'In two or three days. Don't come here again. I'll let you know when I'm transferred. Has the boy gone to sleep?'

'No, he's awake.'

He stared back for a while in silence.

'Aziza!'

Again there was silence. The face alongside his smiled, then slowly slid back inside and disappeared. Her husband remained silent, his arms around the bars.

Suddenly he glanced behind him and quickly drew in his arms. He signalled to her to move away, then disappeared from the window.

She stepped back, though she remained standing looking up at the window.

After a while she seated herself on the stones and stretched out her leg. Taking out her breasts, she suckled her child.

The shadow advanced halfway across the street. She saw that its fringe was touching her foot. She drew her foot back a little. The place was quiet and the washing that had been hung out gently swayed in the breeze.

When she looked at her foot again; she saw that the shadow clothed the tips of her toes. She stood up.

The soldier was still inside the tower; the toe of his boot could be seen at the edge of the wooden platform. Before reaching where the horse stood she glanced behind her, but the window was empty.

She looked quietly at the policeman: his eyes were closed, his hands on the pommel of the saddle. The horse stood motionless.

She walked down the narrow passageway towards the main street.

■ Amos Oz (1939–) *Israel* (story)

TRANSLATED BY AMOS OZ

Amos Oz is among Israel's finest writers, a prolific novelist and short story and essay writer. He was born Amos Khausner to a strict Zionist family in Jerusalem but moved to a kibbutz and changed his name in rebellion. He has served in the military in two wars, and the conflict between Arab and Jew, and between ideals and realities, is a central concern of his work. "Nomad and Viper" is a representative story in this sense, and it is a good example of his ability as a masterful prose stylist. He continues living on the kibbutz today. His books in English translation include *Black Box* (1988); *Elsewhere, Perhaps* (1973), his fine novel about kibbutz life; *The Hill of Evil Counsel: Three Stories* (1978); *In the Land of Israel* (1983); *My Michael* (1972); *A Perfect Peace* (1985); *The Slopes of Lebanon* (1989); *Soumchi* (1980); *To Know a Woman* (1991); *Touch the Water, Touch the Wind* (1974); *Unto Death* (1975); *Where the Jackals Howl, and Other Stories* (1981); and *Until Daybreak: Stories from the Kibbutz* (1984).

Nomad and Viper

1

The famine brought them.

They fled north from the horrors of famine, together with their dusty flocks. From September to April the desert had not known a moment's relief from drought. The loess was pounded to dust. Famine had spread through the nomads' encampments and wrought havoc among their flocks.

The military authorities gave the situation their urgent attention. Despite certain hesitations, they decided to open the roads leading north to the Bedouins. A whole population—men, women, and children—could not simply be abandoned to the horrors of starvation.

Dark, sinuous, and wiry, the desert tribesmen trickled along the dirt paths, and with them came their emaciated flocks. They meandered along gullies hidden from town dwellers' eyes. A persistent stream pressed northward, circling the scattered settlements, staring wide-eyed at the sights of the settled land. The dark flocks spread into the fields of golden stubble, tearing and chewing with strong, vengeful teeth. The nomads' bearing was stealthy and subdued; they shrank from watchful eyes. They took pains to avoid encounters. Tried to conceal their presence.

If you passed them on a noisy tractor and set billows of dust loose on them, they would courteously gather their scattered flocks and give you a wide passage, wider by far than was necessary. They stared at you from a distance, frozen like statues. The scorching atmosphere blurred their appearance and gave a uniform look to their features: a shepherd with his staff, a woman with her babes, an old man with his eyes sunk deep in their sockets. Some were half-blind, or perhaps feigned half-blindness from some vague alms-gathering motive. Inscrutable to the likes of you.

How unlike our well-tended sheep were their miserable specimens: knots of small, skinny beasts huddling into a dark, seething mass, silent and subdued, humble as their dumb keepers.

The camels alone spurn meekness. From atop tall necks they fix you with tired eyes brimming with scornful sorrow. The wisdom of age seems to lurk in their eyes, and a nameless tremor runs often through their skin.

Sometimes you manage to catch them unawares. Crossing a field on foot, you may suddenly happen on an indolent flock standing motionless, moon-struck, their feet apparently rooted in the parched soil. Among them lies the shepherd, fast asleep, dark as a block of basalt. You approach and cover him with a harsh shadow. You are startled to find his eyes wide open. He bares most of his teeth in a placatory smile. Some of them are gleaming, others decayed. His smell hits you. You grimace. Your grimace hits him like a punch in the face. Daintily he picks himself up, trunk erect, shoulders hunched. You fix him with a cold blue eye. He broadens his smile and utters a guttural syllable. His garb is a compromise: a short, patched European jacket over a white desert robe. He cocks his head to one side. An appeased gleam crosses his face. If you do not upbraid him, he suddenly extends his left hand and asks for a cigarette in rapid Hebrew. His voice has a silken quality, like that of a shy woman. If your mood is generous, you put a cigarette to your lips and toss another into his wrinkled palm. To your surprise, he snatches a gilt lighter from the recesses of his robe and offers a furtive flame. The smile never leaves his lips. His smile lasts too long, is unconvincing. A flash of sunlight darts off the thick gold ring adorning his finger and pierces your squinting eyes.

Eventually you turn your back on the nomad and continue on your way. After a hundred, two hundred paces, you may turn your head and see him standing just as he was, his gaze stabbing your back. You could swear that he is still smiling, that he will go on smiling for a long while to come.

＊ ＊ ＊

And then, their singing in the night. A long-drawn-out, dolorous wail drifts on the night air from sunset until the early hours. The voices penetrate to the gardens and pathways of the kibbutz and charge our nights with an uneasy heaviness. No sooner have you settled down to sleep than a distant drumbeat sets the rhythm of your slumber like the pounding of an obdurate heart. Hot are the nights, and vapor-laden. Stray clouds caress the moon like a train of gentle camels, camels without any bells.

The nomads' tents are made up of dark drapes. Stray women drift around at night, barefoot and noiseless. Lean, vicious nomad hounds dart out of the camp to challenge the moon all night long. Their barking drives our kibbutz dogs insane. Our finest dog went mad one night, broke into the henhouse, and massacred the young chicks. It was not out of savagery that the watchmen shot him. There was no alternative. Any reasonable man would justify the action.

2

You might imagine that the nomad incursion enriched our heat-prostrated nights with a dimension of poetry. This may have been the case for some of our unattached girls. But we cannot refrain from mentioning a whole string of prosaic, indeed unaesthetic disturbances, such as foot-and-mouth disease, crop damage, and an epidemic of petty thefts.

The foot-and-mouth disease came out of the desert, carried by their livestock, which had never been subjected to any proper medical inspection. Although we took various early precautions, the virus infected our sheep and cattle, severely reducing the milk yield and killing off a number of animals.

As for the damage to the crops, we had to admit that we had never managed to catch one of the nomads in the act. All we ever found were the tracks of men and animals among the rows of vegetables, in the hayfields, and deep inside the carefully fenced orchards. And wrecked irrigation pipes, plot markers, farming implements left out in the fields, and other objects.

We are not the kind to take such things lying down. We are no believers in forbearance or vegetarianism. This is especially true of our younger men. Among the veteran founders there are a few adherents of Tolstoyan ideas and such like. Decency constrains me not to dwell in detail on certain isolated and exceptional acts of reprisal conducted by some of the youngsters whose patience had expired, such as cattle rustling, stoning a nomad boy, or beating one of the shepherds senseless. In defense of the perpetrators of the last-mentioned act of retaliation I must state clearly that the shepherd in question had an infuriatingly sly face. He was blind in one eye, broken-nosed, drooling; and his mouth—on this men responsible were unanimous—was set with long, curved fangs like a fox's. A man with such an appearance was capable of anything. And the Bedouins would certainly not forget this lesson.

The pilfering was the most worrisome aspect of all. They laid hands on the unripe fruit in our orchards, pocketed the faucets, whittled away piles of empty sacks in the fields, stole into the henhouses, and even made away with the modest valuables from our little houses.

The very darkness was their accomplice. Elusive as the wind, they passed through the settlement, evading both the guards we had posted and the extra guards we had added. Sometimes you would set out on a tractor or a battered jeep toward midnight to turn off the irrigation faucets in an outlying field and your headlights would trap fleeting shadows, a man or a night beast. An irritable guard decided one night to open fire, and in the dark he managed to kill a stray jackal.

Needless to say, the kibbutz secretariat did not remain silent. Several times Etkin, the secretary, called in the police, but their tracking dogs betrayed or failed them. Having led their handlers a few paces outside the kibbutz fence, they raised their black noses, uttered a savage howl, and stared foolishly ahead.

Spot raids on the tattered tents revealed nothing. It was as if the very earth had decided to cover up the plunder and brazenly outstare the victims. Eventually the elder of the tribe was brought to the kibbutz office, flanked by a pair of inscrutable nomads. The short-tempered policemen pushed them forward with repeated cries of "Yallah, yallah."

We, the members of the secretariat, received the elder and his men politely and respectfully. We invited them to sit down on the bench, smiled at them, and offered them steaming coffee prepared by Geula at Etkin's special request. The old man responded with elaborate courtesies, favoring us with a smile which he kept up from the beginning of the interview till its conclusion. He phrased his remarks in careful, formal Hebrew.

It was true that some of the youngsters of his tribe had laid hands on our property. Why should he deny it. Boys would be boys, and the world was getting steadily worse. He had the honor of begging our pardon and restoring the stolen property. Stolen property fastens its teeth in the flesh of the thief, as the proverb says. That was the way of it. What could one do about the hotheadedness of youth? He deeply regretted the trouble and distress we had been caused.

So saying, he put his hand into the folds of his robe and drew out a few screws, some gleaming, some rusty, a pair of pruning hooks, a stray knife-blade, a pocket flashlight, a broken hammer, and three grubby bank notes, as a recompense for our loss and worry.

Etkin spread his hands in embarrassment. For reasons best known to himself, he chose to ignore our guest's Hebrew and to reply in broken Arabic, the residue of his studies during the time of the riots and the siege. He opened his remarks with a frank and clear statement about the brotherhood of nations—the cornerstone of our ideology—and about the quality of neighborliness of which the peoples of the East had long been justly proud, and never more so than in these days of bloodshed and groundless hatred.

To Etkin's credit, let it be said that he did not shrink in the slightest from reciting a full and detailed list of the acts of theft, damage, and sabotage that our guest—as the result of oversight, no doubt—had refrained from mentioning in his apology. If all the stolen property were returned and the vandalism stopped once and for all, we would be wholeheartedly willing to open a new page in the relations of our two neighboring communities. Our children would doubtless enjoy and profit from an educational courtesy visit to the Bedouin encampment, the kind of visit that broadens horizons. And it went without saying that the tribe's children would pay a return visit to our kibbutz home, in the interest of deepening mutual understanding.

The old man neither relaxed nor broadened his smile, but kept it sternly at its former level as he remarked with an abundance of polite phrases that the gentlemen of the kibbutz would be able to prove no further thefts beyond those he had already admitted and for which he had sought our forgiveness.

He concluded with elaborate benedictions, wished us health and long life, posterity and plenty, then took his leave and departed, accompanied by his two barefooted companions wrapped in their dark robes. They were soon swallowed up by the wadi that lay outside the kibbutz fence.

Since the police had proved ineffectual—and had indeed abandoned the investigation—some of our young men suggested making an excursion one night to teach the savages a lesson in a language they would really understand.

Etkin rejected their suggestion with disgust and with reasonable arguments. The young men, in turn, applied to Etkin a number of epithets that decency obliges me to pass over in silence. Strangely enough, Etkin ignored their insults and reluctantly agreed to put their suggestion before the kibbutz secretariat. Perhaps he was afraid that they might take matters into their own hands.

Toward evening, Etkin went around from room to room and invited the committee to an urgent meeting at eight-thirty. When he came to Geula, he told her about the young men's ideas and the undemocratic pressure to which he was being subjected, and asked her to bring along to the meeting a pot of black coffee and a lot of good will. Geula responded with an acid smile. Her eyes were bleary because Etkin had awakened her from a troubled sleep. As she changed her clothes, the night fell, damp and hot and close.

3

Damp and close and hot the night fell on the kibbutz, tangled in the dust-laden cypresses, oppressed the lawns and ornamental shrubs. Sprinklers scattered water onto the thirsty lawn, but it was swallowed up at once: perhaps it evaporated even before it touched the grass. An irritable phone rang vainly in the locked office. The walls of the houses gave out a damp vapor. From the kitchen chimney a stiff column of smoke rose like an arrow into the heart of the sky, because there was no breeze. From the greasy sinks came a shout. A dish had been broken and somebody was bleeding. A fat house-cat had killed a lizard or a snake and dragged its prey onto the baking concrete path to toy with it lazily in the dense evening sunlight. An ancient tractor started to rumble in one of the sheds, choked, belched a stench of oil, roared, spluttered, and finally managed to set out to deliver an evening meal to the second shift, who were toiling in an outlying field. Near the Persian lilac Geula saw a bottle dirty with the remnants of a greasy liquid. She kicked at it repeatedly, but instead of shattering, the bottle rolled heavily among the rosebushes. She picked up a big stone. She tried to hit the bottle. She longed to smash it. The stone missed. The girl began to whistle a vague tune.

Geula was a short, energetic girl of twenty-nine or so. Although she had not yet found a husband, none of us would deny her good qualities, such as the dedication she lavished on local social and cultural activities. Her face was pale and thin. No one could rival her in brewing strong coffee—coffee to raise the dead, we called it. A pair of bitter lines were etched at the corners of her mouth.

On summer evenings, when the rest of us would lounge in a group on a rug spread on one of the lawns and launch jokes and bursts of cheerful song heavenward, accompanied by clouds of cigarette smoke, Geula would shut herself up in her room and not join us until she had prepared the pot of scalding, strong coffee. She it was, too, who always took pains to ensure that there was no shortage of biscuits.

What had passed between Geula and me is not relevant here, and I shall make do with a hint or two. Long ago we used to stroll together to the orchards in the evening and talk. It was all a long time ago, and it is a long time since it ended. We would exchange unconventional political ideas or argue about the latest books. Geula was a stern and sometimes merciless critic: I was covered in confusion. She did not like my stories, because of the extreme polarity of situations, scenery, and characters, with no intermediate shades between black and white. I would utter an apology or a denial, but Geula always had ready proofs and she was a very methodical thinker. Sometimes I would dare to rest a conciliatory hand on her neck, and wait for her to calm down. But she never relaxed completely. If once or twice she leaned against me, she always blamed her broken sandal or her aching head. And so we drifted apart. To this day she still cuts my stories out of the periodicals, and arranges them in a cardboard box kept in a special drawer devoted to them alone.

I always buy her a new book of poems for her birthday. I creep into her room when she is out and leave the book on her table, without any inscription or dedication. Sometimes we happen to sit together in the dining hall. I avoid her glance, so as not to have to face her mocking sadness. On hot days, when faces are covered in sweat, the acne on her cheeks reddens and she seems to have no hope. When the cool of autumn comes, I sometimes find her pretty and attractive from a distance. On such days Geula likes to walk to the orchards in the early evening. She goes alone and comes back alone. Some of the youngsters come and ask me what she is looking for there, and they have a malicious snicker on their faces. I tell them that I don't know. And I really don't.

4

Viciously Geula picked up another stone to hurl at the bottle. This time she did not miss, but she still failed to hear the shattering sound she craved. The stone grazed the bottle, which tinkled faintly and disappeared under one of the bushes. A third stone, bigger and heavier than the other two, was launched from ridiculously close range: the girl trampled on the loose soil of the flower bed and stood right over the bottle. This time there was a harsh, dry explosion, which brought no relief. Must get out.

Damp and close and hot the night fell, its heat prickling the skin like broken glass. Geula retraced her steps, passed the balcony of her room, tossed her sandals inside, and walked down barefoot onto the dirt path.

The clods of earth tickled the soles of her feet. There was a rough friction, and her nerve endings quivered with flickers of vague excitement. Beyond the rocky hill the shadows were waiting for her: the orchard in the last of the light. With determined hands she widened the gap in the fence and slipped through. At that moment a slight evening breeze began to stir. It was a warmish summer breeze with no definite direction. An old sun rolled westward, trying to be sucked up by the dusty horizon. A last tractor climbed back to the depot, panting along the dirt road from the outlying plots. No doubt it was the tractor that had taken the second-shift workers their supper. It seemed shrouded in smoke or summer haze.

Geula bent down and picked some pebbles out of the dust. Absently she began to throw them back again, one by one. There were lines of poetry on her lips, some by the young poets she was fond of, others her own. By the irrigation pipe she paused, bent down, and drank as though kissing the faucet. But the faucet was rusty, the pipe was still hot, and the water was tepid and foul. Nevertheless she bent her head and let the water pour over her face and neck and into her shirt. A sharp taste of rust and wet dust filled her throat. She closed her eyes and stood in silence. No relief. Perhaps a cup of coffee. But only after the orchard. Must go now.

5

The orchards were heavily laden and fragrant. The branches intertwined, converging above the rows of trunks to form a shadowy dome. Underfoot the irrigated soil retained a hidden dampness. Shadows upon shadows at the foot of those gnarled trunks. Geula picked a plum, sniffed and crushed it. Sticky juice dripped from it. The sight made her feel dizzy. And the smell. She crushed a second plum. She picked another and rubbed it on her cheek till she was spattered with juice. Then, on her knees, she picked up a dry stick and scratched shapes in the dust. Aimless lines and curves. Sharp angles. Domes. A distant bleating invaded the orchard. Dimly she became aware of a sound of bells. She was far away. The nomad stopped behind Geula's back, as silent as a phantom. He dug at the dust with his big toe, and his shadow fell in front of him. But the girl was blinded by a flood of sounds. She saw and heard nothing. For a long time she continued to kneel on the ground and draw shapes in the dust with her twig. The nomad waited patiently in total silence. From time to time he closed his good eye and stared ahead of him with the other, the blind one. Finally he reached out and bestowed a long caress on the air. His obedient shadow moved in the dust. Geula stared, leapt to her feet, and leaned against the nearest tree, letting out a low sound. The nomad let his shoulders drop and put on a faint smile. Geula raised her arm and stabbed the air with her twig. The nomad continued to smile. His gaze dropped to her bare feet. His voice was hushed, and the Hebrew he spoke exuded a rare gentleness:

"What time is it?"

Geula inhaled to her lungs' full capacity. Her features grew sharp, her glance cold. Clearly and dryly she replied:

"It is half past six. Precisely."

The Arab broadened his smile and bowed slightly, as if to acknowledge a great kindness.

"Thank you very much, miss."

His bare toe had dug deep into the damp soil, and the clods of earth crawled at his feet as if there were a startled mole burrowing underneath them.

Geula fastened the top button of her blouse. There were large perspiration stains on her shirt, drawing attention to her armpits. She could smell the sweat on her body, and her nostrils widened. The nomad closed his blind eye and looked up. His good eye blinked. His skin was very dark; it was alive and warm. Creases were etched in his cheeks. He was unlike any man Geula had ever known, and his smell and color and breathing were also strange. His nose was long and narrow, and a shadow of a mustache showed beneath it. His cheeks seemed to be sunk into his mouth cavity. His lips were thin and fine, much finer than her own. But the chin was strong, almost expressing contempt or rebellion.

The man was repulsively handsome, Geula decided to herself. Unconsciously she responded with a mocking half-smile to the nomad's persistent grin. The Bedouin drew two crumpled cigarettes from a hidden pocket in his belt, laid them on his dark, outstretched palm, and held them out to her as though proffering crumbs to a sparrow. Geula dropped her smile, nodded twice, and accepted one. She ran the cigarette through her fingers, slowly, dreamily, ironing out the creases, straightening it, and only then did she put it to her lips. Quick as lightning, before she realized the purpose of the man's sudden movement, a tiny flame was dancing in front of her. Geula shielded the lighter with her hand even though there was no breeze in the orchard, sucked in the flame, closed her eyes. The nomad lit his own cigarette and bowed politely.

"Thank you very much," he said in his velvety voice.

"Thanks," Geula replied. "Thank you."

"You from the kibbutz?"

Geula nodded.

"Goo-d." An elongated syllable escaped from between his gleaming teeth. "That's goo-d."

The girl eyed his desert robe.

"Aren't you hot in that thing?"

The man gave an embarrassed, guilty smile, as if he had been caught red-handed. He took a slight step backward.

"Heaven forbid, it's not hot. Really not. Why? There's air, there's water. . . ." And he fell silent.

The treetops were already growing darker. A first jackal sniffed the oncoming night and let out a tired howl. The orchard filled with a scurry of small, busy feet. All of a sudden Geula became aware of the throngs of black goats intruding in search of their master. They swirled silently in and out of the fruit trees. Geula pursed her lips and let out a short whistle of surprise.

"What are you doing here, anyway? Stealing?"

The nomad cowered as though a stone had been thrown at him. His hand beat a hollow tattoo on his chest.

"No, not stealing, heaven forbid, really not." He added a lengthy oath in his own language and resumed his silent smile. His blind eye winked nervously. Meanwhile an emaciated goat darted forward and rubbed against his leg. He kicked it away and continued to swear with passion:

"Not steal, truly, by Allah not steal. Forbidden to steal."

"Forbidden in the Bible," Geula replied with a dry, cruel smile. "Forbidden to steal, forbidden to kill, forbidden to covet, and forbidden to commit adultery. The righteous are above suspicion."

The Arab cowered before the onslaught of words and looked down at the ground. Shamefaced. Guilty. His foot continued to kick restlessly at the loose earth. He was trying to ingratiate himself. His blind eye narrowed. Geula was momentarily alarmed: surely it was a wink. The smile left his lips. He spoke in a soft, drawn-out whisper, as though uttering a prayer.

"Beautiful girl, truly very beautiful girl. Me, I got no girl yet. Me still young. No girl yet. Yaaa," he concluded with a guttural yell directed at an impudent goat that had rested its forelegs against a tree trunk and was munching hungrily at the foliage. The animal cast a pensive, skeptical glance at its master, shook its beard, and solemnly resumed its munching.

Without warning, and with amazing agility, the shepherd leapt through the air and seized the beast by the hindquarters, lifted it above his head, let out a terrifying, savage screech, and flung it ruthlessly to the ground. Then he spat and turned to the girl.

"Beast," he apologized. "Beast. What to do. No brains. No manners."

The girl let go of the tree trunk against which she had been resting and leaned toward the nomad. A sweet shudder ran down her back. Her voice was still firm and cool.

"Another cigarette?" she asked. "Have you got another cigarette?"

The Bedouin replied with a look of anguish, almost of despair. He apologized. He explained at length that he had no more cigarettes, not even one, not even a little one. No more. All gone. What a pity. He would gladly, very gladly, have given her one. None left. All gone.

The beaten goat was getting shakily to its feet. Treading circumspectly, it returned to the tree trunk, disingenuously observing its master out of the corner of its eye. The shepherd watched it without moving. The goat reached up, rested its front hoofs on the tree, and calmly continued munching. The Arab picked up a heavy stone and swung his arm wildly. Geula seized his arm and restrained him.

"Leave it. Why. Let it be. It doesn't understand. It's only a beast. No brains, no manners."

The nomad obeyed. In total submission he let the stone drop. Then Geula let go of his arm. Once again the man drew the lighter out of his belt. With thin, pensive fingers he toyed with it. He accidentally lit a small flame, and hastily blew at it. The flame widened slightly, slanted, and died. Nearby a jackal broke into a loud, piercing wail. The rest of the goats, meanwhile, had followed the example of the first and were absorbed in rapid, almost angry munching.

A vague wail came from the nomad encampment away to the south, the dim drum beating time to its languorous call. The dusky men were sitting around their campfires, sending skyward their single-noted song. The night took up the strain and answered with dismal cricket-chirp. Last glimmers of light were dying away in the far west. The orchard stood in darkness. Sounds gathered all around, the wind's whispering, the goats' sniffing, the rustle of ravished leaves. Geula pursed her lips and whistled an old tune. The nomad listened to her with rapt attention, his head cocked to one side in surprise, his mouth hanging slightly open. She glanced at her watch. The hands winked back at her with a malign, phosphorescent glint, but said nothing. Night.

The Arab turned his back on Geula, dropped to his knees, touched his forehead on the ground, and began mumbling fervently.

"You've got no girl yet," Geula broke into his prayer. "You're still too young." Her voice was loud and strange. Her hands were on her lips, her breathing still even. The man stopped praying, turned his dark face toward her, and muttered a phrase in Arabic. He was still crouched on all fours, but his pose suggested a certain suppressed joy.

"You're still young," Geula repeated, "very young. Perhaps twenty. Perhaps thirty. Young. No girl for you. Too young."

The man replied with a very long and solemn remark in his own language. She laughed nervously, her hands embracing her hips.

"What's the matter with you?" she inquired, laughing still. "Why are you talking to me in Arabic all of a sudden? What do you think I am? What do you want here, anyway?"

Again the nomad replied in his own language. Now a note of terror filled his voice. With soft, silent steps he recoiled and withdrew as though from a dying creature. She was breathing heavily now, panting, trembling. A single wild syllable escaped from the shepherd's mouth: a sign between him and his goats. The goats responded and thronged around him, their feet pattering on the carpet of dead leaves like cloth ripping. The crickets fell silent. The goats huddled in the dark, a terrified, quivering mass, and disappeared into the darkness, the shepherd vanishing in their midst.

Afterward, alone and trembling, she watched an airplane passing in the dark sky above the treetops, rumbling dully, its lights blinking alternately with a rhythm as precise as that of the drums: red, green, red, green, red. The night covered over the traces. There was a smell of bonfires on the air and a smell of dust borne on the breeze. Only a slight breeze among the fruit trees. Then panic struck her and her blood froze. Her mouth opened to scream but she did not scream, she started to run and she ran barefoot with all her strength for home and stumbled and rose and ran as though pursued, but only the sawing of the crickets chased after her.

6

She returned to her room and made coffee for all the members of the secretariat, because she remembered her promise to Etkin. Outside the cool of evening had set in, but inside her room the walls were hot and her body was also on fire. Her clothes stuck to her body because she had been running, and her armpits disgusted her. The spots on her face were glowing. She stood and counted the number of times the coffee boiled—seven successive boilings, as she had learned to do it from her brother Ehud before he was killed in a reprisal raid in the desert. With pursed lips she counted as the black liquid rose and subsided, rose and subsided, bubbling fiercely as it reached its climax.

That's enough, now. Take clean clothes for the evening. Go to the showers.

What can that Etkin understand about savages. A great socialist. What does he know about Bedouins. A nomad sniffs out weakness from a distance. Give him a kind word, or a smile, and he pounces on you like a wild beast and tries to rape you. It was just as well I ran away from him.

In the showers the drain was clogged and the bench was greasy. Geula put her clean clothes on the stone ledge. I'm not shivering because the water's cold. I'm shivering with disgust. Those black fingers, and how he went straight for my throat. And his teeth. And the goats. Small and skinny like a child, but so strong. It was only by biting and kicking that I managed to escape. Soap my belly and everything, soap it again and again. Yes, let the boys go right away tonight to their camp and smash their black bones because of what they did to me. Now I must get outside.

7

She left the shower and started back toward her room, to pick up the coffee and take it to the secretariat. But on the way she heard crickets and laughter, and she remembered him bent down on all fours, and she was alarmed and stood still in the dark. Suddenly she vomited among the flowering shrubs. And she began to cry. Then her knees gave way. She sat down to rest on the dark earth. She stopped crying. But her teeth continued to chatter, from the cold or from pity. Suddenly she was not in a hurry any more, even the coffee no longer seemed important, and she thought to herself: There's still time. There's still time.

Those planes sweeping the sky tonight were probably on a night-bombing exercise. Repeatedly they roared among the stars, keeping up a constant flashing, red, green, red, green, red. In counterpoint came the singing of the nomads and their drums, a persistent heartbeat in the distance: One, one, two. One, one, two. And silence.

8

From eight-thirty until nearly nine o'clock we waited for Geula. At five to nine Etkin said that he could not imagine what had happened; he could not recall her ever having missed a meeting or been late before; at all events, we must now begin the meeting and turn to the business on the agenda.

He began with a summary of the facts. He gave details of the damage that had apparently been caused by the Bedouins, although there was no formal proof, and enumerated the steps that had been taken on the committee's initiative. The appeal to good will. Calling in the police. Strengthening the guard around the settlement. Tracking dogs. The meeting with the elder of the tribe. He had to admit, Etkin said, that we had now reached an impasse. Nevertheless, he believed that we had to maintain a sense of balance and not give way to extremism, because hatred always gave rise to further hatred. It was essential to break the vicious circle of hostility. He therefore opposed with all the moral force at his disposal the approach — and particularly the intentions — of certain of the younger members. He wished to remind us, by way of conclusion, that the conflict between herdsmen and tillers of the soil was as old as human civilization, as seemed to be evidenced by the story of Cain, who rose up against Abel, his brother. It was fitting, in view of the social gospel we had adopted, that we should put an end to this ancient feud, too, just as we had put an end to other ugly phenomena. It was up to us, and everything depended on our moral strength.

The room was full of tension, even unpleasantness. Rami twice interrupted Etkin and on one occasion went so far as to use the ugly word "rubbish." Etkin took offense, accused the younger members of planning terrorist activities, and said in conclusion, "We're not going to have that sort of thing here."

Geula had not arrived, and that was why there was no one to cool down the temper of the meeting. And no coffee. A heated exchange broke out between me and Rami. Although in age I belonged with the younger men, I did not agree with their proposals. Like Etkin, I was absolutely opposed to answering the nomads with violence—for two reasons, and when I was given permission to speak I mentioned them both. In the first place, nothing really serious had happened so far. A little stealing perhaps, but even that was not certain: every faucet or pair of pliers that a tractor driver left in a field or lost in the garage or took home with him was immediately blamed on the Bedouins. Secondly, there had been no rape or murder. Hereupon Rami broke in excitedly and asked what I was waiting for. Was I perhaps waiting for some small incident of rape that Geula could write poems about and I could make into a short story? I flushed and cast around in my mind for a telling retort.

But Etkin, upset by our rudeness, immediately deprived us both of the right to speak and began to explain his position all over again. He asked us how it would look if the papers reported that a kibbutz had sent out a lynch mob to settle scores with its Arab neighbors. As Etkin uttered the phrase "lynch mob," Rami made a gesture to his young friends that is commonly used by basketball players. At this signal they rose in a body and walked out in disgust, leaving Etkin to lecture to his heart's content to three elderly women and a long-retired member of Parliament.

After a moment's hesitation I rose and followed them. True, I did not share their views, but I, too, had been deprived of the right to speak in an arbitrary and insulting manner.

9

If only Geula had come to the meeting and brought her famous coffee with her, it is possible that tempers might have been soothed. Perhaps, too, her understanding might have achieved some sort of compromise between the conflicting points of view. But the coffee was standing, cold by now, on the table in her room. And Geula herself was lying among the bushes behind the Memorial Hall, watching the lights of the planes and listening to the sounds of the night. How she longed to make her peace and to forgive. Not to hate him and wish him dead. Perhaps to get up and go to him, to find him among the wadis and forgive him and never come back. Even to sing to him. The sharp slivers piercing her skin and drawing blood were the fragments of the bottle she had smashed here with a big stone at the beginning of the evening. And the living thing slithering among the slivers of glass among the clods of earth was a snake, perhaps a venomous snake, perhaps a viper. It stuck out a forked tongue, and its triangular head was cold and erect. Its eyes were dark glass. It could never close them, because it had no eyelids. A thorn in her flesh, perhaps a sliver of glass. She was very tired. And the pain was vague, almost pleasant. A distant ringing in her ears. To sleep now. Wearily, through the thickening film, she watched the gang of youngsters crossing the lawn on their way to the fields and the wadi to even the score with the nomads. We were carrying short, thick sticks. Excitement was dilating our pupils. And the blood was drumming in our temples.

Far away in the darkened orchards stood somber, dust-laden cypresses, swaying to and fro with a gentle, religious fervor. She felt tired, and that was why she did not come to see us off. But her fingers caressed the dust, and her face was very calm and almost beautiful.

■ Mohammed Mrabet (1940–)
Morocco (story)

TRANSLATED BY PAUL BOWLES

Mohammed Mrabet was born in Tangiers in 1940 when it was an international tax-free city. Mrabet still lives in Tangiers, but his tales often concern the Moghrebi region. In his book *M'Hashish* (1988), he speaks about hashish and the uncertain pleasures of being a habitual user of the drug. He is also concerned with the plight of Muslim women and their virtual imprisonment in the houses of their husbands. In fact, Mrabet's grandfather murdered one of his wives because she was standing in the doorway of his house, gazing into the street. Mrabet is a gripping storyteller. His translator is the American writer Paul Bowles, famed friend of the Beat writers, who has spent most of his life in Morocco. We owe Mrabet's own recognition to Bowles's excellent translations.

FURTHER READING: Mrabet, Mohammed. *M'Hashish*. Taped and translated from Moghrebi by Paul Bowles, 1988; *The Boy Who Set the Fire and Other Stories*. Taped and translated from Moghrebi by Paul Bowles, 1974; *Chocolate Cream and Dollars*. Taped and translated from Moghrebi by Paul Bowles, 1992.

The Canebrake

Kacem and Stito met every afternoon at a café. They were old friends. Kacem drank, and he had a wife whom he never allowed to go out of the house. No matter how much she entreated him and argued with him, he would not even let her go to the hammam to bathe. Stito had no troubles because he was a bachelor, and only smoked kif.

Kacem would come into the café with a bottle in his shopping bag, and soon both of them would go on to Kacem's house. On the way they would stop at the market to buy food, since Kacem would not permit his wife to go to market, either. Stito had no one to cook for him, and so he ate each night at Kacem's house, and always paid his share.

They would carry the food to Kacem's wife so she could prepare it. First, however, she would make tapas for Kacem's drinks, and tea for Stito's kif. Later when the food was cooking she would go in and sit with the two men.

Once when they were all sitting there together, Stito turned to Kacem and said: Sometimes I wonder how you can drink so much. Where do you store it all?

Kacem laughed. And you? You don't get anything but smoke out of your pipe. I get the alcohol right inside me, and it feels wonderful.

That's an empty idea you have, said Stito. Kif gives me more pleasure than alcohol could ever give anybody. And it makes me think straighter and talk better.

Kacem's wife decided that this was a good moment to say to her husband: Your friend's right. You drink too much.

Kacem was annoyed. Go and look at the food, he told her. It ought to be ready. We want to eat.

She brought the dinner in, and they set to work eating it. After they had finished, they talked for a half hour or so, and then Stito stood up. Until tomorrow, he told Kacem.

Yes, yes. Until tomorrow, said Kacem, who was drunk.

If Allah wills, Stito added.

Kacem's wife got up and opened the door for him.

Good night.

She shut the door, and then she and Kacem went to bed. Feeling full of love, she began to kiss her husband. But he only lay there, too drunk to notice her.

Soon she sat up and began to complain. From the day of our wedding you've never loved me, she said. You never pay me any attention at all unless you want to eat.

Go to sleep, woman, he told her.

She had started to cry, and it was a long time before she slept.

The next afternoon when he finished work, Kacem went to the café to meet Stito. They did the marketing and carried the food back to Kacem's house. The evening passed the same as always. Kacem was very drunk by the time Stito was ready to go home.

Kacem's wife opened the door for Stito and stepped outside. As he went through the doorway she whispered: Try and come alone tomorrow. Let him come by himself.

What do you mean? he said.

She pointed at the canebrake behind the garden. Hide there, she said.

Stito understood. But he'll be here, he whispered.

That's all right. Don't worry, she told him. Good night.

Good night.

The woman shut the door. Kacem was still sitting there drinking. She left him there and went to bed.

Again the following afternoon the two friends met in the café. Stito put away his pipe. How are you? he said.

Let's go, said Kacem. He was eager to get home and open his bottle.

I can't go right now, Stito told him. I've got to wait here and see somebody. I'll come later. Here's the money for the food.

Yes, said Kacem. I'll go on to the market, then.

Sit down with me a minute, said Stito.

No, no. I'll be going.

I'll see you later, Stito said.

Stito sat there in the café until dusk, and then he got up and went to the street where Kacem's house was. He waited until no one was passing by before he began to make his way through the canebrake. He was invisible in here. He peered between the canes and saw Kacem sitting in his room with a bottle on the table beside him, and a glass in his hand. And he saw the woman bring in the tailor.

Then she came outside carrying a large basin, and walked straight to the edge of the canebrake. She set the basin down and bent over it as if she were working. She was facing her husband and talking with him, and her garments reached to the ground in front of her. In the back, however, she was completely uncovered, and Stito saw everything he wanted to see. While she pretended to be washing something in the basin, she pushed her bare haunches back against the canes, and he pressed forward and began to enjoy himself with her.

When you're ready, she whispered, pull it out and let me catch it all in my hand.

That's no way, he said. How can I do that?

The woman moved forward suddenly and made it slip out, so that Stito understood that if he were to have anything at all with her, he would have to do as she wanted.

You can do it again afterwards and finish inside, if you like, she whispered.

She backed against the canes again, and he started once more. When he was almost ready he warned her, and she reached back with her hand, and got what she wanted. Keeping her fist shut, she waited so he could do it again the way he enjoyed it. He finished and went out of the canebrake into the street. No one saw him.

The woman walked into the house. She stood by the chair where Kacem sat, looking down at him. Can't I go to the hammam tomorrow? she said.

Are you starting that all over again? cried Kacem. I've told you no a thousand times. No! You can't leave this house.

She reached out her hand, opened it, and let what she had been holding drip into the taifor beside Kacem's glass.

Kacem stared. He had been drunk a moment before, and now he was no longer drunk. He did not even ask her from whom she had got it, or how. He stood up, leaving the bottle and glass, and went to bed without his dinner.

In the morning when he went out to work, Kacem left the door of his house wide open. All day he thought about his wife. When he had finished work, he went to the café to meet Stito.

His face was sad as he sat down. Fill me a pipe, he said.

What? Stito cried.

Yes.

Stito gave him his pipe. What's happened? It's the first time you've ever asked for kif.

I'm through with drinking, Kacem told him. I'm going to start smoking kif.

But why?

Kacem did not reply, and Stito did not ask again.

That evening the two friends arrived at Kacem's house laughing and joking, with their heads full of kif. Kacem was in a fine humor all evening. After Stito had gone, he said to his wife: You went to the hammam?

Yes, she said. Thank you for leaving the door open. I thought you'd forgotten to shut it when you went out.

I'm not going to lock it any more, he told her.

She kissed him and they went to bed. It was the first time in many nights that Kacem was not too drunk to play games with his wife. They made one another very happy, and finally they fell into a perfect sleep.

■ Mahmud Darwish (1942–)
Palestine/Lebanon (poems)

Mahmud Darwish was born in the village of al-Barwa in Palestine and grew up under Israeli rule, writing resistance poems and experiencing prison and house arrest. In 1948, when he was six, his village was attacked and obliterated by Israeli forces, and his family fled to Lebanon where they lived as refugees for a year. He worked as a journalist in Haifa until 1971, when he left for Beirut, where he lived until 1982. He currently resides in Paris and is the editor of the journal *Al-Karmal*. He has been awarded the Lotus Prize (1969) and the Lenin Prize (1983). He has published more than a dozen books of poetry and an autobiographical novel. He is probably the world's most celebrated Palestinian poet.

FURTHER READING: Al-Udhari, Abdullah, tr. and ed. *Modern Poetry of the Arab World*, 1986. Bennani, Ben, ed. and tr. *Bread, Hashish, and Moon: Four Modern Arab Poets*, 1982. Wedde, Ian, and Fawwaz Tuqan, trs. *Selected Poems: Mahmoud Darwish*, 1973.

The Prison Cell

It is possible . . .
It is possible at least sometimes . . .
It is possible especially now
To ride a horse
Inside a prison cell   5
And run away . . .

It is possible for prison walls
To disappear,
For the cell to become a distant land
Without frontiers: 10

—What did you do with the walls?
—I gave them back to the rocks.
—And what did you do with the ceiling?
—I turned it into a saddle.
—And your chain?   15
—I turned it into a pencil.

The prison guard got angry:
He put an end to the dialogue.
He said he didn't care for poetry,
And bolted the door of my cell.   20

He came back to see me
In the morning;
He shouted at me:

—Where did all this water come from?
—I brought it from the Nile.   25
—And the trees?
—From the orchards of Damascus.
—And the music?
—From my heartbeat.

The prison guard got mad;   30
He put an end to the dialogue.
He said he didn't like poetry,
And bolted the door of my cell.

But he returned in the evening:
—Where did this moon come from?   35
—From the nights of Bagdad.
—And the wine?
—From the vineyards of Algiers.
—And this freedom?
—From the chain you tied me with last night.   40

The prison guard grew so sad . . .
He begged me to give him back
His freedom.

TRANSLATED BY BEN BENNANI

Victim No. 48

He was lying dead on a stone.
They found in his chest the moon and a rose lantern,
They found in his pocket a few coins,
A box of matches and a travel permit.
     He had tattoos on his arms.   *5*

His mother kissed him
And cried for a year.
Boxthorn tangled in his eyes.
     And it was dark.

His brother grew up   *10*
And went to town looking for work.
He was put in prison
Because he had no travel permit;
He was carrying a dustbin
     And boxes down the street.   *15*

Children of my country,
     That's how the moon died.

TRANSLATED BY ABDULLAH AL-UDHARI

■ Hatif Janabi (1955–) *Iraq/Poland* (poem)

TRANSLATED BY KHALED MATTAWA

Hatif Janabi was born in Iraq and has lived in Poland since 1976. He writes mainly in Arabic, but also in Polish. He has published five bilingual volumes of poetry and has won many Polish poetry prizes. He earned a Ph.D. in drama from Warsaw University, where he currently teaches Arabic literature and world drama. His poems, essays, and translations have appeared in many Arab literary magazines and he has been a visiting professor in the United States. His poems have a deep philosophical and historical resonance and can be gnomic and evocative or broad, surreal, fantastic, and Whitmanian in scope. They have a dramatic fullness, and a poem such as "Questions and Their Retinue" veers widely through Arabic history and literature with postmodern humor, elegaic wistfulness, and sardonic commentary.

Questions and Their Retinue

... These are the questions
and their retinue of poetry and prose.
There is no difference between one testicle and another
except for swelling. Now I ask all
those who differentiate between one finger and another 5
a catastrophe and another, a woman and another.
They give birth and were born on the banks of paralysis and weeping.
They have pointed hooves. Before they emerge they kick the wombs
    and the midwives' caves collapse. Afterwards everywhere
    becomes a barren place.
They are born in a quilt that quickly turns into a street,
a neighborhood, a lavish yacht, an expensive harem, etc. etc. 10
Thank you, it was you, from the beginning, who forced us
to start writing verse, and because the old meters have calcified
we now are trying a new form of expression
for the violets of failure,
for the swings of despair, 15
for the crumbs of white tombs
(white in wartime)
for the chirping of a bedouin as he leans over a prostitute,
soft and marble-like,
for the garbage heaps of plenty procreating and flying 20
in the air of strange coasts,
always fleeing the holy books and their prohibitions.

This then is the bludgeon of civilization
that forced us to bring prohibited animals to our lands,
pigs to plow our fields, grasshoppers in clinics 25
grasshoppers slapping widows
who give birth now (and forever)
in a landfill-museum ...
This is our heritage.
Let us return to its chains and spears, 30
its freedom and licentiousness.
What a marvelous indigenous cocktail
fortified with promiscuity,
blessed by the computers of friendly allies!
Danke! ça va! Good! 35

Once again we feel our bodies,
our fingers touching and listening attentively
for things, minerals, ores, and stones.
What a blessed magical return to the stone ages! It is
the miracle of our offspring that we now bless with verse: *40*
       As they plough our steps
    as they crack open the horizon
      a grass blade of speech
  and Babylon weeping in refugee camps to a stone
flung at us by witches   *45*
and our feet have yet to reach the Black Stone[1]
    but the winds were generous
    giving us an arm with which we struck
  the archipelago of the dark.
Blackness smears the fingernails   *50*
with burns of light and a querulous wound.
Naked we danced
wiping off the dust of the night.
To the river in the outfit of willows
we moved.   *55*
Fishermen began throwing clubs and dictionaries
and heavy boots into the river
and an idea began to glow—
The naked ones screamed:
Hang her! Hang her!   *60*
For centuries the ropes have been ready
to be used in various ways
in these arid, ravished cities.
—"And now Ibn Munif you must write
the last chapter of your salt mine,"[2]   *65*
said a speaker with obvious contempt!
Everyone laughed then
and a child began
hammering the forehead of a poet
with a stone—the miracle of stone.   *70*
"Now say what you will,"
the child said as though drunk.
Nothing except stone can subdue this metal.
. . . A flurry of stabs
    and behind the crooked statues a woman   *75*
    fell
    (the poet said . . .)
    I said lift your arms and kiss

---

1. A holy stone in the Ka'aba shrine in Mecca.

2. A reference to novelist Abdulrahman Munif and his novel *Cities of Salt*.

her coat, O body
her lacquered chest—   *80*
her knees, a violin
her limbs, reeds.
Now she twists her fingers into a song.
Released from the noose of stabs,
she proudly plants her nails in the dirt.   *85*
These are the questions
and their retinues are funerals
that stretch from door to door.
These are the questions,
stone and childhood,   *90*
and the retinues are a herd
of impoverished streets.
A wide horizon.
No window to shut us from it, no veil.

■ Khaled Mattawa (1964–) *Libya* (poems, written in English)

Khaled Mattawa, born in Benghazi, Libya, came to America in his late teens, took his M.A. in English and Creative Writing at Indiana University, has taught at California State University at Northridge, and has received a Guggenheim Fellowship. He has translated and published the poetry of the Syrian-Lebanese poet Adunis and the exiled Iraqi poet Hatif Janabi. Mattawa's own poems, like the writings of the Indian novelist Bharati Mukherjee and many writers living outside their native country, are composed in English and have been published widely in American literary magazines, including *The Kenyon Review, The Iowa Review,* and *The Michigan Quarterly.* He is one of the most vigorous and sophisticated painters of modern Arab life. His lush, ironic, moving poem, "Watermelon Tales," concerning family and neighbors in Benghazi, Libya, was selected for publication in *The Pushcart Prize Anthology.*

FURTHER READING: Mattawa, Khaled. *Ismailia Eclipse,* 1995.

History of My Face

My lips came with a caravan of slaves
That belonged to the Grand Sanussi.
In Al-Jaghbub he freed them.
They still live in the poor section of Benghazi
Near the hospital where I was born.   *5*

They never meant to settle
In Tokara, those Greeks
Whose eyebrows I wear.
Then they smelled the wild sage
And declared my country their birthplace.   *10*

The Knights of St. John invaded Tripoli.
The residents of the city
Sought help from Istanbul. In 1531
The Turks brought along my nose.

My hair stretches back   *15*
To a concubine of Septimius Severus.
She made his breakfast,
Bore four of his sons.

Uqba took my city
In the name of God.   *20*
We sit by his grave
And I sing to you:
       Sweet lashes, arrow sharp
       Is that my face I see
       Reflected in your eyes?   *25*

Watermelon Tales

January. Snow. For days I have craved
      watermelons, wanted
    to freckle the ground with seeds,
to perform a ritual:
      Noon time, an early   *5*
      summer Sunday, the village
chief faces north, spits seven mouthfuls,
      fingers a circle
around the galaxy of seeds.

               * * *

Maimoon the bedouin visited in   *10*
      summer, always with
    a gift: a pick-up truck load
of watermelons. "Something for the
      children," he explained.
      Neighbors brought wheelbarrows to   *15*
fetch their share. Our chickens ate the rest.

               * * *

His right ear pricked up
   close, my father taps on a
watermelon, strokes as though it were
     a thigh. A light slap.
    "If it doesn't sound like your hands
clapping at a wedding, it's not yours."

20

* * *

Men shake the chief's hand,
   children kiss it. Everyone files
behind him when he walks back. No one
    talks until the tomb
    of the local saint. The rich
place coin sacks at his feet, the poor leave
    cups of melon seeds.

25

* * *

30

Maimoon also brought us meat,
gazelles he rammed with his truck.
    His daughter, Selima,
    said he once swerved off the road
suddenly, drove for an hour until
    he spotted six. He hadn't
    hit any when the truck ran out
of gas. Thirty yards away the gazelles
    stood panting, and he
    ran to catch one with bare hands.

35

* * *

40

Two choices, my father's doctor tells us:
    transplant or six months
    of pain. Outside the office,
I point to a fruit stall, the seller
    waving off flies with
    a feather fan. My father
strokes, slaps, and when I lift the melon
    to my shoulder, says
    "Eleven years in America
and you carry a watermelon
    like a damn peasant!"

45

50

* * *

Uncle Abdallah buries
a watermelon underneath the
    approach of the waves —
    "Like a refrigerator
down there." It's July, a picnic at

55

Tokara Beach. We're
kicking a ball when
my brother trips hard on the hole. He's
    told to eat what he'd 60
    broken too soon. I watched him
swallow pulp, seed, salt, and sand.

         * * *

Her shadow twice her
height, the village sorceress
walks to where the chief spat. She reveals 65
    size of the harvest,
    chance of drought, whose sons will wed
whose daughters, and names of elders whose
    ailments will not cease.

         * * *

Selima told the gazelle 70
story sitting in a tub. With soap,
    my mother scrubbed the girl's scalp,
tossing handfuls of foam against
    the white tile. She then
    poured kerosene on Selima's 75
hair, rubbed till lice slid down her face,
    combed till the tines
    filled with the dead.

         * * *

Selima married. My mother sent her
    a silver anklet, 80
    a green silk shawl, and decided
against an ivory comb. My father paid
    the sheikh to perform
    the wedding. A week later
at his door, the sheikh found three watermelons and a gazelle- 85
    skin prayer rug, a tire mark
across the spot where he would have rested his
    head in prostration.

         * * *

I cut the melon we bought
into cubes, strawberry red. But they were 90
    dry, almost bitter.
    After the third taste, my father
dropped his fork. He gazed at the window
    for a while, and spent
    the rest of his days in bed.

ACKNOWLEDGMENTS

SECTION 1: SUMERIAN, AKKADIAN, AND ANCIENT EGYPTIAN LITERATURES

Enheduanna, tr. Aliki Barnstone and Willis Barnstone, excerpts from *A Book of Women Poets from Antiquity to Now*, edited by Willis and Aliki Barnstone. Copyright © 1980 by Schocken Books Inc. Reprinted by permission of Schocken Books, published by Pantheon Books, a division of Random House, Inc.

"Adapa the Man," tr. N. K. Sandars, from *Poems of Heaven and Hell from Ancient Mesopotamia*, translated by N. K. Sandars (Penguin Classics, 1971). Copyright © N. K. Sandars, 1971. Reproduced by permission of Penguin Books Ltd.

"The Shipwrecked Sailor" and "The Tale of the Doomed Prince," tr. Edward F. Wente, Jr., from *The Literature of Ancient Egypt: An Anthology of Stories, Instructions, and Poetry*, edited with an Introduction by William Kelly Simpson, pp. 50–55, 85–91. Copyright 1972. Reprinted by permission of Yale University Press.

The Book of the Dead, "Spell 26" and "Spell 53," tr. Raymond O. Faulkner, from *Ancient Egyptian Book of the Dead*, edited by Carol Andrews. Copyright the Trustees of the British Museum, British Museum Press. Reprinted by permission of British Museum Press.

From "Pleasant Songs of the Sweetheart Who Meets You in the Fields," from "Garden Songs," and "Love Lyrics," tr. Ezra Pound and Noel Stock. By anonymous, from *Love Poems of Ancient Egypt*, translated by Noel Stock. Copyright © 1962 by Noel Stock. Reprinted by permission of New Directions Publishing Corp.

SECTION 2: BIBLICAL LITERATURE: OLD TESTAMENT, NEW TESTAMENT, AND INTERTESTAMENT

From Job, *Revised Standard Version of the Bible*, Old Testament Section. Copyright 1952 by Division of Christian Education of the National Council of Churches of Christ in the USA. Used by permission. All rights reserved.

"Ecclesiastes, or the Preacher," from *Revised Standard Version of the Bible*, Old Testament Section. Copyright 1952 by Division of Christian Education of the National Council of Churches of Christ in the USA. Used by permission. All rights reserved.

From Isaiah, *Revised Standard Version of the Bible*, Old Testament Section. Copyright 1952 by Division of Christian Education of the National Council of Churches of Christ in the USA. Used by permission. All rights reserved.

From Daniel, *Revised Standard Version of the Bible*, Old Testament Section. Copyright 1952 by Division of Christian Education of the National Council of Churches of Christ in the USA. Used by permission. All rights reserved.

Jewish Apocrypha, "Susanna" and "Bel and the Dragon," from *New Revised Standard Version Apocryphal/Deuterocanonical Books*. Copyright 1989 by Division of Christian Education of the National Council of the Churches of Christ in the USA. Used by permission. All rights reserved.

From Paul, *First Letter to the Corinthians*, *New Revised Standard Version of the Bible*. Copyright 1989 by Division of Christian Education of the National Council of the Churches of Christ in the USA. Used by permission. All rights reserved.

Intertestament from *The Book of Jubilees*, tr. R. H. Charles, adapted by Willis Barnstone from "The Book of Jubilees," translated by R. H. Charles, in *The Other Bible* by Willis Barnstone, editor. Copyright © 1984 by Willis Barnstone. Used by permission of Bantam Books, a division of Bantam Doubleday Dell Publishing Group, Inc.

The Gospel of Thomas, tr. Helmut Koester from *The Nag Hammadi Library in English,* 3rd, completely revised edition by James M. Robinson, Gen. Ed. Copyright © 1988 by E. J. Brill, Leiden, The Netherlands. Reprinted by permission of HarperCollins Publishers, Inc.

On the Origin of the World, "The Raising of Adam from Mud by Eve" and "The Rape of Eve by the Prime Ruler (God) and by His Angels," tr. Hans-Gebhard Bethge and Orval S. Wintermute from *The Nag Hammadi Library in English,* 3rd, completely revised edition by James M. Robinson, Gen. Ed. Copyright © 1988 by E. J. Brill, Leiden, The Netherlands. Reprinted by permission of HarperCollins Publishers, Inc.

Plotinus, "The Ascent to Union with the One" from "The Enneads" tr. A. H. Armstrong from *Plotinus* by A. H. Armstrong. Copyright 1953. Reprinted by permission of Routledge, London.

SECTION 3: EARLY ARABIC LITERATURE

Al-Khansa, "Elegy for Her Brother Sakhr" and "Sleepless," tr. Willis Barnstone from *A Book of Women Poets from Antiquity to Now,* edited by Willis and Aliki Barnstone. Copyright © 1980 by Schocken Books Inc. Reprinted by permission of Schocken Books, published by Pantheon Books, a division of Random House, Inc.

Muallaqat, from "The Ode of Tarafa" and from "The Ode of Imru al-Quays," tr. Tony Barnstone and Beatrice Gruendler. Reprinted by permission of the translators.

Excerpts from the Quran, translated by N. J. Dawood (Penguin Classics 1956, Fifth revised edition 1990). Copyright © N. J. Dawood 1956, 1959, 1965, 1968, 1974, 1990. Reprinted by permission of Penguin Books Ltd.

Rabia the Mystic, "O My Lord, the Stars Glitter and the Eyes of Men Are Closed," tr. Willis Barnstone from *A Book of Women Poets from Antiquity to Now,* edited by Willis and Aliki Barnstone. Copyright © 1980 by Schocken Books Inc. Reprinted by permission of Schocken Books, published by Pantheon Books, a division of Random House, Inc.

Rabia the Mystic, "Miracle Story" and "How Long Will You Keep Pounding," tr. Charles Upton from *Doorkeeper of the Heart.* Reprinted by permission of Threshold Books, 139 Main St., Brattleboro, VT 05301.

Abu Nuwas, "Drunkenness after Drunkenness," tr. Richard Serrano. Reprinted by permission of the translator.

From *The Thousand and One Nights,* "The Tale of the Fisherman and the Genie," "The Tale of the Vizier and the Sage Duban," "The Tale of King Sinbad and His Falcon," "The Tale of the Husband and the Parrot," "The Tale of the Prince and the Ogress," and "The Tale of the Enchanted Prince," tr. Richard Burton, adapted by Emma Varesio. Reprinted by permission of Emma Varesio.

Usamah ibn Munqidh, from "The Book of Reflections," tr. Phillip K. Hitti from *An Arab-Syrian Gentleman and Warrior in the Period of the Crusades: Memoirs of Usamah Ibn-Munqidh,* translated by Phillip K. Hitti. Copyright © 1987 by Princeton University Press. Reprinted by permission of Princeton University Press.

SECTION 5: PERSIAN LITERATURE

Ferdowsi, from *The Epic of the Kings,* "The Reign of Jamshid" and "Faridun," tr. Reuben Levy, revised by Amin Banani from *The Epic of the Kings* by Ferdowsi, translated by Reuben Levy, Persian Heritage Series, Ehsan Yarshater, General Editor (University of Chicago Press, 1967), pp. 9–16, 17–25. Reprinted by permission of Ehsan Yarshater.

Omar Khayyam, *The Rubaiyat,* tr. Peter Avery and John Heath-Stubbs from *The Ruba'iyat of Omar Khayyam,* translated by Peter Avery and John Heath-Stubbs (Allen Lane, 1979). Translation copyright © Peter Avery and John Heath-Stubbs, 1979. Reprinted by permission of Penguin Books Ltd.

SECTION 6: MODERN ARABIC, HEBREW, TURKISH, ALEXANDRIAN GREEK, AND PERSIAN LITERATURES

Copyright © in selection and translation by Denys Johnson-Davies 1978. Reprinted by permission of Lynne Rienner Publishers, Inc.

Joyce Mansour, "In the Gloom on the Left" and "A Mango," from *Prose & Poésie: Oeuvre Complète* (Arles: Actes Sud, 1991). English translation of "In the Gloom on the Left" published in *APR*, Vol. 123.4, 1994, © 1992 Molly Bendall. English translation of "A Mango" published in *Volt*, No. 1, 1993, © 1993 Molly Bendall. Reprinted by permission of Molly Bendall and Samir Mansour.

Adunis, from "The Desert: The Diary of Beirut under Siege," 1982, by Aldonis (Ali Ahmed Sa'id), in *Modern Poetry of the Arab World*, translated and edited by Abdullah al-Udhari (Penguin Books, 1986). Copyright © Abdullah al-Udhari, 1986. Reprinted by permission of Penguin Books Ltd.

Dan Pagis, "End of the Questionnaire" and "Written in Pencil in the Sealed Railway-Car" from *Variable Directions: The Selected Poetry of Dan Pagis*, translated by Stephen Mitchell (San Francisco: North Point Press, 1989). Reprinted by permission of Stephen Mitchell.

Nawal Al-Saadawi, "The Thirst," tr. J. Ryder, published in *Translation*, Vol. XI (Fall 1983). Reprinted by permission of Nawal Al-Saadawi.

Forugh Farrokhzad, "Window" and "The Windup Doll," tr. Leora Baude and Ali Shashaani. Reprinted by permission of the translators.

Reza Baraheni, "Autumn in Tehran." Reprinted by permission of Reza Baraheni.

Dahlia Ravikovitch, "Clockwork Doll," from *The Window: New and Selected Poems by Dahlia Ravikovitch*, translated and edited by Chana Bloch and Ariel Bloch (Sheep Meadow Press, 1989). Reprinted by permission of Chana Bloch.

Haydar Haydar, "The Ants and the Qat," tr. Michel G. Azrak, revised by M. J. L. Young from *Modern Syrian Short Stories* (Three Continents Press, 1988). Reprinted by permission of the publisher.

Mohamed el-Bisatie, "A Conversation from the Third Floor," tr. Denys Johnson-Davies from *A Last Glass of Tea and Other Stories*, translated by Denys Johnson-Davies. English-language translation copyright © 1994, 1998 by Denys Johnson-Davies. Arabic text copyright © 1970, 1979, 1988, 1992, 1993 by Mohamed El-Bisatie. Used by permission of Lynne Rienner Publishers, Inc.

Amos Oz, "Nomad and Viper," tr. Amos Oz from *Where the Jackals Howl and Other Stories*. English translation copyright © 1973 by Amos Oz. Reprinted by permission of Harcourt Brace & Company.

Mohammed Mrabet, "The Canebrake," from *M'Hashish*, translated by Paul Bowles. Copyright © 1969 by Paul Bowles. Reprinted by permission of City Lights Books.

Mahmud Darwish, "The Prison Cell," from *Bread, Hashish, and Moon: Four Modern Arab Poets*, translated by Ben Bennani. Copyright 1982. Reprinted by permission of Unicorn Press, Inc.

Mahmud Darwish, "Victim No. 48," from *Modern Poetry of the Arab World*, translated and edited by Abdullah al-Udhari (Penguin Books, 1986). Copyright © Abdullah al-Udhari, 1986. Reprinted by permission of Penguin Books Ltd.

Hatif Janabi, "Questions and Their Retinue," from *Questions and Their Retinue* by Hatif Janabi, translated by Khaled Mattawa (University of Arkansas Press, 1996). Reprinted by permission of University of Arkansas Press.

Khaled Mattawa, "History of My Face" and "Watermelon Tales." Reprinted by permission of Khaled Mattawa.

I N D E X